LEARNING THE ART OF HELPING

BUILDING BLOCKS AND TECHNIQUES

Fifth Edition

Mark E. Young
University of Central Florida

Boston   Columbus   Indianapolis   New York   San Franciso   Upper Saddle River
Amsterdam   Cape Town   Dubai   London   Madrid   Milan   Munich   Paris   Montreal   Toronto
Delhi   Mexico City   Sao Paulo   Sydney   Hong Kong   Seoul   Singapore   Taipei   Tokyo

Vice President and Editorial Director: Jeffery W. Johnston
Senior Acquisitions Editor: Meredith D. Fossel
Editorial Assistant: Andrea Hall
Vice President, Director of Marketing: Margaret Waples
Senior Marketing Manager: Christopher Barry
Senior Managing Editor: Pamela D. Bennett
Project Manager: Kerry Rubadue
Senior Operations Supervisor: Matthew Ottenweller
Senior Art Director: Diane Lorenzo

Text Designer: Aptara®, Inc.
Cover Designer: Jodi Notowitz
Cover Image: Superstock
Permissions Administrator: Rebecca Savage
Media Project Manager: Rebecca Norsic
Full-Service Project Management: Penny Walker, Aptara®, Inc.
Composition: Aptara®, Inc.
Printer/Binder: STP Courier
Cover Printer: STP Courier
Text Font: ITC Garamond Std

Credits and acknowledgments borrowed from other sources and reproduced, with permission, in this textbook appear on appropriate page within text.

Every effort has been made to provide accurate and current Internet information in this book. However, the Internet and information posted on it are constantly changing, so it is inevitable that some of the Internet addresses listed in this textbook will change.

Library of Congress Cataloging-in-Publication Data

Young, Mark E.
    Learning the art of helping : building blocks and techniques/Mark E. Young. — 5th ed.
      p. cm.
    ISBN 13: 978-0-13-262750-4
    ISBN 10: 0-13-262750-7
    1. Counseling.   2. Psychotherapy.   I. Title.
    BF636.6.Y68 2013
    158.3—dc23   2011050576

10 9 8 7 6 5 4 3 2 1

ISBN 10:   0-13-262750-7
ISBN 13: 978-0-13-262750-4

For Joe, Olivia, Claire, Isabelle and Piper, my riches.

ABOUT THE AUTHOR

Mark E. Young is professor at the University of Central Florida. He received his doctorate from Ohio University. He has trained helpers for more than 20 years and worked in community mental health, private practice, college counseling centers, and corrections for more than 15 years. His professional writing has focused mainly on therapeutic methods and techniques, wellness, and counseling couples. If you have comments or suggestions on what you have read, please send e-mail to *myoung@cfl.rr.com*.

PREFACE

Learning the art of helping is a journey. It is a journey with a beginning but no real ending point. Those who embark on this quest find it to be a lifelong process of discovery rather than a destination. There is always more to learn about human behavior and more to discover about the process of what helps people change. In your journey to become a helper, you bring along your own baggage of life experiences, family history, and cultural background, as well as your biases and prejudices, likes and dislikes. At every stage, you will test your new learning against what you already know. You will accept most readily those things that fit within your present way of looking at the world despite the new information that is flooding in. How can you possibly merge the two worlds of new data and past experiences? Just as travelers keep journals to remember where they went, you need to learn the art of reflection so that new experiences do not pass you by. The reflective process is a connection between what you know and what you are learning.

NEW TO THIS EDITION

- Increased content on the assessment of suicide
- Increased content on positive psychology interventions and strengths-based counseling
- More emphasis on utilizing evidence-based treatment
- New classroom activities to reinforce learning
- New content on the importance of emotions
- New content on the use of questions

In every chapter, there are opportunities to stop and reflect and to engage in additional experiential learning activities. The decision to present the material in this way is based on the philosophy that each person carries with them a set of assumptions about the world that affects what they learn and how they assimilate new learning. New material becomes connected to the storehouse of information you already have collected and the skills that you presently possess. Reflecting on new material not only will help you integrate it with what you already know, but reflection also lays bare your prejudices and untested assumptions. For this reason, the process of reflection is not as benign as it may first appear. If you really become involved in reflecting and make it a habit, you will have made a giant step on your journey. You will have made a commitment to understanding yourself as well as those you are trying to help.

Reflection means thinking about new learning through writing, contemplation, or discussions with others. It is particularly important to reflect on issues that cause you emotional distress, that clash with what you already know, and that you have trouble grasping. Learning to reflect is a skill that will serve you well in difficult situations on the journey to become a professional helper. Helping is filled with difficult diagnostic, ethical, and practical problems. By incorporating a reflective process early in your journey, you will avoid many of the pitfalls caused by making snap judgments. There are several effective methods for reflecting. They include discussing your thoughts with a small group, bouncing your ideas off another person, posting impressions electronically, or e-mailing fellow learners and teachers. One of the best ways to learn to reflect is through the use of a journal. A journal is not just a collection of emotional reactions. A journal should include your feelings about the material, but it should also contain a serious considera-tion of alternative viewpoints or competing voices. In other words, use reflection when you find yourself at a crossroads between two points of view. Learn to state your current thinking on a particular topic and then write down an alternative viewpoint as well. For example, you may have learned that advice giving is a very helpful technique in dealing with friends and families. In this book, it is rather strongly stated that you should consider retiring this skill for now because it is not very effective and can, at times, be dangerous. Before deciding about this dilemma, perhaps you could write a bit on the virtues of each argument before blindly accepting my premise or rigidly sticking to your own point of view. See if there is a way to integrate these divergent positions.

There is a Japanese exercise called "the pillow technique" that illustrates good reflective thinking. Each corner of the pillow represents an area to ponder when a con-troversy arises. The exercise begins when you can identify two contrasting viewpoints on a topic; A is true or B is true. For example, A = giving advice is extremely helpful, and B = giving advice is not helpful. In reflecting on the issue, move methodically from one corner of the pillow to the next, giving each point of view due consideration. In the first corner, think of all the reasons you believe that giving advice is extremely helpful. In the second corner, think of all the reasons why advice is *not* helpful. At the third corner, think of all the reasons why neither A nor B is true, and finally in the fourth corner, list all the ways that A and B might both be true.

Of course, it is not necessary to go through this entire process when you reflect on the material in this book. But reflection should be a conscious process for which you set aside time. That is why journal starters have been included in each chapter. If you wish, you can choose one of the starters and write a new journal entry for each chapter as you go along. Alternately, you can choose to write in your journal when you experience a conflict or wish to test out a new idea. Try to write about those things that interest, excite, or trouble you. Share your writings with others and reflect together.

ORGANIZATION OF THE BOOK

This book contains 14 chapters and teaches 21 basic building block skills as well as sev-eral more advanced skills. Chapters 1 and 2 introduce you to the book, its organization, and its approach. Chapter 3 delves deeply into the therapeutic relationship, perhaps the most important ingredient for producing change. Chapters 4, 5, 6, and 7 teach the basic helping skills, including nonverbal skills, opening skills, reflecting, and advanced reflect-ing. Chapter 8, entitled *Challenging Skills,* teaches how to give feedback and how to confront inconsistencies in a client's story. Chapter 9 is an overview of basic assessment techniques to collect data and gain a clearer picture of the client and the client's prob-lems. Chapter 10 adds goal-setting skills so that you can narrow down the list of client issues and focus on the most important ones. Chapter 11 is called *Change Techniques.* Change techniques are interventions designed to produce action and push and influence the client to develop. Chapter 12, *Outcome Evaluation and Termination Skills,* explains how to set and measure outcomes and how to end a helping relationship. The final two chapters of the book, Chapters 13 and 14 are organized "therapeutic factors." These are the "megaskills" that helpers from different persuasions commonly use to enhance client growth. In this book, we describe six factors. The first is the therapeutic relationship, which is covered in Chapter 3. It is so important that we decided to address this early in the book. The remaining therapeutic factors include enhancing efficacy and self-esteem (Chapter 13); practicing new behaviors (Chapter 13), lowering and raising emotional arousal (Chapter 14); activating expectations, motivation, and hope (Chapter 14); and new learning experiences (Chapter 14). Under each of these therapeutic factors, you will learn more advanced change techniques such as role-playing, relaxation, and reframing. Although these techniques are more complex, once you have established the foundation with the basic building blocks, you will be ready to construct these more elaborate methods.

MyCounselingLab™

Help your students bridge the gap between theory and practice with MyCounselingLab™. MyCounselingLab™ connects your course content to video- and case-based real world scenarios, and provides:

- *Building Counseling Skills* exercises that offer opportunities for students to develop and practice skills critical to their success as professional helpers. Hints and feedback provide scaffolding and reinforce key concepts.
- *Assignments & Activities* assess students' understanding of key concepts and skill development. Suggested responses are available to instructors, making grading easy.
- *Multiple-Choice Quizzes* help students gauge their understanding of important topics and prepare for success on licensure examinations.

Access to MyCounselingLab™ can be packaged with this textbook or purchased standalone. To find out how to package student access to this website and gain access as an instructor, go to www.MyCounselingLab.com, email us at counseling@pearson.com, or contact your Pearson sales representative.

The videos that accompanied the previous edition of **Learning the Art of Helping** *on DVD are now exclusively available online via* MyCounselingLab™.

ACKNOWLEDGMENTS

In my own journey, there have been many who have taught and inspired me to be a better person and a better helper. I must acknowledge my teachers Rajinder Singh, J. Melvin Witmer, Harry Dewire, and James Pinnell, my first supervisor, who took me as a raw recruit in a mental health clinic, sacrificing his time and talent to teach me as an apprentice. We shared a zeal and passion for the profession, and his wisdom infuses every chapter of this book. I must also mention my friends who have encouraged me in my writing: Sam Gladding, Gerald Corey, Jeffrey Kottler, Adam Blatner, John Norcross, and Jerome Frank. I appreciate the feedback from Linda Robertson, and my friends at Ohio State University, Darcy and Paul Granello. Tracy Hutchinson, my colleague, deserves special mention for reading every chapter and giving feedback at every step. I also recognize the helpful comments of those who reviewed various drafts of the manuscript: Beulah Hirschlein, Oklahoma State University; Shawn Spurgeon, University of Tennessee at Knoxville; Sue Stickel, Eastern Michigan University; Barbara Thompson, George Washington University; and Carrie Wachter Morris, Purdue University.

I would like to thank my editor, Meredith Fossel, for her confidence and support. Finally, I recognize the contribution of my wife, Jora, who remains my most demanding critic and my staunchest supporter.

BRIEF CONTENTS

CONTENTS

Helping as a Personal Journey

The Demands of the Journey

Becoming a Reflective Practitioner
- Using Reflection to Help You Overcome Challenging Helping Situations and Enhance Your Learning
- Using Reflection to Help Clients with Backgrounds Different from Your Own
- Using Reflection to Accommodate New Information about Yourself
- Learning to Reflect Through Exercises in This Book

How a Helper Develops: Perry's Stages
- The Dualistic or "Right/Wrong" Stage
- The Multiplistic Stage
- The Relativistic Stage

The Development of Expertise
- Implications of the Concept of Expertise for Training Helpers

The Challenge of Development
- Taking Responsibility for Your Own Learning
- Finding a Mentor

THE DEMANDS OF THE JOURNEY

Learning to be a professional helper is a journey that takes years. Besides gaining a basic fund of knowledge about people and their strengths and challenges, one must be constantly learning and updating knowledge just as a physician needs to know about new treatments and new diseases. But helping is also a personal, "interior" journey because you must be committed to understanding yourself as well as your clients. In this book you will learn the essential counseling skills, but it is not enough to be skilled; at every turn, you face self-doubt, personal prejudices, and feelings of attraction, repulsion, and frustration. You will experience self-doubt when your clients encounter complex and unfamiliar problems; you will experience attraction and repulsion because of your personal needs and prejudices based on your cultural conditioning. Moreover, all helpers become frustrated at times when clients fail to reach the goals we expect of them. These reactions can be roadblocks on our journey if they interfere with the ability to form a vibrant client/helper relationship or when we see the client as a reflection of ourselves rather than as a unique human being. Irvin Yalom, in his book *Love's Executioner* (1989, pp. 94–95), describes his treatment of an obese woman who is depressed. From the moment he meets her, he is disgusted by her body and realizes his reaction is extreme. It makes him think about the rejection he received for being Jewish and white during his childhood in segregated Washington, D.C. He thinks that maybe his repulsion is a historical attempt to have someone to reject as he was rejected. It makes him wonder why he cannot accept fatness even though he was able to easily counsel people who were criminals when he worked in a prison. All of these reactions flood into his mind before the client ever even opens her mouth. Becoming aware of our prejudiced responses to others is part of the journey of the professional helper. This journey is difficult because it requires that we simultaneously try to focus on the client while keeping a close watch on our own tendencies to judge, to boost our egos, or to force our viewpoint on others.

BECOMING A REFLECTIVE PRACTITIONER

Because of the challenges caused by our personal reactions and unique client characteristics, we believe that helpers need a method of integrating new learning and coping with moments of indecision and doubt. In this book, we teach one method of dealing with the dilemma of understanding the client and monitoring the self. This is an approach called the **reflective practitioner**. Being a reflective practitioner means that you make a commitment to personal awareness of your automatic reactions and prejudices by taking time to think back on them and perhaps record them in a journal or discuss them with a supervisor or colleague. In other words, the reflective practitioner consciously reviews what has happened and decides on a plan of action. Jeffrey Kottler (2004) considers reflection to be not only a necessary characteristic of an effective helper but also a form of training. Reflection trains one to be open to contemplation, to consider alternative plans of action, to become resourceful, and to be inquisitive in one's lifestyle as well as in one's work.

You may find that your teachers ask you to use reflective methods in class and on your own. For example, the teacher might use Socratic questioning (asking leading questions), journal writing, watching and then reflecting on video segments, utilizing small groups to react to case studies, or even reflecting teams (Griffith & Frieden, 2000; Magnuson & Norem, 2002; Willow, Bastow, & Ratkowski, 2007). Just as every client will respond to the same technique or skill in a different way, you, as a student, will react to different learning situations based on your history and favored learning styles. Some students learn best by listening and then reflecting, others need to write down what they are learning, and some do best when they can have hands-on experience and then talk about the theory. Thus, you will respond differently to different assignments throughout your program of study based on your individual preferences. Still, reflection can help you even when a teacher's method does not suit your learning style. You can record what is said and then write your reaction and rebuttals in the margins. You can come to class with questions and concerns based on last week's lesson. In short, the method of the reflective practitioner challenges you to be more than a receptacle of knowledge. It asks that you chew everything before you digest it, rather than asking you to remember and give back just what you have heard or read.

Using Reflection to Help You Overcome Challenging Helping Situations and Enhance Your Learning

If you are engaged in a course of study to become a professional helper, you will be confronted with many new experiences both in the classroom and when you actually meet your clients. For example, a client may be hostile and uncooperative. Your training may tell you to encourage clients to articulate their concerns more fully. But sometimes this seems to make the client even madder. The process of reflection can help at such times when tried and true methods are not working. Let me give an example from my own experience. When I was first learning group counseling, I read in several textbooks that clients should never receive both group and individual therapy at the same time. As I began to practice group counseling, I found support for this rule in the fact that when clients received both treatments, they did not contribute to the group, saving their most personal issues for their individual sessions. One day, I received a new client for my group who had undergone a number of very traumatic events and was still in individual counseling with another therapist. She performed beautifully in group, and she felt that individual counseling was a vital support in her life. She seemed to be profiting from both treatments. Normally, I would insist on the client dropping out of individual counseling while she attended my group, but now my rule of thumb was in jeopardy because it did not seem to be limiting her progress or the group. In fact, she was applying the insights of individual counseling to her interpersonal world! I went to my supervisor with my dilemma, and she helped me put my old rule and my new experience together. With her help, I constructed a revised rule: "Most of the time, clients will not benefit from both forms of treatment; however, there are times, especially when the client is in need of a great deal of support or has been traumatized, when both modalities might be beneficial." I have found that the process of reflection allows me to better accommodate new information rather than rejecting it out of hand. You will undoubtedly experience similar moments as you study the skills of helping. You may be shocked when you discover that the methods you have always used to help your friends are not recommended in a therapeutic relationship. At times like these, reflection can help you meld old and new information.

Using Reflection to Help Clients with Backgrounds Different from Your Own

An important and frequent challenge occurs when you encounter people who are completely different from you in one or several ways: culture or ethnicity, socioeconomics, education, race, religion/spirituality, and family rules and relationships. For example, you will encounter family situations where people openly express their thoughts and feelings and others where they rarely if ever reveal their inner lives to each other. Because of your own upbringing, you might be shocked or you might disapprove. If you undertake the challenge of becoming a reflective practitioner, allow yourself to register surprise and all the other emotions as you encounter these novel situations. Later, take time to think back on what you know and what you have learned and compare it with your new experience. Through reflecting, you will be better able to separate your personal prejudices about what seems normal and perhaps look at the situation from an alternate viewpoint. The ability to see another perspective is enhanced when you have the opportunity to reflect with teachers, fellow students, and supervisors. Growth means that we expand and are able to see multiple viewpoints. That is why we think of helpers as *expanders* rather than as "shrinks."

Using Reflection to Accommodate New Information about Yourself

Perhaps more than any other profession, helping requires helpers to become aware of their own personalities, preferences, values, and feelings. Reflection can help you integrate new discoveries that you make about yourself. It allows you to carefully consider the feedback you are getting from supervisors, teachers, fellow students, and even your clients. In the course of your training, others will comment on your interpersonal style (the typical way you interact with others), your words, and even your gestures and posture. You will frequently become defensive, rationalizing your mistakes, discounting the giver of feedback, or blaming the client for a lack of progress. These are natural reflexes to the threat of feeling uncertain, impotent, or incompetent. The reflective practitioner is one who examines and reflects on critical incidents and strong personal feelings in the course of supervision, rather than making excuses or blaming others. He or she learns from difficult clients, unpleasant interactions, failure of a technique, and unexpected successes (Gordon, 2004). So being a reflective practitioner also means having the courage to ask for feedback from others and then to reflect on how you can work more effectively in a particularly difficult situation (Schön, 1983, 1987).

The following discussion describes some ways that you can be proactive in reflecting on your practice, including asking for supervision, developing a support group of fellow learners, becoming a client yourself, and keeping a personal journal. In addition, this book contains a number of exercises to help you learn more about the process of reflection.

ASK FOR SUPERVISION   Supervision is the practice of a helper and a supervisor sitting down to review the helper's problems and successes with his or her clients. In supervision, you will reflect on possible courses of action, ethical issues, and personal reactions. Everyone in the helping field needs periodic supervision whether he or she is a student or a long-time practitioner. Professional helpers are required to be under supervision while they are students and during their postdegree internships. Lawrence LeShan (1996) reported that his own mentor still sought supervision for herself, even when she was in her 80s, indicating that the reflective process is necessary at all stages of the journey. This approach abandons the view of supervision as a dependent relationship and guidance as the main reason for the supervisory relationship. Supervision's real value is that it is a time set aside for you to listen to yourself as you explain it to someone else. As a student, you may have the opportunity to ask supervisors and faculty members to look at your videos and discuss cases with you. Make use of this valuable opportunity to reflect on your work. Schön (1987) indicates that having a "master teacher" is important, but it must be in a setting where you have the chance to face real problems, try out various solutions, and make mistakes. This is called *reflection in action*.

DEVELOP A SUPPORT GROUP OF FELLOW LEARNERS   Another golden opportunity for reflecting on your new learning is to develop a supportive group of co-learners with whom you can discuss your personal reactions. Many therapists in private practice are members of such groups. In some training programs, students are part of a cohort or group that goes through every class together. If you are not part of a cohort, you can still develop a supportive group that meets regularly, shares information, and studies together.

BECOME A CLIENT   Another way of building in a reflective component is entering a counseling relationship as a client. More than half of therapists enter therapy after their advanced training and about 90% consider it to be very beneficial (Norcross, 1990). Many universities offer free counseling to students, and this can be a way for you to experience what it is like to sit in the other chair. You should be aware that some schools restrict their counseling centers to people who are in critical need.

KEEP A PERSONAL JOURNAL   One of the most popular methods for reflecting is to keep a personal journal. Journaling about one's problems, feelings, relationships, and dreams has dramatically increased in recent years. Some helpers even use journals as a therapeutic technique (Stone, 1998). They write their reflections to clients in letters or client and counselor journal together and compare notes. There is also a boom in online Internet journals. For example, the American Association of Retired Persons (AARP) has an online journal for those experiencing grief and loss, which can be downloaded from their website. There is even a magazine called *Personal Journaling*. Personal journaling is also available on your smartphone using applications such as iJournal, Maxjournal, and Momento.

OTHER METHODS FOR REFLECTING   Some researchers (Gordon, 2004; Sax, 2006) have compiled lists of opportunities for reflection. These opportunities, which were submitted by helpers, can become part of one's regular study or during work with clients. Reflecting can take place:

- When writing case notes
- During group supervision
- During individual discussion with a supervisor
- In personal therapy
- While journal writing
- During meditation
- As a part of course assignments such as papers
- While listening to recorded counseling sessions
- When talking informally to fellow counselors
- When suddenly thinking about a client
- In online groups, synchronously or asynchronously

Learning to Reflect Through Exercises in This Book

As you read this book, we will offer several opportunities to develop this reflective habit. In every chapter, we have included "Stop and Reflect" sections that ask you to consider your reaction to real cases or situations. You will also have the opportunity to receive feedback from your fellow students and to reflect on your own progress when you practice new skills. Finally, we have included suggested journal questions at the end of each chapter. These questions are meant to kindle your thinking, but do not feel that answering these questions is your only journaling option. If you do not find the stimulus question to be relevant, design your own, or instead, record your reaction to your practice sessions each week.

Now, let us actually engage in the process of reflecting by responding to an inventory of your attitudes about helping. The key step is to record your answers and then think back on what it might reveal about you. Rather than writing what might impress your teacher or fellow students, in this self-assessment, try to respond as honestly as possible. Toward the middle of your course and again at the end, you may wish to review this inventory, change your answers, reflect on it in writing, and determine if your attitudes have shifted. For the time being, answer the questions and then write down a reflection or two about what you notice in your answers. Remember, the "Stop and Reflect" sections in this book have no right or wrong answers. They ask for personal reactions and hopefully stimulate your thinking. They can make your learning more interactive if you take the time to respond as authentically as you can. When you are asked to agree or disagree, try to be as honest as possible and be aware of any internal censoring that occurs. Just as Yalom did with his obese client, think about where these censoring or prejudicial thoughts are coming from. You may or may not wish to share your answers with others during a class discussion, but by putting your answers on paper, you can take a step back and look at your thoughts from a more objective viewpoint. That is what reflection is really all about: taking yourself out of the situation and looking at it from a more detached perspective. You may find that your implicit viewpoints about human nature, your attitudes about helping, and your personal values come into sharper focus. Let us begin this experiment in reflecting by becoming aware of the basic attitudes you bring to the helping relationship.

STOP AND REFLECT

1. Write A or D next to each of the following statements, indicating whether you agree or disagree. Put down any thoughts on a separate sheet that may clarify or qualify your responses.
   a. In most cases, clients come to me for help because they are in a crisis. They need leadership. In order to help, I should generally be active and directive, have a lot of knowledge, and provide guidance and advice.
   b. Clients may have different values about families, religious principles, and what is important in life. It is not up to me to change clients' values or even talk about such personal issues.
   c. The relationship between helper and client must be a good one. Without "good chemistry," the counseling process will be difficult, if not impossible.
   d. I must remain at a professional distance. Caring too much about a client makes me lose my objectivity.
   e. People are responsible for their own problems. I must get clients to work on themselves rather than blaming others.
   f. If I have not been through an experience personally, I cannot help another person deal with it.
   g. I should never disclose anything personal to a client; the client's issues should be paramount.
2. Answer the following questions:

   As a helper, which do you think you are most likely to focus on helping a client to change? (You may circle more than one.)
   a. A client's feelings
   b. A client's thoughts and perceptions
   c. A client's behaviors

   Why? _____

   _____

   When talking with a client about a problem, which do you think are most likely to interest you?
   a. The history of the problem
   b. The present difficulties caused by the problem
   c. The client's future goals
   d. The client's personality

   Why? _____

   _____

   Do you think a helper is more responsible for helping a client adjust to the difficulties in the world or for changing the society that breeds these problems?

   Why? _____

   _____

3. On a separate sheet of paper, describe briefly a specific circumstance in which you actually displayed each of the following helper characteristics:
   • Empathy (the ability to put yourself in the shoes of another, to understand the other person's subjective reality)

   (Continued)

- Positive regard (the ability to respect another person, even though you may not like what he or she has done)
- Genuineness (the ability to be honest and open with another person, even though what you have to say might be difficult to express)
- Courage to confront (the ability to bring up inconsistent thoughts, feelings, and behaviors displayed by the client and the willingness to address "touchy subjects")

4. The following are some difficult situations helpers face. Rank-order them from 1 to 6, depending on how uncomfortable you might feel in each case. In this ranking system, 6 denotes the most difficult for you, and 1 is the least difficult.
   - A client is considering suicide.
   - A client is suffering from the death of a loved one.
   - A client is struggling over whether to get an abortion.
   - A client has religious beliefs that you feel are wrong.
   - An adolescent client is trying to decide whether he is gay or straight.
   - A married client is having an affair.

5. Stop and Reflect: As you look back on your answers, what life experiences have probably shaped your answers? Which issues are most likely to elicit conflict and personal challenges for you during your training? Which answers were the most difficult for you to answer? Where were you stumped? Where were you most confident?

HOW A HELPER DEVELOPS: PERRY'S STAGES

Susan has known for a long time that she wants to work with people. During her teenage years, a school counselor helped her cope during her parents' divorce. She worked as a camp counselor and really enjoyed helping kids. Since then, she has always hoped to work in a helping profession. She is finally sitting in her first course, a techniques class where she will begin her formal training. Suddenly, she is filled with a combination of excitement and apprehension. What if she can't do it? What if she says the wrong thing in front of the class or to a fragile client? She is confident in her abilities to memorize facts from the textbook and to select the best answers in multiple-choice exams, but can she really learn and demonstrate her skills? Is she in the wrong place?

Three weeks into the class, Susan is still nervous. When her professor calls on her to practice a role play, her stomach is in knots. She feels light-headed as she makes her way to the front of the classroom. She fears that she will forget the skills she has just learned, that she will make a mistake, that her mind will go blank, and that she will appear foolish to her classmates and professor. A few weeks later, Susan feels more confident because she has been practicing and getting better feedback from her teacher and fellow students. She still struggles, but there are moments when she feels more comfortable and effective.

Beginning a new course of study can be simultaneously exciting, overwhelming, and intimidating. Maybe you have even watched an experienced professional at work and thought, "How does he or she know what to say? How will I ever know the right answers?" Perhaps you even feel apprehensive as you read this, wondering whether you will ever learn to help by talking with someone. The desire to learn the "right" answers and to make the "right" interventions, and the nervousness that accompanies it, are a natural part of the process of becoming a helper. It may be comforting to know that students often progress through a series of developmental stages and that this tendency to want answers immediately is normal. Let us begin with an overview of the developmental stages that you can expect to experience during your training. The stages of cognitive development presented here are based on the work of Perry (1970), who studied undergraduate students during a 20-year period. Later research found that Perry's stages are also applicable to graduate students learning a new profession (Simpson, Dalgaard, & O'Brien, 1986) and to counseling students (Fong, Borders, Ethington, & Pitts, 1998; Granello, 2002).

By recognizing these stages as they arise, you may be able to avoid some of the discouragement that may accompany learning new skills when you realize that you are on the expected path. You may also be able to identify some ways to get beyond the thinking patterns that are holding you back. The three stages are the dualistic stage, the multiplistic stage, and the relativistic stage.

The Dualistic or "Right/Wrong" Stage

The first stage is a dualistic or absolutist position that can also be called the "right/wrong" stage. The **dualistic stage** is characterized by the belief that a helper's responses to a client are either right or wrong. In the beginning, trainees often believe that there is only one right way to respond to a client's statement or situation. This black/white, success/failure way of thinking increases the internal pressure and makes helpers overly concerned with their own performance. Moreover, they may fail to listen fully to their clients because they are thinking about what they are going to say next. They may feel that, by planning their next statement, they will be able to construct a better response. Actually, they are missing the boat by ruminating as the flow of the interview sails on by. Students in this stage often ask for direct feedback with questions such as "Was that right?" "How long should I wait before giving advice?" and "What should I have told the client when she asked me that question?" They are frustrated and annoyed when the teacher fails to indicate what is right and what is wrong.

The Multiplistic Stage

As you learn the therapeutic building blocks presented in the early chapters of this book, you will recognize that there are actually many possible responses to each statement a client makes. Eventually, you will become comfortable with the knowledge that there is no one right answer at any moment in the helping process. Because of the diversity in clients' backgrounds, experiences, and worldviews, what is "right" for one client may not be helpful at all for another. For example, a client considering leaving her boyfriend might say something like this: "I think that I should get out of the relationship, and then other times I think that I should stay. Everyone is giving me advice. What do you suggest?" You might react in several different ways:

You could respond with a question: "What aspects of the relationship make you question whether you should continue it?"

You could respond with a reflection of feeling: "You feel overwhelmed and confused, and you would like someone to guide you."

You could respond with a confrontation: "On the one hand, you are saying that you are confused by all the advice; on the other hand, you want me to give my viewpoint. How will another viewpoint help?"

Each of these responses could be helpful, depending on the client's unique situation. When you discover that there are several "right" answers to the same client statement, you will have moved into a multiplistic way of thinking. Unfortunately, at the **multiplistic stage**, all interventions and techniques may seem equally appropriate. You may even find yourself feeling overwhelmed by so many possibilities and wondering what differentiates a good response from a great one.

Students at this stage often report being frustrated and defensive with supervisors who "correct" them, because all roads seem to be equally valid. For example, a student may pose a series of probing questions to a client. The supervisor points out that the questions make the client feel interrogated and that the best course would be to identify and reflect the client's feelings. The student at the multiplistic stage knows that questioning can be a valid approach, but he or she does not yet understand *when* this approach is most appropriate and therefore is confused about what to do. Students at this stage may feel that because there are many possible "right" responses to a given situation, there is no organized system in helping. In fact, the students' ideas may seem just as valid as the instructor's. Here are some common statements students make at this phase of development, indicating their confusion when confronted with several helpful responses:

> "I watched Albert Ellis on film. He was very effective, and he didn't do any of the things you taught us."

> "I can't see why you told me not to ask so many closed questions when you told Ximena that it was all right with her client."

> "I thought you said that we weren't supposed to give advice, and now you're saying that I should have given this client more direction."

The Relativistic Stage

When you have gained some experience through study and practice, you will move into a **relativistic stage**. At that stage, you will recognize that although many types of responses may be appropriate, depending on circumstances, some are relatively better than others. You will become more skilled at choosing from the many possibilities based on the available information and on the goals for the session. Let us reconsider the client we discussed earlier who was asking for help with a relationship problem. The client said, "I think that I should get out of the relationship, and then other times I think that I should stay. Everyone is giving me advice. What do you suggest?" We identified three different possible helper responses, each of which leads in a different direction. The interventions and possible client reactions are as follows:

> **Question:** "What aspects of the relationship make you question whether you should continue it?"

> **Response:** The client will probably discuss the good and bad points of the relationship.

> **Reflection of Feeling:** "You feel overwhelmed and confused, and you would like someone to guide you."

> **Response:** The client will talk about feelings and may indicate why she feels so helpless.

Confrontation: "On the one hand, you are saying that you are confused by all the advice; on the other hand, you want me to give my viewpoint. How will another viewpoint help?"

Response: The client may respond with anger at the helper's perception that she is maintaining her confusion by asking people for advice. The client may also begin to explore her lack of confidence in her own decisions.

Obviously, none of these responses is glaringly wrong, but each will take the session in a different direction. When you reach the relativistic stage, you will judge a response as good or bad, depending on whether it takes the session in the most helpful direction for the client. You will have moved past a belief in right or wrong answers and toward an understanding that your choice of responses will have particular repercussions. This will happen when you have the knowledge and self-confidence to make effective choices among a wide variety of interventions and techniques. As contrasted with the dualistic stage, you will probably not be so concerned with your own performance, and you will be better able to think about the effects of certain responses on the client and the effectiveness of the responses in reaching the desired goals. Achieving the relativistic stage takes time. By becoming a reflective practitioner, you can speed this process along; however, you may not become a comfortable resident of the relativistic stage until long after this course is over. The main value of thinking about stages of development is that it can help you recognize that your struggles are part of a normal progression. In the beginning, try to focus less on grades and "right" answers. Instead, keep your focus on the effects your interventions are having on your clients. Listening to and reflecting on feedback and making changes based on the feedback will be the most helpful tools to spur your development as a helper.

There are three questions that guide the helper in selecting skills at this juncture: *What?, When?,* and *How? What?* refers to which skill the helper should use. What will be the most effective technique with this client's particular problem? *When?* refers to selecting the skill that is most appropriate at this point in the therapeutic relationship. For example, being very confrontational early on in the relationship does not make sense, as you have not yet earned the right to be so direct. *How?* refers to how you say it. In other words, how can the helper frame his or her response to best reach the client and facilitate change?

DO COUNSELORS DEVELOP?

Darcy Granello's (2002) article entitled "Assessing the Cognitive Development of Counseling Students: Changes and Epistemological Assumptions" deserves special attention. In her research, Dr. Granello studied counselors as they progressed through their training (a longitudinal study), and she also compared groups of students who were at different stages in their training (a cross-sectional study). In general, she found that counselors do change in their thinking along the lines Perry suggests (though perhaps not so neatly). The students in her study showed most growth during the later stages of their training—*when they are most involved with clients.* On the other hand, experience in human services, age, and grade point average seemed to have no effect on how quickly students developed. What we can take away from this study is that (1) time may be a necessary factor in training even for those who are older, wiser, and have previous experience, and (2) contact with clients may accelerate our growth when it is in combination with ongoing training.

THE DEVELOPMENT OF EXPERTISE

Another way of thinking about helper development is that it is a matter of developing expertise or mastery. This definition is more skills-oriented than Perry's cognitive system. The concept of levels of expertise is a commonsense approach that has been around for centuries, especially in the skilled trades. For example, we often hear of a master carpenter, master plumber, or master electrician. The terms *master counselor* or *master therapist* have also been used among helpers. For example, the American Association for Marriage and Family Therapy has, for a long time, invited and videotaped master therapists working with real clients. It has long been known that expertise in helping does not come solely from university degrees or from years of experience. Becoming a master is probably the result of training, experience, mentoring, and a passion and zeal for the profession that keeps one a lifetime learner.

Robert Hoffman and his associates (Hoffman, Shadboldt, Burton, & Klein, 1995) have studied the concept of expertise and concluded that mastery comes after a long period of hands-on experience, perhaps even 10 years, during which time one gains at least 50,000 bits of information (Hoffman et al., 1995). Thus, it is understandable that expertise in helping also takes a lengthy apprenticeship because of the vast differences among clients and the immense amount of knowledge needed to assess, diagnose, and treat various disorders and problems. Hoffman and his colleagues use traditional "guild" terminology from the trades to divide expertise into seven stages. In Table 1.1, you will see this concept applied to the development of expertise in helping (Young, 1998).

Implications of the Concept of Expertise for Training Helpers

The first piece of disappointing news that comes from this discussion of expertise is that one cannot master the art of helping in one semester or even 2 years of formal training. Although becoming a master of the helping art is a lifetime journey, we sometimes expect to have some measure of competence quickly. Those feelings may elude you for quite some time. Take comfort in the small victories when your instructor or fellow students notice your progress—even if it is hard for you to see.

A second implication is that, despite what state legislatures allow, a new helper is probably not able to handle all of the day-to-day decisions independent of supervision after 2 years of education and 2 more years of supervised experience. A journeyman still needs ongoing contact with an expert or master counselor. Supervision is a vital part of the journey because when you are a working professional, it may be the only time when you are able to reflect during the day.

Third, people enter this training with varying levels of expertise. A significant number are already journeymen when they register for basic counseling skills training (McLennan, 1994). If you are in this situation, you may feel that your time is being wasted going back over the basic skills. I have frequently taught basic skills to students who have been working as helpers for several years. Invariably, the more experienced students eventually feel that the course has been extremely valuable. They report that it was beneficial to reexamine their basic positions on important questions such as "Under what circumstances should I give advice?" and they feel that they may have not been as thoughtful as needed about treatment alternatives when working in a system that prescribes the way that clients are counseled. If you already have some helping experience, you may find that on-the-job training has not been systematic and that this course can

TABLE 1.1   "Guild" Terminology for Helper Development (Based on Hoffman et al., 1995)

Naivette	One who knows nothing about the practice of counseling or psychotherapy—a layperson. This term was coined by Hoffman to identify a person who is completely naive to the trade.
Novice	The word *novice* means one who is new. The novice is a new trainee who is on probation, for example, someone beginning the first class in basic counseling skills but not yet accepted into the program.
Initiate	A person who has been selected for a program and has begun introductory training—a new student in his or her first semester.
Apprentice	A student still undergoing instruction but who is beyond the introductory level. The apprentice is fully immersed in the practice of counseling and works as an assistant. Students in practicum and internship experiences are apprentices. In the trades, apprenticeship lasts from 1 to 12 years.
Journeyman	The term *journeyman* comes from the French word for day, *journée*. A journeyman is one who can do a day's work unsupervised. A journeyman works on orders from his or her supervisor. In the counseling field, this period may last for many years, even beyond the two to three years postgraduate experience required by the supervisor or the licensing state.
Expert	An expert is an exceptional journeyman who is highly esteemed by his or her peers, whose diagnostic and counseling skills are exceptionally accurate, and who can quickly and effectively deal with normal counseling situations. In addition, the expert is one who can handle "tough cases" and may have some particular area of expertise based on considerable experience with a particular type of problem—for example, substance abuse, crisis intervention, domestic violence, and so on. Expert status is by no means inevitable. Some helpers stay at the journeyman stage for life.
Master	A master therapist is one of a select group of experts who are qualified to teach others. A master is one whose judgments and practices become standards for others to follow. One way to identify a master is that he or she is regarded as an expert by other experts. Frequently, this is because the master is thought of as "the expert" in a particular area within the field.

Source: Young, M. E. (1998). Skills-based training for counselors: Microskills or mega-skills? *Counseling and Human Development, 31*(3), 2. Reprinted with permission of Love Publishing.

help fill in the gaps. You may also discover that your experience allows you to make connections not available to you the first time you learned these skills. If you feel that this course is repetitious, ask your instructor for more challenging assignments. Also, with your instructor's permission, find ways to help other members of your training group by giving them detailed feedback. Encourage them to reflect on their learning. You will be learning supervision skills as you do so.

These suggestions about how to develop expertise in counseling are consistent with the findings of Skovholt, Ronnestad, and Jennings (1997), who state that expertise is not achieved merely by cramming our heads with knowledge. Part of what spurs one to the next level of development is learning to reflect on experiences. Recently I told one of my colleagues that a certain individual should know what he is doing. After all, I said, "he has 15 years' experience." "Yes," said my colleague, "but it is the same year over and over again." I believe he was making this same point, albeit in a more cynical way. The process of becoming a master counselor or master therapist takes experience, but it also needs the catalyst of reflection that you must call on every day if you want to learn from your experience.

THE CHALLENGE OF DEVELOPMENT

Although the major shifts in your thinking may follow some of the predictable stages of development described by Perry or in the discussion of expertise, there are a number of other challenges that arise. During the initial period of instruction, you will encounter frustration and feelings of incompetence that accompany helping skills training, so much so that many students feel like throwing in the towel. By thinking about these issues now, you may be able to recognize them when they arise and you will deal with them more effectively, or at least with less towel throwing.

Taking Responsibility for Your Own Learning

Helping skills training requires you to perform skills in front of other people in practice situations. To receive the maximum benefit from practice sessions, you must open yourself up to feedback and suggestions. There is a strong tendency to compare oneself with others and to view training as a competition. Although that may have been a good strategy in some classes, it can be a detriment in learning helping skills because it may keep you from volunteering to practice in class and receiving the feedback that will help you grow. For example, you may appear to be ahead or behind your classmates as you learn a particular skill in this book. If the class moves ahead, you may need to continue to work on that skill by practicing with fellow students, watching videos of your performance, reading, or getting special help from the instructor. You must take responsibility for educating yourself and request the training that you need, rather than seeing the process of learning as a "mug and jug" phenomenon, in which the teacher pours from the jug of knowledge into the student's mug. You must move from teacher-directed learning to self-directed learning (Caffarella, 1993; Canipe & Brockett, 2003). In your training, this may mean that you face embarrassment if you are honest about what you do not know or cannot do. Although you may be able to keep it hidden for a little while, eventually you will be alone with a client, and you will need these skills to really be effective.

Finding a Mentor

Earlier, we talked about the value of a master therapist for reflecting or supervision. But learning from models is not restricted to only those in the highest altitudes. One of the best ways to learn the helping skills is to watch effective models and to receive feedback from teachers even if they are only a few steps beyond you. It is a challenge, however, to find experienced helpers who have the time to act as mentors. Once I watched one of my own teachers in a session with a client. I remember saying to myself, "He acts like being with that person is the most important thing in the world." Although I had read about "eye contact," "empathy," and "unconditional positive regard," when I saw the quality of his presence, I grasped, for the first time, how powerful such attention can be. How few are the times when someone really stops to listen wholly and solely. Teachers and supervisors are vital guides throughout the journey, especially in the beginning, and you must seek them out. As time goes on, it is true that one learns to have more faith and confidence in one's own judgment and abilities (Skovholt & Ronnestad, 1992), but even then, supervision and mentoring are essential for self-assessment and reflection.

Finding the Perfect Technique

Beginning helpers are extremely anxious to learn specific techniques and interventions. They gather techniques and tricks of the trade at workshops, hoping that one will be the magic pill that cures all clients. When you feel anxious or ineffective, it is normal to experience a desire to learn every method available and assume a sort of "cookbook" approach to helping. There is nothing wrong with learning all you can. It is unlikely, however, that you will find a perfect technique that will work for every client. The pursuit of a silver bullet is characteristic of dualistic or "right/wrong" thinking. In the relativistic stage, you will evaluate a technique to see if it is best for a specific client, with a particular problem, in a particular situation.

In Limbo

As you begin the process of learning to help, you may find that you abandon your "pre-training" natural helping style. Although beginning helpers are often naturally therapeutic, they typically find that they must temporarily set aside their old ways of helping. You may find that the new techniques and interventions feel artificial or "not like me" at first. Do not be surprised to hear yourself say, "I used to know what to do when a friend was upset. Now that I've begun to study helping, I no longer know what to say." Even your attempts to regain your old self seem awkward and artificial. It is a little like the centipede who was asked how she could coordinate those hundred legs and walk. Once she started thinking about it, she couldn't do it. As you consciously learn the helping process, it may be difficult to be natural.

Arnold Lazarus, the founder of multimodal therapy, cautions us that training can sometimes undermine our natural talents (1990). He tells the story of his friend, a dentist, who was a natural listener and was very therapeutic with his patients. But the dentist went back to school to become a therapist. Lazarus felt that the result was a rather phony person who resorted to jargon instead of listening. Perhaps Lazarus's friend was going through a stage characterized by overzealousness and insecurity. But the story is there to remind us that we have much to lose. If we abandon our genuineness, personal warmth, and all the other qualities that make people feel we are listening and caring, our training will be something to overcome rather than to rely on. Hopefully, as you give up old habits and learn new skills, you will find a way to integrate the old "therapeutic friend" with the new "therapeutic helper."

Accepting Feedback and Being Perfect

Your willingness to accept feedback will be another indicator of developmental change. As we have said, students in the dualistic stage accept feedback but feel discouraged at being "wrong." In the multiplistic stage, they may be defensive because they cannot see the superiority of one course of action. When faced with feedback, they attempt to justify their actions rather than listening to critiques and suggestions. As you gain confidence and see how different responses take clients in different directions, it is easier not to take such criticism personally because you feel confident in your basic skills, and it is as if someone says, "There is this path as well. Is it better?"

I experienced just such a crisis when I turned from full-time therapist to textbook writer. Although I was confident in my approach to clients, I was sensitive about how my writing would be seen by others. I also know writers who are afraid to show their work to others. Writing and engaging in a therapeutic relationship are both very personal forms of self-expression, and so we are tempted to hide our work and avoid any damage to self-esteem. It turns out that showing our work to others is the fastest road to growth because we can then learn from the response of our audience—there is no better way to learn.

Following Ethical Guidelines

We are all familiar with errors in medical treatment. However, we may fail to recognize that clients in a helping relationship can also be harmed by inappropriate advice, humiliation, emotionally arousing techniques, and subtle messages of contempt when we do not understand their cultures, religions, families, or beliefs. The Hippocratic challenge to all practitioners of the healing arts is *primum non nocere*—first, do no harm. Ethical guidelines help us avoid harm to clients by asking us to adhere to some general rules.

Ethical guidelines have been proposed by virtually every professional organization in the helping professions. These standards can be found in recent publications, and updated versions are available online. Ethical guidelines and codes largely deal with the work environment; however, ethical dilemmas are also likely to arise in your training group. The following are some guidelines you may wish to adopt as a group during your class. Optimally, you should discuss these thoroughly, so that everyone is in agreement. On the other hand, rules are inadequate to deal with every problem that arises. In many cases, it will be necessary to talk with your instructor about how to handle these conflicts. Although many of the issues described in these guidelines will not surface in your training group, you should still be prepared. Talk with your group about how you might handle specific situations. Make sure everyone is in agreement to abide by the ethical guidelines.

> ### Guideline 1: Do not reveal what other training group members say about themselves during role-playing and practice sessions.
> This means that you should not tell your best friend, your father, or your spouse. Although there may not seem to be any serious harm, forming these boundaries will set up an atmosphere of trust and allow for more freedom for all participants. It may be your first experience in keeping professional secrets. Try thinking of it as a sacred trust, similar to the seal of the confessional taken by Catholic priests.
>
> ### Guideline 2: Avoid giving advice.
> This is a practical suggestion as well as an ethical guideline. From the practical standpoint, you may find that giving advice, especially early on, can damage the relationship and slow down client progress. From the ethical perspective, are you really competent and knowledgeable enough to give advice? Could your advice be dangerous to a person's relationships or his or her academic or professional life? Could it undermine the client's self-confidence? These concerns suggest that you might wish to resist giving advice during this part of your training and develop some alternative skills.

Guideline 3: Do not impose your values on others.

Avoid making value judgments on a person's lifestyle, life experiences, or philosophy of life. Similar to giving advice, your judgments may be based on inadequate knowledge, may reflect your own limited experiences, or may communicate contempt or lack of acceptance of the other person. Learning to be sensitive to the cultural differences and unique experiences of clients helps us to avoid the trap of subtly communicating that a person's values and worldview are unacceptable.

Guideline 4: Be careful with feedback to clients and to fellow students.

Give feedback only when asked and package it in a way that the other person can accept. Give only specific and constructive feedback. Giving vague and very negative feedback can be damaging. Give feedback on areas where the person wants more information. We give feedback not to show how clever we are but to provide something useful to the client. I am sure you have heard of an "empathy sandwich." An "empathy sandwich" refers to giving the bad news in between two positive statements. In fact, this kind of sandwich is not a bad idea for training situations. In couples communication, Gottman (2000) has found that it takes five positive statements to counteract one negative statement in a couple's conversation. Similarly, specific, simple positive feedback will be the most helpful here because one negative statement is heard five times louder than a compliment.

Guideline 5: Stay mainly with the techniques described in the book or those taught by your instructor.

Using an unfamiliar and potentially harmful method should only be attempted with the guidance and permission of your teacher or supervisor. A powerful technique can cut both ways; it may have an equally powerful negative effect when misapplied. Generally speaking, reading about a technique or seeing it demonstrated at a workshop is not sufficient training. Practicing new techniques is only ethical when you are under supervision.

Guideline 6: Notify your instructor or supervisor at once if a member of your training group or a client is contemplating suicide or is considering harming others.

Even if you are relatively sure that the probability of violence is low, it is vital that you discuss any suggestion of violence with someone in authority. A few years ago, Michael Mahoney, one of the most prolific writers and most innovative thinkers in cognitive therapy, committed suicide. It makes us realize that we have the obligation to be sensitive and to receive training in suicide assessment and prevention, and even be aware of these issues in our colleagues (cf. Granello & Granello, 2007). Learning to talk to your fellow students and to those in authority is good training for your later work when you must learn to disclose and consult when an ethical or clinical problem arises.

Individual Differences

If you are a member of a minority group, have a disability, are one of the first in your family to attain higher education, or are going through a particularly stressful life stage (for example, getting married or divorced, leaving home, or having children), you may face additional challenges in the process of becoming a helper. Students facing outside stressors may also have difficulty maintaining the flexible schedule that is required (Gaff & Gaff, 1981; Quimby & O'Brien, 2006). Specifically, consider how the following differences may have an impact:

- Minority students may lack same-race peer interactions and minority role models (Cheatham & Berg-Cross, 1992).
- Female students raised in traditional families may have difficulty trusting in an internal authority (Bernard, 1981; Marx, 1990).
- Some male students may not be as attuned to relationships and feelings as their female counterparts.
- Hypermasculine upbringing may cause male trainees to seek solutions quickly, before understanding the client. They may fail to recognize and accept feelings of fear and helplessness in themselves and may therefore have difficulty recognizing them in others.

Such considerations should serve to illustrate that development is not the same for each person, rather than discourage those with special situations. An individual's progress cannot be confined to a timetable (Barrow, 1987), nor is it necessarily a linear, step-by-step process. Sometimes you may feel that you are taking two steps forward and one step back. Allow yourself time to develop and move at your own pace. Development is not a competition with your classmates; it is a personal journey.

THE PERFECT HELPER, OR WHEN DO I QUIT DEVELOPING?

Your development as a professional helper does not end with graduation; it is a lifelong process toward mastery. Academic training will give you the skills, but practice, supervision, networking, and experience will make you a helper. Neither a Ph.D. nor a certificate from a training institute will mean that you have become the perfect helper. Students develop during their training, and this does not stop when they finish their formal education. In fact, interviews with professionals possessing more than 20 years of experience revealed that these helpers believed most of their development occurred after graduation (Skovholt & Ronnestad, 1992). Equipped with diplomas, but not a lot of work experience, new professionals may feel the effects of the "imposter phenomenon." Even beginning helpers also tend to see themselves as frauds and likely to be found out (Harvey & Katz, 1985). Those professionals who have been out of school more than 10 years speak of a deeper authenticity in their work, the reassurance of accumulated wisdom, and the ability to make individual and personalized interventions with their clients. Do you have to wait 10 years until you can be a good helper? No—you can be the best helper you can be at your particular stage. Keep learning, keep receiving supervision, and do not pretend you know more than you do. One of the best books on this topic is *Counselors Finding Their Way* (Kottler, 2002), a collection of stories by practicing counselors about the issues they face as they develop. Besides making us feel that we are not alone, the writers give us help in thinking about how to get over these hurdles we continue to face.

To address ongoing developmental needs, the concept of lifelong learning is essential for helpers. Our knowledge of new techniques, advances in research in the field, new client populations, and emerging social issues can be updated through workshops, professional journals, classes, study groups, and conventions. The foundation you receive in your formal training is crucial. But it is not enough. You will need to learn about the newest treatments and programs developed by other helpers rather than "reinvent the wheel" each time a new client problem confronts you.

WHO CAN BE AN EFFECTIVE HELPER?

Questioning whether you are really cut out for a job is to be expected when you enter a new field. Are you similar to the professionals you know? What must you know, and what abilities must you possess going in? Although there is no single personality configuration that defines the perfect helper, various writers have looked at specific traits that lead to effective helping. They have also looked at the beliefs and attitudes most conducive to learning and working in the profession. Knowing more about these may help you because many of these qualities can be acquired.

The Legacy of Rogers

The writings of Carl Rogers (1967) have provided much of the framework for the core facilitative conditions that many see as the necessary ingredients for change and growth. More than anyone else, Rogers talked about therapeutic attitudes. Rogers believed that clients would move toward growth and positive outcomes if the helper provided the right environment. This environment, he felt, was more a reflection of the helper than an outcome of prescribed techniques or interventions. He considered three personal characteristics to be essential for a helper: congruence, positive regard, and empathy.

CONGRUENCE **Congruence** is the ability to be completely genuine with another person. Congruency means that there is consistency between what a person feels and says and how he or she acts. When we are congruent, we are not afraid to take risks and to spontaneously share reactions and thoughts with clients. If we are congruent, we react to clients in the here and now and do not hide behind the façade of the professional role. A simple example of incongruence is when our verbal and nonverbal messages conflict. Suppose you tell a client that you will provide support on the phone during a period of crisis, but then you do not regularly return phone calls. The nonverbal action comes across more clearly than the verbal message, and the client likely will not trust an incongruent helper.

POSITIVE REGARD **Positive regard** does not mean that helpers must approve of every client behavior. Rather, the helper must respect the personhood of each client and believe that all persons have inherent worth. Hazler (1988) wrote about finding unconditional positive regard while working with a prison population. He described the insight that occurred when he was able to differentiate the prisoners (as real, valuable persons who had hopes and dreams and goals) from their crimes (which were brutal). A helper who works from unconditional positive regard never rejects a person, although he or she may reject that person's actions.

EMPATHY **Empathy**, or empathic understanding, is the ability to understand another person's feelings or worldview. Responding to another's feelings can be called *emotional empathy,* whereas taking the time to reflect an understanding of a person's motives, intentions, values, and thinking might be called *cognitive empathy*. Helpers suspend their own judgment as they learn the subjective worldview of their clients. Rather than to evaluate the content of client statements, the purpose is to simply understand the client's feelings, beliefs, experiences, and goals. Rogers believed that through empathy, clients feel understood and are empowered to solve their own problems. Again, the habit of reflecting is an activity we can employ to monitor our tendency to judge rather than to empathize.

Courage to Confront

The effective helper has the supportive qualities that Rogers mentions, but he or she is also able to "go for the jugular." Clients come to a helper for more than support. Sometimes the job of a helper is to make the client aware of painful realities. Helpers may be forced to show the client their annoying interpersonal behaviors and be willing to risk the client's anger when delicate issues need to be addressed. Effective helpers are not so dependent on the client's approval that they will fail to bring up touchy subjects. As one moves from dualistic to relativistic thinking, it is easier to think about the client's best interests and not be so focused on oneself.

Other Research on Effective Helping

The writings of 15 different authors described 55 characteristics, attitudes, and beliefs of effective helpers. I have tried to consolidate these into five key elements (Combs, Avila, & Purkey, 1971; Corey, Corey, & Callanan, 2003; Gladding, 2008; Kottler, 2004; McConnaughy, 1987; Patterson & Eisenberg, 1983; Spurling & Dryden, 1989; Truax & Carkhuff, 1967).

First and foremost, an effective helper has a positive, accepting view of other people. He or she accepts people who are different and is not judgmental about other people's lifestyles, values, cultures, and religions. He or she wants to help others and believes that people have the desire to change. The helper must be able to communicate his or her nonjudgmental attitude as well as warmth and caring.

Second, the effective helper has good self-esteem and is a secure and mentally healthy person. Learning to be a helper because of a personal mental disorder is not the correct motivation, nor should it be a way to experience power over others or to feel superior to those with more serious problems. Does this mean that if you have a serious mental disorder you should not be a professional helper? I think the answer is yes. Frequently, clients who have been helped want to return the favor or are interested in the help they have gotten. Although the process of recovery may intrigue the recovering alcoholic or addict, recovery is not the only credential one needs. The addicted client needs to be well beyond the thrall of his or her addiction before becoming a counselor. Similarly, individuals who have been through counseling may be attracted to the field that helped them so much, but before entering the field of professional helping, every person should evaluate his or her own personal mental health and stamina. Effective helpers appreciate their strengths but know their limitations, too. They are able to examine themselves critically. They have the courage to look at themselves under a microscope and can separate helping the client from boosting the ego of the helper. They make reflection and personal growth part of their lifestyle.

Most writers agree that the effective helper has good self-care skills. Many who are attracted to this profession want to help others, but soon find that it can be depleting.

It is easy to become emotionally "bankrupt" and "burned out" if one does not develop techniques for stress management, time management, relaxation, leisure, and personal self-renewal. The effective helper has a stable and fulfilling personal life with close family and friends to provide support as a buffer to the stress of helping.

The effective helper is both creative and intellectually competent, a Renaissance person who appreciates both the science and the art of helping. The effective helper has specialized knowledge of human relationships, human motivation, and human development and understands how to create change. Those who remain vital in the profession have "insatiable curiosity" to learn and grow in their skills and knowledge (Spurling & Dryden, 1989). Creativity and flexibility are equally vital. Helping requires one to devise innovative ideas with different clients in different situations. A helper must be able to deal flexibly with ambivalence, unfinished business, and moral dilemmas. He or she has to allow clients to work through difficult situations without moving them to premature decisions.

When J. L. Moreno, the founder of psychodrama, was once asked what the most necessary quality was for a group leader, his unexpected response was "courage." This fifth characteristic of an effective helper has two facets: First, the helper must be able to listen unflinchingly to stories of great pain. Like a physician who sets a broken arm, he or she must be able to look with a detached eye at human destruction and see where the healing can be started. Second, the helper's job requires risk taking and action, without the security offered by other sciences. Individuals who believe that they can control every circumstance and that there is a procedure and a solution for every crisis have a difficult time as helpers. For example, there are no psychological tests that accurately predict a person's tendency to be violent. Helpers' decisions must be based on experience, training, and even intuition. Because human behavior is relatively unpredictable, effective helpers must be able to live with that uncertainty.

WHAT CAN YOU BRING TO A CLIENT?

There is no one set of personal qualities that makes an effective helper. The profession has room for many types of individuals, each of whom brings significant strengths and simultaneously must be aware of the limitations of his or her own personality style. The example of a former student may help to illustrate this. Maria, a graduate student, got under my skin sometimes because she had little patience for long theoretical discussions and did not like studying anything that did not have immediate application. She seemed to roll her eyes when the discussion became too intellectual. She was practical and concrete and liked people who were "down-to-earth." She wanted to solve problems and make a difference in the lives of children. It seemed to me that sometimes she tended to be too quick to come to closure with adult clients when they became stuck or were indecisive. Sometimes she pushed them to make decisions and seemed insensitive to their turmoil.

However, Maria now works effectively as a school counselor. Her particular strength is that she knows how to manage crises. She instantly grasps what has to be done and takes bold and concrete steps to accomplish it. She has excellent judgment and is indispensable to her school because she knows how to take quick action and exudes calm and poise in times of confusion. Maria's case illustrates that each of us brings strengths to the helping role. Much depends on knowing our own abilities and finding an environment where they can be put to good use.

As you consider the characteristics of effective helpers that we have identified, remember two things. First, many of the characteristics can be developed. They are not necessarily inborn. Second, each person brings unique characteristics to the helping profession and, as in Maria's case, the challenge is to find a place where these gifts will help others. Do not look at the characteristics of effective helpers in order to identify those you do not have. Helpers should not be clones. A client will have a relationship with you, not with a set of skills. By focusing on your strengths, you will have much to bring to a client.

STOP AND REFLECT

The characteristics of effective helpers identified by the experts are listed in brief form in the following statements. Answer the accompanying questions as truthfully as possible, because your answers may point out areas you may wish to address later in your training. Which of these qualities do you presently possess and on which do you want to improve? For those skills you need to develop, think for a moment about what you might do to challenge yourself. What extracurricular activities might help you to grow?

Positive View of Humankind

You believe that most people are basically good and are striving for self-improvement. You enjoy people and believe that people can change.

>   How true is this for you?
>   How can you grow?

Stable and Mentally Healthy

You have good self-esteem and are basically a secure, mentally healthy person. (You may not be able to make a completely unbiased self-assessment, but friends and family can give you feedback on your coping ability.)

>   How true is this for you?
>   How can you grow?

Good Self-Care Skills

You do not become overly involved with those you are helping. You know your limits and are able to set boundaries to protect yourself from burnout.

>   How true is this for you?
>   How can you grow?

Intelligent and Psychologically Minded

You are an intellectually curious person who is interested in the psychological world of other people. You can appreciate both a scientific and an artistic approach to learning about helping.

>   How true is this for you?
>   How can you grow?

Creative

You are a creative person in some aspect of your life. You are not rigid or inflexible in your attitudes. You are not bothered by many prejudices about people, cultures, religions, and family customs that differ from your own.

How true is this for you?

How can you grow?

Courageous

You have enough courage to examine your own personal problems and to seek help and guidance for yourself when you need it. You are willing to admit that you need to change and grow. You are able, for the most part, to deal with the cruelties that other people inflict on each other without being so disturbed that it disrupts your own life or your ability to help.

How true is this for you?

How can you grow?

VIDEO EXERCISES

At this point in most chapters, we prompt you to view video exercises in MyCounselingLab. These segments were unscripted and unrehearsed, and the clients are talking about their real issues. You will be invited to watch a segment and then consider how you might respond, or you may simply be asked to pay attention to certain helper or client reactions. Usually, some answers are provided, but they are not *the* answers. At other times, the video is suggested as a tool for you to use to reflect on what you like and did not like and what you learned from watching.

MyCounselingLab™ Exercises

Go to the Video and Resource Library on the **MyCounselingLab**™ site for your text and search for the following clip: *Segment 8,* in which a helper (Dayle) tries to learn more about a client (Eve) and her issues. Watch the entire segment once or twice, and then write your answers to the questions below on a separate sheet of paper and discuss them with a fellow student.

1. How much of the helper's own thoughts, feelings, and ideas came across during this part of the session? If you had been a client, would you have wanted the helper to be more involved or less verbal? For what reasons?
2. From your viewpoint as an observer, did the helper appear to be listening and involved? If so, how did she communicate this?
3. Identify one thing the helper said that seems to encourage the client to talk about what she wants to do without giving too much guidance.
4. If there is any helper statement you did not like, note it here. What made you uncomfortable?
5. Was there any area of the client's story you would like to have known more about? For what reasons?
6. The helper in this video demonstrated a nonjudgmental attitude. What did she do to convey this?
7. The opinion expressed in this guide is that advice is generally to be avoided. What is your reaction to this guideline with respect to Eve? Does she need advice?

8. Discuss your answers with a fellow student. Identify one thing that surprised you about this video.

Some Answers

1. Not very much. Dayle keeps the focus on the client and her concerns.
2. She maintained eye contact, nodded, and frequently said, "um hmm."
3. 35:42 "Where would you picture yourself as being, if you could wave a magic wand and be right where you think you should be at this moment? What would that look like?" (There are probably other answers here, too.)
4. Answer this for yourself. There is no right or wrong answer.
5. I wish I could have asked Eve if anything happened recently that made her think about moving back home. Maybe this would have thrown her off track, though.
6. One possible answer to this question is that Dayle did not evaluate or question Eve's feelings about returning home.
7. Eve can probably solve her own problems without advice.

Summary and Suggestions

Entering a new field of knowledge brings about uncertainty and challenges us to remain open and nondefensive. One central point of the chapter is that learning the art of helping follows some predictable stages. Knowing this should allow us to be less self-critical when we face the normal developmental hurdles. We need to be patient, considering the time and knowledge that we must gain are significant. One of the ways that we can accelerate our progress is through reflection. Reflection is the process of thinking about what we are learning. Even more, it means identifying discrepancies and problems that do not fit our normal solutions and taking stock of our own reactions. We also need to develop the habit of reflection so that we can separate our clients' goals from our own personal wishes.

Learning the art of helping is a long journey, and everyone travels at a different rate, bringing unique traits and differing gifts. Although experts have identified characteristics of effective helpers, including self-acceptance, cooperation, and the ability to reach out to others, there is not just one kind of person who can practice the helping arts. You might find it helpful to consider some methods for reflection, self-assessment, and self-improvement that other students have found conducive to their own learning and development.

• Many have found it helpful to keep a journal of their thoughts and feelings during this course.

Identify your fears and moments of success and then look back from start to finish, seeing how far you have come. Take the opportunity to journal when you are stuck or have trouble progressing. Write down your frustrations and then talk them over with your instructor or use your journal as a basis for your questions in class.

• Consider getting together on a regular basis with other students to practice new skills and to provide support for each other.
• You may want to keep a record of unrealistic thoughts, self-criticisms, and exaggerated expectations that you may be holding for yourself. Are you focusing enough on what you do well, or is self-criticism becoming a barrier to growth?
• Think about recording your practice sessions and writing down all of your responses. Identify each of your responses and think about how it affected the client.

By now you might be thinking that learning to help is a long journey requiring much of the learner. It is that, but it is also a voyage of personal discovery and an opportunity to encounter and appreciate other people at a level of intimacy that few professions allow. As you begin, remember the adage of the mountain climber: Don't look at the summit; keep your attention on your next step. One day you'll get to the top, but right now appreciate where you are.

Exercises

SMALL GROUP DISCUSSIONS

1. In groups of three, discuss your reasons for wanting to become a professional helper. What are your expectations and concerns?
2. In a small group, discuss the following: You probably were encouraged to study helping by friends or family members. What do you think are the natural helping qualities that you possess and that you do not want to lose during your training?
3. Think of a time when you learned a new skill (for example, playing tennis or learning to sew). What stages did you go through? How did you improve? Were you self-critical at first? If so, what effect did your negative thinking have? Can you identify any particular thoughts that you had during that time? Discuss them with classmates and see if you can relate your previous experience to what you might encounter as you learn helping skills.

WRITTEN EXERCISES AND SELF-ASSESSMENT

In the chapters that follow, we have separate sections for Written Exercises and Self-Assessment of your progress in learning the helping skills. Because you are not yet practicing skills, instead use the "Stop and Reflect" section on p. XX as a self-assessment activity. If you want to extend that activity, look at question 3 about helper characteristics and ask someone who knows you to rate you on a 1–10 scale for each characteristic. Compare their answers with yours.

HOMEWORK

Homework 1: Meet a Professional

Make an appointment with a professional who has been working for only a few years (say, 1–5). Ask him or her the following questions and react briefly in writing to each answer. (Be sure to add a couple of questions of particular interest to you.)
1. Does another helper supervise you? If so, what do you value about these sessions?
2. Thinking about the therapists you have known or observed, what qualities do they possess that you admire?
3. When do you feel least confident in your job?
4. To what theoretical orientation do you subscribe?

5. What kinds of professional reading do you do?
6. Do you benefit from conferences?
7. Did you notice any big "jumps" or stages in your ability to help?
8. Other questions . . .

Homework 2: Review Your Work History

Review your résumé or your past work history, whether paid or volunteer. Include jobs you held in organizations in high school or college if your work history is short. List your jobs and, under each, write significant learnings you gained about working with other people, both clients and co-workers. Even if your job was not in a helping capacity, did you find ways to help others? Has helping been a regular part of your work life, or is it a new development? Summarize your learnings in a final paragraph.

JOURNAL STARTERS

Think about starting a personal journal that chronicles your experiences on the journey to becoming a helper. Development of expertise is sometimes described as gaining knowledge, skills, and attitudes in a particular domain. Through this book, your lectures, and other courses, you are definitely gaining knowledge and skills. The journal, on the other hand, allows you to reflect on your own attitudes about helping and to react personally to what you are learning. Such reflection is the basis for modern approaches to assessment such as the portfolio. By looking back over your work, you can gauge your own development and think about future goals. A journal is not just a record; it should be reread and thought about.

You can use a computer, purchase a blank book, or develop a three-ring binder to construct a journal that allows you to add other information such as articles, poems, pictures, and so on. Bring your reflections to class or share them privately with your instructor. Because this class invites so much personal growth, your instructor may ask you to complete journal entries several times during the semester. Try to be as honest as you can, not only in a journal but also with your classmates. Is it possible to share too much about a particular topic that might overwhelm others? Whether you are asked to share some of your journal or not, approach it with complete honesty and edit it later. Sometimes I suggest that students write everything down and then remove or black out those portions they want to keep private before they hand in their assignment.

The following are three stimulus sentences you can use to provide a warm-up for your journaling. Each chapter contains several of these starters. Because these are warm-ups, continue writing, even if you feel that you have departed from the original stimulus sentences. After writing for a while, reflect on what you are learning in class and focus on the challenges you face. Feel free to modify these journal starters or create your own.

1. Thinking about my previous relationships with significant others in my life, what are the best and worst parts of my personality? How might these show up in my relationships with clients? What fears do I have about my abilities?

2. Reviewing times in my life when I have not been as successful as I wanted to be, how did I react? What helped me to overcome the problem? How can I best deal with setbacks in my basic skills training? What feelings do I have as I start this process?

3. Reflect on a time when you think that you really helped someone. What did you do and say that seemed to have been especially helpful? Contrast this, if you can, with another time when you tried to help but you were not as successful. What was different about the two situations?

The Nuts and Bolts of Helping

MyCounselingLab™

Visit the MyCounselingLab™ site for *Learning the Art of Helping: Building Blocks and Techniques,* Fifth Edition to enhance your understanding of chapter concepts. You'll have the opportunity to practice your skills through video- and case-based Assignments and Activities as well as Building Counseling Skills units, and to prepare for your certification exam with Practice for Certification quizzes.

Defining Some Important Terms
- What Is Helping?
- Psychological Helping
- Interviewing
- What Are Counseling and Psychotherapy?
- Coaching

How Is Professional Helping Different from Friendship?

What Can You Expect from a Helping Relationship?

Learning Basic Skills and Common Therapeutic Factors

- Therapeutic Building Blocks
- The Importance of the Building Block Skills

Stages of the Helping Process: A Road Map
- Relationship Building: The Heart of Helping
- Assessment Stage
- Goal-Setting Stage
- Intervention and Action Stage
- Evaluation and Reflection Stage

Summary

Exercises
- Group Exercises
- Small Group Discussions
- Written Exercises and Self-Assessment
- Self-Assessment
- Homework
- Journal Starters

In this chapter, you will learn the difference between professional helping and other things that people do, such as teaching and coaching. In addition, you will be introduced to the basic skills, or "building blocks," that make up more complicated counseling techniques that you also will be learning. Because beginning helpers often question how basic skills fit into the larger picture, you will study the theoretical concept of "common therapeutic factors." These are the megaskills that underlie all helping methodologies regardless of theoretical persuasion (Young, 1998). The chapter ends by taking you through the process of a basic helping session. After reading and completing the exercises in this chapter, you should have a framework that will help you organize your learning.

DEFINING SOME IMPORTANT TERMS

What Is Helping?

Helping is a broad term that encompasses all the activities we use to assist another person, whether we have a therapeutic relationship or not. For example, a school administrator who takes time to listen to a crying first grader can utilize helping skills. A foster parent can learn to listen to the child and to the biological parents. A teacher's aide in a sixth-grade classroom can take a nonjudgmental stance when a child talks about why homework is late. Marital partners can help each other deal with disappointments and frustrations. Helping does not require a contract or a professional, confidential relationship. Helping only requires a person desiring help (a client), someone willing and able to give help (a helper), and a conducive setting (Hackney & Cormier, 2005). You can learn helping skills and use them whether you are on the way to becoming a professional or you simply want to help those with whom you live and work. In Table 2.1, we identify some of the major ways that we can help another person, whether physically, financially, spiritually, psychologically, or through advocacy. The table provides examples and cautions, and briefly describes the role of the helper. One of the current controversies in counseling is how much emphasis should be placed on advocacy, or seeking to change unfair social and political systems, rather than on merely helping an individual client. Consider the anecdote about a group of people pulling accident victims from the river without sending anyone upstream to see why people were ending up in the river in the first place. The apparent moral is that we need to prevent people falling in rather than just treat the victims. The problem is that there will always be people falling in the river, and someone still needs to pull them out. Efforts to make our social systems more responsive and just will not entirely replace the need to help individual clients. So, we take the stance that while all counselors should have advocacy skills, they must also have the skills to help the individual, couple, group, or family member. Some helpers are better at working with agencies and institutions, and some helpers are better with families or children, but both are equally important.

TABLE 2.1   Ways of Helping

Ways of Helping	Example	Cautions	Help That Is Not Helping	Role of the Helper	Comment
Physically	Joining Habitat for Humanity to build houses	None	Doing things for people that they can do for themselves makes them dependent.	Laborer	
Financially	Giving money to the Red Cross	Not all organizations make the best use of donated funds. Be sure your donations are used effectively.	Giving money to person on the street can assuage your conscience but may not actually be helping.	Donor	
Advocating at agency or school level	Calling social security to understand application procedures and explaining them to the client	This kind of help is only useful if clients then learns more about how to work the system themselves.	The client may be helped in one situation but not empowered to deal with future situations.	Client Advocate	This is a normal part of every helper's daily work.
Advocating at the socio-political level	Writing letters of complaint or concern to the Veteran's Administration about gaps in service; helping client get on Medicaid	You must have client's permission if advocating for a specific client.	Professional helping requires a client. Most clients are not looking for this kind of help.	Activist	More educators are recommending additional training for helpers in this area.
Spiritually	Encouraging client to pray or meditate, read scriptures, go to church, mosque or temple or utilize spiritual beliefs to aid treatment	Helpers must be aware of their client's background and their own personal biases.	Client may be seeking to avoid or oversimplify problems rather than address them.	Spiritual Advisor	Helpers are becoming more aware of their responsibility to consider this aspect of a person's life and help or refer.

(continued)

Ways of Helping	Example	Cautions	Help That Is Not Helping	Role of the Helper	Comment
Psychologically	Counseling or psycho-therapy to aid client in changing, thoughts, feelings and behaviors	This kind of helping requires a commitment to personal growth and a long period of training and supervision.	Clients can become de-pendent on the relation-ship and the helper must stay alert to when the cli-ent needs to go it alone.	Professional Helper	This book is about help-ing psycho-logically.

Psychological Helping

Although *helping* in the psychological realm is the overarching term we use in Table 2.1, different settings and different contracts between helper and client mean that there are a variety of ways that this kind of helping can be defined (see Figure 2.1). To the newcomer, this can be confusing. The following sections will clarify some of the most common terms, including *interviewing, counseling, psychotherapy,* and *coaching*.

Interviewing

According to the simplest definition, **interviewing** is a conversation between an inter-viewer and an interviewee. During the conversation, the interviewer gathers and records information about the interviewee. In essence, during an interview, the interviewer is eliciting data, not trying to improve the situation of the interviewee. Thus, interviewing is one method of assessment, just like giving a client a paper-and-pencil test. Both assess-ment methods can utilize simple and direct questions or use a fill-in-the-blank approach. Interviews can be *structured* with a series of predetermined questions or *unstructured* with the helper fitting questions in during the flow of the session. There are published structured interviews for a variety of psychological conditions and problems, from eating disorders to depression. If you utilize an intake or history form during the first session

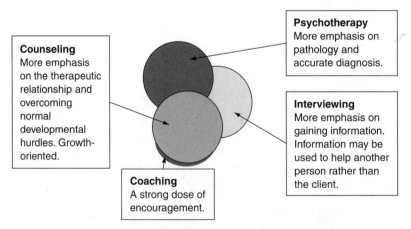

Counseling
More emphasis on the therapeutic relationship and overcoming normal developmental hurdles. Growth-oriented.

Psychotherapy
More emphasis on pathology and accurate diagnosis.

Interviewing
More emphasis on gaining information. Information may be used to help another person rather than the client.

Coaching
A strong dose of encouragement.

FIGURE 2.1   Different Emphases Among Psychotherapy, Counseling, Interviewing, and Coaching Despite these differences, there are many common theoretical underpinnings as well as common skills. The area overlapped by all four circles represents this shared base.

with a client and fill in all the spaces, you are conducting an interview. Interviewing is part of the assessment process that we discuss in more detail later. But it is important to talk about the relationship between assessment and helping early on, so that you can begin to distinguish their separate but complementary roles.

The purpose of an interview may be to help an interviewee or to make a decision about that person. For example, many counseling centers hire intake interviewers who talk with clients and then assign them to the appropriate counselor or refer them to another service or treatment facility. Employers interview applicants for jobs, promotions, or entrance into a special training program. An interview may also be used to test the interviewee's skills, poise, or ability to think in a "live" setting. This is called a *situational* interview. For example, some companies use a stress interview (a type of situational interview) to determine which of their employees can operate best under pressure. The interviewee is "grilled" and even treated disrespectfully to gauge his or her reaction. Many people think that this kind of interview is unethical, but the point is that an interview can provide an opportunity to observe the reaction of a student or employee in a contrived situation similar to actual situations that he or she may encounter. Whenever we interview someone, we want to watch their reaction to the interview because we can learn about how they respond to people.

Helpers interview to determine the appropriateness of counseling for an individual, to assess some skill, or to confirm a diagnosis. These interviews are designed to ultimately benefit the client, but in business settings, the interview is primarily for the benefit of the organization. In clinical settings, interviewing and counseling are rarely separate processes. For example, I was recently seeing a couple for counseling. During the first session, they both wanted to talk about their anger and frustration related to financial difficulties. It seemed clear that they blamed each other for the problem, and each wanted to unload. Although I felt that it was important that they be allowed to express some of these feelings, I had other items on my agenda. I needed to know if financial problems were the only issues. In my experience, couples most frequently complain about the following issues: their inability to communicate, children, in-laws, sex, and finances. I wanted to make sure that I covered each of these areas and that I was not missing something important. It is also essential to know if there has been violence in the relationship, if substance abuse is involved, or if either party suffers from a mental disorder. So I frequently stopped their argument about finances to insert a question about these other areas. In the middle of the session, the wife revealed that she was concerned about her husband's drinking. I immediately took time to ask the husband several questions about his drinking and looked back at the OQ-45, a short test we give to all our clients during the first session. He had marked several of the questions that indicate substance abuse problems. I used the data from the test, from his spouse, and from the client himself to determine the extent of his problem. By the end of the session it was clear that his drinking was a serious problem that needed treatment before we could solve any of the other issues, even their finances. This case demonstrates several important issues. First, helping and interviewing frequently occur during the same therapeutic session. Second, interviewing, as part of the assessment process, can make your helping more effective because it is a way of making sure you are going in the right direction and treating the right problems. Finally, interviewing can be disruptive of the relationship. Clients want to tell you their version of the story, and interviewing is experienced as an intrusion. A helper must go back and forth between helping and interviewing in almost every session because clients bring up new issues as the relationship deepens. It is up to the helper to repair the relationship when clients feel disrupted and to explain the reasons for the interview so the clients understand *your need* to get the whole picture.

In summary, interviewing is utilized in a variety of settings, not all of which are designed to directly help the interviewee. Interviewing is an art whose medium is the relationship; it is not merely a mechanical process of filling in the spaces. A skilled interviewer knows how to quickly develop a working relationship with an interviewee in order to obtain the most relevant information for the decision-making process. The interviewer creates a climate where the interviewee will feel like talking and asks relevant questions to gain vital information. The basic helping skills you learn in this text will help you create this climate of openness, warmth, and acceptance needed for an effective interview. This atmosphere increases the quantity and quality of information obtained. In the assessment chapter (Chapter 10), you will have an opportunity to utilize your helping relationship skills and also learn to interview for key data.

What Are Counseling and Psychotherapy?

Counseling and **psychotherapy** are professional helping services provided by trained individuals who have contracts with their clients to assist them in attaining their goals. Counselors and other psychotherapists use specific techniques to persuade, inform, arouse, motivate, and encourage their clients and to thoroughly assess their issues and backgrounds. Sessions with a counselor or psychotherapist take place on a regularly scheduled basis, usually weekly, and last about 1 hour. A therapeutic relationship will last several months or even several years. Although counselors and psychotherapists may help clients deal with emergencies, they also try to empower clients to address persistent problems in living and make changes that will lead to overall improvement rather than temporary relief. In most states, counselors, social workers, psychologists, marriage and family therapists, and psychiatrists can all practice counseling and psychotherapy in private practice when they have a license. Other individuals without these licenses, such as individuals certified in substance abuse or with a background in human services, can usually practice within an organization under supervision.

In the literature and in practice, the words *counseling* and *psychotherapy* are now used interchangeably. Historically, however, different professional groups have tended to prefer one or the other, creating confusion for professionals and clients. Between 1920 and 1950, *psychotherapy* was used to describe the process of helping clients who were troubled by mental disorders. *Mental disorders* are defined as severe disturbances of mood, thought, and behavior for which there are specific diagnostic criteria. Examples include major depressive disorder, schizophrenia, and panic disorder. For each disorder, there is a list of criteria that the client must meet to possess the diagnosis. The criteria for more than 300 mental disorders are outlined in the *Diagnostic and Statistical Manual* (*DSM*), the American Psychiatric Association's manual, which is the bible of mental disorders (American Psychiatric Association [*DSM-IV-TR*], 2000). Even today, these are the only problems that most health insurance companies recognize as reimbursable. From the beginning, the processes of assessment, diagnosis, and treatment planning have been integral aspects of psychotherapy.

Counseling was invented in the early 1960s as psychotherapy for "normal people." Medical terminology was shunned by counselors, along with words such as *treatment, patient,* and *diagnosis.* Counselors believed in seeing each individual as a unique person, rather than a diagnostic label. For that reason, personality tests and other assessment activities were minimized, and identifying areas of growth rather than dysfunction was emphasized. Counseling was focused more on the counselor/client relationship as the medium for change rather than on the tools and techniques. Although these values are still common among counselors today, the distinctions between counseling and psychotherapy have blurred. Now, counseling includes helping people with mental disorders as well as those experiencing normal developmental problems. Modern counselors routinely use assessment tools, learn diagnostic methods, and engage in treatment planning. By the same token, professionals such as psychologists and marriage and family therapists who prefer the term *psychotherapy* or *therapy* also help clients with difficulties such as adolescent adjustment, marital issues, and the transition to college or work—what we might call "normal problems." Although some may still feel there are good reasons to make distinctions between the terms *counseling* and *psychotherapy,* they will be used interchangeably in this book. Both will refer to the contractual and professional relationship between a trained helper and a client.

Coaching

Coaching is a new term on the mental health scene. Coaching practices are springing up left and right because coaching is not yet regulated by licensing boards and state legislatures, and because there is a market for a helper who is not therapeutic but mostly supportive. Coaching allows individuals without therapeutic degrees to practice professional helping, and it sounds a lot more pleasant than counseling or therapy. But **coaching** is mostly counseling by another name. Here is a definition provided by Whetworth, Kimsey-House, Kimsey-House, and Sandahl (2007): "Coaching is a powerful relationship for people making important changes in their lives" (p. xvii). DuBrin (2005) identifies the following elements of an effective coach: "empathy, active listening, ability to size up people, diplomacy and tact, patience toward people, concern for the welfare of others, self-confidence, non-competitiveness with team members and enthusiasm" (p. ix). About 90% of this definition overlaps with counseling and psychotherapy. What may be different is that the definition of a coach frequently includes a very encouraging cheerleader sort of attitude and the focus on specific achievable goals that the client wants to pursue. Later in this book, we will talk about this issue more. Under what circumstances is this kind of enthusiasm helpful or potentially detrimental? Determine for yourself whether you think coaching is a new approach or merely a marketing strategy (cf. Williams & Davis, 2002).

HOW IS PROFESSIONAL HELPING DIFFERENT FROM FRIENDSHIP?

As you learn the art of **helping,** you will be able to provide friends with a listening ear, a caring attitude, and emotional support, enhancing your relationships and aiding those you care about. There is, however, a difference between friendship and a professional helping relationship; each is built on a distinct contract. A friendship is based on the assumption that we are there for each other—a two-way street. In a **professional helping** relationship, it is the client's issues that are discussed and the client's welfare that is paramount. In exchange, the helper receives compensation for professional services rendered. Consider this analogy: You mention to your friend, who is a dentist, that you have a toothache. She may suggest that you take some aspirin and that you make an appointment with a dentist as soon as possible. Despite her professional capabilities, she probably won't pull out her dental equipment and start drilling in the living room. Although the analogy does not hold completely, helping can also be a painful process best accomplished in a more professional setting. For example, a professional helper is required to identify and articulate issues not normally broached in a friendship, such as painful childhood memories. Moreover, the professional helper is committed to hours of listening, confidentiality, responsibility for the outcome, and disregard for whether the client ultimately likes him or her. The helper's concern, as a professional, is to do a good job, not to maintain a relationship for its own sake.

One reason for drawing the distinction between a professional helping relationship and a friendship is that it is easy to make mistakes in both settings when you begin learning helping skills. You might be tempted to use elaborate techniques on your friends when all they are asking for is support. On the other hand, you might find yourself treating a client as a friend. Remember that with friends you have no agreement or contract for change, but instead you have an opportunity to care, to show concern, and to provide support. In the professional helping relationship, you have a contract to help the client make specific changes in his or her life, not to make a new friend, enjoy each other's company, or discuss the weather, your family, or your favorite hobby. What makes this difficult is that we have learned our natural helping skills in the context of our friendships and family relationships. It is easy to find ourselves being sociable and sympathetic, rather than thinking about how to help the client. It is also easy to act like a therapist with our friends, who may find this behavior intrusive and phony.

Before leaving this topic, let us take a moment to emphasize the importance of a contract in relationships. Eric Berne (1961), the founder of transactional analysis, felt that this was a vital aspect of the helping relationship but was often ignored. Clients must know what they are agreeing to and must participate in the changes that they are about to make. Berne believed that problems in relationships frequently occur because the parties have made assumptions but not outlined their expectations of each other. For example, clients may assume that everything that they say to their counselor is confidential, but it is not. There are several instances where counselors must release information—for example, to prevent harm to others. Some counselors outline the parameters of the helping relationship in a handout that they discuss with their clients. As you become a professional helper, you will recognize how important it is to identify the contract early in the relationship so that people you meet on an airplane and clients you see in your office know if you are a friend or a professional helper.

WHAT CAN YOU EXPECT FROM A HELPING RELATIONSHIP?

Beginners' hopes about what can be achieved in a professional helping relationship are often very grand. When, inevitably, the hopes are dashed, naturally there is disappointment. In this section, we will identify some common unrealistic beliefs about the helping process that many struggle with, and we will examine the corresponding more reasonable expectations.

Unrealistic Belief: I must help clients solve all their problems.

Reasonable Expectation: If all goes well, I may make a good-sized dent in a problem or two and the client will continue to progress when the relationship ends.

Most agencies and private practitioners find that, on average, helpers and clients meet for 6 to 10 sessions. Most clients do not expect long-term relationships, and they come to a helper to deal with specific problems. Indeed, contrary to our expectations, clients who have even just a session or two with a helper are often very satisfied with the results. Helpers must not become disappointed when they want more progress than the client.

Unrealistic Belief: If the client is not motivated, it is my fault.

Reasonable Expectation: Although I can stimulate clients to consider making changes, I cannot force them.

It is estimated that nearly a third of helpers' clients today are involuntary referrals by courts, government agencies, or others. Although clients can be forced to attend sessions, helping is a voluntary relationship. Ethically, we cannot attempt to coerce clients to change. We can supply the opportunities for change, but the client must meet us halfway. We are all ambivalent about change. In the real world, some clients are genuinely opposed to changing their lifestyles, even self-destructive ones. Others know that they need to change but require encouragement. The art of helping involves getting clients to envisage and consider a different kind of life and persuading them to change. For example, when an alcoholic client is sent by the court for treatment, the helper's job is twofold. First, the helper must intensify the client's awareness of the negative consequences of drinking; second, the helper must help the client to see the advantages of sobriety. However, even with detoxification and Alcoholics Anonymous, the odds are less than even that the client will stop drinking.

> *Unrealistic Belief:* If I care about my clients or have good practical experience, that is enough.

> *Reasonable Expectation:* Besides caring and practical experience in the helping field, I must learn all the skills I can.

No matter how good our intentions are, caring about another person is not a substitute for professional knowledge of how to help him or her. A caring physician is, of course, better than one who is indifferent, but the physician must also be well trained and kept fully abreast of his or her specialty through continuing education. Similarly, caring will enhance your helping skills, but it cannot replace them.

Some helpers believe that they are already fully trained. They have practical skills gained in the helping field, and they go on for formal education merely to "have their tickets punched." This is a potentially dangerous attitude. When we see the wide variety and severity of client problems and the new treatments that are cropping up everywhere, it is unreasonable to believe that we can ignore skills training in our formal education or that we can ever really be finished learning.

> *Unrealistic Belief:* If I am a good helper, my client will never need help again.

> *Reasonable Expectation:* If I am successful, the client may consult me again when a similar problem arises.

It is unrealistic to expect that clients will be "cured" in a single encounter with a helper. A family doctor model is a better analogy for the helping relationship. Such a relationship can be revived if the client needs help at a later developmental stage.

> *Unrealistic Belief:* If I am effective with one client, I will be effective with every client.

> *Reasonable Expectation:* I will not be the best match for every client.

Even famous therapists have found that they are not effective with every person who consults them. There are many reasons why a helping relationship may not succeed; some are not under the helper's control. The client may perceive a mismatch because the helper is not of his or her gender, race, or social class. The client may instantly dislike the helper because the helper reminds him or her of someone in the past. It is easy to feel rejected and disappointed if a client does not wish to continue the helping relationship, especially if you feel positive about it.

Unrealistic Belief: It is unacceptable to make a mistake.

Reasonable Expectation: I am a fallible human being who can learn from my mistakes.

If you attend workshops and seminars, you will see well-known counselors and psychotherapists showing videos of their amazing successes. In *The Imperfect Therapist* (1989), Jeffrey Kottler and Diane Blau have suggested that we can learn just as much from our failures, but we rarely talk about them. It is both ego protection and a fear that we are incompetent that keep us from discussing our mistakes with colleagues, supervisors, and teachers. However, if we do not examine these missteps, we are likely to repeat them. This is where reflecting on your learning comes in. Rather than avoiding thinking about mistakes, consider them to be learning opportunities and spend time reviewing them (see the "Stop and Reflect" section in this chapter).

Unrealistic Belief: Sometimes I feel incompetent; therefore, I am not competent.

Reasonable Expectation: There will be many times in my training and work as a helper when I will feel incompetent. It goes with the territory.

No matter how long you have worked as a helper, clients will surprise you. They have problems you have never heard of and problems your supervisor has never encountered. This can be either an assault on your self-esteem or a reminder that you need to keep learning. Although you need to keep abreast of changes in the field and reach the highest level of training that you can, neither a Ph.D. nor a certificate from a training institute will prepare you for everything. Feeling incompetent should motivate you to learn more about a client and his or her problems, but it should not paralyze you. You can seek supervision or possibly refer your client if an honest appraisal of the situation suggests that this would be in the client's best interest.

STOP AND REFLECT

Learning the art of helping is a personal journey that asks you to examine your own ideas and reflect about what you are reading. Try to use the "Stop and Reflect" sections, such as this one, to jot down your thoughts and reactions and then share them with another classmate or small group. You will certainly find other points in the book where your own ideas are challenged. Learn to pause at those moments and contrast the two positions. If you can begin this habit now, you are well on your way to becoming a reflective practitioner.

Start by considering each of the following questions about friendship and helping:

- Have you ever given a friend help that was not well received or that changed the friendship? Discuss with a small group.
- Some people think that our mobile, stressful society has led to a lack of community and has separated us from our extended family. If friendships and family relationships were closer, do you think that professional helping would be needed?
- What would you do if a friend told you that he or she was contemplating suicide? Think about your answer and then discuss it with the class. In what other situations do you think that a professional helper might have an advantage?
- Have you noticed that in group situations you become interested when someone mentions something you agree with or when you have similar backgrounds? This "similar-to-me effect"

has a powerful influence on our connections with people. In a job interview, you may be more apt to hire someone who joined the same sorority, came from your home state, or reminds you of yourself at a younger age. When you look for friends, do you look for someone who is similar to you? Does this search for similarity mean that it is harder to make contact with someone who is quite different? How could one's preference for similar people be a handicap in a helping profession?

LEARNING BASIC SKILLS AND COMMON THERAPEUTIC FACTORS

Basic helping skills are normally taught as small units called microskills (Ivey, 1971). This makes learning easier, but it also creates problems. Individual skills often seem so elementary that students may be confused about why they are important. Students have trouble seeing the big picture because they learn first one piece and then another. One conceptual framework that may help to put these small pieces into the bigger puzzle is understanding that these fundamentals are effective because they evoke common therapeutic factors, or "megaskills" (Young, 1998).

These skills mostly originated as techniques embedded in theories of counseling and psychotherapy. It is estimated that there are between 100 and 500 different theoretical orientations, from cognitive behavioral to psychodrama (Corsini, 2001; Corsini & Wedding, 2008; Herink, 1980; Parloff, 1979). The question is, "Are these different theories calling forth unique healing qualities or are there common things that all helpers do that work?" Common therapeutic factors are thought to be the basic healing properties that underlie all effective counseling theories and techniques (Duncan, Miller, Wampold, & Hubble, 2009; Karson & Fox, 2010). The lifetime work of Jerome Frank (1971, 1981) showed how different theories rely on these factors for their effectiveness. Although helpers seem to be utilizing different techniques, they are actually drawing on similar methods. Frank described six common **therapeutic factors** that seem to cut across theoretical persuasions (Frank & Frank, 1991):

1. Maintaining a strong helper/client relationship
2. Increasing the client's motivation and expectations of help
3. Enhancing the client's sense of mastery or self-efficacy
4. Providing new learning experiences
5. Raising emotional arousal and promoting emotional expression (Later, we make a rationale to include techniques in this category that lower emotional arousal such as relaxation training and meditation.)
6. Providing opportunities to practice new behaviors

Most therapies utilize these therapeutic factors to produce change and are probably more important than theory-specific techniques (Lambert, 2005). One of the best-researched and most potent common factors is the helper/client relationship. Because it is so central to what helpers do, we will examine it in more detail in the next chapter. The therapeutic building blocks or basic skills that you will learn are mainly aimed at helping you maximize this therapeutic factor. By learning to create a climate of openness and listening, you will have the foundation to develop more advanced skills and to implement the other therapeutic factors.

Therapeutic Building Blocks

Therapeutic building blocks is the phrase we use to describe the basic helping skills discussed in the previous section. These are the most fundamental components of the helping interview, such as asking open-ended questions or maintaining eye contact. These building blocks are like the elements of the periodic table we all learned in high school chemistry (I apologize if this brings back traumatic memories). When elements are combined, they form more complex substances, such as oxygen and hydrogen coming together to make water. The therapeutic building blocks represent the foundational behaviors used to create change, but they can be combined into more complex techniques. In this book, we identify 21 therapeutic building blocks. They represent the combined wisdom of many theorists and helpers over time. Although 21 may seem to be an overwhelming number, 9 of the building blocks are quite simple (we call them invitational skills) and very easy to master. The building block skills are divided into six categories (see Table 2.2). Each category represents an important helping activity as follows:

INVITATIONAL SKILLS (NINE SKILLS—CHAPTER 4) Invitational skills are the basic means by which the helper invites the client into a therapeutic relationship. These skills encompass

TABLE 2.2 The Building Block Skills

Skill Category	Building Blocks
Invitational skills	
Nonverbal skills	Eye contact
	Body position
	Attentive silence
	Voice tone
	Gestures and facial expressions
	Physical distance
	Touching
Opening skills	Encouragers
	Door openers
	Minimal encouragers
	Questions
	Open questions
	Closed questions
Reflecting skills	Paraphrasing
	Reflecting feelings
Advanced reflecting skills	Reflecting meaning
	Summarizing
Challenging skills	Giving feedback
	Confrontation
Goal-setting skills	Focusing on the client
	Boiling down the problem
Change techniques	Giving advice
	Giving information
	Alternative interpretation/reframing
	Brainstorming

all the subtle verbal and nonverbal messages that helpers send to encourage a client to open up without applying pressure. For example, imagine how you would feel if the helper constantly checked her watch or looked out the window. You may think that paying attention is only polite, but it is also a skill. Eye contact and attentive body posture are two of the invitational behaviors you will learn and practice in Chapter 4.

REFLECTING SKILLS (TWO SKILLS—CHAPTERS 5 AND 6)   Whereas invitational skills invite clients to tell their stories, reflecting skills let them know that you have heard their stories. Reflections are condensed versions of the facts and emotions the client has conveyed. The helper shares these "snapshots" of the client's story to let the client know that he or she is being understood both in terms of content and at the affective level. When clients feel understood, they disclose more deeply and the important issues begin to surface. These skills take some time to develop. Recognizing and reflecting the gist of the client's story and underlying emotions is something you will practice throughout your training.

ADVANCED REFLECTING SKILLS (TWO SKILLS—CHAPTER 8)   **Advanced** reflecting skills help a client move even deeper than the reflecting skills do. They include **reflecting meaning** and **summarizing**. Advanced reflecting skills are hunches that helpers make and repeat to their clients to see whether they understand the unique impact of their clients' problems beyond the basic facts and feelings. For example, the loss of a job is not just the change in economic status and feelings of loss. Depending on the person, losing a job may also be seen as a sign of failure or evidence of incompetence. Understanding the unique meanings that people assign to events and helping them identify their beliefs about themselves, others, and the world are advanced skills that move clients to deeper self-understanding. Advanced reflecting skills help clients explore.

CHALLENGING SKILLS (TWO SKILLS—CHAPTER 8)   Whereas invitational skills, reflecting skills, and advanced reflecting skills encourage deeper self-examination, challenging skills push clients to recognize discrepancies in their statements. Challenging skills identify incongruities in a client's story and may give information on client strengths and weaknesses. For example, a client who says that he wishes to stop smoking but does not follow any of the suggestions made by the helper might be challenged about the discrepancy between words and behavior. Challenging skills can strain the relationship, but they may also remind clients that the helping relationship is a work project, not a social encounter. **Giving feedback** and **confrontation** are fundamental challenging skills.

GOAL-SETTING SKILLS (TWO SKILLS—CHAPTER 10)   Up to this point, the aim of the skills has been to encourage the client to disclose in as much depth and breadth as possible. Goal-setting skills, however, begin to narrow the focus. The first key goal-setting skill is to keep the client focused on his or her own issues and ask the client to identify the most crucial areas of concern. For example, helpers encourage clients to talk about how they themselves can change, rather than focus on how to change others. The second key helping skill in this area is to "boil down" the problem, which involves shaping a client's vague or unrealistic goals into specific and achievable targets. These building block skills of **focusing on the client** and **boiling down the problem** are needed to help clients develop short- and long-term goals.

CHANGE TECHNIQUES (FOUR SKILLS—CHAPTER 11) Once tentative goals have been collaboratively established, change techniques are employed to help clients achieve those goals. Change techniques outline alternatives for action and press the client to consider new possibilities. **Giving advice** is a commonly misused change technique. Other change techniques include **giving information,** using **alternate interpretation,** and **brainstorming.**

The Importance of the Building Block Skills

We have said that one of the problems confronting most beginning helpers is that they learn elementary skills in isolation and cannot see how the skills fit into a grand scheme. They do not understand how flashy theory-based techniques such as Gestalt's "empty chair" relate to the baby steps they are learning in class. They begin making fun of their own tendencies to say "Um Hmm . . ." and "What I hear you saying is . . . ." They secretly yearn to do what famous therapists do in training films: have a tremendous impact on clients. Just as in basketball or baseball, every helper needs to practice the fundamentals. In sports, when fundamentals are mastered, they are linked into more complex movements, or plays. Without solid fundamentals, the plays are less effective. An example of this principle is shown in the 2010 film, *The Karate Kid.* When the student begins to study karate, his teacher tells him over and over again to pick up his coat and hang it on the rack. At one point, he rebels and angrily confronts his teacher for having wasted his time. The student wants to be Bruce Lee. In a moving scene, the teacher shows him how each of the seemingly unrelated tasks is a fundamental move in the art of Kung Fu. Through repetition, the movements become second nature; when combined in a combat situation, they form an impenetrable defense. Your training in the helping skills will be very similar. You will learn basic helping movements, many of which will seem awkward and repetitive. However, when they are properly learned and put in the appropriate sequence, they form more elaborate and elegant techniques, and they will take on a naturalness that you cannot feel at first. The art of helping begins when the basics have become second nature.

STAGES OF THE HELPING PROCESS: A ROAD MAP

One of the issues beginning counselors face is feeling lost. After listening for a few minutes or a session or two, the student feels that there should be a next step, but what is it? Figure 2.2 presents the stages of the helping process over time. The diagram shows five helper tasks that occur more or less sequentially from the first session to the last. This five-part structure is based on the work of several different writers (Dimond & Havens, 1975; Dimond, Havens, & Jones, 1978; Ivey & Mathews, 1986). The road map shows the typical progression of activities of helper and client through the process. At each stage, for the helping process to progress, something is required from both the helper and the client. For example, at the first stage, *relationship building,* the helper engages in nonverbal activities to build a trusting relationship. The helper does this primarily by using invitational, reflecting, and advanced reflecting skills. If the client is willing, he or she opens up and discloses more fully. Most helpers find that they use a session or two in the beginning just for building the therapeutic relationship and allowing time for the client to open up. Although we have placed this stage at the beginning of the road map, in reality, the relationship is crucial at all the other stages because the strength of the relationship

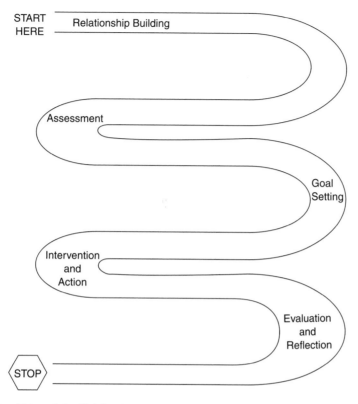

FIGURE 2.2 Road Map of the Helping Process

helps to move the helping process forward and empowers the methods and techniques used later on. For example, a strong therapeutic relationship allows a client to disclose more easily in the assessment stage.

In the second stage, *assessment,* the helper collects information and the client provides it through answers to questions or data from intake forms or tests. In this book, assessment skills are covered in Chapter 9, although we have not included them in the therapeutic building blocks. The reason for not saying more about assessment in this book is that these skills, while important, tend to sidetrack us from our central purpose, which is to learn the fundamentals of a helping relationship. Normally, your course of study will include an entire course on assessment. Many helpers might spend an entire session collecting background data, and some might spend a session or two conducting more in-depth evaluations using tests. However, assessment actually occurs throughout the helping process when a new problem emerges, and the helper takes some time from the session to collect needed information.

The third stage in the helping process is *goal setting.* In goal setting, the client must participate by thinking about and agreeing to the goals that are mutually determined. The helper must use his or her expertise to shape these goals into clear statements and accept only those goals that will lead to real improvement in the client's life. For the client, goal setting can help bring structure when things seem out of control. Goals bring hope and encourage the client to imagine a different future. Still, not all helpers like to set clear, identifiable goals for the helping relationship. Some prefer to let each session unfold and to deal with the issues that arise week to week. Nevertheless, goal setting has become a necessity today because most agencies, hospitals, insurance companies, and managed care companies require detailed lists of goals (called *treatment plans*) for each client. Treatment plans often have specific behaviors that clients must produce in order to accomplish the goal in the expected time frame.

Next, in the *intervention and action* stage, the helper identifies and implements helping techniques to accomplish each of the treatment goals. The helper does this based on his or her theoretical background and training. The client is expected to take action, practice, and do homework to aid in this process. The degree to which this is successful depends largely on three things: the strength of the client/helper bond, the extent to which the goals are really important to the client, and the acceptability of the helper's methods. If the helper implements a technique that is repugnant to the client, is mysterious, or seems to miss the mark, progress will be slowed. Again, the helper must use the therapeutic relationship to make sure that everyone is on the same page and in agreement about goals.

In the *evaluation and reflection* stage, the helper invites the client to think about the progress being made, and together they decide whether to continue the helping relationship. As the client reflects on changes made, the helper also shares his or her evaluation of progress and may utilize standardized outcome measures to give the client feedback.

Evaluation is the last stop in the stages of the helping process depicted in Figure 2.2. Here the helper and client reflect on progress when the problem has significantly diminished. Once a problem has been resolved, the trip either begins again with a new problem or leads to termination of the relationship. The stages of the helping process will become clearer in the case example below. The case is described in the words of Jane, a counselor, whose client, Barbara, was referred by her daughter because of depression.

Relationship Building: The Heart of Helping

Jane: "Barbara is 68 years old with gray hair; she is somewhat slim but apparently in good physical condition. Barbara's husband died 6 months ago, and although she felt that she had handled the first 3 months well, recently she had become depressed and apathetic about life. She reminded me a lot of my grandmother, and I felt an urgency to help her when I realized how much her depression was interfering with her life. She had recently started taking antidepressant medication, but her doctor had insisted that she also receive counseling. Barbara had never seen a counselor before, so I took some time to explain the process to her. She was skeptical—believing nothing could help her—so I spent about half of the first session listening, reflecting, and getting to know her better. I told her a little bit about myself because I sensed that we would not be successful unless she trusted me. Near the end of the session, I told her that we would be working on the feelings of depression that she was experiencing, and I told her about the techniques we might use. We also discussed the issue of confidentiality, and I explained that I could not even discuss our sessions with her daughter without her permission. This seemed to alleviate some of her tension because Barbara saw asking for help as a weakness and was afraid that others would judge her for being depressed. We signed an agreement for treatment that outlined the limits to confidentiality, our goals, and the fees. By the end of the session, Barbara seemed more hopeful about progress, but the work of dealing with her depression was still before us."

At the center of the helping process is the therapeutic relationship, which provides the core conditions or supports for the other activities of the helper. The relationship is the glue or the hub of the helping process. In relationship building, the helper uses invitational skills to convey understanding, to allow the client to open up, and to create a safe environment. This is exactly what Jane did with Barbara during their first session. Jane tried to allay any misgivings that Barbara might have had by developing a personal relationship and by dealing with Barbara's real concern that entering a helping relationship was a sign of weakness. It is obvious in this case that if the relationship were not firmly established, getting needed information in the assessment stage would be extremely difficult.

Assessment Stage

Jane: "When I first saw Barbara, I was a little bit surprised to see that she was well groomed, alert, and talkative. Her depression seemed to have started about 3 months after the death of her second husband, Carl. I took a complete history of Barbara's life and noted a number of losses. Barbara's mother died when Barbara was 20 years old. She had her only daughter at age 28. The next year, she lost a baby through a miscarriage, the complications of which left her unable to have more children. Barbara's first husband subsequently died during military training. In addition to the death of her second husband, Barbara was now coping with financial problems. Carl's will named her as the sole beneficiary, but his children were contesting the will. The family problems and the lack of money were both sources of worry.

"One of the things I did in the very first session was to assess her suicide risk. Barbara denied any suicidal thoughts. She said, 'Sometimes I wish I were dead, but I would never kill myself.' Barbara had strong religious beliefs against suicide, she did not own a gun, and her depression was not so severe that I was worried about her taking her own life. I did call the family physician and asked him to limit the number of antidepressant pills that were issued to Barbara each week to reduce the possibility of an overdose. I diagnosed Barbara's problems as depression stemming from grief and associated stress, with only a small risk of suicide. I also gave her the Beck Depression Inventory and found that she was moderately depressed, which fit with my personal assessment.

"One of the things that I noticed was that any time Barbara identified something she was handling well, she discounted it and seemed to exaggerate the minor deficiencies in her performance. For example, she still went to church twice a week, but she was very discouraged over the fact that it often took her 15 minutes to decide what clothes to wear in the morning. Barbara agreed to keep a journal of her 'negative thoughts' so that we could deal with them in future sessions."

Assessment is the second stage of the helping process. As is apparent in Barbara's case, much of the assessment stage is inseparable from the relationship-building stage because helpers are observing their clients and collecting information from the moment that they first meet. This process continues throughout the helping relationship, but most of the background data pour in during the first few sessions. Some agencies ask that intake forms (sometimes called *psychosocial histories*) be completed and a preliminary diagnosis be made during the first session. The drawback is that a thorough assessment takes several hours, and if the entire first session is spent in gathering information, the client may not return because he or she has not made a real connection with the helper. Clearly, when the relationship is well established, assessment is more complete and easier to accomplish because clients are much better able to freely disclose information about the problem and about themselves.

Assessment includes formal and informal ways that helpers collect information about clients, among them paper-and-pencil tests, client reports, and helper observations. Collecting background data helps us determine whether the services available are appropriate for a particular client and ensures that we are not missing a serious mental disorder such as schizophrenia, a substance abuse problem, or suicidal or violent behavior. Beyond this, assessment is the organizing of data on the client's problem, providing baseline data (the intensity, frequency, and duration of the problem at the beginning), and relevant history.

Goal-Setting Stage

Jane: "In the second session, I started off by giving Barbara a summary of what I had learned so far. She had three major problems as I saw it: feelings of depression that interfered with her life, financial problems, and disruption of family relationships caused by the fight over the will. We both agreed that there was little she could do at the present time to work on the money issues or deal with the legal challenge, as these were longer-term problems. Instead, we decided to focus efforts on reducing her feelings of depression. If she could deal with the depression, she would be better able to move the legal process along. In order to do this, I asked Barbara to think about what she would be doing if the depression lifted and what she would be feeling and thinking. This was easy for her. Barbara said, 'I would be able to play golf again. I would get dressed early every morning, and I would not have these negative thoughts going around in my head.' Using Barbara's ideas, we hammered out some goals for the next few sessions. First, we agreed that we would reduce the negative self-talk by using cognitive therapy techniques. Second, Barbara would become more physically active to overcome her lethargy and help her get back to her old routine. This was more of a challenge than I first expected. Barbara resisted playing golf because she was afraid that friends would notice her depression, and she wanted to appear normal. I encouraged her to accept the fact that being depressed was a normal reaction to the loss of a spouse and that she did not have to expect so much of herself right now. I suggested that by acting 'normal,' Barbara would start to feel 'normal.' "

Once a helper has gained an understanding of the client's problem and the important background issues, it is time to identify the helping goals. Here, Barbara and Jane identified one goal: to reduce Barbara's depression. Two interventions were selected because Jane, the helper, had been trained in these methods. The first intervention was to reduce Barbara's negative self-talk, and the second was to increase her physical activity. In this book, we advance the theory that goals, such as the one set by Barbara and Jane, are a collaborative construction of helper and client. Although goals do not necessarily have to be defined behaviorally, if the desired outcomes are observable, it is easier to know when they have been achieved. For example, if Barbara plays golf three times a week and goes for an evening walk two times a week, we are on target. In the goal-setting phase, professionals draw up treatment plans that state agreed-upon goals and the interventions that will be used to achieve them. This plan instills hope in the client and invites his or her participation as a team player.

Intervention and Action Stage

Jane: "The third session was spent in going over the negative thoughts that Barbara had recorded. When summarized, they seemed to have two persistent themes: 'I should not be depressed,' and 'I am a burden on everyone by being depressed.' These seemed to reflect Barbara's beliefs that she should appear perfect to everyone and that she should not rely on others for help. We discussed the fact that Barbara even felt that she was a burden to me. During the session, we identified some ways of countering her negative thinking by examining the flaws in her negative conclusions. She readily admitted that the thoughts were not logical, but she did not know how to stop them. We suggested that she combat these thoughts in a two-step process. First, stop the thought when she noticed it; second, replace the thought with one that was more constructive. For example, when the thought came up, 'I am a weakling for being depressed,' she was to argue back, 'Feeling this way is a natural part of grieving. I am not perfect; no one is.' We decided to check on how effective these replacement thoughts were at the next meeting. She was to practice 'stopping and inserting' over the next week. During the previous session, I had encouraged Barbara to begin playing golf one time a week as an experiment. I explained that she might not feel 'normal,' but that the exercise would help to reduce the depression. She reluctantly agreed to try it, but at this session Barbara admitted that she had not done so yet."

During the intervention and action stage, professional helpers utilize more advanced skills and ask clients to take active steps to reach their goals. For example, Jane advised Barbara to get some exercise. In this stage, the client is invited to do something to begin solving the problem. As is typical, Jane met with mixed success in getting Barbara to take action. In the case of Barbara and Jane, you might see how important a trusting, confiding, therapeutic relationship is to the success of techniques. At this stage, if Barbara does not have confidence and trust, she will not wholeheartedly engage in the activities suggested by Jane. Barbara is also more likely to complete homework assignments because Jane is expecting her to do so. The relationship becomes a lever to help the client fulfill goals.

Evaluation and Reflection Stage

Jane: "We spent about five sessions working on Barbara's negative thinking and increasing her physical exercise. Although her physician decided to discontinue the antidepressant medication because of severe dizziness, Barbara's depression gradually lifted over this time. Every three or four sessions, I gave Barbara the Beck Depression Inventory and her depression showed a slow but steady decline.

"I asked Barbara to evaluate her progress after about 2 months of counseling. She said, 'Well, I am back to doing most of the things I used to do. I am still very sad sometimes when I think about Carl, and I still have trouble making decisions. That is not totally over. I guess I won't be happy until that is resolved. I am still afraid to be around people too much because I don't want them to see how I feel.'

"I noticed that Barbara's statement still focused on what was missing in her life and underrated the gains she had made. I asked her to give herself a pat on the back for having reduced her depression and increasing her physical activity. She was reluctant to do this, but admitted that things were substantially improved. We also discussed the most recent score on the Beck Depression Inventory, which showed a substantial positive change since her first session.

"I continued to see Barbara for 3 more months. The last month was mainly to monitor her progress and to make certain that changes were lasting. I also referred her to a grief support group at the local hospice, but she declined to attend. At the last session, we set an appointment for 6 months to see how things are going."

Helpers regularly ask their clients to evaluate their progress on goals by reflecting verbally or in writing or by using self-report tests. Also, some time in each session is devoted to gauging the effectiveness of specific techniques and homework. Outcome evaluation also occurs during the final sessions when the helper and client—like Jane and Barbara—review and celebrate the resolution of problems and look at the change from first to last sessions. When client and helper agree that the goals have been reached, either new goals are established or the relationship is terminated.

STOP AND REFLECT

Let us think back for a moment to the case of Jane and Barbara. Jot down your answers to the following questions and discuss them with classmates or your training group.

Relationship Building

Jane was reminded of her grandmother when she first saw Barbara. Because Jane seemed to care about her own grandmother, this created a motive to help Barbara. Can you think of some situations that might arise between Barbara and Jane where Jane's feelings might not have been productive? In your own experience with different age groups, think about whether you feel more comfortable working with children, adults, or older people. Which group will create the biggest challenge for you? Discuss some past experiences that might account for this.

Assessment

One of the first issues Jane assessed was Barbara's suicide potential. All helpers, even those who work with young children, have to make judgments about this in the first few sessions. Because assessing suicide and violent behavior is not an exact science, how do you think you might handle a situation in which you are not certain about a particular client's suicidal intentions? If you were a client, how do you think you would feel about taking tests like the Beck Depression Inventory?

Goal Setting

In the case of Jane, the helper, and Barbara, the client, they both agreed that Barbara needed to deal with her depression, but it was Jane who suggested the goal of increasing physical exercise. Some feel that the helper's job is only to accomplish the client's agenda. Others feel that the helper's expertise and a diagnosis should be the basis of the goals. For example, some would say that because Barbara was depressed, she needed medication and a certain kind of therapy, whether Barbara wished to deal with her depression or not. Who do you think should set the goals in the helping relationship: the helper, the client, or both?

Intervention and Action

In thinking about which techniques to use, Jane mainly focused on cognitive techniques: identifying and replacing negative thoughts. Barbara only reluctantly agreed to the procedure. How do you think you might deal with a client's lack of motivation to work on a problem, do homework assignments, or participate in a particular technique during a session? What might you say?

Evaluation and Reflection

In this stage, Jane highlighted Barbara's successes, but Barbara focused on the fact that she was not 100% back to normal. Why do you think Barbara made this statement? Could she be fearing the termination of the helping relationship? What other issues might be behind her unwillingness to recognize success? How do you think you might deal with her fears about termination or other reasons for her reluctance to celebrate success?

MyCounselingLab™

Go to Topic 2, *Invitational Interviewing*, on the MyCounselingLab™ site (www. MyCounselingLab.com) for *Learning the Art of Helping: Building Blocks and Techniques*, Fifth Edition, where you can:

- Find learning outcomes for *Invitational Interviewing* along with the national standards that connect to these outcomes.
- Complete Assignments and Activities that can help you more deeply understand the chapter content.
- Apply and practice your understanding of the core skills identified in the chapter with the Building Counseling Skills unit.
- Prepare yourself for professional certification with a Practice for Certification quiz.
- Connect to videos through the Video and Resource Library.

MyCounselingLab™ Exercises

Go to the Video and Resource Library on the MyCounselingLab™ site for your text and search for the following clip. *Goal Setting: Mark*, which shows a meeting between Mark and Jackie. Answer the following questions in a sentence or two:

1. The focus of this exercise is on the basic skills of building the relationship. Name two things that Mark does nonverbally that help build this new relationship.
2. Mark is extremely tentative. He says, "Is this right? . . ." "It seems like, you see yourself as a very responsible person." "Am I right? . . ." "I'm wondering if I'm seeing you correctly . . ." "Maybe." Why does he do this?
3. At 1:15:45 Mark makes a thematic summary, tying two or three things together that seem to relate. The client does not see a connection. What response does Mark make to being wrong?
4. What stage do the helper and client reach in this segment? (1) Relationship Building; (2) Assessment; (3) Goal Setting; (4) Intervention and Action; (5) Evaluation and Reflection.

Summary

Helping, interviewing, counseling, coaching, and psychotherapy are all terms that have been used to describe the relationship that identifies goals and brings about positive change. Helping skills are best used within a professional relationship that includes a trained helper and a client seeking help. A therapeutic relationship has special characteristics that differentiate it from other relationships. Among these are a contractual

relationship between helper and client. There are limits to how much one can employ helping skills with personal friends and family.

In this book, you will be learning 21 basic helping skills, or building blocks (see Table 2.2). When combined and elaborated, these building blocks form more complex techniques. It is important to take the time to practice the fundamental skills and gain mastery of them, even if they seem overly simple or awkward.

In the case of Jane and Barbara, we emphasized how crucial this relationship is in accomplishing the goals of the helping relationship. Each of the other stages of helping—assessment, goal setting, intervention and action, and evaluation and reflection—is dependent on the quality of the client/helper bond.

Exercises

GROUP EXERCISES

1. Dividing into Groups and Constructing Questions

Earlier we made the statement that developing an atmosphere that allows the client to feel comfortable and relaxed enhances interviewing. In this exercise, students divide into groups of four or five. Each group develops a list of 20 questions it would like to ask someone about his or her life if the group members wanted to get important information or know the person better.

Structured Interview

When the list is compiled, one member of the group, an interviewer, asks these questions of another person in the group, the interviewee. The interviewee should answer honestly but may pass on any question if it is too personal.

Unstructured Interview

In the second part of the exercise, two new individuals participate in an interview. This time, the interviewer does not use the list. Instead he or she uses 20 interventions to get the interviewee to talk about personal issues in a normal conversational way. The interviewer may want to ask general "open questions," such as "Can you tell me a little bit about your family?" It should be more informal, but the emphasis should be on helping the client feel comfortable and relaxed.

Discussion and Analysis

Finally, the group discusses the two contrasting interviews. What was the effect of each interview style on the interviewees? What are the advantages and disadvantages of each style? In the second unstructured interview, did you obtain the answers to all the questions on the list? What did you get that was new or unexpected in the unstructured situation?

2. One-way versus Two-way Communication

The purpose of this exercise is to become aware of two basic communication forms. An example of one-way communication is when your boss sends you an e-mail or you get a letter from the credit card company. Two-way communication means both people are responding to each other's communication.

For example, you and your friend talk on the phone about a computer problem you are having, and at each step you tell her what you are doing and she helps you solve the problem. This exercise explores these two kinds of communication options. To begin, students find a partner and they sit back to back with one sitting facing the front of the classroom and the other facing towards the back of the room. Using a whiteboard or flipchart, the instructor draws a figure of four connected geometrical shapes, and in the first phase, each front-facing student explains the figure to their rear-facing partner. The rear-facing students draw what they hear their partner describing.

Of course, the rear-facing students *cannot* see the figures and are *not* allowed to speak until they have completed the drawing. When they have completed the drawing, they may stop and show it to their partner and look at the board. In the second part of the exercise, rear-facing students again look away from the board and the instructor draws a different figure of about the same complexity. The rear-facing students still may not look at the board, but this time they are encouraged to stop their partner and ask for specific information. For example, "Is the triangle twice as big as the square? Is the rectangle inside the circle?" When the drawing is complete, each set of partners compares their two drawings. Which took longer? Which one is more accurate? Conduct a class discussion on the advantages and disadvantages of one-way communication. Think about the noise that was going on in the classroom. Did this affect communication?

SMALL GROUP DISCUSSIONS

Discussion 1: Interviewing

Sometimes job interviews are comfortable, and sometimes they are stressful. Do you think there are advantages to making someone uncomfortable in a job interview? Which jobs really require people to react quickly under stress? Discuss some job interviews that you have participated in. What conclusions can you draw about interviewing?

Discussion 2: Energizing

There are a number of high-energy spokespeople who run infomercials and talk about human motivation. Frequently, they suggest that we all have greater potential than we are aware of. Do you think these energizers are helpful? Is this kind of encouragement enough to make people achieve lasting change?

Discussion 3: Types of Helping

Earlier in this chapter, we discussed the various types of helping in Table 2.1. Discuss in a small group the need for counselors to learn advocacy skills. Is this important?

WRITTEN EXERCISES AND SELF-ASSESSMENT

Written Exercise: Stages of the Road Map

To get a better idea of the helping process, let us examine the five stages shown in Figure 2.2. Think about a problem that you are experiencing. It can be a small problem you are now facing or an issue from the past that you can pretend is an issue today. Jot down your answers to the following questions about each stage of the helping process and the helper who might be assisting you.

a. Relationship building:

How important would it be for a helper to be warm and inviting, or would you prefer a more businesslike atmosphere?

How much would you like the helper to say about himself or herself?

How long do you think it would take before you trusted a helper enough to disclose something extremely personal?

What sort of personal characteristics would you want in a helper?

b. Assessment:

What important issues would a helper have to find out about you, your family, your environment, your goals, your cultural and religious background, and your history before he or she could help you?

How would you feel about spending the first session answering questions about your problem?

How might you respond to the helper's request that you complete tests or inventories?

c. Goal setting:

Imagine yourself without the problem. What would you be doing, thinking, or feeling that you are not experiencing now?

Can you turn your problem into a goal? For example, rather than stating the problem, "I bite my fingernails," transform it into a future scenario, such as "I would like to have attractive nails that I would not be ashamed of in public."

d. Intervention and action:

What kind of approach by a helper would you object to? Is there anything that immediately comes to mind that you might want the helper to do? React to each of the interventions below as to whether you would want the helper to use this specific technique. If the problem you have selected does not really fit with a particular technique, just leave it blank.

With my chosen problem, I would most like to:

Listen to advice about how to solve my problem

Write in a journal to express my feelings

Just have someone to listen (no advice)

Keep a record of specific behaviors

Role-play my problem

Enter group therapy and hear the reactions of others

Bring a family member with me to a session

Complete an assignment to say no to others more often

Hear a story by the helper about how he or she handled a similar problem

Other (anything here that you think would help)

e. Evaluation and reflection:

How would you know that you had definitely completed your goal?

How would you be thinking, feeling, and acting when you had accomplished it?

SELF-ASSESSMENT

Efficacy and Self-Esteem

One of the common therapeutic factors mentioned in this chapter involves enhancing client efficacy and self-esteem. Efficacy is the expectation that you can do something well. For example, you may be confident about your ability to sit down at a keyboard and type. If you are considering a career in a helping profession, you probably possess some crucial skills already. Think about what you are good at when it comes to dealing with other people. While you are learning new skills, it is important to remember your present strengths and find a way to incorporate them with your new helping skills. How do you rate yourself on the following skills? I am confident that I can:

1. Talk to people about serious and painful subjects without being overwhelmed.

1   2   3   4   5   6   7   8   9   10

Not at all confident   *Very confident*

2. Chat, make small talk, and keep a conversation going.

1   2   3   4   5   6   7   8   9   10

Not at all confident   *Very confident*

3. Make people feel comfortable.

1   2   3   4   5   6   7   8   9   10

Not at all confident   *Very confident*

4. Allow other people to cry or express emotions.

1   2   3   4   5   6   7   8   9   10

Not at all confident   *Very confident*

5. Help people figure out answers to their problems.

1   2   3   4   5   6   7   8   9   10

Not at all confident   *Very confident*

6. Make people think by posing challenging questions.

1   2   3   4   5   6   7   8   9   10

Not at all confident   *Very confident*

7. Talk about myself, my feelings, and my ideas.

1   2   3   4   5   6   7   8   9   10

Not at all confident   *Very confident*

8. Challenge people when they are not being honest with themselves.

1   2   3   4   5   6   7   8   9   10

Not at all confident   *Very confident*

9. Describe any other skill that you have that you might be able to transfer to the helping relationship.

1   2   3   4   5   6   7   8   9   10

Not at all confident   *Very confident*

HOMEWORK

Homework 1: Unrealistic Beliefs

Go over the list of unrealistic beliefs about helping and the corresponding reasonable expectations given in this chapter. Identify two or three that you think might create difficulties for you in the helping relationship. Write a paragraph about each belief giving your reactions and indicate how you might deal with that thought if it should arise in your interaction with a client. Alternatively, identify some of the beliefs you have about helping that you think are realistic.

Homework 2: Involvement with Clients

You will sometimes hear helpers talk about being "over involved" with clients, and they may sometimes suggest that you "keep a professional distance." What kinds of behaviors do you think would indicate that a helper was too involved in a client's life? What limits should the helper set in the relationship? Does this necessarily mean that the helper should not care about a client? What ethical guidelines do professional helpers rely on to determine whether the professional relationship has become too close? Write down your reaction to these questions in a page or two.

JOURNAL STARTERS

Rescuing is sometimes defined as doing more than 50% of the work in a helping relationship. Have you ever tried to help someone who did not put forth much effort to help himself or herself? How did you end up feeling? As you think about that, how do you believe this affected your relationship with that person? What do you think it would be like to work with someone who may not really want to be helped? Is it ethical?

The Therapeutic Relationship

In the beginning was the relationship.

MARTIN BUBER

MyCounselingLab™

Visit the MyCounselingLab™ site for *Learning the Art of Helping: Building Blocks and Techniques,* Fifth Edition to enhance your understanding of chapter concepts. You'll have the opportunity to practice your skills through video- and case-based Assignments and Activities as well as Building Counseling Skills units, and to prepare for your certification exam with Practice for Certification quizzes.

Summary

Exercises

• Group Exercises

• Small Group Discussions

• Written Exercises and Self-Assessment

• Homework

• Journal Starters

The last chapter talked about the high expectations helpers have for themselves in the helping relationship. It also highlighted the differences between a therapeutic relationship and a friendship. But what is so special about this helping relationship? This chapter digs a little bit deeper into the mystery of the interaction between client and helper, discussing briefly why helpers and researchers place so much emphasis on it. More practically, you will learn how you can build such a relationship with another person. Finally, you will learn about mistakes that can be made that strain or weaken the helping relationship and the knotty problems of transference and countertransference. Before addressing these important issues, though, let us take a look at a real client's recollection of the helping relationship in her own words:

> I came to counseling because my husband was having an affair, and I was devastated over the impending breakup of my marriage. I was anxious, depressed, and having trouble eating and sleeping. I was like a zombie at work. I don't want to give the impression that I am a weak person. I had always been the kind of person others leaned on. This was the first time I had ever been so needy. I felt like the rug had been pulled out from under my life.
>
> I heard that Jim was the best therapist in the area, so I called to make an appointment. Jim was a minister who also had a degree in counseling. Although I am not a Christian, I am very spiritually oriented, and I wanted someone who could understand that side of me. In many ways, Jim fit perfectly my ideas of what a helper should be. He was older than me by 25 years and had gray hair, and I had heard that he had been happily married for many years to another therapist in the area. I had also heard that he studied with some famous teachers. My expectations were high, and I was desperate.
>
> At our first meeting, Jim got up to greet me at the door, shook my hand warmly with both of his, ushering me into his crowded office. Then, I had one of the most powerful experiences of my life. He listened to me for the next half hour as though nothing else in the world was more important. I had talked to a few friends about the situation, but he seemed to make me feel that there was all the time in the world, and I sensed that all my problems were no burden to him. Although I cried through much of the first session, Jim remained calm and at the end offered some hope. First, he asked me the question, "What holds you together?" I then talked about my spiritual beliefs. It made me realize that I could rely on that to help me through this crisis. Later, he commented, "I don't think it is time to give up on this yet." Having that light at the end of the tunnel made a lot of difference. I was able to hold on for a few weeks while things sorted themselves out. I continued to see Jim over the next few months.
>
> Once, I came to a session and found that there was a mix-up in communication and only a half hour of my session remained. I was upset because I really needed to talk to someone. I was bursting with sadness and anger. That night I dreamt that I was sitting in Jim's waiting room and everybody else was allowed to go in except me. Even though it wasn't his fault, I felt displaced. When we talked about it in the counseling session, Jim said, "I guess it was hard for you to face another rejection." This really helped me become aware of how discarded and unwanted I felt in my relationship with my husband. I also felt sick to my stomach when I realized how dependent I had become on my therapist. As time went on, I became stronger and was able to handle my problems much better. Knowing Jim was there was a great comfort sometimes. At other times,

I was frustrated that when I needed to talk to him, it was still 3 or 4 days until our session. For some irrational reason, it made me mad that he was not available when I called.

After 4 or 5 months, Jim told me one day that he thought I had become too dependent on the relationship and that we needed to reduce our sessions to once per month. I agreed that things were better and silently assented to this new arrangement. After that session, I met a friend for lunch, and as we went through the buffet line, I took three knives, three forks, three spoons, and four napkins. I was so disoriented by powerful feelings, I could hardly concentrate. Part of me saw Jim's reducing our sessions as a form of confidence in me. But I also felt suddenly adrift. It took 6 months or so before I was able to really get back on solid ground and feel a sense of confidence.

I feel that I owe Jim a debt that I can never adequately repay. He helped me survive during the lowest period of my life. I don't idealize him any longer, but I recognize his caring and his undivided attention as one of the things that pulled me through.

ALICIA B.

Alicia's story illustrates the power that a therapeutic relationship can have to pull us through difficult times, and it also reveals that strong emotions can be evoked when the relationship is threatened. Not all helping relationships are so intense, and sometimes the relationship does not even gel despite the best efforts of the helper. Still, there are a number of things you can do to make such a relationship possible, and there are also things you can do to repair the relationship when it is strained. Before we address those issues, let us take some time to review the critical nature of the relationship in a time when evidence-based techniques seem to be more valued than are evidence-based relationships (Norcross, 2011).

THE IMPORTANCE OF THE THERAPEUTIC RELATIONSHIP IN CREATING CHANGE

One of the ongoing dilemmas for a helper is the tension between relationship and technique. How much emphasis should be placed on making sure that the helper/client relationship has been established? Is it better to make certain you understand how to utilize a particular method of treatment? Of course, you want to be on the cutting edge by knowing the newest and the most effective techniques available to help your client. Many treatments have now been standardized and recorded in manuals.

For example, there are manualized treatments for various kinds of depression, anxiety, sexual abuse, and so on. This standardization has led to a better ability to evaluate treatments and to devise better ways to teach these techniques to clients. Some argue that too much emphasis has been made on the techniques of helping and too little on the therapeutic relationship, the heart of helping (Erskine, 1998; Kelly, 1994; Norcross, 2011).

There is strong research support for the contention that the relationship is a key factor in client success (Horvath & Bedi, 2002; Ilgen, Tiet, & Finney, 2006). Lambert (1986) and others indicate that utilizing effective techniques accounts for some of the success in helping but that the *therapeutic relationship* accounts for about twice as much as technique. Therapists and researchers have long recognized the importance of a strong working alliance in potentiating change (Bachelor & Horvath, 1999; Belkin, 1980; Fiedler, 1950; Horvath & Greenberg, 1994). From behaviorists Kanfer and Goldstein (1986) to Carl Rogers (1957), helpers have indicated that achieving client goals is much more likely in a good relationship. In fact, the quality of the therapeutic relationship appears to be more predictive of success than the theoretical approach of the helper (Nuttall, 2002). It is truly a common therapeutic factor among all theoretical approaches (Hubble, Duncan, & Miller, 1999). The therapeutic relationship is crucial in all modalities of helping including group work, working with children and adolescents, and working with couples and families (cf. Norcross, 2011).

The helper/client relationship is also an important factor in understanding why clients drop out of counseling in the first few sessions. Often, clients drop out because they feel uncomfortable with the helper, do not like the helper, or decide that the helper is not capable of helping. So the power of the therapeutic relationship not only is vital to creating improvement, but also must be created immediately to prevent attrition. Think about how you might feel if you went to a physician and, although he or she appeared to have a lot of technical skill, the physician showed no warmth or concern and did not seem to listen. You might complain, but more likely, you would "vote with your feet" by not returning. As in any professional relationship, if the helper does not instill confidence and communicate warmth and acceptance in the first few sessions, the client's fragile hopes may be dashed, and he or she will give up on the helper or even give up on seeking professional help altogether.

The central importance of the relationship in the helping process is portrayed in Figure 3.1, which shows the six therapeutic factors which we introduced in Chapter 2. The therapeutic relationship is shown at the center of the diagram to suggest that the other factors depend, to a large extent, on the power of the relationship for their effectiveness. It is also true that each stage on the road map of the helping process—relationship building, assessment, goal setting, intervention and action, and evaluation and reflection—all require the presence of a strong, cooperative relationship between helper and client in order to move through these steps (see Figure 2.2).

FIGURE 3.1 Six Common Therapeutic Factors

Obtaining a full and accurate assessment, for example, requires that the client feel safe enough to disclose the good, the bad, and the ugly. In this chapter, you will learn skills to enhance the relationship, so as to maximize the effectiveness of the other therapeutic factors and to identify and reduce impediments to the relationship that can lead to client dropout and slower progress.

The Unique Characteristics of a Therapeutic Relationship

Professional helping relies on a special therapeutic relationship involving a trained helper and a client wanting help. There is a definite relationship between the client's and the helper's rating of client progress and their confidence in the helping relationship (Clemence, Hilsenroth, Ackerman, Strassle, & Handler, 2005). More importantly, stronger therapeutic alliances are linked with better outcomes (symptom improvement) (Ackerman & Hilsenroth, 2003; Dinger, Strack, Sachsse, & Schauenberg, 2009; Horvath & Bedi, 2002; Horvath, Del Re, Flückiger & Symonds, 2011). But how do you know when such a relationship has been established? In the previous chapter, we talked about the difference between friendship and a helping relationship. Keep this difference in mind as you look over this list of elements in the therapeutic relationship:

There is a mutual liking—or at least respect: A therapeutic relationship has at its base respect. Does the therapeutic relationship have to be one where client and helper have mutual fondness? Perhaps not, but at least the helper conveys respect for the client's autonomy, and the client respects the helper's expertise. Without this, a real alliance may not be possible. This does not mean that the client cannot be helped; it means that one of the therapeutic factors is not being used to its potential and that any change will probably be the result of other therapeutic factors.

The purpose of the relationship is the resolution of the client's issues: Compared with other relationships, the helper/client dyad is unbalanced in favor of the client. Even if the client invites it, the helper does not ask for or receive support from the client. It is a one-way street where the helper is the giver. The helper's own issues are dealt with outside of the client's hour. The helper shares only to aid the client.

There is a sense of teamwork as both helper and client work toward a mutually agreed-upon goal: The client can draw strength from the fact that the helper is there to provide support for change in the mutually decided direction. Just as a friend might become your ally in quitting smoking or maintaining an exercise program, the client feels the helper's presence as a constant nudge to grow.

Safety and trust are established, allowing honest disclosure by the client and feedback from the helper. There is a contract specifying what will be disclosed to others outside of the relationship: Unlike a friendship at work, confidences with a family member, or feelings shared with a neighbor, the client begins to realize that secrets will not circulate. As the client experiences this safety, he or she begins to discuss deeper and deeper issues. At times, the helping relationship requires the helper to give the client honest feedback or nonjudgmental information about the client's behavior.

There is an agreement about compensation for the helper: Although some helpers may be volunteers, most receive credit or money for each client hour. Even the volunteer may benefit by listing the work experience on his or her résumé. At the beginning of the relationship, helper and client discuss compensation. Help from a professional is usually not a gift but a fee-for-services relationship.

There is an understanding that the relationship is confined to the counseling sessions and does not overlap into the participants' personal lives: As a general rule, helpers try to devote regularly scheduled times to a client. Crises are exceptions to the rule, but nearly all helpers have a system for dealing with emergent problems. Most helpers give out a 24-hour crisis hotline number rather than their home phone number. They do not interact socially with clients when it can be avoided so that objectivity is not strained by other considerations.

As a contractual relationship, the relationship can be terminated at any time: A unique aspect of the helping relationship is that once the client has reached the identified goals, the helping relationship is put on hold until some future help is needed. The relationship can be ended by either party at any time. Sometimes agencies specify how many sessions a client may be seen, and frequently insurance companies limit their payments to a certain time frame. Generally, the helper terminates the relationship when sufficient progress has been made or if the client is not making progress at all. Sometimes the relationship is ended by referral to another helper. Referral may be necessary when special needs are detected such as a need for sex therapy or substance abuse treatment.

What Clients Say

A client's judgment about the strength of the therapeutic bond is a better predictor of client progress than the helper's (Bedi, Davis, & Williams, 2005). Thus it is critical to know what clients can tell us that weakens or strengthens the relationship. When clients were asked about incidents that helped establish a solid relationship with the helper, among others, the clients mentioned the following helper behaviors:

1. The helper taught me a technique, such as making a list of goals.
2. The helper showed good nonverbals, such as eye contact and leaning forward.
3. The helper showed good listening behaviors: remembering what was said and paraphrasing.
4. The helper self-disclosed that he or she had had a similar experience.
5. The helper encouraged me by making comments, including pointing out strengths.
6. The helper emphasized that it was my choice and that I knew myself best.
7. The helper was open to my criticism about the structure of the sessions or what he or she said.
8. The helper validated my feelings and gave me support.
9. The helper greeted me, introduced himself or herself, and said goodbye. I had a positive first impression.
10. The helper used humor.
11. The helper's office environment helped to enhance the relationship (including relevant books).
12. I liked some personal characteristics of the helper (well groomed, similar background).
13. The helper normalized the feelings I was having.
14. The helper came highly recommended.

15. The helper was honest and frank.
16. The helper explained how therapy would work.
17. The helper went beyond a business relationship and made extra efforts to help.

Clients in another study (Lilliengren & Werbart, 2005) were asked to identify the most helpful things they experienced in the helping process as a whole. They mentioned:

1. Labeling and expressing feelings.
2. Using the relationship as a nonjudgmental space where they could open up to a supportive person.
3. Becoming more aware of themselves through self-exploration.
4. Finding new ways of relating to people because of their experience in the therapeutic relationship.
5. Having therapists ask questions and summarize to help them find patterns in their lives.

HOW CAN A HELPER CREATE A THERAPEUTIC RELATIONSHIP?

So far, we have examined the therapeutic relationship from the perspective of a client and heard about its importance and special characteristics. But how can a helper create this special experience? Before looking at the following suggestions, remember that you probably already know some of the ways to make a relationship work. You may have found that people naturally seek you out for help already. It is important to recognize your natural abilities and not discount them as you eliminate some behaviors and try out new ones. On the other hand, it is important to recognize that creating a therapeutic relationship is a skill that must be learned (Wachtel, 2011).

Relationship Enhancers

Frederick Kanfer and Arnold Goldstein (1986) identified key *relationship enhancers* or helper behaviors that improve the quality of the therapeutic relationship. They include some nonverbal skills such as posture, as well as empathy and self-disclosure. These helper behaviors lead to the emotional qualities or *relationship components*: liking, respect, and trust. In other words, the relationship enhancers create a favorable emotional climate for helping. Naturally, the presence of liking, respect, and trust has *relationship consequences*. They are communication, openness, and persuasibility. If we like, respect, and trust someone, there is a free flow of information—no holding back—and that person's suggestions hold more weight. Furthermore, when there is communication, openness, and persuasibility, there is the possibility of change. Thus, the very small helper behaviors called *relationship enhancers* cannot be ignored because they lead ultimately to the kind of safe and open relationship that gives the client the courage to change. Because the focus in this part of the chapter is on creating and enhancing the therapeutic relationship, let us look at two relationship enhancers (empathy and self-disclosure) in a little more detail. Nonverbal behaviors such as posture will be discussed in a later, more in-depth discussion.

PHYSICAL CLOSENESS, POSTURE, AND WARMTH   In the next chapter, you will learn the basic skills associated with physical distance, the creation of a warm atmosphere for helping, posture, and other body language skills. These nonverbals invite the client into a safe relationship and lead to greater openness. Although these may seem like small things, the ability to create an inviting relationship can have a powerful effect on others in all kinds of situations (Purkey, 1987). Let us assume that you are going for two different job interviews. In the first case, the interviewer greets you by shaking your hand. Her voice is friendly and informal. When you arrive at her office, she smiles and welcomes you. Then she sits down in a chair next to you, turning it around so she can face you directly. Contrast this scenario with another office in which a secretary ushers you into the interviewer. The interviewer greets you from behind her desk. She spends much of the session staring at a file and making notes as she asks direct questions about your history. Under which circumstances are you likely to feel the most comfortable and to open up about your past? In which situation are you most able to convey information you would like the potential employer to know? If one of these interviewers were to ask you to say something very personal about yourself, to whom would you be most likely to disclose? Although interviewing is not necessarily a helping relationship, even in this circumstance it is easy to see how powerful the small nonverbal enhancers can be in eliciting greater communication, openness, and persuasibility.

EMPATHY   The word *empathy* is related to the German word *Einfühlung*, which means "feeling oneself into" another person's experience. Empathy means that you grasp the facts, the feelings, and the significance of another person's story; more important, empathy involves the ability to *convey* your accurate perceptions to the other person.

There is a vast literature on the importance of empathy. Although much of it focuses on the helping relationship, empathy has proved to be a vital aspect of other interpersonal situations. Empathy training has been found to be an essential in good leadership and parenting (Gordon, 1986). Stephen Covey, in *The 7 Habits of Highly Effective People* (1990), recommends seeking "first to understand then to be understood" as one of the ingredients of personal job success regardless of your profession.

Recent news events have focused on alienated adults and teenagers who seem to lack any recognition of the feelings and needs of others. One group of researchers has suggested that this is due to a trend in young people becoming more and more self-centered and narcissistic (Twenge, Konrath, Foster, Campbell & Bushman, 2008). Reality television shows, Facebook, MySpace, and *American Idol* auditions are filled with examples of exaggerated self-perceptions. The problem is that being overly concerned with one's own success and needs prevents us from focusing with empathy on the concerns of others. The book *Emotional Intelligence*, by Daniel Goleman (2006), suggests training in emotional awareness as the long-term cure for this condition in our society. Goleman's research shows that awareness of one's own emotions and those of others is among the most important predictors of success, mental health, happy families, and friendships. In summary, beyond its uses in helping, the skills of empathy can have a positive spillover into other areas of a person's life.

NEUROSCIENCE AND EMPATHY   There is growing evidence that human beings are biologically attuned to others. Recently there has been a lot of talk about the discovery of mirror neurons, which are brain cells that fire when we see another person performing an action (Decety, & Ickes, 2009). We automatically put ourselves in the other person's position if we pay attention. Note how your facial muscles cringe when you see someone about to fall. Understanding people through empathy gives us a deeper understanding because we are, to some extent, feeling what the other person is feeling (Dimberg, Andréasson, & Thunberg, 2011; Trout, 2010).

In his book, *Social Intelligence*, Daniel Goleman explains how developing our social IQ is vital to interpersonal functioning in our intimate relationships (Goleman, 2006). He also points out one of the prime benefits of empathy—besides perspective taking— is that it soothes the other person's emotional arousal. A spate of other books, bolstered by these findings in neuroscience, have focused on the business (Patanaik, 2009) and relationship advantages of empathy (de Waal, 2009; Iacomboni, 2009).

Helper Empathy   The special thing about empathy in the helping relationship is that here the term encompasses the experiences of both client and helper. Empathy does not occur in this situation if the helper has not communicated understanding to the client. If the helper hears the story only superficially or appears judgmental, even if he or she is accurate about the facts, the client does not experience the helper's empathy. Empathy occurs when the client feels and may even say, "That's it! That's how I feel!" If we further analyze this statement, it could be said that a client experiences empathy when the helper communicates that he or she understands the facts, the emotions, and the special meanings of the client's story.

Empathy and Differences   Empathy is a crucial skill in overcoming cultural, gender, and other differences between client and helper. Empathy means taking a "tutorial stance" rather than an authoritarian position when we are confronted with a person's life experience that clashes with our own. A *tutorial stance* means that the helper becomes a learner, seeking to understand the client—recognizing that the helper must learn from the client what it is like to be that person.

Racism and prejudices about various cultural groups can be seen as a form of narcissism or self-absorption. We become so attached to our own perspective that we have no tolerance for those who do not share it. Of course, we all come to an interpersonal situation with cultural "baggage" and a worldview that contains prejudices of one kind or another. These will show up in our verbal and nonverbal messages. Clients recognize our attitudes not only from the things we say, but also by body language that may signal subtle disapproval. The next chapter takes up the issue of how to deal with these kinds of differences.

Empathy is a first step in moving us away from our ethnocentric narcissism and signals to clients that we are trying to "feel ourselves into" their world, rather than attempting to convert them to our perspective. Although empathy provides a doorway to the inner life of another person, is it really ever possible to enter that world completely, leaving behind the vestiges of our own beliefs? We may not be able to completely grasp another person's reality; however, it is important that our clients recognize that we are struggling to understand and that we care enough to try.

What Empathy Isn't   *Empathy is not merely supporting or agreeing with the client.* Consider the following story related by a school counselor:

> Last week, I saw 17-year-old Monique, a young woman who has been accepted to college with a full scholarship. She has a keen intellect and is especially good in math. She has always preferred older men, and now she has become pregnant by a man, David, who is 15 years older than she is. Recently, she found out that he was lying to

her about his relationships with other women and that he had even lied to her about his job, saying that he was an architect when, in fact, he is a paraprofessional in an architect's office. Her parents have told her she cannot remain in their home because they do not wish to raise another child. Although David will support her, she is afraid of him because she has heard he can become violent. Monique is also afraid to stay with him and feels that if she has a child with him, they will be bonded forever. She is considering an abortion because she feels that she misjudged him and cannot see a good future for herself or the child.

This situation presented a dilemma for the helper because, although she could empathize with the client's situation, she felt that by empathizing she was supporting the client's decision to obtain an abortion. Many helpers are afraid to empathize with a client for fear of taking sides. In fact, though, empathy can help clients examine their feelings at a deeper level and make decisions that are more consistent with their own feelings and values. You can communicate understanding about the circumstances that spawned the problem without supporting or agreeing with the client's subsequent action.

Empathy Is Not Pretending to Understand.   In the next chapters, you will learn some techniques to help you communicate empathy to clients. You will discover, however, that empathy is not effective if it is not sincere. Clients pick up on the nonverbals as well as on what you say. Merely saying the prescribed formula will not help the client if you truly do not understand the situation. The best advice for the beginning helper is to be patient. Spend as much time as you need to hear the story before you tell the client that you understand.

Empathy Is Not Taking on Your Client's Problems.   For the most part, helper fears about being overwhelmed by the client's problems are unfounded. Empathic people try to understand another person's pain in order to relieve it (Johnson, 1990). Consequently, it may be natural to fear that problems are "catching" and that by entering another person's world too deeply, we may become depressed ourselves. Although it is impossible not to be affected in some way by great pain, you learn over time to deal with it within the session and not let it hamper your time with the next person or carry over into your personal life. The great therapist Frieda Fromm-Reichmann (1960) claimed that we must learn to be like skin divers able to go to the depth of a client's problems, but also able to surface when we need to.

Empathy Is Not Sympathy.   Sympathy is a synonym for pity. No one likes to receive pity because it suggests that the sufferer is somehow less than the other person. Nietzsche (1920) contended that pity for someone creates a power imbalance that makes the pitied person resentful, because, in some sense, the person's dignity is being attacked. Thus, sympathy is not compatible with a positive, nonhierarchical relationship.

Empathy Is Not a One-time Behavior.   Although empathy is especially important in the relationship-building stage of the helping process, empathy is crucial throughout. As the relationship develops, the client may disclose more and more deeply. For example, as marriage counseling progresses, instead of talking about the problems the kids are having at school, a couple might begin to examine their attitudes about child rearing and their disagreements about how to discipline. These very personal topics might require the helper to empathize at a deeper level, trying to understand their perspectives and how these were shaped by their own families.

SELF-DISCLOSURE AND THE THERAPEUTIC RELATIONSHIP

> *If we hold that the ideal therapeutic relationship is one of genuineness and authenticity, then shouldn't the therapist be a real person in the therapy process? As real in the therapy hour as outside of it?*
>
> (YALOM, 1999, P. 253).

How can we become *real*, as Yalom recommends, and be helpful at the same time? Should not our authenticity and self-disclosure be tempered with concern for the client? Indeed, Carl Rogers (1972) cautions that disclosure by the helper must be "appropriate" (p. 129). Self-disclosure is not initiated to develop a social relationship or to allow the helper to ventilate feelings (Weiner, 1979). As a strategy in helping, it is high-risk/high-gain (Farber, 2006). It has great potential, yet it must be used with care. For many reasons, some writers feel that beginning helpers should avoid self-disclosure altogether. The point of view of this text is that by discussing its ramifications now, you will be better prepared to disclose appropriately when the opportunity arises.

Helper self-disclosure has been shown to be associated with positive outcomes for clients (Barrett & Berman, 2001; Hill & Knox, 2002; Lilliengren & Werbart, 2005). It has been shown to increase trust in the relationship (Johnson & Matross, 1977; Jourard, 1971), make the helper more attractive (Goodyear & Schumate, 1996), deepen client self-disclosure, and encourage expression of feelings (McCarthy, 2001; Nilsson, Strassberg, & Bannon, 1979; Sermat & Smythe, 1973). It appears that moderate levels of self-disclosure are better than highly personal or only mildly personal disclosures (Bannikotes, Kubinski, & Purcell, 1981; Edwards & Murdock, 1994).

The research on self-disclosure has come to differentiate between *self-disclosing* and *self-involving* statements by the helper (Cashwell, Shcherbakova, & Cashwell, 2003; McCarthy, 1979, 1982). Helper self-disclosure occurs when the helper relates facts about himself or herself. Self-involving statements occur when the helper shares his or her thoughts and emotions about the client. To show this distinction, take a look at the two helper statements below:

> "You said you wanted to know a little bit about me. I have been practicing for the last 7 years in this area, but I grew up in New England where most of my family still lives. I'm married and have three children. My practice here centers on individuals going through divorce. I also run couples groups, which I really like." (self-disclosing statement)

> "I've noticed in the past few weeks that you seem to be irritated whenever I bring up the fact that you have not been looking for work. I am wondering if it is just too stressful a topic, and I find myself being reluctant to mention this even though it is one of the main problems we agreed to work on." (self-involving statement)

In general, research has supported self-involving statements (Curtis, Field, Knaan-Kostman, & Mannix, 2004), but has not always endorsed self-disclosure (Cashwell et al., 2003; Knox, Hess, Petersen, & Hill, 1997; Watkins, 1990). One reason is that much seems to depend on the client's preference for self-disclosure (Cashwell et al., 2003). In other words, clients vary in how much disclosure they can handle without feeling that the helper is too self-focused or unprofessional. Second, it appears that timing is important. Self-disclosing statements (facts about the helper) are more useful early in treatment, whereas self-involving statements may be more effective later on (McCarthy, 2001). Finally, there are all kinds of disclosures, ranging from the superficial "I have a master's degree" to the very personal "I once had a drinking problem."

Too much self-disclosure can be a serious mistake. One of the best discussions of this is contained in Kottler and Blau's book, *The Imperfect Therapist* (1989). According to the authors, "Whether the therapist's ignorance, insensitivity, or narcissism is at fault, more than a few clients have been chased out of treatment because they felt negated by the repeated focus on the therapist's life" (p. 137). Kottler and Blau go on to say that clients are "frightened away" because helpers who talk about themselves make the client feel less important. Clients with low self-esteem do not want to hear about the successes of others. Helpers may lose their authority as transference figures and might be less able to influence the client through modeling. Finally, the client becomes bored with the repetition of therapist stories and anecdotes. The common mistake here is that the helper simply spends too much time in self-disclosure. Taking too much time for helper self-disclosure may put more stress on a client who already feels overburdened. Kottler and Blau contend that the saddest aspect of this situation is that the helper is usually unaware of the problem. To give a concrete example, a couple recently came to me for premarital counseling. They had been dissatisfied with a previous therapist because "She didn't seem interested in us. Instead, she spent the whole hour talking about her relationship with her husband and how they handled their differences. It seemed like they had the perfect marriage. It was a waste of time and money." Later, I found out that this therapist and her husband were getting a divorce because of serious problems. Although one might be tempted to explain the lack of therapeutic connection as a feeling that the couple could not measure up, it is just as likely they felt ignored and bored.

Common Mistakes in Helper Self-disclosure   The purpose of **self-disclosure** is to enhance the relationship, help the client realize that he or she is not alone, help the client see another viewpoint, or convey that the client's experience is normal. However, if the helper's story clashes with the client's, self-disclosure may have the opposite effect. Many of the mistakes are due to the helper failing to realize that the client needs to focus on his or her own issues. Obviously, self-disclosure shifts the focus onto the helper. Once disclosure is made, it is imperative that the helper shift the focus back onto the client. The following are examples of common errors in self-disclosure:

Mistake 1: The helper's self-disclosure is too deep. Thus, the client has to react to the helper, rather than focus on parallels between his or her own story and the helper's.

> *Situation:* The client expresses that she feels like a failure because he or she is going through a divorce.

> *Inappropriate Disclosure by the Helper:* "When I was going through my third divorce, I thought that there was something wrong with me. After all, I am supposed to help other people with their problems. So I went into therapy for over a year."

> *Appropriate Disclosure by the Helper:* "I have been through divorce myself, and I can relate to those feelings. I guess they are pretty common."

Mistake 2: Self-disclosure is poorly timed. When a person has gone through a traumatic event, it is a poor time to get him or her to focus on the helper's story. Rather, the client should be encouraged to disclose more.

> *Situation:* The client's mother died last week. (In this case, the client cannot really appreciate or focus on another person's story.)

Inappropriate Disclosure by the Helper: "I know just how you feel because my mother died about 5 years ago after a long illness. It was a long time before I got over it."

Appropriate Disclosure by the Helper: "I don't know exactly what you are going through, but I know a little bit about what it means to lose someone that close. I can guess that this whole thing has been very painful for you."

Mistake 3: The helper's self-disclosure does not match the client's experience.

Situation: The client has received a basketball scholarship to go to college. No one in her family has ever gone to a university. She is having trouble achieving satisfactory College Board scores for admission.

Inappropriate Disclosure by the Helper: "Once I wanted to go to a prep school that cost $20,000 per year. But I had to go to one that cost a lot less because my family couldn't afford it."

Appropriate Disclosure by the Helper: "I can relate to your story in that I have had some goals in my life that I wanted that badly. It must be frustrating to be almost there and run into this new hurdle."

In summary, self-disclosure is a technique that must be used with caution and at the right time. We discuss it here because it can affect the therapeutic relationship, but we will also reintroduce it as you learn building blocks skills. Self-disclosure can be used to bond with the client. Self-disclosure at the beginning stages of the relationship can help the client feel less alone. Self-involving statements can be used later in the counseling process to (1) inspire hope in the client and (2) provide feedback, confrontation, or an alternative viewpoint. We will learn more about self-disclosure in Chapter 4 when we look at invitational skills and more about self-involving statements in Chapter 8 when we discuss challenging skills.

OTHER FACTORS THAT HELP OR STRAIN THE THERAPEUTIC RELATIONSHIP

In the last section, we examined the effect of helper self-disclosure on the therapeutic relationship. Here, we will talk about some other commonly identified issues that may lead to a stronger or weaker therapeutic alliance. Among these are the environment where helping takes place, the therapeutic blunders that we can try to avoid, and the issues of transference and countertransference.

Facilitative Office Environment

The helper's office should be quiet, comfortable, orderly, and well lit. Most professionals and clients prefer soft lighting to bright fluorescence. Decorating that is comfortable rather than "clinical" is helpful, especially at the beginning of a therapeutic relationship. People prefer rooms that are decorated and "warm" (see Pressly & Heesacker, 2001). Sigmund Freud called his office a "consulting room." In other words, it should not be the therapist's living room, nor should it look like a laboratory (Bloom, Weigel, & Trautt, 1977). The office should not be merely an outgrowth of the helper's personality but a workplace. Generally, it is recommended that the helper face away from the desk so that there are no obstacles between client and helper (Pietrofesa, Hoffman, & Splete, 1984; Gass, 1984). Side tables are useful for a clock and the indispensable boxes of facial tissue.

Although it is easy to depict the ideal, not all helpers today have the model facilitative environment. Some helpers now work primarily on the telephone or on conduct counseling online. Sometimes school counselors see students in the hallways and in the lunchroom in 5-minute snatches. Other helpers work in cubicles without soundproofing. Many work out of their cars, doing home visits and actually conducting sessions in their clients' homes. For them, the issues of distractions and privacy must be dealt with creatively. Many have traveling kits that can be unpacked to create a "therapeutic space," with clocks, tissues, and play equipment for working with children.

Distractions

Noise from outside can interfere with the session, disrupting a delicate moment or giving the client the feeling that he or she may be heard by persons outside. A "Quiet Please" sign or one that says "Session in Progress" should be placed on the outside of the door. In some cases, it may be necessary to purchase a mechanical white-noise or ocean-sound device that can act as a "sound blanket." Position office seating to provide the most freedom from glaring lights, noise, and the possibility of being overheard.

Other disturbances to be avoided during the session include knocks on the door and phone calls (Benjamin, 1969). Beier and Young (1998), in their classic book on therapeutic communication, *The Silent Language of Psychotherapy*, make the point that a helper communicates the importance he or she places on the relationship by the way in which these distractions are handled. If you were a client, how would you feel if I answered the phone during our sessions or ate a bag of potato chips? What would you conclude about the importance I place on the session?

Appearing Credible and Taking a Nonhierarchical Stance

Certainly, the helper must be seen as credible (Ritter, Bowden, Murray, Ross, Greeley, & Pead, 2002), but how do you, at this stage in your training, appear credible to the client? You may be still training and you may be inexperienced, but the following suggestions can help you feel self-assured:

1. Remember what you do know and use the skills that you have. Review your strengths that we discussed in Chapter 1. There is no need to exaggerate your experience or downplay your ability. Don't communicate your own lack of confidence to the client. Sometimes, under the guise of honesty, helpers level with their clients and reveal their feelings of inadequacy. Clients have enough going on without having to deal with your issues.
2. Don't use emotional distance as a way of being professional. Sometimes beginning helpers will be overly formal with clients in an attempt to hide their uneasiness. This is where the nonhierarchical therapeutic relationship comes in. Just forming a one-to-one working relationship is therapeutic.
3. Remember that credibility is enhanced by appearing confident, organized, and interested and exhibiting nonverbal behaviors associated with attentiveness. These are behaviors that you can develop.

TABLE 3.1   Roadblocks to Communication

1. Ordering, Directing, Commanding
You must do this.
You cannot do this.
I expect you to do this.
Stop it.
Go apologize to her.

2. Warning, Admonishing, Threatening
You had better do this, or else . . .
If you don't do this, then . . .
You better not try that.
I warn you, if you do that . . .

3. Moralizing, Preaching, Imploring
You should do this.
You ought to try it.
It is your responsibility to do this.
It is your duty to do this.
I wish you would do this.
I urge you to do this.

4. Advising, Giving Suggestions or Solutions
What I think you should do is . . .
Let me suggest . . .
It would be best for you if . . .
Why not take a different approach?
The best solution is . . .

5. Persuading with Logic, Lecturing, Arguing
Do you realize that . . .
The facts are in favor of . . .
Let me give you the facts.
Here is the right way.
Experience tells us that . . .

6. Judging, Criticizing, Disagreeing, Blaming
You are acting foolishly.
You are not thinking straight.
You are out of line.
You didn't do it right.
You are wrong.
That is a stupid thing to say.

7. Praising, Agreeing, Evaluating Positively, Buttering Up
You usually have very good judgment.
You are an intelligent person.
You have so much potential.
You've made quite a bit of progress.
You have always made it in the past.

8. Name-Calling, Ridiculing, Shaming
You are a sloppy worker.
You are a fuzzy thinker.
You're talking like an engineer.
You really goofed on this one!

9. Interpreting, Analyzing, Diagnosing
You're saying this because you're angry.
You are jealous.
What you really need is . . .
You have problems with authority.
You want to look good.
You are being a bit paranoid.

10. Reassuring, Sympathizing, Consoling, Supporting
You'll feel different tomorrow.
Things will get better.
It is always darkest before the dawn.
Behind every cloud there's a silver lining.
Don't worry so much about it.
It's not that bad.

11. Probing, Questioning, Interrogating
Why did you do that?
How long have you felt this way?
What have you done to try to solve it?
Have you consulted with anyone?
When did you become aware of this feeling?
Who has influenced you?

12. Distracting, Diverting, Kidding
Think about the positive side.
Try not to think about it until you're rested.
Let's have lunch and forget about it.
That reminds me of the time when ...
You think you've got problems!

Source: "Skills That Help Subordinates Solve Their Problems," from *Leader Effectiveness Training L.E.T.* by Thomas Gordon, copyright © 1977 by Thomas Gordon. Adapted by permission of G. P. Putnam's Sons, a division of Penguin Putnam Inc.

Therapeutic Faux Pas

Faux pas is a French term meaning "false steps" or "wrong turns." It is better to think of **therapeutic faux pas** not as mistakes, but as detours that can be corrected later. Thomas Gordon (1986) identified 12 such "wrong turns," known as the "dirty dozen," that may occur in the development of a helping relationship. These are listed—with examples—in Table 3.1.

Gordon feels that there are two general messages communicated by the 12 roadblocks. First, they suggest that the client is incapable of solving his or her own problems. Second, they indicate that the client needs another person to solve the problems for him or her. Both are disempowering messages that take the responsibility for change away from the client and place it in the hands of the helper. Besides these 12 common detours, Wolberg (1967) has identified some other helper responses that can weaken or disrupt the therapeutic relationship. These include:

EXCLAMATIONS OF SURPRISE

CLIENT: "I spanked the living daylights out of my kids last night."

Not Helpful: "You what?!"

"That's awful!"

Helpful: "Sounds like you're feeling guilty about it now."

"You must have been really frustrated to have resorted to that."

BEING PUNITIVE

CLIENT: "I don't think that you are giving me the help I need."

Not Helpful: "Then I will just refer you to someone else." "You are not making progress because you are not working on the problem."

Helpful: "You feel stuck and that you are not making any progress."

"You're wondering if I am the right person to help you."

"What kind of help do you think would be useful to you at this time?"

GIVING FALSE REASSURANCE   Sometimes clients want us to give them hope that the helping process will be successful. This can backfire if the helper makes promises that cannot be kept.

CLIENT: "Will I ever get over this completely and be normal?"

Not Helpful: "Of course you will."

"I think that you are normal now!"

"You will be better in 6 weeks. I guarantee it."

Helpful: "First, tell me how you would like your life to be. If you were normal, how would you be feeling and acting?"

"Right now, you are feeling unsure about whether you can conquer this problem. I am hopeful that we can make a significant change if we work together."

PSYCHOBABBLE AND PREMATURE INTERPRETATIONS *Psychobabble* is a word describing the overuse of psychological terminology. When the helper identifies a technical term for every issue, the client feels that his or her problems are trivialized or that they have become clinical syndromes. *Premature interpretation* is suggesting deep meanings before adequate data have been collected to support these interpretations.

> CLIENT: "My father was an alcoholic and my mother seemed to tolerate it. We lived in denial our whole lives."
>
> Not Helpful: "That's because your mother was codependent and that makes you ACOA (adult child of an alcoholic)."
>
> "That is why you are a dependent personality."
>
> "How does that make you feel?"
>
> Helpful: "Tell me more about what you mean by denial."
>
> "Tell me something about your family relationships."

PROBING TRAUMATIC ISSUES WHEN THE CLIENT STRONGLY RESISTS Respecting the client's wish to avoid a topic can be handled by noting it, reflecting, and suggesting that it can be put off until later. Damage to the relationship can take place when the helper mercilessly pursues a topic. It is often a question of timing. Sometimes it is best to nurture the relationship and address the topic later.

> CLIENT: "I don't want to talk about sex."
>
> Not Helpful: "We have to talk about it sometime."
>
> "Then, let's talk about your past sex life."
>
> Helpful: "It is a painful subject for you."
>
> "All right, we can come back to that another time if you want."

Transference and Countertransference

As the relationship develops, a sort of intimacy grows. An atmosphere of openness, liking, respect, and trust is hopefully developing. This kind of therapeutic intimacy is generally seen as a positive state of agreement and mutual caring. It creates favorable conditions for change (Rogers, 1957) and increases client involvement and compliance with treatment. However, intimacy also tends to elicit strong feelings—feelings that may have had their genesis in previous relationships (Wachtel, 2011). *Transference* and *countertransference* are terms that originated among psychoanalysts to denote these powerful feelings that develop when client and helper bond. As client and helper grow closer, a client may experience the same emotions of self-doubt, fear of abandonment, and other residue from parental or love relationships. This is called **transference**. On the other hand, the helper may also see the client as a reflection of a past or present relationship or may experience strong emotions for the client. This is called **countertransference**. When the helper finds that the client's progress is stymied by the relationship itself, the helper must be trained and willing to examine the therapeutic relationship as a living model of the client's social world. When the helper finds personal needs spilling over into the therapeutic setting, he or she needs to consult with a supervisor and deal with these issues privately.

STOP AND REFLECT

Transference is not confined to the helping relationship; it is a part of everyday life (Andersen & Berk, 1998). A recent book, *Blink* (Gladwell, 2005), tells us that we rely on snap judgments about people and the world every day. It is said that we can form our first impressions of someone's personality in less than 4 seconds (Bar, Neta, & Linz, 2006). In other words, we are constantly experiencing transference reactions at our very first meetings with people. Most of us are familiar with automatic feelings of liking or disliking a person on sight. These emotional reactions are most likely due to experiences with a similar person in the past, and they may be vague and impressionistic, in other words, unreasonable. One simple way to categorize such reactions is to label them positive, neutral, or negative.

As an experiment, take a look around at your classmates and mentally note your feelings for each one—especially for those you have never met before this class or know only slightly. List each person's name or indicate some memorable feature such as "blue shirt." Next to each person, put a plus sign (+) next to those for whom you feel a positive attraction and a minus sign (−) if you have a negative feeling. If there is neither attraction nor a negative feeling, write *N* for neutral. You may think that it is unfair to assign a value to your feelings without taking into account the fact that you do not really know all your classmates well. That is true, but these impressions, like all first impressions, can be powerful. As mentioned earlier, we experience these first impressions within the first 4 seconds and act on them whether or not they are valid. Are there any real reasons for the positives and negatives you recorded? Are they the result of experiences with similar people? Think about the names of your classmates. Do any evoke an emotional reaction? If you had to choose two people in the class to play your parents in a role play, whom would you choose? Are you transferring any of your experiences with your parents or significant others to these people?

WHAT IS TRANSFERENCE? **Transference** is a client's carryover of feelings from past relationships into a new one—the client/helper relationship. Relationship-building activities, such as listening and providing conditions of safety, increase feelings of intimacy and enhance the possibility of transference. Clients' feelings can be described as positive, ranging from liking to sexual attraction, or negative, ranging from suspiciousness to hatred (Watkins, 1986). Negative transference reactions are thought to be an important reason for treatment failures (Basch, 1980; Spinhoven, Giesen-Bloo, van Dyck, Kooiman, & Arntz, 2007), because clients often drop out of therapy rather than face them. Although it may be impossible to avoid transference altogether (Gelso & Carter, 1985), in many helping relationships, transference never endangers the relationship or the client's progress. For others, it is vital to examine the therapeutic relationship as a first step in setting other relationships straight. A client may experience such strong feelings toward the helper that they become a roadblock that must be overcome in order for treatment to continue. When issues of transference interfere with the attainment of goals, they must be dealt with, either in an isolated fashion or in conjunction with other relationship problems the client may be experiencing.

Why are we looking at a complicated issue like transference so early in your skill training? Dealing with such issues is certainly an advanced skill. But this is a chapter about all the things that can delay or prevent the formation of a therapeutic relationship, and it is crucial to address some of the initial challenges that you will face as you learn the art of helping. You may find that this chapter is most helpful when you start seeing clients in a school, agency, or clinical setting, although it is background for the basic skills you will learn and something to refer to when real relationship breakdowns occur.

PSYCHODYNAMIC CONCEPTIONS OF TRANSFERENCE   Some believe that transference is caused by unfinished business from the past. This notion is central to psychoanalysis, which asserts that issues surface from the unconscious because they are unresolved (Corradi, 2006). Freud believed that resolution of transference was the most important aspect of therapy because it allowed the client to address emotional issues about parents and siblings. One alternative viewpoint that has emerged is to conceptualize transference as a set of cognitive distortions, rather than as unresolved conflicts or unfulfilled needs (Sullivan, 1954). These distortions are learned patterns of thinking, not unlike the irrational ideas that have been described by Albert Ellis (1985). Still, there is a common thread that binds the modern viewpoint to the psychoanalytic idea. In both conceptualizations, the client is seen as focused on the outside (external causes of behavior) versus the inside (self-direction). The client is thinking about the attributes of the helper, rather than focusing on self-awareness. Even if it is a positive distortion (the helper as ideal), it is not reality. Hero worship may damage self-esteem if one compares oneself in a negative way to the helper (Singer, 1970).

To summarize, on the one hand, the client may have distorted ideas about the helper and the helping relationship that should be addressed. These may appear as inflated expectations about the helper, believing that he or she will solve all the problems single-handedly. Alternatively, the client may have strong negative feelings for the helper, especially when overblown expectations are not met. Watkins (1986) has identified five major transference patterns that are based on the concept of transference as cognitive distortion. Table 3.2, adapted from Watkins, shows these patterns along with the client's attitudes and the helper's reaction to them.

COUNTERTRANSFERENCE: DEALING WITH THE HELPER'S FEELINGS   **Countertransference** is defined as the helper's strong emotional reactions to a client. To give an example of this, consider this true story that a practicum student tells about one of her first clients:

> My client is a 35-year-old woman who owns her own business. She showed up for her first session 5 minutes late. When I came to the waiting room, she complained loudly that she had been waiting for 10 minutes and then followed me to my office in a huff. Although I was pretty sure that she had been late, not me, I was on the defensive from the beginning, and I felt very uncomfortable and intimidated by her. As I watched the video, I saw the many unreasonable demands she made. For example, she said that she needed to change seats with me because there was too much glare in her eyes. She criticized the decorating and quizzed me about whether or not I had read the notes of the previous counselor. I watched myself just back down and become silent. I talked this over with my supervisor, who also noticed my passive behavior. I think that I reacted this way partially because this was my typical behavior with my previous boyfriend. Although he was not violent, he was verbally explosive,

and I learned to become quiet and back off during his rages. Now I am doing the same thing with this client.

Countertransference is an issue not fully appreciated by the beginning helper. When intellectualizing about the therapeutic relationship, one can hardly imagine the powerful feelings that some clients may elicit. In the example above, it would be easy to blame the client for her behavior and label her as uncooperative. Although her interpersonal behavior may have to be addressed later in the helping process, the helper's reaction merits examination too. In practice, helpers need ongoing supervision to monitor the tendency to be too helpful and to deal with feelings of sexual attraction, as well as fear and insecurity. Anger toward clients is one of the most common issues (Dalenberg, 2004; Fremont & Anderson, 1986). Normally such issues are dealt with between helper and supervisor and not in the presence of the client. However, because countertransference can seriously disrupt the client/helper bond, it merits discussion in this chapter on the therapeutic relationship.

TABLE 3.2 Major Transference Patterns

Client Behaviors/Attitudes	Helper Experiences
Helper as Ideal Compliments helper profusely Imitates helper Wears similar clothing General idealization	Feels pride, satisfaction, and all-competent Feels flattered Experiences tension, anxiety, confusion, anger, and frustration
Helper as Seer Ascribes omniscience and power to the helper Views helper as expert. Sees self as incompetent Seeks answers, solutions, and advice	Experiences "God complex" and self-doubt Feels incompetent and pressure to be right and live up to client's expectations
Helper as Nurturer Experiences profuse emotion and sense of fragility Cries Feels dependent, helpless, and indecisive Desires to be touched and held	Experiences feelings of sorrow, sympathy, depression, despair, and depletion Has urge to soothe, coddle, and touch
Helper as Frustrator Feels defensive, cautious, guarded, suspicious, and distrustful Tests helper	Feels uneasy, on edge (walking on eggshells), tense, hostile, and hateful Withdraws and becomes unavailable Dislikes and blames client
Helper as Nonentity Shifts topics Lacks focus Is voluble and desultory Meanders aimlessly	Feels overwhelmed, subdued, taken aback, used, useless Feels bored Experiences resentment, frustration, and lack of recognition Characterizes self as a nonperson

TABLE 3.3 Common Patterns of Countertransference

Helper Emotional Response to Client	Helper Behavior	Client Seen as
Paternal/maternal nurturing	Overprotective	Fragile
	Failure to challenge	
Fear of client's anger	Reduction of conflict	Aggressor
	Attempts to please	
Disgust, disapproval	Rejection	Needy
		Immoral
Need for reassurance	Socializing	Friend
Need for liking	Failure to challenge	
Anxiety	Avoidance of emotionally charged topics	
Insecurity		
Feelings of identification	Advice giving	Self
	Overinvolvement	
	Failure to recognize client's uniqueness	
Sexual	Seductive behavior	Sexual object
Romantic	Inappropriate self-disclosure	Romantic partner
	Reduced focus on presenting problems	
	Inappropriate exploration of sexual topics	
Frustration	Extreme confrontation	Product
Anger	Scolding	Success
	Criticizing	

Some helpers try to deal with their own feelings simply by disclosing everything to the client. Such disclosure is a mistake if motivated by the helper's need to relieve his or her own discomfort. The therapeutic relationship is based on a contract that implicitly agrees that the helper should disclose information only if it is beneficial to the client. The therapeutic relationship is not a friendship, nor is it a two-way street. It involves a helper and the person being helped. The helper agrees to set his or her own needs aside and to do what is best for the client. Table 3.3 describes common helper emotional reactions, based on information collected by Corey, Corey, and Callanan (2003). The essential point of the information in the table is that countertransference issues are generally emotional reactions to clients, which can then lead to certain behaviors on the part of the helper. Instead of helping the client achieve mutually derived goals, the helper develops a second (you might say unconscious) agenda that changes the helper's view of the client as a contractual partner in the therapy process. The helper has come to see the client as a project, as a sexual object, as a friend, or even as a reflection of the self.

Countertransference is as common as transference, and most helpers regularly have strong feelings about their clients. Much of the unethical behavior in which helpers indulge is probably due to the strong emotions elicited in the therapeutic relationship, which make us forget our "asocial," contractual role. This is one reason why a supervisory relationship is so crucial for every helper. The supervisor's role is to appeal to the helper's professional and ethical sense, provide insight and support, and remind the helper to act in accordance with therapeutic goals.

DEALING WITH TRANSFERENCE FROM A CLIENT A client's strong emotional reactions to the helper may be the result of transference or may be honest reactions to the helper's behavior. In both cases, the task of the helper is the same: to help the client gain more awareness and to nondefensively explore the source of these feelings (see Dalenberg, 2004). Let us look briefly at how a helper can react therapeutically when a client expresses strong feelings of anger.

Step 1: Convey Acceptance of the Client's Remarks But Don't Retaliate. Dealing with an angry client is one of the most difficult and delicate issues in helping. One reason is that it tends to evoke anger or fear in the helper. Retaliation or a defensive response can be perceived by the client as a weakness, as an admission of guilt, or as a punishment. The client's anger may be triggered by frustration over lack of progress or by the perception that the helper is unfriendly, inept, or destructive. After having expressed this hostility, the client may be concerned about angering or hurting the helper or may fear abandonment.

Example (conveying respect):

CLIENT: I don't think we're getting anywhere. When are we going to deal with the real issues? I'm sick of coming in here and paying all this money.

HELPER: I can tell you're angry. I'm glad you had the courage to be so honest. I can't think of anything that will be of more help to you than dealing with this issue.

Step 2: Explore the Client's Feelings. Following an expression of hostility toward the helper, the client may retreat, fearing he or she will be punished, lose control, or hurt the helper. Exploration of a client's hostile feelings involves continuing to encourage the expression and labeling of feelings while trying to clarify the source of the anger.

Example (exploring):

CLIENT: I don't think this is working, and I am tired of coming in here and being told that it is entirely my fault.

HELPER: What made you feel that it was all your fault?

or

HELPER: Do you have the sense that I am blaming you for not changing?

or

HELPER: You wish I would be more supportive.

Step 3: Utilize Self-involving Statements to Help the Client Become Aware of the Helper's Genuine Thoughts and Emotions about the Client and the Client's Behavior. Self-involving statements are the helper's thoughts and feelings that are shared with the client as information about the relationship.

Example:

CLIENT: You are darn right you should be more supportive. Nobody supports me, not my wife, not my boss. I have to blow my top before they will even listen.

HELPER
(SELF-INVOLVING
STATEMENT):
I can tell you're angry with me because you think I am siding with these other people. I don't see it that way. I feel very much on your side, but I also feel a duty to help you look at what you are doing. And I can see where your anger is hurting your relationships.

Here is another example of a self-involving statement given by a helper when his client expressed feelings of romantic attraction:

Example:

HELPER: I must say I am flattered and a little uneasy when you say you feel this way about me. I am uneasy because I don't want this to interfere with the progress we're making. At the same time, I need to tell you I don't share your feelings. I don't want to hurt your feelings, and I don't want to make you feel embarrassed. I also don't want to lose the closeness that we have felt going through all the crises over the past year.

Step 4: Use the Experience to Help the Client to Find New and Better Ways of Expressing Feelings and Meeting His or Her Needs. If the helper can avoid blaming, embarrassing, or shaming the client, the client's expressions of strong emotions such as anger or attraction can be used to examine the client's interpersonal life. Clients who exhibit excessive anger or who are indirect or revengeful may be alienating others and thereby engaging in self-defeating patterns. Clients who romanticize all close relationships may need to find ways of developing more intimate friendships that are not sexual in nature. Dealing with transference by listening, exploring, and disclosing has the effect of making clients aware of these patterns, but clients still may need assistance either individually or in a structured group to learn new and more productive ways of behaving. These interpersonal patterns are automatic and reflexive. Clients need to utilize the therapeutic relationship as a tool to examine new situations as they arise and to design alternative responses.

Example (using the therapeutic relationship to consider alternative behaviors):

CLIENT: I don't know why I blow up. But I don't know what else to do.

HELPER: In this session, you have mentioned a number of situations besides this relationship in which you feel that you have to explode in order to be heard. I am not at all sure that is your only alternative. I think it would be helpful to learn and try out some new ways of relating, and you can practice on me. How do you feel about that?

MyCounselingLab™

Go to Topic 1, *Establishing the Therapeutic Relationship*, on the **MyCounselingLab™** site (www.MyCounselingLab.com) for *Learning the Art of Helping: Building Blocks and Techniques*, Fifth Edition, where you can:

- Find learning outcomes for *Establishing the Therapeutic Relationship* along with the national standards that connect to these outcomes.
- Complete Assignments and Activities that can help you more deeply understand the chapter content.
- Apply and practice your understanding of the core skills identified in the chapter with the Building Counseling Skills unit.
- Prepare yourself for professional certification with a Practice for Certification quiz.
- Connect to videos through the Video and Resource Library.

MyCounselingLab™ Exercises

Go to the Video and Resource Library on the **MyCounselingLab™** site for your text and search for the following clip: *Paraphrasing: Samantha*. Answer the following questions about what you see:

Exercise 1: Not Agreeing but Empathizing

1. Consider the statement, "Empathy is not merely agreeing with the client." Samantha (the helper) appears to empathize with Stacey (the client) without agreeing with her statements that her boyfriend is the problem. What words did Samantha use to communicate this neutral stance?
2. At times Stacey implies that the helper has an easy job just like the client's boyfriend. If this were a social situation, how might you respond to this challenge? How did Samantha respond to this innuendo?
3. Notice the décor of the office shown on the video. What words would you use to describe it? Do you consider this to be a facilitative office environment? What do you like or dislike about it?

Summary

In this chapter, we discussed the therapeutic relationship as a keystone in the process of change. In the road map of the helping relationship, we said that it empowers all the other activities that a helper uses to aid a client, including assessment, goal setting, intervention, and evaluation. There are a number of helper behaviors that can enhance the relationship, including nonverbals such as physical closeness, posture, and warmth. In addition, empathy, self-disclosure, and a good helper/client match can make the helping relationship stronger. The attribute of empathy was discussed in some detail because it seems to be a foundational skill, as well as an attitude that allows us to enter more deeply into relationships.

There are also issues and behaviors that can strain the budding alliance. Among these are Thomas Gordon's 12 roadblocks, a number of therapeutic faux pas, a poor office environment, and the challenges of transference and countertransference. This chapter also dealt with the issue of how to handle differences between client and helper when they seem to weaken the relationship. Differences in culture, gender, socioeconomic status, family background, and ethnic origin have their greatest impact in the initial sessions. Unless the therapeutic bond is forged quickly, there may be slow progress or clients may simply drop out. Although it may be impossible to cross all the barriers between people, because of the changing nature of our world, the helpers of tomorrow must possess the skills, knowledge, and attitudes that help them appreciate different people, different families, and different cultures. One of the subtle points of this chapter is that a helping relationship is not a social relationship. It is more important that there be a working alliance than a friendship. The social skills of making clients feel comfortable, talking about the weather, and being a friendly person can reduce anxiety in the beginning stages, but the helping relationship should not be constrained by the social forces of politeness and cultural tendencies to avoid certain topics for fear of embarrassment or controversy. Entering a helping relationship requires you to boldly go where few have gone before, using the relationship as the fuel to explore more and more deeply into the mystery of another person.

Exercises

GROUP EXERCISES

Exercise 1: Getting Feedback on Your Natural Helping Style

In groups of four or five, students take turns as the helper and client with two observers. The client talks about any problem he or she wishes to disclose. After about 5–8 minutes, the conversation stops, and the helper receives feedback from the group including the client about the helper's natural style. Try to give the helper honest feedback about your reaction to him or her manner. What did the group see as strengths or things to work on? Was the helper warm or cold? Was the helper light or serious, friendly or professional, formal or informal? If you wish, you may use a metaphor to describe how the conversation felt.

Exercise 2: Barriers to Communication

Divide into groups of three to five students. The instructor will assign each group one of Thomas Gordon's roadblocks in Table 3.1. (Roadblocks 4, 7, 10, and 12 are especially effective.) Each group is to put together a presentation that demonstrates its roadblock to the class in a role play between a helper and a client and then show helper behaviors that could enhance the relationship in that situation. Following each demonstration, the class can discuss the effects of the roadblock on the helping relationship. It is especially useful for the "clients" to describe what it felt like when the helper used one of these roadblocks.

Exercise 3: Dealing with Strong Feelings from a Client

In groups of three, role play a scenario in which the client expresses strong feelings toward the helper. As the "client" fumes, the "helper" is to try to use the four steps given in the section "Dealing with Transference from a Client":

Step 1 Convey acceptance of the client's remarks but don't retaliate.

Step 2 Explore the client's feelings.

Step 3 Utilize self-involving statements to help the client become aware of the helper's genuine thoughts and emotions about the client and the client's behavior.

Step 4 Use the experience to help the client to find new and better ways of expressing feelings and meeting his or her needs.

The observer in the group keeps track of any helper statements that seem to help the client explore this issue.

SMALL GROUP DISCUSSIONS

Discussion 1: Case Study

In a small group, read and discuss the following example: Ricardo is a counselor in private practice. The following is his discussion of a client who was referred for counseling by her family physician when she came to the medical office crying and needing to talk.

> The client began the therapeutic relationship with much enthusiasm and high expectations for achieving her goals. She was a 23-year-old only child who felt that she could not maintain a serious relationship. After a few weeks, her enthusiasm waned, and she expressed disappointment in me as a helper. By this time, enough assessment had been done to identify this denouement as being

similar to her history of intimate relationships. She began relationships with an idealized picture of her boyfriends and then was quickly disappointed. She came to the session one day indicating that she was angry that I had not been able to give her an earlier session. During her earlier phone call, she had said it was important but not urgent that she see me soon. She admitted that she expected me to know how upset she was and to set up an emergency appointment. When we examined our relationship, the client was able to pick out several times when she left hints and clues about her needs but failed to ask for things directly.

I shared my feelings of surprise, being unaware of her real feelings. Naturally, this led to a discussion of how her behavior might have affected other relationships. It was a very significant insight when she realized that she was undermining relationships by her failure to send clear messages about her needs. In her case, this pattern of behavior could be traced back to her upbringing, which did not require that she state her needs and rewarded indirect suggestions. In therapy, she was able to learn some assertiveness skills and practice them in a group setting.

a. Do you think it was necessary to examine the client's past to help her with the problem in the helping relationship?
b. Is it possible that the client has a legitimate gripe and that Ricardo is "saving face" by making it the client's problem?
c. In a case such as this, how much responsibility should the helper take for the miscommunication about the client's needs? Would it have helped the client if the helper had apologized or assumed partial responsibility for the misunderstanding?
d. If you were Ricardo, how would you have handled the client's expression of anger?

Discussion 2: Transference

PART 1. Take a look at the common transference reactions in Table 3.2. Now think back on the case of Alicia B. that introduced this chapter. Which of these reactions did she experience in her relationship with Jim?

PART 2. Have you ever experienced any of these feelings for someone in authority? Think for a moment about the concept of authority. You have probably heard it said that a person has "authority issues." How is this similar to or different from transference reaction discussed in this chapter? Discuss your findings with a small group.

DISCUSSION 2: SELF-DISCLOSURE Pretend that you are a helper working in a public agency. Tell members of your small group a few things about you that you might disclose to a client. Get feedback from the group about the appropriateness of your disclosures. Recall that the appropriate uses of self-disclosure are to (1) enhance the relationship; (2) help the client realize that he or she is not alone; (3) help the client see another viewpoint; or (4) convey that the client's experience is normal.

WRITTEN EXERCISES AND SELF-ASSESSMENT

Exercise 1: Identifying Appropriate Helper Self-Disclosure

Below are some examples of inappropriate helper self-disclosure. For each, write a more appropriate helper disclosure. The first problem is completed as an example.

1. Situation: The client feels anger toward her boss because she believes he is mistreating her.

   Inappropriate helper self-disclosure: "I remember once being so mad at my boss that I thought about letting the air out of her tires."

   Appropriate helper self-disclosure: "I've had challenges with bosses too. It's frustrating not having much control."

Now, you try it.

2. Situation: The client is dealing with grief from the death of a spouse.

   Inappropriate helper self-disclosure: "When my grandmother died about 2 years ago, I found I got over it reasonably quickly."

   Appropriate helper self-disclosure:

3. Situation: The client has problems with excessive alcohol use.

   Inappropriate helper self-disclosure: "I am a recovering alcoholic. I used to drink a bottle of whiskey a day and I was often drunk at work."

Appropriate helper self-disclosure:

4. Situation: The client is suffering with depression.

Inappropriate helper self-disclosure: "I am lucky, I've never been depressed."

Appropriate helper self-disclosure:

5. Situation: The client is hoping to be accepted into graduate school.

Inappropriate helper self-disclosure: "Exams can be important. I failed an exam once because I overslept."

Appropriate helper self-disclosure:

Exercise 2: Roadblocks Exercise

A roadblock is a response by the helper that cuts off communication. Read the client situations below each roadblock. First create a "roadblock response," and then follow this with an appropriate helping response that encourages the client to open up. As an example, the first roadblock is filled out for you. Note that the Roadblock Response we have supplied exemplifies Ordering, Directing, or Commanding, a statement that disrupts helper/client communication. When it comes to creating a more appropriate helper response, do not worry too much about creating the perfect intervention. The aim of the exercise is to recognize that there are alternatives to these common obstacles.

1. Ordering, Directing, Commanding.

CLIENT: "I am thinking of leaving my wife."

Roadblock response: "You'd better get to marriage counseling right away."

Appropriate helper response: "Sounds like you have been having serious trouble with your relationship. Can you tell me more about it?"

Now, it's your turn. For each of the following roadblock categories, write a typical "roadblock response" and an alternative.

2. Moralizing, Preaching, Imploring.

CLIENT: "I am confused about whether or not to stop drinking alcohol; it relaxes me after work."

3. Advising, Giving Suggestions or Solutions.

CLIENT: "I want to lose weight; I'm just too fat."

4. Judging, Criticizing, Disagreeing, Blaming.

CLIENT: "I decided not to go to work today. I spent all morning in bed reading magazines."

5. Interpreting, Analyzing, Diagnosing.

CLIENT: "My son Bobby took some money from my purse the other day. He's done it before, but I don't say anything as I might hurt his feelings."

6. Reassuring, Sympathizing, Consoling, Supporting.

CLIENT: "She left me again last night after a big fight. I think she is staying at her lover's house."

7. Probing, Questioning, Interrogating.

CLIENT: "This is my third speeding ticket this month."

8. Distracting, Diverting, Kidding.

CLIENT: "I don't know if things will ever improve for me."

HOMEWORK

Homework 1: Favorite Teachers

Make a list of your five favorite teachers from elementary school to present. List the traits or qualities of these persons. Identify any similarities. Are there also glaring differences? Now contrast them with some teacher or learning situation that was either very unpleasant or simply unhelpful. What do these experiences say about how you like to learn? Based on your experiences with teachers, what kind of helper do you think might be the best fit for you? What kind of helper is likely to "push your buttons" and elicit some of the feelings you have had in previous helping relationships? Summarize your reactions to this exercise in two or three paragraphs.

Homework 2: Your Reactions to Clients

One of the most common countertransference reactions is to feel sorry for a client and help the client too much. Another reaction is strong feelings of attraction for a client. Research the ethical codes of one of the helping professions. What guidelines can help you determine ethical action in such situations? In each case, what could be harmful about this particular counter-transference reaction? In two or three paragraphs, discuss how you would handle each of the two situations, ethically and therapeutically.

JOURNAL STARTERS

Remember that these starters are designed to warm you up to the issues. You may take them in whatever direction you like.

Recall a relationship, past or present, where the other person was significantly different from you, either in age, culture, or ethnicity. Discuss the experience. Was the development of the relationship more challenging than with someone more similar to you? In what ways? How did you your differences enhance or deter from the relationship? How did you overcome any obstacles to communication? What did you learn from the experience?

Invitational Skills

*Yes, there is no doubt that paper is patient and as I don't
intend to show this cardboard covered notebook . . .
to anyone, unless I find a real friend, boy or girl,
probably nobody cares. And now I come to the root of
the matter, the reason for my diary: it is that I have no
such real friend.*

ANNE FRANK (IN MOFFAT & PAINTER, 1975, P. 15)

MyCounselingLab™

Visit the MyCounselingLab™ site for *Learning the Art of Helping: Building Blocks and Techniques,* Fifth Edition to enhance your understanding of chapter concepts. You'll have the opportunity to practice your skills through video- and case-based Assignments and Activities as well as Building Counseling Skills units, and to prepare for your certification exam with Practice for Certification quizzes.

Listening to the Client's Story

Nonverbal Communication Between
Helper and Client

Nonverbal Skills in the Helping
Relationship
- Eye Contact
- Body Position
- Attentive Silence

- Voice Tone
- Facial Expressions and Gestures
- Physical Distance
- Touching and Warmth

Opening Skills: How to Invite
- Encouragers
- Questions

Summary

Exercises
- Group Exercises
- Small Group Discussions
- Written Exercises

- Self-Assessment
- Homework
- Journal Starters

This entry from Anne Frank's diary reminds us of the great human need to be understood and to communicate. This desire to explain oneself has been met in various ways through the ages such as by keeping journals and diaries, by taking part in religious confession, by confiding in friends, and by praying. In the same way, the therapeutic relationship, described in the previous chapter, offers the client a way to hear themselves in a nonthreatening atmosphere with the safeguards of confidentiality. It is not enough to think about one's life, it must be disclosed verbally or in writing. The act of disclosing can be a great relief and is the first step in the healing process.

James Pennebaker (1989, 1990, 2002) has conducted some of the most interesting research on the benefits of self-disclosure and confession. He became interested in the phenomenon while talking to polygraph operators who gave lie detector tests to people suspected of crimes. These technicians told him stories of suspects who admitted their guilt under questioning and who even thanked the operators. Some operators said they had even received Christmas cards from some of those they helped to convict! This suggested to him that there is a powerful need to confess. Pennebaker found in his own research that college students who regularly wrote diaries about their most troubling experiences showed better immune system responses and significantly better health compared with those who did not write. Pennebaker's work exemplifies a growing body of evidence that opening up is good for the soul *and* the body (Frattaroli, 2006).

Pennebaker's work about disclosure also underlines the fact that when clients come for help, they are seeking to explain themselves to a nonjudgmental listener (Pennebaker, 1990). Clients want to untangle the knots of traumas, miscalculations, and resentments that are troubling them. However, they do not simply want absolution; they desire to understand how things got so mixed up and how to deal with the unfinished business. The therapeutic relationship can provide the opportunity to heal the body and the mind if the helper can get out of the way and allow the client to open up and investigate all the nooks and crannies of the problem.

In this chapter, you will learn and practice the first set of techniques you need in the art of helping. They are called *invitational skills*. Invitational skills are broken into two general categories: nonverbal skills and opening skills (see Table 4.1). Nonverbal skills such as using eye contact and body position set the stage for an open and confiding relationship. Opening skills are verbal catalysts that consist of encouraging statements and questions. Together, these two categories of invitational skills will allow you to convey to clients that you are listening to them and that they are invited to open up. The invitational skills are especially useful early on in the helping session when they do not interfere with the client's recitation of the story. However, these skills are used throughout the entire helping process, session after session, as the helper listens to the client relate his or her progress, report setbacks, and describe new issues as they emerge.

TABLE 4.1	**The Building Blocks for Invitational Skills**

Nonverbal Skills

Nonverbal skills are the use of attentive silence, eye contact, appropriate voice tone, body position, and nonverbal encouragers such as head nodding or hand gestures that invite the client to talk.

Nonverbal Skill	Example
Eye contact	Direct eye contact with occasional breaks for client comfort
Facilitative body position	"Open" attentive body position, squarely facing the client
Appropriate use of silence	Allowing the client to fill in the "voids" in the conversation
Voice tone	Using a voice tone that reflects the client's and is appropriate in volume and rate and shows warmth and support
Gestures	Encouraging the client to open up with appropriate gestures and head nodding

Opening Skills

Opening skills are verbal encouragers. They ask the client to explore a little deeper but are not very invasive. They also reassure the client that you are following the story.

Opening Skill	Example
Encouragers	
Door opener	"Say some more about that."
Minimal encourager	"Uh, huh." "Okay."
Questions	
Open question	"Could you tell me what has been going on?"
Closed question	"Is she your ex-wife?"

LISTENING TO THE CLIENT'S STORY

"My wife says I don't listen to her ... at least I think that's what she said."

LAWRENCE PETER

The quote by Peter points out how often we fail to fully listen to those around us—even those closest to us. Most people do not expect others to solve their problems, but they do want someone to listen, and they want to have a chance to hear themselves as well. Can listening all by itself have a powerful effect on another person? Is it possible that merely giving someone your full attention is healing? Some writers have called this *active listening*, a way of attending and encouraging without intruding on the client's telling of the story. It is called active because the listener is fully absorbed and communicates this to the other. But listening is difficult. A number of competing thoughts and urges assail us.

One of the biggest distractions is the need to help. A client's story can create tremendous pressure on the listener. We want to ease the client's pain, help him or her decide upon a course of action, and create a change. It is this impulse that prompts friends to offer quick advice to difficult problems. Frequently, however, the best approach in the professional helping relationship is to allow clients to completely describe the situation to you and to themselves before jumping into an instant solution. If you think about it, the client has probably heard a lot of advice already. What makes you think that your ideas are likely to be any better than a close friend's? It is through listening to the client's story that client and helper are able to find the keys to change, not by attempting to solve the problem in the first few minutes. In fact, quick advice tends to disqualify the helper in the client's eyes.

Sheldon Kopp (1978) emphasized the importance of clients needing to "tell their tales." The tale is a full recitation of the problem from the client's unique perspective. It is the client's story of his or her life. Michael White, the Australian therapist, calls these stories "narratives" (White, 2000). Hidden in each story are the keys to understanding how that person views the world. Helpers who take the time to let the client's story unfold will design helping interventions that fit the unique client and his or her special worldview (cf. Goldberg & Crespo, 2003). So besides the therapeutic effects of allowing the client to disclose, we also gain greater insight into the client's world.

STOP AND REFLECT

Many beginning helpers get stuck because they feel that they have heard the whole story in the first 5 minutes. They become nervous because they think that if they spend more time listening, they will end up covering old ground. They also anticipate the client's unspoken question, "What should I do?"

Consider the first few minutes of this actual counseling session between a 30-year-old woman, Tia, and her counselor, Renee. Tia is living with her mother and her 4-year-old son.

> "My mother wants everything done her way. I can't do anything right, even with my son. For example, I have to call her at the end of today's session and let her know I came. She thinks I need counseling. But really I just need her to get off my back. I have a job possibility, and it's walking distance from home. But my mother thinks that it doesn't pay enough. But I have to start somewhere, and I think I would like it. If it weren't for her, I would probably be living on the street. But when I try to get more independent, it's like she doesn't want me to. There are so many things I want to do. I want to go to school, have my own place, but she just won't let me."

After the session, Renee met with her supervisor, Marcy, to discuss the case:

> RENEE: "I had a hard time in the session because I just wanted to tell her to take the job and move out. I also wanted to agree with her that her mother is overbearing."
>
> MARCY: "Do you know enough yet to make that kind of statement to her?"
>
> RENEE: "I guess not, but I wanted to help her figure out what to do."
>
> MARCY: "Resist the temptation to intervene until you know more about the situation and about her."
>
> RENEE: "So I just listen? For how long?"

- How would you answer Renee's question? As you look back at Tia, what more would you like to know about her before you feel that you have enough information to help? As you look at Tia's story, do you see any way in which the helper might actually be hurting the client by intervening?
- What cultural, family, and religious factors are in the background of this client's story? How important are these things in understanding the client? What assumptions have you already made about Tia based on her background? How can you test them?

- In this situation, would you be tempted to find ways for the client to change her mother?
- Why is Marcy cautioning Renee to listen more? What other issues does Tia struggle with besides her relationship with her mother?
- What parts of Tia's story would you like to hear more about? Why do you think that would be helpful?
- What specific issues does Tia need to address in herself? Would encouraging her to take a job or move from her mother's house solve her problems?

Like Tia, in the "Stop and Reflect" section, some clients will open the floodgates of the story during the first session, pausing only to take a breath and perhaps ignoring most of the helper's questions and comments. It often seems that a client wants to get the story told as completely as possible before he or she will allow the helper to make an intervention. For others, it is a grueling process as the client's story is extracted drop by drop. In either case, the role of the helper *seems* passive, waiting for the client to finish the tale. Actually, the helper is listening with full attention so as to understand the facts, the feelings, and the unique perspective of the client. At times the helper is stopping to clarify a very important point of fact. Many client stories are as ironic and full of twists and turns as a Shakespearean comedy or tragedy. You cannot make a comment that a client will respect until you know the names of all the players and their relationships. It is difficult for many beginning helpers to listen to all these details. They cannot see where the story is going, and their own personal anxiety and desire to help propel them to fall back on the skills they have used all their life: offering praise, giving advice, and trying to track the client's problems back to some original cause. The art of helping, however, requires the helper to initially place his or her own concerns, questions, and theories on the back burner and to focus on the client's story, waiting until all the wrinkles have been explored.

NONVERBAL COMMUNICATION BETWEEN HELPER AND CLIENT

Nonverbal communication is also called *body language*. We generally talk about seven nonverbal ways that we speak to others without words: eye contact, body position, silence, voice tone, facial expressions and gestures, physical distance, and touching (Gladstein, 1974). Some writers have suggested that as much as 80 percent of communication takes place on the nonverbal level. It has been estimated that only 7 percent of emotions are conveyed by verbal means, whereas 38 percent are conveyed by the voice and 55 percent by the face (Mehrabian, 1972). Nonverbals can be compared to the musical score in a movie. They can affect us tremendously, but we may not notice their presence. For example, researchers studying couples communication were at first confused when they examined written transcripts of troubled marriages. Everything appeared normal. It was not until they watched the videos that they were able to see the subtle nonverbal signals of contempt such as rolling of the eyes. Even very minor movements and expressions can set off an argument. For example, it has been found that a raised eyebrow takes only a sixth of a second, but it can be detected at distances of over 150 feet (Blum, 1998).

Nonverbal behavior communicates has three functions that affect the content of what we say; nonverbals regulate the interaction (indicates pauses and stopping points), they can enhance intimacy, and they can be persuasive (cf. Argyle, 1987). From this, it is obvious that nonverbals add crucial information to messages, but we often fail to recognize their power.

REGULATION Occasionally, we are required to interact with others without having access to all the nonverbal cues that the person is sending. Have you ever participated in a conference call on the telephone? In face-to-face conversations, cues about when to speak and when to listen are communicated nonverbally. Without access to these regulators, everyone talks at once or there are long periods of silence.

INTIMACY Where strong emotions are being expressed, nonverbals are even more significant. For example, we might prefer e-mail from family members if we are merely exchanging information, but when we want to hear their voice to feel close to them we call or Skype to get access to their nonverbals. Think about the difference between sending a sympathy card and placing your arm around the shoulder of a grieving friend. To increase intimacy, we increase proximity and use touch.

PERSUASION Nonverbal communication is also a powerful component of persuasion. The gestures and voice tone of famous orators such as Martin Luther King Jr. are evidence of this. Certainly the most persuasive communication takes place when we can see another person's face and when we are in the same room. It is much easier to say "no" to the salesperson on the phone than to the one who is standing right in front of you. The art of helping also relies on persuasive nonverbal messages to encourage the client to open up. Helpers use specific nonverbal behaviors to persuade their clients that they are listening nonjudgmentally and, that the client is in a safe environment. Your willingness to take the time to provide the most inviting nonverbal atmosphere will ultimately affect your client's perception of you and his or her willingness to open up.

NONVERBAL SKILLS IN THE HELPING RELATIONSHIP

One maxim says that you can't *not* communicate. Our bodies are not very good liars (Archer & Akert, 1977; Ekman, 2009; Vrij, Akehurst, Soukara, & Bull, 2004). Folded arms and drooping facial muscles tend to give us away. Astute helpers learn to read the body language of their clients as clues to the depth and meaning of the client's problems. However, helpers must be aware of the signals that they are sending, too. The client is interpreting and reacting to the nonverbal messages of the helper. Clients react to helper nonverbals from the very first contact by voice tone on the phone and even by the arrangement of the office where client and helper meet. This discussion brings up an important caution about nonverbal messages. They are *ambiguous*. A client whose voice seems monotonous and depressed may actually be suffering from a cold. Crossed arms may be a better signal that the air conditioning is too high than that the client is "closed" to what you are saying. Although many emotions come through loud and clear regardless of culture, there is a wide variation in gestures and facial expressions because of one's upbringing (Ekman, 2009; Kim, Liang, & Li, 2003). Because of the ambiguous nature of nonverbal communication, most helpers are cautious about interpreting a client's posture, facial expressions, or voice tone, or about drawing serious conclusions about a client's mental state from a single piece of data. On the other hand, we have no control over what conclusions clients may draw from inadvertent nonverbal signals that we as helpers send. For this reason, from the initial meeting, helpers try to present the most welcoming, nonthreatening, and facilitative nonverbals that encourage the client to talk and do not interfere with the client's telling of the story. Recall that there are seven ways to communicate nonverbally: eye contact, body position, attentive silence, voice tone, facial expressions and gestures, physical distance, and touch. In the sections that follow, we will address each of these as they are best used in the helping relationship.

Eye Contact

Eye-to-eye contact is the first and most important indicator of listening. It conveys the helper's confidence and involvement (Ridley & Asbury, 1988). In Western culture, we normally associate lack of eye contact with dishonesty, indifference, or shame (see Kleinke, 1986). By contrast, those who sustain eye contact are seen as more ambitious, confident, assertive, intelligent, independent, and decisive than those who do not (Brooks, Church, & Fraser, 1986; Droney & Brooks, 1993).

Further, speakers who maintain eye contact with their audience are considered to be more credible and create more interest than those who do not. One study showed that graduate students in a seminar class are more likely to participate when they receive more eye contact from the professor (Caproni, Levine, O'Neal, McDonald, & Garwood, 1977). This suggests that eye contact can have an important interpersonal effect. It can stimulate involvement.

Clearly, eye contact is a powerful communication tool, but one should also be cautious in making assumptions about eye contact made by clients, especially those from different cultural backgrounds (Timm & Schroeder 2000). For example, some African American clients may have been trained to look away when listening (LaFrance & Mayo, 1976; Majors, 1991), and in many cultures, it is common to lower the eyes as a gesture of respect to superiors (Galanti, 2004). Care must be taken when interacting with people from cultures (such as some Asian cultures) in which direct eye contact may be considered offensive. In some situations, such as in the military and with some cultural groups, direct eye contact can be considered an act of defiance, a rude gesture, a sexual invitation, or a sign that you consider yourself to be superior. If cultures seem to clash, it might be useful to discuss this with the client. Depending on the situation, it might be best merely to respect the client's own way of using eye contact and try to mirror it. Discussing it with the client might be distracting and make the client feel overly self-conscious.

There is also evidence to suggest that eye contact may be more effective in some situations than others. When people discuss difficult situations, are struggling for words, or do not trust the other person, they tend to look away (Brooks et al., 1986; Droney & Brooks, 1993). In addition, looking at the other person's face takes a lot of mental energy, and when thinking deeply, a person breaks eye contact. Sometimes, the helper's fixed stare may be disconcerting and should be broken naturally and intermittently if the client becomes uncomfortable. A rule of thumb is to maintain a moderate amount of eye contact while closely monitoring its effect on the client. Still, eye contact by the helper can be a powerful tool because it forces intimacy on the client and increases the helper's ability to persuade (Goldman & Fordyce, 1983). During times when the helper wants to be heard, eye contact will make his or her message more potent.

Body Position

Actions speak louder than words. Posture may be the most often noticed aspect of body language, so it becomes important to have a "posture of involvement." A relaxed alertness communicates "I am comfortable with myself and I have time to listen to you." A relaxed and attentive posture is one of the fundamental tools for putting the client at ease (Maurer & Tindall, 1983). Lounging or sprawling in the chair might add an air of informality, but it may also communicate that the level of the helper's involvement is minimal. It is suggested that the helper lean the torso *slightly* forward (not the limbs), because leaning forward conveys attentiveness. Helpers normally maintain an open posture—no crossed arms or legs. Open postures seem to relax the client and encourage less defensiveness. In general, this kind of posture has been supported by research because it tends to increase rapport with the client (Sharpley, 2001).

Attentive Silence

Silence is a powerful tool in the helping session, whereas in social settings silence is deadly. When there is a gap in social conversations, people talk to fill the awkward void. If the helper is able to endure the discomfort caused by these silences, the social expectation to keep the discussion going may prompt the client to open up (MacDonald, 2005). Words often seem somehow to deny the validity of a person's grief or are perceived as attempts to sweep feelings under the rug. At these times, the helper falls back on **attentive silence** in order to be present without interfering. Allowing for small periods of silence gives the client moments for reflection and the helper time for processing. At times, silence is often the most appropriate response, such as when a client has experienced a great loss. If used too much or too early, it can make the client too uncomfortable and unsupported. Helpers tend to use silence more as they gain experience (Hill, Thompson, & Ladany, 2003). Thus, using silence is something of an art.

Experienced helpers use silence to allow the client to reflect, to communicate empathy, and to take time to think (Ladany, Hill, Thompson, & O'Brien, 2004). They do not use silence when a client is experiencing a great deal of anxiety or anger or if the client suffers from a psychotic disorder such as schizophrenia (Ladany et al., 2004). In addition, clients feel more rapport with the therapist when the therapist allows for intermittent silence (Sharpley, 2005). Clients also feel more positive about a session if the helper talks about one third of the time or less (Kleinke, 1986).

Voice Tone

A client's voice can give clues to his or her emotional state. We can tell from the client's tone which issues are the most painful and which are the sources of the greatest motivation and excitement. Similarly, clients respond to the helper's voice tone. Helpers attempt to show calm concern and empathy with their voices, and at times they try to mirror the client's emotional tone. When clients come to counseling, whether they are adults or children, they may be in a state of emotional turmoil. The helper who conveys a sense of calm and empathy with the voice can help stabilize the situation and give the impression that the helper will not be overwhelmed by the problem (cf. Tepper & Haase, 1978).

Sometimes, helpers use the voice to communicate that they understand how intensely the client is experiencing the problem. When a helper uses his or her voice to mirror the client's emotion, the helper does not try to *match* the intensity of the client's feelings but, instead, raises the voice slightly or gives emphasis to words that convey that the client's experience has been understood. Let us suppose, for example, that a client describes a situation in which he or she did not get an expected promotion at work. The helper may respond to the client's situation by saying, "You were really angry," or by saying, "You were *really* angry." In the second sentence, the helper's voice tone emphasizes the word *really* to more closely reflect the intensity of the client's feelings. This slight lifting of the voice can quickly let the client know you are listening very closely, not just to the facts but to the emotions as well.

Facial Expressions and Gestures

All human beings express the six primary emotions of sadness, joy, anger, surprise, disgust, and fear with the same basic facial expressions regardless of culture (Ekman, 1975), but interestingly, many of these expressions have cultural "accents." In other words, although Americans can identify sadness in pictures of Japanese people, there is something culturally distinct about their expression as well (Marsh, Elfenbein, & Ambady, 2003). Setting aside the basic emotions, human beings can also discern about 5,000 different facial expressions, many of which are culturally specific (Blum, 1998). Thus helpers must pay close attention to facial expressions, especially when it is important to determine if these signals match the clients' words. Incongruities between facial expression and verbal messages are clues to deceit, lack of self-awareness, and conflict.

Besides carefully attending to a client's expressions, the helper must consider what messages he or she is sending through facial gestures (Hackney, 1974). The first Freudian analysts were trained to avoid reacting to the client's expressions of emotion, whereas those trained in the client-centered approach of Carl Rogers felt that facial expressions shown by the helper should be genuine responses to the client's emotions. Regardless of one's theoretical persuasion, it is clear that facial expressions that convey the helper's reactions to the client's joy or sadness, anger or fear, excitement or boredom can serve as invitations to greater disclosure or potentially close the door if the client detects disdain, laughter, or boredom (Fretz, Corn, Tuemmler, & Bellet, 1979; Maurer & Tindall, 1983).

Gestures are physical motions we use to convey emotion or emphasize important points. At the two extremes, excessive movement may signal anxiety, whereas a motionless statuelike pose communicates aloofness. Fidgeting, playing with a pencil, drumming one's fingers, frequently shifting body position, checking a watch, and other such movements can be read by the client as nervousness, impatience, or disinterest. The listener who is moderately reactive to the client's content and feelings is more likely to be viewed as friendly, warm, casual, and natural. Specifically, this includes occasional head nodding for encouragement, a facial expression that indicates concern and interest, and encouraging movements of the hands that are not distracting.

Physical Distance

One's personal space, or "bubble," varies considerably from culture to culture. You may have noticed that people from Northern Europe require more space during a conversation than do Southern Europeans or Middle Easterners. It has been said that some Italians, for example, are perfectly comfortable with a conversation that is almost nose to nose (4 inches or less). Most one-on-one dialogues among Americans take place at a distance of 1 to 4 feet. Normally, about 3 feet is a comfortable space for personal interaction. In general, the smaller the physical distance, the more personal the interaction. While little research has been done on physical distance in helping settings, in general, we can say that a culturally appropriate distance enhances disclosure (Hazlewood & Schuldt, 1977).

Physical barriers such as desks increase distance and add a feeling of formality to the relationship. On the other hand, extremely close quarters can also feel intimidating and create anxiety. Stone and Morden (1976) suggest 5 feet (knee-to-knee sitting down) as an optimal distance between client and helper in a Western setting; however, most social situations are closer, with people sitting about 18 inches apart. Many helpers like to set up office chairs at about this distance, allowing the client to rearrange the chair in a comfortable way if it feels too close or too distant.

Touching and Warmth

We usually greet our clients by shaking hands in Western society. It signals that we are harmless and friendly (just as dogs roll over on their backs and stick their tongues out to communicate the same thing). Shaking hands conveys our willingness to connect. Touch has a long history in the helping professions, dating back to Freud's "pressure technique," which involved placing a hand on the client's forehead to encourage free association (Smith, Clance, & Imes, 1998). Touch can communicate caring and concern, especially during moments of grief (Driscoll, Newman, & Seals, 1988; Eyckmans, 2009). There are several writers who contend that helpers need to use appropriate touch (Swade, Bayne, & Horton, 2006; Willison & Masson, 1986) and that, at times, it might be antitherapeutic to avoid it. Holroyd and Brodsky (1980) recommend touch with socially immature clients to foster communication and bonding and with clients who are grieving, depressed, or traumatized as a way of showing support. They also encourage the use of touch as a greeting or at termination. In addition, touch may be used to emphasize or underline important points (Older, 1982). Touching another person does increase one's ability to influence that person (Goldman & Fordyce, 1983).

Although there is much to be said for the healing power of the human touch, certain taboos must be observed (Bonitz, 2008; Goodman & Teicher, 1988; Hunter & Struve, 1997; Phelan, 2009). Touch can also engender powerful sexual and transference reactions in the client (Alyn, 1988). For a client who has been sexually abused, a good deal of anxiety may be aroused, and any kind of touch might be inappropriate (Hunter & Struve, 1997). Perhaps fears about physical contact are overblown in the literature, but many writers have cautioned that it is important to know the client well before initiating even the safest forms of touch, such as a pat on the shoulder or back (Eiden, 1998). One guideline is to use touch only sparingly to communicate encouragement and concern, with the knowledge that even slight gestures may evoke sexual or fearful feelings in the client (Stenzel & Rupert, 2004). The helper must be prepared to recognize this reaction in the client and be willing to discuss it.

Fisher, Rytting, and Heslin (1976) established three useful guidelines for helper touch: (1) Touch should be appropriate to the situation; (2) touch should not impose a greater level of intimacy than the client can handle; and (3) touch should not communicate a negative message (such as a patronizing pat). It must be recognized here that there is a "pro-hug" school of thought among some helpers. A hug may be a special gesture at the end of the counseling relationship, but it may be experienced as forced intimacy

TABLE 4.2   Nonverbals That Communicate Warmth or Coldness

Nonverbal Cue	Warmth	Coldness
Tone of voice	Soft	Hard
Facial expression	Smiling, interested	Poker-faced, frowning, uninterested
Posture	Lean toward other; relaxed	Lean away from other; tense
Eye contact	Look into other's eyes	Avoid looking into other's eyes
Touching	Touch other softly	Avoid touching other
Gestures	Open, welcoming	Closed, guarding oneself, and keeping other away
Spatial distance	Close	Distant

Source: David W. Johnson, *Reaching Out: Interpersonal Effectiveness and Self-Actualization*, 7/e, Copyright 2000. Reprinted with permission of Allyn and Bacon.

when used routinely. An embrace may be seen as phony, and the helper may actually be seen as less trustworthy (Suiter & Goodyear, 1985).

Because touch has its dangers, most beginning helpers should probably avoid it at first. The helper can still convey caring nonverbally by communicating warmth. Warmth is not a skill but a synthesis of nonverbal communications that can have a powerful effect on a client's willingness to open up. Warmth is difficult to define, but when it is present, we recognize it and respond by opening up. In Table 4.2, David Johnson (2000) shows how nonverbal messages can communicate either warmth or coldness.

STOP AND REFLECT

Differences in nonverbal communication can be a stumbling block in forming a relationship with someone from a different cultural background. We make assumptions about people based on the way they talk, look, or dress. In this section, Dr. Andrew Daire, who worked in a university counseling center, describes how talking about these perceived differences can lead to a better helping relationship and turn a negative first impression into a source of growth for helper and client.

I was the only black counselor at a small, private, predominantly white institution in the South. Once I was called to the office to meet a new client named Ray. When I came downstairs, I saw a burly young man in Western wear and cowboy boots who possessed a strong Southern drawl. He seemed very guarded initially, which I attributed to his discomfort in talking about his relationship problems. Soon I realized that we were not talking about the obvious differences between us, so I made the decision to cautiously open a discussion about his upbringing and how it differed from my own.

During that first session, he talked about his father being a racist and then admitted that he had almost walked out the door when he saw that his counselor was black. Despite this first encounter, we were able to form a good counseling relationship, and over the next nine sessions, we talked about his relationship issues as well as stereotypes and prejudice. When I saw my client for the first time, based on his clothing and accent, I expected him to be racist, and I was tempted to pull back and not even address our differences. I now believe that treating him in that way would probably have reinforced his stereotypes and prejudice, rather than providing an opportunity for him to examine them. I also began to understand a little about the fears that drive the attitudes of people like Ray and his father. Most important, we were able to develop a relationship that helped

(Continued)

him deal with the issues he had come to work on. Had I not brought up the impressions we shared of each other, he probably would not have come back after the first session.

- Have you ever thought about attitudes you might have about people from various parts of the country? Do certain accents lead you to make unfair assumptions about people? What does a Southern, New York, Appalachian, or British accent imply about someone?
- Have you ever thought of clothing, hairstyle, or jewelry as a form of communication? All of these can be culturally influenced. For example, many people wear religious jewelry, giving a glimpse of their background. What customs can you identify in your own culture that help you decide what clothes or jewelry to wear? Are certain colors best for certain occasions, such as black for funerals?
- What can you really tell about a person from his or her clothing? Is there a risk of "pigeonholing" people based on their clothing choice or the kind of car they drive?
- Think for a moment about your experience with people from different cultural backgrounds. Which cultural groups do you have the most experience with through friends or family? Which groups do you know the least about? How important do you think it is for a helper to experience a variety of cultural groups during his or her training? Do you think it is always possible for a helper to cross over cultural lines, as Andrew did, and help someone who seems to be so different?
- In Andrew's story, both helper and client reacted to the nonverbals of the other person—clothing, accent, skin color, and probably many other tiny cultural differences—but they were hesitant to mention them. When do you think it might be important in a helping relationship to notice these and talk about them? When do you think it is best to ignore them? Is part of your job as a counselor to open up areas of discussion that are traditionally taboo? Is broaching difficult topics a separate skill? Discuss this with your classmates.

We have now seen that nonverbal communication can invite or discourage a client from self-disclosure. Next, we turn to opening skills, which are verbal prompts that encourage clients to disclose themselves even more deeply.

OPENING SKILLS: HOW TO INVITE

The nonverbal skills say to the client, "I am ready to listen," but the opening skills say, "Tell me more." Because opening skills are actually demands that the helper makes of the client, they must be presented in a way that the client feels that he or she has the opportunity to refuse. They are soft commands. Opening skills include two broad skills: encouragers and questions.

Encouragers

Encouragement means "to cause to have heart." Encouragers are words the helper uses to bolster the client's courage to confide. We have divided these encouragers into two categories, but both types—door openers and minimal encouragers—are brief interventions to kindle the fire of self-expression. We will discuss them separately here, but later in the book, we will simply refer to them both as encouragers because both serve the same basic function: to spark disclosure without taking over the conversation.

DOOR OPENERS The first kind of encourager is called a **door opener**, which is "a noncoercive invitation to talk" (Bolton, 1979, p. 50). The door opener is initiated by the helper, but the client determines the depth of the response. More than a passing social response or greeting, the door opener signals availability on the part of the listener and encourages exploration and discussion. By contrast, evaluative or judgmental responses are "door closers." Some parents and teachers use door closers and wonder why their children or students clam up. Here are some examples of door closers:

"I suppose you are going to sulk again this morning, aren't you?"

"When will you ever learn?"

By contrast, a door opener is generally a positive, nonjudgmental response made during the initial phase of a contact. It may include observations by the helper such as the following:

"I see you are reading a book about Sylvia Plath [observation]. How do you like it?"

"You look down this morning [observation]. Do you want to talk about it?"

"What's on your mind?"

"Tell me about it."

"Can you say more about that?"

"What would you like to talk about today?"

Door openers are invaluable to helpers because they can be used to get clients to expand on what they have been saying, to begin conversations in the first place, and to allow helpers additional time to formulate a response.

MINIMAL ENCOURAGERS   **Minimal encouragers** are brief supportive statements that convey attention and understanding. Most of us are familiar with minimal encouragers from the media's image of the Freudian analyst behind the couch, stroking his beard and saying, "Mm-hmm." Minimal encouragers are verbal responses that show interest and involvement but allow the client to determine the primary direction of the conversation. They are different from door openers in that they communicate only that the listener is on track (Hill, 2004). Such phrases reinforce talking on the part of the client and are often accompanied by an approving nod of the head. Examples of minimal encouragers include:

"I see."

"Yes."

"Right."

"Okay."

"Hmm."

"I've got you."

"I hear you."

"I'm with you."

Of course, these responses are not sufficient to help a client achieve the goals of therapy, but if they are *not* used frequently enough (especially in the beginning of the session), the client feels stranded and uncertain. Minimal encouragers tell the client, "I am present," but they do not interrupt the story's flow.

Questions

Be patient toward all that is unresolved in your heart.
Try to love the questions themselves.
Do not seek the answers which cannot be given,
Because you would not be able to live them.
And the point is to live everything.
Live the questions now.
Perhaps you will then gradually without noticing it,
Live along some distant day into the answers.

                               Rainer Marie Rilke

The great poet's words underline our common tendency to think that questions provide the ultimate road to understanding. Frequently, we can learn the most by patiently living with our questions until the answers come of themselves. We fall back on questioning when silence fails or when we feel uncertain about the direction of the conversation with someone we are trying to help. Sometimes questions get in the way of understanding for both helper and client.

Of all the opening skills, *questions* are the most easily abused. Excessive questions distract us from listening, and on the other side, the client may feel interrogated and evaluated (Brodsky & Lichtenstein, 1999). Questions can sidetrack the client from the story that is emerging because a question is a demand. In the beginning, questions interfere with the need the client has to tell the tale. Even more important is the fact that we are training our clients to answer questions rather than express themselves. Clients learn what helping is from the helper. Therefore, we want to be very careful, especially in the beginning, not to convey the impression that helping is an inquisition into what is wrong. Some of the most useless questions helpers ask are:

"How are you doing?"

"How have things been this week?"

"How do you feel about that?"

"Why do you feel that way?"

Still, the helper must ask some questions in order to gain key information. So the problem is to know when to ask questions and which questions to ask. In general, specific questions about facts are best used (1) when an important part of the story is unclear and (2) as a means of encouraging the client to open up. In my experience, beginning helpers tend to ask too many questions, and they ask the wrong kinds of questions. Research suggests that helpers ask fewer questions as they gain experience (Ornston, Cichetti, Levine, & Freeman, 1968). The next section takes aim at two common pitfalls: "why?" questions and leading questions. The following section talks about the appropriate use of questions in the beginning stages of helping.

"WHY?" QUESTIONS Asking the client *why* they behaved or felt a particular way is very enticing because this inquiry seems very psychological and appears to be getting to the root of a problem. The assumptions here are (1) that the client knows why and (2) that knowing why will be helpful. In fact, asking a client, "Why did you get a divorce?" may put him or her on the defensive rather than stimulating deeper thought (Brodsky & Lichtenstein, 1999). Adults tend to respond to "why?" questions with intellectualizations and rationalizations.

On the other hand, if you ask a 5-year-old why he or she stepped in the mud, the inevitable and truthful answer is "I don't know." In reality, a few decisions people make, such as buying a car or a house, may have been the result of a lengthy, rational process, but the best answer to most "why?" questions is usually "It seemed like a good idea at the time." This may be true even for important life decisions such as getting married or changing jobs. Over time, helpers learn to ask fewer "why?" questions and learn to extract the motivations, or "why," of the client's behavior from the whole of the story.

Frequently the reason for asking questions is that the helper feels stuck. When you encounter a sullen, reluctant, silent, or angry client, you may find the almost irresistible urge to revert to questioning because listening alone does not seem to be working. This feeling generally leads to desperate measures that do more harm than good. At such times, the helper should fall back on attentive silence and encouragers to keep the door open.

LEADING QUESTIONS Leading questions have an embedded message. The message usually is "If you follow my logic, you will soon see the answer to your problem." Leading questions are usually grouped together as a subtle argument or a secret way of giving the client advice (Hargie & Dickson, 2004). Consider this example:

RAYMOND (CLIENT): "Since I was diagnosed with cancer, my entire life has changed. People have started looking at me differently. They look down on me like I can't do the job anymore. I am sick of being pitied."

LEILA (HELPer): "Are you letting other people affect your mood?" (leading)

RAYMOND: "I guess so."

LEILA: "Would you let other people affect you so much if you had more faith in yourself?" (leading)

RAYMOND: "No, probably not."

LEILA: "Do you think that if your self-esteem were higher, you would feel better?" (leading)

RAYMOND: "Yeah."

These questions are *leading* because they are really disguised attempts to push through the client's acceptance of the helper's agenda. Can you see that in this example the helper is trying to get the client to acknowledge that his lack of self-esteem is the cause of his problem? Notice that the client tacitly agrees, but does not respond with more information or real enthusiasm. Unfortunately, this type of questioning is very common among those who are trying to work with children and adolescents, but the evidence suggests that this approach shuts down the conversation (Sternberg et al.1997).

OPEN AND CLOSED QUESTIONS While leading and "why?" questions are to be avoided, there are two other categories of questions that you will want to use: open and closed.

Closed Questions **Closed questions** ask for specific information and usually require a short factual response. Some closed questions can be answered with a "yes" or "no"; others demand information such as when you ask someone's age. Closed questions are important when you need to get the facts straight—especially when there is an emergency situation or when an understanding of the complicated facts is crucial to your understanding of the client's story. This became apparent in a recent demonstration session during which a client discussed the trauma and aftereffects of a serious two-car accident. The helper, using door openers, minimal encouragers, and appropriate nonverbals, was able to get the client to talk about many of the important issues. However, the student helper failed to ask if the other victim of the accident had been killed or injured, an event that was the key to the client's shame and remorse about the incident. The student helper felt that the client should have volunteered this vital piece of information, but clients often talk about a problem on a superficial level at first. Sometimes, the helper must delve and pry to get the important facts. The difficulty is in knowing which aspects of the story are likely to be important. In this incident, for example, it was the seriousness of the accident that needed to be explored. Many beginning helpers might ask about less relevant details. They might ask when the accident occurred, how bad the damage was to the cars involved, where the incident took place, and so forth. These are the sorts of questions that sidetrack the client from the important issues.

Although there are times when closed questions are called for, they can have a dampening effect on the relationship and on the conversation. If a helper begins with a series of questions such as name, address, and phone number, the client may begin to believe that his or her job is to respond to the helper's questions rather than to tell the story. The client can become passive, waiting for the right line of questioning before speaking. Sometimes the deadly silence in the session is due to the fact that you trained the client to wait for questions rather than initiate conversation. It may also be true that, depending on a client's cultural background, the helper is viewed as an authority. The client might feel that it is only respectful to wait for a question. At such times, the helper should not let the client suffer in silence, but instead let the client know that helping means a partnership in which both people have the opportunity to contribute. The use of open questions will help these clients make a transition to greater involvement.

Open Questions   Compared with closed questions, **open questions** allow more freedom of expression and are perceived as more helpful (Elliott, 1985). Open questions do not request specific information but encourage one to speak about the general topic. Because open questions are less coercive than closed questions, clients who are reluctant to seek help may respond better to open questions (Brodsky & Lichtenstein, 1999). Here are some examples. Consider how you might respond to them.

> "Could you tell me about the kinds of problems you have been having?"
>
> "Last week, we discussed your relationships with men. Would you mind going into that again?"
>
> "Can you tell me about your problems with math?"
>
> "You say you have self-esteem problems. What do you mean by that?"

Now consider the following *closed* questions:

> "How old are you?"
>
> "What school do you go to?"
>
> "Are you planning to go to college?"
>
> "Would you describe your marriage as happy?"

The difference between the two question types is something like the comparison between multiple-choice and essay exams. Multiple-choice tests check your knowledge of the facts, but essays ask you to show a deeper level of understanding. Here are some pairs of open and closed questions that each explore a similar topic. Note the differences in the client's typical response to open versus closed questions.

Closed

HELPER: "Are you getting along with your parents these days?"

CLIENT: "Yeah. Pretty good."

Open

HELPER: "Can you tell me how you and your parents have been dealing with your differences recently?"

CLIENT: "Well, we haven't been, really. We're not fighting, but we're not talking, either. Just existing."

Closed

HELPER: "Are you married now?"

CLIENT: "No, divorced."

Open

HELPER: "Can you tell me a little about your personal relationships during the past few years?"

CLIENT: "Well, I've been divorced for 6 months from my second wife. We were married for over 7 years, and one day she left me for this guy at work. Since then, I haven't really been up to seeing anyone."

As these examples suggest, open questions eventually elicit more information than closed questions, even though they may not seem as direct (Johns Hopkins University, 1998). Open questions enhance the therapeutic relationship (Boyd, 2003). Open questions also persuade the client to answer by giving the client the opportunity to refuse. They do not box the client in by forcing him or her to answer directly. When you feel the need to ask a closed question, try to transform it into an open one first.

In summary, there is a tendency for beginners to ask too many questions including "why?" questions, leading questions, and unnecessary closed questions. Yet it is also important to get crucial information. Good questioning is an art (Goldberg, 1998), and we will consider it in greater detail when we discuss its use in the assessment stage of the helping process. For the time being, keep a close watch on the overuse of questions in the exercises and practice sessions. See if you can do without closed questions, and let your nonverbal skills and other encouragers be the workhorses of your helping conversation.

STOP AND REFLECT

Are You an Opener?

The Opener Scale was developed by Miller, Berg, and Archer (1983) to identify individuals who are good listeners and are able to get others to disclose information about themselves.[*] If you score yourself as low on this scale, it does not mean that you cannot learn the basic helping skills in this

(Continued)

book. It is a self-assessment of where you are right now, not what you can become. When you have finished this book, write down your answers again to see what changes you have made. As you fill out the scale, try to be as honest as you can. Do not compare your score with other people's results—this scale was not devised for that purpose.

Rate each statement as it applies to you on a scale of 1–5 (4–5 strongly agree, 3 agree, 2 disagree, 1 strongly disagree).

1. People frequently tell me about themselves.
2. I've been told that I'm a good listener.
3. I'm very accepting of others.
4. People trust me with their secrets.
5. I easily get people to "open up."
6. People feel relaxed around me.
7. I enjoy listening to people.
8. I'm sympathetic to people's problems.
9. I encourage people to tell me how they are feeling.
10. I can keep people talking about themselves.

Although the Opener Scale does not have any guidelines about what constitutes a high or low score, let us arbitrarily set 0–10 as a low score and 30–40 as a high score. It has been found that people with higher scores on the Opener Scale are more successful in eliciting self-disclosure, even in people whose self-disclosure is normally low. High scorers are also able to take the viewpoint of others (be empathic) more easily than low scorers. Purvis, Dabbs, and Hopper (1984) found that high scorers show more comfort, enjoyment, and attentiveness than low scorers and are more verbally and nonverbally engaged.

What reaction do you have to your results? Some beginning helpers wrongly believe that everyone has these interests and skills. In other words, they take their "opener" skills for granted. They are surprised to find that the opening abilities tapped by this scale are not as common as they thought. Discuss this idea with classmates or record your reactions in your journal.

---

*Used with permission of the authors.

MyCounselingLab™

Go to Topic 2, *Invitational Interviewing*, on the MyCounselingLab™ site (www. MyCounselingLab.com) for *Learning the Art of Helping: Building Blocks and Techniques*, Fifth Edition, where you can:

- Find learning outcomes for *Invitational Interviewing* along with the national standards that connect to these outcomes.
- Complete Assignments and Activities that can help you more deeply understand the chapter content.
- Apply and practice your understanding of the core skills identified in the chapter with the Building Counseling Skills unit.
- Prepare yourself for professional certification with a Practice for Certification quiz.
- Connect to videos through the Video and Resource Library.

MyCounselingLab™ Exercises

Exercise 1: Focusing on Body Language

Go to the Video and Resource Library on the MyCounselingLab™ site for your text and search for the following clip: *Invitational Skills*, a video showing Chris, a helper, and Kevin, her client. Watch the entire video first, and then answer the questions below.

1. Would you describe Chris's body posture as attentive and open? If so, what gives you this impression?
2. At one point, the helper touches the client's arm. Would you, as a helper, have touched the client at this point? Why or why not? How did the client react?
3. Chris is able to convey warmth. How does she do this?
4. Even though Chris did not add any new information, was she able to get the client to talk more deeply about his problem? If so, what do you think allowed him to do this?
5. List a couple of encouragers Chris used.
6. Were all of Chris's questions open questions? Write down one of her open questions.
7. If you were to ask a relevant closed question, what would it be?
8. What closed questions would not be relevant?

Summary

Every client has a story to tell, and invitational skills let the client know that you are interested in that story. Invitational skills have two basic components: nonverbal skills and opening skills. Nonverbal skills are messages used by helpers to provide the right conditions for the client to open up. The skills are eye contact, body position, attentive silence, voice tone, facial expressions and gestures, physical distance, and touching. Opening skills are the verbal messages the helper sends to facilitate the client's disclosure. Opening skills include encouragers and open and closed questions. Invitational skills are relatively simple to learn, but they count for so much in the relationship between client and helper. A summary of suggestions about how to use invitational skills effectively is presented in the following "Quick Tips."

- After an open question or two, use the first few minutes to listen to the client, using minimal encouragers and head nodding.
- When a silence occurs, don't rush to fill the void. Wait for the client to do it first.
- Rely on door openers such as "Go on" and "Say some more about that," rather than asking too many questions at first.
- Use closed questions sparingly, but ask yourself if you have understood the most important facts. If you are unsure, stop the client and ask a closed question or two.

Getting the relationship off on the right foot means establishing the norm that the client has free rein to explore his or her deepest issues in a nonjudgmental atmosphere. Besides their importance in the beginning, invitational skills are needed at all stages of the helping process. As each new issue comes to the surface, the helper relies on invitational skills and a nonjudgmental attitude to provide the atmosphere of warmth and safety that allows for the deepest exploration of the client's needs, fears, and dreams.

QUICK TIPS:

Invitational Skills
- Once you have adopted a **facilitative body position,** take a deep breath and relax.
- Remember that the ball is in the client's court: Invite the client to talk and to tell the story.

Exercises

GROUP EXERCISES

Exercise 1: First Encounters

In this activity, the instructor selects two or three people to demonstrate a first encounter with a client. These may be students who have had some experience in the helping field or even individuals who have worked in the professional or retail world. These "helpers" each select a student to play their clients and one by one demonstrate, in a role play, how they establish conditions in which the client feels comfortable talking. For example, one student might role-play a school counselor bringing an elementary student from the playground to his or her office. The helpers should demonstrate in the role play how they greet the person and how they begin the helping conversation. After each role play, students in the class discusses what they liked about each helper's approach. Does the class think that this first impression is crucial? What skills did you observe in each helper's vignette?

Exercise 2: Practice and Feedback Session Using Invitational Skills

Some Notes on the Helper/Client/Observer Training Group

For many of the practice sessions in this book, we will be asking you to break into groups of three or four. This works in a circular fashion, with person A counseling person B, then person B counseling person C, and finally person C counseling person A. Depending on how your instructor likes to work, you may be assigned to the same groups for all practice sessions, or you may frequently change groups. Practicing on fellow students is a method used in medical and dental schools as well as in the training of mental health professionals. Recently, I met a dental student who told me that he and his fellow students practice giving each other numbing shots. Just as in giving an injection, there is some risk involved in role-playing, but one of the prime benefits is that you learn something about being in the client role. You learn how it feels to be challenged or supported. You also get a feeling about what is too invasive or too superficial. On the other hand, in the role of observer you are able to step out of the helping situation and look at the situation more objectively. All three roles are instructive. Finally, as a member of a practice group, you will be challenged ethically, too. Although you may be role-playing part of the time, some of the situations are real; you should have an agreement for confidentiality just as if it were an actual problem. It has been our experience that students respect this confidentiality and take it very seriously. Still, confidentiality and its limits need to be explicitly discussed in each group.

Instructions for Group Exercise 1

Break up into groups of four. One person is the helper, another the client, and two act as observers. Before the "session" begins, the helper should take time to review the "Quick Tips: Invitational Skills" section. Meanwhile, the client decides on the topic he or she wants to discuss, and the observers look over their checklists. Observer 1 will use Feedback Checklist 1 to give the helper data on his or her nonverbal skills. Observer 2 will use Feedback Checklist 2 to rate the helper on opening skills. If there are only three in your group, the observer should try to give feedback on checklist number 2 and the client can comment on the helper's nonverbals. For 5 to 8 minutes, the helper invites the client to discuss one of the following topics:

- How I chose my present job
- A trip I took that was very important to me
- My relationship with a close friend
- A topic of the client's choice
- The problem of a friend or acquaintance whose role the client assumes

Feedback

At the end of the time period, the observers and client give feedback to the helper. The client is encouraged to give qualitative feedback that may include general impressions of the helper's manner. The client should indicate whether or not he or she felt genuineness, empathy, and respect from the helper. The observers then give feedback based on their checklists. The participants switch roles, giving each person a chance to experience helper, client, and observer roles. The entire process will take about 45 minutes.

Feedback Checklist 1 (to be completed by Observer 1)

During the practice session, try to work through the checklist systematically, recording your comments for each skill on a separate sheet as you observe it. If you have time, start at the beginning and review each skill, at the end of the conversation, to check your observations. When you are finished, write down any suggestions for improvement. Be as honest as possible so that the helper can benefit from feedback.

1. Draw a stick figure sketch of the helper's body position.
   What does the body position convey? (Circle all that apply)

Openness	Relaxation	Tension
Stiffness	Interest	Aloofness

Suggestions for improvement:

2. Evaluate the helper's ability to maintain appropriate eye contact (circle one).

   Avoids
   Occasional
   Constant with breaks
   Stares
   Suggestions for improvement:

3. Evaluate the helper's voice tone (circle all that apply).

Too loud	Cold
Too soft	Soothing
Confident	Clipped
Hesitant	Interested
Moralistic or smug	Bored
Warm	Other

Suggestions for improvement:

4. Evaluate the helper's gestures and facial expressions (circle all that apply).

Gestures:
Nervous movement or distracting movement
Occasional
Inviting gestures
Rigid

Nodding:
Head nodding appropriate
Head nodding too frequent
Head nodding too infrequent

Expression:
Helper's face shows concern and interest
Face shows disinterest
Face reflects client's feelings
Face is unchanging/masklike
Other (e.g., warmth or use of touch)
Suggestions for improvement:

Feedback Checklist 2 (to be completed by Observer 2)

You are to give feedback on the helper's use of encouragers (door openers and minimal encouragers) and questions (open and closed). Your task is to write down everything the helper says during the interview. At the end, categorize each response and give the helper feedback.

Categories

Encourager (E)—include door openers and minimal encouragers under this same category
Open question (OQ)
Closed question (CQ)

Helper Question or Statement	Category
1.	
2.	
3.	
4.	
5.	
6.	
7.	
8.	
9.	
10.	
11.	
12.	
13.	
14.	
15.	

Feedback on the Use of Encouragers

1. Did the helper supply enough encouragers during the initial 2 minutes of the interview to let the client know he or she was listening?

2. Were minimal encouragers used too often, instead of open questions that might have given more depth to the discussion?

Feedback on the Use of Questions

1. Look at the list of closed questions used by the helper. Based on the client's response, were they vitally important or merely asked out of curiosity? How many "why?" questions did you detect?
2. Were there more open or closed questions? Does this helper need to increase the use of open questions or decrease the use of closed questions?

SMALL GROUP DISCUSSIONS

The following activities can be done in a small group or as a whole class.

Discussion 1: Open Versus Closed Questions

Each member of a small group (two or three students) should individually turn the following closed questions into open questions. Write your answers on a separate sheet. Remember, an open question can expand a topic beyond the original closed question. For example, the closed question "Are your parents still married?" can be "opened" by changing it to "Can you tell me something about your family?" Share your open questions with others in a small group. Think how you might answer your own open questions. Does it give you room to expand and disclose?

- Where are you from?
- What is your problem?
- Why do you need help?
- When did all of your problems begin?
- Do your mom and dad fight?
- Did you have fun on the class trip?
- How old is your daughter?

Discussion 2: Watch a Video of a Practice Session Between Another Helper and a Client

View 10 to 15 minutes of a video that shows a client/helper interaction. While watching, write down any observations you may have concerning the client's body posture, gestures, and movements. Afterward, discuss the relationship of these nonverbal messages to the client's concerns. Alternatively, half of the class can observe the client and the other half can focus on the helper. Check the helper's invitational skills against the list in Table 4.1.

Discussion 3: Eyes Closed

Form dyads (groups of two) and sit facing each other with your eyes closed. Discuss your activities over the past week for about 4 to 5 minutes. In the class discussion that follows, take turns giving your reactions to the experience. What nonverbal behaviors did you and your classmates find it most difficult to do without?

Discussion 4: The Effect of Distance

Set up a simulated office for a role-playing situation. Provide one chair for the client and another for the helper. Use a third chair to represent a desk if one is not available. Place the chairs about 10 feet apart and ask two participants to hold a conversation at that distance concerning a minor problem one of them is having. Ask the group to comment on how the distance has affected the conversation. Next, allow the participants to move the chairs to a comfortable distance. Once the chairs have been moved and the participants are seated, measure the distance from knee to knee with a yardstick or tape measure and see if it is approximately 18 inches, an average social distance. Does it seem too close or too far away? Next, move the chairs so close that the participants feel uncomfortable. Measure that distance. If participants from diverse ethnic backgrounds are members of the group, interesting variations can occur. Try the exercise with participants standing instead of seated. You will find that some people will feel comfortable with an interpersonal distance of 6 inches or less.

Discussion 5: Touch with Caution

Conduct a group discussion on the implications of touching clients. What constitutes sexual touching? Whose needs are being fulfilled by touching? Is it all right for the helper's emotional needs to be met by hugging a client? Under what circumstances would a hug be beneficial or harmful? What about hugging in group therapy?

Discussion 6: Try a 15-Minute Video Session

Make a 15-minute video of two trainees, one of whom acts as the client and the other as the helper. The client discusses a minor problem he or she is having at work or at school. Focus the camera for half of the session on the helper's face and the other half of the session on the helper's whole body. Replay the tape and ask the helper to evaluate his or her own facial expressions, body position, and gestures. While this is a very simple exercise, it may help students who are feeling camera shy. Our experience is that the more opportunities students have to be recorded, the better their final sessions will be. As the normal fear of being observed lessens, the helper's responses become more natural and more attention is focused on the client.

Discussion 7: Sustained Eye Contact

In this exercise, students form dyads. The leader or instructor will keep time and signal the completion of the activity at the end of 2 minutes. Maintain eye contact with your partner and assume the appropriate helper's posture while remaining completely silent. Afterward, discuss your personal reactions to this exercise with your partner and then with the larger group.

WRITTEN EXERCISES

Written Exercise 1: Practice in Classifying Opening Skills

Learning to identify skills is the first step. The second step is performing the skills aloud. We have found that the more practice you have in identifying skills, the more rapidly you will be able to produce the skills yourself. Read the following excerpt from a counseling session between a helper, Mrs. Henderson, and her new student, Maryann and then classify each of the eight helper responses as a door opener (DO), minimal encourager (ME), open question (OQ), or closed question (CQ).

		Skill Used
Mrs. Henderson:	It looks like you've been crying, Maryann.	1. _____
Maryann:	Yes, that is why I came to see you.	
Mrs. Henderson:	Can you tell me what's upsetting you?	2. _____
Maryann:	Everything! I hate this school!	
Mrs. Henderson:	Go on.	3. _____
Maryann:	I hate the other kids, and I hate my teacher.	
Mrs. Henderson:	Tell me some more about what has been happening.	4. _____
Maryann:	Well, ever since I moved here, Joe and Maggie have been calling me names.	
Mrs. Henderson:	And how long ago was that?	5. _____
Maryann:	About half a year now.	
Mrs. Henderson:	What are they saying?	6. _____
Maryann:	That I'm stupid and ugly. Someone called me dummy today.	
Mrs. Henderson:	I see.	7. _____
Maryann:	It happens a lot. It's not fair.	
Mrs. Henderson:	What has it been like—having to deal with this?	8. _____
Maryann:	Horrible! I feel like I want to go back to my old school. I had lots of friends there.	

SELF-ASSESSMENT

One simple way of evaluating yourself is "Did Well" and "Do Better." This consists of recognizing what you liked about your performance and what you want to improve. Based on your feedback and experience in the group exercise or other exercises so far, write down one or two things that you did well in your first practice sessions:

1. _____
2. _____

Now, based on your feedback, write down one or two things you could do to improve your skills:

1. _____
2. _____

HOMEWORK

Homework 1: Sound Off

Record a television show or movie and replay it with the sound turned off. Try to see if you can guess emotional content by examining the characters' body language. Write a half-page reaction to this assignment. If you want to have the voice tone added, try watching a program in another language and see if you can still get the gist of the story without understanding the words.

Homework 2: Hug Survey

Conduct a survey among a few friends or family members. How would they feel about being hugged or touched by a professional helper? Try to be objective and prepare a one-page summary of their answers and your conclusions.

Homework 3: Experiment with Silence

In conversations with coworkers, family, and friends, instead of immediately responding to what they say, build in attentive silence and notice the effect. The purpose of the assignment is to observe the effect of silence on the communication of others. Make notes and report findings to the group. Write a one-paragraph reaction to this exercise. If your silence is too long, your friends and family will complain or look at you strangely. If it is just right, it should have the effect of encouraging them to talk.

JOURNAL STARTERS

Think about a secret that you have not shared with anyone. How do you think you would feel if a helper urged you to share this private information? Would it be easier to share it with a close friend? What kind of response would you expect if you told a close friend about this issue? How do you think you would feel after sharing this information? What are your fantasies about what might happen if you disclosed this secret to a helper? Do you imagine the helper telling others, or is it simply disquieting to think about the secret? Would any of these expectations affect your willingness to share the information with a professional helper?

Reflecting Skills: Paraphrasing

The unexamined life is not worth living.

SOCRATES

MyCounselingLab™

Visit the MyCounselingLab™ site for *Learning the Art of Helping: Building Blocks and Techniques,* Fifth Edition to enhance your understanding of chapter concepts. You'll have the opportunity to practice your skills through video- and case-based Assignments and Activities as well as Building Counseling Skills units, and to prepare for your certification exam with Practice for Certification quizzes.

The invitational skills you learned in the last chapter send this message to the client: "I am ready and willing to listen." Although invitational skills, such as eye contact, convey that you are present and available, they do not adequately indicate that you really understand what the other person is trying to convey. Invitational skills are commonly used by friends, family, and acquaintances, as well as by helpers. Reflecting skills, on the other hand, are specialized interventions used by helpers to stimulate deeper exploration of the facts, feelings, and meanings that coexist in the client's presentation of the problem.

REFLECTING CONTENT AND THOUGHTS, REFLECTING FEELINGS, AND REFLECTING MEANING

Every client message has three basic components: (1) the client's understanding of the facts and his or her thoughts (a cognitive level), (2) the client's underlying feelings (an emotional level), and (3) hidden meanings (existential level) (see Figure 5.1). Each of these three dimensions of experience can be evoked by specific skills. As Figure 5.1 suggests, you might want to think of them as three separate boxes that have to be unpacked if you are to really grasp the whole story. Frequently, students feel that they have reached a point with a client where there seems to be "nowhere to go." In most of these cases, it is because he or she has not examined all of the boxes.

In this chapter, you will learn about the first box, reflecting story content and client thoughts, a skill that is called *paraphrasing*. Chapter 7 focuses on learning the skill of *reflecting feelings,* and Chapter 8 addresses the skill of *reflecting meaning.* You will learn these skills separately and then practice putting them together in a complete helping session. Table 5.1 gives examples of these three building block skills.

To gain a clearer idea of the distinction between the parts of the client's message, consider the following story in which a helper describes how he began to recognize that parts of a story are suppressed and must be reflected.

> Once I ran a private practice in a small town. The house next door to my office was guarded by a huge German shepherd dog that frequently growled at my clients when they approached the front door. When I greeted my clients, I was always interested

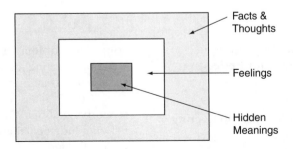

FIGURE 5.1 Components of the Client's Message

TABLE 5.1	**Three Building Blocks in Reflecting Skills**
Skill	**Examples**
Paraphrase	Topic A: "So this week has been very difficult, at work and at home."
	Topic B: "If I understand, an old friend contacted you about getting together, and you are not looking forward to it."
Reflection of feeling	Topic A: "You felt discouraged about your job and sad about the problems at home."
	Topic B: "After all that had happened, you were wary about continuing your friendship and perhaps you are still angry."
Reflection of meaning	Topic A: "You began looking at yourself as a failure because neither of these two important areas of your life are fulfilling at the moment."
	Topic B: "You want to see yourself as a forgiving person but the fact that you harbor some resentment after all this time makes you doubt this view of yourself."

in how they framed their reaction. They often said, "That is the biggest dog I've ever seen." If I had responded to the content of the message, I might have said, "Yes, that is exceptionally large for a German shepherd," or, "Actually, I've seen bigger," or even, "Yes, he weighs over 100 pounds and has excellent teeth!"

This example illustrates that every communication has at least two dimensions: the explicit and the implicit. In this case, the hidden message is an emotional one concerning the fear that the dog evoked but that very few people felt comfortable in expressing. From culture to culture, people vary in their willingness to reveal their feelings. Gender also affects what a person feels is permissible. For example, many men will not acknowledge feeling fearful or weak. In general, we are all much more comfortable talking about content or facts. That is why weather but not politics or religion is most likely to be an early conversation starter.

In helping conversations, the content and the emotional side are equally important if we are to really know someone. A response that recognizes both will lead to the deepest communication of understanding. At the beginning of the helping relationship, clients usually find it more comfortable if the helper is able to reflect the content of their stories. Later, a helper can show that he or she also grasps the other layers of the story.

It is not usually possible to understand the deeper layers of the story right away. During a session, the helper makes a series of reflections. As the client responds to the reflections, the helper gets more information about what has happened and the client's emotional response to the events. Eventually, the helper begins to grasp the meaning, which involves the client's values and beliefs about the self, others, and the world in general.

To demonstrate how a helper can lead a client to fully explore a story, let us look at the case of Philippe, a single father who has come for help with his adolescent daughter.

PHILIPPE (CLIENT): "I am having trouble with my daughter. She has just started driving. I think she is a good driver, but I am not so sure about the kids she hangs around with. My wife says I am overreacting, that I don't want her to grow up."

TRACY (HELPER):   "So the main reason you're here is to think about how you are handling the conflict you are having with your daughter, and it sounds like driving is an important part of that." (paraphrase)

PHILIPPE: "Yes, I guess it is. When I was 16, I stole a car with some other kids. We went joyriding and had an accident. The driver was drunk, and one of the kids in the car was killed. Every time my own kid goes out on Saturday night, I think of that. I yell and scream, and maybe I am too strict with her."

TRACY: "You remember that incident and worry that the same kind of thing might happen to her." (reflecting feeling—worry)

PHILIPPE: "Yes, sometimes I get really scared. My own parents didn't care what I did. I don't want to keep her at home all the time, but I don't want her doing something stupid."

TRACY: "It seems that you're wondering, 'Am I being a good parent.'" (reflection of meaning—being a good parent and not repeating his parents' mistakes is a deeper level of meaning)

The reflecting skills in this example go beyond invitational skills by bringing out a deeper level of the story—the emotional reactions of the client and the potential meanings. To use a metaphor, recognizing these deeper levels adds color to the black-and-white facts. With the example of Philippe and Tracy in mind, we are ready to explore what reflecting involves and what functions are served by reflecting skills in helping.

REASONS FOR REFLECTING

In general, reflecting entails repeating back to the client his or her own thoughts and feelings and implied meanings in a condensed way, using different words and in a manner that communicates nonevaluative, nonjudgmental understanding.

Four functions are served by reflecting skills in helping:

1. ***Reflecting is a verbal way of communicating empathy.*** In Chapter 3, we discussed the concept of empathy, or trying to "feel oneself into" another's experience. We indicated then that the helper tries to share a client's deeper experiences and that it is also important to convey this understanding to the client. Reflecting feelings communicates, "I hear your deeper thoughts and emotions as well as the facts." In the preceding example, Tracy does not have to say to Philippe, "I understand what you are going through." Instead, she communicates his worry, confusion, and fear, trying to understand the situation through his eyes rather than a similar experience of her own.

2. ***Reflecting is a form of feedback or a mirror that enables the person to confirm or correct the impression he or she is giving.*** In Tracy's second response to Philippe, she uses the word *worry*. For a number of reasons, this word might not have exactly fit what Philippe was trying to communicate. He might have responded, "No, I don't worry that the same thing will happen. I just get mad at her for not listening to me!" This demonstrates that a reflecting statement, even if inaccurate, can give the client an opportunity to clarify the experience to others and to oneself (Hill, 2004). In other words, beginning helpers should try

to reflect without being concerned that every reflection is perfect. If the helper does not hit the bull's-eye, in many cases the client will expand and explain the situation more clearly.

3. ***Reflecting stimulates further exploration of what the client is experiencing.*** Notice that when Tracy identifies Philippe's feelings of worry in the first reflection, Philippe begins discussing his own upbringing and talks about the conflict between being overprotective and too lenient. This shows that accurate reflection has an "opening effect", bringing out more facts and deeper feelings. Reflecting could also be compared to the soliloquy in a Shakespearean play or in an opera where the main character turns to the audience and expresses what is going on inside of him. Because clients do not always express or even recognize these deeper thoughts and feelings, the helper primes the pump with reflections.

4. ***Reflecting captures important aspects of the client's message that otherwise might remain camouflaged.*** In Philippe's opening statement, he makes no mention of the fact that he is scared or worried about his daughter. Many people have difficulty admitting to negative feelings such as fear and anger. Perhaps, at this first meeting, Philippe does not wish to appear foolish in his concerns. It is the helper's reflection that extracts this feeling that is hidden in his first statement.

THE SKILL OF PARAPHRASING: REFLECTING CONTENT AND THOUGHTS

In the discussion of invitational skills, you were warned not to ask too many questions at the beginning stages of the helping relationship. Questions, especially closed questions, can interrupt the flow of the client's story and make the client feel that he or she is under a microscope. However, it is important to have a clear grasp of the facts relating to the client's problem and also, at times, to repeat some important thoughts or intentions embedded in the client's statements. So how can we get more information without quizzing the client and also let the client know we are on board? Paraphrasing is a reflecting skill that serves both purposes.

The paraphrase is *not* a word-for-word reiteration. The **paraphrase** is a distilled version of the content of the client's message that restates the facts and thoughts in different words and in a nonjudgmental way. As a client tells his or her story, the paraphrase is used as a mirror to let the client know that you are following but does not pressure the client by asking a question. It is short and sweet and therefore does not slow the client down while he or she is disclosing. It does not take sides with the client by supporting his or her version of the story but, rather, points out that this is the client's perspective.

Paraphrasing means reflecting what the client knows to be factual, but these facts are those that are uniquely perceived by the client. Facts and the client's thoughts and perceptions are intertwined. To accurately reflect them and at the same time remain nonjudgmental, the helper must take a neutral stance. Here is an example of a typical helper/client exchange:

> CLIENT: "Okay, I came in 2 hours late. And then my mom sent me to my room for the rest of the day. I am 17 years old. She treats me like a baby just because she likes to be in control all the time."

HELPER (PARAPHRASING):   "So you were punished again for breaking curfew. You think it is unfair and that she is doing it to control you."

Can you see that the helper is not taking sides in this paraphrase? Instead, the aim is to convey that the message was heard and to make the client aware of his or her perceptions of the events. This exchange illustrates some of the differences between social communication and therapeutic communication. The helper is not merely supportive but asks the client to reflect on his or her own words.

How to Paraphrase

Paraphrasing involves two steps: (1) listening carefully to the client's story and then (2) feeding back to the client a *condensed,* nonjudgmental version of the facts and thoughts. The second step in paraphrasing involves finding the important information in a large volume of client material and repeating it in a succinct summary. If the paraphrase goes on too long, it can fatally disrupt the client's story, and he or she will not stay on track. Using a boxing analogy, the paraphrase is more like a jab. The helper gets in and out quickly. The paraphrase is actually a miniature version of the client's story. A good paraphrase keeps the client's story on track by mentioning only the important aspects, not issues that sidetrack the client.

Here is an example of a conversation between a helper and a client in their first meeting. Notice how paraphrase assists the helper in understanding the facts of the story and also allows the client to feel the helper is on track:

SWATI (HELPER):   "So what brought you in today?" (door opener)

FRED (CLIENT):   "Well, I am a teacher, and I have been having some problems at school recently."

SWATI: "Okay, can you tell me about that?" (door opener)

FRED: "I have a group of sixth graders this year that are just wild. They won't listen, and they constantly challenge me. I've sent more kids to the office this year than I can ever remember. I've sent notes home and scheduled a lot of parent conferences."

SWATI: "Uh-huh. Okay." (encouragers)

FRED: "I guess you get a bad group sometimes. I've been teaching for 13 years, and I am used to working with rowdy kids. But this year it seems like it's getting on my nerves even more."

SWATI: "So you are not sure if it's just a wild class or if you are overreacting." (paraphrase)

FRED: "For some reason, I am really feeling the stress. This year, one of the teachers was fired during the first week for some unknown reason."

SWATI: "I see." (encourager)

FRED: "That has left a lot of people upset. With that kind of support from the principal, I just don't know what this year is going to be like."

SWATI: "So on top of the new students, you're dealing with a new atmosphere at work." (paraphrase)

FRED: "I guess this atmosphere isn't new. But it never really affected me before. I tried to stay out of all the politics and the complaining in the teachers' lounge. This year, all the teachers do is gripe. At meetings and after school, somebody is always talking about it."

SWATI: "So for the first time, it's hard to escape the gossiping." (paraphrase)

FRED: "Yeah. And I am wondering if the gossiping is worse or if it is me. There are a lot of other things happening in my life."

SWATI: "You are wondering if the things going on in your life are coloring your whole viewpoint about work." (paraphrase)

FRED: "That's it. That's what is so confusing."

Now that you have read the dialogue between Swati and Fred, take a look at Swati's reflections. Do you notice how Swati does not repeat Fred's statements exactly? Swati rewords Fred's statements to show that he grasps the essence. This is the art of distilling or collapsing the client's words into a brief statement. It is tempting to think that paraphrasing is just mimicking the client, but as you can see in Swati's paraphrase, "You are wondering if the things going on in your life are coloring your whole viewpoint about work," Swati is also picking out something said and very softly guiding and highlighting a key issue. Now Fred is being asked to talk about what is going on in his life outside of school that may be contributing to his feelings.

STOP AND REFLECT

Secrets

"You are only as sick as your darkest secret." In Alcoholics Anonymous, this aphorism is used to remind those in recovery that being truthful and open about themselves is much healthier than putting on a false front. The positive consequences of disclosing to others include the following:

1. We may see a reduction in psychological and physical problems.
2. We may be better able to quit smoking or other addictions. Social pressure does affect the ability to conquer addictions.
3. The secret does not have to be suppressed and therefore it loses its power to dominate one's life.
4. When we reveal secrets, we may gain insight and see the issue in a different light (Kelly & McKillop, 1996).

Although it may be difficult and potentially dangerous to disclose one's intimate secrets, about half of long-term therapy clients reported that they kept secrets from their counselors (Hill, Thompson, Cogar, & Denman, 1993; Robey, 2011; Kelly & Yuan, 2009). When a client comes for help to a mental health professional, how important is it that he or she be completely honest? Is it all right for a client to retain some privacy and under what circumstances? How can we invite clients to share but show respect for their refusal to examine every nook and cranny?

The notion of secrets is an important issue for helpers to grapple with (Kottler & Carlson, 2011). Many of the ethical guidelines of professional organizations deal with the issue of secrets

(continued)

because of the notion of confidentiality. Compelling or forcing people to deal with all their secrets could be considered as undue pressure and therefore unethical. Certainly there are risks to revealing oneself to others, and it is not always a good idea to disclose, as it may lead to rejection (Kelly & McKillop, 1996).

It is a paradox that we are to keep our client's secrets, yet we cannot force them to be completely honest with us. Consider the following scenarios and think about how you might handle them. If possible, discuss them with a small group of fellow learners.

- Your client is a 43-year-old married man who has just returned from alcohol treatment. He does not want to attend Alcoholics Anonymous for aftercare but comes weekly for counseling. During his sessions, he is open about his substance abuse issues but is very quiet about his family relationships and his feelings about everyone. Apparently he has no friends and confides in no one. How would you deal with this issue? How far would you go in insisting that he learn to open up?
- You are conducting outpatient group therapy for 12 women. One of the rules of the group is that there will be no socializing outside of the group. One evening while shopping, you happen to see two of the women sitting together at a restaurant in the mall. They are deep in conversation, and they do not notice you. How do you think their secret relationship might affect their interactions with each other and with the group? As the group leader, what should you do? Should group leaders have rules about keeping secrets?
- You have been seeing Isabel for 4 weeks for individual counseling. At first, she discussed her dissatisfaction with her job and concerns about her parenting of her teenage son. On the fifth week, Isabel admits she is having an affair with a co-worker, unbeknown to her husband. Isabel says that her husband senses something is wrong in the relationship and wants marriage counseling. Isabel believes they could benefit by being seen as a couple and asks you to do the counseling, but not to reveal the affair. What would be the best response to Isabel? Can you agree to keep this secret? What are the consequences if the secret is uncovered?

When to Paraphrase

Paraphrases can be used early on in any helping session, as soon as the helper gets a grasp of the facts or, conversely, needs to clarify the facts. Later in the session, paraphrases go a little deeper by reflecting the client's thoughts and perceptions of the event. Paraphrasing should follow a sequence of opening and invitational skills. Figure 5.2 shows the typical sequence of a helper's using invitational skills and paraphrasing in the beginning of a session. The helper begins with door openers and minimal encouragers, perhaps going on to an open question before paraphrasing. Paraphrasing after every client statement would be excessive and might seem to make the helper's responses trivial. It is therefore better to wait until the client has gone on at some length.

A general guideline is to use a sequence of invitational and reflecting skills from encouragers to open questions to paraphrasing. This slowly allows the client to open up and discuss more difficult issues.

In this book, I use the term *topic* to refer to a specific subject that the client is discussing. In Figure 5.2, all the helper responses are on a single topic. It is quite possible to discuss more than one topic in a given session. For example, a client might, in 1 hour, discuss the topic of her relationships, the topic of her problems at work, and the topic of

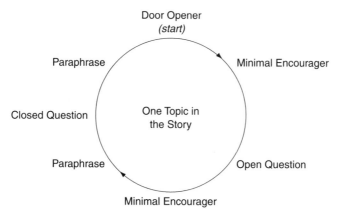

FIGURE 5.2 A Typical Sequence of Helper Responses in the First Few Minutes of a Session

her family. In early assessment-oriented sessions, a large number of topics are explored because the helper is trying to get a grasp of all the different issues that a client is dealing with. However, when these assessment sessions are completed, helpers tend to focus on a particular subject until the *topic* has been fully explored. These topics are those that are associated with the client's key issues or problems.

As a beginner, you might have the tendency to rush a client through a topic without discussing all the facts, feelings, and meanings, going on to the next issue and then the next. More experienced helpers take time to ask open questions, check out key facts with closed questions, and paraphrase to make sure the story is being understood. They try to have a clear understanding of the surface issues and then use reflecting feelings to go even deeper. Beginning helpers become impatient at this point. They would like to do something to alleviate the client's discomfort and to solve the problem, and they quickly find themselves at the end of a topic. It turns out that trying to solve the client's problems prematurely is one of the quickest ways to lose a client. As you practice, see for yourself how a gradual buildup can lead to deeper sessions.

One way of understanding the process of easing into a topic is to take a look at the typical sequence of skills (see Figure 5.2). In the following conversation between a child and a school counselor, a paraphrase is shown in the normal examination of a topic. Later, you will have a chance to identify these elements and to practice paraphrasing along with all the other skills you have learned thus far.

CHRIS:	"The teacher said I have to tell you what happened yesterday."
SCHOOL COUNSELOR:	"Do you want to give me an idea about what went on?" (encourager)
CHRIS:	"Well, I was walking around the playground, not really looking at anything, you know? I was bored."
SCHOOL COUNSELOR:	"Yes; um-hmm." (encouragers)
CHRIS:	"And then these three second graders came around the corner and started calling me names. I said, 'Shut up.' And later I punched William in the nose. It was bleeding, and he was crying, but I didn't care because he's mean."

SCHOOL COUNSELOR: "Can you tell me more about what you mean when you said, you didn't care that William was hurt?" (open question)

CHRIS: "Well, I didn't mean to hurt him, but I am not saying 'Sorry' because he started it."

SCHOOL COUNSELOR: "So, you got into a fight with William. He got hurt but you don't think it was your fault." (paraphrase)

Can you see how the counselor used encouragers and an open question before paraphrasing? These invitational and opening skills allowed more of the story to come out. Notice that the counselor's paraphrase is not just a restatement of what Chris said. It is a summary of the child's story, giving its essence in a nonjudgmental way. The paraphrase is brief and therefore does not interrupt the child unduly as he talks. It does not take sides by supporting one version of the story, but recognizes instead the child's perspective. It also identifies the child's thoughts, "You don't think it was your fault." Let us now look at the importance of understanding and reflecting the client's thoughts as well as what the client says happened.

COMMON PROBLEMS IN PARAPHRASING

Simply Reciting the Facts

A common mistake (Corey & Corey, 2006; Corey, Corey, & Corey, 2010) is to simply list the major points the client has made in exactly the same way that the client said them. This is sometimes called, "parroting." The best way to illustrate this mistake is to take an example from Swati and Fred's dialogue in the earlier section "How to Paraphrase." Below is a statement by Fred (the client) followed by two alternative paraphrases by Swati (the helper). The first one is copied from the actual dialogue, and the second is a less effective paraphrase that merely recites the facts.

FRED: "I guess this atmosphere isn't new. But it never really affected me before. I tried to stay out of all the politics and the complaining in the teachers' lounge. This year, all the teachers do is gripe. At meetings and after school somebody is always talking about it."

SWATI 1: "So for the first time, it's hard to escape the gossiping." (paraphrase)

SWATI 2: "So this atmosphere isn't new, but now it is affecting you. You don't like to get involved in all this backbiting, but the teachers are complaining, and it is everywhere you go, at meetings and after school. You can't escape it."

Besides the fact that this last reflection is too long and tends to parrot the client's words, the helper would be merely reflecting the content without recognizing the thoughts and perceptions of the client. Remember the deeper paraphrase that was made by Swati in the "How to Paraphrase" section, "You are wondering if the things going on in your life are coloring your whole viewpoint about work." This gets at the essence of the story.

Difficulty Hearing the Story Because of "Noise"

A second problem is caused by distractions. Of course, helpers must select quiet environments so that listening is not impaired by external noises. However, the biggest distractions come from "mental noise." You cannot grasp the client's message when you are listening to your own thoughts. Helpers sometimes experience mental noise when the client's story evokes a personal memory of a similar situation. Internal noise may interrupt because the client is expressing something you find distasteful or evokes moral outrage. When you realize that you have lost track of the client's story because of mental noise, stop and request that the client repeat the last part of the story again. Then respond with an appropriate paraphrase. Even though it is a distraction, it is better to stay on track than to miss the key elements of the story. If you find a client boring, morally repugnant, sexually attractive, or pitiful, you are probably going to have difficulty really listening. You can start now to identify those issues that trigger mental noise and discuss or write about them in your journal.

Worrying about What to Say Next

Worrying about what to say next is perhaps the biggest source of mental noise. Rather than responding to the client's statement, the helper is sidetracked into thinking about what his or her response ought to be. This is especially true when you are being observed by others, such as your instructor. One thing to remember is that almost everyone becomes less anxious as time goes on. Practicing in front of others may expose your weaknesses, but it is also the best way to get feedback and to learn. Still, there are a few things you can do to cope with this kind of worry.

The first antidote is to shift your attention to the client. Because it is difficult to do two things simultaneously, when you become focused on your own thoughts, you lose track of the client's story. This happens to everyone at some time. Your mind will go blank! The remedy is to refocus your attention keenly on the client's story. One other helpful hint is to remember that your job is to respond to *the last thing the client said,* rather than stimulate a new topic or ask a question. This will lead to greater exploration of the topic rather than shifting topics. If you cannot remember the client's last statement, ask them to repeat it.

Being Judgmental and Taking the Client's Side

Beginners are often too quick to take the client's side and to agree that the problem is caused by other people. You may think you are being supportive, but you may be accepting the client's version of the story prematurely. For example:

RACHEL (CLIENT): "At work, the other women ignore me because I don't go drinking with them on Friday night, and they think I am the boss's favorite. The boss always compliments me on my work. I can't help it if they don't work as hard as I do."

SANTIAGO (HELPER): "Things aren't going very well at the job because your co-workers mistreat you." (judgmental paraphrase)

With a judgmental paraphrase, the helper has essentially agreed that the co-workers are at fault. Shifting the blame to other people will not widen the client's perspective or help the client change his or her behavior. The following is a nonjudgmental response to Rachel's problem:

SANTIAGO: "So you see yourself as a hard worker, but you think your co-workers may be critical of you because of your dedication."

Here Santiago is subtly telling Rachel that his mind is open about who is causing the problem and that this may be Rachel's perception. It is possible that her co-workers have no such thoughts.

Being Judgmental of the Client

This error is made when the helper feels strongly about the client's behavior and thinks the client ought to correct it. This is an error, especially in the early sessions, because it will undermine the trust that has been building.

> RACHEL: "At work, the other women ignore me because I don't go drinking with them on Friday night, and they think I am the boss's favorite. The boss always compliments me on my work. I can't help it if they don't work as hard as I do."
>
> SANTIAGO: "You're having trouble at work because you haven't been a team player." (judgmental)

Sometimes helpers show a judgmental attitude when they try to sneak in a little advice. In the previous example, there is a hidden message, "If you want to be liked, be more a part of the team." A nonjudgmental response would be:

> SANTIAGO: "So you're saying that your boss appreciates you, but in your mind, your co-workers don't accept you." (nonjudgmental)

In summary, the purpose of a paraphrase is to make sure that you understand the facts and the client's thoughts rather than to supply a solution or place blame.

QUICK TIPS: PARAPHRASING

- Don't paraphrase too early. Wait until you have a firm grasp of the important details and thoughts, and then compress them into a short paraphrase.
- Early on, use encouragers liberally to invite the client to supply essential information.
- Don't repeat the client's exact words. Give a distilled version in slightly different words.
- Don't add a moral tone to your paraphrase.
- When you can, paraphrase the client's thoughts and intentions as well as the basic facts.
- If you get lost, ask the client to repeat his or her last statement and try another paraphrase.
- Keep on track by responding to the last thing the client said.

MyCounselingLab™

Go to Topic 2, *Invitational Interviewing*, on the MyCounselingLab™ site (www. MyCounselingLab.com) for *Learning the Art of Helping: Building Blocks and Techniques,* Fifth Edition, where you can:

- Find learning outcomes for *Invitational Interviewing* along with the national standards that connect to these outcomes.

- Complete Assignments and Activities that can help you more deeply understand the chapter content.
- Apply and practice your understanding of the core skills identified in the chapter with the Building Counseling Skills unit.
- Prepare yourself for professional certification with a Practice for Certification quiz.
- Connect to videos through the Video and Resource Library.

MyCounselingLab™ Exercises

Using Questions and Paraphrasing to Understand the Problem

Go to the Video and Resource Library on the MyCounselingLab™ site for your text and search for the following clip: *Paraphrasing: Nicole*. The video shows a conversation between Nicole, the helper, and her client, Mike. While Nicole uses a few minimal encouragers, her primary method at this early stage is to vary between questions and paraphrases. After viewing the video, answer the questions below.

1. During this segment, Nicole makes about 17 interventions. See if you can label each as a closed question, open question, or paraphrase.
2. Many beginning helpers offer only a couple of paraphrases at this stage and then start asking closed questions. Do you think that Nicole is better able to connect with the client and understand the problem through the use of paraphrases?

Next, search for the clip entitled, *Paraphrasing: Samantha*. This video shows Samantha (the helper) demonstrating paraphrasing with Stacey (the client). Watch the whole segment first, and then go back and look at specific parts as directed by the questions below. Here, and in later chapters, you are asked to identify skills by their names. Learning to identify helper responses will help you when you watch your own videos or go over your transcripts. It will also assist you in giving useful feedback to your fellow students because you will be using a common language. At other times, you will be asked to examine the client's response to the helper's intervention. Examining a client's reaction is one way to check the effectiveness of your statement. Did it achieve what you hoped? Did it confuse or silence the client?

1. Samantha used the skill of paraphrasing five times in this segment. See if you can identify the five paraphrases. Write them out on a separate sheet. Underneath each, indicate how the client reacted to the paraphrase. Did they tend to move the client along to the next part of the story?
2. Write down one door opener used by Samantha.
3. In this video, Samantha does not seem interested in Stacey's boyfriend. Why doesn't she ask about him? What effect do you think this might have had on the conversation?
4. After watching the video, try to write a one-sentence paraphrase, in your own words, that captures the major facts in Stacey's story.

Summary

Paraphrasing is the first of three reflecting skills, all of which involve feeding back to the client a distilled version of the story. The challenge is to construct the paraphrase so that it does not mimic the client's words but encapsulates the essence in a slightly different way. At the same time, the paraphrase should be non-judgmental, not implying any advice or taking sides.

Good paraphrases will let a client know that you really understand the facts and the client's thoughts but will not stifle the client's attempts to get the story out. Paraphrasing may seem like a very minor skill, but it is deceptively simple. A good paraphrase can convey understanding and even push the client to examine his or her version of the story more objectively.

Exercises

GROUP EXERCISES

Exercise 1: Practice Using Invitational Skills, Opening Skills, and Paraphrasing

In groups of three, divide into helper, client, and observer. The helper should review the "Quick Tips" section while the client takes a moment to think about a story that is often told in his or her family. Alternatively, the client can talk about career goals from childhood to the present. The exercise begins with the client

relating his or her story. As the client talks, the helper will try to demonstrate all of the opening and invitational skills first and then try to paraphrase once or twice during the practice session. The observer will use the *Feedback Checklist: Paraphrasing* to record the helper's responses or may simply write the responses on lined paper. Following the session, all three participants join in labeling the helper responses as indicated in the *Category* column of the checklist.

Feedback Checklist: Paraphrasing

Observer Name:_____ Helper Name:_____

During the session, the observer records the helper's responses verbatim. After the session, the group categorizes the responses with the following symbols: E for an encourager (either door opener or minimal encourager), CQ for closed question, OQ for open question, or P for paraphrase.

Category	Helper Response	Client Feedback
_____	1. _____	_____
_____	2. _____	_____
_____	3. _____	_____
_____	4. _____	_____
_____	5. _____	_____
_____	6. _____	_____
_____	7. _____	_____
_____	8. _____	_____
_____	9. _____	_____
_____	10. _____	_____

Exercise 2

Earlier we talked about reducing questions and trying instead to use encouragers and paraphrases. This exercise asks students to replace questions with encouragers and paraphrases and to take turns as helper, client and observer. The client's topic is "a brief history of my life," and the helper's job is to use encouragers and paraphrases but not questions of any type. The observer notes any questions that the helper asks and also identifies how many times the helper's voice rises at the end of a sentence (which is a nonverbal cue that a question is being asked). After everyone has had a chance to be the helper and receive feedback, the class discusses the activity. Was it difficult to withhold questioning? What is the difference between "Are you and your mother not getting along?" and "I'm picking up that things between you and your mother are rather strained"?

SMALL GROUP DISCUSSIONS

Following are parts of three clients' stories. Try to paraphrase the facts of the stories as well as unspoken thoughts. See if you can use slightly different words than the client did. In your responses, leave out the client's feelings for now. Compare your paraphrases with those of your small group, and discuss any differences in your approaches.

1. "I had to tell one of my co-workers he couldn't go on the trip. He had not put in enough time with the company. I was forced to follow the rules. It wasn't really my fault, and I couldn't do anything about it. When I told him, he didn't say much. He just walked away."
2. "I met this woman. She seems too good to be true. I don't know too much about her. We only met last week. But since then, everything I find out about her makes me feel more like she is 'the one.' I believe there is only one person out there for everyone, you know. But how can I be sure?"
3. "I was recently laid off from my job as vice president in charge of purchasing. They said it was a layoff, but it feels like being fired. They have farmed my work to my subordinates, many of whom were not let go. My friend wants me to go into business with him, but there is a big part of me that feels that I gave my heart and soul to that company, and I don't feel ready to move on."

After you have read and responded to these short stories, answer the following questions for yourself:

- Do any of these stories challenge your ability to be nonjudgmental?
- What feelings are aroused in you?
- Which one is the most challenging to remaining nonjudgmental? Why?
- What might you be tempted to say that would indicate that you are taking sides?
- How well were you able to distill the story, including the client's thoughts, rather than just reiterating the facts?
- Did you find it hard to leave out the feelings? Is there a time for listening to the facts of a story without reflecting the feelings?

WRITTEN EXERCISES

Exercise 1: Making Your Paraphrases Nonjudgmental

The following client statements test your ability to be nonjudgmental—neither agreeing nor criticizing. On a separate sheet, paraphrase the content of the following client statements without taking sides.

1. "I am so excited; I am getting married in 2 weeks. We met over the Internet and she just sounds great. Even though we've never met, I know she is the one for me. In fact we aren't going to meet before the wedding. Isn't it romantic?"
2. "I've just started a relationship with a co-worker. It's the best thing that's ever happened to me. But here's the thing, she's married and has a kid. I don't want to be the kind of person who breaks up a relationship, but I guess she wouldn't be seeing me if everything was fine between her and her husband."
3. "My best friend and I are both seniors and heading off to college next year. SATs are over and I am partying a lot. She looks down on me because I started drinking. She says I'm an alcoholic. We can't even talk anymore because she's so down on me."

SELF-ASSESSMENT

Now that you have had the opportunity to practice paraphrasing, look at the aspects of paraphrasing below and indicate with a checkmark if you have been able to:

1. listen carefully using invitational and opening skills *before* paraphrasing. _____
2. supply a distilled version of the facts and the client's thoughts. _____
3. make the paraphrase in slightly different words. _____

4. make paraphrases that are nonjudgmental. _____
5. respond to the last thing the client said. _____

What part of the skill do you need to work on? _____

_____

HOMEWORK

In the last chapter, it was suggested that you watch a television program with the sound off to see if you could guess the emotional content based on body language alone. For this assignment, watch a television program where one individual is speaking. An interview on a news program works well for this activity. Using a remote control, listen to a couple of minutes of the dialogue, and then press the mute button. See if you can paraphrase the content of the last 2 or 3 minutes in a couple of brief sentences. This activity can provide anxiety-free practice because you can turn the "client" off while you are paraphrasing.

JOURNAL STARTERS

Reread the "Stop and Reflect" section in this chapter about secrets. Dostoyevsky says in *Notes from the Underground* that there are things that we are afraid to tell even to ourselves and that every decent person has several of these things stored away. Can you mentally identify one of these issues for yourself? Instead of describing the secret in writing, imagine telling your secret to a nonjudgmental listener. What reaction do you imagine? Do you think such confessions are helpful?

Reflecting Skills: Reflecting Feelings

MyCounselingLab™

Visit the **My**CounselingLab™ site for *Learning the Art of Helping: Building Blocks and Techniques,* Fifth Edition to enhance your understanding of chapter concepts. You'll have the opportunity to practice your skills through video- and case-based Assignments and Activities as well as Building Counseling Skills units, and to prepare for your certification exam with Practice for Certification quizzes.

THE IMPORTANCE OF UNDERSTANDING EMOTIONS

Daniel Goleman, the author of *Emotional Intelligence* (2006), describes an incident in Iraq when a group of soldiers who were distributing relief supplies were surrounded by an angry mob of people who thought the soldiers were there to arrest one of the villagers. Using social intelligence, the officer in charge ordered his men to kneel, point their guns at the ground and smile, all of which defused the situation without anyone being hurt. The officer, Lieutenant Colonel Christopher Hughes, was able to transmit the message through nonverbal means that the soldiers were nonthreatening and friendly.

Goleman's story is in support of his thesis that there is a kind of intelligence that is quite different from what IQ tests capture (Goleman, 2003). If the soldiers had attempted to explain their mission to the villagers, it might have been a logical move, but not emotionally smart. **Emotional intelligence** has been described as the "ability to monitor one's own and other's feelings and emotions, to discriminate among them, and to use this information to guide one's thinking and action" (Salovey & Mayer, 1990, p. 189).

There is little doubt that helpers must possess this emotional intelligence in the same way that an engineer must have the intellectual ability to understand higher mathematics. The point is that many helpers go into the profession because they have this basic emotional intelligence about people and want to use it, but they may not realize that they possess it. We undervalue this ability, probably because it is not widely acclaimed, because it does not show up in standardized achievement tests, and because we think everyone has it. In addition, we may not recognize that emotional intelligence can be enhanced by paying attention to emotions in the stories we hear.

THE SKILL OF REFLECTING FEELINGS

Although being aware of emotions is important, being able to recognize them in others and convey that you understand their feelings is a special ability. This is the skill of **reflecting feelings** that conveys to your client that you recognize how they are affected by their problems. The building block of reflecting feelings involves essentially the same technique as paraphrasing. This time, however, the focus is on emotions rather than on content and thoughts. Reflecting feelings involves listening and then expressing in one's own words the emotions *stated or implied* by the client. Feelings can be reflected from both verbal and nonverbal responses of the client.

A number of therapeutic events occur when feelings are reflected. For one thing, the client becomes more keenly aware of the emotions surrounding a topic. Let us suppose that the helper makes a reflection such as, "I can tell that you are terribly angry about that." The client's response may be one of surprise, "Yes, I guess I am." Because a reflection is done in a nonevaluative manner, it communicates understanding of feelings—anger, guilt, and sadness—that the client may not be conscious of and that the client may even think he or she has no right to feel.

More importantly, reflecting feelings brings the client to deeper and deeper levels of self-disclosure. An accurate reflection focuses the client on emotions and teaches the client to become aware of and to report feelings. Even if the reflection is not quite accurate, the client will provide a correction that is more on target. Many clients underdisclose, and any method or technique that allows them to more fully experience and express their feelings is thought to be therapeutic (Young & Bemak, 1996). In addition, an accurate reflection of feelings has the almost magical power to deepen the relationship between client and counselor. Nothing transmits nonjudgmental understanding more completely. This is why this technique, which originated in the client-centered tradition of Carl Rogers (1961), has gained such wide usage. It taps the enormous healing properties of the therapeutic relationship. A beginning helper who can accurately reflect feelings can provide supportive counseling and understanding without any other tools.

Finally, reflecting feelings brings on genuine relief from emotional pressure. Take, for example, the client who found his wife in bed with another man. He came to counseling crying about his loss of the relationship. He ran the gamut, on an emotional roller coaster, from shock to disgust to affection to rage. Experiencing all these conflicting emotions in one session can make anyone feel "crazy." Even though there were still conflicting feelings, by the end, the client felt more in control simply because he had sorted out his feelings and labeled them. Untangling the emotional knots seems to be healing even if no real action is taken. Somehow we can accept our feelings as normal reactions when we bring them to the surface and sort them out. Reflecting feelings by saying, for example, "You feel so betrayed, and yet you still feel a bond of affection," can help to normalize what the client perceives as a deeply conflicting emotional experience.

Why It Is Difficult to Reflect Feelings

Reflecting feelings is one of the most valuable tools of the helper, but it is not an easy one to learn. Theodore Reik, the famous analyst, claimed that in order to hear deeply, one must learn to become sensitive to the unexpressed and listen with the "third ear." Referring to the fact that the client may not even be aware of these feelings, Reik said, "The voice that speaks in him speaks low but he who listens with a third ear, hears also what is expressed almost noiselessly, what is said *pianissimo*" (Reik, 1968, p. 165).

One reason that feelings may be hard to hear is that our upbringing, family background, and culture affect the way we express them (Matsumoto, 2009; Tsai, Levenson, & McCoy, 2006). For example, many individuals with Appalachian and English roots may tend to express emotions in very subtle ways. Some Native Americans, East Indians, and Europeans may come from cultures where open expression of feelings is rude or is a sign of weakness. For instance, a recent conference was held in Amsterdam on the "underexpression" of emotions as a mental health issue in Europe.

When a client's family background or culture is constantly sending the message "Don't let anyone see your feelings," the job of helping is more difficult because the helper can only guess what the client is experiencing. Getting to feelings may require more time and effort, and even then expression may seem faint by comparison. This can be frustrating when the client does not seem to respond to your reflections. For some clients, though, even a small crack in the voice may be quite a strong emotional sign and should be valued as a deep disclosure.

Gender also has a bearing on emotional expression. Men, more than women, have been trained to "never let them see you sweat" and to believe that "big boys don't cry" (Kottler, 1997; Wong, Steinfeldt, LaFollette & Tsao, 2010). Consequently, it may be difficult for some men to openly display feelings in the helping relationship and in their other relationships too. When feelings leak out, a man may feel weak or out of control. Feminine socialization, on the other hand, is more relationship-oriented and is more likely to encourage telling another person how you feel (Madrid & Kantor, 2009; Workman, 1993). However, women, too, are asked to repress certain emotions, such as anger or even confidence, that are not considered feminine. In summary, do not be discouraged if you do not instantly uncover the emotional theme in the client's story because there may be a number of barriers that only a strong therapeutic relationship can overcome. We have found that if you strive to understand, eventually you will.

HOW TO REFLECT FEELINGS

Like paraphrasing, reflecting feelings involves two steps. The first step is identifying the client's feelings; the second step is articulating the underlying emotions that you detect in his or her statements. You can learn the first step in your practice sessions as you listen intently to the client. Imagine how he or she feels in this situation, and then, first try to label the feeling. The best way to do this is to think of yourself as the client, taking into account all the facts and also thinking about what you know about the client's personality and history. In other words, do not try to think about how *you* would feel in this situation; instead, become the client and think about how he or she might feel. For practice in identifying feelings, read the three client stories in the "Stop and Reflect" section in Chapter 5. See if you can spot the main emotions. Take a look at the feeling words in Table 6.1 to see if another word is closer to what the client seems to be expressing. Do not forget that nonverbals are major clues to the client's feeling state. Although reading and responding to vignettes in this book will be a good training exercise, practicing with classmates will be more realistic as you must pay attention to the nonverbal expressions as well as the words.

The second step in reflecting feelings is making a *statement* (rather than asking a question) that accurately mirrors the client's emotions. The client may not have actually shared the emotions; the feelings may be hiding in the client's story. Although this sounds easier than the first step, it is actually more difficult because you must *accurately* express emotions in words.

In my experience, these two steps to reflecting feelings are often learned independently. Identifying feelings seems to be a precursor to actually reflecting them. Take some time to practice identifying feelings, and then it will be easier to put them into words. Later in this chapter you will find more opportunities to identify feelings before you try to actually reflect them to a person.

A Formula for Reflecting Feelings

Statements that reflect feelings take two forms. The simple version of reflecting feelings is a helper statement with the structure "You feel _____." As you look at the following

TABLE 6.1 Feeling Words

Feeling	Mild	Moderate	Strong
Joy	at ease	glad	overjoyed
	pleased	happy	jubilant
	satisfied	peaceful	elated
	content	delighted	thrilled
Sadness	down	glum	depressed
	sad	downhearted	dejected
	low	melancholy	despondent
		blue	dismayed
Anger	annoyed	angry	furious
	irritated	mad	outraged
	miffed	resentful	enraged
	ticked	indignant	bitter
			fuming
Guilt/shame	responsible	guilty	ashamed
	at fault	embarrassed	humiliated
	chagrined		mortified
Fear	apprehensive	anxious	frightened
	restless	scared	terrified
	uneasy	worried	panicked
	wary	afraid	
	insecure	nervous	
	on edge	unnerved	
Disgust	offended	turned off	repulsed
	put off	disgusted	sickened
			revolted
			nauseated
Surprise	perplexed	amazed	awed
	puzzled	bewildered	stunned
	stumped	baffled	astonished
		surprised	shocked
Interest/excitement	bored	amused	excited
	interested	curious	stimulated
		inspired	fascinated
		engaged	intrigued
Feelings Associated with Power and Confidence			
Weakness	unimportant	inadequate	worthless
	awkward	incompetent	helpless
	unsure	inept	dependent
	confused	powerless	impotent
		weak	discouraged

(continued)

TABLE 6.1   Feeling Words (Continued)

Feeling	Mild	Moderate	Strong
Strength	able	confident	self-assured
	capable	strong	potent
		authoritative	powerful
		secure	optimistic
		competent	
Feelings of General Distress			
	upset	frustrated	distressed
	concerned	disturbed	pained
	troubled	perturbed	miserable
	bothered	distressed	anguished
	uneasy	restless	agitated
			overwhelmed
			miserable

interactions between helper and client, think about what the reflection of feelings brings to the client's story and to the relationship.

> LATRICE (CLIENT): "You can imagine how everyone in the family reacted when Grandpa got married 6 months after Grandma's death."
>
> RYAN (HELPER):   "It must have been quite a shock." (simple reflection of feelings)

After one or two reflections of feeling, a helper may then use a reflection of feelings that connects emotions and content. The format of this combination response is "You feel _____ because _____." The first blank is a reflection of the client's feeling. The second blank *explains* the feeling by paraphrasing the content while, at the same time, showing the connection between the feeling and the content (Carkhuff, 1987). As the conversation between Latrice and Ryan continues, Ryan begins to understand and articulate the reason for Latrice's resentment and anger:

> LATRICE: "I was floored. I always thought that they had the perfect marriage."
>
> RYAN: "You felt let down because you didn't think he was honoring his marriage to your grandmother."

The reflection of feeling "You feel let down" is connected to the paraphrase "You didn't think he was honoring his marriage to your grandmother." This last phrase explains why she feels let down. The connection is the word *because,* which demonstrates to Latrice that Ryan understands what has happened. Can you see that Ryan's statement is essentially a mirror image of Latrice's, containing both a paraphrase and a feeling?

Not every reflection has to contain a paraphrase. Sometimes it is sufficient to reflect the feeling using the simple "You feel _____." When you understand the connection between feeling and content, you can then utilize the combined form to convey deeper understanding of the *reasons* for the client's feelings.

Students report that they often feel phony when they use a response such as "You feel _____ because _____." The formula is merely a training tool that you can modify later when reflecting feelings has become second nature. Later, you will want to vary the way you reflect so that it feels natural to you and sounds natural to the client.

Improving Your Feeling Vocabulary

To learn the first step in reflecting feelings—identifying feelings—it is important to recognize that emotions have many shades and variations. They also vary in strength. Table 6.1 categorizes feelings in a way that will help you recognize the basic emotions. They could be compared to the primary colors in the light spectrum, red, orange, yellow, green, blue, indigo, and violet. The color analogy is used here because the emotions of clients are often mixed together, producing a completely unique hue, and your job is to identify the particular shade. The primary emotions are listed top to bottom on the left-hand side of Table 6.1. They are *joy, sadness, anger, guilt/shame, fear, disgust, surprise,* and *interest/excitement.* People around the world can recognize facial expressions of these primary emotional states whether the people are from remote parts of New Guinea or New York City (Izard, 1977). These facial expressions appear to have deep biological roots. In addition to the primary emotions, three other categories of emotions are indicated in the table: *feelings of weakness, feelings of strength,* and *feelings of general or nonspecific distress.* Normally, the helper should be trying to identify the specific feeling that a client is experiencing. Sometimes though, especially in the beginning of a client's story, you may only be able to reflect these nonspecific emotional states before homing in on the target feelings.

Across the top of Table 6.1, the emotions are categorized by intensity (mild, moderate, and strong), much as colors can be described in terms of brightness. Take a look at the emotion of fear in the table. Suppose you had a client who was a little nervous about an upcoming exam, and you reflected "terrified" in the *Strong* category. Can you see that the client would feel misunderstood? Besides finding precise words that suggest different intensities, you can qualify your reflections by using terms like *a little, somewhat,* and *very* to zero in on the client's exact feeling. In fact, some clients do not have large feeling vocabularies, and it is better to say, "You were very angry," rather than, "You were filled with consternation." Use Table 6.1 to familiarize yourself with a wider variety of words. The more closely you express the exact shade of feeling, the more the client will sense that you understand his or her emotional experience.

STOP AND REFLECT

Let us take another look at the distinction between content and feelings. Read the following excerpt from a client's story and see if you can respond as a professional helper would, answering the related questions and comparing your responses with those of your classmates.

> TERESA: "First, we went to the drugstore; then we went to the grocery. We went to two or three other places and ended up in a bad part of town. All because he wanted this particular kind of candy. I had a lot to do that day. And this wasn't the first time this kind of thing had happened. He's a lot of fun most of the time; other times, he is a pain! What can you do?"

- What might Teresa be feeling? Identify as many emotions as you can. Try to pinpoint her feelings using Table 6.1. My answers are provided at the bottom of this section. Use qualifiers

(Continued)

like "a little" or "very" as needed to try to get the right shade of emotion. My answers, your answers, and those of your classmates may vary because in a written example we cannot hear the client's voice tone to cue us in on how strong her emotions are.

- Why do you think Teresa does not express her feelings about the situation in this opening statement?
- Try to summarize the content of Teresa's message (not the feelings) in a single sentence. Remember that the content includes thoughts, intentions, and facts that she relates.
- Try to make a connection between what Teresa is feeling and the content of her story: Teresa feels _____ (emotion) because _____ (reason you identify from content).

My Answers: Some of the things Teresa *might* be feeling:

1. Annoyed or irritated because she had to spend so much time on a minor errand
2. A little angry and rather scared because she ended up in a bad part of town
3. A little troubled about the relationship because there are both highs and lows, and perhaps hopeless when she says, "What can you do?"

COMMON PROBLEMS IN REFLECTING FEELINGS

Learning to reflect feelings is one of the most challenging skills you will develop in this course. For this reason, you will want to practice as much as possible. In your practice sessions, you may find it easy to use opening and invitational skills and even paraphrase; however, you may find that some practice sessions seem to have gone by without a single reflection of feeling. At these times, you may wish to review the following common problems. Under each problem are some suggested ways of dealing with that issue. If you find that you are having difficulty with one of these typical hurdles, let your instructor and fellow students know so that you can receive specific feedback during practice sessions.

Asking the Client, "How Did You Feel?" or "How Did That Make You Feel?"

When you are not able to reflect the client's feeling, you may be tempted to ask the question, "How did you feel?" When you ask a *closed question* like this, the client does not feel that you understand—empathy is lost. To make matters worse, frequently the client can't pinpoint the feeling when asked and the conversation stalls. At such times, the best advice is to use your opening skills, asking open questions and door openers to keep the client talking. Eventually you will realize what the client is feeling and be able to reflect. I often suggest that students try working without this question for a while.

Waiting Too Long to Reflect

In the opening minutes of the helping session, utilize invitational skills to help elicit the client's story, but don't wait too long. A common mistake is to wait 10 or 15 minutes before going on to reflect the client's feelings. You may want to reflect a feeling after 2 or 3 minutes of listening if you can. It is better to reflect inaccurately than never to reflect at all. To avoid the mistake of waiting too long, work first on becoming proficient at identifying feelings. Make full use of the written exercises in this chapter. Look at exercises in previous chapters, read the client statements, and see if you can pick out the feelings.

Also, watch television shows, particularly daytime dramas, to see if you can listen to people's statements and then reflect their feelings immediately after they speak, picking up on nonverbal as well as spoken cues.

Turning the Reflection into a Question

Another error is when we are able to reflect the client's feeling but state it as a question. This is usually because we lack confidence in our reflection. When we ask a question, we are giving the client the option of saying, "No" instead of agreeing or correcting us. In the conversation below, the helper is correct but waters down her reflection by making it a question. The result is that the client does not have to expand her answer, but merely has to answer the question.

> XIOMARA (CLIENT): "I've had a very difficult time. My mother died about 1 month ago, and now my dad is in the hospital with pneumonia. I'm here 2,000 miles away, and I am running out of sick leave at my work."
>
> TORI (HELPER): "Are you feeling sad over the death of your mom and a sense of helplessness as you worry about your dad?"

Can you see how a client might respond with a simple "yes" or "no"? The question suggests that the helper is confused, and it does not provide as many options to explore. Had the helper reflected the client's feelings with a statement, he or she could have said, "It must be a very helpless feeling for you to be so far away when you are worried about your dad and still trying to deal with the sadness of your mom's death." Such a statement more effectively communicates understanding of the client's situation and is more compassionate. Rather than responding to a question, the client can go on to explore whatever issues seem important to him or her. If you have the tendency to turn statements into questions by raising your voice at the end of a sentence, let your fellow students know and see if they can alert you to this habit.

Combining a Reflection and a Question: The Error of the Compound Response

In the early stages, it is tempting to add a question after the reflecting statement. We might call this a *compound response*. A compound response confuses the client because he or she has been asked to do two things: respond to the reflection of feeling and answer the question. For example, a helper might say, "You feel really alone since your best friend moved away. Do you have any other close friends?" When confronted with two options, clients usually respond to the last thing the helper said. In this example, the client may go on to tell you about his or her close friends but fail to return to "feeling alone" that the helper reflected. If you have this tendency to add a question to your reflections, try eliminating questions altogether for a while in your practice sessions and try to keep your reflections simple.

Focusing on the Wrong Person or the Wrong Topic

In a therapeutic conversation, there are four domains that can be a topic of discussion between helper and client: (1) talking about what is going on inside the client, (2) talking about the helper, (3) talking about the relationship between helper and client, and

(4) talking about external factors such as the environment and other people. The first domain, the client, is where you, as a beginning helper, should focus most of your conversation. It is the domain of the client's story including their thoughts, feelings, and meanings. Because this is the area that a client can control, you should keep bringing your attention back to the client's viewpoint. Consider the following interchange between client and helper:

CLIENT: "I am sick and tired of my sister butting into my life when she knows I need to make my own decisions."

HELPER: (Focusing on client through reflection of feeling and content) "So, you are frustrated by her calling a lot and look forward to being able to run your own life."

A second domain of discussion is the helper. These originate either from the client or are self-disclosure by the helper. As we said before, these may activate transference and are useful only if they help the client to feel more trust or if the client gets insight into his or her reactions to others. Even here, while the helper tries to respond genuinely, we keep returning to the client's needs and reactions. For example:

CLIENT: "Do you have a family?" (focus on the helper)

HELPER: (reflecting). "Yes I do. Sounds like you're thinking that someone who has a family will be more likely to help you with your parenting problems."

The third domain of client/helper dialogue is talking about the helping relationship. This is an important and useful subject because the therapeutic alliance is the backbone of client improvement. Still, it is often neglected. Consider the following questions that a helper might ask a client to shift the focus to the relationship:

"How do you think our relationship is going? Do you think this is going to be helpful?"

"Last week, I noticed that when we talked about your past marriages, things between you and me seemed a little strained. Can you talk about that a little bit?"

The fourth domain of client/helper discussion is other people, environmental aspects of the client's problems and the world outside. There are many times when helpers need to discuss the external forces that a client is facing and how they might react to them. There is problem solving to be done, but this is by far the most common place where beginning helpers can get off track. Save this until after the relationship is well established. Instead, try to focus on the client's view of the problem.

As we try to uncover the story through reflection, clients may lead us away from painful topics by focusing on other people and launching into long stories about them. In the first statement below, the helper takes the bait by agreeing to talk about someone who is not present and whom presumably the client cannot change.

Client (focusing on an absent person): "My best friend, Hope, and I are not as close as we used to be. Sometimes I think she just wants to neutralize our relationship. It seems like she has no time for me, like she doesn't care."

One way to get off track is paraphrasing in a judgmental way by focusing on the client's friend: "She neglects you," or "She must not be a really good friend." If the helper wants the client to go deeper he or she keeps attention centered on the client: "You miss the relationship you used to enjoy so much." Can you see how focusing on the other person can send a judgmental message about the friend? Because you do not know anything directly about the other person, such a statement is unfair and perhaps inaccurate. Unfortunately, this is a rather subtle problem and you may not be aware that you are doing it. To eliminate this problem, record your practice sessions and go over your responses and write Wrong Focus or WF next to your response when you see it. When the client makes statements about other people, check to see what you are reflecting: the client's thoughts and feelings, or the issues of the third party?

Letting the Client Ramble

Many helpers tend to let their clients talk too long without responding. In social situations, it is not polite to interrupt. However, clients need paraphrases and reflections in order to know that their story is making sense to the helper. Because they are talkative or anxious, some clients leave little room for the helper to reflect and the important issues just fly past. The main cure for this error is to give yourself permission to stop clients when they are rambling and make reflections. You may have to do this several times during a session. Surprisingly, stopping and reflecting often serves to reassure clients that each aspect of their story is being heard in a systematic way. Here is one example of a way that a helper politely requests a pause to verify that the right message is being received:

HELPER: "Let me stop you here for a second and see if I understand correctly. You feel both angry and hurt that your friend is not spending time with you, but you are afraid to mention it because you are afraid that she may simply terminate the friendship."

or

HELPER: "I'm sorry to interrupt, but let me tell you what I know so far. You resent the fact that you and your friend don't get together much anymore, but it is too scary to think about bringing it up."

A footnote to this discussion is that a helping relationship needs to have both people actively participating. By stopping the flow of the client's story to catch up, the helper is becoming involved with the client, creating a connection and *actively* listening, rather than becoming a "listening post."

Using the Word *Feel* Instead of *Think*

When you watch a recording or view a transcript, you may believe you are reflecting feelings when you are actually paraphrasing. For example, when the client says, "I feel that I am making progress," and you reflect, "You feel you are getting somewhere now," you have made an accurate paraphrase but it is not a reflection of the feeling. Can you see that in this client's statement, he or she might be feeling optimistic or confident but that "getting somewhere" is not a feeling? We simply cannot take the client's word that they have a feeling. We have to look beneath the surface of their words and reflect if we want to empathize. This is where practice in identifying feelings can help. The alter-ego technique is one of the best methods for practicing this skill (see Group Exercise 1).

The second error is when the helper wrongly uses the word *feel* instead of *think*, and as a result believes he or she is identifying an emotion. In the beginning, you may hear yourself or your classmates make an error along these lines: "You feel that your husband should have been more respectful of your need for privacy." This is not a reflection of feeling because the client's underlying emotions are not being identified. In this helper's statement, the word *think* may be substituted for *feel*: "You *think* that your husband should have been more respectful of your need for privacy." If you can substitute the word *think* without changing the meaning, you have not reflected a feeling; rather, you have paraphrased the client's thoughts, which are part of the content. In the preceding example, a true reflection of feeling would be "You feel angry (or hurt) because you think that your husband should have been more respectful of your need for privacy."

Some people use *feel* instead of *think* a great deal in their daily conversations. If you have this tendency, try to become aware of it and change your *feel* to *think* whenever you can. By being accurate in your word choice with clients, you are subtly teaching them to recognize the differences between thoughts and feelings.

Undershooting and Overshooting

Undershooting and overshooting are two common mistakes in reflecting feelings (Gordon, 1975). **Overshooting** means that the helper has reflected a feeling that is more intense than the one expressed by the client. **Undershooting** is reflecting a feeling that is too weak to adequately mirror the client's emotion. Consider this client statement and three possible responses:

> CLIENT: "Becky told Mrs. Gordon that I was not a fast worker, so she started giving the most interesting work to Rolando instead of me."
>
> HELPER: "You must have been mad enough to kill!" (overshooting)
>
> HELPER: "You were a little annoyed." (undershooting)
>
> HELPER: "You were angry." (accurate intensity)

Overshooting and undershooting are beginners' mistakes; this tendency normally corrects itself as you gain a larger feeling vocabulary. Like playing darts, you learn to hit the bull's-eye more often as you recognize your mistakes. In your practice sessions, note the difference between a polite "Yes, that's right" and "Yes!" from the client when you hit the mark. If you undershoot, in your next statement, you can raise the intensity a notch, and you can lower it when you overshoot. If your feeling vocabulary seems limited at present, study lists of feeling words like those in Table 6.1. You may also try using qualifiers such as *a little angry, somewhat angry,* or *very angry* to convey various shades of emotional intensity.

Parroting

Parroting is another common mistake caused by an inadequate feeling vocabulary. **Parroting** means repeating back to the client the very same feeling words he or she has just used. For example, a client might say, "The whole party I planned was rather frustrating because no one came for the first hour and then people stayed past the time limit we had indicated in the invitation." The helper then responds (parroting): "You were frustrated that they disregarded your instructions." The paraphrase in this case is pretty good since it distills the facts. However, the feeling is an exact reproduction. The tendency to parrot arises when the client seems to have beaten you to the punch and to have already expressed a feeling in his or her story before you had the chance. What do you do? The answer is to discern what other feelings the client might have experienced at the same time or to identify a feeling more accurate than the one the client has expressed. Forget about the feeling of frustration that the client has expressed and ask yourself, "What else would I be feeling in this situation?" Here are two possible ways of responding after imagining yourself in the client's shoes:

CLIENT: "The whole party I planned was rather frustrating because no one came for the first hour and then people stayed past the time limit we had indicated in the invitation."

HELPER: "I'd guess you were also a little angry that they didn't seem to get the message after all the planning you put into it."

HELPER: "If I had been in your shoes, I guess I might have felt a little hurt that very few of the people seemed to have honored my wishes."

Letting Your Reflecting Statements Go On and On

Sometimes helpers tend to continue to reflect and paraphrase, not in sentences, but in chapters. This is a kind of shotgun approach that we use to make sure we reflect everything. In reality, the important aspects of your response are lost in the verbiage. The student thinks, "If I reflect several different things, one of them is bound to be right." Instead, try thinking of reflecting as a form of gambling, like playing poker. You must wait until you think you understand and then you place your bet on a single brief reflection, paraphrase, or combination. If you are wrong, the client will correct you and proceed to describe the accurate feeling, helping you to find the bull's-eye. You will become more aware of this tendency when you record your sessions and transcribe them. When you notice that you are saying more than the client, it is a good indication that you are saying too much. Try sticking to the formula, "You feel _____ because _____," which will help you limit the length of your interventions.

MyCounselingLab™

Go to Topic 2, *Invitational Interviewing*, on the MyCounselingLab™ site (www.MyCounselingLab.com) for *Learning the Art of Helping: Building Blocks and Techniques,* Fifth Edition, where you can:

- Find learning outcomes for *Invitational Interviewing* along with the national standards that connect to these outcomes.
- Complete Assignments and Activities that can help you more deeply understand the chapter content.
- Apply and practice your understanding of the core skills identified in the chapter with the Building Counseling Skills unit.
- Prepare yourself for professional certification with a Practice for Certification quiz.
- Connect to videos through the Video and Resource Library.

MyCounselingLab™ Exercises

Exercise 1: Practice in Identifying Feelings in Context

Go to the Video and Resource Library on the MyCounselingLab™ site for your text and search for the following clip: *Reflecting Feelings: Mark.* Watch the video and respond to the following questions:

1. Write down each of the emotional states that Mark (the helper) identified in Alisa's (the client's) story.
2. If you were Alisa, what additional feelings might you be experiencing? This technique of imagining yourself as the client may help you identify the emotions that the client has not openly expressed but are hidden in the story.
3. At one point Mark reflected the feeling of frustration and later, resentment. Since the client has not mentioned these feelings, review the video and see if you can identify one or two nonverbal or verbal cues that led Mark to suspect these emotional states.

Exercise 2: Waiting to Reflect Feelings

In the video *Reflecting Feelings: Muthoni* in MyCounselingLab™, Muthoni, the helper, lets Nivischi talk about her grandmother's illness. Watch this video and consider the following questions:

1. Muthoni waits to reflect feelings because she does not immediately grasp what Nivischi is feeling. She reflects "confused," which is not exactly on target. What is Nivischi's response?
2. What does Muthoni do next to "buy time" until she is able to find the feeling?
3. Write the next two reflections of feeling that Muthoni makes.
4. Later when we talked about this video segment, Muthoni indicated that she was having difficulty reflecting feelings because she had recently lost close relatives of her own. What effect do you think this had on her ability to respond?
5. Use your intuition and guess what other emotions Nivischi might be feeling but has not yet expressed.

Exercise 3: Practice in Reflecting Feelings

The video in MyCounselingLab™ entitled *Reflecting Feelings: Bryce* is a conversation between Kara and Bryce.

1. First, listen to the following two statements by Kara and then compose a reflection of feeling using the formula, "You feel _____ because _____."
   a. 25:21: "It's just frustrating . . . "
   b. 25:59 "I probably haven't addressed it enough, but I'm scared that he will be scared away if I do."
2. List the feelings that Bryce is able to reflect in this segment.
3. What else might Kara be feeling?

Summary

The reflecting skills are a quantum leap from the invitational skills because they do much more than encourage clients to tell their stories. The reflecting skills move clients to greater self-awareness and encourage the client to address deeper issues beneath the surface. They forge an empathic bond between client and helper because the client senses that someone has taken the time to really understand.

Reflecting feelings involves identifying and labeling the client's feeling, whether or not such feelings have been openly expressed. The feeling component of the message is often hidden because disclosure of feelings is bound by cultural and family rules. The emotions that helpers identify when reflecting feelings have many nuances and variations. Helpers need to improve their feeling vocabularies in order to convey understanding of the client's message. Labeling and reflecting feelings can be one of the most difficult processes to learn. There is a great variability in how quickly students learn to reflect feelings. Some come to it very naturally and quickly. Others take longer but can learn the skill eventually through persistence and practice.

Exercises

GROUP EXERCISES

Exercise 1: The Alter-Ego Technique for Identifying Feelings

Identifying feelings precedes reflecting them. One of the best action methods for learning to identify feelings is the *alter-ego technique,* which comes to us from psychodrama (Moreno, 1958). The alter-ego technique asks the student to pretend that he or she is the client in order to imagine the client's feelings. This group exercise requires four members: the client, the helper, the alter ego, and the observer. It is in the role of alter ego that the student learns most about how to identify feelings.

The Client

The client discusses an experience with either positive or negative ramifications, such as a good or bad vacation, a relationship that ended abruptly, a missed opportunity, or another minor problem.

The Helper or Listener

The trainee who plays the part of the helper has little to do in this exercise. The job of the helper is to listen with appropriate body position, using only open questions and minimal encouragers, providing a focus for the client but rarely intervening.

The Alter Ego

The third student, the alter ego, stands *behind* the client and speaks for the client, identifying anything the client might be feeling but has left out. It is very important that the alter ego speaks using the word *I* as if he or she were speaking for the client; "I am angry," "I am embarrassed," and so on. Sometimes as the alter ego, you might find it easier to close your eyes to reduce distractions.

The Observer

The fourth member of the group is an observer who records the alter ego's remarks on a blank sheet of paper. In the discussion phase, the client gives the alter ego feedback on the most accurate and the least accurate reflections and paraphrases. The observer should gently correct the alter ego if he or she forgets to speak as the client and lapses into "you feel" rather than "I feel."

Action Phase

Once roles have been assigned, the client tells his or her story to the helper/listener. The alter ego, standing behind the client, expresses underlying feelings in the client's story. The client should be directed to ignore the alter ego, except when the alter ego really hits the mark. At that point, the client should incorporate the alter ego's comment into his or her statements. For example, if the alter ego says, "I am angry and embarrassed," the client may then respond, saying, "I *am* embarrassed." The client always directs his or her response to the helper/listener, even when reacting to the alter ego. Although client and helper/listener may find this exercise frustrating, it allows the alter ego to stand outside the relationship and he or she can learn to hear feelings, imagining himself or herself as another person.

Discussion Phase

After 5 to 8 minutes, the group members discuss their experiences, and the observer gives the alter ego feedback. Members then exchange positions until everyone has had a chance to experience the role of alter ego.

QUICK TIPS: REFLECTING FEELINGS

- You will probably need to use invitational skills and paraphrasing before you have enough information to reflect feelings. Don't expect to hear feelings immediately. When you have heard enough of the client's story to grasp the emotional content, stop the client and make a reflection.
- If you don't know how the client is feeling, imagine yourself in the client's shoes. What would you be feeling if you were the client?
- Use slightly different feeling words than those used by the client to avoid parroting.
- Don't agree with the client when he or she is placing blame on someone else. Keep your focus on the client's viewpoint. Convey that you understand the client's perspective without taking sides.

Exercise 2: Using the Feedback Checklist in a Practice Session

The alter-ego technique is a good way to develop the initial skill of imagining oneself as the client and identifying thoughts and feelings. The next step is to incorporate the skill within the helping interview. Break into groups of three with a helper, client, and observer. During a 5- to 8-minute session, the client describes a small problem he or she has been having with a friend, a family member, or someone at work. The helper uses invitational skills, paraphrases and, whenever possible, reflects feelings. The helper's goal is to reflect *at least three feelings* during the practice session.

The observer makes certain that the time limits are observed and, during the period, records every helper statement on the Feedback Checklist. At the end of the time, he or she shares feedback with the helper. The client gives the helper feedback on which responses on the checklist were most accurate and which were least accurate. The client makes a check next to those that seem to hit the mark. The group exchanges roles until everyone has had a chance to practice the role of helper and receive feedback.

Feedback Checklist: Reflecting Feelings

Observer Name: _____ Helper Name: _____

During the session, the observer records the helper's responses verbatim. After the session, the group decides on a category for each response: E for an encourager (either door opener or minimal encourager), CQ for closed question, OQ for open question, P for paraphrase, ROF for reflecting feelings, and P/R for a response that paraphrases *and* hits the feeling. Were any of the helper's responses focused on the wrong person? If so, note WF for wrong focus.

Category	Helper Response	Client Feedback
_____	1. _____	_____
_____	2. _____	_____
_____	3. _____	_____
_____	4. _____	_____
_____	5. _____	_____
_____	6. _____	_____
_____	7. _____	_____
_____	8. _____	_____
_____	9. _____	_____
_____	10. _____	_____

Exercise 3: Reflecting More than One Feeling

Clients are usually not experiencing a single emotion associated with their problem. Emotions are tangled like spaghetti. When you are trying to reflect all of the feelings a client is experiencing, it helps to untangle the problem and it begins to feel more manageable. In this exercise, you will try to identify more than one emotion in a client statement from the Written Exercises in this chapter (Exercise 1).

First, form circles of four students. Each student reads one of the eight client statements in turn as if he or she were the client, using voice tone that expresses the client's feelings. The student across from the client reflects the feeling the client seems to be experiencing using the, "You feel . . . because . . ." format. But this time, the student attempts to identify two or more feelings that might be associated with the problem. For example, "You felt angry *and* hurt because you thought management cared about the workers." In groups of four, each student will have two chances to reflect more than one emotion. Following each round, the group should discuss the accuracy of each student's reflections. You may want to consult the list of feeling words in Table 6.1.

WRITTEN EXERCISES

Exercise 1: Practice in Identifying Feelings and Reflecting Feelings in Writing

Listed below are eight client statements. First go through and identify the major feeling or feelings in each client statement. Then write down, "You feel _____." If more than one feeling exists, reflect all that you can. If you have identified the right primary emotion but differ on the exact shade of emotion, you could be right depending on the context and nonverbals of the client.

1. "There I was, standing in front of the entire assembly, and I froze. Everyone was staring at me. My heart was pounding and I started to shake. I thought I was going to die right there on the spot. I can never show my face again after that."
2. "And for the third time in a row, he failed to show. What a jerk! My daughter looks forward to these times with her father, and I hate to see him treat her this way. But I can't seem to do anything to make him listen."
3. "I can't wait to go to Europe with the French club. It's the opportunity of a lifetime! Yet it is going to be expensive. In addition to the obvious things, I'm going to need spending money, too. I would have to bring my boyfriend something. I don't know how I am going to come up with all the money I need."
4. "The more I do, the more the boss seems to expect. He's never satisfied and is always finding fault. I think I should start looking for another job because I can't take it any more."
5. "I can't believe I trusted my sister-in-law. She is such a backstabbing witch. I hate her. She'd start badmouthing my mother-in-law and get me going. Then after she got me saying negative things, I found out she was going back and repeating everything I said to her! Now my mother-in-law hates me."
6. "We just moved here, and I'm working two jobs. But somehow I've got to find time to take my kids to their schoolmates' houses so they can get to know people and have some friends. I just don't seem to have time."
7. "My son keeps staying out late at night with his friends. He won't tell me where he goes. I'm afraid he'll get hurt. He's probably able to take care of himself. I don't know what to do."
8. "My best friend was hoping that Glenn would invite her to the formal, but he invited me. She's not talking to me and I don't know what to say. It's not my fault."

Exercise 2: Connecting Feelings and a Paraphrase

Using the stem "You feel _____ because _____," create statements that reflect feeling and the related reason for the feeling, which comes out of the content of the story. Write your reflection + paraphrase down on a sheet of paper and compare your answers with mine. Make your paraphrase brief. Remember, the word *because* must logically connect the feeling and the content.

1. "My husband and I keep fighting. We argue over very minor things. I didn't really mind before, but I think its having a big impact on the kids."
2. "I think my girlfriend likes someone else. Whenever I turn around, I see her talking to Kent. She seems to laugh a lot when I see them together."
3. "I've always wanted to be an actor. But my mom and my teacher have told me it's a crazy idea and I need to get a proper job. Acting is all I want to do."
4. "I told my best friend something that was top secret. I found out yesterday that she told my worst enemy in the whole school."
5. "My sister's boyfriend is just terrible. He drinks too much and never works. I don't know, but I think he may be cheating on her."

SELF-ASSESSMENT

Practice reflecting feelings with a fellow class member who plays the role of the client. This practice can be as short as 10 minutes. Following the practice session, ask your client to fill out the following feedback.

To the Client:

Please respond as honestly as possible to the following statements, using the 5-point scale below:

1	2	3	4	5
Strongly Disagree	Disagree	Neutral	Agree	Strongly Agree

1. ____ The helper's nonverbal and opening skills seemed appropriate.
2. ____ The helper allowed me to talk too long before reflecting.
3. ____ The helper showed warmth.

4. ____ The helper's responses seemed concise.
5. ____ The helper seemed to understand the facts.
6. ____ The helper at times reflected using the original words I used (parroting).
7. ____ The helper identified one or two primary feelings accurately.
8. ____ The helper reflected a feeling of which I was unaware.
9. ____ Overall, the session helped me think a little more deeply about the situation.

Please identify one or two things the helper did well in the session.

1. _____
2. _____

Please identify one or two things the helper can do to further improve his or her skills.

1. _____
2. _____

To the Helper:

Based on the feedback you received, identify one or two things you hope to work on in upcoming practice sessions.

1. _____
2. _____

HOMEWORK

Keeping an Emotions Diary

Make a copy of Table 6.1 and keep it with some blank paper on a clipboard near your bed. Think about an emotion you experienced today. For example, if you felt angry at work, at school, or with family, record that feeling as the answer to the first question below. Fill out this diary for 2 successive days and then write a one-paragraph reaction recording your discoveries.

- What was the emotion?
- Think of a synonym for the emotion as you experienced it today.
- Describe the situation in which you experienced the emotion.
- Who was present when you experienced the emotion?
- What do you think caused your emotion? Do you blame other people for your emotion? Which of your personal values and beliefs might have given rise to this emotion? In other words, what did you say to yourself that seemed to spark this emotional response?
- How did you express the emotion?
- What societal rules come to mind when you think about expressing this emotion?
- Record any other thoughts you have about your experience today.

JOURNAL STARTERS

Think about the ways emotions are commonly expressed in your own family. Do you think that, in your family, some emotions are more acceptable than others? How do you think your family or ethnic background might affect your willingness to listen to a client's feelings?

Reflecting Skills: Reflecting Meaning and Summarizing

It is not just what we inherit from our mothers and fathers that haunts us. It's all kinds of old defunct theories, all sorts of old defunct beliefs, and things like that. It's not that they actually live on in us; they are simply lodged there and we cannot get rid of them. I've only to pick up a newspaper and I see ghosts gliding between the lines.

HENRIK IBSEN, *GHOSTS*, ACT 2

MyCounselingLab™

Visit the MyCounselingLab™ site for *Learning the Art of Helping: Building Blocks and Techniques,* Fifth Edition to enhance your understanding of chapter concepts. You'll have the opportunity to practice your skills through video- and case-based Assignments and Activities as well as Building Counseling Skills units, and to prepare for your certification exam with Practice for Certification quizzes.

Ibsen's quote brings home that in every situation, human beings are imprinting their previous conclusions about the world onto the present situation. Human beings are meaning-makers by nature. Making meaning is a higher order skill that allows us to make generalizations and rules so that we learn from our experiences. Unfortunately, many of these conclusions are faulty and self-defeating; more importantly, we are trapped by our own perspective and cannot understand how another person is reacting to a situation because we do not understand the cognitive map that he or she is using. Let me give two examples of the importance of understanding meaning. Both focus on couples' relationships where each person is trying to understand the other person's worldview and try to find a way to live with it. The first example is in the remake of the movie *Father of the Bride,* when the bride-to-be calls off the wedding because her fiancé buys her a blender for the 6-month anniversary of their meeting. She is tearful and angry because, for her, the blender is a sexist symbol. She interprets the present as an expression of his wish for her to take on a traditional female role—in the kitchen. Her husband-to-be responds with bewilderment because that is not what he intended. This example illustrates two points about the perceived meaning of an event. First, each person's interpretations, values, and perceptions are unique. They are formed by the person's history, current needs, values, and beliefs. Two people experiencing the same event will have different takes on its significance. As many cognitive therapists like to quote, "It is not what happens to us, but what we make of it." Second, the meaning of an event for an individual can be uncovered only with some deeper knowledge of that person. Had the fiancé understood that being independent and being recognized as more than wife and mother were very important to his fiancée, he would have been able to anticipate her reaction to the gift of a blender!

The second example relates to Gary Chapman's book, *The Five Love Languages* (1992). Based on his experiences, Chapman identified five ways in which people express and want to be loved. He claims that many relationship problems are due to the fact that we do not speak the language of our significant others. This breakdown was evident at a birthday party, when a woman named Jessie left early because her friend, Joyce, bypassed opening the birthday cards and instead cut the cake and opened the presents. Jessie was sad and angry that her friend did not read the carefully chosen card and additional sentiments she had written. Jessie's love language, according to Chapman, was "words of affirmation," and Joyce's language was, "receiving gifts." Sadly, we are very often ships passing in the night. We like to give to others what we like to receive. The reason for relating this story is that the meaning of the event for Jessie was deeply concealed in her own story. It involves how Jessie likes to be acknowledged, through affirming words; to really understand *why* Jessie was upset, we have to discover this hidden meaning.

Similarly, if a helper wants to really understand a client, he or she must be willing to go beyond facts and feelings and uncover the deeper meaning that the client assigns to life events. We must understand the client's implicit theories about life. Research studies have suggested that people tend to consistently bring their own beliefs to a situation (cf. Robins, Mendelsohn, Connell, & Kwan, 2004). These beliefs alter how we perceive others, what we focus on in a situation, and what we remember. Understanding that what really happened is not as important as how the client interprets it is consistent with the ideas behind **constructivism**. Constructivism posits that human beings actively work with their experiences, and based on their language and acquired beliefs, construct reality in concert with others (Mahoney, 2004). The main implication for the helping profession is that each person's situation can only be understood by examining his or her way of looking at the world, his or her culture, and the way he or she talks about issues. Later, we will identify some techniques aimed at helping a person change perspectives, including "reframing" and "countering." For now, perhaps you can accept the idea that each person's "take" on a situation is likely to be unique, and if we want to help, we need to understand how that person sees it rather than on just knowing the so-called facts. In this chapter, we will look at how a helper can identify and respond to the meanings behind a client's story by using advanced reflecting skills. Reflecting meaning communicates that we understand at a very deep level. We will also look at summarizing, a method of binding together the parts of the story into a capsule account. Summaries are ways of pulling together the loose ends of a client's story and communicating that the helper has grasped the totality of content, feelings, and meanings.

MEANING, UNCOVERING THE NEXT LAYER

> *We don't see things as they are; we see things as we are.*
>
> ANAÏS NIN

Understanding the content of the client's story gives us an outline or picture in our minds about what has happened. The emotions add color to the story and help us imagine the sometimes overwhelming feelings that he or she is experiencing. On the other hand, when we understand a person's meaning system, we begin to grasp how they view the world. Meanings are built from a person's past experiences, which are "alloyed with firm beliefs, fuzzy ideas, and unconscious schemes and prejudices" (Leontiev, 2007, p. 244). Thus, reflection of meaning is a significant step beyond content and emotion, because it helps us understand the unique perspective of the client. It also allows clients to become aware of the lens through which they are seeing themselves and others.

Client problems are frequently clashes between new experiences and the client's worldview (the collection of personal meanings). For example, we are frequently troubled by the discrepancy between our expectations and our partner's actual behavior. Our partner should be like our ideal. Our parents should love us in the way we want them to. I should be successful because I have worked hard. These are all meanings derived from how we think the world should be. If we know the meaning of the story, we will have learned why the client is troubled by it. It answers the question, "Why are we talking about this topic?"

Consider the case of Joan, who had been having problems at work for 2 years. Her co-workers had split into two factions that everyone on the job called "the redbirds" and "the bluebirds." There was considerable animosity because of a power struggle between the leaders of the two groups. Joan found herself allied with the bluebirds. During one of their after-work gripe sessions, she revealed that she knew one of the redbirds, Bob, had sought treatment for alcoholism. Bob had told her this several years ago when they were on good terms. Somehow this information leaked to the administration; Bob's boss called him "on the carpet" because the company was working on several government contracts, and Bob was investigated as a security risk. A couple of weeks later, Joan went to the company's employee assistance program and asked for counseling. During the interview, she and the counselor (Lynn) had the following exchange.

JOAN: "There is just so much turmoil. It used to be a good place to work. Now it's 'dog eat dog'."

LYNN: "You are sad because things have changed and now there is so much competition." (reflection of feeling and paraphrase)

JOAN: "Yes, that among other things."

LYNN: "Okay, say more." (door opener)

JOAN: "Well, Bob told me about his treatment for alcoholism one night when we were working late, sort of offhand. I even thought of him as a friend."

LYNN: "You're afraid of his reaction when he finds out that you leaked the information." (reflection of feeling and paraphrase)

JOAN: "Not really. It just seems a nasty thing to do to someone who was trying to be friendly."

LYNN: "In other words, you are disappointed in yourself for having betrayed a confidence." (reflection of feeling and meaning)

JOAN: "Yeah, that's the thing. I think I did it just to be part of the club. I don't like that about myself. I wish I were secure enough to have my own opinions about people."

LYNN: "It sounds like it has always been very important for you to be approved of, and sometimes, to be part of the group, you find yourself doing something you don't agree with." (reflection of meaning)

If Lynn had merely paraphrased the story of Joan's problems at work, her thoughts, and her underlying feelings, they would have had a productive session. However, Lynn chose to dig more deeply, not only paraphrasing Joan's feelings about recent events but also looking at the underlying meaning—the perceptions and values her client attributed to the self, the office situation, and the other workers involved. Notice how Lynn understands Joan's disappointment in herself and how this leads to a deeper response by Joan. Previous paraphrases and reflections of feeling were not nearly as effective as when the helper keyed in on what was really bothering Joan.

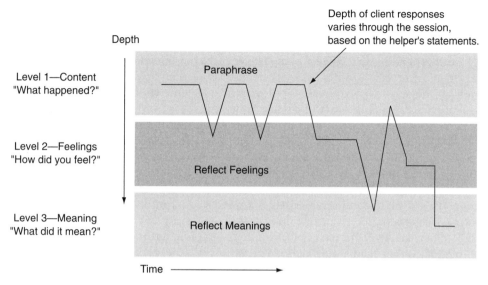

FIGURE 7.1 Levels of Disclosure

Figure 7.1 shows that every client story, like Joan's, has several layers. As if peeling an onion, a client is likely to give us first the content of the story, then the feelings it evokes and, finally, its personal meaning. The figure also portrays the fact that as the client's story becomes deeper over time, there are occasional returns to more superficial material. Increasing depth is due to the development of trust, but at the same time, more threatening material emerges, such as feelings and meanings that evoke embarrassment and shame. Therefore, depth varies as the client discloses. If the helper can keep the client focused on deeper issues and provide a safe environment, the full meaning of the story starts to emerge.

Why Reflect Meaning?

The events in Joan's story clearly have a deeper significance than Joan herself is able to identify at first. Meaning is the background against which the client's story is projected, but meaning needs to be noticed and brought into awareness. Why is it important for the helper to bring this deeper level of meaning to the surface? One reason is that the client takes these backdrop issues for granted. When the helper highlights them, the client begins to realize their significance in shaping the story and begins to understand that these meanings are part of the unique way he or she constructs the world. Letting the client know that you understand the way that he or she views life forms an empathic bond between client and helper.

Besides increasing the helper/client bond, reflection of meaning allows the client to recognize that the story they are telling is not necessarily the facts but is, instead, a perspective. The helper holds up a mirror to the client, "reflecting" rather than agreeing with what the client says. The helper lets the client get a good look at his or her own values and viewpoint about the self, others, and the world. When a client sees himself or herself through the eyes of another, he or she begins to envision how to make constructive changes. In Joan's case, by opening up to the meaning of the story, she begins to see that her actions were due, in part, to her long-felt need for approval. When she makes this connection, it paves the way to set a goal for becoming more self-directing.

Besides shifting the client's perspective, reflecting meaning inevitably has the effect of getting the client to discuss even deeper issues than those brought out in the first version of the story. Can you see how Joan's next statements in her dialogue with Lynn might progress? Perhaps she will discuss how she was raised, where her values came from, and how she is going to interact with her colleagues in the future. Although reflecting meanings leads to more disclosure and exploration of a topic, by the same token, a helper's inability to tap meaning results in more superficial conversations.

Beginning helpers are often confused when the client's story seems to have run its course. They feel that once the basic facts are known, where else can the conversation go? This is because the helper has not gone deeper into the meaning of the story. Figure 7.1 shows the concept of depth in a client's story over time. According to this model, superficiality is the result of traveling too rapidly through the story in a horizontal direction, rather than going deeper or vertically. The depth that a client is willing to reveal depends on a number of factors. Among these are helper responses, client readiness and willingness, and whether or not the client feels safe in the therapeutic relationship.

Encouragers like "Uh huh" and "Go on," do not necessarily nudge the client to go deeper. They tend to keep the client at whatever level the discussion has reached. If the helper does not invite the client to reach deeper levels by reflecting feelings and meanings, the client will normally remain at level 1 (Figure 7.1). Of course, some clients are very psychologically minded and will quickly discuss the deeper aspects of a problem with little prompting, but even insightful clients will frequently miss the importance of meaning because they take their meanings for granted.

On the other hand, some clients are not very talkative and are uncomfortable with expressing feelings and uncovering personal issues. In that case, going deeper takes a much longer time, even if the helper is very inviting and uses reflecting skills. Such clients may have trouble getting to the feelings level and meaning, and when they do, they only visit briefly. As we discussed in Chapter 3, clients are more likely to disclose deeply if the helper is perceived as competent, trustworthy, and nurturing.

Obviously, the only factors that the helper can control are his or her own actions. The helper cannot always break through a client's reluctance to open up. To increase the likelihood of greater depth in the client's explorations, the helper must avoid the overuse of closed questions and an interrogating attitude and must also rely on reflecting skills to enhance empathy in order to deepen the client's story whenever possible.

Challenging the Client to Go Deeper: The Inner Circle Strategy

In Joan's case, the helper used questions and reflections of meaning to get at the deeper levels of the story. Sometimes clients have difficulty recognizing that their stories have these deeper layers, and it is useful to challenge them to move from a superficial recounting to the area of personal meanings, secrets, and core beliefs (see Shaughnessy, 1987). Arnold Lazarus, the founder of multimodal therapy, used what he called an "inner circle strategy" for getting clients to identify deeper, more personal issues (1981, p. 55). Using

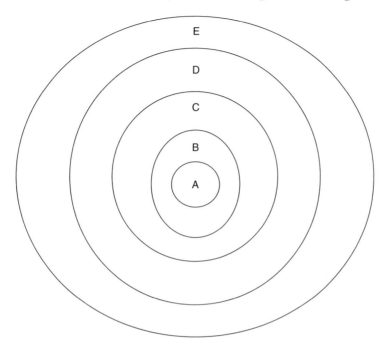

FIGURE 7.2 Inner Circle Strategy

the **inner circle strategy**, the helper draws a series of concentric circles labeled A, B, C, D, and E (see Figure 7.2). At ring E are issues that are essentially public and might be discussed with almost anyone on first meeting, including one's appearance and occupation. At ring A are very personal issues such as sexual problems, anger and resentment toward people, negative views of the self, and secrets that the client feels are immoral or dishonest. Most relationships start at D and move towards A as the relationship grows. However, some relationships remain very close to D, and deeper topics are never broached. To illustrate this tendency, the helper might ask the client to write in the names of individuals, including the helper, who have access to the various rings from A to D. Lazarus likes to use the diagram to confront the client when therapy has become too superficial. For example, the helper might say, "It seems to me that we are discussing issues that fall in the D or C category. The most effective work occurs at levels A or B. I am wondering if you do not feel comfortable talking about these deeper levels yet."

STOP AND REFLECT

We have been talking about the fact that the most productive therapeutic relationships are developed when clients feel free to reveal their deepest thoughts, feelings, and perceptions. Clients who venture to this level of disclosure are, however, risking a great deal. One way to realize this is to imagine yourself in the client's position. Think for a moment about what is unique about you. What

(Continued)

would a person need to know about you before you would feel that he or she was sufficiently informed to help you? How long would you have to know someone before discussing your deepest secrets? Read each topic in the following list, and identify something relevant about yourself that you would be willing to discuss with a helper during the first session and something else that you probably would not discuss. Write down brief notes under each heading. What do you fear might happen if you disclosed the thoughts, feelings, and perceptions that you would prefer not to discuss?

Topic	I Would Disclose	I Would Not Disclose
• Your family values and family history • Your religion or spiritual beliefs • Your sexual history • Your personal dreams and ambitions • Happy and unhappy childhood memories • Physical limitations, disabilities, and illnesses • Times when you were dishonest or unethical		

Draw an inner circle for yourself like the one in Figure 7.2 and write down the names of people who have access to the deeper issues in your life. Now think of one or two issues that you would not discuss with anyone, even a professional helper. What would stop you? Are there also issues at rings B and C that would be difficult but not impossible to discuss with a helper? What issues would you discuss only if there were safeguards of confidentiality? Share your inner circle with a small group of classmates if you feel comfortable in doing so. There is no need to discuss the issues at each of the levels. However, it might be interesting to compare the numbers of people who have access to the various levels of your life. Who are these people, and how did they gain this kind of trust?

Worldview

Worldview is a term that refers to a person's view of self, others, and the world (Koltko-Rivera, 2004). Language, gender, ethnicity/race, religion/spirituality, age, physical abilities, socioeconomic status, and trauma all influence the development of one's worldview (Ivey, Ivey, & Simek-Morgan, 1997). In addition to worldview, a client's personal **values** (what is important in life) are sources of meaning that can be brought to the surface. Recall the discussion between Lynn and Joan. The issue boiled down to Joan's feeling that she had strayed from what she believed was right. Violations of one's personal values are frequently background issues in client's messages. The helper's job is to understand both the client's worldview and his or her values so that the client's viewpoint—and the meaning of his or her story—can be appreciated and an appropriate solution to the client's problems found. Without understanding Joan's moral dilemma and disappointment in herself, do you think it would be possible to help her deal with her situation at work? The appropriate solution must be consistent with her ideas of what is right and healthy. In other words, it must take into account her worldview.

Following are some other examples of client statements that give a window to worldview or values. A helper can listen for these kinds of statements as avenues for reflecting meanings.

View of Self

"I am essentially . . . (a good person) (evil) (selfish) (okay/not okay) (smart/dull) (damaged) (unlovable)."

"Nothing I do seems to work out."

"I always land on my feet."

"I am unlucky."

"I am a victim."

"I am a bad parent."

Notice that these statements express general notions about the self, rather than defining specific abilities such as being a good piano player or having a good sense of direction.

View of Others

"People are . . . (unreliable) (essentially good) (selfish) (trustworthy) (kind)."

"Men are all alike."

"People will take advantage of you if they can."

"White people are . . ."

"Asians are . . ."

Beliefs about the Environment or the World in General

"It's a jungle out there."

"Life is a vale of tears."

"You can't get ahead."

"It's bad luck."

"God punished you."

"God rewarded you."

"Things always turn out for the best."

Values

"People should treat each other fairly."

"Men should be the head of the family."

"Family secrets should be kept in the family."

"Conflict is bad."

"You should always try to do your best."

HOW TO IDENTIFY MEANING ISSUES WITH A CLIENT

Reflecting Meaning

Reflecting meaning is a technique that counselors use to attempt to restate the personal impact and significance of the event the client is describing. Some investigations into the transcripts of Carl Rogers have found that 70% of his responses were reflections of meaning, not feeling (Elliott, Bohart, Watson, & Greenberg, 2011). While helpers of all kinds use reflection of meaning, it is very difficult to learn.

Reflection of meaning is difficult to learn because each person's take on a situation is unique. For example, much work was done in the 1960s and 1970s on the effect of stressful life events (Holmes & Rahe, 1967). If you have ever been in a stress workshop, you may have taken a "stress scale" that lists life events such as moving, changing jobs, divorce, and so on. Each event is given a weight based on its predicted impact on your life. Initially it was thought that, by adding up the scores, one could anticipate how much stress a person would feel based on the number of changes during the past year. It turns out that the number of events is not very predictive of stress or illness, but the meaning and importance you place on the events is significant. For example, while divorce is highly stressful to most people and gets a high score on the stress scale, in conflict-ridden relationships, divorce may actually lead to a reduction in stress. It is not really possible to know how an event has affected someone until you understand his or her experiences, basic beliefs, and values.

Because meaning is even deeper below the surface than feelings, meanings are harder to detect. The meanings are implicit in the client's story, but one must learn to read between the lines to unearth them. This sometimes involves employing intuition or hunches. The more you know about a client, the greater the likelihood that your hunches will be correct. Therefore, helpers are encouraged to be patient, using invitational skills, paraphrasing, and reflecting feelings to help the meanings emerge. Helpers generally use two methods to get at meaning in a client's story. First, helpers can *pose open questions* that ask the client to focus on the perceived significance and meaning of the story. Second, helpers can *reflect meanings* by listening carefully and taking educated guesses about why the story is important to the client.

In Chapter 6, you learned to reflect feelings using the formula or algorithm: "You feel _____ because _____." The first blank was to be filled in with the client's emotion and the second with paraphrased content—for example, "You feel angry because you didn't get the promotion." To reflect meaning, we use the same formula, but in this case, we place an accurate reflection of feeling in the first blank and a reflection of meaning in the second blank, as in the statement, "You feel disappointed in yourself because being a good daughter is an important value to you." Sometimes it may be necessary to include both a reflection of feeling and a short paraphrase of content in the first blank so that the client knows exactly which event you are referring to—for example, "You were excited (feeling) when you received your driver's license (paraphrase) *because* it meant you were becoming an adult (meaning)." The word *because* shows the connection between the content and feelings of the story and their relationship to the underlying meaning for the client. In other words, it is quite possible, as one goes deeper into the story, to choose among reflecting meaning, reflecting feelings, and paraphrasing as needed. They can be delivered alone or in combination. How do you know when to use each one? The answer is that you try to reflect as deeply as you are able. If you can only grasp the feelings, then reflect those feelings and wait until you know more before playing a hunch about meaning. Here are some examples of reflections of meaning. Assume that each reflection of meaning comes after a longer period of listening during a helping session.

Example 1

CLIENT: "I don't know what to do now. Everything I worked for is going down the drain."

HELPER: "You must feel pretty lost because the dream of having your own business was so important to you."

Here the helper reflects the feeling of being lost. The helper then ties this feeling with the unique meaning that the client's dream has died. Notice that the word "because" connects the feeling and meaning logically: The client feels lost because the dream was so important. The helper may only make a reflection like this when he or she has adequate knowledge of the client's hopes and ambitions from previous statements.

Example 2

CLIENT: "My daughter isn't living right. She stays out late, and now she's moved in with that boy, and I don't have the heart to tell anyone where she's staying."

HELPER: "You are a bit ashamed about your daughter's living situation because you think you have failed as a parent to convey your values."

The helper reflects the client's feeling of being ashamed and briefly paraphrases by mentioning her "daughter's living situation" in a nonjudgmental way. Then the helper connects the feelings to the underlying meaning: The client feels that she has failed.

Example 3

CLIENT: "When my mom died, at first I was disoriented, like I was in a haze. Now, my high school graduation is coming up, and she won't be there."

HELPER: "In a way, your feelings have changed from shock to sadness, and because she will not be there for graduation, it seems less special."

Can you see that the helper took a risk and played a hunch? The helper intuitively grasped what the client might be feeling now and what it meant not to have her mother at this milestone event.

Reflecting meaning requires that the helper think intuitively, and it also means that the helper must fully comprehend the client's unique situation and values. Although we can guess what meaning most people might derive from a situation to accurately reflect the meaning of an event, we frequently must have some understanding of its cultural context. The surest route to reflection of meaning is to patiently and persistently use the basic invitational and reflecting skills. These provide the best atmosphere for clients to tell their stories. The more fully we understand the content and feelings, the easier it will be to reflect the underlying meaning. We must patiently plod away at our reflecting until the light bulb comes on and we see the meaning. The main difference between a beginner and an experienced helper is that the experienced helper knows the light bulb will come on and that reduces anxiety considerably.

QUICK TIPS: REVIEW OF REFLECTING FEELINGS AND MEANINGS

- The formula for reflecting feelings is "**You feel** (specific emotion) **because** (the facts of the situation that account for the emotion)."
- For example, "You feel embarrassed because you really didn't want your teacher to know that you were getting a free lunch."

- The formula for reflecting meanings is **"You feel** (specific emotion) **because** (the personal meaning behind the situation that accounts for the feeling)."
- For example, "You felt embarrassed because you don't want to be singled out as someone that needs help."

Using Open Questions to Uncover Meaning

Open questions focusing on meaning can be useful, especially when a client is not very forthcoming. You are already familiar with open questions as a building block from Chapter 4. There, open questions were recommended as a way to delve deeper into some aspect of the client's story and to invite greater disclosure. Open questions can also be employed to facilitate a client's identification and expression of meaning. Consider the following exchange between a client, Sonia, and a helper, Chris:

SONIA: "There was a big family problem because I didn't pick up my sister at the airport. Everyone in the family jumped on me. I guess I was wrong, but I was busy and no one seemed to understand. Now my mom is mad at me and so is my brother."

CHRIS: "You feel confused about what happened." (reflection of feeling)

SONIA: "Yeah, and I am mad!"

CHRIS: "What is it about this situation that makes you so angry?" (open question focusing on meaning of the event)

SONIA: "My time isn't important. The family is important. My sister Camilla is important, but I am not important to my parents."

In this interaction, Chris correctly reflected a feeling of confusion, but Sonia added that she also felt angry, letting Chris know that she had only understood part of her emotions. Getting at these feelings seemed to pave the way for the client to expose more about the deeper significance of the problem. Because Chris could not quite identify the meaning in the client's statement, she used an open question to try to understand the deeper issue. The client responded by revealing the meaning of the event: She does not think her family cares about her needs.

STOP AND REFLECT

The Ultimate Meanings Technique

Leontiev (2007) devised a creative technique for identifying the meaning. The technique consists of writing down your answer to a question with the stem, "Why do people . . . ?" and then following up with more "why questions" to the answers. For example, "Why do people watch TV (smoke cigarettes, get married, buy a house, etc.)?" Below is an example using the question "Why do people travel?"

ANSWER: "To see new things."
QUESTION: "Why see new things?"
ANSWER: "Because you can see different ways of doing things."

QUESTION: "Why see other ways of doing things?"
ANSWER: "Because then you will be able to think of new ideas."
QUESTION: "Why think of new ideas?"
ANSWER: "So that you can create new products at work and get an edge on other people."

This example is truncated but perhaps you can see that this person may value creativity, success at work, and competing with others. Of course, you would need a longer series of questions and different topics to get a clearer insight. But perhaps you can see that each person's answers to the questions will be different and based on what he or she believes to be important.

If you would like to try the Ultimate Meanings Technique for yourself, respond to the following question: "Why do people work?" Write down your answer. Then ask a series of "why questions" based on your answers. Try to put down 20 or so answers, then look through your answers and see if you can spot some key values and meanings for yourself.

SUMMARIZING

Summarizing is the final reflecting skill you will need to learn. Although it is easier to learn than reflecting meaning, we place it here because you cannot really use summarizing until you have paraphrased and reflected feelings and meanings in a client's story. Summarizing pulls together everything a client has said in a brief synopsis of the session up to that point. The summary helps the client make some sense of the tangle of thoughts and feelings just expressed in the session. In other words, it serves a reflecting purpose, letting the client hear his or her viewpoint in a more organized way. The summary ties some of the major issues that have emerged into a compact version of the story. It may include any of the following: (1) content, (2) major feelings, (3) meaning issues and themes, and (4) future plans. Of the reflecting skills, it could be considered the broadest brush, bringing together main content, themes, and feelings in the client's story by concisely recapping them. But summaries are not to be used only at the end of a session. Summaries may be used at all points—beginning, middle, and end. This is because summaries have different purposes. Based on the reason for using the summary, they can be divided into four types: focusing, signal, thematic, and planning.

Focusing Summaries

At the beginning of a session, a summary may help to focus the conversation before it begins. A **focusing summary** is an intervention that brings the discussion to bear on the major issues and themes, places the spotlight on the client's responsibility for the problem, and reminds the client of the goals. For example:

"In the last few sessions, it seems like we have been dealing with two major issues. The first is the way that you are trying to renew your social network and find some supportive friends since your breakup with Alicia. The other issue is your mixed feelings about living back home with your parents."

Focusing summaries are not only to remind clients about their goals from previous sessions. They can even be used at the first session with a new client. For example, a helper says:

"Let's review what I know so far. Your mother called and made this appointment for you because you were arrested about a month ago for public intoxication. One of the conditions of your probation is that you receive help for your drinking problem. Your probation officer referred you to our agency. So you're here to do something about the problems you've been having with alcohol. Is this about right?"

Brammer (1973) points out that a focusing summary at the beginning gets the client on track immediately. Contrast this with the normal opening statements such as, "How have things been going this week?" or "What would you like to talk about today?" When a client begins the session by reacting to a focusing summary, he or she immediately begins talking about the key issues and goals.

Signal Summaries

In the middle of a session, the **signal summary** tells the client that the helper has digested what has been said and that the session can move on to the next topic. If the helper does not summarize occasionally, the client may feel that it is necessary to go over an issue several times until full understanding is communicated. A good time for a signal summary is when the client seems to have come to the end of a story and pauses.

CLIENT: "So that's about it . . . (pause)."

HELPER: "Before we move on, let's just summarize where we've been so far. You have tried to get professional help for your daughter's drug problem, and she has rejected it. Because she is an adult, there is not much force you can apply. This makes you feel helpless, and when you see her, your relationship is very superficial because you can't talk about the drug issue without getting into a fight. You've always been the kind of person who likes to leap into action when a problem arises, and here is a situation where there is little to do. That's what makes it especially frustrating." (summary)

CLIENT: "Yes, but that's the way it is. Now I guess I need to talk about how I can go on with my life under these circumstances."

HELPER: "Okay, let's talk about that." (door opener)

Thematic Summaries

A theme is a pattern of content, feelings, or meanings that the client returns to again and again (Carkhuff, 1987). The **thematic summary** is an advanced reflecting skill because it means that the helper has to be able to make connections among the content, emotions, or meanings expressed in many client statements or even during many sessions. When this kind of reflection is made, it often provides new information to the client, who may be unaware that the issue is resurfacing so often. Rather than signaling a transition to a new topic, the thematic summary tends to push clients to an even deeper level of understanding or exploration. Here are some examples of thematic summaries:

• "There seem to be two issues that keep coming up. One of them is the anger you feel in a number of different close relationships (emotional or feelings theme), and the other is your sense that you haven't been able to reach your potential in your career (content theme)."

- "As you have been talking, I seemed to notice a pattern, and I'd like to check it out. You seem to want to end relationships when they begin to lose their initial excitement and romance (content theme)."
- "From everything we've talked about over these past few weeks, one major issue seems to be that, over and over again, you hesitate to make a commitment to a career or to a relationship or to take any important action because you are afraid you might let your parents down by failing (meaning theme). Is this right?"

It is difficult to practice using thematic summaries because it presumes that you have seen a client for some time and usually for more than one session. It takes time for important themes to emerge. Identification of themes is an intuitive process. The helper must think back on the whole of his or her experience with the client and try to cull the big issues. Even though identifying themes is an advanced skill, it is placed here because it is possible you may notice these themes as you practice. You may also have the opportunity to see advanced practitioners identify these themes in recorded sessions. Remember too that themes are constructions or interpretations of the helper; they should be used only when you have enough information to be fairly certain that you have identified a theme. It is best to propose themes tentatively, because if incorrect, a thematic summary can have the effect of making the client feel analyzed.

Planning Summaries

Planning summaries entail a review of the progress, plans, and agreements made during the session. The planning summary brings a sense of closure and ends the session on a hopeful note. Here are two examples:

- "Well, it seems like we've identified several things in this first session that we want to pursue. First, you are unhappy with the way you tend to become overly dependent on your friends. You want to follow your own interests. In fact, you want to get to know yourself better. With this in mind, we thought about your entering a counseling group at the local mental health center. Besides that, you'd like to identify some goals for your career. That is something you and I can begin to work on right away. We'll set up an assessment program and talk more about this in the next several weeks. How does all this sound?"
- "Let's recap what we have talked about so far. On the one hand, you have accomplished your financial goals, but you are far from satisfied with your relationships with friends and family. You have said that this is because you are not very assertive. It sounds as if this is the area we need to discuss in our next session. What do you think?"

THE NONJUDGMENTAL LISTENING CYCLE

When Do You Use Each Skill?

Up to this point, you have been learning what to say to a client needing help. You have also been learning how to say it with the appropriate body language and voice tone. The next question you might ask is, *When? When* refers to selecting the skill that is most appropriate at this point in the therapeutic relationship. Should I ask a question or reflect a feeling? One way of thinking about it is "Where do I want the conversation to go right now?" Table 7.1 shows how you might select skills on this basis.

TABLE 7.1 Where Do You Want the Session to Go Next?				
What do you want to do?	Listen to the client's story until you understand it better	Find out crucial information	Move the client to deeper exploration of the topic	Transition to a new topic
Skill You Might Use	Invitational and Opening Skills including open questions and encouragers	Closed Questions	Reflect Feelings and Meaning	Summaries

Of course, each client tells his or her story in a particular way and at a particular pace, depending on personal history, previous experiences with helpers, and present emotional condition. So it is not possible to predict the exact order of the skills you will use. However, we can assume that, in general, helping sessions will follow a fairly similar path. We call this the **nonjudgmental listening cycle (NLC)**, or just the *listening cycle*, to emphasize that it is a repeating pattern of basic helping skills. The nonjudgmental listening cycle is a way of conceptualizing a normal or average helping session during which you use the most common building blocks. The listening cycle is repeated with each major topic the client presents. The helper switches gears and begins a new listening cycle whenever the client opens a new topic, encounters difficulty, has a crisis, or needs to explain.

The nonjudgmental listening cycle can be thought of as a set of sequential procedures to be followed as each topic emerges, is discussed, and comes to closure. As shown in Figure 7.3, each topic forms a circle from open question to summary. The invitational skills open the topic, and the reflecting skills move the discussion to deeper levels. A summary normally makes the transition from one topic to another or ends the session. Because each person and each helping relationship is different, this map of the average session should not be seen as the way every helping session must unfold. Instead, it is designed to help you think about the whole session and give you an idea about what the pattern should look like. A cycle like that shown in Figure 8.3 is typical of an interchange that would occur later in a helping session or after a session or two.

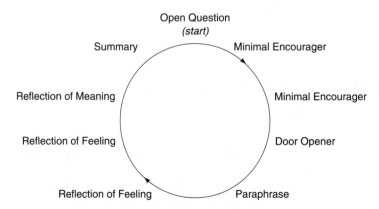

FIGURE 7.3 A Complete Nonjudgmental Listening Cycle Moving from Open Question to Summary

It is deeper and more mature because it shows reflections of feeling and meaning. Early on, a client and helper move through several more superficial cycles, as the client gives information and the helper paraphrases, asks questions, and collects data for the assessment process.

Following is an example of helper responses to client statements that represent a complete nonjudgmental listening cycle. Although the helper summarizes here, actually, it may take more than one such cycle before the helper is able to summarize. The session is condensed here to illustrate the major components in sequence:

1. *Open question:* "Would you tell me more about the accident?"
2. *Minimal encouragers:* "Okay," "Uh-huh," "Yes," "Can you tell me more about that?"
3. *Closed question (important facts):* "How badly were you hurt?"
4. *Paraphrase:* "So you had to be in the rehabilitation center for several weeks and you're still unable to work."
5. *Reflection of feeling:* "You're embarrassed about what has happened and a little afraid that people blame you."
6. *Reflection of meaning:* "Your identity has always been tied up with your job. Now that you cannot work for several months, it is hard to feel good about yourself."
7. *Summary:* "Though you're recovering on a physical level, there are several issues that continue to worry you, including how you might perform at your job and how other people will see you."

At this point, some students become restless to learn more advanced skills, thinking that their teachers are promoting the listening cycle as sufficient for all situations. The listening cycle is not the only set of skills used by helpers, but the listening cycle provides a safe pathway for the client to tell the story and builds openness and cooperation in the client/helper relationship. Without this foundation, the later processes of assessment, goal setting, and implementing advanced techniques are much more difficult.

Why Is the Cycle Described as Nonjudgmental?

We have focused a great deal on the skills that a helper uses to understand a client's story, but the attitudes displayed by the helper can make a great difference in the willingness of the client to open up. Carl Rogers (1957), a pioneer in counseling and psychotherapy, identified unconditional positive regard as one of these important attitudes. Positive regard, as the name suggests, is not a neutral stance. The helper actively demonstrates a nonjudgmental approach to the client by showing respect and interest in the unique life of the client. It is a continual challenge to hold such an attitude, especially when we are confronted by clients who have perpetrated violence or engaged in self-defeating behaviors or have committed what we consider to be immoral acts. Positive regard means responding in an accepting and nondefensive way to others who are different in culture, language, ethnicity, or religion. The listening cycle is called nonjudgmental because the attitude of positive regard must be in place when the helping skills are being employed. Without this underpinning, the skills are perceived as cold and robotic. The client will feel dissected rather than understood. How can one develop such a nonjudgmental attitude? One way is through vicarious learning. By watching videos or live demonstrations by helpers who have this nonjudgmental attitude, you may be able to acquire it. If you are a very judgmental person, you will have trouble learning advanced reflecting skills.

Judgments come from your own perspective and what you believe to be true. The ability to be nonjudgmental can be developed by putting yourself in situations where you can see another person's perspective.

A Questioning Cycle Typically Found Early in Training

In direct opposition to the nonjudgmental listening cycle, early on it is easy and perhaps inevitable that you will fall into an unproductive spiral, a *questioning cycle.* Figure 7.4 shows a *questioning cycle,* typically found in the beginning of training. In this cycle, the helper starts well with an open question and is able to paraphrase the content. Unable to use reflecting skills yet, the helper relies on a closed question to keep things moving. The question focuses the client back on content, and the helper follows this with a series of questions or minimal encouragers. After several such cycles, the helper is tempted to give advice because he or she has understood essential facts and expects that the client is simply in need of direction. In fact, because the helper is engaging the client's intellect with questions, the discussion does not deepen and the helper is surprised to find that the client has not really even scratched the surface.

One way of getting away from this trap is to *respond to the client's last statement* directly, using a paraphrase or an open question. This will buy a little time as you search for a reflection. Closed questions, however, will lead to short answers that do not allow you this breathing room. In the example below, the helper has fallen into a questioning spiral. Note the client does not stay on the topic because the helper's questions do not respond to the client's last statement.

HELPER: "Tell me more about the accident."

CLIENT: "It was horrible—what can I say? It was a financial problem, I felt terrible for months, and there were the physical problems, too."

HELPER: "Can you tell me more about the wreck itself?"

CLIENT: "I ran into another car, and that car hit some people on the sidewalk."

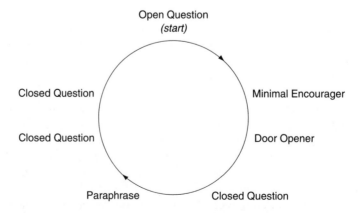

FIGURE 7.4 A Questioning Cycle Typically Found Early in Training

HELPER: "How badly were you hurt?"

CLIENT: "I spent 2 weeks in the hospital with a broken femur and a broken ankle. I had to go to the rehab center for the month of May. I'm still using a cane to walk. I don't know when I can go back to my job."

HELPER: "Do you think you are getting better?"

CLIENT: "Yes, but I am in no hurry to face people. I am a little afraid to see everybody."

HELPER: "What is it like being out of work for so long?"

CLIENT: "I am bored, and I focus a lot on the pain in my legs."

HELPER: "Are they giving you some medication for that?"

Can you see that the helper's fifth question, "What is it like being out of work for so long?" is not responsive to the client's statement, "Yes, but I am in no hurry to face people. I am a little afraid to see everybody"? Here the helper has a golden opportunity to reflect the client's feelings of fear and embarrassment. Instead, the helper falls back on questioning, taking the client to a more superficial level. When the helper is struggling to understand but cannot make a quick response, he or she is better off using a paraphrase or open question as a delaying tactic. It is crucial that the helper respond to the client's last statement rather than ask a question that sidetracks the conversation.

Here is an example of how responding to the client's last statement using encouragers, reflecting feeling, and reflecting meaning in that sequence can deepen the client's self-examination.

HELPER: "How badly were you hurt?" (closed question)

CLIENT: "I spent 2 weeks in the hospital with a broken femur and a broken ankle. I had to go to the rehab center for the month of May. I'm not walking yet without a cane. I don't know when I can go back to my job."

HELPER: "So you had to be in the rehabilitation center for several weeks, and you're still unable to work." (paraphrase)

CLIENT: "Yes, but I am in no hurry to face people. I am a little afraid to see everybody."

HELPER: "Go on." (door opener)

CLIENT: "Well, I don't know what they are thinking."

HELPER: "Okay." (minimal encourager)

CLIENT: "I think that everyone blames me for what happened."

HELPER: "You're worried that some of your friends will reject you because of the injuries to the other people." (reflection of feeling and paraphrase)

CLIENT: "I guess it is not rational."

HELPER: "When you think about it, it doesn't seem sensible, but all the same, it worries you." (paraphrase and reflection of feeling)

CLIENT: "Sure. I guess I would feel even worse if my own friends blamed me."

HELPER: "So it sounds like sometimes you blame yourself for what has happened." (reflection of meaning)

CLIENT: "Sometimes I think like that."

HELPER: "So, as I understand it, you are still recovering from your accident, and you are still a little unsure about how others will feel about the accident. More importantly, you feel guilty about what happened." (summary)

MyCounselingLab™

Go to Topic 2, *Invitational Interviewing*, on the MyCounselingLab™ site (www. MyCounselingLab.com) for *Learning the Art of Helping: Building Blocks and Techniques*, Fifth Edition, where you can:

• Find learning outcomes for *Invitational Interviewing* along with the national standards that connect to these outcomes.
• Complete Assignments and Activities that can help you more deeply understand the chapter content.
• Apply and practice your understanding of the core skills identified in the chapter with the Building Counseling Skills unit.
• Prepare yourself for professional certification with a Practice for Certification quiz.
• Connect to videos through the Video and Resource Library.

MyCounselingLab™ Exercises

Go to the Video and Resource Library on the MyCounselingLab™ site for your text and search for the following clips: *Reflecting Feelings: Muthoni* and *Reflecting Feelings: Mark*.

Exercise 1: Reflecting Meaning I

Reflecting meaning is a difficult skill. One way to improve your ability to identify meanings is to go back and watch other segments on the video and see if you can sense the underlying significance of client's stories, world view, and values. Try not to focus on the helper's statements because they are demonstrating other skills. Instead, listen carefully to the client.

Remember that there are two ways to get at meaning: (1) Reflecting meaning by rephrasing the client's statement, indicating that you understand the values, worldview, or hidden meanings in the client's words; and (2) asking a closed question of the client that elicits the client's values and meanings. In both of the video segments devoted to meaning, the helpers use both methods.

Search for the video clip *Reflecting Meaning: Mark* which shows a conversation between a helper, Mark, and a client, Santiago. Watch the entire segment and then respond to the following questions on a separate sheet.

1. Mark uses a question early on to focus Santiago on the meanings. What is it?
2. Later, Mark reflects a value implied in Santiago's story. What is it?
3. To get a sense of meaning, it is often useful to reflect feelings for some time before reflecting meaning. There is at least one significant feeling that the helper failed to identify. Of the following categories, which do you think Mark missed? Circle your first choice.

Sadness/Depression	Anger
Guilt/Shame	Interest/Excitement
Joy/Happiness	Fear/Anxiety
Surprise	Disgust

Exercise 2: Reflecting Meaning II

Video Segment 8, *Reflecting Meaning II*, in MyCounselingLab˘ shows Dayle, the helper, talking with Eve, the client. Before watching the entire segment, listen to Eve's first statement beginning at 33:20 and ending at 34:20. Try for a moment to put yourself in Eve's situation.

1. What feelings might you be experiencing?
2. Why might you be feeling this?
3. Does the answer to the question above give you a possible clue to the meaning behind this decision? Guess what might really be troubling her or why this is so important.
4. Now listen to the remainder of the segment. Dayle asked a number of insightful questions that gave Eve clues to the significance of this decision. List two questions that you think were especially useful in getting Eve to dig deeper.

Exercise 3: Summarizing

In Video Segment 8, *Reflecting Meaning II,* in MyCounselingLab˘ Dayle summarized her session with Eve beginning at 40:35. Watch that summary and answer the following questions.

1. Dayle's summary is brief. Does it capture the essence of the entire conversation? Are facts, feelings, and meanings included? If you do not think so, what would you add?
2. Of the summary types described in the book—focusing, thematic, signal, and planning—how would you categorize Dayle's?
3. Now take a look at Mark's summary in Segment 17, Advanced Change Techniques: Countering. The summary begins at 1:42:13. Marks begins to summarize then changes his mind and asks the client to summarize what she got out of the session. How did you like this approach to a planning summary? Are there any pitfalls to letting the client summarize?

Summary

Reflecting feelings and content are important tools for communicating to a client that you understand the story, but for a client to deeply sense understanding from the helper, it is also important to identify and reflect the meanings behind the client's experiences. Meanings consist of the worldview and values that arise from upbringing, culture, family, and life experiences.

The inner circle strategy is a method to indicate to clients that they are not disclosing at the deepest levels. The diagram also helps us to recognize that everyone maintains some secret areas. When we consider how scary it might be to expose these to others, we can begin to understand a client's need for a therapeutic alliance built on trust and time before deep disclosure can be expected.

Reflections of meaning are helper responses that go beyond the superficial, getting at the implicit messages rather than the explicit. This means that the helper must use intuition to go beyond the surface of what the client says, extrapolating the underlying meanings. When the facts, feelings, and meanings of a client's story are reflected, he or she feels that the helper has understood at a very deep level.

Summarizing is the second building block skill described in this chapter. Summaries pull together the content, feelings, and meanings in a distilled form. Summaries serve to focus the client on the major issues, identify themes, signal a transition in the session, and provide a basis for planning the next steps.

The nonjudgmental listening cycle is a way of explaining the deepening sequence of skills that a helper uses. Understanding the NLC can help new learners decide which skills to use at various points. By analyzing the NLC in transcripts or in classroom practice, a helper can determine if he or she is responding to the client's statements with deepening responses or is falling into the mistake of shifting topics by the overuse of questions.

Exercises

GROUP EXERCISES

Exercise 1: Reflecting Meaning

Form groups of three with a client, helper, and observer. The client is to pick a topic that is likely to evoke some deeper meaning such as:

"My greatest ambition is . . . "

"My biggest disappointment has been . . . "

"Something I am not very proud of is . . . "

"My ideas about divorce are . . . "

"What I like about this country is . . . "

"Something I would like to improve about myself is . . . "

The helper is to use encouragers and open questions to keep things moving, but the main goal is to advance hunches about the personal meanings that lie behind the client's disclosures. The helper should review the "Quick Tips: Reflecting Meaning" section that follows and make reflections of meaning to the client's story.

As the helper reflects, the observer is to write down all helper responses on a sheet of paper. Later

the helper can record any useful feedback on this same sheet and take this record home for further examination. After 5 minutes or 10 attempts at reflection of meaning, the observer calls time. Together, look at the helper's responses and see how many of these are accurate reflections of meaning. The client, in particular, should give the helper feedback on key meaning issues that were missed. Group members should then change roles and continue until each person has had a chance to play the role of the helper.

QUICK TIPS: REFLECTING MEANING

If you are having difficulty identifying the meaning behind the client's story, consider these tips:

- Use the following plan in your practice sessions: Ask an open question to start, use minimal encouragers as you get the details, and then strive for reflection of feelings. Whenever possible, make a reflection of meaning.

- Ask yourself, "Why is this story important to the client?" "Why is he or she telling me

this?" "What is it that bothers the client so much about the event?"
- Be patient! Wait until you have heard enough of the story to understand its importance, and then reflect meaning.
- Think about the client's background, and then tie in what you know about his or her unique viewpoint from previous topics.
- Are you responding to the last thing the client said, or are you looking ahead to what you are going to say? If you stay with the client's statements, one by one, they will lead you to meaning.
- When you have established a good reflecting relationship, and the client knows you understand the situation, take a risk and play your best hunch about some deeper underlying meaning.

Exercise 2: Using Summaries

Students form groups of five individuals with two volunteer playing client and helper. The helper tries to use opening, invitational and reflecting skills but does not summarize. The topic is "a brief history of my family." The other members of the group listen to the entire dialogue, and after 12 minutes, they each write down a summary of the client's history. Group members read their summaries to the client, who evaluates them based on their thoroughness. Did they capture content, feelings, and meanings? Were the summaries distilled or were they too lengthy?

SMALL GROUP DISCUSSIONS

Discussion 1: Planning and Focusing Summaries

Look back in this chapter to the scenario of Joan and Lynn. After reading that dialogue again, write down a brief planning summary and share it with your classmates in a small group. Next, write down a focusing summary that you might use to begin the next session. Summaries should be about two or three sentences in length. They should contain a brief synopsis of the thoughts, feelings, and meanings expressed by the client. Use the following criteria to give each other feedback on the summaries:

- Was the summary no longer than two or three sentences?
- Did the summary essentially capture the major points?

- Did the summary include the key events, feelings, and meanings expressed?
- Is there a hopeful tone to the planning summary?

Discussion 2: Create a Presenting Problem

For this discussion, form groups of four. Each member is to write down a three- or four-line statement that a fictitious client might give as a statement of a presenting problem. It should be written in the first person, as follows: "I am having trouble getting my children to mind me. That's not all. I've been very depressed, and I'm not going to be able to pay my bills this month. I try as hard as I can. What am I supposed to do?" When writing the example, students should remember to include enough information so that a reflection of meaning is possible. The trainer or leader reads each one anonymously, and the training group takes turns giving a reflection of meaning using the formula "You feel _____ because _____." A good response to the preceding problem might be, "You are feeling really discouraged because your best does not seem good enough." The trainer or leader asks for feedback from the group concerning the accuracy of the reflection. Another option is to ask one participant to reflect the meaning using the formula and the next participant to rephrase it in more natural terms.

QUICK TIPS: SUMMARIZING

- Use a summary when the client appears to be stuck. This will tend to get things back on track.
- At the end of a summary, it is often useful to finish with a quick "checking question" such as, "Have I got that right?" or "Am I correct?"
- When you feel like asking a question, try summarizing to signal the client to move on to the next topic.
- Use a summary when the client is moving too quickly and you want to slow the session down.
- Try to finish every session with a planning summary.

WRITTEN EXERCISES

Exercise 1: Identifying Meanings

In this exercise, you are asked to separately identify only meanings in a client's statement. Take into account that there may be more than one possible answer because, in practice, inflection or word emphasis would certainly change the meaning of these statements.

1. "I am extremely depressed and have been for about 6 months. I am now taking medication, and things are a little better. But every day I go to the refrigerator and look in. I can't decide what to eat. In the morning, I can't decide what to wear. This isn't me. If a friend calls on the phone, I am not sure what I will talk about, so I dread anyone calling. How long do you think this is going to last? Never has anything like this happened in my family. I feel so bad that my daughter has to come and take care of me. She has a life, too. I even feel like I am a burden to you."

Client's underlying meanings or hinted, unspoken assumptions (why is this important?):

_____

_____

Your reflection of meaning (content, feeling, meaning):

_____

_____

2. "I am a 31-year-old construction worker. Lately I've had thoughts of hitting my child, Barbie. She is the light of my life. But she doesn't mind me. I have to yell and scream. My wife and I don't seem to see eye to eye on how she should be raised. Maybe we don't agree on a lot of things. When I tell my daughter something, my wife rolls her eyes and belittles me. So, of course, Barbie won't do what I say. I tried to talk to my wife, but she won't listen any better than my daughter does. Now, I was brought up with a belt. But only when I needed it. I don't necessarily think she has to be spanked, but she needs to learn to mind. I am embarrassed when I have to take her to my mom's house or anywhere else because she won't listen."

Client's underlying meanings or hinted, unspoken assumptions:

_____

_____

Your reflection of meaning (content, feeling, meaning):

_____

_____

3. "My main problem is that I am overweight. I know that. And I want to lose weight. Look at the television and magazines. Everybody's skinny! I guess I am supposed to go along with the crowd. But

my husband doesn't realize that I have tried everything. He never says it, but I know he doesn't find me attractive anymore. But is a slim body all that is important? How about unconditional love? If I lost weight, what would I have to do next? Dress some particular way? He says he is concerned about my health, but do you believe that? Last week, my 7-year-old son and I went to the mall, and one of his classmates was there. In front of everyone, the other kid said to my son, "You have a big fat mom!" Children can be so cruel. And his mother didn't even correct him. Don't you think she should have?"

Client's underlying meanings or unspoken assumptions:

_____

_____

Your reflection of meaning (content, feeling, meaning):

_____

_____

Exercise 2: Constructing a Nonjudgmental Listening Cycle

After each client statement, there is space for you to write a specific response. Record your answer as if you were actually talking to the client. Your final response will be a summary. After you have completed the assignment, go back and look over your responses and indicate how they could be improved.

Background: Jennifer, age 15, a high school sophomore, has problems with motivation. She is about to fail her social studies class, requiring her to attend summer school. Her main goal is to pass social studies, and you have agreed to help.

Identify an open question or door opener to start the interview:

_____

JENNIFER: "You probably know I'm failing social studies. That's all my mom talks about. I am not studying as hard as she wants me to. But I can't sleep very well. So I sleep in class sometimes. It's really boring and I'm not going to need social studies, I am going to be a flight attendant. I can't wait until I get out of high school and can run my own life for a change."

Your paraphrase:

_____

_____

JENNIFER: "It's like this all the time, people telling me what to do. I want to pass but I just can't sleep. Maybe if everybody would leave me alone. My friends are having trouble with Mr. Robinson, the social studies teacher. Everyone in the class is probably failing."

Your reflection of feeling:

_____

_____

JENNIFER: "Yeah, that's how I feel. But why can't I be treated like an adult? At home, my mom is always after me. She and my dad are divorced. When I go to his house, he doesn't pressure me. He lets me do what I want. I would go and live with him but when I bring it up, he changes the subject. If they make me go to summer school, I will really be hard to live with. They have no idea."

Your reflection of meaning (or part of the meaning):

_____

_____

JENNIFER: "The main thing is I have got to pass this class 'cause I can't handle the whole summer in school again. The summer is when you're supposed to go to the mall and the beach. If they make me go to summer school, I'll probably sleep in class."

Your summary:

_____

_____

_____

_____

SELF-ASSESSMENT

A Midcourse Checkup

You have now learned most of the building blocks skills presented in this book. Although you have probably not mastered all of them, it is time for a brief review and checkup. Try to be as honest as possible. This will help you identify areas where more practice is needed. Review the feedback you have received during group exercises. Then take a look at the building blocks that follow and rate your current level of mastery for each skill.

> 1 = I understand the concept.
>
> 2 = I can identify it and give examples.
>
> 3 = I can do it occasionally.
>
> 4 = I can do it regularly.

_____ Eye contact
_____ Body position
_____ Attentive silence
_____ Voice tone
_____ Gestures and facial expressions
_____ Door openers and minimal encouragers
_____ Open and closed questions
_____ Paraphrasing
_____ Reflecting feelings
_____ Reflecting meaning
_____ Summarizing

Examine the pattern of your responses. If you are like most beginners, your invitational skills are strong. You may also be doing fairly well with paraphrasing, but you may well be at level 2 or 3 on reflecting feelings, reflecting meanings, and summarizing.

HOMEWORK

Homework 1: First Transcript

Now that you have read about and practiced the building blocks of the helping relationship, it is time to make a record of your present skill level by recording a longer session (20–30 minutes). The next task is to convert the recording to hard copy, or as we will call it, a _transcript_.

Your goal as a helper in this transcript is to demonstrate your ability to move from cycles of questioning and paraphrasing to the use of the higher skills of reflecting feelings and meanings. Rather than asking questions, fall back on paraphrasing, encouragers, and even silence until you are able to make a reflection.

STEP 1: With a partner from your training group, conduct and record a session based on a concern that he or she is willing to discuss. Alternatively, your fellow student may role-play the problem of a friend or acquaintance or fabricate a problem he or she might someday encounter in real life.

STEP 2: Choose the best 15 minutes of the video you made and transcribe every word of both client and helper using the format shown in Table 7.2. It is important that the client's comments appear directly *below* your helping responses, so that the connection between the two can be examined. Be sure you have permission to record from the client. You should do this aloud on the recording *and* in writing.

STEP 3: Listen to the recording or read the transcript and make comments, naming each of the skills that your response exemplifies. Sometimes students describe their responses rather than categorizing them. It is important to identify the skills you are using to determine their frequency and appropriateness. Use only the names of the building blocks you have learned. The comments section is a place for you to reflect on your responses. Do not just note weaknesses; identify strengths as well. In the comments section, you may also wish to identify any other issues that come to mind as you review the transcript.

Homework 2: Alternative to the Transcript—Making a Video

Make a video as described in Homework 1. Instead of making a full transcript of the video, watch it again and classify each of your skills as you watch. The process of identifying skills can be a form of practice. Get feedback from fellow students and your instructor on your progress. Try not to be judgmental. One of the biggest mistakes at this point is to notice weaknesses. For example, many students see themselves on video and do not like what they see. They see mistakes in body position or facial expression. Rather than reacting on a purely emotional basis, try to think about the following questions: "Did I help the client to go deeper into the problem? In the brief encounter, did we form the basis for a therapeutic relationship?" Build on your strengths before focusing too much on your weaknesses. Here are some questions to ask yourself:

- Was I able to get the client to open up?
- Are any of my gestures distracting to the client?
- Are my body position, facial expression, and voice tone inviting?
- Do I allow silence sometimes to urge the client to open up?
- Do I appear relaxed?
- Do I seem engaged with the client, or am I too passive?

TABLE 7.2   Transcript Example

In your write-up, include a short description of the client and the nature of the issue to be discussed. Note that each helper and client response is numbered so that the instructor can refer to them.

Client and Helper Responses	The Skill You Used	Comments
H1: "What would you like to talk about today?"	Open question	Looking at this now, it seems a little trite. I think I will try something else next time.
C1: "Well, I have been having a problem with a nosy neighbor."		
H2: "Really? Tell me more."	Minimal encourager and door opener	Seems appropriate at this stage.
C2: "Well, she comes over every day. I can't get anything done. I need to work on the computer. I need to do some work around the house. But she won't let me."		I notice that the client is blaming the neighbor. She is not owning the problem. Maybe next time I will get the client to focus more on that.
H3: "She doesn't have anything else to do?"	Closed question	Whoops, I missed the boat. I think it might have been better to reflect the client's frustration.

- How many paraphrases and reflections of feeling did I use?
- Did I rely too much on questions?
- Did I reflect soon enough?
- Did I overuse minimal encouragers rather than reflecting?
- How many reflections of meaning was I able to attempt?
- Are my words responsive to the client's last statement or to my own thoughts?
- What are my natural strengths as a helper?

JOURNAL STARTERS

Think about a strong personal value you hold and think about how you might react to a client who holds the opposite value. For example, let us say you value health and you encounter a client who smokes, drinks excessively, and takes other substantial health risks. In the value that you chose, under what circumstances would you confront the client or expose your own values? What ethical issues should concern you?

Challenging Skills

My experience is what I agree to attend to.
Only those items I notice shape my mind.

WILLIAM JAMES

MyCounselingLab™

Visit the MyCounselingLab™ site for *Learning the Art of Helping: Building Blocks and Techniques,* Fifth Edition to enhance your understanding of chapter concepts. You'll have the opportunity to practice your skills through video- and case-based Assignments and Activities as well as Building Counseling Skills units, and to prepare for your certification exam with Practice for Certification quizzes.

Evaluating Confrontation and Client Response
- The Client Acceptance Scale: Gauging the Client's Response to Confrontation
- Problems and Precautions

Summary

Exercises

- Group Exercises
- Small Group Discussions
- Written Exercises
- Self-Assessment
- Homework
- Journal Starters

In his book *Vital Lies, Simple Truths,* Daniel Goleman (1998) relates the following story told by a woman at a dinner party:

> *I am very close to my family. They were always very demonstrative and loving. When I disagreed with my mother, she threw whatever was nearest at hand at me. Once it happened to be a knife and I needed ten stitches in my leg. A few years later, my father tried to choke me when I began dating a boy he didn't like. They really are very concerned about me.* (pp. 16–17)

Goleman claims this tale is a good example of how people deceive themselves. Because the client cannot face the fact that she was the victim of child abuse, she changes the story to its exact opposite, one of caring and concern. If a helper points out this inconsistency, he or she is using a challenging skill. Another way of looking at challenging skills is that clients have multiple voices or stories that need to be told. By challenging, the helper is asking if the client is denying some aspect of the story. In the excerpt above, the client perceived her parents as caring, but she also must have been aware of the other voices. It is a human tendency to block these voices out and smooth out the competing ideas. Life is simpler that way. The helper awakens the client to this defensive maneuver through challenging skills. Irvin Yalom goes so far as to compare this duty to that of an executioner (Yalom, 2000). The client has found a refuge, and the helper's revelations kill off protective fantasies, potentially arousing resentment and discomfort. Sometimes it becomes necessary for helpers to "dare" clients to examine the inconsistencies in their stories by *giving them feedback* and, at other times, by *confronting discrepancies.* Making clients aware of uncomfortable information motivates them to act and change their circumstances. For most helpers, this step in the journey is a giant one. While the invitational and reflecting skills are supportive and convince a client to open up, these two challenging skills, feedback and confrontation, push the client to examine critically his or her choices, feelings, and thoughts. When the helper uses challenging skills, he or she is giving the client an honest reaction or pointing out warring factions in the client's story. Invitational and reflecting skills do not necessarily encourage the client to dig deeper or follow through with plans and commitments, but challenging skills do.

Consider Figure 8.1, which depicts the relationship between support and confrontation. Depending on the mixture you use, the client will see you as someone who is critical, as someone who is apathetic, as a helper person, or as a friend. The ideas behind Figure 8.1 are based on research in organizational settings that have identified managerial styles (Hersey, Blanchard, & Johnson, 2007). Supervisors in business situations can be roughly described as supportive or nonsupportive and challenging or not challenging. It appears that good managers have a balance of pushing and supporting. Similarly, in the helping

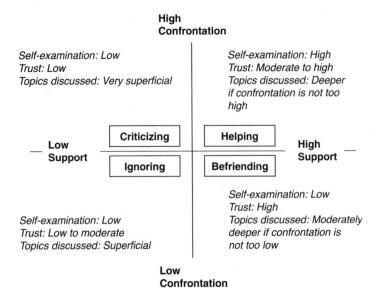

Self-examination: Low
Trust: Low
Topics discussed: Very superficial

Self-examination: High
Trust: Moderate to high
Topics discussed: Deeper if confrontation is not too high

High Confrontation

Low Support — **High Support**

| Criticizing | Helping |
| Ignoring | Befriending |

Self-examination: Low
Trust: Low to moderate
Topics discussed: Superficial

Self-examination: Low
Trust: High
Topics discussed: Moderately deeper if confrontation is not too low

Low Confrontation

FIGURE 8.1   Effect of Helper Interventions Based on the Ratio of Confrontation and Support

professions, much of what we do can be described as a combination of confrontation and support (Keen, 1976) or "joining" and "kicking" (Minuchin, 1974).

The ratio of confrontation to support has an effect on the client's willingness to *explore* his or her own thoughts, feelings, motives, and actions. This ratio also affects the client's willingness to *trust* the helper and to *discuss deeper or more superficial topics.* On the bottom half of the chart in Figure 8.1, you can see that when a helper does not use enough confrontation, the client does not engage in very much self-examination; yet in the high-confrontation conditions, the client's trust in the helper is reduced. When confrontation is high, the helper is bringing up topics and inconsistencies that may be painful for the client, and this strains the relationship. On the left-hand side of the figure, it also becomes clear that without support, the client does not engage in self-examination, nor does the client wish to discuss deeper issues because the trust level is so low. This figure suggests that the worst conditions for helping are high-confrontation, low-trust situations, and that high support conditions along with challenge lead to the best conditions for change.

WHEN SHOULD WE USE THE CHALLENGING SKILLS?

When challenging skills are used, the aura of safety and support, so carefully constructed by the helper, is at risk. There is a fundamental shift from relationship building to a focus on the goals set by the client and helper, conveying to the client that the helping relationship is not a friendship but a business partnership during which the helper may have to hold the client's feet to the fire in order to attain the agreed-upon outcomes.

During the initial stages of the relationship, the helper strives to understand the client's unique worldview by getting the client to open up. As a client tells the story, the helper listens attentively using the nonjudgmental listening cycle (NLC). After several cycles, the helper begins to detect distortions, blind spots, and inconsistencies. He or she may then use feedback and challenging skills, not so much to straighten out the client as to teach the client the method of self-challenging. This based on the assumption that self-delusion is no way to live. The essential aim of the challenging skills is to help clients operate with unclouded information about themselves. With heightened self-awareness, they are better able to make decisions and to operate free of illusions and "vital lies." This is consistent with the goal of helping: to empower clients by encouraging them to explore their own thoughts, feelings, and behaviors and to take steps toward their dreams and goals. Clients need to be challenged when:

- They are operating on misinformation about the self. For example, a client may underestimate her intelligence, feeling that she is not capable of attending college when there is evidence to the contrary.
- They are operating with mistaken ideas and irrational beliefs. For example, the client believes she must be perfect.
- They misinterpret the actions of others. This tendency is called *mind reading* and is a common problem among couples. A client may act on assumptions without confirming them, making statements such as the following: "I could tell by the way he acted that he did not want to date me anymore."
- They are blaming others rather than examining themselves. For example, a client may blame the boss at work but refuse to look at his own responsibility for the poor relationship or his own work performance.
- Their behavior, thoughts, feelings, and values are inconsistent. For example, a client talks about how much she values honesty but, at the same time, discusses how she hides her financial difficulties from her husband.
- They are not operating according to their own values.
- They are not working on the goals that they participated in setting.

In this chapter, we will focus on two building blocks, or basic skills, used to challenge clients and help them deal with problems more consciously. The first of these is giving **feedback:** your honest reaction to the client. The skill of giving effective feedback is one that has wide application in helping, including group work, couples counseling, and individual and family therapy. Second, we tackle the skill of confrontation itself, which is the art of pointing out inconsistencies and blind spots in the client's story. Confrontation is a powerful technique that must be used with great caution.

GIVING FEEDBACK

Why Is Feedback Important?

Disclosing oneself to others and receiving feedback from others are the twin processes of personal growth. The invitational, reflecting, and advanced reflecting skills that you have already learned are the primary methods helpers use to encourage client self-disclosure. The mere act of confiding in another person seems to have many health benefits (Pennebaker, 1990, 2004), and the ability to be "transparent" to others has been linked with mental health (Jourard, 1971). Learning to receive feedback is the other key to self-awareness and growth. Clients need accurate feedback in order to confront inconsistencies in their own attitudes and to know how they are affecting others. Most problems that people face are "people problems." People usually come for help when they experience pain in their interpersonal worlds. Unfortunately, we often receive conflicting messages about ourselves from other people because even family members and close friends may be afraid to give honest feedback. A friend or family member may say, "You look like a lunatic when you dance," or "Your driving makes me nervous." Our significant others withhold feedback because they do not wish to jeopardize the relationship. Rosen and Tesser (1970) called this unwillingness to transmit bad news the "mum" effect. Thus, we are often operating with incorrect or inadequate information.

The Johari Window

The *Johari window* (Luft, 1969) is a visual way of explaining that information about the self comes from two sources: things we observe about ourselves, and feedback from those around us (Figure 8.2). The Johari window (named by *Joe* Luft and *Harry* Ingram, who invented it) helps to explain how we can gain greater self-awareness through the two tools of personal growth: self-disclosure and feedback. The window is created by two axes: the amount of information known to self and the amount of information known to others. The intersection of these axes creates four "panes" in the window.

The helping relationship reduces the size of the unknown area (Area IV). Clients have moments of insight or "aha!" experiences that occur when they consolidate information gained through both self-disclosure and feedback. Invitational, reflecting, and challenging skills help clients gain more information about themselves and reduce this unknown area.

HOW SELF-DISCLOSURE AND FEEDBACK SHRINK OR EXPAND THE FOUR "PANES" According to the model, self-disclosure widens the public area (Area I) and shrinks the hidden area (Area III). A client who has a broader public area is able to disclose more deeply, will experience greater relief, creates better relationships, and supplies the helper with more complete information about problems. The relative size of this windowpane compared with the other three areas and the information disclosed vary depending on how open or transparent an individual is. Overdisclosure can also be a problem when a person monopolizes conversations and drives people away. So, it is possible that this pane may be too large and clients need to learn how to avoid overdisclosure.

Feedback, on the other hand, shrinks Area II, the blind spot. One example of a blind spot is the fact that, even when we look in a mirror, we are not seeing ourselves exactly. We are really seeing the reverse image. We often do not know if we have bad

	Known to self	Not known to self
Known to others	I Public area	II Blind spot
Not known to others	III Hidden area	IV Unknown area

FIGURE 8.2 The Johari Window

Source: From J. Luft. (1969). *Of human interaction* (p. 13). Palo Alto, CA: National Press. Reprinted by permission.

breath, if we are annoying someone, if we appear judgmental, or if we have a whining tone to our voice. Conversely, we may miss our positive traits as well, unaware that others see us as attractive, kind, or a good listener.

Finally, the helping processes assist clients discover new things about themselves, insights and "aha!" experiences of which neither they nor others were aware (Area IV). These come about as the client discloses and receives feedback from the helper. A number of counseling techniques such as imagery, the use of creative arts, monitoring thoughts and feelings, dream analysis, and even free association have been used to help clients learn more about themselves.

HOW TO GIVE FEEDBACK

In the helping relationship, giving feedback means supplying information to a client about what you see, feel, or suspect about him or her. Feedback helps people grow when they are receiving constructive, specific information about themselves. When a professional helper gives feedback, the sole purpose is to help the client. Feedback from a professional—unlike that from family and friends—does not take into consideration the needs of the helper or concern itself with whether or not this will produce a strain on the relationship. Helpers only give feedback when clients ask for it or when the client needs information to progress. They give feedback for three purposes:

1. To indicate how the client's behavior affects the helper

   Example: "You say you want to be assertive, but I experience your behavior as passive when you look away and avoid eye contact."

2. To evaluate a client's progress toward the goals

   Example: "As I see it, you have now been successful in overcoming your anxiety by facing the situations you have been avoiding."

3. To supply a client with information based on the helper's observation

   Example: "I notice that you never seem to talk about your father."

Feedback may be rejected by clients because "the truth hurts," or because it is incorrect in the client's eyes, or because it is too harsh. Clients use defense mechanisms to avoid accepting the information they receive. Therefore, helpers endeavor to present feedback so that it will be more palatable. Here are some suggestions about how to give effective feedback in a way that others may accept. These are good rules for trainees, who may be giving feedback to each other in group exercises.

1. Use I-messages

   In his classic book about raising children, *PET: Parent Effectiveness Training* (1975, 2000), Thomas Gordon described the process of delivering feedback as "I-messages." Most feedback statements delivered by helpers are I-messages because using the word *I* conveys that the helper is expressing his or her own perspective. When a person starts a conversation by saying, in effect, "This is my viewpoint," we are more likely to listen nondefensively. For example, consider the following pieces of feedback:

   "I am uncomfortable when you talk that way about women."

   "I am hurt that you did not seem to acknowledge my sister's birthday."

   "I am concerned about the fact that you don't seem to have any friends."

2. Do not give people feedback on their personality traits. It is hard to see how one can change a description of one's character and such general remarks are easy to reject.

   Poor feedback (boss to subordinate): "You are a procrastinator."

   Good feedback: "For the past 3 months, your report has been late."

3. Be specific, concrete, and nonjudgmental.

   Poor feedback: "You're bugging me."

   Good feedback: "I find it annoying when you whistle during my favorite music." (I-message with specific content)

4. Ask permission before giving feedback.

   For example: "You say that people at work are angry about your behavior. Would you like some feedback?"

   or "I would like to give you some feedback on something I have noticed. Is that all right?"

5. Sometimes feedback about touchy subjects is accepted more easily if it is offered tentatively. You do not have to dilute the feedback; rather, find an acceptable route to get the client to think about what is being reported.

   Poor feedback: "Last time, we talked about your feelings that you deserted your father when he was ill. This time, you avoid the topic when I try to reopen it."

   Good feedback: "I got the impression last time that talking about your father was difficult for you and you seemed to steer away from that topic. Maybe it is because you think you deserted him when he was ill. Am I right about this?"

6. Give only one or two pieces of feedback at a time. When too much feedback is given, client defenses rear up like impenetrable walls and little gets through.

   Poor feedback: "I think you should improve your appearance at work. You look disheveled, and you need to wear a more formal shirt. By the way, you left the copy machine on again last night, and you forgot to call Dodie back."

   Good feedback: "I think you should improve your appearance at work. For example, your pants are wrinkled, and a t-shirt really is not appropriate."

7. Do not forget to give feedback that emphasizes the client's strengths. It is easy to assume that clients are aware of their strengths and to focus on their foibles. Identifying strengths is "positive psychology" and engenders hope, a common therapeutic factor (Lopez & Kerr, 2006; Ward & Reuter, 2011). We tend to give more feedback to uncover unknown weaknesses rather than to point out assets. More often, clients need to know what is going right, what is working, and what resources the client has to bring to the problem [see Wong's (2006) strength-centered therapy and Ward and Reuter's (2011) strength-centered counseling]. Try focusing on the positive aspects first and bringing up the negative later if needed.

   Poor feedback: "You asked someone out for a date, but you did not work on the other part of the assignment, where you were to confront your friend about her behavior. Let's talk about that."

Good feedback: "Based on what you've said today, I'm picking up that you have made real progress. Even though it was a little scary, you asked two people for a date and one of them said yes."

8. Use an open question to determine whether feedback was received and how it was accepted.

Helper: "A minute ago, I pointed out that you have spent the last few weeks talking only about your ex-husband. What is your reaction to that feedback?"

STOP AND REFLECT

There is a parallel in our own optic system that can demonstrate the existence of blind spots or holes in our view of the world, at least from a physiological viewpoint. You may know that the optic nerve attaches to the back of the eyeball. Where it connects, there is a small gap in the picture your brain sees. Because we have two eyes, the other eye takes over and corrects for this tiny blind spot and we never know that it exists. Take a look at the X and the large dot shown in Figure 8.3. Now hold this book with your right hand and stretch it out to arm's length. Stare directly at the X on the left side of the page. Close your left eye and slowly move the book straight toward your face. At about 12 inches, the dot on the right side disappears.

The physical blind spot is only an analogy of the psychological phenomenon identified in the Johari window (Area II). Still, it alerts us to the fact that our knowledge about the world and ourselves is not complete. Because we are unaware of these hidden parts of ourselves, it takes some convincing before we believe. Consider the following questions:

- In this experiment, you learned about your blind spot through actual experience. Suppose I had merely told you about the blind spot? Which information is the most powerful in convincing you of its existence?
- How can we help clients have experiences of their psychological blind spots rather than merely telling them?
- Suppose you gave the client some feedback that you were 98% sure was true and accurate, and the client's response was to dismiss it completely. How do you think you might react? How could you get the client to consider it further without damaging the relationship?
- Suppose that a client feels rejected in her personal relationships. In her interactions with you and with other personnel, you notice that she talks constantly, rarely allowing anyone else to control the conversation. First, write down a nonjudgmental feedback statement exactly as you would deliver it. Next, identify one or two other situations where the client might get this kind of feedback. What assignments might you give the client to make her more aware of this tendency?

FIGURE 8.3   Blind Spot

CONFRONTATION

Confrontations are interventions that point out discrepancies in client beliefs, behaviors, words, or nonverbal messages. As a result of confrontation, client awareness of inconsistencies is stimulated, and the client moves to resolve them. In essence, it is an educational process that brings information to the client's attention that has been previously unknown, disregarded, or repressed. The most powerful confrontation urges the client to resolve the inconsistencies. Confrontation creates emotional arousal and can lead clients to develop important insights and motivate them to change their behavior. A **discrepancy** is an inconsistency, a mixed message, or a conflict among a client's thoughts, feelings, and behaviors. In fact, every problem a client presents contains discrepancies. For example:

- A client says that she wants an equal, sharing relationship, but she only dates domineering men.
- A client says that she loves her job, but she complains about it constantly.
- A client states that he wants to improve his marriage, but he forgets to go to marriage counseling sessions.
- A client is intelligent and tenacious but is convinced he will not do well in school.

Why Should Inconsistencies Be Confronted?

Ivey and Simek-Downing (1980) say that "the resolution or synthesis of incongruities may be said to be a central goal of all theoretical orientations" (p. 177). In fact, most well-known therapeutic systems use confrontation to some degree. The Gestalt therapist Fritz Perls confronted clients about incongruities in their nonverbal and verbal behavior (which he labeled "phony"). Albert Ellis, the founder of rational emotive behavior therapy, liked showing clients the gap between their beliefs and rationality by directly exposing them to the "nuttiness" of their ideas. Albert Ellis used loud voice tones or even curse words to intensify confrontations. Some early group therapy methods for substance abuse (the Synanon approach, Straight Inc.) used personal attacks and abusive confrontation to create movement in dealing with deeply ingrained behavior patterns. There is little evidence to support the use of such strong confrontation. In fact, it appears that, even with substance abusers, a consistent highly confrontational therapist style is not as effective as a moderately confrontational one (Miller, Benefield, & Tonigan, 1993).

These examples of negative confrontation are cited because many helpers feel they must emulate these master therapists who seem to be highly critical and judgmental toward their clients. Confrontation need not be a hammer. It can be a gentle push. In this chapter, we urge you to consider how to raise inconsistencies in a client's mind without alienating him or her. I believe that confrontation is a skill that should be developed after the early helping building blocks are well established, namely invitational and reflecting skills. Research confirms that highly trained (doctoral) counselors used confrontation more often than students (Tracey, Hays, Malone, & Herman, 1988). At the same time, doctoral-level counselors demonstrated less dominance and verbosity than student helpers. It appears, then, that experience and training teach helpers to use confrontation more frequently, to talk less, and to simultaneously provide support.

Cognitive Dissonance and Confrontation: Why Confrontation Works

Do you remember the concept of cognitive dissonance from your first Introduction to Psychology class? **Cognitive dissonance** theory states that we are motivated to keep cognitions such as values, beliefs, and attitudes consistent (Festinger, 1957). When people experience inconsistencies in their thoughts, feelings, and behaviors, this creates tension, and they are motivated to reduce the tension. We can either convince ourselves that the incongruity is unimportant or change one of the incompatible elements. For example, a client, Donna, describes her job as good-paying but also as repetitive and boring. She needs the job to help her mother, who is struggling to survive on social security. Donna is aware that she wants to go to college because she is not intellectually challenged in her present position, but the costs are too great. This creates dissonance. She deals with the tension caused by these conflicting thoughts by telling others and herself that education and intellectual challenge are not really important. We all use such defense mechanisms to distort reality so that we can reduce anxiety. In this case, the distortion masks the fact that Donna does really want to go to college: It may not be possible, but pretending that her desire to go to college does not exist is creating a giant "blind spot" in her life. Many times, clients use defense mechanisms to escape tension, rather than making choices based on thinking and planning. When helpers confront people with these discrepancies, anxiety often resurfaces but so does awareness of choices. Donna may realize that there may be nontraditional and incremental ways of taking classes she has not considered.

Kiesler and Pallak (1976) reviewed dissonance studies and found a link between dissonance and physiological arousal (Cooper, Zanna, & Taves, 1978; Croyle & Cooper, 1983; Pittman, 1975; Zanna & Cooper, 1974). It seems that clients actually change their attitudes in order to reduce the arousal caused when the helper makes the client aware of the two incompatible elements. The confrontation causes anxiety because the client must become aware of this split, which is normally kept out of awareness by his or her defenses. This sudden awareness of a conflict is what Ernst Beier calls "beneficial uncertainty" (Beier & Young, 1998). The client's frozen position had provided some security, but now the client is acutely aware of his or her mixed feelings. In this state of beneficial uncertainty, the client becomes open to a shift. In the case of Donna, the helper might encourage Donna to become more aware of her need to be intellectually stimulated and ask her to talk about it, explore it, and even investigate options to use her mind. Without blind spots and defense mechanisms, we make decisions that are more reality-based and personally satisfying (Claiborn, 1982; Olson & Claiborn, 1990).

Although we may use confrontation to bring buried elements into consciousness, we must remember that clients do not really like it (Hill et al., 1988). If the helper's confrontation is too powerful and the client's emotional arousal is too great, the client will not only reject the message, and may be less willing to explore feelings and to trust the helper (Hill et al., 1988). Thus, therapists tend to use confrontations sparingly because it is strong medicine; and they should combine it with a liberal helping of support, or else they risk alienating the client (Barkham & Shapiro, 1986; Strong & Zeman, 2010).

Types of Discrepancies

There are five elements of a client's story that can come into conflict: the client's worldview or beliefs, the client's previous experiences, the client's verbal messages, the client's nonverbal messages, and the client's behavior. They can occur in many possible combinations, but the six most common forms are illustrated in the following dialogues.

Incongruity between Verbal and Nonverbal Messages

CLIENT: "It's been hell. This whole thing. It's almost funny [laughs]. You know. Sometimes he loves me, sometimes he hates me."

HELPER: "Your laughing and smiling make me think the problem is not serious, and yet I can tell by what you've said that it has been very painful for you." (confrontation)

Incongruity between Beliefs and Experiences

CLIENT: "I do the best I can. But I'm not really good-looking. I've been dating the same two guys for about 4 months now. They say I'm pretty, but I don't believe it."

HELPER: "You tell me that you believe you're not attractive and then you describe going on a lot of dates." (confrontation)

Incongruity between Values and How the Client Behaves

CLIENT: "My son is the most important thing in the world to me. But I just don't have time to see him every week. I need some recreation, too. If I want to get ahead at work, I have to put in the hours."

HELPER: "If I understand you, you say that your relationship with your son means a lot to you, but somehow you've let other things get in the way." (confrontation)

Incongruity between What the Client Says and How the Client Behaves

CLIENT: "I've been going to Cocaine Anonymous as I said I would. But it's not really helping. Every time I see one of my old friends, I'm back into it again."

HELPER: "I'm confused. You say that you want to give up cocaine, and yet you continue to see your old drug friends." (confrontation)

Incongruity between Experiences and Plans

CLIENT: "Sure, my girlfriend and I have been having a lot of problems lately. But if we moved in together, I think things would improve."

HELPER: "Isn't one of the problems that whenever you spend any length of time together, you fight violently for days? How will living together and spending even more time together help the relationship?" (confrontation)

Incongruity between Two Verbal Messages

CLIENT: "My wife makes twice as much money as I do. It doesn't bother me. But I always feel that she looks down on me because of it. I should be making a lot more than I do. I often think about starting a new career."

Helper: "Okay, on the one hand, you say that it doesn't bother you, and yet you also say that you feel inadequate in her eyes and talk about a career change!" (confrontation)

ETHICAL ALERT

In our previous discussion of confrontation, some guidelines were given for the most effective use of confrontation. But a few of these issues also point to ethical issues as well. The codes do not specifically identify confrontation, but there are guidelines for use of emotionally arousing techniques and the training you should receive before using techniques. Consider the following:

1. It is unethical according to the codes of helping professionals to use a technique that you are unfamiliar with unless you are under the supervision of someone who is adept in its use. Confrontation, being a potent method, is a technique that should be discussed with a supervisor before it is applied.
2. Most ethical codes point to considering the cultural, religious, and spiritual background of a client before applying a technique such as confrontation. Consider the research and check with a supervisor.
3. Using confrontation as a way to vent your frustration would not be ethical. The needs of clients must take precedence over those of the helper.

    For more information, consult the following codes of ethics on association websites:
    American Counseling Association's 2005 Code of Ethics
    http://www.counseling.org/resources/CodeofEthics/TP/Home/CT2.aspx

    American Psychological Association's Ethical Principles and Code of Conduct
    http://www.apa.org/ethics/code/index.aspx

    National Association of Social Workers
    http://www.socialworkers.org/pubs/code/default.asp

    National Organization for Human Services (NOHS)
    http://www.nationalhumanservices.org/index.php

HOW TO CONFRONT

The helper's confrontational statement usually takes one of the following forms:

"You said _____, but your nonverbals said _____." (verbal versus nonverbal)

Example: "You said you were happy, but I don't see that in your face."

"You believe _____, but you possess _____." (negative beliefs about oneself versus strengths)

Example: "You say that you believe you aren't very strong or tough, but your tenacity in dealing with the Veteran's Administration does not seem to fit with that belief."

"You value _____, but you act _____." (values versus actions)

Example: "You obviously value your family, but you spend nearly 60 hours at work each week."

"You said _____, but you acted _____." (verbal versus actions)

Example: "You said you were excited about coming to counseling, but you haven't been making your appointments."

"You plan to do _____, but your past experiences tell you _____." (plans or beliefs versus experiences)

Example: "You plan to try to become more socially active, but there is a part of you that says you'll be rejected like before."

"You said _____, but you also say _____." (verbal versus verbal)

Example: "Sometimes you say you are happy with your job, and other times you threaten to quit."

As you begin to identify discrepancies and present them to a client, you might find it helpful to memorize the following phrase: "On the one hand, _____; on the other hand, _____." Although you do not wish to overuse this statement with clients, this formula or template will help remind you to identify the conflicting aspects of a client's story.

Steps to Confrontation

Step 1 First, take time to understand the issue and listen carefully, making sure the relationship is well established before confronting. Move through the nonjudgmental listening cycle to fully understand the client's message and reflect feeling and meaning. Ask yourself if the timing is right or if a confrontation will prematurely place stress on the relationship. In other words, have you earned the right to confront?

Step 2 Present the challenge in a way that the client will most likely accept it. The following example shows a helper using open questioning and reflection of feeling to gently usher in confrontation and reduce the negative impact.

VEENA (HELPER): "You say that this hasn't been a good school year for you and you are thinking about dropping your Advanced Placement class." (paraphrase)

OLIVIER (CLIENT): "Yeah, it's not going too well."

VEENA: "Well, if I understand it right, you're discouraged because you are getting a 'B'." (reflection of feeling)

OLIVIER: "Yeah, obviously I am not going to make it."

VEENA: "Okay, I'm confused. On the one hand you say it's been a terrible year but at the same time a lot of good things have happened this year. We've talked about the fact that you've become more organized and gotten along better with your teachers. You're doing better than passing in your AP class but you don't want to recognize that." (confrontation of client's negative view of self and strengths)

OLIVIER: "I guess so. But I still have a long way to go."

> VEENA: "Sounds like it's hard for you to pay attention to the strengths you have and the gains you've made this year. In a way, you seem to prefer to focus on what you're not achieving."
>
> OLIVIER: "I'm afraid I would slack off if I patted myself on the back all the time."

Step 3 Observe the client's response to the confrontation. In this case, the client does not fully accept Veena's first confrontation. She notes this and repeats her confrontation in a slightly different way.

Step 4 Follow up the confrontation by rephrasing or retreating. When the client does not accept or rejects the confrontation outright, the helper should try another tack. Because clients often respond to confrontation either by denial or by superficial agreement, the helper must be ready to follow up with additional exploration, another confrontation, or clarification. Veena's second confrontation seems to be more acceptable to the client. He gains some insight into his situation.

Other Ways of Confronting

Besides pointing out discrepancies, there are other methods for getting clients to pay attention to discrepant, irrational, or troubling issues and focusing the conversation in that direction. Among these are relationship immediacy, challenging irrational beliefs, and humor. These are more advanced skills but we mention them here because you will likely run into them early in your training through films or reading. We hope that you will place them in the category of challenging skills and get supervision as you learn to use them.

RELATIONSHIP IMMEDIACY   When you meet someone for the first time, think about what issues are the most difficult to discuss. It is easier to talk about *past* problems and previous relationships rather than present issues and relationships. It is easier to discuss issues that are positive and uplifting rather than negative or depressing. It is easier to talk about issues that concern neither of us, such as the weather, rather than talking about what is going on between us right now. By the same token, it is sometimes difficult for the helper to bring up issues affecting the helper or the relationship between helper and client. However, the ability to give honest feedback and discuss openly the helper/client relationship gives it a special meaning that separates it from other social interactions. Nothing is taboo. The relationship can be a laboratory where the client can learn about his or her effect on others. Relationship immediacy (Kiesler, 1988) is a technique that helpers use to give clients immediate feedback of their effect on another person—the helper.

Relationship immediacy is a comment by the helper about what he or she thinks or feels at a given moment about what is happening in the relationship. Immediacy statements by the helper should have three characteristics:

1. The helper uses the word *I* in the statement to indicate that this is the helper's perspective.
2. The helper describes the client's behavior or the helping relationship issue in nonjudgmental terms.
3. The helper expresses his or her feelings in a way that does not overload or burden the client.

These three characteristics are illustrated in the following helper statement: (1) "I am aware that (2) when I make a suggestion, such as the one just presented, we seem to end up in a struggle and the issue gets dropped. (3) I am a little concerned about this."

Helpers use relationship immediacy because interactions with the helper tend to mirror those that happen with others, but more importantly, confronting something that is happening right now is more powerful than something that happened last session. For example, a client might talk incessantly, not leaving room for the helper to respond. Using an immediacy challenge, the helper might say, "You tell me that other people say you don't listen to you. As I am sitting here, I don't feel listened to either. Can we talk about that?" In this vein, Murray (1986) cites the example of a young woman who came to therapy because she felt she was overly dependent on her father. For example, whenever she had car trouble, she turned it over to him. After a month of therapy, she brought in her auto insurance policy, which she was having trouble deciphering, and handed it to the therapist who began reading it. After a moment, the therapist laughed and exclaimed, "Look, I'm behaving just like your father."

Relationship immediacy is "you-me" talk. It challenges the client to focus on the helper's impressions of the therapeutic relationship. Relationship immediacy can enhance intimacy in a relationship because it acknowledges the mutual bond and gives the client liberty to also look at his or her feelings toward the helper. Relationship immediacy is one of the best ways of dealing with so-called resistance and transference reactions. Relationship immediacy is also an invitation to examine the client/helper relationship as a microcosm of the client's difficulties. It should only be used if it seems that the relationship issues between client and helper relate to the client's goals or if the therapeutic relationship is strained and needs to be repaired.

Relationship immediacy can be of the "here-and-now" variety such as, "Right now, I feel a lot of tension between us because we brought up the alcohol issue. What is your reading on that?" Alternately, relationship immediacy can ask the client to reflect on the relationship as it has progressed up to that point, for example, "Over the past few weeks, I have found that our relationship seems to have changed. My experience is that the sessions are much more fun and productive. What do you think?"

While immediacy can be extremely valuable, caution must be taken not to give oneself liberty to dump feelings on the client or vent frustration. Expressing feelings of disappointment, disapproval, or anger can produce a rupture in the relationship that may be impossible to repair. Several therapeutic *faux pas* such as exclamations of surprise and being punitive can masquerade as immediacy. Before a helper uses immediacy, he or she must ask, "Am I doing this for myself or to help the client?"

CHALLENGING IRRATIONAL BELIEFS   Some cognitive therapists challenge clients' strongly held beliefs when they are responsible for a client's emotional suffering. Challenging beliefs involves making the client aware of their irrational nature and teaching them to dispute these disturbing thoughts when they arise. Thus, while the helper highlights the irrational ideas in session, disputing and replacing irrational thoughts is ultimately a form of self-confrontation. Below is a short list of irrational beliefs adapted from Ellis and Velten (1992). Ellis has longer lists of common irrational beliefs, but this will give you a feel for the general categories.

1. *Shoulding and musting.* "I must be the best in my class." "I should have learned this by now."

More rational challenge: "Have you ever tried saying, 'I would like to be the best in my class without laying a 'must' or 'should' on yourself? I think it is those words that cause you to feel so upset when you can't reach perfection."

2. *Awfulizing.* "When I don't get it right the first time, it is a tragedy, a catastrophe, and it is awful."
    More rational challenge: "Isn't it more accurate to say that it's unpleasant, but not the end of the world?"

3. *Low frustration tolerance.* "I can't stop myself from calling my ex-girlfriend." "I can't wait to buy things when they are on sale, and I get myself into big credit card debt."
    More rational challenge: "So, it's uncomfortable for you to wait, right? But is it really true that waiting is impossible or just annoying?"

4. *Blaming.* "No one even tried to help me. It's their fault that I wasn't able to register for classes, not mine. This is the worst school."
    More rational challenge: "I wonder about this idea that it is the responsibility of other people to get you registered and help you when you didn't even request assistance."

5. *Overgeneralizing—"always" or "never" attitudes.* "I went to one AA meeting and all they did was drink coffee and smoke cigarettes. The organization is crazy. No one gets helped there."
    More rational challenge: "I'd like to take issue with this idea that attending one AA meeting gives you enough information to make this blanket statement. Isn't it possible that there were some positive aspects of the meeting? Tell me why you think you must look at this in black and white. Is it really true that you get nothing from a meeting like this?"

You can probably see how confronting a person's beliefs can feel like a very strong intervention. It takes a great deal of skill to challenge a client's beliefs in a way that does not alienate him or her personally. The goal is for both client and helper to gang up on the irrational beliefs while maintaining a good working relationship.

HUMOR AS CONFRONTATION   Later we mention that humor can be one way of relating to clients and teaching them to view situations in a different way. But humor can also be a way of making a confrontation, especially through exaggeration. Both stories and humor seem to bypass the client's defenses. Clients tend to accept humorous stories because they are not seen as preachy or mean. Once, a client told me about her fears that, as a divorced woman, everyone would be looking at her and treating her differently. I responded by agreeing that although she lived in a city of one million people, that, at first, rumors would be spreading like wildfire. There would be newspaper headlines and, of course television news. I reassured her that after the requests from talk shows were rebuffed, she would be able to resume her private life once again. She laughed with me and admitted that her fears were overblown as usual. I was able to get away with this because I knew the client well, and she did not perceive me as laughing at her. That is, of course, the primary precaution of using humor as confrontation. It could belittle the client or convey that you think their concerns are unimportant. Again, there is no substitute for knowing your client and having the kind of relationship where you can talk about ruptures when they occur.

EVALUATING CONFRONTATION AND CLIENT RESPONSE

The Client Acceptance Scale: Gauging the Client's Response to Confrontation

Unfortunately, many confrontations "bounce off" because the client is not ready to look at the discrepancy or the confrontation either is worded too strongly or is too vague. The **Client Acceptance Scale (CAS)** is a training tool to help you gauge the client's reaction to a confrontation. While you would not use the CAS in normal practice, in the beginning stages it can make you aware of how the client is reacting to your confrontations. Clients can react to a confrontation in three basic ways. Each represents a different level of acceptance of the confrontation, and each reaction gives the helper important feedback and direction. A client response on the CAS can be rated as a 1, 2, or 3, depending on the extent to which a client agrees to the existence of a discrepancy pointed out by the helper. A client who fails to agree with a confrontation is not necessarily "resistant," because the confrontation may have been inaccurate, may have been delivered without support, or may be at odds with the client's experience. Very often, a client will tentatively respond at levels 1 and 2 before fully accepting a confrontation.

The three levels of acceptance on the CAS are:

1. *A client may deny that a discrepancy even exists.* Examples of denial include attempts by the client to discredit the helper, to change the topic, to seek support elsewhere, or to falsely accept the confrontation. The helper must decide whether to pound away continually until the confrontation is accepted or to bring the topic up again at a later date. The more combative approach is likely to be detrimental to the relationship.

2. *The client may choose to accept one part or aspect of the confrontation* as being true, while rejecting another part. For one thing, the helper might be inaccurate. Having the client disagree with some of the confrontation but accept part can clarify this issue and lead to further dialogue. At such times, the helper is encouraged to focus the discussion on the areas of agreement.

3. *The client appears to fully accept the confrontation* and agrees to try to change his or her behavior to resolve the inconsistency that has been pointed out.

Previously, an example was given in which a helper confronted an individual (a) who stated that he wanted to give up cocaine and (b) who continued to associate with his old, drug-using friends. The continuation of their conversation is presented here to show how the helper can promote exploration even when the client does not fully accept the confrontation (responds at CAS level 2). The dialogue also shows how a confrontation can lead to the setting of a new goal when the helper points out a discrepancy and then asks the client to resolve it.

CLIENT: "I've been going to Cocaine Anonymous as I said I would. But it's not really helping. Every time I see one of my old friends, I'm back into it again."

HELPER: "I'm confused. You say that you want to give up cocaine, and yet you continue to see your old drug friends." (confrontation)

CLIENT: "I do want to stop using. But what am I supposed to do? Stay by myself all the time?" (Client Acceptance Scale—2)

HELPER: "So what you really need is to be around people, socialize, have friends. How could you do this—stay away from cocaine and still have friends?" (helper moves on to Goal Setting)

CLIENT: "You tell me."

HELPER: "Hold it. I don't have all the answers to this. But you said you want to have friends and you want to stop using. Is this possible?" (paraphrase)

CLIENT: "It must be. People do it."

HELPER: "Yes, but how do they do it?"

CLIENT: "I don't know. I guess they have new friends that don't use. But it's hard to start all over again."

HELPER: "I'm not an expert on this. But some people who have been off cocaine for a while must be familiar with this problem. It seems like it might be fairly common. Between now and when we next meet, would you be willing to think about this? Go to your next Anonymous meeting and ask one or two people about this. Then let me know what they have to say."

CLIENT: "All right. And I'll talk to my friend Michelle. She's been sober for a year now."

SELF-CONFRONTATION   In the last chapter, we discussed the idea of constructivist philosophy, which says that clients actively construct meaning in their lives and that they are continually changing the meanings they assign to events. One approach to confrontation is for the client to direct it rather than relying on the helper to point out discrepancies. For one thing, the helper's input is biased by his or her theoretical or implicit theories of what is mentally healthy. Although it is good to have the input of others, it may be more useful to have the client learn to self-confront, a skill that could provide lasting benefit when the helping relationship is over. Motivational interviewing is a method that was recently developed in substance abuse treatment as a more collaborative method of identifying obstacles to treatment. In motivational interviewing, instead of attacking the client, the helper asks a series of questions about the client's substance abuse. There is confrontation because the client is exposed to his or her continued substance abuse despite the self-reported problems associated with that abuse (Polcin, 2006).

Self-confrontation has been studied as a complex assessment and research tool (Hermans, Fiddelaers, de Groot, & Nauta, 1990; Lyddon, Yowell, & Hermans, 2006). But the method can be applied more simply as a research project that the client conducts on himself or herself with the assistance of a helper. One way to do self-confrontation is for the client to write down everything that he or she considers to be a conflict in life. For example, "I am in love with this woman, but she has made it clear I am only a friend," or "My parents want me to get better grades, but I really don't want to go to college." If given as a writing assignment, the client might be asked to respond to questions such as:

What is it that I don't really want to do?

What would it say about me if I changed in the way people want me to?

In what ways am I lying to myself?

What possibilities in my life am I not paying attention to?

What conclusions am I drawing about life that have no evidence to support them?

The helper then guides the discussion of these issues in the past, present, and future and helps the client explore the issues collaboratively. Together client and helper try to identify key themes in the client's life that come from this discussion. Finally, client and helper identify a plan to solve the dilemmas.

STOP AND REFLECT

The following is a story by Cindy Yee Fong about how she was brought up and how her family and cultural values helped her become a nonjudgmental listener and also presented a challenge when she was forced to confront her clients.

Respect is a core value in Chinese culture. "Respect your parents and do as they say." "Respect your teachers and don't question or challenge them." "Respect your family and don't discuss concerns or problems outside the family circle." "Respect your elders and don't talk back to them." These were the values and expectations instilled in me by my parents, especially my mother. She was born in China and believed strongly in these rules.

When I first began working as a counselor, my job was to facilitate a group for court-ordered drunk drivers, one of the most angry and difficult client populations. You can imagine the challenges I had to face. For someone who is assertive, open, and willing to confront others, regardless of age or status, this would be a difficult job. For someone like me who was taught to listen, not interrupt, and agree with others, especially older people and those in higher positions, it was a daunting task.

Frequently, there were older clients in the group who tended to "ramble on" in their discussions. Interrupting them, in Chinese eyes, would have been very disrespectful. When doctors, lawyers, and teachers were in the group and expressed opinions contrary to my curriculum, it was nearly impossible for me, at first, to disagree with them. It has taken quite a while for me to overcome this reluctance to be what my culture would consider "disrespectful" and to develop the necessary skills as a counselor to be assertive in confronting others. This is still an area I am trying to improve. My cultural style of passive acceptance has helped me develop unconditional acceptance regardless of differences. This has helped me in developing rapport with clients and getting to the point in a relationship where they can accept confrontation. Chinese cultural values and beliefs have been both helpful and challenging to me as an emerging helper.

- Cindy Yee Fong indicates that respect is one of the core values in Chinese culture. Thinking back on your own upbringing, what cultural or family values would you describe as "core"?
- What were your family's values about contradicting others, keeping the peace, and disclosing weaknesses? Was family business to be kept within the family? Do you think any of your own core values might have an effect on your willingness either to talk with clients about their deepest issues or to confront certain individuals?
- One of the most common difficulties for most of us is overcoming the "mum" effect, the social rule that says to keep feedback to yourself. As a helper, your contract with the client implies that you will give honest feedback despite your personal discomfort. Think about some specific situations that will create discomfort for you such as refusing an expensive gift from a client, informing a client that his or her personal hygiene is poor, dealing with tardiness, talking about sexual problems, discussing whether the client is having an affair, or asking if the client

is being honest with you. Which do you think will be the most difficult for you? How might you increase your comfort with these topics?

• Would you find it more difficult to confront someone of a different ethnic or racial background, someone older or younger than you, someone who has a high-status profession, or someone of the same or opposite sex? How do you plan to overcome these limitations? Discuss with a small group some strategies for overcoming some of these roadblocks to feedback and confrontation.

Problems and Precautions

One writer called confrontations the "thermonuclear weapons" of helping. They are powerful, and their force can help or harm. Confrontation may arouse the defenses of the client or damage self-esteem, rather than increase awareness and motivate action. Although the force of the confrontation should not be watered down with qualifiers, confrontation must be presented in a way that does not shame the client by saying "Gotcha!" We are aiming to deliver moderately confrontational statements with the client's best interests at heart.

Earlier we mentioned that timing the confrontation could be important. Timing means knowing when in the relationship and when in the course of therapy confrontation will do the most good. Obviously, the time for confrontation is when the client/helper relationship is well established and the client trusts your motives. It has been my experience that frequent and premature confrontations based on very little information tend to erode the credibility of the helper. If you wait to confront an issue until after it has been raised on several occasions, the chances of acceptance by the client are high.

Before confronting, the helper must be clear that the reason for the intervention is to increase client awareness, not just to unload a sense of frustration. Helpers feel like confronting when they are stuck. This may or may not be a good idea. A cool head is required for confrontation, and the client's interests, not the helper's exasperation, should be the motive. Forcing one's viewpoint onto the client could be considered unethical.

A general caveat is that any helper intervention that is in opposition to the client's social and cultural values may be not only disrespectful but also ineffective. Confrontation is an excellent example of a technique with important cultural and developmental implications. For example, Lazarus (1982) discusses how this technique backfired with some Native American children in a school counseling setting. Others have recommended a gentle approach in using confrontation with African American and Asian American clients (Ivey, 1994). Schectman and Yanov (2001) found that confrontation was not effective with children in groups.

MyCounselingLab™

Go to Topic 2, *Invitational Interviewing*, on the MyCounselingLab™ site (www.MyCounselingLab.com) for *Learning the Art of Helping: Building Blocks and Techniques*, Fifth Edition, where you can:

• Find learning outcomes for *Invitational Interviewing* along with the national standards that connect to these outcomes.

- Complete Assignments and Activities that can help you more deeply understand the chapter content.
- Apply and practice your understanding of the core skills identified in the chapter with the Building Counseling Skills unit.
- Prepare yourself for professional certification with a Practice for Certification quiz.
- Connect to videos through the Video and Resource Library.

MyCounselingLab™ Exercises

Go to the Video and Resource Library on the MyCounselingLab™ site for your text and search for the following clips: *Confrontation: Mark* and *Confrontation: Dayle*. Watch the videos and then answer the questions that follow.

Exercise 1: Analyzing Confrontations and Client Responses

The video *Confrontation: Mark* in MyCounselingLab™ shows Mark (helper) and Nasundra (client) discussing her wedding plans. Watch this entire segment and answer the questions below on a separate sheet.

1. At 50:09 Mark says, "I don't want to say this too strongly, but it sounds like you're more afraid of embarrassing your family than doing what you would like to do." Watch this section and look at Nasundra's reaction to this confrontation. Make note here of any nonverbal communications that might signal the degree of her acceptance of Mark's confrontation.
2. Using the Client Acceptance Scale, how would you rate Nasundra's reaction at 50:24 beginning with, "Um. Wow . . . "

| (1) *Denial of Discrepancy* | (2) *Partial Acceptance* | (3) *Full Acceptance* |

3. What, in Nasundra's response, prompts you to make this assessment?
4. Twice Mark says, "I don't want to say this too strongly." What effect does this have on the confrontation?
5. Do you like this statement? Why or why not?
6. At 50:41 Mark uses the cliché, "You want your cake and eat it, too." Do you think this is too strong? How might you have responded instead?
7. What discrepancy is Mark trying to bring out at 51:13 when he says, "You don't want to let everyone down"?

Exercise 2: More Work on Confrontation

Watch the video, *Confrontation: Dayle* in MyCounselingLab™ which shows Dayle (helper) and Catherine (client) talking about Catherine's difficulty in completely stopping smoking. After watching the entire video answer the questions below:

1. At 53:34, Dayle identifies three elements in Catherine's story that form the basis of her conflict. What are they? How would you describe Catherine's reaction to

Dayle's description? Does it push her to explore more deeply or does she become defensive?

2. At 56:06, Dayle says, "When you talk about that internal struggle, I notice you looked away. You looked a little sad." Is this a confrontation?

3. Write down all of Dayle's confrontations during this segment.

Summary

In this chapter, the Johari window was introduced as a way of envisioning the big picture in the helping process. This diagram highlights self-disclosure and feedback as twin principles of growth. There are two main ways that a helper can facilitate growth. The helper can provide the client with information through feedback and confrontation, and create a conducive relationship that allows the client to open up. Much of the material in previous chapters has been devoted to learning how to use the nonjudgmental listening cycle and adopting the attitudes that will create this ambience and allow the client to tell his or her story. However, the story also has inconsistencies and conflicts, or else the client would not be seeking help. The problems the client is experiencing may be due to incompatible ideas and motivations. The helper must give feedback and use confrontational skills to help the client become aware of these discrepancies and also encourage the client to act to resolve them. Paradoxically, this places a strain on the therapeutic relationship because the client becomes uncomfortable, blames the helper for entering unsafe territory, and may feel that the helper has abandoned his or her supporting role.

Compared with feedback, confrontation is a serious challenge to the client's version of the story, and the client feels a strong push from the helper. Confrontation is an art because one must point out these discrepancies clearly, yet kindly and with respect for the client's worldview. In this chapter, we describe the Client Acceptance Scale, which rates client reactions to confrontations so that you can determine how much of an impact your confrontation is having or whether another tactic should be tried. One reason that so much time has been spent on confrontation is that it is the stuff of therapeutic legends. Videos of famous therapists show them making startling confrontations. The beginning helper is advised to use confrontation sparingly, when you really know the client and only when the relationship is firmly established.

Exercises

GROUP EXERCISES

Exercise 1: Feedback—The Fishbowl Activity

This exercise works best with groups of eight to ten people. Four or five people sit in chairs facing each other to form an inner circle. The same number of participants forms an outer circle. Each member of the outer circle is paired with an inner-circle member. The outer-circle members sit behind the inner circle and across from the members they are paired with so they can observe them (see Figure 8.4). For 10 to 15 minutes, the inner-circle members engage in a leaderless discussion on a topic such as "What are the most important personal characteristics of a helper?" or "What do you see yourself doing, personally and professionally, 5 years from now?" It is important that members do not take turns talking but just hold an open discussion.

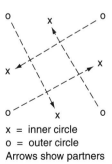

x = inner circle
o = outer circle
Arrows show partners

FIGURE 8.4 Fishbowl Activity Diagram

During the discussion, outer-circle members are instructed to carefully observe nonverbals and listen to the words of their partners in the inner group. At the end of the discussion, the groups break down into dyads of the inner-circle members and their outer-circle partners. Outer-circle members give feedback to inner-circle members about *interpersonal style*.

Interpersonal style means the verbal and nonverbal ways that a person communicates and includes the amount the person talks and how much he or she discloses. The outer-circle members offer their counterparts feedback using the tips given in the "Quick Tips: Giving Feedback" section. Feedback should take about 5 minutes. Finally, inner-circle members identify, for their partners, any feedback that was especially accurate or helpful. Time permitting, the exercise can be repeated with inner- and outer-circle members changing places. Following the feedback in dyads, a class discussion can be held in which members compare their experiences of giving and receiving feedback. Which role was more difficult, giver or receiver of feedback? Were you surprised by the accuracy of the feedback on your interpersonal style?

QUICK TIPS: GIVING FEEDBACK

- Do not give people feedback on their personality traits.
- Be specific, concrete, and nonjudgmental.
- Ask permission before giving feedback.
- Sometimes feedback about touchy subjects is accepted more easily if it is offered tentatively.
- Give only one or two pieces of feedback at a time.
- Give feedback that also emphasizes the client's strengths, not just his or her weaknesses.
- Use a checking question to determine whether feedback was received and how it was accepted.

Exercise 2: Confrontation

Break into groups of three trainees, who will assume the roles of helper, client, and observer. As the exercise continues, each member should have the opportunity to assume each of the three roles.

The Client's Role

Discuss a problem that is causing an internal conflict or moral dilemma. The problem might be the result of:

- Conflict about a job or whether to relocate.
- Conflict about whether or not to be honest in a relationship, for example, whether to tell a friend she depends on you too much.
- Conflict about something you have done that you do not feel good about, that you regret, or that you wish you could change.

The Helper's Role

Review the list of quick tips for confrontation in the "Quick Tips: Confrontation" section. Use the nonjudgmental listening cycle to get the basics of the client's story. Do not spend too much time on setting up the relationship. Although this is critical in real helping situations, in this exercise the main purpose is to practice identifying discrepancies and delivering them to a client. As soon as possible, identify discrepancies by pointing them out, and then encourage the client to resolve the inconsistency.

QUICK TIPS: CONFRONTATION

- Wait until you have heard the client's whole story before you identify discrepancies. What seems to be a discrepancy may be a minor point once you know more about the situation.
- If you are having trouble identifying discrepancies, remember that there would not be a problem if there were no discrepancy. Ask yourself, "What makes this a dilemma?" or, "What are the two sides to the client's problem that make this situation so bothersome?" Use the memory aid, "On the one hand, _____; on the other hand, _____."
- Note the impact of your confrontation on the client. Does he or she deny, partially accept, or fully accept your identification of the discrepancy? Follow up denial and partial acceptance with invitational and reflecting skills.
- After you identify a discrepancy, try using a question such as, "Am I on target?" Often the client will correct you and clarify the discrepancy.

The Observer's Role

Write down verbatim the helper's responses and then evaluate the helper on his or her ability to use confrontation. Code the helper's responses using P for paraphrase, ROF for reflection of feelings, ROM for reflection of meaning, OQ for open question, CQ for closed question, and CON for confrontation. Do not include encouragers.

Feedback Checklist: Confrontation

Observer Name: _____ Helper Name: _____

Helper Statement	Coding	CAS (1–3)
1.		
2.		
3.		
4.		
5.		
6.		
7.		
8.		
9.		
10.		
11.		
12.		

Post-exercise Discussion

The observer shares feedback with the helper, based on the Feedback Checklist. The client gives feedback to the helper concerning the effectiveness of the confrontations and the degree of discomfort they caused. For example, were the confrontations presented as observations rather than accusations? Were they presented nonjudgmentally? Helper and observer can also attempt to recall the client's reaction to the confrontation by scoring them 1, 2, or 3 on the Client Acceptance Scale.

SMALL GROUP DISCUSSIONS

Discussion 1: Collaborating to Identify Effective Confrontations

In groups of four, one member (the client) describes a problem situation to the group (use the suggestions described in Group Exercise 2). After the client has spent a few minutes describing the situation, each re-maining member writes down a confrontation and delivers it verbally to the client. The client responds to each confrontation in turn. As the client does so, the member who gave the confrontation uses the Client Acceptance Scale to evaluate the client's response. Following the client's responses, the group discusses which confrontations seem to be the most effective and acceptable to the client. After this discussion, members trade roles and continue until each has had a turn as client.

WRITTEN EXERCISES

Exercise: Identifying Discrepancies

Following are five client situations. Try to identify the discrepancy in each, using the formula "On the one hand, _____; on the other hand, _____." This will help you get a feel for identifying discrepancies.

In some of the situations below, the conflict is implied rather than actually stated. Imagine what conflicts you might be experiencing if you were in that situation. When you have written your answers, meet with a small group and discuss them. Looking at both the clients and the issues, which would be most difficult for you to actually confront?

1. An 18-year-old client describes how sad she is that she has to leave her parents and go off to college. She smiles as she talks about this.
2. The client is very religious and is very judgmental about nonbelievers. At age 22, he has only a few friends and has never had a longstanding romantic relationship. He comes for help because he has become "addicted" to Internet pornography.
3. The client says that he loves his sister and that she is very important to him. During their last encounter, she "exploded" because he did not attend her wedding.
4. The client states that she has just been offered a job as a manager at a new company. They are very excited about having her because of her years of experience. She has worked at her current company on weekends and during the summer since she was 17. She says that she feels the owner relies on her, but her pay and responsibilities are unlikely to improve. She feels that she has made as much advancement as she can and would like a new challenge.
5. The client is a 17-year-old high school student in an alternative school. She has worked hard and improved her poor grades to Bs and Cs. She failed

her high school equivalency examination by 1 point. She is discouraged and has decided to drop out of school. She plans to continue working at her job, even though her boss has indicated she must have a high school diploma.

SELF-ASSESSMENT

1. Go back and look at the exercises for this chapter. Indicate where you are having the most difficulty. Circle Yes or No to the following questions.
   a. I generally follow guidelines for giving good feedback. Yes No
   Problems? _____
   b. I can identify discrepancies in a client story. Yes No
   Problems? _____
   c. Sometimes I am judgmental when I point out discrepancies. Yes No
   Problems? _____
   d. I can point out discrepancies in a way that is acceptable to the client. Yes No
   Problems? _____
   e. Every time I practice, I use confrontation at least once during the session. Yes No
   Problems? _____

HOMEWORK

Homework 1: Identifying Discrepancies

In a single page, identify an incongruity or discrepancy in your own life that you are willing to talk about. Alternatively, you may write about, in a disguised fashion, a discrepancy you have noticed in another person. Write down the two sides of the dilemma. How deeply does this discrepancy affect your life (or the other person's)? Do all problems contain discrepancies? Can you think of ways that you have used defense mechanisms or other methods of self-deception to decrease your discomfort? What action steps would be needed now to resolve the discrepancy? Do you think this method of self-confrontation would work for an adult client? What about an adolescent?

Homework 2: Receiving Feedback

Think about a particularly difficult piece of feedback you have received. It may have been about a weakness in your appearance, a job evaluation, or perhaps even feedback you received in this class. How did you respond emotionally to the feedback? Did it make you angry, hurt your feelings, or just make you feel incompetent? Did you try to protect yourself by denying or discounting the feedback? Did you learn anything constructive from the negative feedback?

Now think about a time when you received some positive feedback on a personal strength, for example, about a job well done or some aspect of your appearance or personality. What made the feedback positive?

Finally, have you ever had an experience where you received no feedback after expending considerable time and effort? What effect do you think a lack of feedback would have on a person's behavior in the long run?

Of the three kinds of feedback mentioned here—positive, negative, and none—which helped you the most? How might you apply your reactions to your future dealings with clients? Summarize your reactions in two or three paragraphs.

JOURNAL STARTER

Carl Rogers said that the greatest harm one can do to the self is to deny one's own thoughts, feelings, and perceptions in order to gain the love of another. Reflect on Rogers's idea. Can you think of an example of when you were not true to yourself in order to stay in the good graces of others? How do you think you might have responded to a confrontation that highlighted the discrepancy between your actions and what you truly believed? How important do you think it is for a helper to confront clients when they are not being true to themselves?

Assessment and the Initial Interview

A question not asked is a door not opened.

M. C. GOLDBERG, 1998, P. IX

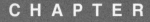

Visit the MyCounselingLab™ site for *Learning the Art of Helping: Building Blocks and Techniques,* Fifth Edition to enhance your understanding of chapter concepts. You'll have the opportunity to practice your skills through video- and case-based Assignments and Activities as well as Building Counseling Skills units, and to prepare for your certification exam with Practice for Certification quizzes.

Summary

Exercises
- Group Exercises
- Small Group Discussions
- Written Exercises
- Self-Assessment
- Homework
- Journal Starters

WHY ASSESSMENT?

Assessment means gathering information about a client and the client's problems. Helpers collect information in a variety of ways, beginning with the first contact as the helper observes the client's behavior and listens to the story. Formal assessment methods include testing and filling out questionnaires and forms. Informal assessment encompasses all the other ways a helper learns about a client, including observing and listening. Formal assessment may occur at a specific time in the helping relationship, but informal assessment is an ongoing process. In this book, I recommend that the helper set aside time for assessment during the second stage of the helping process (Figure 9.1).

Because each client situation is unique, it is impossible to be precise about how much time to give to each stage of the helping process. Still, a rule of thumb is to spend one session primarily in relationship building, with the only assessment activities being the collection of basic demographics, observation of the client's behavior, and whatever else you

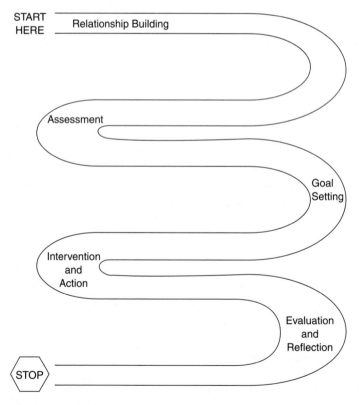

FIGURE 9.1 Road Map of the Helping Process

can glean from the client's story. The second and possibly a third session are spent in more in-depth assessment before moving on to a goal-setting phase, which might include testing. Therefore, if a client is seen for 10 sessions, about 10% may be devoted to assessment.

In many places, it is common practice to have a formal period of assessment before the client and helper actually meet. In some agencies, the assessment may be done by an intake worker or a clerical person before the client has any opportunity to talk about his or her problem. The decision to employ such an approach is based primarily on saving time and money, but it may also be a way of finding out if the client matches the services being offered. Beginning a relationship with formal assessment can be a mistake, even if it is conducted by a professional, because the initial moments of any human encounter are so important. Imagine how you would feel if you went for a doctor's appointment and were asked only to fill out forms, contribute blood samples, and answer questions, but you did not see the physician or receive any help for your problem.

Here are actual statements from two different client satisfaction forms at a community counseling clinic that relate the experiences of clients who underwent formal assessment in their first sessions:

> "I only came to two sessions. We had to fill out 21 sheets of paper before we could get started. It didn't seem worth it."

> "The helper didn't seem to care about my problem. He just kept writing on his papers."

The recommended approach is to focus on the relationship first and ask questions later.

When clients have been invited to tell their stories, they give much more information during the formal assessment period that follows. They leave the first session believing that they have made a start on solving problems, instead of feeling dissected by tests and probing questions. Key data need to be collected at the first interview, but there are several ways to handle this. For clients who can read and write, asking clients to come in early or stay later than the session can be an effective way of collecting information about the client's background and current status.

Time must somehow be set aside for assessment in the first sessions, but assessment continues through the duration of the relationship and overlaps with every other stage (Drummond & Jones, 2010; Whiston, 2004). As time goes on, the helper learns more and more about the client, the environment, and the client's problem. Moreover, the helper needs different kinds of information later in the relationship. For example, assume that a child is referred to a school counselor for excessive school absences that may be linked to problems at home. At first, the counselor spends time getting to know the client in the office (*relationship-building stage*, see Figure 9.1) and later becomes familiar with the cumulative folder concerning the child's academic progress and behavior at school (*assessment stage*). At this point, the child and counselor might set goals such as decreasing absences by 50% during the next grading period (*treatment-planning stage*). To achieve the goal, the counselor contacts the parents for more information, and together they identify a course of action to solve the problem. During this process, the counselor learns a great deal about the client's family and begins to understand which interventions will work and which will probably fail. Next, the school counselor suggests a plan involving parenting skills training for the parents and a change in math teachers for the child (*intervention and action stage*). Once the plan has been established, the counselor regularly contacts the child, the teacher, and the parents to determine if the intervention is working (*evaluation and reflection stage*). During each stage, information has to be collected. If not, the helper may set inappropriate goals, implement techniques that are rejected, or be unable to recognize success. In short, assessment is not a one-time activity but a continuous process that accompanies all the therapeutic skills that the helper is employing.

TESTING AS AN ASSESSMENT TOOL

Testing has gone through several phases of popularity and decline within the helping professions. Some of the ups and downs have been due to the enthusiasm and criticism associated with psychological testing. Psychologists embraced testing after World War II, just as other professionals also became enthralled with testing around this time. By the 1960s, some realistic skepticism was directed at testing, as some of its abuses were uncovered. Many tests were found to be culturally biased (Anastasi & Urbina, 1997). At that time, personality testing with instruments such as the Minnesota Multiphasic Personality Inventory and the Rorschach test were routinely administered to all kinds of clients despite the fact that they could not accurately predict behavior. Now they are used more judiciously.

Carl Rogers's client-centered approach was at its height in the 1960s and 1970s; its adherents rejected testing as being antithetical to the goal of seeing the client as a unique person. Family therapy proponents have also been leery of instruments that focus on a single person rather than on the family system (Gladding, 2010). Both of these theoretical positions lent impetus to the anti-testing forces within the helping professions. Perhaps today we can look at testing with a more balanced perspective. We see testing as a tool, rather than as the only way of getting at the truth. Testing can certainly be valuable when diagnosis is difficult. Testing can alert you to dangerous behavior, substance abuse, and psychotic symptoms such as hallucinations and delusions. Testing can also give you insights into a client's functioning in areas you may not have inquired about, uncovering topics for discussion with the client (Hood & Johnson, 2006; Palmer & McMahon, 1997). At its worst, testing can be a waste of valuable time, label the client, and reveal little beyond what could be found in a couple of sessions of talking with the client. Testing can be inappropriate for those who are different culturally than those for whom the test was intended (Paniagua, 2005).

ASSESSMENT IS A CRITICAL PART OF HELPING

Sometimes you will hear that gathering a lot of historical information about a client is not worthwhile. Some theories emphasize the present and the future rather than the past, and so they ignore history and personality data. It is true that some helpers do spend an inordinate amount of time gathering background information and administering tests. On the other hand, by failing to collect critical data, one takes the chance of making a serious mistake. You must know your customer thoroughly (Lukas, 1993).

Once I interviewed a 65-year-old man who had been a shoe salesman in Cleveland. He had led an interesting life before retiring about 2 years before we met. He reported no real difficulties, and, as he was very convincing, I couldn't understand why he had consulted me. As a courtesy, I talked separately to his 28-year-old son, who had waited patiently outside. The son told me his father had been a physician in Texas and 5 years ago developed a syndrome, which was thought to be Alzheimer's disease, a severe brain disorder with a deteriorating course. The client had simply filled in the gaps of his history with very convincing fiction. That incident taught me that it is best to get as much information about a client as possible *and* information from a variety of sources. If I had tested the client's memory or talked to his son first, I might have saved some time. More importantly, had I only relied on the client as the sole source of information, I might have sent him away without treatment.

Conducting superficial assessments, however, does not always lead to such spectacular embarrassment. It is very common, though, for helpers to accept the client's story without a critical thought. Even the most astute helper can make drastic mistakes. It is important to listen to what clients leave out and where they minimize or deny. Also, it is easy to forget to ask specific questions. Because someone is well groomed and comes from a prominent family does not mean that he or she should not be asked about drug abuse or suicidal thoughts. Our prejudices and worldview color our definition of pathology. Even the *Diagnostic and Statistical Manual* (*DSM*) of the American Psychiatric Association, the diagnostic bible, recognizes that misdiagnosis can occur when the helper is not familiar with a client's cultural background and interprets symptoms within his or her own cultural context (Paniagua, 2005).

Because of these common lapses in good assessment habits, helpers need to conduct a regular screening procedure. A systematic assessment assures us that we are helping the client with the most important issues, such as serious mental disorders, substance abuse, and danger to self or others (Drummond & Jones, 2010; Granello & Granello, 2007). Perhaps you are thinking that you will never encounter serious problems like these in your future workplace. The reality is that nearly every helper comes into contact with these kinds of serious problems. Even school counselors deal with students with eating disorders and learning disabilities, depressed parents, and alcoholic co-workers.

Reasons to Spend Time in the Assessment Stage

ASSESSMENT HELPS YOU DETERMINE IF THE CLIENT IS A GOOD CANDIDATE FOR THE HELP YOU CAN PROVIDE Therapeutic help from a trained professional is not the best treatment for everyone. The client must have the capacity to form a relationship, be motivated to change, and be able to attend sessions and understand what is going on (see Truant, 1999). For example, there may be other avenues of help for the client that are better than "talk therapy." For example, clients with less verbal skills might benefit from art or music therapy. There are educational, online learning, occupational, chemotherapy, and other alternatives to consider. When a client arrives for treatment, the first thought should be: Is this the right place for this client?

ASSESSMENT GIVES CRUCIAL INFORMATION TO PLAN USEFUL AND REALISTIC GOALS The main purpose of assessment is to gather information that will be useful in planning the goals that will guide the helper and client. Assessment must have both breadth and depth. As far as breadth is concerned, the helper must throw the net broadly enough to make sure nothing crucial escapes. Depth refers to focusing on specific issues such as suicide, the existence of mental disorders, and the crucial problem that acted as a catalyst for the client's decision to seek help.

ASSESSMENT HELPS CLIENTS DISCOVER EVENTS RELATED TO THE PROBLEM A woman came to a community clinic asking for help in dealing with problems at work. She recognized that her job was stressful, but she found that she was unusually irritable with her coworkers and wanted to work on that problem. After some reflection and homework by the client, we discovered that her angry outbursts all happened between 1 and 2 p.m. on days when she did not eat lunch. The client knew that she became grumpy when she was hungry, but she had never connected this with her behavior on the job. A physician helped the client to deal with a problem of low blood sugar, and her extreme irritability diminished.

ASSESSMENT HELPS US UNDERSTAND THE IMPACT OF THE CLIENT'S ENVIRONMENT ON HIS OR HER MENTAL HEALTH For example, is the client living with family, in a shelter, or alone. Does the client suffer isolation because he or she does not speak the dominant language or belongs to a religious minority? If the client is a child, what is happening at school every day that might be affecting the problem? Is the child bullied, rejected by classmates, encouraged by a teacher, and so on?

ASSESSMENT HELPS US RECOGNIZE THE UNIQUENESS OF INDIVIDUALS We all have the tendency to generalize and stereotype. Unless we ask clients about family and cultural background issues, we make assumptions about them through our own cultural lens. People from a different cultural group may be judged as more pathological than are those who share our own background. A systematic assessment helps us be less manipulated by these strong social influences and more objective because we are recording the answers to standard questions rather than merely relying on our own impressions. Assessment can also be useful in helping clients recognize their unique personality, values, and interests (Armstrong & Rounds, 2010).

ASSESSMENT UNCOVERS THE POTENTIAL FOR VIOLENCE Some clients are prone to harm themselves or others. Assessment can identify individuals who are at risk for violence. Although it is not possible to always accurately predict violent behavior, a history of self-inflicted injury or harm to others can cue us to examine the client's situation more thoroughly and take precautions (see Granello & Granello, 2007; Junkhe, Granello, & Granello, 2011). (See Table 9.1). School counselors are recognizing the need to assess for violent behavior in the aftermath of Columbine and in the wake of renewed interest in bullying (Bernes & Bardick, 2007; Felix, Sharkey, Green, & Tanigawa, 2011).

ASSESSMENT REVEALS CRITICAL HISTORICAL DATA Figure 9.2 shows a simple assessment device called a *timeline*. Rafael was asked to fill in the boxes with critical life events in sequential order. His choice of key interpersonal events gave a glimpse of his worldview and his major concerns.

ASSESSMENT CAN HIGHLIGHT STRENGTHS, NOT JUST WEAKNESSES AND PATHOLOGY More and more helpers are using assessment tools that identify client strengths and competencies (Flükiger, Wüsten, Zinbarg, & Wampold, 2010; Kiselica & Englar-Carlson, 2010; Lopez & Snyder, 2009; Snyder & Lopez, 2002; Ward & Reuter, 2011). Strength-based assessment instruments such as the Behavioral and Emotional Rating Schedule (Epstein, 2004; Epstein, Harniss, Pearson, & Ryser, 1999) have been developed in recent years in response to this need. Strength-based assessment is, in part, a reaction to medical models based on pathology. It is also being recognized that building on client strengths enhances client self-esteem and helps client and helper use time more effectively (Miller, Hubble, & Duncan, 1996). Another direction is to base assessment on a wellness philosophy. A wellness philosophy also emphasizes strengths, but it is an holistic philosophy that advocates evaluation of client physical, mental, emotional, social, cognitive, occupational, and spiritual resources (Myers & Sweeney, 2005; Witmer & Sweeney, 1992).

ASSESSMENT HELPS CLIENTS BECOME AWARE OF IMPORTANT PROBLEMS Frequently, painful issues are pushed out of awareness or remain unrecognized until brought to the

TABLE 9.1   Is Path Warm?

IS PATH WARM is an acronym that was developed by the American Association of Suicidology. It is a set of symptoms that can be used to assess suicide risk (see Junkhe, Granello, & Lebrón-Striker, 2007). They are:

Ideation: Does the person think, talk or write about a desire to self-destruct or purchase the means to do so? Does the person show an intention to carry out the plan?

Substance Abuse: Is the person intoxicated or has she been abusing alcohol or other drugs?

Purposelessness: Is the person adrift, without a sense of meaning and purpose in life, seeing no meaning to keep living?

Anxiety: Is the client experiencing anxiety that interferes with sleep and daily functioning?

Trapped: Does the client feel there is no way out of the present situation and that he or she is better off dead?

Hopelessness: Does the client have a negative view of the future and feels that he or she is a lost cause or beyond help?

Withdrawal: Has the client withdrawn from family, friends, and other supportive people?

Anger: Is the client's mood angry or hostile? Is he or she feeling vengeful towards someone?

Recklessness: Does the client engage in risky behaviors, such as driving at high speed or taking other chances?

Mood: Is the client experiencing drastic mood swings? Is the client feeling depressed?

It must be remembered that these are guidelines based on risk factors and that there is no foolproof method of determining how suicidal a client might be. However, the rule of thumb is to err on the side of caution and a client who is exhibiting any of these symptoms should be further evaluated.

surface through assessment procedures (Granello, 2010). A common example of this is substance abuse. When clients are asked to discuss the problems that alcohol has caused, the resulting list can be an eye-opener. Many alcohol treatment centers take thorough histories and use motivational interviewing as a beginning step in breaking down the alcoholic's denial system (Miller & Rose, 2009).

ASSESSMENT HELPS THE HELPER CHOOSE WHICH TECHNIQUES TO USE   When you think about learning helping techniques, chances are that you did not consider assessment as a critical part of that process. Yet how do you know which techniques to use? The answer is derived from two sources of knowledge: information about your client and information about the client's problems. If you know that your client is very religious, for example,

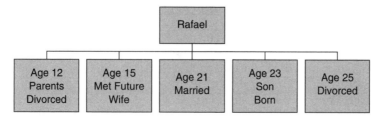

FIGURE 9.2   Timeline Assessment

you will be able to select techniques that the client will embrace. If you know when and where your client has panic attacks, you will be better able to identify an effective plan. Thus, it is difficult to discuss helping techniques without thinking about how we choose which methods to use with which clients for what particular problem (Paul, 1967).

CATEGORIZING CLIENTS AND THEIR PROBLEMS

Although helpers realize that each person is unique, the irony is that in order to simplify our work, we like to categorize and label clients as having this personality or that mental disorder. We construct pigeonholes so that we have some way of deciding how to help people with similar problems. However, with this simplification, we lose some of the important information we need. Labeling a child as possessing ADHD (attention deficit hyperactivity disorder) may illustrate something important to know about the client, but soon every action of the child is seen in light of this classification. Although diagnostic systems can paint humanity in broad brushstrokes, when it comes to an individual, so often the person does not seem to fit neatly into any of the categories we devise, and his or her unique strengths are lost behind a powerful and popular label.

Recently a magazine advertisement showed a photograph of people of many different nationalities wearing the company's T-shirts. The essence of the advertisement was that though people may look different and come from many cultures, from the company's perspective, there are only three types of people—small, medium, and large. While the clothing firm was trying to portray the oneness of the human family, the ad made me realize that by trying to see everyone as the same, we are probably ignoring something important. There must be many people who fall between small and medium and are not comfortable in either size. Compared to differences in clothing, the helping process is even more personal and must be tailored to each client.

This T-shirt metaphor also applies to the area of assessment and diagnosis, especially in cases where a helper becomes enamored with a specific tool. For example, if you use the Myers-Briggs Type Indicator (a commonly used test), there are only 16 types of people based on the configuration of preferences. Although 16 is quite a few, it is also not nearly enough to encompass all human differences. As the saying goes, "When the only tool you have is a hammer, everything looks like a nail." A familiar instrument can help you quickly summarize a person, but it will also limit your ability to describe an individual accurately, fairly, and in a culturally appropriate way. Instead of relying on a single test or intake form, it is suggested that you first listen carefully and gather information from any source that fills in the missing colors in the client's unique portrait. The more complete the picture, the better you will be able to design a treatment that really fits.

Organizing the Flood of Information: Making a Diagnosis

Professionals use paper-and-pencil tests, questionnaires, drawings, and similar instruments to gather data about clients and their problems. Besides *formal testing,* there are six other important sources of information to consider. Key information comes from *things the helper observes,* from *information provided by friends and family,* from *what the client supplies* (verbal descriptions, journals, recordings, and genograms)*,* from *medical history,* from *other agencies,* and from *the legal system.* Because there is so much information that can be collected, it may be confusing to know which sources to tap and how to manage the incoming data. As you learn to be a helper, you will take a course in evaluation and assessment or tests and measurements and probably diagnosis. These courses will provide you with a more complete background. However, it is still important that you recognize that all assessment tools are attempts to simplify the process by placing clients in categories based on a theoretical system.

Figure 9.3 shows the downpour of information from the seven sources of information entering a funnel that narrows as the data are examined and summarized into catego-

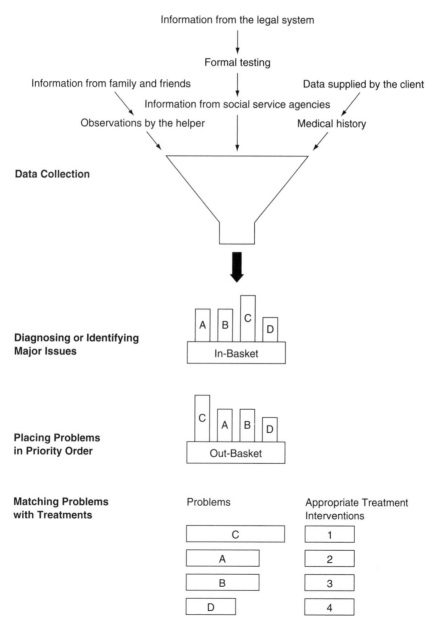

FIGURE 9.3 Process of Gathering, Sorting, and Matching Problems with Treatments in the Assessment Stage

ries. **Diagnosis** is the simplifying process we use to organize the results of our examination. Diagnosis is identifying the overriding issues or problems that seem to encompass a large number of the client's complaints. Using this broad definition, all helpers engage in some form of diagnosis (Hohenshil, 1996).

Figure 9.3 also shows how the client's problems or diagnoses are placed on a treatment planning list, something like an in-basket to be sorted out during the goal-setting stage of the helping process. For example, a typical client's in-box might contain marital problems, career confusion, and low self-esteem, which become the focus of the client/helper discussions. Once the client's problems are identified, it is the helper's job to consult with the client and place them in order of priority, noting those issues that will take precedence and those that will be placed at the bottom of the box. The helper selects methods and techniques to treat each problem on the list. These methods might include referral to a physician, assertiveness training, group therapy, or any other method that the helper suggests. Typically, the treatment plan is constructed in conjunction with the client, who signs an agreement.

BEGINNING ASSESSMENT METHODS

The Mental Status Examination

One way of systematically organizing an interview is by starting with the Mental Status Examination (Daniel & Gurczynski, 2010; Doverspike, 2009). This examination normally includes recording observations and the responses to questions during an initial interview. The Mental Status Examination is a snapshot of the client's *current* mental functioning and usually does not tap historical data (Sommers-Flanagan & Sommers-Flanagan, 2008). The examination can be criticized for dragging the client through many unnecessary questions, and because diagnoses have changed significantly in the past few years, the Mental Status Examination does not directly help the clinician make a *DSM* diagnosis (Othmer & Othmer, 2002). The Mental Status Examination can also be criticized as sometimes being too culturally specific. In the past, the mental status evaluation included asking the client about past U.S. presidents or explaining proverbs such as "strike while the iron is hot." Answers to these questions can be indicators of intelligence or psychosis or simply confusing to a person from a minority group. Still, many helpers in clinical settings use the Mental Status Examination as the basis for their initial screening of a client (Polanski & Hinkle, 2000; Sommers-Flanagan & Sommers-Flanagan, 2008). It is mentioned here and shows you the basic categories. Learning to conduct a Mental Status Examination may be part of your basic training in assessment at some point, but it is too detailed for the present discussion. It is included so that you are aware of its existence as an important assessment tool. Table 9.2 shows the major categories of the Mental Status Examination. They are sometimes grouped differently depending on the examiner. Short versions are available.

The following sections present four beginning methods of assessment: observation, questioning, genograms, and interviews using a brief intake form. With these four basic techniques, you can be confident that you have made a concerted effort to screen for major problems and to determine if the help you have to offer fits the needs of the client.

TABLE 9.2   Mental Status Examination

Category	Description	How Assessed
Appearance	Physical description and clothing	Observation For example, race and ethnic background
Behavior	In the interview	Observation For example, odd gestures
Attitude	Toward the helper and the examination	Observation For example, very submissive or passive or suspicious
Motor behavior	Possible neurological problems or agitation/retardation	Observation For example, shaking the foot, or sitting "stone still"
Reliability	Is the client too impaired or guarded to be a good source of information?	Observation For example, not answering questions in a detailed way and unable to elaborate
Mood and affect	Mood = client's report of emotions over time	Questions For example, "How have you been feeling lately?"
	Affect = predominant emotion at the time of the interview	Observation and inference For example, monotonous voice indicating sadness
Orientation	Is the client oriented as to place, person, and time?	Questions For example, "Do you know where you are right now? Do you know the name of this place?"
Speech processes	Ability to express and receive, including unusual speech patterns suggestive of certain mental disorders	Observation For example, amount, volume, and speed of speech
Thought processes	Including psychotic processes such as delusions	Questions and observation For example, "loose associations" such as "the scandal in the White House has ruined the fishing!", and when asked, cannot make a logical connection between these ideas.
Perceptual abnormalities	For example, hallucinations	Questions For example, "Do you sometimes see things that are not there?"
Memory, attention, and concentration	Impairments in this area may be symptoms of a number of mental disorders or brain dysfunction.	Questions There are many questions designed to measure each of these areas. One example for memory is to ask the client to recall both recent and remote experiences. "What did you have for breakfast?" "Where did you grow up?"
Intelligence	A client's intelligence tells us what he or she is capable of intellectually and in therapy.	Questions and inference This is a difficult and controversial area. Intelligence may not be a single concept. But it may be possible to infer extremes of intelligence from academic achievement, ability to cope, vocabulary, and abstract thinking.
Judgment and insight	Insight is recognizing that one has a problem. Judgment is the ability to make decisions and solve problems.	Questions and inferences When a client denies the existence of problems, insight is absent. On the other hand, when a client's choices appear to be poor and he or she is impulsive, judgment is thought to be poor.

Observation

Yogi Berra once said, "You can observe a lot just by watching." His statement underlines the fact that **observation** is something of a lost art. It also emphasizes that observation is not a passive process, but a conscious, concerted effort. Experienced helpers are able to detect patterns from a number of small clues that, on the surface, may seem inconsequential. For example, some helpers can catch signs of alcohol abuse from a client's hand tremors, jaundiced and dry red skin, finger swelling, and changes in the nose. Some time ago, a cardiac surgeon called the national offices of a television network because he had seen an interview with a national figure on a talk show. He encouraged the broadcasters to inform the speaker that he was in imminent danger of a heart attack. Although the surgeon had not examined the person, he had seen hundreds of cardiac patients over a 20-year period. Unfortunately, the information was not passed along, and the individual died before seeking treatment. Through experience and training, observation can be just as crucial in the helping professions. Clients often carry the clues to their problems on their faces and in the way they walk and speak.

THE HELPER AS DETECTIVE The fictional detective Sherlock Holmes relied on inferences (which he called deductions) to solve mysteries. These inferences were based on his keen powers of observation. In *The Sign of the Four* (Doyle, 1929), Holmes discusses with his partner, Watson, the two different processes involved in his art—observation and deduction:

> Observation shows me that you have been to the Wigmore Street Post Office this morning but deduction tells me that when there you dispatched a telegram. . . . Observation tells me that you have a reddish mold adhering to your instep. Just opposite to the Wigmore Street Office they have taken up the pavement and thrown up bare earth which lies in such a way that it is difficult to avoid treading upon it . . . the earth there is of this particular reddish tint which is found, so far as I know, nowhere else in the neighborhood. So much for observation, the next is deduction. . . . Why of course I know that you had not written a letter since I sat opposite you all morning. What could you go into a post office for but to send a wire? Eliminate all other factors and what remains is the truth. (pp. 7–8)

Like Holmes, Sigmund Freud was aware of the importance of observation and a thinking process (deduction). Freud also believed that evidence of unconscious motivation was available in the everyday activities of clients, including unconscious movements and slips of the tongue (parapraxes). For example, Freud described clients with marriage problems who twisted their wedding rings throughout the session. From *observing* unconscious acts, underlying problems could be *deduced*.

The helper can learn much about observation from Holmes and certainly from Freud, but, unfortunately, human behavior is too complex to take the next step and conclude that we can leap from our observations to accurate predictions about people based on only a few clues. In this age, helpers are a little less inclined to jump to conclusions without validating them against data from the client. In the case of the wedding ring, there are several possible reasons for ring-twisting behavior, including weight gain, itchiness, or anxiety. Therefore, helper hypotheses are guesses, not deductions. Instead of arriving at Holmes's single inescapable conclusion, the assessment process of observation involves documenting observations and forming a list of hypotheses which, when linked to other information, may show a general pattern or theme. Instead of drawing swift conclusions, the helper confirms or disconfirms hypotheses more slowly through discussions with the client. By questioning and listening, a helper can determine if a client's disheveled appearance is due to depression, poverty, or apathy. Observation skills should be practiced, but conclusions should be drawn only when there is confirming evidence from the client and from other sources.

AVOIDING BIAS IN OBSERVATION AND RESISTING CULTURAL ENCAPSULATION Our own cultural biases, assumptions, worldview, and experiences color what we observe. One of these biases is the human tendency to see and remember the things we are searching for. For example, if you are thinking about buying a new car, suddenly you may begin noticing more of them on the road than ever before (Goleman, 1998). Similarly, some mental health professionals see pathology everywhere because of their training in a particular theoretical orientation (Kirk & Hsieh, 2004).

Our expectations and experiences can also distort our observations. In a landmark article entitled "On Being Sane in Insane Places," Rosenhan (1973) recruited individuals for an experiment who then faked their way into a mental hospital by reporting auditory hallucinations. Once admitted and labeled psychotic, all of their subsequent behavior was seen as abnormal. For example, hospital personnel classified one man's diary writing as "obsessive." Our professional experience and training sometimes keep us focused on weaknesses and pathology. In addition, our own family background and culture shape what we remember and pay attention to. We see clients through our own cultural lens and judge their behavior based on our standards. Freeing ourselves entirely from this conditioning is nearly impossible, but we can become more aware of our own limited cultural vision. Again, supervision allows us to reflect on our observations and involves another person who can help us identify our own lenses that may be coloring our vision. The reflective process described in this book suggests that you should think about and record your reactions to your learning. Keeping a diary and obtaining supervision can help us become aware of the tendency to judge other people's behavior from our own narrow perspective.

Furthermore, helpers need to have firsthand contact with people from different backgrounds. Only by experiencing different cultures can we even begin to understand client behavior within the context of the client's own culture. Every helper should consider finding ways to have extended experiences or immersion in another culture (Canfield, Low, & Hovestadt, 2009). Although it is enlightening to be a visitor to another culture, we can also learn about other cultures by being curious and becoming students of every culture we encounter. For example, on a trip to Europe, my companions and I met a large group of Japanese tourists taking hundreds of pictures of a Dutch windmill. We found this to be, on the one hand, amusing, and on the other, excessive and annoying. I began talking with the Japanese tour guide about this. She explained that living on an island means that travel is more restricted, and off-island vacations are relatively rare for most people. In addition, she indicated that pictures are a way of sharing experiences with family and friends back home, who may expect and eagerly await a slide show. When we heard these explanations, my colleagues and I were embarrassed by our cultural encapsulation, and we began to see the behavior in a completely different light. Since then, I have tried to take special care in recording and reflecting on my observations when a client is culturally different. In the following sections, remember that your impressions come through your own cultural lens. When you have the chance to record your observations with real clients, revisit this section and reflect on what you may be bringing to the picture you are painting.

WHAT TO OBSERVE

Speech. Note all aspects of a client's speaking voice. Does the client's voice annoy or soothe? Is the client's tone slow and monotonous or excessively labile? Does the client have an accent of any kind? Does it reflect alcohol abuse or smoking? Is the client's speech hurried or forced? Does the client have a speech impediment of any kind? Does the client speak without listening?

Client's Clothing. Does the client wear expensive, stylish, well-coordinated, seductive, old, or outmoded clothing? Is there anything odd or unusual about it? Does the client reflect a particular style (artistic, conservative, etc.)? Is clothing inappropriate to the weather (several layers on a hot day), and is it appropriate to the occasion? Does the client wear jewelry? A lot of jewelry? Does the client wear appropriate amounts of makeup? Does the client wear glasses or a hearing aid? Does the client's clothing suggest a different cultural background?

Grooming. Is the client clean? Does the client exhibit body odor and a general disregard for personal hygiene? Even if the client shows concern for cleanliness, is there a disorganized appearance to the hair and clothing, perhaps suggesting disorderliness, depression, or lack of social awareness? Do cultural differences in grooming account for the client's appearance? If the client is a child, what does grooming suggest about family environment?

Posture, Build, and Gait. What is the client's posture during the session? What is the position of the shoulders and head? Does the client sit in a rigid or a slouched position or with head in hands? Does the client's posture reflect the present emotional state, or is the client's posture indicative of a more long-term state of anxiety, tension, or depression?

Build refers to the body habitus. Is the client physically attractive? Is the client obese, muscular, or thin? Are there any unusual physical characteristics, such as excessive acne, physical disabilities, or prostheses?

Gait means the person's manner of walking. Does the client's manner of walking reflect an emotional state, such as depression or anxiety? Does the client's walk seem to indicate confidence or low self-esteem? Is the client tentative and cautious in finding a seat?

Facial Expressions. Facial expressions include movements of the eyes, lips, forehead, and mouth. Do the client's feelings show, or are the client's expressions flat, devoid of any emotion? Does the client maintain direct eye contact or avoid it? Do the eyes fill with tears? Does the client smile or laugh during the session? Is the brow wrinkled? Could the client's facial expressions be due to cultural injunctions about eye contact or posture in the presence of an authority figure like the helper?

Other Bodily Movements.   A client may show anxiety by twisting tissue or by tapping restlessly with fingers, toes, or legs. One important way in which people express themselves is through their hand movements. Fritz Perls, the founder of Gestalt therapy, was fond of making clients aware of how bodily movements expressed their inner conflicts and impulses (Perls, 1959, p. 83).

General Appearance.   In recording an assessment of the client, it is sometimes useful to note initial holistic impressions, which may become less noticeable as treatment progresses—for example, "The client appeared much older than his stated age," "The client appeared to be very precise and neat and seemed to carefully consider all of his statements before speaking," "I had the feeling that the client was a super salesman." Many of these holistic impressions can be stereotypes, although sometimes they give insight into the impression the client is trying to make. Are you judging the client based on your own upbringing?

Feelings of the Helper.   Basing his observations on Harry Stack Sullivan's theories, Timothy Leary (1957) (before he took LSD) hypothesized that we react automatically and unconsciously to the communications of others. Our reaction, in turn, triggers the other person's next response. We tend to instinctively react in a positive, friendly manner to individuals whom we find attractive and friendly. Similarly, we instinctively respond negatively to individuals who are combative or aloof. They, in turn, become more abrasive and the cycle continues. These *interpersonal reflexes* (Shannon & Guerney, 1973) occur outside of awareness and are rarely discussed, but they can be very important in the helping relationship and in the client's social world.

If the helper finds himself or herself becoming annoyed with the client, is it possible that most of the client's social contacts have the same response? What would motivate the client to push people away? Is the client even aware of his or her effect on others? According to Ernst Beier (Beier & Young, 1998), the helper can learn to use his or her personal feelings as an assessment instrument. It requires detaching and not reacting to the client's overtures. Instead, think about how others in the client's world must feel about the client and record this information.

Questioning

Asking too many questions was cautioned against earlier as being apt to strain the relationship between client and helper. In fact, the most common mistake for beginning helpers is relying on questions in the relationship-building stage, rather than taking the necessary time to understand the client and provide an atmosphere of openness and trust. But there are many kinds of questions. Questioning is an important part of the assessment process because answers to direct and indirect questions expedite taking personal and sexual histories, structuring genograms, and allowing the client to elaborate on his or her construction of the problem. It is not that questions are inherently bad; it is just that they are used too often by beginning helpers and at the wrong time.

Questioning is an art (Goldberg, 1998). When used artfully, questions can even be therapeutic devices to spur the client's thinking or stimulate action. Questions can also be used to gain valuable information and to focus the client on the agreed-upon goals. They serve an "orienting" function in that they tell the client what is important (Tomm, 1988).

Following are some orienting questions frequently asked by helpers early in the assessment stage in order to begin focusing on a client's concerns.

"How can I help you?"

"Where would you like to begin?"

"What prompted you to make today's appointment?"

"Has something happened in the last few days or weeks that persuaded you that help was needed?"

"What is it that you want to stop doing or do less of?"

"What is it that you want to begin to do or do more of?"

Here are some more sophisticated questions that push a client to dig deeper:

"What effect do you think your depression has on your spouse?"

"What would your life be like if the problem were solved?"

"What does that do to the relationship between you and your stepfather?"

"Where did that idea come from, that you are not capable of being a good father?"

Genograms

The **genogram** is a pictorial representation of the client's family tree. It quickly shows a family's history by depicting current and past relationships. Figure 9.4 shows the symbols used to construct the genogram, and Figure 9.5 is an example of a completed genogram for a client, Bob. It is for a real family, but a rather traditional one with no divorces. In fact, most genograms are more complex, with stepfamilies and unmarried people living together. Figure 9.6 is a skeletal genogram you can use as a template. As you use this template, remember that the bonds between people may be cohabitation (dotted line) and that current households are likely to be more diverse than the example.

When a client comes from a large family or one with many siblings or stepsiblings, the genogram can assist the helper in identifying the individuals involved instead of continually quizzing the client. The genogram is therapeutic when a client's main concerns are family problems because the client gains insight into the issues by describing them to the helper as the genogram is constructed. Finally, the genogram is a tool to explore specific issues such as family influences on career choice (Dickson & Parmerlee, 1980; Okiishi, 1987; Malott & Magnuson, 2004), alcoholism, substance abuse (Armstrong, 2004), or physical and sexual abuse (Armsworth & Stronck, 1998; Long & Young, 2007).

Reasons to Consider Using the Genogram

1. To identify cultural and ethnic influences on the client (Lim & Nakamoto, 2008; Yznaga, 2008)
2. To represent the strengths and weaknesses in relationships between family members
3. To understand the present household composition and the relationships among the client's household, previous marriages, and past generations
4. To discover the presence of family disturbances that might be affecting the client, including alcoholism, abuse, divorces, suicides, sexual abuse, schisms and skews in marital relationships, mental illness in the family, and so on
5. To uncover gender role and other family expectations on the client

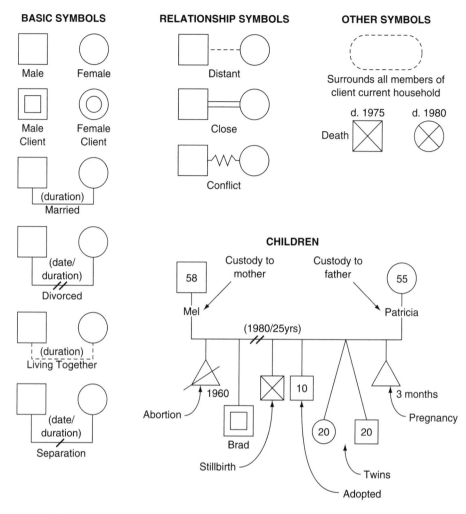

FIGURE 9.4 Genogram Symbols

Adapted from Figure 4.2, page 93, *Counseling Methods and Techniques: An Eclectic Approach* by Mark E. Young. Columbus, OH: Merrill/Macmillan, 1992.

6. To assess economic and emotional support resources for the client
7. To identify repeated patterns in the client's relationships
8. To determine the effects of birth order and sibling rivalry on the client
9. To make the client and helper aware of family attitudes concerning health and illness
10. To identify extrafamilial sources of support
11. To trace family patterns of certain preferences, values, and behaviors, such as legal problems, sexual values, obesity, and job problems
12. To identify problem relationships
13. To document historical traumas, such as suicides, deaths, abuse, and losses of pregnancies
14. To understand the role of religion and spirituality in the client's family (Wiggins-Frame, 2001)

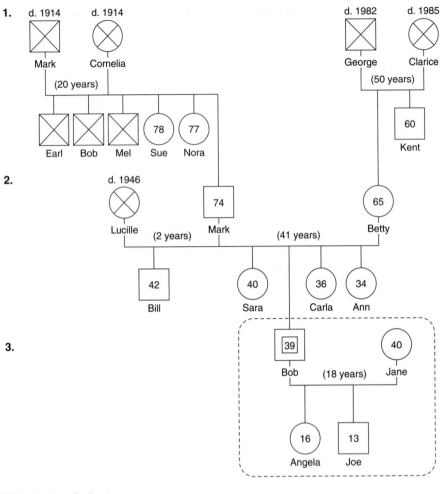

FIGURE 9.5 Sample Genogram

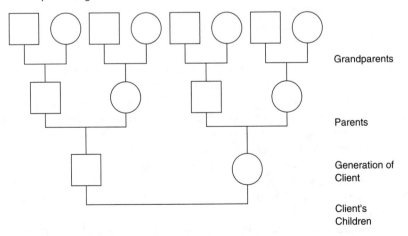

FIGURE 9.6 Skeletal Genogram

STOP AND REFLECT

Construct your own genogram using Figure 9.6. Copy the skeleton on a separate piece of paper and begin by filling in your grandparents' names and ages in the appropriate row. Note that men are squares and women are circles. Now fill in your parents' names in the boxes of the "parents" row and then bring down a line for each sibling in your original nuclear family along the line that connects your parents. When a person has been married more than once, his or her previous spouses are connected to that person horizontally. In the sample genogram in Figure 9.5, Bob is the third of five children. His box is dropped so that we can identify him as the person of interest and show a fourth generation, his children. For this exercise, drop your own box, below that of your siblings, if you wish to show your own marriage or children. Indicate your present nuclear family by encircling it with dashes as shown in the example in Figure 9.5.

Check your drawing to make sure you have not missed any family members in the three generations. If parents or grandparents have been married more than once, place their other spouses to the side (see the example of Lucille and Mark in Figure 9.5). Put an X in the box or circle of anyone who is deceased. Place the ages of each person in his or her box or circle. Place the approximate years of marriage (or committed relationship) and make slashes to indicate divorces or separations. Put this information on the lines between spouses as shown in Figure 9.5 (see also Figure 9.4, which shows a divorce). Now review the genogram symbols in Figure 9.4. Add any additional symbols that you wish to include in your family genogram. Specifically, you may wish to depict relationships within your family as shown in the section entitled "Relationship Symbols."

When you have completed the genogram, answer the following questions:

1. What cultural or ethnic background characterizes each person in your family tree?
2. How do you think culture and history affect the values and rules around which your family functions?
3. Are differences in backgrounds ever the source of conflict in the family? Does cultural heritage beget closeness or conflict? If there are different cultural influences in your family, are you more a part of one specific side of the family, or do you embrace more than one culture?
4. Check out free or shareware online genogram programs such as GenoPro.

Conducting an Interview Using a Brief Intake Form

One way of getting started in the assessment process is to systematically record your impressions about a client on some kind of standard form. A form is a good training device because it ensures that you have not missed the big problems. In this chapter, you will find a prototype form to use for reflection, case presentation, and treatment planning. The form asks you to jot down your evaluation of the client's (A) affective or emotional issues and status; (B) behavior deficits, excesses, and strengths; and (C) thinking or cognitions. These three items will be referred to as A, B, and C, for short. In addition, you are asked to accumulate data about the client's (1) developmental level, (2) family history, (3) cultural and religious/spiritual background, and (4) physical challenges and strengths.

Within this brief assessment questionnaire, several trigger questions are embedded in each area. Trigger questions prompt the helper to reflect on the client's answers and

seek assistance from a supervisor or consider referring the client to a more qualified practitioner. The trigger questions are:

1. Does the client meet criteria for a major emotional disorder such as anxiety or
   depression? Such a diagnosis might require referral or special treatment, including
   medication.
2. Does the client show any evidence of suicidal thinking, have a history of self-
   destructive behavior, or indicate thoughts or history of harming others? If so, an
   assessment must be made by a qualified practitioner.
3. Does the client show any evidence of thought disorders, highly unusual thought
   processes, hallucinations (seeing things that are not here), or delusions (bizarre or
   fixed false beliefs)? If so, the client may require a medication evaluation and specific
   support groups.
4. Is the relationship between helper and client moving toward a healthy alliance?
   Have cultural differences been addressed? Does the client feel the helper is a trustworthy and credible resource for helping to achieve treatment goals?
5. Could any medical problems or organic brain syndromes be causing or contributing
   to the client's problem?
6. Does the client need treatment for substance abuse?

Let us now take a brief look at each of the seven elements (ABC-1234) and why it is
critical to collect these data on each client during a screening or intake interview.

A. AFFECTIVE ASSESSMENT   Clients come for help because of overwhelming and confused emotions. They are seeking relief from anxiety, grief, depression, and anger.
Whether these are disabling conditions or merely uncomfortable, the helper assesses the
intensity, frequency, and **duration** of these negative emotions in order to plan effective treatment. It is similarly important to identify the client's positive affective states. If
clients can identify the times when they feel satisfied and happy, they can attempt to re-create
those states.

B. BEHAVIORAL ASSESSMENT   Many people are seeking assistance for *excessive* behaviors, ranging from smoking to sexual addiction. Others need help in learning and increasing new behaviors such as social skills or time management. Clients also have "positive
addictions" or healthy habits that should be noted. If a client has a regular exercise regime, meditates, or is very organized, these behaviors can be identified and encouraged.

C. COGNITIVE ASSESSMENT   Cognition includes the client's thinking, images, and meanings (the client's worldview). For example, a client may be engaging in negative thinking
and negative imagery about an upcoming event. By uncovering this in an assessment
interview, the helper can help the client find specific constructive thoughts and images as
an antidote. In this section of the intake form, the helper records intellectual deficits and
strengths, any specific learning problems, or head injuries.

1. DEVELOPMENTAL ISSUES   Helpers must have a basic knowledge of human development as major theorists such as Piaget, Erikson, Loevinger, and Kohlberg have described
it. Then assessment and helping techniques can be modified to deal with life-stage differences. In this section, people are grouped according to the common age-related categories

of children, adolescents, adults, and older people. The descriptions of these life stages are generalizations about groups of people. The discussion is meant to urge you to consider critical **developmental** issues. However, it is important to remember that each person is unique. There are some octogenarians who are physically and intellectually younger than their chronological ages; some 7-year-olds demonstrate an unusual amount of intellectual and emotional maturity.

Children.   There are many specialized assessment and helping techniques that are specific to children (Sattler & Hoge, 2006). School functioning for children is analogous to occupational functioning in adults and is an indicator of overall adjustment. Contact a teacher for insight into a child's behavior toward adults and peers. To understand a child's family and his or her relationship with parents, interview parents, grandparents, and siblings.

Adolescents.   Adolescents are challenging but also intriguing and rewarding to work with. Issues of trust and betrayal, freedom, autonomy, dangerous behavior, and anger are just beneath the surface of their words. When assessing adolescent problems, it is particularly important to touch on drug and alcohol abuse, sexual behavior, and relationships with parents and siblings. Most adolescent deaths are due not to medical problems but to automobile accidents, suicide, homicide, and substance abuse. These areas must be carefully addressed in the assessment stage.

College Students.   College students are characterized by their focus on issues of self-esteem, separation from their family of origin, and their strong need to form close bonds with others. The helper who works with college students deals with alcohol and drug abuse, suicide attempts, eating disorders, intense love relationships and their dismal aftermath, problems with parents, pregnancy, and sexually transmitted diseases.

Older People.   Understanding the problems of older people requires consideration of their unique histories. The oldest people today lived through the Great Depression and World War II. These two events shaped their thinking and worldview. It instilled in them a cautious approach to life, especially where money is concerned. When choosing a career, for example, they might counsel, "Have something to fall back on!" In short, to know an older person, it may be important to get a sense of the time they grew up in because it affected their perspective on life and is the basis for their view of the future. Helpers who work with older people deal with issues of loss, deteriorating health, thoughts about lost opportunities, and fears associated with loneliness. Helpers frequently also assist older people who are trying to create new lives following the death of a spouse, who need to let go of past experiences, or who have disappointing family relationships.

2. FAMILY HISTORY   Our family histories provide a deep insight into who we are. Our ideas of gender roles, parental roles, and what is normal and good all come from our original family group, or our *family of origin*. The visual nature of the genogram makes it an efficient way to understand a client's family history. In the absence of a genogram, you may simply want to question clients concerning important stressors in their family now and in the past.

A family history of depression, suicide, anxiety disorders, substance abuse, and sexual abuse is valuable information, as it may shed light on the client's current concerns. Our ideas about normal family functioning, what it means to be a spouse and parent, are based on our own families. Taking the time to get a sense of the client's family will be rewarded by insights into the forces that shaped the client's worldview.

3. CULTURAL AND RELIGIOUS/SPIRITUAL BACKGROUND Besides identifying a client's ethnicity, race, or class, it is important to understand the client's acculturation. A client's acculturation is the degree to which he or she personally identifies with a particular culture. For example, two children in a bicultural family may feel close to one parent's culture but not the other's. In addition, a girl whose parents are Russian Jews but who was born in the United States might conceivably have a minimal relationship to her family's culture and religion. Following are some additional questions that stimulate thinking about the degree of a client's cultural identity and its impact on the helping process:

- What is the client's cultural/ethnic identity?
- What is the client's religion or spiritual orientation? How closely do they follow that belief?
- How much does the client identify with his or her cultural or ethnic background?
- According to the client, how is seeking help from a helper viewed within his or her culture?
- How can the client's goals and problems be viewed in a way that is compatible with his or her cultural background?
- How does the client's upbringing regarding appropriate gender roles relate to the presenting problems?
- Is the client's culture a source of pride or shame?

4. PHYSICAL CHALLENGES AND STRENGTHS For our purposes, physical challenges include medical diagnoses, physical disabilities and limitations, and drug and alcohol use and abuse. All these may have physical, social, and psychological effects. Focus on the client's physical assets and abilities in this category, too.

Medical Diagnoses. A number of physical disorders have psychological effects. A helper can go wrong by trying to work on a symptom that turns out to be the result of a treatable medical condition (Pollak, Levy, & Breitholtz, 1999). For example, a brain tumor or other serious problem, rather than stress, may be the cause of a client's headaches. Symptoms of depression, anxiety, sexual disorders, irritability, weight gain or loss, headaches, and fatigue suggest that the client should receive a thorough medical checkup as part of the helping process. It is irresponsible and unethical to treat someone for these symptoms until medical causes have been ruled out. When in doubt, helpers should refer clients for medical evaluation. On the other side of the coin, be sure to note positive health and wellness behaviors such as good diet and physical exercise.

Physical Disabilities. The term *physical disabilities* suggests that there are normal and disabled people. Perhaps the term should be "physical differ-abilities," because abilities are probably better described on a continuum rather than within a disabled/abled dichotomy. It is not as important to know that a person is in a wheelchair as it is to know how he or she sees himself or herself in relation to other people, how he or she functions, and how this way of getting around affects that person socially and professionally.

TABLE 9.3	Some Key Interview Questions for Substance Abuse

"Do any of your friends and family think you have a substance abuse problem?"

"Have you ever been arrested for driving under the influence?"

"Have you ever been physically injured or had an accident while using?"

"Have you ever broken any bones as an adult? If so, how?"

"How much do you drink or use each day?"

"Have you ever had a blackout or amnesia while using?"

"Has your substance abuse changed any of your close relationships or affected your work?"

"Looking back at your family tree, which relatives have had a substance abuse problem?"

"Have you ever felt the need to cut back on your use of substances?"

Not all disabilities are as obvious as a prosthesis or wheelchair. Heart conditions, multiple sclerosis, arthritis, diabetes, and a myriad of other problems have an effect on mood, behavior, and thinking. It is helpful to know the normal psychological effects of common diseases, and it is important to explore with a client the impact of the disease on his or her overall functioning.

Drug and Alcohol Use and Abuse.   Alcohol and other drug use is difficult to assess because clients consciously and unconsciously minimize the amount they report. Prescription and nonprescription drug taking must also be recorded because the mental, emotional, and behavioral effects can make other issues worse. Even medically necessary medication can affect school or work functioning and family relationships.

When substance abuse is identified, many helpers try to treat this first because continued substance abuse undermines progress on other issues. Because clients may not want to bring up substance abuse, one way to start a discussion and gain important information is by asking direct questions or by asking the client to fill out a questionnaire on substance use and history (see Evans, 1998). Table 9.3 contains a list of additional questions that you might use to follow up on suspected substance abuse.

SUMMARIZING IMPORTANT BACKGROUND INFORMATION   Figure 9.7 shows a blank copy of the ABC-1234 **Intake Form.** It can be used as a worksheet to summarize data collected about the client in the initial interview. Figure 9.8 shows a completed form on a fictitious client. Each section should contain problems and strengths. It is important to emphasize the client's abilities as well as disabilities, because strengths give the helper useful information about what methods and techniques might be most effective. For example, a client who is an excellent reader and enjoys books might profit from bibliotherapy. A client who has a strong religious background can be implored to use this strength in understanding and dealing with fear or depression.

The intake form begins with a statement by the client, indicating what issue(s) propelled him or her to seek help and what he or she hopes to achieve. It is useful to record this statement in the client's own words because the client's view of the problem is critical to treatment planning. Let us say, for example, that in the client's statement she indicates that she is mostly concerned with her adolescent son's marijuana abuse. Even if the helper focuses on what seem to be more critical problems, the client may not feel that she has received the treatment she has asked for.

Demographic Data

Name: _____

Age: _____

Date of Birth: _____

Street Address: _____

City: _____ State: _____ Zip: _____

Home Phone: _____

Work Phone: _____ Okay to call at work? Yes/No

Level of Education: _____

Occupation: _____

Marital Status: _____

Children's Names and Ages: _____

Reason for Referral: _____

Referral Source: _____

Client's Statement of the Problem
Write down a paragraph in the client's own words that describes why he or she came for help.

A. Affective Assessment

What major and minor emotions are troubling the client? _____

Is the client sad? Angry? Fearful? Anxious? _____

Are these due to the helping interview or longer-term states? _____

What emotional states does the client wish to reduce? _____

How does the client normally handle negative emotions? _____

What emotional strengths does the client have? _____

Trigger: Does the client require treatment for depression, mania, or severe anxiety?

_____

B. Behavioral Assessment

What does the client want to do that he or she is not doing? _____

What behaviors does the client wish to reduce or eliminate? _____

What behaviors does the client need to increase? _____

What behaviors does the client want to learn? _____

What habits does he or she want to eliminate? _____

What positive behaviors does he or she want to strengthen? _____

Has the client ever engaged in violence toward self or others? _____

Identify the client's strengths and positive social and health behaviors. _____

Trigger: Does the client now require treatment for dangerous behavior toward self or others? _____

C. Cognitive Assessment

Does the client show any signs of memory problems or other problems in thinking? _____

Does the client succeed in a typical classroom environment? _____

Does the client report *negative or positive* imagery about the problem? _____

What rational and irrational thoughts were detected in the client's statements? _____

Does the client show distorted thinking patterns such as overgeneralization, black-and-white thinking, etc.? _____

How would you characterize the client's worldview and values? _____

What positive thinking patterns exist? _____

Trigger: Does the client show any evidence of thought disorders, highly unusual thought processes, hallucinations, or delusions (bizarre fixed false beliefs)? Does the client think about hurting self or others? _____

FIGURE 9.7 ABC-1234 Intake Form Worksheet

1. Developmental Issues

How did the client handle major maturational milestones of childhood? _____

Compared with the client's peers, how is the client adjusting to normal developmental issues? _____

Describe the client's maturational level in terms of career, intellectual, sexual, moral, and social development. _____

Do any of the client's developmental issues relate to the statement of the problem? _____

2. Family History (Attach Genogram if Possible)

What does the genogram reveal about the client's family history as it relates to the statement of the problem? _____

How many brothers and sisters does the client have? What is the client's birth order? ____

What problems in family relationships are revealed by the genogram or by questioning? ___

What family support does the client have? _____

Is the client on good terms with family members? _____

Has the client achieved a healthy interdependence with family compared with others of the client's culture? _____

What traumatic events have affected the family? _____

What family changes have occurred recently? _____

What strengths has the client gained from his or family background? _____

3. Cultural and Religious/Spiritual Background

What is the client's cultural/ethnic identity? _____

What is the client's religion or spiritual orientation? _____

How closely does the client identify with his or her cultural or ethnic background? _____

How culturally acceptable is it for the client to seek professional help? _____

Does the client's attitude regarding appropriate gender roles relate to the presenting problems? _____

Is the client able to identify the positive and healthy aspects of his or her culture and the part they might play in solving problems? _____

Trigger: Does the client appear skeptical that the helping process and the helper are credible methods for achieving the stated goals? _____

4. Physical Challenges and Strengths

Does the client report any medical issues or disabilities? _____

How does the client view himself or herself in relation to diseases or disabilities? _____

What is the extent of the client's current use of alcohol and drugs? Previous use? _____

What is the client's level of knowledge about substance abuse? _____

Does the client have a family history of substance abuse? _____

Does the client have a good diet and physical self-care habits such as exercise? _____

Trigger: Could any medical condition be causing or contributing to the client's statement of the problem? _____

Trigger: Does the client need treatment for substance abuse? _____

Treatment Goals (Mutually Agreed Upon)   Treatment Plans (Proposed Interventions)

1. _____   1. _____

2. _____   2. _____

3. _____   3. _____

Signatures: _____   Date: _____

FIGURE 9.7 (*Continued*)

Demographic Data

Name: Claudia O'Reilly

Age: 35

Date of Birth: 11/13/69

Street Address: 132 Shade St.

City: New Brunswick   State: OH   Zip: 45123

Home Phone: 614-555-2194

Work Phone: None   Okay to call at work?   Yes/No

Level of Education: H.S. diploma

Occupation: Homemaker

Marital Status: Married

Children's Names and Ages: Amber age 6, Heather age 4

Reason for Referral: Pastor felt she needed individual help to deal with feelings of depression.

Referral Source: Pastor, R. Brown, Central Community Church

Client's Statement of the Problem

"My main problem is learning to accept my husband for the way he is. I get very depressed over the fact that he does not seem to want to spend time with me and the kids. He is not motivated at work. He smokes marijuana and drinks with his friends. Because I don't work, I have no say-so about the money. I go to church and to Alanon and that is my total social life. I would like to go out more with him and have a life."

A. Affective Assessment

Client reported lack of direction in her life. She feels ineffective in her work taking care of the children and her home. Client also indicated feelings of sadness over her marital problems. At times, she reported feelings of "frustration" with her husband that would best be described as anger and resentment. She did not meet *DSM-IV* criteria for a mental disorder associated with her feelings of depression.

On the positive side, the client reports that religious activities, including attending church and reading her Bible, have helped her during her worst "down" periods.

B. Behavioral Assessment

Client admits that she lacks assertiveness skills. She believes that she "sulks" at times as a way of getting her husband to respond. She wants to "go out more and have a life." By this, she means that she would like to return to school, eventually go to work, and have some free time outside of the house. The client has no history of harming herself or others and does not appear to be a danger to herself or others. The client appears to be ready to return to school and has an interest in reading and learning.

C. Cognitive Assessment

The client shows no apparent problems with memory. She reports being an A and B student in high school. In fact, the client is aware of her above-average scholastic abilities, but sometimes berates herself for not developing her mind earlier in life. In assessing the client's thinking about herself, she reports low self-esteem. She is perfectionistic in her thinking and often engages in black-and-white thinking. For example, she said that she was not a good housekeeper because her home is rarely spotless like her mother's. She had difficulty seeing that her expectations were rather high for someone with two young children. She believes that expressing her feelings and stating her preferences is "generally rude."

FIGURE 9.8 ABC-1234 Intake Form Sample

1. Developmental Issues

The client is approaching midlife and feels unfulfilled in her work as a wife and mother. She was married at 25, but says she lived a sheltered life before that, living at home with her mother. She wants to work outside the home and wishes to begin training of some kind.

The client and her husband have been married for 10 years. The marriage was apparently a happy one in the first 2 years, but there have been major problems and upheavals over the last 5 years. Although the marriage is now stable in that there is no talk of divorce, apparently both partners are dissatisfied with the way they interact.

The client and her family are in transition because the youngest child is now entering preschool and will be gone most of the day. With two children in school, there are new pressures, including transportation. Because the children are in school, the client will also have some additional free time on her hands and conceivably might have enough time to take classes. She has received career testing at the community college and is interested in becoming a dental hygienist.

2. Family History

The client's parents were divorced 20 years ago. She has two older sisters, both of whom work in professional occupations. The client's mother is a retired bookkeeper, and her father is still working as a building contractor. The client related that as she was growing up, both of her parents, but especially her mother, had high, even impossible, standards for all the children. She feels that she has let them down by not achieving.

Today, Claudia and her mother are closer. Her mother helps with the children, and Claudia can talk to her about most problems. Both of Claudia's sisters live out of state, but she receives some support via telephone.

The client is most disturbed by the lack of support she receives from her husband. Her opinion is that he does not wish to be a part of the family. The family has little money, and she is angry that he spends any amount on alcohol and drugs. He gives her money with which she pays the bills. She regards him as her "third child." About 1 year ago, she began attending Alanon. She claims that his drinking is not as much of a problem as it was a year ago, but that he smokes marijuana daily and this bothers her a great deal.

3. Cultural and Religious/Spiritual Background

The client's family members consider themselves to be "Southern." Her grandparents and even her father at one time worked as peanut farmers in Georgia, where the family originated. The client had a strict religious upbringing, a fundamentalist Protestant denomination. She has continued to be a member of this church, and she takes her daughters every Sunday, although her husband does not attend. Her religion is definitely a support for her. Besides the time she spends at church, she also prays regularly and feels that her depression is reduced by both activities.

One of the cultural/gender issues surfaces when the client talks about "not being lady-like." She sometimes describes other people in this way and has indicated she has trouble standing up for herself because she does not want to "act like a man." In addition, the client has very traditional views about the roles of husband and wife that may clash with the mainstream of society and her own goals to have a more personally fulfilling life.

4. Physical Challenges and Strengths

The client has suffered from periods of chronic fatigue. Her physician indicates that this is not solely the result of feeling depressed, but is associated with an endocrine dysfunction. She takes medication for the condition but occasionally has periods when she is unable to do much for 2 or 3 days.

FIGURE 9.8 (*Continued*)

The client has no regular exercise regime and eats a diet that is very high in fat, salt, and sugar. She claims that she has to cook what her husband likes and so she cannot really change her eating patterns. The client has never used drugs or alcohol.

Treatment Goals (Helper and Client Contract)	Treatment Plans
1. Increase assertive behavior	1. Client will be referred to assertiveness training class.
2. Decrease depression, increase self-esteem	2. Individual sessions will decrease depression and increase self-esteem.
3. Improve marital relationship	3. Following treatment for items 1 and 2, client will be referred with husband to couples counseling.

Signatures: _____ Date: _____

FIGURE 9.8 (*Continued*)

Each section of the intake form contains a trigger question. This question, when answered positively, prompts a referral to specialized treatment or, at the minimum, identifies an issue that should be discussed with a supervisor. The trigger question is a reminder to look for serious issues that should be dealt with first or that might jeopardize the helping relationship.

When to Refer Someone for In-Depth Testing

During the assessment process, you may find, just as I did, that observation and questions may not be enough to determine what kind of help a person needs. You and the client may be confused about the source of his or her problems and testing by an expert might be called for. In some states, the ordinary helper may administer tests; in others, extensive experience and credentials are required. To use a medical analogy, most of us are General Practitioners (GPs). When in-depth testing is needed, it should be referred to someone who does this on a daily basis. Continuing my analogy, you probably would like specialized medical treatment by someone who has years of experience in your particular problem. Here are some guidelines that might help you recognize when you need additional testing:

1. When a trigger question in the initial interview indicates that you need to discuss the situation with your supervisor (for example, violence, severe mental disorder, substance abuse, or suicide). The result of your discussion may be that the client is referred to a testing specialist.
2. When the client is evasive or unreliable. There are tests that can identify a person's tendency to exaggerate or understate their problems. There may be longstanding personality issues that suggest a pattern of antisocial behavior. There may be a long history of incarcerations or hospitalizations. There may be drug or alcohol abuse or domestic violence.
3. When the client has a physical condition that might be causing the problem. For example, is the client's memory problem due to depression or to a more severe issue such as Alzheimer's?
4. When a client's problems seem to stem from the ability to remember things. The client might be anxious or might have neurological difficulties.

5. When the person has difficulty reading or writing. While this may be due to lack of education, it might also indicate learning disabilities, attention deficit, or some pervasive developmental disorder such as a problem on the autism spectrum.
6. When the person seems to be functioning poorly but does not provide enough information to make a diagnosis or conversely appears to have symptoms of several disorders. Testing might assist the helper in determining which issues are the most central.
7. When you are unconvinced about a previous diagnostic label based on your experience with a client.

MyCounselingLab™

Go to Topic 3, *Diagnostic Assessment,* on the MyCounselingLab™ site (www. MyCounselingLab.com) for *Learning the Art of Helping: Building Blocks and Techniques,* Fifth Edition, where you can:

• Find learning outcomes for *Diagnostic Assessment* along with the national standards that connect to these outcomes.
• Complete Assignments and Activities that can help you more deeply understand the chapter content.
• Apply and practice your understanding of the core skills identified in the chapter with the Building Counseling Skills unit.
• Prepare yourself for professional certification with a Practice for Certification quiz.
• Connect to videos through the Video and Resource Library.

MyCounselingLab™ Exercises

Go to the Video and Resource Library on the MyCounselingLab™ site for your text and search for the following clip: *Confrontation Dayle.* Watch the video and answer the questions that follow.

Using Questions for Assessment

Questions are one important method for gaining information about a client's problems. This segment shows Catherine (a client) and Dayle (the helper). In this interview, Catherine talks about her problems with smoking. An assessment of Catherine's current smoking behavior and her desired goals would likely be useful.

1. Write three questions you would like to ask Catherine. Make sure your questions shed some light on the problem itself rather than merely satisfying your curiosity.
2. Compare your answers with those of another student. Of all the questions you have considered, which one is most likely to reveal crucial information?
3. How important is it to gain specific data about a client's troublesome behaviors? For example, would you have asked Catherine to record the number of cigarettes she smokes? Why or why not?
4. Catherine mentions something about her father. What relevance does this have to her problem? Is it worth exploring? If so, how might you do so?

Summary

Assessment means gathering information about a client. The gathering begins the moment a client walks through the door. We observe, ask questions, review tests, and receive medical data and reports from social service agencies. We may even interrogate family and friends. One of the pressures from the beginning is to organize the flood of information from multiple sources. This process involves listing and then organizing problems in priority order. This is the process of treatment planning.

Assessment helps both client and helper. Assessment helps the client discover events that may be related to the problem which they may never have identified or recognize issues that were previously hidden. The helper uses assessment data to plan useful and realistic goals, identify the best treatment for the client's particular problem, determine whether the client is suicidal or dangerous, and become aware of client strengths and unique attributes. Sometimes referral to a testing expert is called for.

The final section of this chapter presents four beginning assessment tools in some detail: Observation, Questioning, Conducting an Interview Using a Brief Intake Form, and the Genogram. Also, the Mental Status Examination, a time-honored method of acquiring basic data about a client, is outlined here.

Exercises

GROUP EXERCISES

Exercise 1: Practice Interviewing

In groups of three, one student acts as the helper, another is the client, and a third observes. The helper interviews a fellow student using the intake form (Figure 9.7). Before the interview, the client and observer identify and agree on a problem that the client is hoping to work on or that is fabricated for this exercise. The client should take a moment to look over the intake form and think about answers to key questions. The client should retain his or her real identity so that the other aspects of the intake are authentic even if the problem itself is concocted. An ethical alert is necessary at this juncture. Collecting information about another person requires a reassurance that what you say will not be passed on to anyone else. Still, you must warn even a fellow classmate that you would have to report to your instructor any potential danger to self or others, the commission of a crime, or abuse to a child or elder. States vary slightly on what must be revealed but giving your fellow student this warning will be good practice and will protect you and others. After the exercise, the client gives specific feedback to the helper on the following issues:

1. Was the helper able to intersperse questioning and listening? Or did the client find that the interview was too businesslike or too familiar?
2. Did the helper find the key problems? If not, why not?

3. What other suggestions do you have for the helper in terms of the quality of the interview?

Within your group, discuss the following questions:

- What is your reaction to the use of a standardized form such as this one?
- What important areas do you think are missing that you would have liked to explore?
- How long did it take to complete the interview?
- Did the client react negatively to answering so many questions? If so, how might this be handled better?

SMALL GROUP DISCUSSIONS

Discussion 1: Religious and Spiritual Beliefs

Religion is the social body associated with a set of beliefs while spirituality is an individual's beliefs and experiences of a higher power. This chapter recommends asking clients about religious and spiritual beliefs. In a group of four or five, react to this suggestion. How comfortable would you feel assessing this area? How would you approach a client who is antireligious or simply nonreligious? Under what circumstances would you refer a client to clergy? If you were a client, how important would it be to discuss spirituality? For more information see the website of ASERVIC, the Association for Spiritual, Ethical and Religious Values in Counseling (www.aservic.org).

Discussion 2: Gender Issues in Assessment

Conduct a classroom discussion on gender issues in assessment. How does the interpretation of data vary based on gender? Are some behaviors seen as more pathological depending on the person's gender? Are women generally seen as unhealthier than men? In your group, discuss the importance of including a discussion of gender-role issues in the assessment process. As you look at the intake form for Claudia (Figure 9.8), how important are these issues for her? If you were helping Claudia, would you bring up her perceptions about gender role? Why or why not?

WRITTEN EXERCISES

Exercise 1: Constructing a Genogram

Draw a basic genogram for a client named Bren. Bren is the second of three children. Both of his parents are alive. He has always had a difficult relationship with his father whom he feels he cannot please. His mother is supportive and has a better relationship with Bren than she has with her husband. Bren has a strained relationship with his wife, Heather (age 32), and a closer relationship with his younger sister, Muthoni (age 28). He does not talk much about his older brother.

Bren is 31 and has come to individual counseling because he is about to lose his job as a salesman. Bren says he does not like being a salesman but has never considered another line of work. He is avoiding his boss as much as possible because he is afraid the boss will want some concrete plans for improvement. He is having trouble with his wife, who feels he is unmotivated; she wants to quit work to stay with their 2-year-old son, Mike. They have been married for 3 years. Bren does not tell his wife much about how he feels or thinks. They seldom fight and when they do, Bren just leaves the house and goes to see his parents for a few hours. Bren is unhappy but he is most upset about the pressure from his boss and wife and is not sure how to handle it. Draw Bren's genogram. For simplicity, we will omit Bren's grandparents from consideration. In Appendix A, you will find our version of the basic genogram. Compare yours and our example. Now use a colored pen to draw in lines that depict the relationship between Bren and Heather, Bren and his sister, Bren and his mother, and Bren and his father. Draw a dotted line showing who lives in Bren's household.

1. Write down two questions you would ask Bren about his genogram.

2. As you look at the questions you have elected to ask, evaluate each of them. Indicate on a 10-point scale how important the question is. A 10 would represent a crucial question, which unasked might lead to improper or inadequate treatment. A 1 on the scale indicates that you have asked the question more out of curiosity than out of need or relevance to the client's goals.

Exercise 2: In-Basket–Out-Basket

It is important to reduce assessment data to a set of major issues, which are then placed on a problem list or in-basket. When a list has been compiled, the helper arranges the issues in order of importance and places the list in an out-basket. Items arranged in the out-basket list represent a treatment plan or goals placed in priority order. Consider the following issues in a client's in-basket. Arrange them in the order that you would address them in an out-basket list. One guide for treatment planning is to think about Maslow's hierarchy of needs. Maslow suggested that basic physiological issues such as food, clothing, and shelter must be dealt with before higher needs such as belongingness, love, and self-actualization.

In-Basket
  a. The client wishes to develop a *better relationship* with his two children who live with his ex-wife.
  b. The client is a *recovering alcoholic* but has not been attending support group meetings.
  c. The client has been experiencing *mild depression*.
  d. The client has *difficulty with his supervisor* and is considering changing jobs.
  e. The client has an *interest in drawing and painting* and would like to consider a career in this area.
  f. The client indicates he *feels lonely and isolated since his divorce* one year ago.

Defend your choices in a sentence or two.

SELF-ASSESSMENT

In reviewing my assessment skills, I feel I need more work on (check all that apply):

1. Using questions
2. Observing
3. Working with a genogram
4. Interviewing and recording information
5. Using standardized tests

For those items that you checked, indicate how you might gain additional experience or training.

Cultural Encapsulation

Think for a moment about one population that you hope to work with in the future. Define the population either by ethnicity or culture, problem area (such as family problems), or developmental level (such as children). Answer the following questions:

How certain are you that you would enjoy working with this group of people?

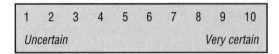

1	2	3	4	5	6	7	8	9	10
Uncertain									Very certain

How familiar are you with this population?

1	2	3	4	5	6	7	8	9	10
Just beginning to know this population									Several years of experience

Think for a few minutes about how people in this group might vary. For example, if you chose children, could you also work with children with a wide variety of ethnic backgrounds, learning disabilities, or physical handicaps? What preparation should *you* make in your training to become more aware of assessment issues with this population?

HOMEWORK

Homework 1: Your Genogram

Complete a genogram for yourself using the skeletal form in this chapter. Use the instructions in the "Stop and Reflect" section as a guide. Next to each person in your genogram, list his or her jobs or careers. If you do not know this information, do some research by asking other family members. Can you identify a family pattern in the selection of vocation? To go into a bit more depth, look up the Holland codes for each occupation in the *Dictionary of Holland Occupational Codes* (Gottfredson, Holland, & Ogawa, 1996) and see if you can see a family transmission of certain traits (Kakiuchi & Weeks, 2009).

The Holland codes match your personality and the work environment according to the following categories: Realistic (practical and mechanical, such as a firefighter), Investigative (such as a scientist), Artistic (such as a musician), Social (such as a teacher), Enterprising (such as a business person), and Conventional (such as an accountant). Usually a person is described by the top three codes. By the way, most helpers are Social, Artistic, and Investigative although not necessarily in that order. The *Self-Directed Search* is a fun and interesting career assessment using the Holland Codes that is even available online if you would like to become familiar with this important area of career assessment.

Homework 2: HIV-Positive Client

Search the Internet for resources for dealing with people who are HIV positive. What limitations do such people experience? What mythologies affect the way people look at them? What challenges would this present socially and professionally for an affected person? Looking at the various websites, what must a helper know about current treatment, testing, and prevention? How would you feel about working with someone who tested positive for HIV? What issues might you expect them to bring to the helping session?

Homework 3: Assessment of Children

Do a brief research study on the symptoms of depression in children. Use articles, books, and Internet sources. What is different about the way that children express and experience depression?

JOURNAL STARTERS

Think back on assessment experiences in your own life. These may range from encounters with a high school guidance counselor to an intake interview at the college counseling center to a College Board Examination (GRE, SAT). What important decisions have you made based on testing or assessment results? What decisions have others made about you based on testing? Discuss any negative or positive experiences. How do these affect your views and feelings about testing clients?

CHAPTER 10

Goal-Setting Skills

Until one is committed, there is hesitancy, the chance to draw back, always ineffectiveness. There is one elementary truth, the ignorance of which kills countless ideas and splendid plans. That the moment one commits oneself, then Providence moves too. All sorts of things occur to help one that would never otherwise have occurred. A whole stream of events issues from the decision, raising in one's favor all manner of unforeseen incidents and meetings and material assistance which no man could have dreamt would come his way. Whatever you do, or dream you can, begin it. Boldness has genius, power and magic in it. Begin it now.

ATTRIBUTED TO GOETHE

MyCounselingLab™

Visit the MyCounselingLab™ site for *Learning the Art of Helping: Building Blocks and Techniques,* Fifth Edition to enhance your understanding of chapter concepts. You'll have the opportunity to practice your skills through video- and case-based Assignments and Activities as well as Building Counseling Skills units, and to prepare for your certification exam with Practice for Certification quizzes.

I have always had Goethe's quote hanging in my office because it reminds me that my job is all about the power of new beginnings. If we are to really help, not only must we understand a client's problems, but we must also decrease demoralization and ignite hope. Identifying and achieving goals help the client gain confidence even if the objectives are rather modest. If one can achieve a small goal, then discouragement, the biggest enemy of change, is diminished (Frank & Frank, 1991).

Goal setting separates the tangled mass of a problem into manageable units. Once a few goals have been identified, helping has a focus and the client begins to see the light at the end of the tunnel. Hope begins to dawn because the client now views the amorphous mass of trouble as a set of solvable problems. Figure 10.1 shows the client's difficulties as they

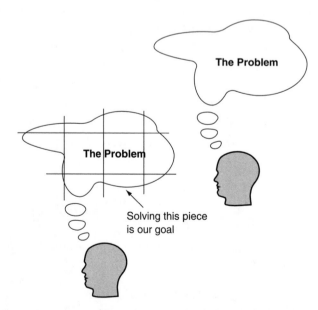

FIGURE 10.1 Breaking the Problem into Parcels and Working on One Part

first appear in the opening sessions and later after the assessment and goal-setting stages. Through this process, the intangible cloud of problems has been broken into identifiable segments.

The second reason I like Goethe's quote is that it reminds me that commitment is required for success. To use an analogy, frequently clients have started a number of dry holes in their life, never sticking with something but trying many different solutions, digging several shallow holes. If you commit to a goal, you are digging deeply in the same place, and you will eventually hit water.

By setting goals and sticking to them, the helper mobilizes the magic of the beginning and also receives the benefit of persistence. Thus, every helping session should focus on the client's goals. When every session begins with a review of goals, the client is much more likely to think about those goals and to work on them between sessions. In this chapter, you will be learning about when to set goals and how to know if the goals you and your client devise are constructive. In addition, we will look at two building block skills that narrow the discussion and help client and counselor identify the key issues, which are (1) focusing on the client and (2) boiling down the problem.

WHERE DO I GO FROM HERE? SET GOALS!

At this point in training, many students make the following statement: "I seem to be able to empathize with the client through the nonjudgmental listening cycle, but where do I go from here?" The helper feels that after a session or two, he or she has exhausted the client's story and explored the client's distress, but the helper does not feel that he or she has really helped. More than ever, the helper is tempted to give the client advice or introduce a new technique of some kind. The best answer to the question "Where do I go now?" is "Set goals!" When you have set goals, the techniques that you choose will make sense to the client. Much of the confusion about the purpose of the helping sessions will be alleviated. If these goals are mutually formed, the client will feel that he or she is part of the team and a partner in the therapeutic project. Partners are much more likely to make contributions than patients.

Why Must We Set Goals?

Steve de Shazer says that one of the most important questions a helper can ask is, "How will we know when we are done?" (de Shazer, 1990). This question can be answered in several ways. Some helpers use a time-limited approach, where the client attends for a certain amount of time or a specific number of sessions. Helping is finished when the time is up, typically between 6 and 20 sessions (Grayson, 1979). One of the reasons that time limits help, as Ben Johnson pointed out, is that the threat of execution tends to focus the mind. Setting a date for termination of the relationship motivates helper and client to work quickly to solve problems.

The problem with the time-limited approach is that we terminate the relationship regardless of success or failure. On the other hand, allowing the client to discontinue the helping process unilaterally makes the process seem haphazard as the relationship just peters out. If we have formulated goals at the beginning of the helping relationship, client and helper will have a shared vision throughout the relationship and will know when it is time to end. The best measure of whether the work is done is to determine whether the treatment goals have been reached. In a later chapter, we discuss issues associated with termination.

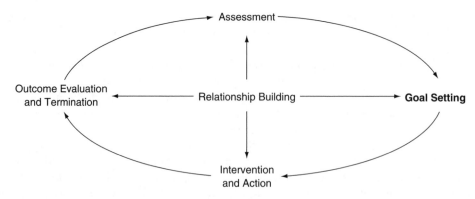

FIGURE 10.2 The Counseling Relationship: Goal Setting

When to Set Goals

Certainly goal setting can be entered into prematurely when you have neither the client's trust nor a clear understanding of the problems. First, the helper must establish a relationship and conduct a thorough assessment. We have said that helping progresses through five basic stages, as shown in Figure 10.2. At the initial relationship-building stage, most of the helper's activities are based on the invitational, reflecting, and challenging skills, which invite the client to open up and engage in self-examination within the confiding relationship. Early in the relationship, the helper does not narrow the field of discussion, but dares the client to go deeper and disclose more about a number of topics. In the assessment stage, the helper gets in-depth information about the client, the client's problems, and the environment. Without this knowledge, the goals might turn out to be irrelevant or efforts ineffective if the client is not motivated, is being influenced by others, or is in a nonsupportive environment. As was mentioned in the last chapter, hidden areas of a client's life might not come to light without a thorough look at the client's history. These secrets, such as substance abuse, could seriously undermine the therapeutic plans.

While invitational and reflecting skills encourage clients to open up and assessment provides crucial data, the skills of the goal-setting stage are methods for narrowing down the information into a few specific tasks and goals. In other words, helping begins with wide-ranging discussions, but eventually it narrows to focus on some particular areas. Goal setting is the stage when the helper begins to change the focus of counseling sessions from the introduction of new topics and assessment to the identification of the most crucial issues to be addressed in later sessions.

WHAT ARE THE CHARACTERISTICS OF CONSTRUCTIVE GOALS?

This section is an argument for selecting goals that are specific, simple, stated positively (reflecting the presence of something rather than the absence of something), important, collaboratively developed, and realistic. Each of the following sections covers one of these topics, and each contains a set of questions or statements the helper can use to refine the goal with a client.

Goals Should Be Specific

Before a client and helper can agree on goals, the client must be questioned about which goals he or she wants to work on. Unfortunately, some clients have difficulty in selecting clear projects. Their goals when stated are vague and elusive (Rule, 1982), as in this type of client statement: "I don't really know what's wrong; it's just that I am uneasy with everything," or, "I haven't been feeling right for about a year." A specific, clear, and easily restated goal sounds more like this: "I want to be able to be more assertive with my friends and coworkers."

When clients have clear goals, they make better progress (Borelli & Mermelstein, 1994; Hart, 1978). For example, having specific goals, even if they are difficult, is more likely to lead to progress than having fuzzy goals in the form of suggestions that you "do your best" or having no goals at all (Ponte-Allan & Giles, 1999; Smith, Hauenstein, & Buchanan, 1996). Specific goals make the direction of the helping process clear to the client. Clients then begin to feel that they have a handle on how to begin making changes. The client who is clear about goals will be able to work on them in and out of session.

It is not only clients who have trouble setting goals. For one reason or another, some helpers prefer to focus on the process of helping, letting the client deal with issues as they arise, rather than establishing landmarks of progress. This book argues that helping has changed radically in the last decade. Nearly all helping is brief. Focusing on specific issues allows helpers to make the best use of therapeutic time. Besides these general advantages, at least five other favorable outcomes accrue from negotiating specific goal statements:

1. When based on specific individual goals for the client, the helping process is more likely to be aimed at the client's needs rather than derived from the helper's theoretical orientation alone. A client who has the goal of overcoming shyness in work situations will perceive this as more relevant than "becoming self-actualized."
2. When goals are clearly understood by client and helper, the helper can determine if he or she possesses the requisite skills to continue with the counseling or if a referral is needed. Sometimes it is only during the goal-setting process that the helper realizes that the client needs some specialized assistance such as sex therapy, couples counseling, or substance abuse treatment.
3. Many clients have problems imagining or envisioning success. Thinking about and imagining specific, positive outcomes have the effect of focusing the client's resources and energies and increasing hope. For this reason, goals that are stated positively such as the acquisition of skills are considered to be more useful than goals that are only focused on eliminating a negative behavior.
4. Identifying specific goals provides a rational basis for selecting treatment strategies that agencies, third-party providers, and supervisors can understand. Specific goals reassure others that the outcomes of helping will result in measurable changes.
5. Specific goals enable helpers to determine how successful helping has been for the client. Goal statements allow the client to gauge their progress as helping progresses. At termination, the helper can realistically evaluate the client's achievements.

INTERVENTIONS TO HELP A CLIENT MAKE A GOAL MORE SPECIFIC The following are helper statements that might help a client transform a vague goal into a clear objective:

- "I understand that you want to be 'happy,' but if you were happy, what would you be doing that you are not doing now?"

- "When you say things are not going well, specifically what things are you talking about?"
- "You say you want things to be better in your relationship with your husband. Specifically what would you like to be better?"
- "You have said that you want higher self-esteem. How would you like to see yourself exactly?"
- "Once you said that you live in the past. Where would you like to live?"

Goals Should Be Stated Positively

Frequently you will hear clients say they want to get over depression, stop drinking, stop binging on food, stop feeling anxious in social situations, reduce arguing, and so on. When goals are stated as negatives, they have less power to influence and motivate us. For example, I have heard it said that the goal of Alcoholics Anonymous is not "stopping drinking." AA's goal is to help people lead happy lives without alcohol. If you think about it, if we focus all our attention on "not drinking," we are still focusing on drinking! Instead, setting a goal to lead a happy life without alcohol allows us to consider what things we would like to have in our lives, what people we would like to interact with, and many other possible futures.

Another way of looking at this is that the helper should try to turn problems into goals. It seems like a small difference, but it would be much better to develop a list of goals than a list of problems. Although we must be willing to understand what problems brought a client for help, we should eventually focus on where we want to go. We spend too much time mapping the prison and too little time planning our escape. When a clear vision of success is formulated, it is easier to see the steps needed to attain it (O'Hanlon & Weiner-Davis, 1989). Below is a list of client problems and then a goal that a client might pursue.

Client Problem	Changed to a Goal
Shyness	I will be able to meet people and operate comfortably in social situations.
Low self-esteem	I will be able to develop a list of positive mental sentences and encourage myself when needed.
Feelings of hopelessness	I will pay attention to signs of hope and recognize that the negative feelings are fleeting. I will be able to ignore negative thoughts and dispute them so that feelings of hopelessness are prevented.
Nervousness	I will be able to calm myself in anxiety provoking situations by relaxing. I will be able to recognize nervousness as a normal reaction and give myself positive messages to help cope with these feelings.

QUESTIONS TO HELP A CLIENT TURN A PROBLEM INTO A GOAL   We are now seeing that questions can be more complex than the open and closed varieties we discussed in an earlier chapter. These questions can be used to focus away from the problem and onto a future without the problem.

- "If a miracle occurred while you were asleep and during the night your problem just vanished, what would be some of the things you would first notice that let you know that the problem had disappeared?" (the miracle question) (O'Hanlon & Weiner-Davis, 1989).

• "You say that you and your husband argue constantly. If you were not arguing, what would you like to be doing?"
• "If the problem were solved, what would you be feeling, doing, or thinking that you are not now?"
• "If you were not procrastinating, what kinds of things would you be doing to get your work in on time?"
• "Suppose I gave you a job with all the money, benefits, and resources you required. Think about this for a moment and design your own job. Where would it be? With whom would you be working, and what would you be doing?" (Beck & Hoppock, 1998).

Goals Should Be Simple

A rule of thumb in developing a goal is that it should be extremely simple, so simple that "an eight-year-old could understand it" (Steiner, 1976). Developing simple goals that have a high probability of success is especially important when the client is demoralized. Whenever small goals are achieved, the client will be encouraged to continue with more difficult or more time-consuming projects (Dyer & Vriend, 1977). As the famous therapist Milton Erickson once said, "Therapy is often a matter of tipping the first domino" (Rossi, 1980, p. 454).

Many agencies require that helpers set quantifiable behavioral goals. Behavioral goals are concrete, measurable, and observable. They indicate the client's current behavior (baseline) and the target or goal behaviors that represent success. Here is an example of how you can develop a behavioral goal:

Client's Stated Goal (Client's Description of the Goal) The client would like to increase comfort and decrease anxiety in social situations. The client's job entails several social functions each week, and they are necessary for his employment.

Target Behaviors (Described in Frequency, Duration, and Intensity) The client would like to be able to attend a social gathering, hold two or more conversations (frequency), at least one of these with a woman, stay for a period of more than 1 hour (duration), and maintain a subjective distress level (SUDS) of 3 or 4. (The SUDS level is the client's feelings of discomfort in the situation and is measured on a 10-point scale of intensity, with 10 being the most uncomfortable and 1 being mildly uncomfortable.)

Baseline (Current Level of Target Behaviors) The client states that he can currently remain at a party for only about 15 minutes before he leaves. He can hold a brief conversation with a male co-worker, but has not recently talked to a woman in this setting. He currently experiences a SUDS level of 8 or 9 during social conversations with any woman.

Behavioral goals have advantages in that they specify exactly what must be achieved in the helping process. Many helpers will be required to set behavioral goals at their place of work because agencies use the numbers to quantify success. Other agencies look at goal attainment in other ways, including client feedback forms and helper and reduction in symptoms. Even when helping goals are not quantifiable, they can still be simple and concrete (Goodyear & Bradley, 1986). For example, the helper might not want to accept the following goal: "I want to improve my relationship with my mother." The helper might be willing, though, to accept the following revision: "Well, I would like to be able to politely stop her when she starts trying to give me advice." Whether goals are described behaviorally or not, simple goals make it easier for both helper and client to identify when helping is on the right track.

QUESTIONS TO HELP SIMPLIFY A GOAL   The questions that simplify a goal are those that try to pin a client down to specific behaviors that the client would like to achieve and that would demonstrate success in a way that would be recognizable. For example:

- *Client's Goal:* "To decrease stress in my life."

Helper's questions:
- "What activities would help you reduce stress?"
- "How often would you like to engage in stress-reducing activities?"
- "How long would you like to meditate?"
- "If your stress level at work is a 10 now, what level of stress would represent an improvement to you?"

Goals Should Be Important to the Client

Clients will be successful when they are pursuing goals that are important to them (Barbrack & Maher, 1984; Bruce, 1984; Evans, 1984; Goodyear & Bradley, 1986; Hart, 1978; Lee, Uken, & Sebold, 2007; Miller & Rollnick, 1999). It seems obvious that clients will work harder when they are focusing on a goal that really matters to them. However, many people are referred by friends, families, courts, principals, or student judiciary boards to solve problems that the client has little or no interest in solving. In cases where the court orders treatment for a particular problem, neither client nor helper has participated in the goal-setting process, and neither may feel personally involved or motivated to achieve the aims. Clearly, the likelihood of success in these conditions is low. The third-party problem is evident in the example of a client who has been referred by a probation officer following an incestuous relationship. The probation officer wants the client treated for sexual dysfunction to ensure that this kind of thing does not happen again. The client is divorced now and has had no contact with his teenage daughter, the incest victim. At this point, the client's concerns center on forming new relationships and dealing with family members' rejection. He is not willing to rehash the incestuous relationship and is resentful of the helper's intrusions. I use the example of incest because it seems so clear that this client has a problem that needs to be treated, and yet we have little hope of making a difference if the client is not a partner in the process (Ritchie, 1986). Goal setting that involves the client has ethical advantages as well because we are doing not only what we think is best for the client but what the client wants to do as well (Tjeltveit, 2006).

SAMPLE QUESTIONS TO GAUGE A GOAL'S IMPORTANCE   Hidden in each of these questions about a goal's significance is a message from the counselor to the client. The message is, "We need to set goals that make a difference in your life."

- "How likely are you to follow through with this goal?"
- "How important is this goal to you?"

- "If we accomplished this goal, what difference would it make in your life?"
- "How are you likely to talk yourself out of trying to accomplish this goal?"
- "Is this your goal, or is it something other people want you to accomplish?"

Goals Should Be Collaboration between Helper and Client

While helping should focus on what is important to the client, the evidence is clear that when helpers and clients reach consensus and collaborate on goal achievement, the chances of success are greatly enhanced (Tryon & Winograd, 2011). This means that the helper and client have developed a joint project upon which they both agree (Strong, 2009). Still, agreement upon goals is not a one-time event. Throughout the helping process, the best practice is to continually see information from your client about his or her progress and the current relevance of the goals (Tryon & Winograd, 2011).

MORALLY OBJECTIONABLE GOALS   Students often raise the question, "What if the client's goals are morally unacceptable to the helper?" Although helpers are generally nonjudgmental and accepting of differences, there are times when a helper cannot help a client to set and achieve a goal because of personal religious convictions or ethics. For example, many helpers will refuse to take sides in custody cases when they have seen a couple for marriage counseling. Some helpers may not choose to help clients achieve goals related to sexuality, such as sexual preferences or conducting extramarital affairs. Professional helpers inform clients early in the counseling process about issues they will not address, so that the relationship does not develop too far before a referral is needed.

SAMPLE QUESTIONS AND STATEMENTS TO ENHANCE COLLABORATION ON GOAL SETTING

"I believe that it very important that both of us be of the same mind when it comes to the goals we set. That is our best chance for success."

"I believe we both agree on the goals now, do you think so?"

"Can you put the goals we have agreed upon into words so we both are on the same page?"

"How do you think we could work together as a team on your goals?"

"Now that we have set some goals, what additions or corrections do you have to the goals we have agreed on?"

Goals Should Be Realistic

The helper's expertise is important in defining goals when a client has unrealistic aims. Sometimes the client has insufficient information about the self or about the issue. At other times, the client wants to accomplish two incompatible aims. For example, a client recently said, "I want to be better paid at my job, but I don't want to work harder and give up my free time." One method of dealing with unrealistic goals is to confront the client with the discrepancy. Another way is to invite him or her to explore the goal and collect information to see if the goal is really possible. In some cases, it may be necessary for the helper to express doubts about the goal. Consider the following client statements and possible helper responses:

Example 1

HIGH SCHOOL SENIOR: "I don't like science or math, and I am not very good at them. My aptitudes in those areas are not very good, according to the national exams. I want to be a doctor because I need to have a good salary and I want to be respected as a professional."

HELPER: "It sounds like you want the status and the money that being a physician might bring, but you are not sure you have the ability or the interest needed for the training. Perhaps we need to look at both of these things a little closer."

Example 2

CLIENT: "I want to get my girlfriend back. She's living with someone else right now, and she won't even return my calls. She hates me because I was dating other people behind her back while we were going out. I still have a problem with being faithful to one person, but I know if I got her back, we could make it work."

HELPER: "I'm not sure that reuniting with your ex-girlfriend is a realistic goal. For one thing, you say you're having trouble being with only one person, and, second, she is showing no interest in getting back together."

Example 3

CLIENT: "I want to stay married and enjoy the safety and security of the married relationship. Myra and I have a problem with communication, and that is something we can work on. But there is someone else that I am seeing right now. The excitement and romance is something that is missing in my marriage. I can't hurt Myra or the kids by letting it come out in the open. So I have decided to keep it a secret. When Myra and I come in for marriage counseling, I don't want to bring up this other relationship."

HELPER: "I would like to help, but I don't believe you can improve your marital relationship while you are carrying on a secret affair."

When a client is operating with faulty information or is engaging in self-deception, as in the preceding cases, the helper uses challenging skills and helps the client gain self-knowledge or information about the problem that will help him or her set better goals. For example, in the case of the student who wants to be a physician, the helper might help the client gain experience and knowledge of medicine in several ways, including volunteering in a hospital, looking at the courses medical schools offer, and asking physicians directly about how important it is to enjoy and do well in math and science.

Resources for Identifying and Clarifying Goals

Before leaving this discussion about the properties of goals, let us mention some tools that you might use if you are having difficulty identifying goals. These assessment techniques have a common purpose, to assist clients and helpers in evaluating and choosing clear, positive goals.

1. Personal Projects Analysis (Little, Salmela-Aro, & Phillips, 2007; Salmela-Aro, 1992). Personal projects analysis is a fascinating system for analyzing and selecting one's own personal goals. These goals may range from "being a better husband" to "improving my score on a video game." Using a template, you select goals that you want to work on and then evaluate them based on their importance to you, the emotions involved, the effect on others, and other categories. For more information see http://www.brianrlittle.com.
2. Identifying and Measuring Positive Life Goals.
   a. A measure to elicit positive future goals and plans (see Vincent, Boddana, & MacLeod, 2004).
   b. The Self-Development Project List–90 (Braaten, 1989).
3. Measures That Help in Finding and Monitoring Goals for Counseling and Psychotherapy.
   a. Simplified Target Complaints Measure (Deane, Spicer, & Todd, 1997).
   b. Bern Inventory of Treatment Goals (Berking, Holtforth, Jacobi, & Kroner-Herwig, 2005).

STOP AND REFLECT

There is a saying among career- and life-planning counselors that if you do not know where you are going, you will arrive somewhere else. The meaning is that if we do not set goals for our lives, other factors besides our own plans will intervene. A well-known football coach, Lou Holtz, has said, "Write down everything you hope to achieve in life, then make sure you do something every day to realize one of your dreams. You are going to encounter adversity but you will also . . . take big, satisfying bites out of life" (1998). Holtz set several hundred personal goals over 20 years ago. Recently he indicated that he had completed over three-fourths of them. Think about the following areas of your own life and write down a goal under each heading that you would like to accomplish in the next 5 to 10 years:

1. A job I would like to have:
2. A project I would like to be involved in:
3. The kind of friendship or intimate relationship I would like to develop:
4. An area of learning I would like to master or a formal degree program I would like to complete:
5. A hobby or interest I would like to develop:
6. A way I would like to improve myself:

   Next evaluate each of the goals that you have identified according to the following criteria:

a. Is the goal specific?
b. Is the goal stated in positive terms?

(Continued)

    c. Is the goal simple enough for an 8-year-old to understand?
    d. How motivated are you to accomplish the goal?
    e. Is the goal realistic considering your abilities?

- Choose one of the goals that appears to meet some or all of the preceding criteria and rewrite it in a simple, specific sentence or two. List the steps you must go through to accomplish this goal.
- As you look at the steps that you have identified, does the goal seem more manageable or more difficult now that it has been broken down into parts?
- Discuss this exercise with a friend who knows you well. Ask him or her to evaluate the goal as to how realistic it is and how clearly it is stated.

WHO OWNS THE PROBLEM? THE TECHNIQUE OF FOCUSING ON THE CLIENT

Thomas Gordon (1975) suggested that helpers think about a key question as they help clients set goals: Who owns the problem? The question can be most clearly answered by determining who is emotionally upset by the problem. The emotional reaction not only provides the motivation to seek help, but acts as a red flag for the helper by identifying the person most affected. For example, if both members of a couple are unhappy with the relationship, the couple will "own" the relationship problem and may seek counseling together. On the other hand, the man who complains about his employer's stinginess "owns" the problem and must decide how to solve the problem by seeking another job, becoming more assertive, or modifying his feelings and perceptions to better handle the situation. It is unlikely that the employer "owns" the problem, since he or she is probably not upset by stinginess toward others.

How to Focus on the Client

A recent cartoon depicted a couple coming to their first counseling session. As they sit before the counselor, you can see the wife thinking, "Now, the counselor will find out how crazy he really is!" Meanwhile, the husband is thinking the same thing about her. As we discussed in the example of alcoholism in the family, one of the major issues we face in dealing with clients is getting them to deal with issues that they can control and trying to coax them to give up on the project of reforming others. The technique of focusing on the client is the skill of asking the client to take responsibility and ownership for his or her problems, rather than trying to convert everyone else. Nearly all major theoretical orientations agree that effective helping involves empowering clients to change themselves. The skill of focusing on the client is the elementary method for shifting the focus away from others and the environment and onto the issues that the client owns. The following is an example of a helper who has been seduced into listening to Bradley's story—a story that seems to point out that Bradley's life would be better if only others or the world would change:

    BRADLEY: "With the economic slowdown and my bills, I can't change jobs right now, no matter how angry I get with my boss."

    HELPER: "Your boss makes the job miserable, but you can't leave because of money. You don't have many options right now." (Here, the helper is paraphrasing with a focus on others and the environment. This may be less useful because the helper is buying into the client's pessimism and external focus.)

BRADLEY: "Yeah, my boss is a jerk, and all around me I see other people getting ahead because either they have connections or maybe they have a boss who helps them."

HELPER: "You feel angry because your boss is unfair." (Here the helper is reflecting feelings with a focus on others and the environment. He has tacitly agreed to the client's viewpoint about his boss.)

BRADLEY: "Yeah, sometimes I get pretty steamed when he starts criticizing everyone."

HELPER: "What does the boss do that makes you angry?" (Here the helper asks a closed question, with a focus on others as the cause of Bradley's anger. The helper has agreed that the boss is the cause of the client's anger.)

BRADLEY: "He is always on me, micromanaging my work and he never has a good word to say."

This dialogue may seem exaggerated, but, in fact, it is typical of what can occur when the helper keeps the focus on external issues such as the boss and the economy. When the client responses center on others or the environment, he or she becomes dispirited and disempowered and does not gain any personal awareness of emotions or engage in thoughtful self-examination. In effect, when the helper asks the client to focus on others or the environment, the helper is agreeing that other people or external events are the cause of the client's problems.

On the other hand, focusing on the client is empowering and prevents the client from blaming other people and external circumstances, a time-draining sidetrack. Focusing on the client does not encourage passive acceptance of the behavior of others or the vicissitudes of life; rather, it challenges the client to become responsible for his or her own happiness and do something to change the world.

Let us take a look at how the dialogue with Bradley might be handled, this time keeping the focus on the client. Note that keeping the focus on the client is a general technique that uses many of the skills you have already learned, including reflecting feelings, asking questions, and reflecting meaning.

BRADLEY: "With the economic slowdown and my bills, I can't change jobs right now, no matter how angry I get with my boss."

HELPER: "It is a difficult situation you find yourself in, caught up in a stressful situation at work, financial pressure, and fewer job opportunities." (Here the helper is paraphrasing with a focus on the client. By paraphrasing, the helper is acknowledging that life is not easy right now.)

BRADLEY: "I really hate my job, but I need the money. One thing I would like to work on is getting rid of some of my bills so that I have more freedom."

HELPER: "You feel trapped in your job right now, and you're experiencing stress from financial problems, too." (Here the helper is reflecting feelings with a focus on the client. Note that "You feel trapped" is different from "You are trapped," which suggests an external locus of control.)

BRADLEY: "I don't feel like I have one place in my life where things are calm and going right. I feel like everything is out of control."

HELPER: "It's always been important for you to feel that you have a handle on things. Now, without that, you can't seem to find many peaceful moments." (Here the helper is reflecting meaning with a focus on the client.)

BRADLEY: "It's hard to feel in control when everyone else is putting pressure on you. I go from one pressure cooker to the next."

HELPER: "In what part of your life do you experience the most pressure?" (Here the helper asks a closed question with a focus on the client. The client is urged to think about which problem pinches the most. The purpose is goal setting.)

BRADLEY: "I have a big car payment, student loans, and a lot of credit card bills."

Can you see that with these interventions the helper is keeping the focus on the client as the one who needs to make decisions and deal with the pressure? The helper acknowledges that external forces are at work and that they affect the client's decisions, but by keeping the focus on the client, the helper indicates that the client can be the one who does something about the situation. Focusing on the client rather than on other people and circumstances leads in a more productive and positive direction, with more client self-examination and empowerment.

THE TECHNIQUE OF BOILING DOWN THE PROBLEM

Earlier we identified some of the characteristics of constructive goals. Goals should be specific, stated positively, simple, important to the client, agreed upon collaboratively and realistic. As you might expect, though, clients do not normally arrive with clearly defined questions and problems. More often, they present tangled stories of feelings, people, and events that spiral in different directions. At some point, the helper must choose areas to develop and others to set aside for the moment. Just sorting the work into "piles" or cutting the job into "pieces" reduces client anxiety and offers fresh hope. Most of us are aware of the experience of motivation and relief that accompanies making a to-do list when we feel overwhelmed. Similarly, clients need to narrow down the list of issues and focus on one or two to begin with.

One therapist used to say to clients, "Well, we've chased a lot of rabbits out of the bush; now let's track down one or two of them." This metaphor worked well to signal that a more specific focus was needed. Boiling down the problem is also a metaphor for this process. First, the client is encouraged to open up, and then specific issues are identified and evaluated. Finally, the list is narrowed to a couple of the most critical. The steps in boiling down the problem are as follows:

Step 1: Summarizing and enumerating all the issues.   The helper uses summaries, reflecting skills, and paraphrasing to determine agreement on the overall content of the counseling session to this point.

> HELPER: "So let me pull this together a little. You're living at home and feel embarrassed because you think that you should be out on your own. The man you have been dating for a year has called it quits, and in the middle of all this upset, your teenage sister is causing turmoil in the home. Meanwhile your mother's illness worries you. You're feeling overwhelmed since everything has happened at once."
>
> TRICIA: "That's about it. I'm living at home. My life is going nowhere, and right now everyone needs me to be strong."

Step 2: Asking the client to identify the most crucial problems.   Next the helper uses one or more closed questions to ask the client to evaluate which problems are the most critical, thereby narrowing down the number of issues to be addressed.

> HELPER: "I realize that all these issues—your mother's health, your sister's problems, getting over your boyfriend, and becoming financially able to have your own place—are important issues to you. Of these, which do you think are the most critical and are ones that we can deal with in these sessions?"
>
> TRICIA: "There is nothing I can do about my mother's illness, and, unfortunately, there is not much I can do about my sister, either. But I want to get on my feet financially and emotionally. I need help in thinking about where I am going in my career so I can earn enough to live on, and I've got to think about how I am going to make it through the next few months without my boyfriend. I need to focus on myself for a little while."

Step 3: Selecting the focal problem.   In this activity, the helper uses a mental checklist to evaluate client goals and advocates for those that are:

- Specific
- Simple and easily restated
- Important to the client
- Mutually agreed upon by helper and client
- Realistic

> HELPER: "So it sounds like one of the emergency issues is to help you find some ways to take care of yourself emotionally so that you can cope with your loss. At the same time, you want to look at the future a little bit, too. You want to explore some career ideas."
>
> TRICIA: "I know I can get some help with the career thing. You've already offered to do the tests and talk about that. The main thing is how I can deal with my angry and depressed feelings all the time. I am bored and angry and alone. I feel like a baby."

Step 4: Changing the problem to a goal.   In this step, the helper encourages the client to think about success. What will the problem look like when it is solved? This step helps us make sure that the goal is stated positively, one of the criteria for constructive goals.

HELPER: "You have told me that you are in a lot of distress about losing your boyfriend, and we have discussed that topic pretty thoroughly. As you think about the future, I wonder if you can envision your life when this is no longer a problem. What would you be doing then that you are not doing now? What would you be feeling and thinking?"

TRICIA: "I would be going out with my friends and enjoying life again. I wouldn't be thinking about him all the time, sitting there waiting for him to call. I would be able to concentrate at work."

HELPER: "So these are the goals that you would like to work toward."

TRICIA: "Sure!"

Step 5: Making sure client and helper are clear and in agreement.   Here the helper summarizes the mutually agreed-upon goals. In addition, the helper may ask the client to state them aloud or write them down, so that the agreement is clear. At this point, clients often need encouragement and a message from the helper that the goals are reachable.

HELPER: "Let's see if I can restate them: You would like to go out with friends and enjoy life again, instead of spending so much time thinking about your ex-boyfriend. Is that about right?"

TRICIA: "Yes, but it is not that easy."

HELPER: "I agree. It won't be easy. Are we on the right track though? Are these your goals?"

TRICIA: "Yes."

HELPER: "Would you mind restating the goals as we talked about them so that I am sure we are both operating with the same understanding?"

TRICIA: "Okay, I am going to find a way to have fun again and spend time with friends again."

HELPER: "Like you said, it won't be easy, but I am confident that you can make this happen. Let's talk some more about how you can actually go about making this happen."

CONSTRUCTING MEASURABLE GOALS

After you have boiled down the problem to a specific issue, you may want to set measurable goals. Breaking down complex goals into measurable units is not always necessary but sometimes your workplace may require it. Moreover, by using measurable goals, the client gains hope as they see the problem fading. For example, if you were trying to lose weight, you might weigh yourself regularly or measure your waistline. Unless you audit the problem regularly, you will not know if you are gaining or losing weight. You will not know if giving up desserts is enough to shrink your middle. Thus, implicit in setting measurable goals is the idea that you need to monitor the goal regularly to see if progress is being made. Sometimes it is difficult in the psychological realm to identify measurable goals because the goal is a change in thinking; however, there are resources if you get stuck. A number of books are available that can help you find reasonable goals for all sorts of problems. For example, the *Child Psychotherapy Treatment Planner* by Jongsma, Peterson, and McInnis (2000) lists a variety of problems that the helper might have identified during assessment, including depression, fire setting, low-self esteem, and school refusal. The process of developing a measurable goal is to think about what you hope to achieve, how you will measure it, how you will know when success is achieved, and the approximate time frame. Here is a list of key questions to help you think about a goal and how to make it measurable:

- What are the goals you are hoping to achieve?

  What intended behavior, knowledge, or skill changes should result from the treatment?

  Example: "The couple's goal is to improve their communication."

- How will a client's progress be measured?

  What data will we use to gauge progress? Will it be from a test; the number of times a client attempts a certain behavior; the frequency, duration, or intensity of a symptom that you want to increase or reduce?

  Example: The couple will demonstrate improved communication skills by decreasing the number of "communication roadblocks." This will be assessed during a conversation the couple will hold in the first ten minutes of the session.

- How will the success level be determined?

  Success level is the point at which the short-term or long-term goal is achieved.

  Example: "The couple will be considered to be proficient in the listening technique when they can conduct a 10-minute discussion during which each partner talks and no roadblocks are noted by the observer. Their current average is three roadblocks per 10-minute session."

- When will the outcome occur?

  Identify the time frame when success is expected.

  Example: "Within six sessions, the couple will reduce 'roadblocks' to zero."

Long-Term and Short-Term Goals

You can probably see that improving a couple's interaction might be more complex than just decreasing the "roadblocks to communication." It might also mean helping them learn to deal with conflict, express feelings, and accomplish several other subgoals. These short-term goals are all in the service of the larger goal we called "improved communication." These short-term goals might not seem important by themselves. For example, a short-term goal might be to weigh myself each night, but when combined with other short-term goals (such as eating less and exercising more), the larger goal of weight reduction is served. To see how this works, take a look at the long-term and short-term goals of a client who suffers from social anxiety and becomes very nervous when she has to meet or perform in front of others. This includes things such as signing her name at the bank or accepting a glass of water from a friend. When required to do these things, she begins to shake and tells herself she is abnormal. Ultimately the client wants to be able to speak to a group of her colleagues at a staff meeting. To achieve this long-term goal, she broke it down into smaller steps (short-term goals) and finally into specific measurable goals:

> Long-Term Goal: Present a proposal at a staff meeting.
>> Short-Term Goal 1: Be able to talk with people around the office.
>> Short-Term Goal 2: Make a presentation to a friend or family member about a topic at work for 5 minutes.

Here are some other examples of measurable goals that a person with social anxiety might set:

> "Purchase something at a store and then return it."
> "Decrease my negative self-talk."
> "Politely disagree with someone."
> "Sign my name once in front of family members."

Note that in these examples of goals, the exact method of how they will be achieved is not specified. That occurs in the next step of the helping process, called Intervention and Action. At this stage, the client is encouraged to set goals that can be achieved and measured.

MyCounselingLab™

Go to Topic 4, *Formulating Goals*, on the MyCounselingLab™ site (www.MyCounselingLab.com) for *Learning the Art of Helping: Building Blocks and Techniques*, Fifth Edition, where you can:

- Find learning outcomes for *Formulating Goals* along with the national standards that connect to these outcomes.
- Complete Assignments and Activities that can help you more deeply understand the chapter content.
- Apply and practice your understanding of the core skills identified in the chapter with the Building Counseling Skills unit.
- Prepare yourself for professional certification with a Practice for Certification quiz.
- Connect to videos through the Video and Resource Library.

MyCounselingLab™ Exercises

Go to the Video and Resource Library on the MyCounselingLab™ site for your text and search for the following clip: *Goal Setting: Linda, Goal Setting: Dayle, Goal Setting: Samir*, and *Listening Cycle*. Watch the videos and answer the following questions.

Exercise 1: Boiling Down the Problem

The video *Goal Setting: Linda* shows Linda, the helper, working with her client, Jennifer. Linda rather rapidly moves through the five stages of boiling down the problem. Can you identify Linda's statements that sequentially take the client through these steps?

Step 1: Summarizing and Enumerating All the Issues
Step 2: Asking the Client to Identify the Most Crucial Problem
Step 3: Selecting the Focal Problem
Step 4: Changing the Problem to a Goal
Step 5: Making Sure Client and Helper Are Clear and in Agreement

Exercise 2: Goal Setting

In *Goal Setting: Dayle*, Dayle talks to Dyan about her struggle with finding enough time to spend with everyone she cares about. As you view the video, answer the following questions:

1. What does Dayle identify as the main issue that worries Dyan?
2. What does Dayle say that gets Dyan to think about what the future would be like without the problem (changing the problem to a goal)?
3. The client finally articulates something that sounds like a fairly clear goal at the end of the session. What is the goal?

Exercise 3: Nonjudgmental Listening Cycle

For this exercise, go to MyCounselingLab˜ and find the video called, *Goal Setting: Samir*, in which John talks to Samir, the helper. Although this interview does not neatly show the five steps of boiling down the problem, there are two aspects that it demonstrates very well. Samir is able to get the client to **change the problem into a goal** and to **select a focal problem.**

1. See if you can determine the point on the video where Samir helps the client identify a goal by thinking about the future.
2. Indicate a time or two where Samir tries to get the client to identify a focal problem.
3. What does the client eventually state as a goal?
4. At the beginning and later on the client mentions another goal to Samir that is not really encompassed by the goal of getting some "me time." What is it?

Exercise 4: Keeping the Focus on the Client

In the video *Listening Cycle*, Mark (the helper) attempts to keep the focus on the client, Anna, rather than her boyfriend.

1. List one helper statement that keeps the client focused on herself when the conversation could easily have moved to a discussion of her boyfriend's insensitivity.
2. Do you think that it would have been productive to say, "It sounds like your boyfriend doesn't try to make you feel comfortable at these parties"? Why or why not?

Summary

In this chapter, we have provided the following guidelines about appropriate goals: They should be specific, positively stated, simple, realistic, important to the client, and set collaboratively between helper and client. In order to reach workable goals, we identified two methods: keeping the focus on the client and "Boiling Down the Problem." Keeping the focus means centering our efforts on problems that the client "owns." This eliminates trying to change other people not in the session and keeps the session from meandering into fruitless areas. "Boiling Down the Problem" is the step-by-step process for deconstructing a larger problem and targeting the most important aspects. This can also be helpful when it is necessary to construct measurable goals.

Not all helpers agree that goal setting should be such an integral part of the helping process. We have tried to argue that goals provide structure for helper and that identifying goals makes problems seem manageable. When helper and client agree upon the goals they will know when it is time to end the helping relationship is at an end. They are also creating a vision of success that will guide and motivate them.

Exercises

GROUP EXERCISES

Exercise 1: Boiling Down the Problem

The purpose of this exercise is to practice the process of boiling down the problem to a workable agreement between helper and client. The activity involves a helper and client and one or two observers.

To complete this exercise in a short period of time, the helper and client should spend only a little time of the interview (perhaps 5 minutes) on the invitational and reflecting skills—just enough to enable the helper to understand the basics of the problem. The helper should then jump immediately into a discussion of goals. While client and helper are engaged in goal setting, one observer (see "Instructions to Observer 1" below) can write down any of the helper's interventions that seem to help the client in setting the goal. A second observer (see "Instructions to Observer 2" below) writes down the final goal verbatim and facilitates a discussion about how closely the goal matches the ideal characteristics.

Part I: Instructions to Observer 1

Record what you believe are the key statements by the helper that help the client boil down the goal to a workable contract.

1. _____
2. _____
3. _____
4. _____
5. _____

Part II: Instructions to Observer 2

In the space provided, write down your understanding of the goal finally arrived at by client and helper.

Read this to the client and helper to determine if your articulation of the goal is accurate. Then give the helper feedback on how closely the goal matches the following characteristics. Is the goal:

- Specific?
- Positively stated? (the presence of something versus the absence of something)
- Simple?
- One that the client is motivated to achieve?
- Set collaboratively?
- Realistic?

Exercise 2: Keeping the Focus on the Client

Keeping the focus on the client means constantly returning the client to how the problem is affecting him or her. It means identifying which part of the problem the client owns. In this exercise, a group of three students take turns being helper, client and observer. Each client/helper interaction lasts about 10–12 minutes.

ROLE OF THE CLIENT   The client in this situation is asked to use one of the following suggestions as a basis for their role-play character:

- A client who lives with a large extended family and who interfere in the client's life
- A client who has had a number of serious relationships, none of which have been successful,

and the client is trying to find out what is wrong with the people he or she has dated.

* A client who tells a number of stories all of which involve how other people have taken advantage of the client in business relationships, financially, in familial situations, and so on.

Unlike most exercises in this book, here the client is not being cooperative and instead continually focuses on external factors through storytelling.

ROLE OF THE HELPER   The role of the counselor in this exercise is to continually try to return the focus to how the problem is affecting the client or what the client can do about it. For example, if the client goes off on a tirade about the inadequacies of the boss at work, the helper paraphrases, reflects feelings or meanings or asks a question that keeps the focus on the client. Here are some examples:

1. As you see it, your work situation has deteriorated and it's no longer a happy place to work. (paraphrase)
2. You feel discouraged because whatever you do, nothing seems to change. (reflection of feelings)
3. Losing your good relationship with your boss was upsetting because you relied on him, not just at work, but as a friend. (reflection of meaning)
4. What effect has this new vision of your boss had on your attitude about work? (question)

ROLE OF OBSERVER   In this exercise the observer's job is to write down the helper's comments and review them following the role play. Together client, helper, and observer identify those comments that kept the focus on the client.

SMALL GROUP DISCUSSIONS

Discussion 1: Constructing Measurable Goals

In a small group, see if you can set one measurable goal for each of these clients. Use the guidelines given earlier in the chapter. To do so, you may have to invent some additional details.

1. Jack, age 11, is doing poorly in school, and his grades have dropped to "Ds." He has difficulty paying attention for long periods and often gets out of his chair at inappropriate times. Jack says that he does not want to get into so much trouble in class and get at least "B" grades at school.
2. Mike came to see his helper due to problems managing his anger. He loses his temper with his wife, often yelling at her during disagreements over minor issues. His wife is considering separation. Mike wants to learn anger management and conflict resolution skills.

Discussion 2: Ethical Issues in Setting Goals

There is an ethical principle that suggests we should respect a client's *autonomy* or ability to decide for themselves what treatment to receive and what choices to make (Kitchener, 1984). Some helpers believe that no one should be forced by the legal system or those in authority. In your small group, discuss whether the helper has the right to set goals for the client. What if the person is ordered into treatment by a judge for a particular problem such as alcoholism or domestic violence? What is the ethical thing to do in such situations?

WRITTEN EXERCISES

Exercise: Focusing on the Client

In the helper/client interview, one of the mistakes beginners make is to ask too many closed questions that focus on others and the environment. Examine the client situations listed here and formulate one question or reflection (paraphrase or reflection of feeling) that focuses on the client and another that would take the client off track.

1. High school student: "I don't know where I am going with my life. My grades are good enough to get into college, and my parents want me to go. But I am more interested in music. My music teacher thinks I should go that route. What do you think?"

   Client Focus: _____

   Other Focus: _____

2. Student who doesn't do homework: "In study hall, it's too distracting. There are these three guys who sit next to me, and all they do is talk. The teacher doesn't even try to stop them. I never have time to do it at home. My parents have a lot of chores for me."

   Client Focus: _____

   Other Focus: _____

3. Parent of a teenager: "He smokes pot continually. I am caught between him and his father. I found some pot under his bed. He says that he is not smoking now, and I am afraid to tell his father.

He will blow up. What am I going to do about his drug problem?"

Client Focus: _____

Other Focus: _____

4. Client who has accepted a job out of state: "My family is upset with me. They can't see that this is my best chance for success. They want me around to come over for Sunday dinner. I want that, too, but it is so hard to balance these things."

Client Focus: _____

Other Focus: _____

SELF-ASSESSMENT

1. On a scale from 1 to 10 (1 = just beginning and 10 = mastery) indicate how well you think you have developed the skill of keeping the focus on the client. When answering, think about your practice sessions as well as your answers to the exercises in this chapter.

1   2   3   4   5   6   7   8   9   10

Just beginning   *Mastery*

2. Indicate how well you think you are able to narrow the client's story to simpler goals or "boil down" the problem.

1   2   3   4   5   6   7   8   9   10

Just beginning   *Mastery*

3. Now rate yourself on your ability to write constructive goals.

1   2   3   4   5   6   7   8   9   10

Just beginning   *Mastery*

4. State two things you feel that you were able to improve upon this week. Recall feedback from fellow students or instructors and write it down.

Include all feedback even if it does not relate to the skills of this chapter.

5. Which skills are you finding to be the most difficult to understand and practice?

6. Identify two steps you can take to help you improve your skills further. Identify concrete actions you are willing and able to take.

HOMEWORK

Homework 1: Changing a Problem to a Goal

When you are learning to boil down a problem, one aspect that takes practice is changing a problem into a goal. Create two short dialogues between client and helper whereby the client is helped through the five steps of boiling down the problem. The five steps are (1) summarizing all the issues, (2) asking the client to identify the most crucial problems, (3) selecting the focal problem, (4) changing the problem to a goal, and (5) making sure that the client and helper are clear and in agreement. After each dialogue, identify the problem as stated by the client and the goal as reformulated by the helper.

Homework 2: Short-Term and Long-Term Goals

Talk with two friends about their personal goals. See if you can get each friend to identify five short-term and five long-term goals. In a single page, describe your experiences. Which friend has the clearest goals? Be sure to describe the reactions of your friends to this exercise. Do you think that most people have defined their life goals?

JOURNAL STARTERS

Consider a personal problem that is currently troubling you. Respond to the question "How will I know when the problem is gone?" Reflect on what you will be doing differently, what you will be thinking and what others will notice different about you. How will you feel when the problem is gone? Comment on this exercise. Do you think it might be helpful in goal setting for a client to imagine a future without the problem?

Change Techniques

MyCounselingLab™

Visit the MyCounselingLab™ site for *Learning the Art of Helping: Building Blocks and Techniques,* Fifth Edition to enhance your understanding of chapter concepts. You'll have the opportunity to practice your skills through video- and case-based Assignments and Activities as well as Building Counseling Skills units, and to prepare for your certification exam with Practice for Certification quizzes.

In a recent set of television commercials, the Royal Bank of Scotland has adopted the slogan, "Make it happen." In one of these commercials (which you can view online) a group of business people are eating lunch when one of them begins to choke. His companions consider the Heimlich maneuver, but rather than employ it, they discuss the proper pronunciation of "Heimlich" and how the technique is performed. Meanwhile, a nearby diner gets up and performs the Heimlich before the man chokes. Some helping situations might suffer from this same problem—too much talk, too little action. The change techniques presented here and in later chapters are action methods introduced by the helper once goals have been identified and agreed upon. They are the specific tools to combat specific problems. These fundamental interventions spark the client to consider new alternatives, break out of old patterns, and may involve moving out of the zone of comfort and safety. In general, change techniques help the client to "change the viewing" or "change the doing" of the problem (Guterman, 2006; O'Hanlon & Weiner-Davis, 1989).

Properly applied, however, change techniques stimulate clients to work toward resolving their own problems, aid clients in getting in touch with creative ideas, and help them to examine their self-limiting assumptions. When clients begin to focus on solutions, they become more hopeful because they are living in the future rather than ruminating over the past. Thus, change techniques are not merely techniques applied by the helper but also ways of teaching clients how to approach problems.

Change techniques are implemented during the Action and Intervention Stage in the Roadmap of the Helping Process (See Figure 11.1). To use an analogy, these stages are

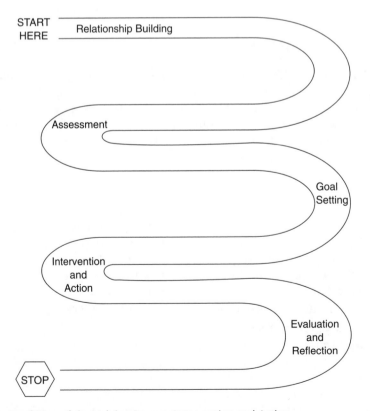

FIGURE 11.1   Road Map of the Helping Process: Intervention and Action

a bit like mountain climbing. Assessment is identifying all of the mountains you want to climb. Goal setting is deciding on which mountain to climb. Change techniques are the means that we use to climb those mountains. In this chapter, we will introduce four new building block skills: giving advice, giving information, brainstorming, and alternate interpretation.

GIVING ADVICE AND INFORMATION

Giving Advice

Like salt, advice is beneficial, but only in the right amount. Giving advice can be crucial in emergency situations such as when a client is engaging in dangerous behavior, like practicing unsafe sex or using drugs, or when a client is being exposed to physical violence.

Because beginning helpers like to give advice too liberally, many teachers ban it outright in the initial stages, and, as a consequence, textbooks often have little to say about it. There is no doubt that it is a complex subject (Couture & Sutherland, 2006). However, because advice giving is rarely addressed, students tend not to be aware of its drawbacks and may find it an easy habit to fall back on. For example, when college students come for counseling, they typically expect advice, and they freely dispense advice to their friends in an attempt to help. They view it as tangible assistance. In fact, advice giving is a veritable minefield. It lures us into thinking that we are actively helping a client. The next section explains some of the reasons for leaving this skill out of your practice sessions for the present. If you have a tendency to give advice, we urge that you consider "retiring" that skill at this point and develop other alternatives.

WHY ARE PROFESSIONAL HELPERS RELUCTANT TO GIVE ADVICE?   In the *Peanuts* cartoons, Lucy sits at the psychiatrist's booth with a sign that says, "Advice: 5 cents." Generally, this is how the media portray the helping professions. The client pays, and the helper gives a good dose of advice. If helping were merely giving advice, we could set up such a booth at the local grocery store. However, as one writer notes, "Clients can get all the advice they want from acquaintances, friends, and family members. They hardly need to pay a therapist to tell them what to do" (Kleinke, 1994, p. 9). To give exactly the same advice as everyone else in the client's world makes the helper seem impotent.

Another reason that professional helpers avoid giving advice is that while they may listen politely, people simply do not act upon our suggestions. There is not very much research on advice giving, but even in medical settings it seems to have a rather small effect (Sutton & Gilbert, 2007; Tymms & Merrell, 2006). About 50% of all medication prescribed by doctors is not taken. It is thought that a major reason that medical patients do not follow physician recommendations is that they have private medical beliefs that are more influential than the doctor's suggestions. Similarly, when helpers give clients advice and homework assignments, the helpers can expect no better than 50% compliance. Are we then to blame the clients or to recognize that the art of helping is more challenging than this?

Real helping is an art that involves getting people to solve their own problems and is much more difficult than supplying solutions by giving advice. Sometimes advice does stimulate a client's thinking about the problem, but more often it is simply disregarded (Mallett, Spokane, & Vance, 1978). Eric Berne (1963) identified a "game" that illustrates this point. Games are sequences of behavior that are frequently repeated and involve a payoff for at least one of the players. This advice-giving game involves a routine set of transactions between client and helper called "Why don't you . . . ? Yes, but . . . ," or WDYYB. The game goes like this: When the helper gives advice, he or she begins, "Why don't you . . . ?"; the client responds, "Yes, but. . . ." and then gives reasons why the advice will not work. Most of us are familiar with this "game" from work and social situations, and we may feel confused and frustrated when good suggestions are rejected. What we need to remember is that while a client may appear to be asking for advice, he or she is really looking for opportunities to think aloud, be understood, explore the options, and find his or her own solutions.

Another crucial drawback to advice giving is that if the client follows the helper's advice, the helper is responsible for the resultant change. If the helper gets the glory for having supplied good advice, how has this empowered the client to solve future life problems? There is an aphorism that states, "Give me a fish and I will eat today; teach me how to fish and I will eat forever." The long-term goal of helping is not to supply a quick fix, but to help the client, even when the helper is no longer in the picture. Sometimes advice may be needed to solve emergent problems, but when clients resolve their own difficulties, they gain confidence and skills.

By solving a client's problem through advising, you may also be sending the client an embedded message. Thomas Gordon (1975, 2000) considers lecturing and preaching to be one of the "dirty dozen" of bad communication practices because it communicates to a client that he or she is incapable of solving the problem. Lecturing and preaching are advice giving in disguise (Patterson & Eisenberg, 1983). For example, during the goal-setting phase, a client identifies excessive anger as one of the areas she wishes to work on. Frequently, beginning helpers launch into a "sermonette" on expressing anger and self-acceptance. The effect on the relationship is that the helper moves into the role of expert and begins to speak in generalities, rather than focusing on the client's unique situation. If you can identify a sermonette in your practice sessions, you are probably using disguised advice giving.

Another persuasive argument against giving advice is that the consequences of giving the wrong advice can be severe, both to the client's life and to the client's faith in the therapeutic relationship. A final reason to avoid advice giving is that it may violate the values of an individual's family, culture, or religion. Such advice will probably be rejected, and it may also harm the therapeutic relationship. Consider these examples of potentially inappropriate advice:

"I advise you to quit your job and go back to college."

"I suggest you learn to be more assertive with your mother."

"If you don't like all the arguing, why don't you get a divorce?"

WHEN IS IT APPROPRIATE AND INAPPROPRIATE TO GIVE ADVICE? A helper who gives advice must have the following knowledge or experience:

- Special knowledge and training in the specific issue the client is facing
- Firsthand experience or experience helping many people deal with the particular issue
- Understanding that the helper's experiences are not the same as the client's experiences
- Ability to give advice in a way that outlines the risks as well as the opportunities that following a certain course of action entails

- Thorough understanding of the client's history, including the client's ethnic, religious, and cultural background
- Ability to see advice as a two-way interaction between helper and client (Couture & Sutherland, 2006)

Appropriate advice is concrete and invites reaction and discussion. It is presented as one alternative along with other solutions generated by the client. It suggests that the client should alter the instructions to fit the circumstances. Advice about what to expect from certain courses of action may be quite helpful. Advice is also appropriate when the client is in some physical danger and a helper's directive can reduce the risk.

Here are some examples of advice that might be appropriate:

"Your statement that you are drinking too much has me concerned, especially since you drive in that condition. If you continue to drink, you can expect to be in an accident or in court. I want you to go to an alcohol treatment center for an assessment interview. Would you be willing to do that?" This advice to get an assessment is designed to inform the client about the likely outcomes of drinking and also identifies potential physical danger.

"You know, my partner and I always try to spend 20 minutes together every morning over coffee, talking about the upcoming day. It has been a way of building in a moment of contact in our hectic lives. Do you think something like that might work for you?" This advice invites discussion and asks the client to tailor the advice to fit his or her particular situation (see Butler, Potter, Danby, Emmison, & Hepburn, 2010).

"You've outlined several possibilities. Let me add one more. Have you considered directly confronting your co-worker about her unsafe behavior on the job? What effect do you think that might have?" This advice asks the client to think and to discuss the alternative suggested by the helper.

On the other hand, here are some situations in which advice is inappropriate and could be harmful to the therapeutic relationship:

- When the client seems to be dependent on others to make decisions and needs to learn to choose his or her own course of action. He or she might ask, for example:
  "Do you think I need a new haircut?"
  "Do you think I should go home this weekend as my parents ask, or should I do what my boyfriend wants?"
- When the client has not heeded advice previously.
- When the client is asking for assurance on issues with unpredictable outcomes, such as:
  "Should we have a baby?"
  "Should I get married?"
  "Should I move to Saudi Arabia?"
- When the purpose of obtaining advice is to influence another person:
  "My husband believes in spanking our child, but I don't. What do you think?"
  "My mother thinks I am too young to date. Do you agree?"
- When the client has information available and is capable of solving the problem without advice.

• When the advice conflicts with a client's basic values, upbringing, or culture. The helper is giving inappropriate advice, for example, when he or she says: "You may come from an East Indian culture, but you live in America now. You have to do what you want, and your parents will have to understand."

Clearly, the times when advice giving is useful are quite limited. Giving advice is appropriate only at carefully considered moments rather than as standard procedure. If advice giving is something you rely on in your natural helping style, try this experiment: Avoid advice giving altogether until you have learned to conduct an entire session using invitational and reflecting skills. There is an analogy in boxing training in which a left-handed puncher ties that hand behind the back in order to learn to operate only with the right arm. By letting go of an old way of responding, a new set of skills has the chance to take hold and become stronger. Similarly, if you can let go of your tendency to sermonize and give advice, you will have the chance to develop the subtler skills of helping the client find his or her own solutions.

STOP AND REFLECT

Think back for a moment on pieces of advice you have received from teachers, school counselors, friends, parents, grandparents, or other family members. It might have been about the purchase of a car or house, about which college to attend, or about what to do in a relationship. Identify one piece of good advice and one that was not very helpful, and then consider the following questions:

• What was it about each piece of advice that made it helpful or not helpful?
• When considering the helpful advice, did the person giving it have particular expertise in that area?
• What other characteristics did the person giving the advice have that encouraged you to accept it?
• If you cannot recall any advice given by friends, teachers, professional helpers, parents, or family members, what conclusions might you draw from this?
• When you have a problem, do you want advice, or is it more important to have someone listen so that you can figure things out for yourself?
• Have you ever given a friend advice that was really heeded? How did it turn out?
• What can you conclude about the role of advice in helping you to make decisions in your own life? Will your conclusions have a bearing on your willingness to give advice as a helper?

Discuss your answers with a small group of classmates.

Giving Information

Giving information means supplying data or facts to help a client reach his or her goal. Information giving might include making referrals to social services or community resources. It differs from advice giving (Prochaska & Norcross, 2009) because it is factual rather than an opinion. It can include correcting erroneous ideas about topics such as sexuality, drugs, parenting, and stereotypes about different ethnic groups. Information giving can also take the form of a planned **psychoeducational** program such as teaching the client assertiveness training.

Like advice giving, a helper uses information giving sparingly because too much data will overload the client who is already struggling with ideas from significant others. Information at those times will likely be ignored. Information giving can also subtly change the relationship between client and helper by emphasizing the helper's superior knowledge. Here is an example of an appropriate use of giving information:

> "Based on what you have told me, your financial problems are significant and you could use some professional help. I would like to refer you to the Consumer Credit Counseling Service. They can help you make the decision about whether bankruptcy is a good answer for you. Would you be willing to go?"

Recently, a student intern referred one of her clients to Alcoholics Anonymous after helping him identify his alcohol problem. She was elated after the session because "It really felt like I did something for a change instead of just listening." I tried to point out that it was really the relationship that she had so painstakingly constructed rather than the referral that was helping. If she had referred him for treatment at their first session, he would never have accepted the referral. It took time and trust to bring him to that realization. Like advice, giving information feels as if we are really accomplishing something. But the proof is in the pudding. Most information we give clients does not sink in. Although the helper feels effective when referring or providing information, it is important to find out if the client has really been helped. Therefore, the helper *must* follow up with clients to see if information or referrals have had an impact. We will talk more about the topic of referral and follow-up when we discuss termination of the helping relationship in the next chapter.

BRAINSTORMING

Creativity and the Art of Helping

Helpers are often creative people. They are flexible and open to a variety of options when a problem arises (Gladding, 1995). They try to help clients devise novel ways of thinking and problem solving. Indeed, they may at times use artistic media—drama, poetry, painting, sculpture, and music—to help clients express themselves (Gladding, 2005, 2010). Helpers also encourage their clients to think creatively when they have problems. A major difficulty in problem solving is that we tend to see things through the lens of our outmoded ideas, social conventions, and personal history. As Emerson noted, consistency can be a hobgoblin, leading us into foolish repetitions when what we need is to break out of our old ways of thinking.

Perhaps you have heard the story of the man who takes his son to the emergency room, and the doctor exclaims, "I can't operate on this child, he's my son!" We do not automatically recognize that the doctor must be the child's mother. Because of our training and the pervasive influence of the media, we unconsciously fall back on our usual way of thinking, that a doctor must be a man. During crisis states, we become even more conservative and less creative. A sort of tunnel vision develops that convinces us that we have very few options. For example, people with suicidal thoughts may have concluded that killing themselves is the only option available. The concept of learned helplessness has been advanced to explain why people fail to look for alternatives following experiences of failure (Seligman, 1991). When people seem to find that nothing works to solve their dilemmas, they stop trying, even when circumstances change. The job of a helper is to be an "expander" (not a "shrink") who urges clients to enlarge their viewpoint, jump-start their thinking, and engage their creativity.

What Is Brainstorming?

Brainstorming originally was developed by Madison Avenue advertising firms to increase the creativity of staff members responsible for commercials. To brainstorm, a group of people sit around a table and generate ideas. The conditions and ground rules, however, are a little different from those of an average meeting: The atmosphere is relaxed and even playful. Cooperation rather than competition is encouraged. Everyone in the group is called upon to participate, and no one is allowed to dominate. All ideas are recorded, but the focus remains on a specific problem that the group wants to solve. Beyond these general conditions for brainstorming, there are some specific rules that differentiate it from other problem-solving activities:

1. No ideas generated by brainstorming are evaluated. They are simply brought before the group and recorded. Evaluation involves a critical function of mind rather than a creative one. Creativity flows best in a nonjudgmental atmosphere.
2. **Freewheeling** is encouraged. Practical considerations are not brought up during a brainstorming session. In fact, the wilder the ideas the better, so that the limits of creativity can be reached. A playful attitude by the facilitator can increase freewheeling.
3. The quantity of ideas is more important than the quality. A large pool of ideas is needed as a source of good solutions. Seemingly unimportant ideas actually can spark thoughts from other members of the group, and small ideas can be used to improve bigger ones.
4. Hitchhiking is encouraged. Hitchhiking, or piggybacking, is building on the ideas of other people. By combining ideas, a concept grows and develops. Thus brainstorming is a creative and cooperative process that has the power to unearth hidden solutions and engage both helper and client.

Research has suggested that sometimes when two or more people brainstorm together, they do not generate as many new ideas as they do when they compile their lists separately (Diehl & Stroebe, 1991; Mullen, Johnson, & Salas, 1991). The reason is "production blocking." Production blocking means that people are sometimes too polite in a group situation to spontaneously blurt out their ideas while others are talking. They are also taking time to listen to the ideas of others instead of formulating new ideas. The flow of ideas dries up. Brainstorming requires that each person be allowed to express his or her ideas without having to wait for others to stop speaking (Johnson & Johnson, 2008). The contributions of women may be limited in brainstorming sessions because men tend to interrupt more. To get around the problem of production blocking, a technique called "brainwriting" can be used; "brainwriting" requires everyone in a large group to write a creative solution to a problem on an index card, and then the group selects the best ideas from the anonymous submissions.

Production blocking can also occur in a therapeutic relationship. The client is reluctant in that setting to really think in a spontaneous and freewheeling way because of the weight that he or she places on the helper's ideas. Sometimes it is more effective for both helper and client to write down their ideas or to have the client generate ideas and the helper record them. This allows for more freewheeling than the start-and-stop approach that a conversation entails.

How to Brainstorm

Brainstorming between a helper and a client involves the same basic activities that groups use, with only slight modifications. The helper acts as a facilitator and participant, but a major aim is to help the client develop skills of creative thinking, which can generalize to other situations. While we are trying to help the client arrive at a solution, we are also teaching a valuable life skill.

In the helping relationship, brainstorming should not be an activity that merely keeps a client talking about options rather than taking action. Brainstorming is a change technique. At the end of a brainstorming session, both helper and client should have a clear idea about the next steps to take to solve the problem. Its aim is to help the client arrive at a practical first step. Brainstorming takes a client through three basic phases:

1. Challenging the client's assumptions and asking the right question
2. Generating ideas
3. Evaluating and agreeing upon potential solutions

Brainstorming with a client does not differ much from the steps in group brainstorming except that, at the outset, more attention is devoted to identifying and challenging assumptions. The client considers the assumptions he or she has about the problem and tries to shake free of them. Otherwise, preexisting ideas will color the next idea-generating step, leading the client to substitute previous solutions rather than to think creatively.

One tactic for dealing with assumptions is to reverse them. For example, while designing an innovative program for training school counselors, participants listed all their assumptions about school counselors. One of them was "School counselors work during school hours." This assumption was then reversed and rewritten, "School counselors do not work during school hours." Ideas based on this new concept were then generated. Participants began thinking about how school counselors should be available to parents after school and in the evenings. This led them to include family counseling training as part of the curriculum. A nearby public school system is now incorporating this idea in its new school. The plans allow flexible working hours for school counselors so that they can meet with parents several evenings per week.

Another story illustrates how assumptions about problems can be challenged and how, in turn, creative thinking leads to better solutions.

> David and Gloria have been married for 5 years. David's job requires that he move to another state for a 2-year period to work on an exciting project. If David refuses the assignment, he risks losing his job. The couple came for help because they have come to an impasse in their decision-making process. David wants Gloria to quit her job as a part-time graphic designer and move with him. Gloria wants to stay where she is, and she wants David to stay, too, even if he gets demoted or loses his job. Neither wants to live alone for the 2-year period.

Acting as a facilitator, the helper took them through the three basic steps of brainstorming to help them arrive at a solution.

Step 1: Challenging Assumptions and Asking the Right Question.   The first step is to ask the right question. This can be determined by asking what is to be achieved in the end. What is the goal? The reason this step is so crucial is that often clients are examining previous solutions rather than the current problem. A good example of how this happens comes from the food industry. For several years, the question was often asked in this way: "How can we make a better can opener?" This formulation generated a number of new can openers, both manual and electric; however, a can opener is a previous solution, not the real problem. Someone ultimately was able to ask the question in a different way: "How do we open a can?" When the problem was stated in this way, a whole new set of creative opening features developed. Helpers assist clients in identifying the key issues by asking closed questions such as:

"What do you want to achieve by solving this problem?"

"What is it you are afraid of losing?"

"What is the most important thing you want to accomplish?"

Similarly, David and Gloria might argue over who is going to move, but what is the real question? With the assistance of the helper, the couple realized that the question that really needed to be asked was, "How will we be able to spend enough time together and feel close to each other if David goes out of state for 2 years?" Previously, the couple had assumed:

"Someone is going to have to move."

"Someone is going to be unhappy."

"Someone is going to lose his or her job."

Once the problem assumptions had been put aside and the real problem identified, the couple were ready to start generating ideas.

Step 2: Generating Ideas.   In a freewheeling and cooperative atmosphere, David and Gloria took a few minutes to identify creative answers to the question "How can we remain close if David takes the job for 2 years?" Since quantity is wanted, the helper insisted that they generate at least 10 ideas. They came up with the following list:

1. We will e-mail every day.
2. We will Skype every day.
3. We will meet halfway every weekend.
4. David will come home once a month and Gloria will travel to see David once a month.
5. We will spend our vacations and holidays with each other for the next 2 years, not with other family members.
6. We will Skype every evening.
7. We will send video recordings to each other.
8. Gloria will take some of her work with her to David's place and stay for a week at a time.
9. David will ask the company for time off to come home.

10. We can take pictures of things that happen and share them with each other.

11. We could both take a class to fill our time and discuss it with each other.

12. We can send smoke signals.

13. We can meet halfway in Mexico.

As the ideas got crazier, they began to hitchhike on each other's ideas. When Gloria said, "We could take a class," David suggested that they take a Spanish class and share their learning when they meet in Mexico.

Step 3: Evaluating and Selecting a Solution.   The final step of brainstorming is evaluating and selecting a solution. David and Gloria went through the list at this point and discussed each possibility. They settled on four or five suggestions to implement that best fit the goal of keeping their relationship vital while they lived separately.

Although the case of David and Gloria may seem too good to be true, many clients and helpers have learned to use brainstorming in just this way. When a client and helper devise a creative solution to a knotty problem, the therapeutic relationship is enhanced and the client's confidence and sense of hope is increased. Not only have the clients been fully involved in the solution, but they have learned or relearned an important problem-solving skill.

THE SKILL OF ALTERNATE INTERPRETATION

The skill of brainstorming encourages clients and helpers to collaborate and create new solutions to old problems. When we challenge our assumptions in the first steps of brainstorming, we begin to recognize that there are many different ways to frame a problem and that the way we conceptualize it has important implications for the eventual solution. **Alternate interpretation,** or *alternative interpretation*, is another method to help clients recognize that problem situations can be seen in many different lights (McMullin, 2000). It is a way of changing the viewing of the problem. The method of alternate interpretation does not attempt to reach into the past to find the correct interpretation or meaning of an event. Rather, its sole purpose is to convince the client that there are several possible alternatives to a negative first impression or catastrophic appraisal. For instance, many people continue, in adulthood, to misinterpret, minimize, or exaggerate events that happened when they were children. The method of alternate interpretation tends to loosen the hold of outmoded ideas and to convince clients that there are many possible ways of looking at a problem, some of them helpful and some of them self-defeating.

HOW TO TEACH A CLIENT TO USE ALTERNATE INTERPRETATION

The decision to use alternate interpretation usually comes within a session when a client describes an event that has occurred and then begins to catastrophize about it. *Catastrophizing* is the tendency to expect that an event will be devastating before one really knows what the outcome will be. In this case, the helper stops the process and asks the client to stop imagining the worst-case scenario and examine the premises that led to the conclusion that a catastrophe has occurred or is imminent. Consider the case of Jane, who has been working at a new job for only a short while.

She was recently fired from another position and is feeling very insecure about her new situation:

> JANE: "On Monday, my boss mentioned that I had not finished last week's reports. My boss is criticizing me. Things are starting all over again. I know I'll lose this job now."

Step 1: Using the skill of alternate interpretation, the helper proceeds as follows: The helper listens to the client's problem and then previews and explains the concept of alternate interpretation.

> HELPER: "I recognize that you are concerned about losing your new job, but I wonder if I could stop you for a moment and ask you to try something."
>
> JANE: "Okay."
>
> HELPER: "This technique is called alternate interpretation. The way it works is that we take the situation and try to identify some different conclusions than the one that you have drawn. As I understand it, your boss stopped you and mentioned you had not done last week's reports, right?"
>
> JANE: "Right."
>
> HELPER: "And your first conclusion was that the same thing is happening that occurred at your old job and that you will probably be fired, right?"
>
> JANE: "It sounds kind of silly when you say it that way."
>
> HELPER: "Well, what I would like to do is get you to try and generate some other interpretations of the facts. For example, perhaps your boss needed that information for some reason and was more interested in the content of the reports than in firing you."
>
> JANE: "All right, I see."
>
> HELPER: "Good, but I want you to come up with some ideas that make just as much sense as your first impression, okay?"

Step 2: The helper asks the client to make a list of three or four other interpretations that fit the facts at least as well as the catastrophic conclusion of the client.

> HELPER: "I am wondering if you would try and think for a moment about some other ways of interpreting the same situation."
>
> JANE: "Well, in this job, I have not received this kind of criticism. It is unfamiliar. Perhaps she—my boss—is trying to help me improve and become a better employee."
>
> HELPER: "That's good. What else?"
>
> JANE: "Um, I guess I could realize that I have just received feedback that will help my performance. Maybe it will actually help me keep the job."
>
> HELPER: "Very good. Can you think of any other way to interpret this situation?"

JANE: "Like I said, this is the first time that my work has been criticized. My boss probably doesn't place that much importance on a single instance like this. She's probably forgotten about it. I am just nervous because of my past history."

Step 3:   The helper assigns a homework task of developing three or four alternate explanations to the first interpretation of any disturbing event that occurs between sessions. The only requirement for the alternatives is that they have as much likelihood of being true as the first impression. The helper does not try to "sell" any particular interpretation but is trying to loosen up the client's automatic, catastrophizing response.

STOP AND REFLECT

1.   Think about the following scenario and consider how you might help the client develop alternate interpretations of the same situation.

    "My best friend Pam isn't talking to me. We were out together on Friday night. Well, I met someone that I knew from work and wanted to spend more time with. He and I left the coffee shop. It was crowded, I didn't see Pam, and so I didn't say good-bye. When I saw her at church, she waved but didn't stay to talk. I know she hates me now. We have been so close for 2 years, and now it's over."

2.   Now take a moment to consider an event in your own life where your first impression was incorrect. Might the skill of alternate interpretation have been helpful in your situation? As you think about it, list two or three other possible interpretations you might have made had you been able to be more objective.

3.   What client problems do you think might respond best to the technique of alternate interpretation? Compare your ideas with those of your classmates.

MyCounselingLab™

Go to Topics 4 and 5, *Formulating Goals* and *Cognitive Interventions*, on the MyCounselingLab™ site (www.MyCounselingLab.com) for *Learning the Art of Helping: Building Blocks and Techniques,* Fifth Edition, where you can:

• Find learning outcomes for *Formulating Goals* and *Cognitive Interventions*, along with the national standards that connect to these outcomes.
• Complete Assignments and Activities that can help you more deeply understand the chapter content.
• Apply and practice your understanding of the core skills identified in the chapter with the Building Counseling Skills unit.
• Prepare yourself for professional certification with a Practice for Certification quiz.
• Connect to videos through the Video and Resource Library.

MyCounselingLab™ Exercises

Go to the Video and Resource Library on the MyCounselingLab™ site for your text and search for the following clip: *Brainstorming*. Watch the video and then answer the following questions.

Exercise: Brainstorming

In the video *Brainstorming*, the helper, Tyson, is assisting Bryan in brainstorming solutions to the problems associated with Bryan's inability to drive. Review the three basic steps of brainstorming below and answer the questions that ask you to evaluate the success of this brainstorming session.

Steps in Brainstorming

- Challenging the client's assumptions and identifying the problem
- Generating ideas
- Evaluating and agreeing upon potential solutions

1. At 1:27:05 Tyson and Bryan begin to agree upon a definition of the problem. What is it?
2. Do they examine any assumptions or presuppositions about the problem?
3. What assumptions might they have overlooked?
4. At 1:29:21, the client and helper have a last interchange. Would you say they are moving toward selecting a potential solution?

Summary

Up to this point, we have looked mainly at skills for developing the therapeutic relationship, exploring client problems, and setting goals. In this chapter, we talked about four building blocks that help move clients toward solutions: giving advice, giving information, brainstorming, and alternate interpretation. Giving advice is the most controversial skill presented and the one that can potentially create the most harm to the therapeutic relationship. It is discussed because helpers need to understand the few appropriate and many inappropriate uses of advice. In addition, we mentioned the need for helpers to, at times, supply information. Helpers possess facts that may enhance the client's safety and also can identify referral sources where clients can receive additional help or information.

The major focus of this chapter, though, was on the skills of brainstorming and alternate interpretation. Both skills are aimed at getting clients to free themselves from their first interpretations of events or the mental constraints that keep them from developing creative solutions to their difficulties. They are valuable because when clients learn these skills, they can utilize them in their daily lives to solve problems and to bring events into perspective.

The change techniques are the final building blocks in the art of helping. Along with challenging skills, the change techniques, if properly applied, are collaborative attempts to move clients out of their current frames of reference and to have them consider new alternative ways of thinking and behaving.

Before leaving this set of skills, let us recognize again the importance of the helping relationship in making change happen. The nonjudgmental listening cycle allows the client to develop a sense of trust, and that begins to pay off as the client takes tentative first steps in changing his or her life. More importantly, as the client encounters obstacles on the path to solutions, the basic relationship skills will be needed again and again. You must go back and forth between listening nonjudgmentally and working on solutions as long as a helping relationship lasts. Thomas Gordon (1975) used to call this "shifting gears." There are times to push forward and break new ground, and there are times to "downshift" and return to a listening stance. In other words, be patient when using change techniques. One cannot go full speed ahead at all times. The therapeutic relationship requires that the helper abandon forward progress at times and reestablish the vital therapeutic bond.

Exercises

GROUP EXERCISES

Exercise 1: Practicing Brainstorming

Students work in groups of three or four. One student takes on the role of a client, another becomes the helper, and the others act as observers. The client discusses a dilemma with a helper. The dilemma should be a situation in which the client is forced to make a difficult choice between two alternatives. It may be a current dilemma or one that the client faced in the past. Suggestions of possible topics for the client to discuss include:

- Whether or not to commit to a relationship
- Whether or not to end a relationship
- Whether to move or stay in the same place
- Whether or not to begin an academic degree program

Before beginning the brainstorming process, the helper first reviews the "Quick Tips: Brainstorming" section below. Then the helper uses the nonjudgmental listening cycle for several minutes to understand a little more about the client's problem. Next the helper moves with the client through the three steps of brainstorming:

1. The helper challenges the client to review his or her assumptions about the problem and to identify the real issue.
2. The helper and client brainstorm solutions.
3. The helper and client agree on a solution.

Following the brainstorming session, the client and observer(s) give the helper general feedback on:

1. The handling of the nonjudgmental listening cycle.
2. The helper's success in getting the client to think creatively.
3. The final solution. Was it realistic and appropriate for this client?

QUICK TIPS: BRAINSTORMING

- Use closed questions to help the client pinpoint the real problem.
- Create a playful and cooperative atmosphere in the session by modeling freewheeling.
- Come up with a few unusual ideas yourself to encourage the client's creativity.
- The helper should take the role of facilitator and write down all the ideas that are generated.
- Make sure that the final creative solution between helper and client meets the "reality criterion": It must effectively address the problem.

Exercise 2: Giving Advice

This activity can be used as a whole-class activity or for groups of at least six or eight students. One student acts as the client and describes a real problem to the group. The client is asked to identify a problem that is not too personal so that he or she does not feel uncomfortable discussing it in some detail. The helper (student or teacher) uses the nonjudgmental listening cycle to understand the issue. When the story has been fully articulated to the helper, the group thinks about the client's story, and each person writes down a piece of advice.

In the second part of the exercise, the helper collects the written advice and reads each student's advice to the client. After hearing the advice, the client discusses with the class which advice he or she is most likely to follow and why.

In the third part of the exercise, the helper uses a brainstorming approach to get the client to think about the issue and to come up with his or her own plan. Finally, the client is asked to review both the advice-giving and brainstorming sessions and indicate what course of action he or she is most likely to take. The class or group discusses the results. If possible, on the following week, the student client is asked to report on what action he or she actually took.

Exercise 3: Reversing Assumptions and Brainstorming

This exercise can be done by the whole class facilitated by the instructor. Its purpose is to challenge basic premises we have about common objects as a way of highlighting the importance of thinking creatively.

Begin by generating a list of ideas about how to improve a common household item such as a clothes hanger or a microwave or any other product of the group's choosing. The task is to produce as many ideas as possible in 2 minutes. These are recorded on a piece of paper. For this first part of the activity, remember that it is important to let go of the mind's evaluative function and allow creativity to flow. Do not think about how practical the ideas are at first. Give equal time to wild ideas.

Next list on the board the assumptions you have about the item—for example, clothes hangers are made of wire, hang in a closet, are for hanging clothes, and so on. Next to each assumption write a *reversal of the assumption*—for example, "Clothes hangers are not in a closet," "They are not made of wire," and so on. Then brainstorm any ideas that arise as a result of the reversal. For example, if they are not wire, they are made of hardened paper and can be recycled. Add any new ideas to the list of improvements. Now see whether you can force-fit any two ideas on the list together, or hitchhike (combine ideas), to devise any new creative ideas. If so, add them to the list.

As the final step in the process, evaluate each idea and select the best. Can any of the good ideas be combined to create a new product? The final design should meet the reality criterion: Is the product really an improvement? How likely would it be to sell?

SMALL GROUP DISCUSSION

Discussion: In this chapter we discussed techniques that involve getting clients to act (advice giving and creative problem solving) and also a technique that encourages a client to see the situation differently (alternate interpretation). Under what circumstances do you think it is useful to help the client change perceptions and when should the client be encouraged to act to change the situation?

Creativity

It has been said that creativity is an important trait of helpers. According to Witmer (1985), creative individuals are said to possess the following characteristics:

- Curiosity
- Openness to new experience
- Independence
- Sense of humor and playfulness (spontaneity)
- Persistence
- Flexibility
- Originality
- Ability to accept that opposing points of view may both be right

Do you see yourself as a creative individual? Is this something you would like to develop? Explore with your small group how you might employ creativity in session or in homework assignments for clients.

WRITTEN EXERCISES

Exercise: Alternate Interpretation

Practice creating alternate interpretations to the client statements below. The goal is not to find the correct interpretation, but instead to let the client know there are other possible and perhaps more hopeful interpretations of the events.

1. *Client:* "This morning I burnt the toast, broke a cup, and then car wouldn't start. This is the beginning of a lousy week."
2. *Client:* "He didn't call me when he said he would. He doesn't love me."
3. *Client:* "I had a panic attack yesterday. I thought things were getting better and I was getting over this problem. The anxiety is never going away."
4. *Client:* "I failed the exam. My father was right, I am stupid."
5. *Client:* "My wife found out I lied to her. I will never be forgiven for this. She will probably divorce me."
6. *Client:* "The new guy at work seems so efficient and intelligent. I'll never get that promotion now."
7. *Client:* "Monica looked at me today. She probably wants to go out with me."
8. *Client:* "My Dad left when I was 6 years old. Everyone says I was a difficult child. I think that had something to do with my parents' divorce."

SELF-ASSESSMENT

Take a moment and think about the building block skills in this chapter (excluding advice giving). Indicate any success or difficulty you had in learning each of them, either in the exercises in the book or in your practice sessions with fellow students.

- Giving information: (successes and difficulties)
- Brainstorming: (successes and difficulties)
- Alternate Interpretation: (successes and difficulties)
- Which of the change techniques presented were most useful or appealing to you?
- Which of the skills would you feel most comfortable using with clients?
- Identify two ways you could learn more about the building block skills in this chapter.

1. _____

2. _____

HOMEWORK

Homework: Knowing Sources of Information and Referral in Your Community

Helpers regularly give clients information about other sources of help. They refer clients to agencies and to other individuals who have specialized services or knowledge. Review the following list of services. See if you can identify someone in your community who delivers them or provides information.

1. A crisis hotline, suicide prevention service, or 24-hour emergency line
2. A nonprofit consumer credit organization that provides help for people with financial problems
3. Parenting classes
4. Help for domestic violence
5. Treatment for substance abuse
6. Couples and relationship education classes
7. Information for families who have a child with cerebral palsy

JOURNAL STARTERS

Some helpers use a technique in which the client sits in the helper's chair and gives advice as if he or she were sitting in the empty client chair. This is a way of tapping into that wise person in each of us. Think for a moment about your relationships, family, money, children, or career. Imagine yourself as this older, wiser self and write down your advice. When you have finished writing, react to the activity by sharing your evaluation of the advice.

Outcome Evaluation
and Termination Skills

*What we call the beginning is often the end. And to make
an end is to make a beginning. The end is where we
start from.*

T. S. ELIOT

MyCounselingLab™

Visit the MyCounselingLab™ site for *Learning the Art of Helping: Building Blocks and
Techniques,* Fifth Edition to enhance your understanding of chapter concepts. You'll
have the opportunity to practice your skills through video- and case-based Assignments
and Activities as well as Building Counseling Skills units, and to prepare for your
certification exam with Practice for Certification quizzes.

**Evaluating the Effectiveness of
Helping**

Basic Outcome Evaluation Methods

- Use Progress Notes to Track
  Improvement on Goals
- Use a Global Measure to Detect
  Overall Improvement
- Use a Specific Measure
- Use Subjective Scaling and Self-Report
  to Measure Improvement

- Use Another Person to Monitor
  Change
- Use Client Satisfaction Scales
- Use Goal-Attainment Measures
- Use Program Evaluation

Termination

- How to Prevent Premature Termination
- How to Tell Whether Termination Is
  Needed
- How to Prepare a Client for Termination

Dealing with Loss at Termination
- The Helper's Reaction to Termination

How to Maintain Therapeutic Gains and Prevent Relapse Following Termination
- Follow-up
- Fading
- Contracts with Paraprofessionals
- Self-Help Groups
- Self-Monitoring Activities
- Self-Management Skills

- Role-Playing for Relapse Prevention
- Letter Writing

Summary

Exercises
- Group Exercises
- Small Group Discussions
- Written Exercises
- Self-Assessment
- Homework
- Journal Starters

How will we know when the helping relationship should end? Our answer has been that helping is complete when helper and client agree that goals have been reached. The final phase of the road map of the helping relationship (Figure 12.1) is a time when helper and client look at progress and make this determination. One outcome is that more work needs to be done or that additional goals should be pursued. Another possibility is that helper and client feel that the relationship should be terminated because a problem has

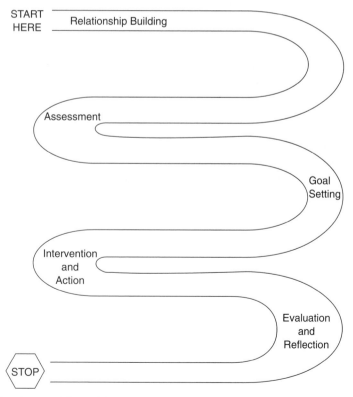

FIGURE 12.1 Road Map of the Helping Process: Outcome Evaluation and Termination

been resolved or because the sessions have not been fruitful. If goals have been reached, and termination is necessary, both helper and client may experience strong feelings about the ending of the contract. In this chapter, we look at methods for monitoring progress and goal completion and also at the emotional and practical aspects involved in terminating the helping relationship.

EVALUATING THE EFFECTIVENESS OF HELPING

Because of the emergence of managed care and a growing awareness that many unsound treatments are being applied, there has been a burgeoning interest in outcome evaluation in the medical and other helping professions (Asay, Lambert, Gregersen, & Goates, 2002; Norcross, 2011; Sexton, 1996; Sexton, Whiston, Bleuer, & Walz, 1997). In other words, insurance companies and researchers are asking clinicians to be more scientific, to show that they are using proven practices and that the client was actually helped by the therapeutic process. Today, whether you work in a school, hospital, agency, or private practice, someone wants to know if you can demonstrate that what you do is actually working (Granello & Granello, 1998).

Outcome research is at the heart of this new trend toward scientific helping. *Outcome research* is the general term for studies that look at whether what we do actually benefits the client. Surprisingly, these studies are conspicuous by their absence. For example, relatively little research has been conducted that looks at the efficacy of the basic helping skills you have learned in this book. Most of the studies suggest that helpers can learn these skills and that some training methods are better than others. But very little has been said about how clients react to these skills. In other words, research confirms that the operation is a success, but nobody asks whether or not the patient survived. Many of our ideas about effective therapy and good training in the helping skills are based on clinical observation. The proponents of outcome research are quick to point out the limitations of this "seat-of-the-pants" approach. We need to find out if the client is better off due to our efforts.

The extremists in this "evidence-based practice" camp suggest that we only use treatment methods that we can back up with research. This is using research as a *prescription* for practice. Unfortunately, this idea is also limited. We know from medicine that two clients will react to the same prescription differently. Second, we also know that two depressed people are depressed in different ways. No treatments (including medications) work for 100% of the clients. So the helper's task is a complex one: to determine "what treatment, by whom, is the most effective for this individual with that specific problem or set of problems, and under which set of circumstances" (Paul, 1967, p. 111). We must be able to adjust the treatment based on the individual person and circumstance (Roth & Fonagy, 2005). This is why we value research as a reflective tool rather than as a prescription. Third, we have only studied a fraction of thousands of available change techniques. Sticking to what has been fully studied would handicap the helper as promising strategies emerge. Still, this does not exonerate the helper from recognizing that some approaches have been better studied than others and have more to recommend them and that the helper need to stay abreast of current research.

Let me give an example. For more than 2 years, I utilized relaxation procedures to help clients with panic disorder because I had been trained in stress management and it seemed logical to do so. I had very little success. These clients had trouble reaching deep states of relaxation through Jacobsonian relaxation procedures. I did not know whether to attribute this to the technique or to the intransigence of the mental disorder. Years later, research confirmed that other techniques are likely to be more effective (Beamish, Granello, & Belcastro, 2002). The competent, ethical helper must stay abreast of research and be constantly watching the professional literature.

But you do not have to wait for research to inform you. You can regularly monitor progress and make adjustments. This might be called using **practice-based evidence** (McLeod, 2007). You are already familiar with practice-based evidence, because in this course you have been trying out the basic helping skills using a partner or small group. We have also encouraged you to get feedback, both qualitative and quantitative, from fellow students. This feedback is a kind of evidence you can also obtain from clients. You can ask, "Are we going in the right direction? What has changed since we started meeting? What is not working for you?" This kind of questioning assists the helper as well as the client. It keeps us from wasting our time or from potentially damaging the helping relationship.

Another reason for collecting practice-based evidence is to maintain helper self-confidence. Because of the wide variety of clients, disorders, problems, and treatment options, it is hard to feel effective, especially as a beginner. Frequently, clients have very high expectation of the helping relationship and may not recognize when changes have been made. Outcome evaluation can give you periodic encouragement, and you can grow in confidence as you see the actual data accumulate, rather than only listening to your fears and discouraging thoughts. If you track outcomes, you can gain a personal sense of power and confidence that you are doing something that works.

Even if you are not particularly attracted to the scientific or research aspects of the helping profession, you can utilize some very simple methods to keep track of what works. In the first section of this chapter, we discuss the use of progress notes, global measures, specific symptom measures, client satisfaction forms, and goal-attainment measures. All of these are minimally intrusive in the helping process and push both client and helper not just to dream but also to fulfill dreams.

BASIC OUTCOME EVALUATION METHODS

Use Progress Notes to Track Improvement on Goals

When you begin seeing clients in a clinical, agency, hospital, or academic setting, you will be asked to document progress by the client using some sort of **progress note** form. There are a variety of systems for note taking including the SOAP format (subjective, objective, assessment, and plan) (Cameron & Turtle-Song, 2002). There are also many computer programs such as *Athena* and *TheraScribe,* which keep records for individual therapists or large organizations. However, I recommend a system that centers on the goals that the client and helper have initially agreed to. The notes should (1) restate the goals, (2) indicate what progress has been made during the week (outside of the session) that was relevant to the goal and the results of any **homework** assignments, (3) include any new information or relevant events that occurred this week, (4) state what was talked about in the session that relates to the goal, and (5) specify what plans have been made for the coming week and next sessions as they relate to the goal. In short, the progress note should keep the helper on track, focusing on the agreed-upon aims and not becoming waylaid by

---

Client Name __John Doe__   Session No. _3_   Date _4_/_18_/_2005_

Client/Counselor Negotiated Goal Statements

1. Decrease depression and suicidal thoughts.
2. Resolve family problems. Increase brief contacts.

Any Progress in Goals Since Last Session

1. Client indicates that depression decreased significantly but still having suicidal thoughts 1 time per day.
2. No effort or progress toward this goal.

New Information (Changes in Client's Situation or Mental Status)

Denied that suicidal thoughts were intense or increasing.
Denied any planned method or available suicide means.

Counseling Activity During This Session

Goal 1. During session, client was confronted on self-downing and was taught to challenge negative self-statements.
Goal 2. We did not address this goal except for client to indicate that he is not quite ready to work on this issue. I suggested he consider attending Adult Children of Alcoholics as a preliminary step. He agreed.

Homework Assignments, Referrals, and Plans

Goal   Plan

1.   Client to challenge negative self-statements as homework and call if suicidal thoughts increase.
2.   Will call friend to accompany him to first ACOA meeting.

Counselor Signature B. B. James   REPLAN date _6_ / _9_ / _2005_

FIGURE 12.2 Sample REPLAN Record and Case Notes

tangential conversations. Figure 12.2 shows a sample case note that utilizes this method of evaluating client outcomes relative to goals at each session. Using this system, the helper evaluates progress toward the goals at every session. A goal-oriented note also reduces the time it takes to do paperwork because the focus is so specific. It is not a blank page that the helper must puzzle over. It should be noted that there is also a case to be made for *co-documentation* when client and counselor both regularly record their ideas about progress (Albeck & Goldman, 1991). This goal-oriented approach helps avoid some of the pitfalls to writing case notes. There are things that should be left out of case notes. For example, do not include your personal reflections or reactions to the client. If you want to keep a journal of "process notes" or reflections, keep them separate (Moline, Williams, & Austin, 1998). You should also omit personal opinions, discussions about a third party that might be embarrassing if revealed, or any sensitive information that is not relevant to treatment. If the client is trying to quit smoking, his or her sexual preferences are probably not relevant.

Use a Global Measure to Detect Overall Improvement

There are a number of global measures of psychological distress and psychopathology. Utilizing these measures periodically can help you chart whether the client is generally improving or deteriorating. The Brief Symptom Inventory (BSI) (Derogatis, 1975) and the OQ-45 (adult and youth versions) (Lambert et al., 1996) are two well-established paper-and-pencil instruments used to identify global change. Both can be administered and scored in just a few minutes. In our clinic we give every client the OQ-45.2 every 4 weeks and track the results over the course of treatment using a computer program. This gives us another way of making sure we do not miss a positive or negative change.

Use a Specific Measure

Sometimes you are looking for a specific change such as a decrease in depression. There are a number of specific brief measures such as the Beck Depression Inventory II that can be used routinely (Beck, Steer, & Brown, 1996). The 21-item Beck has been used extensively in research, and many clinicians like to administer it every week when they are seeing a depressed client because it appears to be sensitive to improvement in mood.

Use Subjective Scaling and Self-Report to Measure Improvement

A SUDS, Subjective Units of Discomfort Scale, was described earlier in this book. Basically SUDS asks the client to indicate on a scale of 1 to 10 or 1 to 100 how uncomfortable (depressed, anxious, stressed, unhappy) he or she currently feels. The clinician regularly requests an update from the client and records changes in SUDS on the progress notes. Besides the fact that helpers can see and inform clients of improvement, keeping track of SUDS gets the clients thinking about their goal and about the changes they are making.

The helper might also ask the client to make a note of specific behaviors in frequency, intensity, or duration such as:

- How many cigarettes did you smoke?
- How many times did the child pull out his or her hair (trichotillomania)?
- How many times was the teenager able to start a conversation with peers?
- How many times did each member of the couple give the other a compliment during the counseling session?
- How intense was this marital argument (on a 10-point scale)?
- How intense was your fear of dogs in this situation (on the SUDS)?
- How long were you able to meditate today?

In a later chapter, we show how monitoring, recordkeeping, and journaling can be used as a treatment and not just an evaluation of progress. When a client tracks his or her own problems or successes, he or she learns what is working and changes behavior accordingly. There are also free online symptom tracking and journaling systems such as MyPsychTracker (www.psychtracker.com).

Use Another Person to Monitor Change

Frequently, someone in the environment is better able to see changes than the client. For example, suppose a college student is trying to become more outgoing and talk more in class and in social situations. The counselor may utilize an ally of the client—a friend who will give the client periodic feedback when the friend sees the client behaving in a different manner or sees evidence of avoidance. There are pitfalls to the use of allies or **aides,** including the fact that they may take too much responsibility or they may not respect confidentiality.

In addition, if the ally is a spouse or parent, his or her own needs and wants for the client can complicate matters. Still, having someone in the client's daily life report on a specific change can be extremely useful and can also motivate the client. Obviously whether or not to use an aide or ally and the choice of the ally should be the client's.

Use Client Satisfaction Scales

Client satisfaction scales are measures of how happy the client is with the services rendered. Most of these are developed by agencies and schools to answer specific questions, but others are nationally normed and can give feedback on how satisfied clients are compared with those around the United States. It may be useful to look at overall satisfaction from a program evaluation standpoint, but helpers can also look at client outcomes by including a few useful statements to be rated (say, on a scale from 1 to 7), such as:

- I was able to achieve my goals as a result of these sessions.
- My relationship with the counselor was important in helping me improve.
- I have a more positive view of the future because of these sessions.

Use Goal-Attainment Measures

One graphic method for evaluating progress is **goal-attainment scaling** (Kiresuk & Sherman, 1968; Newton, 2002). Goal-attainment scaling has been advocated for demonstrating accountability, but its best use may be that it can provide helpful information to the client and counselor about progress (see Table 12.1).

The goal-attainment guide in Table 12.1 is used in the following way:

1. Each goal is briefly described in the goal statement section.
2. Specific indications of success are noted in the sections just beneath the goal statement. A simple example of a goal is to "maintain social support for sobriety." The specific success indicators might be "regular attendance at support meetings."
3. The least and best outcomes for each goal are then described on the goal-attainment guide. These descriptions should be as specific as possible since they will be used as a means for judging client progress. In this case, the best outcome might be "three meetings per week," and the least, "one meeting per month."
4. The client's current functioning is recorded on each of the goal-attainment scales at the bottom of the guide. First the client's initial or baseline functioning should be arrived at by the helper and the client. Let us say that the helper and the client agree that the client, at intake, is functioning at less than expected outcome concerning attendance at support groups. Using the letter B for beginning or S for start, the helper records this information on the goal-attainment scale on the Goal no. 1 line at the 2 position.
5. At various points in therapy, additional notations can be made on the scale showing progress or relapse.
6. Besides the ability to monitor progress, the goal-attainment guide provides a tool for review of therapy during the termination process. At times, the client may be discouraged because one of the goals has not been achieved. The guide may be able to show that even if the best outcome was not achieved, some progress was made (Blocher, 1987).

TABLE 12.1   Goal-attainment Guide

Case of _____

Goal Statement No. 1	Goal Statement No. 2	Goal Statement No. 3
_____	_____	_____
_____	_____	_____
Specific success indicators	Specific success indicators	Specific success indicators
_____	_____	_____
_____	_____	_____
_____	_____	_____
Outcome Description	Outcome Description	Outcome Description

Least favorable likely outcome
Less than expected level of attainment
Expected goal-attainment
Better than expected outcome
Best outcome

Goal-Attainment Scale

	1	2	3	4	5
	Least Favorable Outcome	Less Than Expected Outcome	About Expected Outcome	Better Than Expected Outcome	Best Probable Outcome
Goal scale					
Goal no. 1					
Goal no. 2					
Goal no. 3					
Average goal-attainment with this case					

Source: Reprinted by permission of Donald A. Blocher.

Use Program Evaluation

Program evaluation means looking at the effectiveness of an entire program rather than the outcomes of a particular student, couple, or family. Helpers are routinely asked to begin and participate in treatment programs, but frequently the reason these programs are begun and continued is that they sound like good ideas without regard to whether or not they work. Let us take an example in a school setting. Recently a first-year school counselor, Robb, was asked to set up a "character education" program at his elementary school. In the state where Robb lived, character education was mandated, and this seemed like a good enough reason to implement the program. Most schools bought posters and instructed teaching faculty to discuss a particular value (such as "responsibility") with their students each month. When the school principal asked Robb to design and operate this treatment, the principal insisted that the counselor build in a system of evaluation. Together principal and counselor agreed that the program, if effective, ought to have an effect on the behavior of students, and so together they developed a set of outcomes that they hoped would reveal the effectiveness of the character education project. When the participants know what the outcomes should be, they work in a more focused way. In this case, Robb identified a decrease in disrespectful behavior toward fellow students (those that resulted in a referral to the office) as the hoped-for outcome. Instead of a monthly class discussion, Robb conducted sessions on respectful behavior over the entire school year. The treatment involved role-playing and discussion geared to each grade level. During the school year, the principal and the counselor tracked all the referrals to the office and kept a tally of the reasons for the referral. Over the school year, they were able to see a decrease as the character education program took hold. At the end of the year, the counselor received a grant from the school district to continue this work and teach it to others. The point of this story is clear. Helpers who can prove that they are having an impact will benefit professionally. More important, we will be able to feel that we are administering treatments that are effective, and we can have more confidence that our clients are being helped.

TERMINATION

Termination is a term helpers use to denote the period of time when client and helper negotiate the end to the helping relationship. Much of the literature on termination is somewhat dated. This is probably because helping relationships do not last as long as they did two decades ago. Termination may be less disruptive these days because treatment is typically brief. In addition, many helpers have now adopted a "family doctor" model that allows for periodic return checkups rather than a final end.

Even the word *termination* evokes dread or at least an Arnold Schwarzenegger movie. The practical difficulties in termination include how to manage premature termination, when to bring it up, and dealing with the emotional reaction of both helper and client. If handled well, termination is a time for celebration as the client reviews progress made and together helper and client make plans to keep the momentum going when they are no longer meeting on a regular basis. Termination can also be a catalyst for growth (Gelso & Woodhouse, 2002).

How to Prevent Premature Termination

Frequently our issue is not how to exit the relationship but rather how to restrain the client from terminating until real progress has been made. In a meta-analysis of 125 studies of psychotherapy, the average dropout rate was 49% (Wierzbicki & Pekarik, 1993). No single client characteristic can predict premature termination (Connell, Grant, & Mullin, 2006). Unplanned endings appear to be associated with a deterioration of the therapeutic relationship, or they may be the result of a client feeling a sense of relief after only a few sessions (Connell et al., 2006).

It is discouraging to a helper when a promising client does not return after the first or second session, and the helper may think of this as a failure. Yet, there is evidence that even one-session counseling is often viewed as helpful. Clients also expect a shorter duration in therapy than their counselors (June & Smith, 1983). Yalom (1995) has suggested that early termination by the client may be a good thing since it acts as a safety valve when the client/counselor match is not correct (see also Epperson, 1983). Still, an argument can be made that it is preferable to complete therapy in a formal way or to refer the client after a few sessions rather than letting the relationship wind down. A positive ending may pave the way for the client to return to therapy (Kramer, 1986, 1990). A petering out may cast the helper as ineffective or the client as a failure (Ogrodniczuk, Joyce, & Piper, 2005).

Certainly clients "vote with their feet"; that is, they leave the helping relationship when they feel it is not helping them meet their goals. But there are a number of reasons that clients terminate prematurely that have little to do with how much progress they are making. They also leave the helping relationship due to dissatisfaction with the helper or the process and because of circumstances such as travel time and financial constraints (Roe, Dekel, Harel, & Fennig, 2006). If the helping process is not seen as helpful or if there is a mismatch between helper and client, there is little the helper can do except identify this problem as early as possible and perhaps make a referral to another helper or setting. The suggestions listed below are a combination of observations and recommendations from the literature concerning ways of preventing clients from terminating prematurely (Joyce, Piper, Ogrodniczuk, & Klein, 2007; Mennicke, Lent, & Burgoyne, 1988; Ogrodniczuk et al., 2005; Pekarik, 1985; Piselli, Halgin, & MacEwan, 2011):

1. Avoid delays in seeing clients. Although some clients seem to come only during emergencies and fail to follow through, clients who must wait 2 or 3 weeks for an appointment may not arrive at all or may be hostile and less motivated.

2. In cases and settings where clients might be expected to drop out early, make contracts with clients for completing a small goal or a small number of sessions (6–10).

3. Do not process clients through several channels. Clients who are interviewed by an intake counselor or clerical person for screening and then referred to their permanent helper may not return because they have been treated impersonally. It is difficult enough for many people to reveal their need for help by making the phone call for an appointment. Asking them to disclose their problems to several people may be too much.

4. Provide an orientation to the helping process and offer information about the qualifications of the helper. If it is written as a handout, the client can read it as they wait for their first appointment. Orienting the client to the process can develop positive and realistic expectations and diminish client fears. Fees, billing procedures, expectations of client behavior, confidentiality, and other issues can be included in the handout. It is also a good idea to go over this again in the first session. If clients are not appropriate for the services you are offering, they should be referred to the appropriate setting.

5. Use reminders to motivate client attendance. Obtain the client's permission to call or to write a brief reminder just before the next session. This simple suggestion can improve attendance significantly. Think about your dentist. Do you get a call the night before reminding you of the appointment? A phone call midweek may also serve to remind the client of homework and encourage the client to work on therapeutic issues without the helper even mentioning them.

6. When a client terminates early, call him or her and find out why. There may be several unexpected reasons for the client's termination other than a feeling that the therapy is unproductive. These reasons range from the embarrassment of having

seen an acquaintance in the waiting room, difficulty with transportation, or rudeness from support personnel. Help the client overcome these barriers.

7. In cases where the client decides to terminate before goal completion, the helper should try to go the extra mile (Kaplan & Sadock, 1998) by making it easy for the client to return at a later time. This may mean agreeing with the client's idea to interrupt therapy and directly inviting the client to come back later by setting a follow-up date.

8. Provide a safe environment so that clients can talk about the therapeutic process and how it is fitting their needs. Create a strong working alliance early on and fix ruptures as they occur.

9. Consider negotiating a treatment plan with the client that includes time limits. Brief treatment tends to have fewer dropouts.

How to Tell Whether Termination Is Needed

Clients should be terminated when they have attained their goals, when they have been receiving counseling or psychotherapy for some time and have not made progress, or when there are signs that they can handle their issues independently. Most professional organizations, including the American Counseling Association, the American Psychological Association, the American Association for Marriage and Family Therapy, and the National Association of Social Workers, state in their codes of ethics that a client should be terminated if he or she is not making progress. In such cases, the client should be made aware of alternative sources of help, and a referral should be made. The decision about whether a client is making progress is not always easy. Some of the signals that suggest a client is ready for termination, such as missing sessions, coming late for sessions, or failing to do homework, can also be due to contextual factors such as a change in working hours. In addition, all helpers have a duty not to abandon clients seeking help, and therefore terminating a client who does not seem to be making progress is a delicate process.

How exactly do we know when helping has been successful? Should we consider success from the standpoint of the client or from the standpoint of the helper? Should we define success in terms of societal standards (dangerousness, employment, school grades) or from some ideal of mental health advanced by theorists? Mathews (1989) suggests reviewing one's caseload and asking oneself, "If I had a waiting list right now, would I be seeing this client?" (p. 37). Based on Maholich and Turner (1979), Sciscoe (1990) identified five questions a helper might consider in order to assess a client's readiness for termination:

1. Is the presenting problem under control?
2. Has the client reduced the initial level of distress by developing better coping skills?
3. Has the client achieved greater self-awareness and better relationships?
4. Are life and work more enjoyable for the client?
5. Does the client now feel capable of living without the therapeutic relationship?

The first four of Sciscoe's questions highlight improvements that have been made and goals that have been achieved. The last question is especially important, because it asks the helper whether or not the client is able to maintain the gains of helping without the therapeutic relationship. Answering these questions in a dialogue with the client and arriving at a mutual decision can help in working out the knotty question of termination.

How to Prepare a Client for Termination

Most experts agree that sudden termination is not advisable (Brammer, Shostrom, & Abrego, 1989; Knox et al., 2011; Macneil, Hasty, Conus, & Berk, 2010), but how soon should the topic of termination be brought up? Dixon and Glover (1984) recommend that at least three sessions in advance of termination be devoted to issues of termination, while Lamb (1985) recommends at least seven sessions. As much time as was spent in relationship building in the beginning of the therapy should be devoted to termination, say Cormier and Cormier (1985); and one-sixth of the time spent in therapy should be devoted to termination, according to Shulman (1979). In other words, there should be a period of preparation. How long this should take is a matter of judgment and should be determined by the length and quality of the therapeutic relationship.

During the preparation period, the helper leads the client in a discussion that reviews the counseling process and progress made. In general, it is important to emphasize the client's strengths and to end on a positive note; however, areas left untreated or unresolved must also be discussed (Anderson & Stewart, 1983). One way to review is simply to compare before-and-after client functioning from the viewpoint of both helper and client. This is where outcome evaluation using client goal-attainment or testing can be extremely informative. At times, it is useful to discuss an early session when the client was at a different stage of functioning in order to examine the contrast. Some helpers like to read case notes that they wrote early on and other notes written later in the relationship to highlight changes. Any unfinished business between client and helper should be addressed, and the client should be encouraged to think about how he or she will look back on the counseling experience in the future. How will the client evaluate himself or herself if a return to see the helper is needed?

DEALING WITH LOSS AT TERMINATION

The general strategy to help clients deal with their feelings of loss at termination is to take time to prepare them and to ask them to identify both positive and negative feelings associated with the end of the relationship. Clients may be upset by termination because it is associated with other historical losses (Macneil et al., 2010; Ward, 1984). Some suggestions to help prevent, explore, and resolve these feelings include (Cavanagh, 1982; Dixon & Glover, 1984; Hackney & Cormier, 1979; Macneil et al., 2010; Munro & Bach, 1975):

1. Bring termination up early.
2. Help the client think of termination as an opportunity to put new learning into practice.
3. Specify the number of counseling sessions at the very beginning, so both helper and client are prepared for termination.
4. Use a fading procedure; that is, space appointments over increasing lengths of time (MacCluskie & Ingersoll, 2001).
5. Help the client to see his or her own actions that led to success and that they have personal resources to deal with future issues.
6. Play down the importance of termination; play up the sense of accomplishment and the value of independence.
7. Use reflective listening to allow the client to express feelings of loss.

The Helper's Reaction to Termination

Kanfer and Schefft (1988) suggest that helpers need to accept the fact that termination inevitably occurs at a point far short of perfection. Many clients leave with the helper feeling that the solutions are still under construction. Besides the fact the helper must frequently let go of what seems to be an incomplete project, the helper may have also become deeply involved in the client's life. Helpers may even postpone termination because of their own attachments and feelings of sadness and loss (Gladding, 2008).

Goodyear (1981, p. 348) lists several possible reasons that helpers have trouble letting go:

1. The relationship may be quite significant to the helper.
2. The helper may feel uncertain that the client will be able to function independently.
3. The helper may believe that he or she was not effective.
4. The helper may feel that his or her professional identity is challenged by the client's premature termination.
5. The termination may represent a loss of continued learning for the helper, who was looking forward to gaining experience from the client's peculiar problem.
6. The helper may miss the vicarious excitement of the client's exploits.
7. The termination may uncover historical events associated with loss in the counselor's life.
8. A helper's feelings of loss at termination may also be due to a reliance on helping relationships to meet needs for intimacy (friendship) as well as a conscious or unconscious sexual attraction.

Krantz and Lund (1979) feel that trainees may have special difficulty with termination. Beginning helpers may keep clients too long because they like the client or because they hope that the client will accomplish even greater goals. They may also be unprepared for their own feelings or for the powerful loss experienced by the client, no matter how much they are intellectually informed. A supportive supervisory relationship is the best way to help trainees through difficult terminations (Sciscoe, 1990).

HOW TO MAINTAIN THERAPEUTIC GAINS AND PREVENT RELAPSE FOLLOWING TERMINATION

Helpers use a variety of techniques to help clients maintain the progress and avoid falling back into old patterns. Relapse prevention is another name for activities that the helper and client engage in to anticipate situations that are likely to lead to a return to former behaviors. Relapse prevention has been studied extensively in relation to addiction (Marlatt & Donovan, 2005). Listed below are a number of techniques designed to help maintain therapeutic gains and avoid setbacks (Cavanagh, 1982; Perry & Paquin, 1987):

Follow-up

The term *follow-up* refers to a brief contact the helper makes a few weeks or months following termination. The purpose of the contact, which might be a phone call, is to determine how the client is progressing and to remind the client that the door is open if counseling is needed in the future (Wolberg, 1954).

Fading

Fading means scheduling follow-up sessions with longer and longer intervals spaced over a 1-year period. The client can be informed of the follow-up system during the final sessions. For example, a helper can make brief phone calls to the client at 6 weeks, 6 months, and after a year. In other cases, it may be useful to actually have the client return for a single session at each of these times. When clients are learning specific skills, such as assertiveness training, stress management, and communication, these follow-ups can be called "booster sessions" or "refreshers," with the stated aim of reviewing learning and dealing with problems. One benefit of planning for follow-up as the relationship is winding down is that the client need not later feel a sense of failure if a return to counseling is needed. If the client decides to cancel the later visits, this can be construed as a sign of success. These planned follow-up sessions are particularly useful with children and adolescents, because they may benefit most from reminders and may see them as a sign of the helper's continuing interest.

Contacts with Paraprofessionals

Some agencies provide follow-up services with a paraprofessional for clients on a free or inexpensive basis. Mental health clinics, for example, may provide home visits by caseworkers to monitor medication and identify areas of continuing need in those suffering from severe mental disorders.

Self-Help Groups

Self-help groups, if improperly conducted, can be a case of the blind leading the blind, but they can also be extremely powerful supports for clients following treatment. The quality of such groups is quite variable, and so the helper must be familiar with groups in the client's vicinity before making a recommendation. Because clients are sometimes reluctant to attend self-help groups, helpers must strongly encourage clients to become involved. Sometimes clients do not want to attend self-help groups because it forces them to admit they have a problem. For example, college students who have alcohol problems rarely attend Alcoholics Anonymous because they do not see themselves as alcoholics and do not want to be different from their peers. It is crucial that the helper support attendance at support groups in these cases and encourage the client to attend a few sessions (perhaps three times) before giving up. The composition of these groups varies tremendously, and it is important to find one that suits the client.

Self-Monitoring Activities

Self-monitoring means that the client is asked to keep records of progress on the treatment goals. These reports can be reviewed at the follow-up sessions. In Chapter 13, we show how a client named Joe charts his emotions and subjective discomfort. While a client may continue to self monitor using charts, a less formal way to encourage self-monitoring and self-reflection is teaching the client to use a personal journal to explore thoughts and feelings. In addition, self-monitoring can be achieved when the helper gives feedback to the client through email or text-messaging (Bauer, de Niet, Timman, & Kordy, 2010).

Self-Management Skills

Self-management allows clients to make contracts with themselves for the change they are seeking. Clients can learn to use behavioral principles to reward their own positive behaviors and to punish negative ones (Kanfer, 1975; Kazdin, 1980; Rudestam, 1980). For example, students can learn to make watching a 1-hour television show contingent on completing several hours of study. A helper can assist a depressed client to develop a system of rewards for engaging in physical activity. During follow-up sessions, helpers can monitor client progress and help clients develop new strategies and reward systems. Clients can send both printed and recorded materials back to the helper as evidence of practice.

Role-Playing for Relapse Prevention

At the outset, the client is advised that relapse is a normal part of change and that most progress occurs as "two steps forward and one step back." The client may discuss temptations or even write them down. For example, couples in marriage counseling are asked to talk about what might lead to a disagreement and brainstorm ways of preventing it from occurring.

The technique of role-playing is described in detail in the next chapter. Role-playing can make these relapse opportunities more realistic. If the client is in an individual setting, the helper can assist the client in constructing a scene that the client feels is somewhat challenging. The client is then coached as he or she plays various parts. For example, a client who is trying to quit smoking role-plays sitting at a bar when a friend offers her a cigarette. The helper may need to play the part of the client if she needs assistance in finding the language to refuse. The goal is to have the client discover a satisfactory way of dealing with a situation that could trigger a relapse.

Letter Writing

Young and Rosen (1985) describe a group therapy activity in which clients write a letter to themselves during the last group session before termination. In their letters, clients remind themselves of their goals and also excuses they may use to try to avoid achieving their goals. The group facilitator mails the letters to clients about a month after the completion of group therapy.

Letter writing by the helper is an underutilized but powerful way to spark the client's motivation to continue working on goals as well as to remind the client that the helper is concerned and available. Narrative therapists, in recent years, have been the main champions of letter writing (Andrews, Clark, & Baird, 1997). Through letters, a helper can reinforce the client's new life story and help the client continue to see the new perspective developed in therapy (White, 2000).

MyCounselingLab™

Go to Topic 11, *Maintaining Clinical Gains, Preventing Setbacks, and Relapse Prevention,* on the MyCounselingLab™ site (www.MyCounselingLab.com) for *Learning the Art of Helping: Building Blocks and Techniques,* Fifth Edition, where you can:

- Find learning outcomes for *Maintaining Clinical Gains, Preventing Setbacks, and Relapse Prevention,* along with the national standards that connect to these outcomes.
- Complete Assignments and Activities that can help you more deeply understand the chapter content.
- Apply and practice your understanding of the core skills identified in the chapter with the Building Counseling Skills unit.
- Prepare yourself for professional certification with a Practice for Certification quiz.
- Connect to videos through the Video and Resource Library.

Summary

This chapter began by advocating that helpers stay current with emerging *outcome research* or research about client changes that accrue because of the therapeutic relationship. Using outcome measures such as tests, SUDS scales, and goal-attainment scaling, assures us that clients are working towards their goals. We also recommended using *practice-based evidence* or clinical data like progress notes evaluate clients' progress. The last part of the chapter dealt with termination or the ending of the helping relationship. A major problem is determining when a client has reached the maximum benefit or whether the client is terminating prematurely. Suggestions were made to assist helpers in reducing the probability of early termination and to develop a positive end to the relationship. When clients reach their goals, helpers should first prepare them for termination and then deal with the client's feelings of loss (and their own) that might accompany the ending. Even after the helping relationship is over, helpers can build in some ways of maintaining the client's progress while leaving the door open for booster sessions.

Exercises

GROUP EXERCISES

Exercise 1: Develop a Goal-Attainment Scale

The purpose of this exercise is to allow students to fill out the goal-attainment scale form (Table 12.1). In pairs, students each take a turn as helper and client identifying a real or fictional problem that they could imagine changing. Complete the form, using the six steps contained in this text under the heading, *Use Goal-Attainment Measures.* When you have both had the opportunity to fill out the form with your client, discuss how useful it was to analyze the goal in this way.

Exercise 2: Role-Play a Termination Session

In a small group, two members role-play client and helper discussing termination, which is to take place in a week's time. The client and counselor agree that most goals have been met, but the client feels that there are some issues that are still unresolved. In this scenario, the other members of the small group act as observers and give the helper feedback on the following:

- Did the helper review the history of the helping process and the therapeutic relationship with the client?

- Did the helper help the client celebrate success in attaining the goals?
- How did the helper handle unresolved issues?
- Did the helper leave the door open while expressing confidence in the client's readiness to terminate?

SMALL GROUP DISCUSSIONS

Discussion 1: Research as Reflection

In this chapter, you are told that research is important but should be used for reflection rather than prescription. What does the author mean by this? How do you plan to keep current on new findings in the field when you are no longer a student?

Discussion 2: Sample Case

Discuss the following case with a small group. Your client is a 17-year-old high school senior who has been discussing suicidal thoughts with his classmates. His grades have slipped over the last semester and his interest in going on to training as a chef has diminished. On what goals would you want to focus? What sort of assessment techniques would you use to determine if he or she is making progress? What sort of outcomes would you likely be tracking? How would you determine that helping is nearing completion?

WRITTEN EXERCISES

Exercise 1: Functional Analysis and Self-Management

One obstacle to change is overcoming the force of habit. A bad habit can be frustrating because we seem to persist in it even when we do not want to. One way of attacking bad habits is to scientifically identify what factors are supporting the behavior. This is called conducting a *functional analysis*. Clients can learn functional analysis and then devise self-management strategies to eliminate bad habits by building in rewards (positive reinforcement) for new behaviors. Self-management was mentioned earlier as a method to maintain treatment gains. To understand this process better, select a behavior of your own that you would like to change. Label a blank sheet of paper "Functional Analysis" and follow the instructions below:

1. Begin by identifying the behavior or bad habit you would like to change with as much objectivity,

simplicity, and specificity as you can. For example, "I bite my fingernails about four times a day for 5 minutes at a time."

2. Indicate things that occur simultaneously with or around the same time as the problem behavior, for instance, "I bite my fingernails when I am watching television or when I am reading a good book."

3. List everything you can think of that is usually *not* associated with the bad habit. For example, "When I am biting my nails, I am not around other people."

4. What happens right before the problem behavior? For example, "I am nervous or excited."

5. What happens right after the problem behavior? Do you get a reward or is something negative eliminated? For example, "I am angry at myself for biting my nails and I call myself an idiot." "I feel a little less nervous when I bite my nails during a scary show."

6. Based on your answers to questions 2, 3, 4, and 5, describe, nonjudgmentally, the chain of events that leads up to and follows your bad habit. For example, "When I am biting my nails, it seems to distract me and I feel less nervous. Then I engage in negative self-talk when I realize what I am doing."

7. In this step, identify a hypothesis about the problem behavior. Based on this exercise, what do you think is maintaining (rewarding) the problem behavior? For example, "Biting my nails makes me feel less anxious when I am alone watching television or reading a book."

8. How could you manipulate the environment to reduce the problem behavior? For example, "I could make an agreement with myself not to watch television by myself for a while. When I am reading or watching TV, I could wear gloves or coat my fingers with something that tastes bad. That way, I won't bite my nails without thinking."

9. How could you use rewards to change the behavior? For example, "If I can make it through one day without biting my nails, I will treat myself to an ice-cream cone. If I can make it through a week, I will go and get a manicure."

10. Devise a plan to manipulate the environment and to reward alternative behavior. In this final step, state your plan for changing the environment and reward system. For example, "I plan to only watch television with other people for the next 60 days or wear gloves if I am alone. In addition, for every week that I succeed in refraining from nail biting, I will reward myself with a new article of clothing or a manicure."

Questions to Consider When Utilizing Functional Analysis

When applying these techniques with clients, how will you know which rewards will be the most effective?

What kinds of clients and client problems might work best with a functional analysis and positive reinforcement?

Exercise 2: Writing a Progress Note

Using Figure 12.2 as a model, write progress notes on a fictitious client. Then, evaluate them according to the following criteria:

1. Did the notes capture the client's progress toward goals?
2. Did you report how you worked on the goals in today's session?
3. Were your homework assignments and plans also related to the goals?
4. Did you include any random thoughts, personal opinions, or sensitive information that might be harmful to the client?

SELF-ASSESSMENT

Before you record and transcribe a final session with a client, take some time to review the feedback you have received from teachers and fellow students during group exercises and in your individual practice. Think about each of the following building block skills, and for each, rate your current level of mastery.

1. I understand the concept.
2. I can identify it and give examples.
3. I can do it occasionally.
4. I can do it regularly.

_____ Eye contact
_____ Body position
_____ Attentive silence
_____ Voice tone
_____ Gestures and facial expressions
_____ Door openers and minimal encouragers
_____ Open and closed questions
_____ Paraphrasing
_____ Reflecting feelings
_____ Reflecting meaning
_____ Summarizing
_____ Focusing on the Client
_____ Boiling Down the Problem

Compare the scores with your answers in Chapter 7. Where have you improved? Where do you still need improvement?

HOMEWORK

Homework 1: A Final Recording and Transcript

Previously, you recorded and transcribed a session with a client. Now you might want to make a final video and evaluate it in the same way.

Step 1

Record 20–30 minutes with a classmate who is discussing a real problem or who is role-playing. During the recording, your goal as a helper is to:

- Demonstrate the nonjudgmental listening cycle
- Demonstrate challenging skills
- Demonstrate goal-setting skills including boiling down the problem to a specific goal and focusing on the client

Step 2

Choose the best 15–20 minutes of the recording and transcribe every word of both client and helper, using the format of Table 7.1. It is important that the client's statements appear directly *below* your helping responses so that the connection between the two can be examined. Be sure you have permission to record from the client. You can do this aloud on the recording and/or in writing.

Step 3

Listen to the recording or read the transcript and make comments, naming each of the skills that your response exemplifies. Sometimes students describe their responses rather than categorizing them. It is important to identify the skills using the terminology in the book so that you can count and evaluate their appropriateness. The comments column is a place for you to reflect on your responses. Do not just note weaknesses; identify strengths as well.

In a separate paragraph, reflect for a few minutes on your progress from the start of your training until now. Make some comments about what you have gained. What impact has it had on you personally or on your professional goals or your relationships with others?

TABLE 12.2

(1) Skills	(2) Tally	(3) Comment and Reflect on Depth of Client's Exploration	(4) Questions and Problems
Invitational skills			
Nonverbal skills (checkmark if okay)			
Opening skills			
Questions			
Encouragers			
Reflecting skills			
Paraphrases			
Reflections of feeling			
Advanced reflecting skills			
Reflections of meaning			
Summaries			
Challenging skills			
Feedback			
Confrontation			
Goal-setting skills			
Focusing on the client			
Boiling down the problem			

What steps have you taken so far? What must you do now to go further?

Homework 2: Video Evaluation Form

In some training situations, a final transcript may not be required. Some instructors want to watch and evaluate the videos alone, while others prefer to watch the video with the student. Using the recording you made for the previous assignment, watch the video twice.

During the first viewing of the video, use Table 12.2 to evaluate your basic skills:

- Make tally marks in column 2 next to the skill in each of the first five skill areas. A tally mark is made each time you see a particular skill demonstrated.
- Stop the video, and in column 3 make any comments or reflections about "depth." How deeply have you been able to allow the client to explore? Does your discussion touch on meaning?
- In column 4, list any question or problems you wish to share with your instructor. Make note of the video counter number or a quotation. That will help you find the exact spot again.

JOURNAL STARTERS

Reflect on your termination experiences. They may be associated with leaving a job, a girlfriend or boyfriend, school, family, or a group of friends. How do you think these experiences might affect how you deal with clients who are ending the helping relationship? Are goodbyes hard for you? If these transitions have always been smooth for you, do you think you will be able to relate to someone who has difficulty letting go?

Therapeutic Factors and Advanced Change Techniques: Part I

MyCounselingLab™

Visit the **MyCounselingLab** site for *Learning the Art of Helping: Building Blocks and Techniques,* Fifth Edition to enhance your understanding of chapter concepts. You'll have the opportunity to practice your skills through video- and case-based Assignments and Activities as well as Building Counseling Skills units, and to prepare for your certification exam with Practice for Certification quizzes.

REPLAN and the Therapeutic Factors
- R = Establishing and Maintaining a Strong Helper/Client Relationship
- E = Enhancing Efficacy and Self-Esteem
- P = Practicing New Behaviors
- L = Lowering and Raising Emotional Arousal
- A = Activating Client Expectations, Hope, and Motivation
- N = Providing New Learning Experiences

Treatment Planning and the REPLAN System
- Steps in Treatment Planning Using the REPLAN Model

The Therapeutic Factor of Enhancing Efficacy and Self-Esteem
- Sources of Low Self-Esteem

Silencing the Internal Critic: The Technique of Countering
- How to Counter
- Problems and Precautions When Teaching the Countering Technique
- A Variation on Countering: Thought Stopping

Practicing New Behaviors

Role-Playing
- Elements of Role-Playing

There comes a stage in the development of every helper when we begin to search for the perfect technique or "silver bullet" that will work for all clients, or at least for the client that is confounding us right now. At this juncture, the helper begins a search of literature and attends conferences to find the answer. The helper begins to wonder if what he or she learned in school is really relevant to the real world of unique individuals, where one technique or theory does not seem to work for every client. If you are comfortable working with a particular theory, the change techniques you select will most likely be associated with the theory. But if you want to utilize techniques from other theories, you must find a way to incorporate them in a rational and systematic way. So, how can one choose what is best from a variety of sources without being haphazard?

One metaphor for this comes from quilt making. There are two ways to make a quilt. Either you pick up the pieces nearest to you and sew them together, hoping they will fit when the quilt is done, or you start with a pattern and find the pieces that fit into your design. Starting with a design is the systematic kind of treatment planning recommended by this book. It begins with the agreed-upon goals chosen by helper and client and leads to selecting methods and techniques that are aimed at those goals. This is not a trial-and-error method that begins when we hear about a new technique and just start experimenting with it. In this method, called the REPLAN system, the helper looks to the six therapeutic factors that we discussed in Chapter 2 as a way of fulfilling the client's goals. The REPLAN method of treatment planning recommends that the helper consider the background of the client and the client's problems by reflecting on which of the therapeutic factors are most needed.

REPLAN AND THE THERAPEUTIC FACTORS

As we discussed in Chapter 2, a therapeutic factor is a common or underlying element that explains why many different therapy systems seem to be effective. This viewpoint suggests that the hundreds of change techniques that helpers use are all evoking the healing potential in one or more of these common factors. The concept of therapeutic factors is useful simply because it provides a way of organizing the techniques you are learning and because it will help you to think about the purpose of the techniques you are choosing. The whole range of helping skills and techniques can be linked to one or more of these six factors, and this provides you with a rational way to home in on the special techniques that might be effective for your client. For the sake of convenience, we refer to each of the factors by a letter. Together, they form the acronym REPLAN, which is a way of remembering them when we think about planning the course of helping.

R = Establishing and Maintaining a Strong Helper/Client Relationship

The therapeutic alliance was discussed in Chapter 3 and in later chapters when you learned invitational and reflecting skills. Enhancing the helper/client bond involves both the nonjudgmental listening cycle on the part of the helper and the client's willingness and ability to enter the relationship. Differences between the two people also affect the therapeutic alliance. Not only must the helper provide a therapeutic atmosphere, but he or she must also take into account the unique background, family, religion, and culture that can influence the client's reaction to the helper and to the helping process. In addition, the helper must deal with transference and countertransference issues and other ruptures in the relationship that might sidetrack the helping process.

E = Enhancing Efficacy and Self-Esteem

In this chapter, we will look at techniques that improve a client's confidence in his or her abilities and also deal with an underlying lack of self-worth. Nearly all helpers agree that improved self-esteem is a desired goal, but changing long-held beliefs about the self is a challenge.

P = Practicing New Behaviors

Later in this chapter, we will look at ways of helping clients practice a new behavior once it has been learned. For example, clients may learn communication techniques to improve the couple relationship, but they need to practice both within sessions and between sessions so that the new skills are firmly established. Many practice techniques are available to strengthen fragile new learning.

L = Lowering and Raising Emotional Arousal

The next chapter (Chapter 14) introduces change techniques that include methods used to quiet strong emotions as well as to arouse hidden emotions. Quieting techniques involve such activities as relaxation training, whereas arousing techniques include asking clients to become more aware of suppressed feelings.

A = Activating Client Expectations, Hope, and Motivation

Chapter 14 also introduces ways that a helper can motivate a demoralized client. Here you will learn more about the use of encouragement. That chapter also discusses ways of identifying the techniques that match the client's level of motivation.

N = Providing New Learning Experiences

The number of techniques in this category far surpasses all the other groupings. A great deal of what helpers do involves stimulating new learning by provoking insight, directly teaching social skills, and reframing. These will be discussed in Chapter 14.

TREATMENT PLANNING AND THE REPLAN SYSTEM

There are many different methods for treatment planning. Most people are familiar with the diagnostic treatment planning method. It is the medical methodology that begins by assessing the client and arriving at a diagnosis. The diagnosis becomes the basis for determining what treatment the client will receive. If you have major depression, for example, you receive a certain treatment; if you have obsessive-compulsive disorder, you receive another (cf. Antony & Barlow, 2010).

Alternatively, many clinicians construct treatment plans based on the theory to which they subscribe. The techniques one eventually chooses may come from the person-centered, Gestalt, Adlerian, psychodynamic, or behavioral theories. As indicated earlier in the book, there is good reason to think that an integrative approach to treatment planning is useful, particularly early in training. Even before one is entrenched in a particular theoretical viewpoint, one can utilize the techniques of different theories with a systematic framework as a guide.

This brings us to how the concept of therapeutic factors can aid us in setting up a general treatment plan. The first step in treatment planning is to make a list of problems that have been identified by the counselor, the client, or both. The next step is to order the problems in priority, choose one or more problems to focus on, and then identify techniques to address these problems (Woody, Detweiler-Bedell, Teachman, & O'Hearn, 2003). REPLAN is the goal-oriented, treatment-planning model using six therapeutic factors. The REPLAN system does not conflict with making a *DSM-IV* diagnosis or using theoretically oriented models, but it does assert that nearly all clients with the same diagnosis need different treatments. Therefore, treatment strategies must be tailored to the client's goals and the unique characteristics of the client rather than to a specific diagnosis.

The REPLAN system is distinguishable from other forms of treatment planning because it focuses on a relatively few number of client goals, using strategies associated with one or two therapeutic factors. This makes it a brief treatment model. This approach has the benefit of focusing clients on a few goals at a time, rather than planning an elaborate treatment regimen that may collapse over time as the client's situation changes. The approach is not incompatible with long-term therapy, but it approaches client problems as distinct goals that must be regularly evaluated and replanned. Replanning occurs frequently during the helping process because client goals shift as some problems are resolved and new insights on old problems emerge.

Steps in Treatment Planning Using the REPLAN Model

The three basic steps in REPLAN treatment planning are:

1. Formulate mutually agreed-upon treatment goals, as a result of assessment, that are understandable to both client and helper. These goals are then boiled down to a workable, solvable form and placed in priority order.
2. Use the therapeutic factors (maintaining a strong helper/client relationship; enhancing efficacy and self-esteem; practicing new behaviors; lowering and raising emotional arousal; activating client expectations, hope, and motivation; and providing new learning experiences) to generate a list of possible treatment strategies or techniques to achieve the goals.
3. Replan the treatment on a regular basis, say, every 6 weeks, to move new problems into focus as old issues are resolved.

Once an overall treatment plan has been constructed, the helper generates a list of potential techniques by asking two questions: "What therapeutic factors are most likely to help the client reach the goals?" and "What strategies, methods, or techniques will be

TABLE 13.1   Treatment Plan for Matthew

Long-Term Goal	Short-Term Goal	Therapeutic Factor	Change Technique
Possess better interpersonal skills	Be able to demonstrate nonverbal listening skills	New Learning Experiences	Teach basic communication theory, listening, and self-disclosure
Be able to handle social situations with moderate anxiety levels	Use slow deep breathing to reduce anxiety at the supermarket checkout	Lowering Emotional Arousal	Use a basic relaxation technique to reduce anxiety before entering social situations
Be able to ask someone out for a date	Role-play asking someone out for coffee	Practicing New Behaviors	

most effective and acceptable to the client?" To illustrate how this works in practice, let us look at the case example of Matthew, a 25-year-old single, white male, a chemist, who is shy and wishes to meet and date women but has not been successful. Matthew's main problem is anxiety in social situations. Together he and the helper, Nadia, identify the following positive goal: to be able to go out with a woman and have fun.

To initiate the REPLAN method, Nadia asks herself, "Which therapeutic factors would be most helpful for Matthew in achieving his goal?" Based on her knowledge of Matthew's situation, it seems clear that practicing new behaviors and new learning experiences would be the most useful place to begin. Now that Nadia has identified the major therapeutic factors, she asks herself a second question, "What specific methods under these therapeutic factors would be most effective with Matthew?" She then selects strategies to evoke the therapeutic factors. Table 13.1 shows the first draft of the treatment plan that she developed for Matthew using the REPLAN method.

In summary, the notion of therapeutic factors is a way of identifying what the client needs and selecting a general approach to the client's problems. The use of therapeutic factors is a heuristic, a method for stimulating thinking about possible techniques to employ. Then the helper narrows down the list of potential techniques based on the client's needs and the client's background. The rationale for this kind of approach is that it encourages the helper to weigh a wider variety of planned interventions than a theoretically oriented or a diagnostically oriented treatment planning model, and it asks the helper to be culturally sensitive, thinking about what will work for this particular client. In the remainder of this chapter, we present two of the therapeutic factors in more detail, **E**nhancing Efficacy and Self-Esteem and **P**racticing New Behaviors, and describe some techniques associated with each.

THE THERAPEUTIC FACTOR OF ENHANCING EFFICACY AND SELF-ESTEEM

Although the REPLAN system starts with "R" for relationship, we have already discussed the importance of the therapeutic alliance in Chapter 3. The next therapeutic factor we take up is "E," which stands for enhancing efficacy and self-esteem (see Figure 13.1). There is wide agreement that a positive self-concept is a keystone of mental health

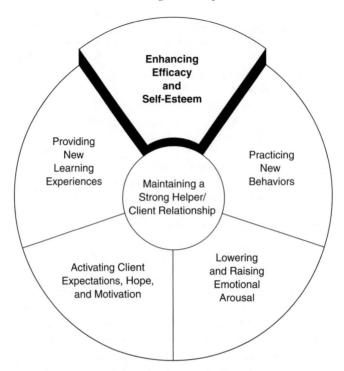

FIGURE 13.1   Therapeutic Factors in the REPLAN System: Enhancing Efficacy and Self-Esteem

and that raising self-esteem is a fundamental task of helping (Bednar & Peterson, 1995; Carlock, 1999; Kurpius, Rockwood, & Corbett, 1989; Schiraldi, McKay, & Fanning, 2005; Walz, 1990). Humanistic theorists have identified the helper's task as increasing "can-ness." For example, Carl Rogers focused on reducing the gap between one's perceived self and one's ideal self. Adler felt that a clear sign of mental health was "faith in oneself." Likewise, low self-esteem has long been identified as a cause or contributing factor in many psychological diagnoses and symptoms, especially anxiety (Rosenberg, 1962), depression (Beck, Rush, Shaw, & Emery, 1979; Burns, 1999b; Michalak, Teismann, Heidenreich, Ströhle, & Vocks, 2011; Wilson & Krane, 1980), stress, dependency, patho-logical guilt, borderline personality (Ingham, Kreitman, Miller, & Sasidharan, 1986), and substance abuse (Brehm & Back, 1968).

Still, the concept of self-esteem has been attacked as too vague, as overpopularized, and as a cure-all for problems ranging from addictions to misbehavior (Kaplan, 1995). One way of clarifying the concept is to recognize that self-esteem has two aspects: effi-cacy (competence) and self-worth (Branden, 1969, 1971, 1994; Witmer, 1985). Efficacy is an expectation that one can perform a specific task (Bandura, 1982, 1997). For example, when an experienced driver sits behind the wheel of a car, he or she feels a sense of con-fidence or expectation that driving a car is a manageable task. Efficacy is tied to specific activities, though it may generalize to similar situations. It is also subject to modification by experience. Having an auto accident could undermine one's sense of efficacy as a driver. Many clients are afraid to try new activities because of past failures. In addition, individuals with low self-esteem often do not pay sufficient attention to successes and improvements, tending to focus on their losses and failures. They may possess needed skills but do not recognize these abilities and strengths. The helper, by focusing on strengths and competencies, enhances the possibilities for success and improved self-esteem (Thompson, 1991).

In contrast to efficacy, **self-worth** is a global feeling that one has the right to exist, that one is basically good and is worthy to live. In short, it is self-approval. It is the sum total of one's attitudes about the self: the fundamental belief that one is "okay" or "not okay" (Berne, 1972). It is possible to have efficacy (feel competent) in a number of skills and still experience low self-worth. As helpers, we often meet intelligent, attractive, and talented individuals whose major problems are deeply held negative beliefs about themselves, despite their obvious competence.

STOP AND REFLECT

Ten Things I Can't Do

Self-esteem can be improved by increasing client self-efficacy and self-worth. For a moment, let us focus on efficacy, the feeling of competence. Efficacy is increased when clients recognize their current abilities or learn new skills. Helpers give clients these opportunities in session and in homework. The chances that a client will attempt a new activity are increased if he or she engages in **warm-up** activities, including thinking about, talking about, and visualizing the new behavior. To become more familiar with this process, try the following:

1. Make a list of 10 things you *cannot do* at the present time but would like to be able to do. For example, your list might include:

    "I would like to learn to swim."

    "I would like to ask someone out on a date."

    "I would like to be able to use a spreadsheet on the computer."

    "I would like to be able to learn ballroom dancing."

    "I would like to be able to speak a little Spanish."

    For this exercise, do not include personal qualities that you would like to develop or global statements about self-worth such as "I would like to be more patient" or "I would like to be a better person."

2. Once you have developed a list of 10 items, place the letter *T* next to each item if you have talked to a friend or family member about engaging in this activity. Place the letter *V* if you have ever visualized or daydreamed about yourself performing this task. Place the letter *M* for "models" if you have seen other people perform this task on several occasions. Place the letter *A* next to each task that you have attempted to perform in the last year.

3. It is thought that a person is more likely to engage in a new behavior if he or she gets ready by talking about it, visualizing it, and watching the behavior modeled. Conversely, when we have not readied ourselves through these activities, we are farther away from actually attempting the behavior. Look at your list and decide if your answers confirm this "readiness hypothesis." Identify one or two behaviors that have the fewest letters next to them. Which letters are

missing? The missing letters should indicate which activities you can initiate if you wish to increase your readiness.

4. Do you think you might experience any change in your self-esteem if you were able to engage in all the activities on your list?
5. Compare your answers and your reactions with those of others in your training group.

Sources of Low Self-Esteem

IRRATIONAL BELIEFS Irrational beliefs are self-destructive ideas that lead to low self-esteem (Daly & Burton, 1983). They cause us to suffer emotionally, but they are so firmly entrenched that they are difficult to challenge and expunge. Albert Ellis (1973) ascribes low self-esteem to a set of "nutty beliefs" about the self and the world. It is not our experiences that keep us in a state of low self-esteem, but our ideas that hold us there. For example, Ellis asserts that it is not a black cat that makes us afraid but the belief that a black cat causes bad luck. If we rid ourselves of **irrational beliefs** and develop more realistic ones, we reduce our emotional turmoil.

Although we each probably have something unique about our belief systems, Ellis found that most people's irrational ideas fall into some broad categories, and he has identified seven of the most common:

1. The idea that it is a dire necessity for an adult human to be loved or approved of by virtually every significant other person in his or her life
2. The idea that one should be thoroughly competent, adequate, and achieving in all possible respects to consider oneself worthwhile
3. The idea that certain people are bad, wicked, or villainous and that they should be severely blamed or punished for their villainy
4. The idea that it is awful and catastrophic when things are not the way one would like them to be
5. The idea that human unhappiness is externally caused and that people have little or no ability to control their terrors and disturbances
6. The idea that it is easier to avoid life's difficulties and self-responsibilities than to face them
7. The idea that one's past history is an all-important determinant of one's present behavior and that, because something once strongly affected one's life, it should definitely continue to do so (Ellis, 1973, p. 37)

In order to improve client self-esteem, helpers assist clients to identify and challenge irrational beliefs and to replace them with more reasonable and realistic ideas. Try to counter the above ideas with something more rational. For example, one would substitute Idea 1 with "I would like it if most of the people I value, loved or approved me in return, but that is not something I can control."

BODY IMAGE Psychological literature tells us that attractiveness is a valuable social asset (Adams, 1977) and that feeling unattractive is often equated with low self-esteem (Greenspan, 1983). Those with high self-worth generally feel good about their bodies. Those who do not like their bodies tend to be negative about themselves as a whole. An individual may have **poor body image** because of a physical disability, a difference, or a lack of attractiveness by media standards. Although, in the past, low self-esteem associated with body image may have been mainly the province of women, men's magazines now reflect that society has chosen some male ideals as well. Today men are expected to have "washboard abs" and other perfect features that provide a negative comparison for the average person. Body-image dissatisfaction is a particular problem of adolescent girls because of weight gain at that time of life (Choate, 2007). Group support for individuals with poor body image can be of benefit (Hall, 2006).

Helpers must also become aware of their evaluations of individuals who are unattractive. Helpers like attractive clients and feel less hopeful about those who are overweight and unattractive. We are all products of our culture and cultural ideas about mental health. Frequently, beginning helpers are unforgiving of clients who do not want to lose weight or who dress unattractively. Some clients view themselves as too fat or unattractive despite evidence to the contrary. This kind of distorted body image might be a symptom of more serious psychological syndromes, especially eating disorders (Baird & Sights, 1986; Choate, 2008). The belief that one must be perfect is probably behind this powerful dissatisfaction that propels starvation, causes self-induced vomiting in extreme cases, and engenders low self-esteem, anger, and distress even in those without major emotional problems (Thompson & Thompson, 1986).

STOP AND REFLECT

One way to increase self-esteem is to ask clients to pay more attention to their strengths and abilities. Because helping is a profession where results are not often immediate, even helpers need to pause and reflect on their accomplishments and positive qualities from time to time. Take this moment to reflect on your own personal assets.

A Self-Esteem Personal Inventory

1. Write down eight personal characteristics that you are proud of. For example, you may be creative, organized, humorous, goal oriented, and so on.
2. List eight things that you do well.
3. Write down a few compliments about yourself that you hear from friends and family. What are the good things people say about you?
4. List three occasions when you feel that you have truly helped another person.
5. List the top three accomplishments of your life so far.
6. Write down three things that you like about your body.

Keep your answers in mind when you answer this next set of questions:

- Now that you have completed this exercise, conduct a brief scan of your emotional state. Do you notice any difference in the way you feel?
- Were there any answers you felt reluctant to write down? Were you apprehensive about "bragging"? What are the rules in your own family or culture governing when it is all right to give yourself a compliment?
- If you were given this assignment as a client, how do you think you might have reacted?
- Which question was the most difficult to answer? Why? If you had been asked to list your negative qualities, would it have been easier or more difficult?

SILENCING THE INTERNAL CRITIC: THE TECHNIQUE OF COUNTERING

In this section, we will learn one key method for increasing client self-esteem: *countering*, a cognitive behavioral method for decreasing the internal, negative voices that depress performance and focus on failure. Certainly many clients will also benefit from assertiveness training and other behaviors that silence *external* critics, but the first step is to decrease the disapproval that is coming from our own mental activity. Countering means finding alternative thoughts to combat self-disapproval.

Before one can experience self-worth, it is often necessary to silence the **internal critic,** the "voice in the head" that reproaches and finds fault. This critic is probably created early in life through interaction with family and failure to meet self-imposed standards (McKay & Fanning, 1987). These irrational beliefs persist as silent sentences that the individual repeats in the mind and sometimes even aloud. Characteristically, these thoughts tend to occur automatically. For example, before giving a speech, the following thought might occur: "I am going to get up and make a fool of myself." The negative thought leads to negative emotions of anger, depression, and lowered expectations of the self. Thus, before self-esteem can be built, it is often necessary to reduce the power of the internal critic and to modify these self-statements (Dowd, 1985). As we mentioned earlier in this chapter, Ellis's method (called Rational Emotive Behavior Therapy or REBT) helps clients classify their beliefs as one of about seven major persistent irrational ideas. Then the helper uses rational argument to try and convince the client to abandon their "nutty thinking." The technique of countering is a constructivist version of Ellis's technique. Instead of indicating that the client must find rational replacements, the countering technique uses the idea that each person's belief structure is different and the most effective arguments will be found in the client's unique worldview.

How to Counter

Countering is a term coined by McMullin (2000). Countering means identifying the discouraging or self-downing statements a person says to himself or herself and replacing them with equally powerful affirmations. The countering method has five steps:

    Step 1: Do a Brief Assessment. Once helper and client have agreed that negative self-talk is a problem, it is critical to determine the frequency of the negative self-statements and their effects on the client. For this purpose, ask the client to engage in self-monitoring activities to determine the frequency and types of self-downing thoughts. Typically, the client carries an index card in a pocket, wallet, or purse and notes each time a self-criticism is made. The client writes down the exact words of each self-criticism and the negative emotions these thoughts provoke. The client brings the card back to the next session and discusses the thoughts he or she has noticed. The self-criticism card serves three functions: It gives client and helper more data about the problem; it helps the client make the connection between negative self-statements and the feeling states they produce; and it makes the client become aware of the thoughts. Just as noting the number of calories per day can decrease snacking, becoming aware of self-downing can lead to less negative thinking. Clients begin to "catch" themselves.

    Step 2: Identify the Negative Thought Patterns and Core Beliefs. Once the client has completed at least a week's worth of self-monitoring, the major negative thought patterns and core beliefs about the self may be identified. Together, helper and client look at the self-monitoring material and choose a few negative patterns to focus on. Often three or four general ideas (or core beliefs) about oneself come to the surface—for example:

"I am not disciplined and never get anything accomplished."

"I am disorganized."

"I'll never be able to reach my goals."

Step 3: Identify Effective Counters.   The counter can be a phrase, a sentence, or a single word such as "nonsense." The counter is a way of talking back to oneself and disputing the self-criticism. A counter is considered to be effective if it neutralizes the criticism. Effective counters are usually those that are consistent with the client's own beliefs rather than a list supplied by the helper.

Together, client and helper brainstorm a number of possible counters, and the client selects several with which to experiment. Here is an example of a self-criticism and a list of counters generated by client and helper:

Self-Criticism	Counters
"I am stupid."	1. "I have always performed well in school; there's no evidence for this."
	2. "Feeling stupid doesn't mean I am stupid."
	3. "That's something my dad always told me. But it's not true!"
	4. "Not true!"

Step 4: Test Counters and Modify Them.   The next stage in the process of eliminating self-criticism is to evaluate the effectiveness of the counters that the individual has practiced since the last helping session. One method for evaluating the potential effectiveness of a counter is for the helper to test the counter with the client during a session. First the client selects a statement from a list of self-criticisms and reads it aloud to the helper. After making the self-criticism, the client rates his or her emotional reaction to the criticism on a 10-point or 100-point SUDS (Subjective Units of Discomfort Scale). On the SUDS, a score of 100 (or 10) equals high emotional distress and 0 equals no emotional distress. Next the client reads a counter from the list that was brainstormed earlier and again rates his or her feelings of distress after saying the counter. In the following example, the client learned that this self-criticism was very disturbing (80) and that the counter was very effective because it reduced the strength of the emotional reaction to about 20.

Self-Criticism	Counter
"I am stupid."	"I have always performed well in school; there's no evidence for this."
SUDS after self-criticism—80	SUDS after counter—20

Step 5: Practice and Report.   Once the client has identified some effective counters for one or two negative thoughts, the client is asked to practice countering and report at the next session. At follow-up sessions, the helper and the client gauge progress and continually seek more effective counters. The client is asked to notice if negative thoughts have become less frequent.

Problems and Precautions When Teaching the Countering Technique

Ineffective counters should be discarded, and the client should be prepared for the fact that some counters are more potent than others. The client can be asked to modify the counter slightly in any way that might refine it or make it more effective. The helper should also suggest any personal words or phrases that might produce more self-confidence. For example, one client found that introducing each counter with "Clearly . . . " gave the counter more power for her.

Counters should be realistic. They should not be simply positive thinking or "affirmations," but should actually dispute the negative ideas. A statement such as "Every day, in every way, I'm getting better and better" is a "pep talk" without real substance; it is not tied to any particular self-criticism. Also, some negative self-statements are quite persistent, and it may take months to eliminate these insidious automatic thoughts.

McMullin (2000) suggests that the counter should be in the same mode as the thought it is disputing. Negative visual images should be countered with positive visual images. Angry thoughts should be countered with compassionate ones and "passive thoughts with assertive ones" (p. 5). Also, shorter counters tend to be more effective than longer ones.

A Variation on Countering: Thought Stopping

Sometimes clients are troubled by unwanted thoughts and images that create anxiety and depression and damage self-esteem. Unwanted thoughts and images may be memories of failure or concern about upcoming events. We are all familiar with lying in bed at night thinking about all the upcoming responsibilities. Once such thoughts get started, they snowball, creating more and more anxiety unless we have the skills to suppress our thinking when it gets out of control. Thought stopping has been used to treat all kinds of recurring thoughts, including smoking (Dodgen, 2005) and obsessive-compulsive disorder (Hannan & Tolin, 2005). Experienced therapists use thought stopping to treat distracting thoughts, boredom, and negative self-talk during therapy sessions (Williams, Polster, Grizzard, Rockenbaugh, & Judge, 2003).

Compared with the developing of counters, thought stopping can be considered more of an emergency measure to halt the flow of negative messages. The helper teaches the client the technique in the office, and the client practices it whenever a severely disturbing thought arises. Three steps in the thought-stopping technique have been identified (Davis, Eshelman, & McKay, 2000; Lazarus, 1971; Witmer, 1985):

1. Stating the thought
2. Creating a startling interruption
3. Substituting a new thought

Once the troubling thought has been identified, the client is asked to label and state it either mentally or aloud—for example, "I have to get an A on this paper!" This repetition brings the thought into clearer focus. The client then creates a startling response strong enough to interrupt the negative thinking pattern. One practical method when practicing thought stopping privately is to yell "Stop!" as loudly as possible. In public, it is best to use "the tongue of thought" and say "Stop!" mentally. You also might want to imagine a huge red stop sign. Some helpers suggest wearing a rubber band around the wrist and snapping it along with a mental "Stop!" to produce the startle effect.

The final step in thought stopping is to insert a positive thought to replace the irrational, self-downing thought. This can be either a spontaneous or a planned counter that the client produces to counteract the negative thought. In this case, the substituted thought might be something such as, "I'm not going to worry about the grade. I'll do the best that I can."

PRACTICING NEW BEHAVIORS

The next therapeutic factor in our list is practicing new behaviors (see Figure 13.2). Practice has always been a part of a "psychoeducational" approach to helping (Guerney, Stollack, & Guerney, 1971; Schutz, 1981; Young & Rosen, 1985). The major idea is that many client problems are due to skill deficits. Clients need to gain some basic knowledge about the problem, see models of the behavior they are trying to acquire, and then rehearse. They may use imagery as a rehearsal (Pierce, 2006; Suinn, 1996; Witmer & Young, 1985) or even technology such as video and computer simulation (Smokowski, 2003).

Some of the skills that clients need to practice include parenting, communicating better as a couple, facing fearful situations, dealing with anger, and developing more effective ways of thinking. As an educator, the helper cannot be content for the client to

FIGURE 13.2 Therapeutic Factors in the REPLAN System: Practicing New Behaviors

temporarily eliminate a problem behavior or merely gain insight into the fact that he or she is operating in a self-defeating manner. Clients must overcome the force of old habits by establishing a new pattern of behaviors through practice and rehearsal.

The best instruction for any skill includes the following sequence: (1) the helper explains a little theory or rationale for learning the new skill, (2) the learner views a model (helper or group member) who correctly demonstrates the skill, (3) the learner demonstrates the behavior in the real or simulated situation by practicing in class, and (4) the learner practices through homework assignments. For example, if you were learning to play the guitar, the instructor might explain the fingering using a chart or graph. Then the instructor would probably demonstrate how the piece is to be played, or you might listen to a recording of the selection. You would then attempt the music with the instructor present, and later you would be sent home to practice. The process of acquiring a new behavior or a new thinking pattern in the helping relationship takes place in much the same way. Helpers use each of these steps when teaching a new skill: explanation of theory, modeling, in-session practice, and homework. In this chapter, we will focus on two specific methods used to aid clients in practicing new skills: role-playing and homework.

ROLE-PLAYING

Role-playing is a technique commonly used by helpers for social skills training and in helping clients face situations they are avoiding (Kipper, 1986, 1996). It involves practicing a behavior in a contrived situation with the helper playing an auxiliary or observer role. It may also take place in a group setting with other participants who can give valuable feedback and act as auxiliaries or actors in the play. For example, clients might wish to learn to refuse requests, express themselves to others, talk in front of an audience, confront someone, or tell someone their true feelings. Role-playing can be used as a rehearsal for these new behaviors. It has been used in a variety of settings with many different types of clients from group work with children (Borbely, Graber, & Nichols, 2005) to training students in family therapy (Browning, Collins, & Nelson, 2005) to working with phobias (Martinez, 2002). Virtual role plays utilize computer technology or video and allow clients to learn in a simulated environment about issues such as how to cope with anxiety (Powers & Emmelkamp, 2008) or respond to sexually threatening situations (Jouriles, Rowe, McDonald, Platt, & Gomez, 2011).

Role-playing was introduced by the creative genius J. L. Moreno, a Viennese psychiatrist who formulated the **psychodramatic** method (see Blatner, 2000). On one occasion, following a lecture by Freud, Moreno is said to have responded, "Well, Dr. Freud, I start where you leave off. You meet people in the artificial setting of your office. I meet them on the street and in their home, in their natural surroundings. You analyze their dreams. I try to give them the courage to dream again . . . " (Moreno, 1964, pp. 5–6). Moreno's response reflects his belief that helping should involve learning in as naturalistic a setting as possible. Part of what Moreno objected to in traditional therapies was the separation of a client's problems from the natural environment, just as a religious sculpture or painting cannot be fully appreciated in a museum but must be seen in a church or temple. Since it is not always possible to see individuals in their natural contexts, the psychodramatic method proposes to re-create an individual's joys and sorrows on the psychodramatic stage (Starr, 1977). Moreno's famous dictum was, "Show me, don't tell me!" He felt that most "talk therapies" relied on the client's descriptions of problems.

Since we cannot reach into the subjective experience of the person through words, we should transfer the mind onto the stage where the person's total behavior, including thoughts, feelings, and intuitions, are observable and changeable. Those who want to learn more about the basics of psychodrama should consult Adam Blatner's book, *Acting-In: Practical Applications of Psychodramatic Methods* (1996). Kipper and Ritchie (2003) have summarized research on the effectiveness of psychodramatic techniques.

Elements of Role-Playing

The technique of role-playing is a limited form of psychodrama, and an understanding of the whole theory of psychodrama is not necessary. Role-playing can be performed by a single individual (the protagonist), who plays all the roles in the drama, or with the help of other individuals called auxiliaries. Role-playing has always been conceived of as having three phases: warm-up, action, and sharing and analysis (Yablonsky, 1976).

Three Phases of Psychodramatic Role-Playing

WARM-UP The warm-up is any activity that helps the client get in touch emotionally with the experience he or she is trying to express. The warm-up decreases stage fright and allows the protagonist to develop **readiness** and involvement in the process. If you think about it, most of us have warm-ups, or rituals, we use to prepare for action. For example, the runner does stretching exercises, the actor rehearses lines, and the competitive skier mentally runs the course. In role-playing, proper warm-up is crucial to the success of the technique. Warm-up might include asking the protagonist to discuss the situation or encouraging some physical activity, such as pacing back and forth.

Another way of warming up is to use role reversal. In role reversal, the helper instructs the client to pretend to be the other person and respond as he or she might. For example, the client changes places and sits on the chair that previously represented his mother. He responds as his mother might in a similar circumstance. Role reversal is one of the most effective ways of getting the client involved in the role play. Besides, role reversal makes the situation more real. The client is required to construct possible responses of a significant other and devise strategies to cope with them.

"Move from the periphery to the center" is a tip for helpers about how to get a client more involved in the role play. It is a suggestion to begin with tangential events before moving to more significant or central issues. For example, if the role play involves returning home to see a dying grandfather, the helper would not begin with the deathbed confrontation, but would move the client through several less potent scenes. In this case, these scenes might include driving to the house while reminiscing about the relationship or replaying previous encounters between grandparent and grandchild. This method also gives the helper more information about the client and the client's relationships and life circumstances. With sufficient warm-up, the client overcomes stage fright and is more in tune with the actual role play when it takes place.

ACTION After the warm-up, the helper asks the client to take on his or her own role and enact the situation. Scene setting is the preliminary step of this action phase. It involves asking the protagonist to set up the stage to resemble the actual setting where the incident took place or where the behavior will possibly occur in the future. The client is given free rein to use available props and to orient the stage in whatever way feels comfortable. The helper assists the client in defining the stage, designating the time of day and date, describing the situation verbally, using props, and identifying important people to be portrayed.

SHARING AND ANALYSIS   In group therapy, the sharing phase of role-playing allows the individual to reenter the group situation, that is, to get out of the spotlight. Instead of the client sharing more about his or her experience, the other group members use this opportunity to relate personal experiences evoked by the client's role play. This technique reinvolves the audience and helps the client feel less alone and exposed. At some later time, a feedback or analysis session is held, during which members give feedback to the client and the role play is discussed, but not immediately after the action phase.

How to Conduct Role-Playing

Role-playing is one of the most effective ways of practicing a new behavior. The immediate observation and feedback allow for actual practice, not simply talking about problems. At a deeper level, role-playing and role reversal can help the individual to become more fully aware of feelings and to explore the phenomenological worlds of the significant people in his or her life. The method described here is a generic role-playing technique for practicing new behavior. To make the method easier to understand, a hypothetical example unfolds throughout the explanation; for the sake of simplicity, this example will show what it is like for a helper to conduct role-playing in an office setting rather than in a group session. The client, Martin, is anxious because he has to give a presentation to his board of directors concerning progress on his yearly goals. The helper, Patrick, suggests that they role-play the situation to rehearse his talk.

Step 1: Warm-Up.   In the warm-up, Patrick previews and explains the purpose and the elements of role-playing. Using the principle of proceeding from the periphery to the center, Patrick begins the warm-up by asking Martin to discuss aspects of his job that he will be presenting, details of the workplace, and other tangential topics. The most important aspect of this step is for Patrick to get Martin to describe the target behaviors very specifically. In this case, Martin wants to:

1. Maintain eye contact with his audience
2. Speak from notes in a loud, clear voice
3. Smile when questions are asked
4. End the session by thanking the audience

Step 2: Scene Setting.   After Martin has discussed the situation, he appears more relaxed. Patrick then invites him to describe his own office (peripheral) and later the board meeting room (central). Patrick lets Martin set the scene, rearranging Patrick's office furnishings to approximate the setup of the boardroom. Patrick encourages Martin to point out various features, such as the color of the walls and the furniture, to establish the scene.

Step 3: Selecting Roles and Role Reversal.   In this step, the client identifies important people in the scene and briefly describes them. In a group setting, other members of the group would be assigned to these roles. In an individual session, empty chairs represent these significant persons. For example, Patrick asks Martin to reverse roles and pretend to be his boss to get a sense of his demeanor and attitude. She also asks him to point out the chairs of some of the other board members and briefly describe them.

Step 4: Enactment.   At this point, the helper asks the client to briefly portray the target behaviors as described during the warm-up. In Martin's case, the scene begins in his office and culminates with his entrance into the "boardroom." Patrick acts as a coach during the first run-through, prompting Martin to display each identified behavior. The helper is dissatisfied with Martin's portrayal of the final behavior, thanking the audience. Patrick stops the action and takes on Martin's role to model an effective closing statement. Following the modeling, Patrick asks Martin to try the closing a second time in his own way using whatever parts of Patrick's closing he liked.

Step 5: Sharing and Feedback.   In this step, the helper shares feedback with the client. The feedback should be specific, simple, observable, and understandable to the client. It should mainly reinforce positive aspects of the behavior. In our example, Patrick tells Martin, "Your voice was very strong and clear. I think you got your points across very well. I would like to see even more eye contact with the board members during the next run-through."

Step 6: Reenactment.   Reenactment is a repetition of the target behavior from entrance to exit. The sequence is repeated until the client is confident that each of the behaviors in the target list has been mastered.

Step 7: Homework and Follow-Up.   At the next session, the client is asked to report practice results. Martin has practiced the behavior by giving the presentation to some family members, and he describes this to Patrick. Further role-playing practice may be given during the session, if necessary. When the helper feels that the client has consistently demonstrated the target behaviors, the helper urges the client to attempt the behaviors in a real situation.

Problems and Precautions with Role-Playing

1. The most frequently encountered difficulty with the role-playing technique is stage fright. Resistance to the technique is ordinarily the result of insufficient warm-up, inadequate preparation time, the client's lack of confidence, or inadequate reassurance by the helper.

2. Because of the power of the technique, both the helper and the client may be unprepared for the strength of the emotion that is sometimes evoked. This is unlikely when using role-playing for practicing a new behavior. Beginning helpers should not attempt to reenact traumatic scenes from the past.

3. Because most helpers focus on the client's thoughts and feelings, we sometimes have trouble thinking in dramatic terms. In the usual session, the client is encouraged to describe an encounter with another person by saying, "I was angry because she neglected me." In a role-playing session, the client would be instructed, "Show me how you expressed your anger to her." By creating a dramatic situation, the helper learns a great deal about the quality and context of the behavior, rather than just the client's description of it.

GIVING HOMEWORK ASSIGNMENTS

Homework has been identified as a crucial tool in effective helping (Kazantzis & L'Abate, 2011). Homework refers to any tasks or assignments given to clients to be completed between sessions (Last, 1985). More than 80% of mental health practitioners in one study used between-session homework (Kazantzis, Busch, Ronan, & Merrick, 2007). Some tasks are used for assessment purposes; others are used to increase client awareness of the behavior (Martin & Worthington, 1982); still other homework assignments are designed as independent practice sessions. In this section, the main emphasis will be on homework that is used to practice new behaviors. These new behaviors are normally learned during the therapeutic session and may be modeled or rehearsed in the office before they are assigned as homework. Review of homework provides a starting point for each new session with a review of progress made and problems encountered in the assignment.

Reasons for Using Homework

A major advantage of using homework assignments is that they provide follow-up or treatment continuance between sessions. When one realizes that a client spends 1 hour out of about 112 waking hours per week in counseling, it is easy to see how helping can be diluted by other activities. Homework assignments, especially if they require some daily work, can enhance treatment (Shelton & Ackerman, 1974; Shelton & Levy, 1981; Strong & Massfeller, 2010).

In addition, homework assignments turn insights and awareness into tangible behaviors and prevent helping from being only a place to unload one's feelings. Transfer of training or generalization of learning is facilitated by applying descriptions and models of behavior to real-life situations as soon as possible. Homework practice also begins the shift of control from the helper to the client. If the client attributes progress to his or her own effort in outside assignments, greater efficacy and self-esteem will result.

Examples of Homework Assignments

BIBLIOTHERAPY **Bibliotherapy** means assigning readings to clients to help them achieve their goals. Numerous studies have found it to be an effective treatment for disorders ranging from alcohol addiction to sexual disorders (McKenna, Hevey, & Martin, 2010). In general, bibliotherapy has been supported for clients with mild to moderate problems. Bibliotherapy should be contrasted with merely recommending a self-help book. Many of the offerings in trade books are oversimplified, unscientific, and based on opinion or a few anecdotes. Before recommending a book to a client, the helper should have read the book and should carefully think about whether it will be acceptable to the client's frame of reference and is in tune with the client's goals. Once a helper has recommended a book or audio assignment, he or she should follow up in subsequent sessions to discuss the client's reading and go over important points, perhaps even asking a few relevant questions about how the assignment fits the client's current dilemma.

Although it is not possible to provide an exhaustive list of good bibliographic materials here, resources for selecting books and manuals are available (cf. Gladding & Gladding, 1991; Jackson, 2001). Many children's libraries, such as the Carnegie Library of Pittsburgh, have online bibliotherapy booklists for kids on special topics such as divorce, adoption, fears, bullies, and so on. One good self-esteem book for kids is called *Sticking Up for Yourself* (Kaufman, 1999), while Schiraldi, McKay, and Fanning's (2005) *Self-Esteem Workbook* is better for adults. *Courage to Heal* (Bass & Davis, 2008) is often prescribed to women who survived child sexual abuse. A very good stress management workbook, *Kicking Your Stress Habits* (Tubesing, 1981), is older but useful for a broad audience. Many clients with marital problems have benefited from Michele Weiner-Davis's (1992)

Divorce Busting and *The Divorce Remedy* (2001), while David Burns's (1999a) *Feeling Good* contains an excellent cognitive approach to depression that the average person can easily grasp. A number of these books, are now available in audio formats and can be listened to while driving or relaxing.

Besides informing the client, bibliotherapy can provide covert practice by exposing the client to a fictional or historical model of a desired behavior. Clients may identify with case studies or with fictional characters who face similar problems. The Harry Potter books and other fictional materials have been used to help grieving children (Markell & Markell, 2008). The "Big Book" of Alcoholics Anonymous contains a number of true accounts of individuals who have successfully overcome drinking problems.

AIDES One way to increase the efficacy of homework practice is to enlist the help of a client's friend, spouse, or family member as an aide who provides either feedback or support for completing assignments. Generally, an aide comes to sessions with the client. The helper specifically identifies the aide's role as either support or feedback. Let us say that the client is attempting to become more assertive. The aide would be given specific verbal and nonverbal behaviors to observe and would report observations to the client. Alternatively, the aide might simply be enlisted to provide support or to accompany the client while he or she completes assignments. The client who is attempting to exercise regularly may use an aide as a regular walking partner. The aide would help the client increase regularity and provide encouragement from session to session. The major pitfall of using aides is that they must be supervised by the helper. Sometimes aides are too helpful and wish to take excessive responsibility for the client. If this behavior cannot be modified, the client should proceed alone.

JOURNALING AND RECORD KEEPING Nowadays therapeutic blogs are common (Lent, 2009), and e-journals are used in counselor training to reflect on personal growth experiences (Haberstroh, Parr, Gee, & Trepal, 2006). Journaling is a daily writing assignment given to the client by the helper. Ordinarily, the client brings the journal to the next session for the helper's reaction. Journals usually serve one of two purposes. Sometimes journals are assigned as an open-ended writing assignment to help the client do more in-depth examination of his or her thoughts, feelings, and behaviors. Helpers use this kind of journaling for spiritual issues (Wiggins-Frame, 2011), in school counseling (Zyromski, 2007), and even in couples work (Lemberg, 1994).

The helper may also encourage the client to use journaling to record practice sessions. The client engages in self-monitoring and also reflects on progress. This might include keeping track of countering skills (cognitive), recording the amount of emotional discomfort (affective), or noting the number of times a new behavior was actually practiced (behavioral). In that light, consider the following case study of Joe, a 29-year-old administrator for an insurance company who has come for help to deal with problems associated with "stress." He has borderline high blood pressure, is often tense and angry after work and, as a result, sometimes becomes rude to his fiancée, alienating her. He plays racquetball competitively, and last week he purposely broke an expensive racquet after a bad shot. He wishes to control his anger and feel less "stressed" at work. During the assessment, the counselor identified negative self-statements as a major cause of the client's stress and felt that, in general, the most useful path for Joe was to increase self-esteem. Joe agreed, but also felt he needed better organizational skills. The initial plan

TABLE 13.2   Self-Criticism Homework Card for Joe

No.	Time	Self-Statement	Feeling	SUDS
1.	8:15	I'll never get all this work done.	Discouraged	85
2.	9:00	I didn't do a good job on that report.	Disgust	50
3.	10:00	I'll never be good at this job. I'm just average and that's all.	Self-pity	60
4.	10:35	I'm daydreaming again. Why am I so lazy?	Anger	35
5.	12:00	I offended the secretary again. Why can't I just keep my mouth shut?	Anger	45
6.	1:00	I feel fat after eating so much. I'm turning into a blimp.	Disgust	35
7.	2:40	Another day almost done, and I've completed nothing.	Anger	40
8.	3:30	My desk is a mess. What a slob!	Discouraged	50
9.	5:15	Even my car is full of trash. I wish I were more organized.	Anger	25

SUDS = Subjective Units of Distress Scale

0..100

No emotional distress   Extreme emotional distress

Emotions = fear, anger, sadness, guilt, interest-excitement/boredom, joy, disgust, surprise

Summary 9 = negative self-statements; average SUDS = 47 (approx.)

Most prevalent emotion = self-anger/disgust

was negotiated as a two-pronged attack: to decrease self-criticism and to develop better time management and organizational skills. Joe enrolled in a 3-day time management workshop sponsored by his company and, at the same time, began keeping a journal, as shown in Table 13.2. Figure 13.3 contains two graphs. The first is of Joe's SUDS levels, and the second shows negative self-statements over the first 10 days. (As noted earlier, SUDS is an acronym for the Subjective Units of Discomfort Scale.) In this case, 0 represents no discomfort, and 100 represents extreme distress. Using a homework card, Joe found that he was producing anger by his self-statements, which were first aimed at himself and sometimes directed at innocent bystanders. Joe agreed to continue to monitor his self-statements for 2 more weeks and noticed a marked diminishing of his self-criticism. In Joe's case, there seemed to be a correspondence between his self-criticism and his emotional discomfort. Although the major purpose of keeping this journal was to encourage practice, the client also developed insight into the way he maintained his anger. Notice also that, like most people, Joe's improvement did not take a steady downward course but shows the normal ups and downs of the change process.

Problems and Precautions with Homework

1. Homework assignments that have a high probability of success should be chosen (Dyer & Vriend, 1977). This is true especially early in the helping relationship in order to keep the client's hope alive. Also, by promoting small, easily completed goals, the client begins to learn that most change is gradual, not an overnight phenomenon.
2. Homework strategies should be individually tailored for each client (Miller, 2010; Scheel, Hanson, & Razzhavaikina, 2004) and should be co-created with the client whenever possible. Too often, the helper uses a standard homework assignment that, to the discouraged client, may feel impersonal. By stretching one's creativity,

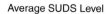

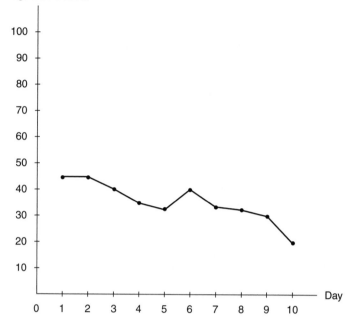

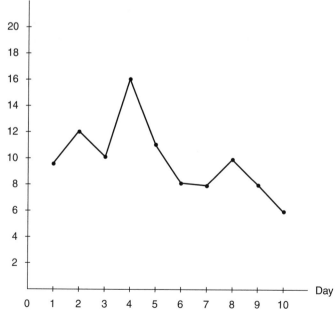

FIGURE 13.3   Graph of Daily SUDS Levels and Critical Self-Statements for Joe

some assignments can incorporate more than one of the client's goals. If the client likes to read, recommending self-help books as homework might work well. If the client enjoys writing, assign a journal.

3. Practicing regularly is important. It would be better, for example, if the client performs a rehearsal for 10 minutes once per day, rather than practicing for an hour one time per week.

4. Homework should be simple and fit easily into the lifestyle of the client. Complicated homework involving extensive record keeping may not be completed.

5. As the client progresses, homework should increase in difficulty or discomfort. Clients usually have a feel for when they are ready for more challenging tasks and for tasks that are presently beyond them.

MyCounselingLab™

Go to Topics 5 and 6, *Cognitive Interventions* and *Behavioral Interventions,* on the MyCounselingLab™ site (www.MyCounselingLab.com) for *Learning the Art of Helping: Building Blocks and Techniques,* Fifth Edition, where you can:

• Find learning outcomes for *Cognitive Interventions* and *Behavioral Interventions,* along with the national standards that connect to these outcomes.
• Complete Assignments and Activities that can help you more deeply understand the chapter content.
• Apply and practice your understanding of the core skills identified in the chapter with the Building Counseling Skills unit.
• Prepare yourself for professional certification with a Practice for Certification quiz.
• Connect to videos through the Video and Resource Library.

MyCounselingLab™ Exercises

Go to the Video and Resource Library on the MyCounselingLab™ site for your text and search for the following clips: *Reflecting Feelings: Mark* and *Countering.* Watch the videos and then answer the following questions.

Exercise 1: Identifying Irrational Beliefs

1. The video entitled *Reflecting Feelings: Mark* shows a session between Alisa (the client) and Mark (the helper).
2. What irrational ideas can you identify in the client's story based on Ellis's irrational beliefs?
3. Construct a counter for one of the irrational beliefs you find.

Counters

1. If I worry about making everyone happy, I will lose touch with my own needs.
2. If everyone is not happy, it's not the end of the world, and I can't control everything.

Exercise 2: Countering

The video called *Countering* shows the technique of countering in an interchange between a client, Letitia, and the helper, Mark. Countering has five steps listed below. List one thing that Mark did under each of these steps:

Step 1: Do a brief assessment.
Step 2: Identify the negative thought patterns and core beliefs.
Step 3: Identify effective counters.
Step 4: Test counters and modify them.
Step 5: Practice and report.

Summary

In this chapter, you were introduced to the idea of using therapeutic factors as a method for understanding the reasons for the effectiveness of various therapeutic techniques, and we described a method of treatment planning called the **REPLAN system** that utilizes six therapeutic factors to organize our therapeutic efforts. Next, we examined two of these factors more closely: (1) enhancing efficacy and self-esteem and (2) practicing new behaviors. Self-esteem has two components: self-worth and efficacy. Enhancing both is critical for boosting self-esteem. Clients with better self-esteem are more likely to succeed in accomplishing other goals. Clients can learn to enhance efficacy by attempting new behaviors and by paying attention to their present strengths and skills. Low self-worth is a general attitude that the self is "not okay," worthless, or ineffective. Low self-worth is responsible for a number of serious psychological conditions, negative emotions, and a demoralized attitude toward life. We have explored causes of low self-worth and identified injunctions learned early in life, including irrational ideas and negative body image. We also looked at one method for enhancing self-esteem called countering. Countering is aimed at reducing negative self-talk.

Practice is a method that helpers promote to help clients put insights into action and try out new behaviors experimentally. In this chapter we looked at two techniques for practice: role-playing and homework. Role-playing is a practice technique that involves re-creating the context of a desired behavior right in the helper's office and then acting out that new behavior as practice. Major contributions to this technique have come from psychodrama and the behaviorists (Lazarus, 1985). This technique allows the helper to obtain firsthand knowledge about the client's behavioral style, while the client benefits from rehearsal and feedback. Finally, we described the use of homework assignments to prolong treatment between sessions as well as to establish new behaviors. Assignments should be individually tailored to the client and may involve journaling activities, lay helpers as aides, and bibliotherapy. Helpers who regularly utilize practice in the office or as homework are more likely to increase the transfer of training to real-life situations.

Exercises

GROUP EXERCISES

Exercise 1: Identifying Irrational Beliefs

The technique of countering described in this chapter involves identifying specific thoughts and finding effective arguments. That countering process is difficult to simulate in class because it is time-consuming to ferret out the specific thoughts and identify effective counters. Yet, you can learn a first step in **cognitive therapy.**

You can learn to listen for errors or counterproductive thinking in a client's story. In this exercise, we will be trying to find irrational beliefs in the client's statements. Do not be afraid to share a real story; we all have irrational beliefs and engage in irrational behavior.

Part I

First, form groups of four, with each student, in turn, taking on the roles of client, helper, and two observers.

The client discusses one of the following topics with the helper:

- A time when the client was very angry at someone
- A time when the client was very angry at himself or herself
- A time when someone disappointed the client
- Something the client has a difficult time forgiving

The helper's job is to listen, using all the skills in the nonjudgmental listening sequence, for 5 to 10 minutes. The helper is not asked to specifically identify irrational beliefs but simply to try and get the client to talk about the beliefs behind his or her actions. Neither is the helper to make an effort to challenge the client's beliefs, just to simply draw them out.

Observer 1 writes down all the helper's interventions verbatim. Observer 2 reviews the list of Ellis's seven irrational beliefs described in the "Sources of Low Self-Esteem" section of this chapter. Then, during the session, observer 2 listens carefully to the client's statements and records the gist of those that seem to indicate an underlying irrational belief.

Part II: Debriefing

1. Take a couple of minutes to allow client, helper, and observers to share their thoughts about this exercise.
2. Then observer 1 gives the helper the list of interventions and feedback about his or her performance on the nonjudgmental listening sequence. Was the helper able to remain in a nonjudgmental stance, neither supporting irrational thinking nor judging the client for these ideas? The helper can keep the list of interventions and review them later. At this point, the list of interventions should include several paraphrases, reflections of feeling, and perhaps a reflection of meaning or two, depending on the depth of the client's story. If questions predominate, the helper should return to previous chapters for review and should schedule additional practice sessions with classmates.
3. Observer 2 indicates any irrational ideas that he or she identified in the client's statements. As a group, the helper and the two observers can identify some counters that might be used by the client as an antidote to these beliefs. The client either confirms or disagrees with the observer's ideas and then indicates which ones he or she feels might be the most effective.

Exercise 2: Role-Playing

Role-playing as a rehearsal technique sometimes focuses on situations in the past that clients would like to resolve. By attempting to bring them to closure in a role-play situation, the client is rehearsing for a later time when the issues can be addressed in real life. Issues from the past are addressed in terms of how similar situations can be handled in the future.

The exercise begins with the client, who identifies an individual in the past or present with whom he or she has "unfinished business." Unfinished business refers to a relationship or an issue that he or she was unable to adequately resolve in the past, but would like to bring to a positive conclusion. Then, the helper directs a role play in which the client encounters this person and tries to express himself or herself in a positive way. It is recommended that participants use one of the following situations or a minor issue in their own lives such as:

> "My friend did not invite me to her wedding."
>
> "My boyfriend criticized me in front of his mother, but I did not mention it."
>
> "A teacher treated me unfairly, and I was never able to explain."
>
> "I was attracted to someone in the past, but I never told her."

For this exercise, students form groups of four with roles of helper, client, observer 1, and observer 2. Observer 1 gives the client feedback, and observer 2 gives the helper feedback on his or her ability to demonstrate the skill of role-playing.

Briefly, this exercise has the following phases:

1. The roles of helper, client, observer 1, and observer 2 are assigned.
2. The client thinks of a situation involving unfinished business.
3. The helper directs the client through the first five steps of role-playing (see the earlier section called, *How to Conduct Role-Playing*) including a reenactment where the client practices a new behavior.
4. Observer 1 and the helper give the client feedback; the client reenacts the role play if more practice seems advisable.
5. Observer 2 gives the helper feedback and discusses the exercise.

STEP 1: WARM-UP. As a warm-up, the helper invites the client to explain the situation and uses the nonjudgmental listening cycle to get a clear understanding of the situation.

STEP 2: SCENE SETTING. The helper asks the client to briefly describe where and when a meeting with the affected individual might take place. The client sits in one chair, and the other chair is left empty for the person with whom the client has unfinished business.

STEP 3: SELECTING ROLES AND ROLE REVERSAL. In this exercise, the client will play both himself or herself and the other person with whom the client has unfinished business. To begin, the helper asks the client to reverse roles and sit in the empty chair while completely taking on the identity of the other person. The helper asks this significant other to describe himself or herself and to give a little bit of background about the situation from that person's perspective.

STEP 4: ENACTMENT. Once the client has presented the other person, the helper asks him or her to return to the original chair and resume his or her natural identity. Now the client expresses some of the thoughts and feelings that he or she has wanted to get out into the open. The helper facilitates the client to express this in any way the client wishes. The client speaks these thoughts and feelings to the empty chair as if the other person were actually present.

Once the client has had the opportunity to express his or her thoughts and feelings, the client reverses roles again and becomes the other person, responding to the charges leveled against him or her. The enactment ends when the client returns to his or her natural role and original seat and responds to the other person's reaction.

STEP 5: SHARING AND FEEDBACK. In this step, the helper and observer 1 give the client feedback on how well the client was able to finish the unfinished business. For example, was the client able to express everything he or she intended in an assertive and straightforward way? Was the client overly aggressive or too tentative and passive? What behavior does the client need to practice in the reenactment step to cope with similar situations in the future?

STEP 6: REENACTMENT. Reenactment follows sharing and feedback if the client needs to make improvements. In reenactment, the client stays in the client chair and has another opportunity to clearly and assertively make complaints and requests. Following this, the helper and observer 1 give the client feedback.

STEP 7: HOMEWORK AND FOLLOW-UP. The final phase of this group exercise is for observer 2 to give feedback to the helper on how well he or she was able to assist the client in practicing the new behavior.

Observer 2 should have notes on each of the steps of role-playing and give specific feedback. Both client and observer 1 may also have feedback to share.

QUICK TIPS: ROLE-PLAYING

- Help the client overcome stage fright and initial discomfort by using a warm-up process such as a discussion of the situation before the role play begins.
- Getting the client to physically move around, arrange chairs, and set the scene helps to warm up the client.
- If clients resist the role-play technique, you may have to abandon it until trust is better developed. On the other hand, your confidence in the procedure will encourage them, and reassurance that "you'll get into it" may help them to get over their initial reluctance.
- Repeat the action phase several times if needed to help the client feel comfortable with the new role.
- If clients experience emotional arousal as a result of the role play, the helper may find it necessary to implement the nonjudgmental listening cycle instead of continuing with the role play.

SMALL GROUP DISCUSSIONS

Discussion: Selecting Rehearsal Methods

Consider the following case studies in a small group of fellow students. What does each client need to practice? Which issues would you address first? What kind of rehearsal seems best suited to each of these client's problems? In a small group, brainstorm one in-session rehearsal idea and two creative homework assignments for each client.

1. Carol is a 37-year-old married woman with one child. She and her counselor agree to work on her extreme reluctance to leave home even for a few hours to go to the grocery store. She experiences fear and panic attacks in public situations. She has not been shopping in 2 years and has lost respect for herself as a contributing member of her family. Following two sessions of history taking and a medical evaluation (the client incorrectly believes she has a heart condition), the counselor and client,

following a complete assessment, agree that she needs assistance in dealing with low self-esteem and that she needs to practice going out in public. The client has a number of dysfunctional beliefs, including "I am weak," that seem to contribute to her inability to attempt new behaviors.

2. Maureen is a 20-year-old college student, the only child of parents who appear to be on the verge of divorce. She comes to the college counseling center complaining that she is always in the middle of her parents' quarrels and that each parent calls to tell her about the other's failings. In her attempts to placate both sides, Maureen has become anxious and depressed and has trouble studying. She experiences periods of crying and expresses sympathy for both parents. Maureen initially frames her problem as "how to help my parents cope with their divorce." In the second session, Maureen agrees that what she wants is to maintain a relationship with both parents, to be supportive of both, and not to listen to their complaints about each other.

3. Kent is an 11-year-old boy who has been diagnosed with autism but who has been mainstreamed at school, meaning he is in class with typical students, most of whom have not been given a diagnostic label. Kent has very poor social skills. He has difficulty carrying on a conversation and maintaining eye contact. He forgets to greet people and say goodbye and cannot work with other students on projects. With Kent, what would you start with and what homework assignments would you give?

SELF-ASSESSMENT

On a scale from 1 to 10 (1 = just beginning and 10 = mastery) indicate how well you think you have developed the skills described in this chapter. Consider your practice sessions as well as the exercises in this chapter.

Rate yourself on your ability to identify irrational beliefs.

1   2   3   4   5   6   7   8   9   10

Rate yourself on your ability to identify practice techniques for clients.

1   2   3   4   5   6   7   8   9   10

Now rate yourself on your ability to direct a client in a role-playing activity.

1   2   3   4   5   6   7   8   9   10

Finally, how well were you able to implement the technique of countering?

1   2   3   4   5   6   7   8   9   10

Identify two things you learned while practicing these skills. You may include things that others may have noticed you doing well that indicated your progress. Include positive comments from instructors or class members.

HOMEWORK

Homework 1: Diary

Select a personal goal for yourself that involves practicing a new behavior. For example:

> "I would like to play my guitar every day."
>
> "I would like to cook regular meals to combat my tendency to snack throughout the day."
>
> "I would like to take time every day to improve my relationship with people at work."

- At the end of each day, for 1 week, write down the number of times you engaged in the behavior, or indicate if you did not practice during the day. Use a blank journal, your smartphone or a secure journal online. Write down any ideas you have about why you did or did not practice the behavior during the day.
- At the end of a week, summarize your conclusions in a half-page reaction. Do you think that self-monitoring by keeping a journal was helpful to you? What kinds of clients might benefit from this approach? What kinds of problems are best suited to keeping a diary such as this?

Homework 2: Practicing a Skill

Select a building block skill from this book that you would like to improve.

1. Write down the name of the skill.
2. Does the skill need to be broken down into small components? If so, list them here.
3. Spend 5 minutes imagining yourself successfully demonstrating each part of the skill. (This could be called "imaginal rehearsal.")
4. Ask a fellow student who is proficient in the skill to model it for you.
5. Watch a video of the skill.

6. Ask a student partner to act as an observer and practice the skill with a third student, who will serve as the client.
7. Get feedback and rehearse again, incorporating the suggestions you received.
8. With help from your training group, select several situations in real life where you might practice this skill.
9. Make an appointment with a fellow student to call him or her and report on your progress in a week.

Homework 3: Personal Experiments

Personal science is a way of getting more additional data about a client's problems. Personal science asks you to test your perceptions by getting feedback from others or by conducting an experiment. Try to apply this to yourself by thinking about something that you don't do very well, or think about a part of your body that you do not feel is very attractive. Get opinions from eight friends or family members. How accurate is your self-concept? If they do not agree, why do you cling to this belief? In what ways have you distorted your view of the self? Write a half-page reaction to this exercise. Do you see how clients might benefit from personal science?

JOURNAL STARTERS

Sometimes helpers ask clients to consider incidents in their lives in which low self-esteem might have originated. For example, was the client affected by excessive criticism or perfectionistic expectations? Harry Stack Sullivan said that self-concept is the reflected appraisals of others. On the other hand, Eleanor Roosevelt believed that no one can make you feel bad about yourself without your permission. Think about your own life experiences and decide which view is closest to your opinion on the subject. Are both true for you?

Therapeutic Factors and Advanced Change Techniques: Part II

MyCounselingLab™

Visit the MyCounselingLab™ site for *Learning the Art of Helping: Building Blocks and Techniques*, Fifth Edition to enhance your understanding of chapter concepts. You'll have the opportunity to practice your skills through video- and case-based Assignments and Activities as well as Building Counseling Skills units, and to prepare for your certification exam with Practice for Certification quizzes.

This chapter completes our description of the REPLAN, a treatment-planning model that focuses on six common therapeutic factors. In Chapter 3, we tackled the most complex and powerful element, "R," the therapeutic relationship. In Chapter 13, we delved into "E," Enhancing Efficacy and Self-Esteem and "P" Practicing New Behaviors. Here, we address the three remaining therapeutic factors: Lowering and raising emotional arousal (L), Activating Expectations, Hope, and Motivation (A), and Providing New Learning Experiences (N). The therapeutic factors in the REPLAN model provide a basis for understanding the common purposes that lie at the roots of the various theoretical systems. As we saw in Chapter 13, the therapeutic factors also provide one way to reflect upon what factors are most likely to be useful in helping a client reach his or her goals. Figure 14.1 shows these therapeutic factors and emphasizes the next factor we will take up: lowering and raising emotional arousal.

FIGURE 14.1 Therapeutic Factors in the REPLAN System: Lowering and Raising Emotional Arousal

LOWERING AND RAISING EMOTIONAL AROUSAL

The fourth therapeutic factor in the REPLAN system is lowering and raising emotional arousal. The overall purpose of this set of techniques is to reduce the impact of negative emotions. This is accomplished in three different ways:

1. ***Reduce negative emotions.*** Helpers are called upon to help clients reduce overpowering feelings of depression, anger, stress, and fear, primarily through methods of stress reduction and cognitive techniques.

2. ***Facilitate expression of strong emotions.*** At other times, helpers arouse emotions to act as catalysts for change: for example, helping a client get in touch with repressed anger or sadness and allowing them to recognize the powerful nature of unresolved feelings.

3. ***Activate positive emotions.*** Helpers also facilitate positive emotions such as joy, gratitude, serenity, interest, hope, pride, amusement, inspiration, awe and love (Frederickson, 2009). Positive emotions also tend to weaken negative ones.

In this section, we will address each of these methods for raising or lowering emotional arousal and identify some key techniques that helpers use in each circumstance.

Reducing Negative Emotions

The three most common negative emotions that clients seek help for are depression/guilt, anxiety, and anger. In Chapter 13, you learned the countering technique, which is used to help clients reduce self-criticism. Reducing negative thinking also tends to reduce depressive feelings, and cognitive therapy has been the primary method for treating depression, by psychological means, since the early 1990s.

Although depression, anger, and anxiety are treated differently, we only have room here to talk about one of these troubling emotional states, so we have chosen to present techniques for coping with anxiety. Anxiety is a very common complaint, and there are several basic anxiety reducing techniques that can be learned and applied rapidly. In this section, we present two methods, muscle relaxation and meditation, which are both effective and low-risk.

Reducing Anxiety and Stress

Although a little anxiety may actually enhance performance at times, it can easily run out of control, causing distress and interfering with relationships and job performance. Modern life, with more crowding, more work pressure, and more choices, has led to greater stress levels for just about everyone. The emotional arousal associated with anxiety or fear may have been useful in more primitive times because the "fight or flight" syndrome chemically sparked physical readiness to deal with potential harm. What once may have increased the chances for survival now threatens our health, because the physiological by-products of stress cannot be easily dissipated in a sedentary lifestyle. Today's helper is frequently called upon to help clients learn to reduce the causes of stress by helping them acquire time management skills and developing habits for self-care, including exercise and good nutrition, and gaining a healthier outlook on life. In addition, helpers assist clients to lower stress by reducing emotional arousal through quieting techniques. Helpers also need to sustain their own mental health by utilizing stress reducing resources (Lawson & Myers, 2011).

Some of the better known methods for reducing anxiety and stress are systematic desensitization for phobic anxiety (Wolpe, 1958), applied relaxation (Clark et al., 2006; Öst, 1987), progressive relaxation (Jacobson, 1938), coping skills training (Frydenberg & Brandon, 2002; Tubesing, 1981), guided imagery (Apóstolo & Kolcaba, 2009; Overholser, 1991; Singer, 2006; Witmer & Young, 1985, 1987), confession/ventilation (Menninger, 1958; Pennebaker, 2002), enhancing social support (Gilliland, James, & Bowman, 1989), stress inoculation (Israelashvili, 1998; Meichenbaum, 1993; Novaco, 1977, 1983), biofeedback training (Fair, 1989; Fedotchev, 2010; Stevens, Hynan, Allen, Beaun, & McCart, 2007), and meditation (Aftanas & Golosheykin, 2005; Bogart, 1991; Burns, Lee, & Brown, 2011; Carrington, 1998; Shapiro, 1994; Singh, 2003a, 2003b; Young, de Armas DeLorenzi, & Cunningham, 2011). These techniques are frequently combined and offered in a psychoeducational format as stress reduction or coping skills training courses (Nickel, 2007). In a group setting, participants also benefit from the support of fellow participants, which also helps to reduce stress.

The most fundamental method for helping clients reduce arousal is deep muscle relaxation. Muscle relaxation training brings about relief from troubling symptoms of anxiety and lets clients experience the positive sensations associated with lowered muscle tension. This technique is explained in detail here because it is part of most stress reduction courses and forms the basis of systematic desensitization and biofeedback training.

RELAXATION TRAINING Edmund Jacobson's progressive relaxation technique (1938) was, for many years, the favored method for teaching clients deep muscle relaxation. Muscle relaxation had been found to reduce anxiety in clients with phobias by pairing relaxation with exposure to fearful stimuli, a process called *systematic desensitization*. Jacobson's method, if faithfully followed, enables the client to identify and relax every major muscle group in the body. The traditional training process may actually take several months in weekly sessions, although abbreviated versions have been used successfully (Gatchel & Baum, 1983; Harris, 2003). Following is a simple and even briefer format developed by Witmer (1985), which can be learned in three or four sessions, each lasting about 20 minutes. Every session is identical and provides a complete tensing and then relaxing of all the major muscle groups (see Table 14.1). Please note that for most problems, relaxation alone is probably not as effective as a treatment program that also includes mental or cognitive control of anxious thoughts (Hinton, Hofmann, Rivera, Otto, & Pollack, 2011; Stevens, Hynan, Allen, Beaun, & McCart, 2007). Still, relaxation training has been consistently shown to work as a treatment for various kinds of anxiety and can easily be included as an adjunct to other helping strategies.

THE TECHNIQUE OF DEEP MUSCLE RELAXATION

Step 1: Preparation. Ask the client to find the most comfortable position with eyes closed. This may be sitting or lying down, but in either case, there should be support for the head. The legs and arms should not be crossed. The procedure is best practiced without the distractions of noise or glaring lights. Instruct the client to speak as little as possible and to avoid moving except as necessary to achieve a more comfortable position. The client may be instructed to raise one finger to indicate when an instruction has been understood or completed.

Step 2: Tighten and Relax. Ask the client to progressively tighten and then relax each muscle group, using the instructions in Table 14.1. Encourage the client to hold each

TABLE 14.1   Instructions to the Client for Tensing and Relaxing Muscle Groups

Major Muscle Group and Area of Tension	Tensing and Relaxing Instructions
1. Hands and Arms	
Hand: The back of your hand, fingers, and the wrist	Tense the muscles in the right hand and lower right arm by making a tight fist. Hold for at least 5 seconds. Feel the tension. Now relax. Notice the difference between the tensing and relaxing. Repeat the same procedure. Now do the same thing with your left hand. Finish by tensing and relaxing both hands together.
Lower Arm: The forearm and the wrist	Hold both arms out in front of you with palms up, bend the hands down. Feel the tension in the hand, wrist, and forearm. Then relax. Repeat the same procedure. Now extend your arms out in front of you but with palms down. Bend your hands up. Feel the tension. Relax. Repeat the same procedure. Now let both arms hang loosely at your side.
Upper Arm: The bicep muscles	Start with your right arm. Bend the elbow, touch your shoulder with your fingers, and tense the bicep just like you want to show off your muscles. Feel the tension, then relax and notice the contrast. Repeat the same procedure. Now do the same thing with your left arm. Finish by tensing, then relaxing both arms together. Now let both arms hang loosely at your side.
2. Head, Face, and Throat	
Forehead and Scalp: The entire forehead and scalp area	Wrinkle your forehead by raising your eyebrows as high as you can. Feel the tension in the forehead and scalp area. Now relax, notice the difference between tension and relaxation. Repeat the procedure. Next frown by pulling your eyebrows down as far as you can. Feel the tension, then relax. Repeat the same procedure. Let go of all tension, then relax. Repeat the same procedure. Let go of all tension in the forehead and scalp area. Feel the smoothness of the muscles.
Eyes and Nose: The eyelids and muscles around the eyes, nose, and upper cheeks	Squeeze your eyes shut and at the same time wrinkle up your nose. Feel the tension, then relax. Repeat the procedure. Next roll your eyes left and right, up and down or rotate them in both directions. Finish by opening your eyes as widely as you can, then relaxing them. Now feel the relaxation of muscles around your eyes.
Mouth and Jaw: The area around the mouth and the lower face	Bite your teeth together and pull the corners of your mouth back. Feel the tension, then let go. Now press your lips tightly together and extend them as though you are sucking a straw. Feel the tension and relax. Next open your mouth widely, then relax. Now pull your mouth to the left side of your face, then to the right. Repeat any of the above exercises until this part of your face is deeply relaxed.
Throat and Jaw: Muscles inside the mouth and throat	Push your tongue against the roof of your mouth. Feel the tension, then relax. Clench your jaw tightly, then relax.
Entire Head and Facial Area	Try a final tensing and relaxing by making a face. Scrunch up your face so your eyes squint, your nose is wrinkled up and your mouth is pulled back. Now your face feels smooth and relaxed as you let go of any tension left over.
3. Neck and Shoulders	
Neck: The muscles in the back of the neck, at the base of the scalp, and across the shoulders	Drop your chin down against your chest. Press down hard enough so you feel tension under your chin and at the back of your neck. Now lift your head and press it backward. Roll your head to the right, then forward to your chest, then to the left and back to where you started. Go slowly and gently. Repeat this at least twice in the same direction. Next, do the same exercise in the other direction. Relax with your head in a normal position, stretching it in whatever way you need for working out remaining tension spots.

Major Muscle Group and Area of Tension	Tensing and Relaxing Instructions
4. Chest, Shoulders, and Upper Back	
Muscles in the Chest, Shoulders, and Upper Back Area	Take a deep breath, hold it and at the same time pull the shoulders back, trying to make the shoulder blades touch. Feel the tension around your ribs, shoulders, and the upper back. Exhale slowly and feel the relaxation as you return to a natural position. Now pull your shoulders as far up as you can, then as far up, as far back, and as far down as you can, making a kind of circular motion. Repeat this at least twice. Feel the tension and relaxation. Next go in the opposite direction in your rotation of the shoulders. Sense the looseness and relaxed feeling in this part of your body.
5. Lower Back, Stomach, and Hips	
Lower Back: The muscles across the lower back area	Begin by taking a deep breath and sitting up straight. Pull your shoulders back and arch your back so your stomach sticks out. Exhale and let all the air and tension flow out. Repeat this procedure. Next bend forward arching your back the other way with your head down to your knees and your hands touching the floor. Feel the muscles stretching. Return to a normal sitting position and feel the relaxation. Repeat the procedure.
Stomach and Hips: The muscles in the abdominal area and hips	Take a deep breath and hold it as you make your stomach muscles hard. Just tighten them up as though you were going to hit yourself in the stomach. You should feel a good deal of tightness in the stomach area. Breathe out and feel the relaxation as you do. Let go of this tension. Repeat the procedure. Next breathe out as far as you can, feeling the tension in your stomach area as you hold your breath. Now let go and allow yourself to breathe naturally, noticing the difference between tension and relaxation.
6. Hips, Legs, and Feet	
Hips and Upper Legs: The muscles in the upper and lower parts of the thighs	Gently hold fast to the bottom of your chair. Press your heels down hard on the floor. Feel the tension around your hips and the hardness of the large upper leg muscles. Relax and notice the difference between tension and relaxation. Repeat the procedure.
Lower Legs: The muscles from the knees to the ankles	Hold both legs straight out in front of you. Point your feet and toes away from your head. Feel the tension in your legs and on top of your feet. Relax and drop both feet on the floor. Now extend your legs again, but point your feet and toes toward your head. Feel the tension in the calf muscles and around your ankles. Relax and drop both feet. Notice the relaxed feeling.
Feet: The muscles around the ankles, over the top of the feet, the arch and ball of the feet, and the toes	Extend both feet, toes pointed away from you. Then turn both feet inward and at the same time curl your toes. Gently tense the muscles just enough to feel the tension and relax. Now try moving each foot in a circular motion, feeling the stretching and tensing. Relax. Repeat but reverse the direction and relax! Try spreading your toes, then relaxing, letting all the tension go out of your feet. Now put both feet flat on the floor, take a deep breath, and relax.
7. Body Review	
	Scan your whole body and recognize how it now feels more relaxed. Let the muscles of your body relax even more as you do a body scan from head to toe. Muscles that still feel a bit tight can be tensed, then relaxed.

(Continued)

TABLE 14.1 *(Continued)*	
Major Muscle Group and Area of Tension	**Tensing and Relaxing Instructions**
	Next, try tensing your whole body at one time. Take a deep breath and feel the tension all over your body. Hold for several seconds, then let go. Let all the air out and feel the deep relaxation coming over your entire body. The tension is flowing out like the air escaping from a balloon. Enjoy the relaxed feeling.

Source: Witmer, J. M. (1985). *Pathways to personal growth*. Muncie, IN: Accelerated Development. Copyright J. M. Witmer. Reprinted with permission.

tensed muscle about 6 or 7 seconds until the experience of tightness is fully felt. If the posture is held too long, cramps and spasms may result. While a muscle group is tensed, ask the client to focus attention on that area, simultaneously relaxing other parts of the body and holding the breath.

Step 3: Relax Fully and Breathe. Following the tensing of a muscle group, instruct the client to exhale and relax fully and completely. This relaxation is to be accompanied by slow, deep, diaphragmatic breathing and should last 20 seconds or so. The tension and relaxation of the same muscle group is then repeated before moving on.

Diaphragmatic breathing consists of inhaling and exhaling below the ribs rather than in the upper chest. It is the relaxed breathing demonstrated by sleeping babies and practiced by singers. Help clients learn diaphragmatic breathing by placing one hand on the chest and the other on the diaphragm/stomach area. Diaphragmatic breathing occurs when the stomach hand goes up and down but the chest hand remains relatively immobile.

Step 4: The Body Scan. The most important phase of the lesson is the body review, or **body scan.** This phase is critical because the client is learning to self-monitor. In this step, the client is asked to return to specific, discrete areas of tension during the relaxation procedure and to relax them. This allows the helper to individualize the relaxation so that the client can spend time on the areas that he or she tends to tighten. Tell clients that a body scan can be used on their own, at any time during the day, to check bodily tension.

Step 5: Assign Practice. The first administration of the relaxation technique should be recorded for the client, or a standardized commercially available version of the technique should be provided. Ask the client to practice the relaxation technique twice daily, usually once upon arising and once in bed before falling asleep. Have the client note which of the six bodily areas show the greatest sources of tension during the day, and ask the client to report this information at the next session.

MEDITATION Meditation may be one of the most effective means for decreasing anxiety, panic, and persistent anger (Brooks & Scarano, 1985; Lane, Seskevich, & Pieper, 2007; Kabat-Zinn et al., 1992). Moreover, meditation is not merely a method for reducing tension; it actually produces positive states of happiness, alertness, improved concentration, fearlessness, optimism, joy, and feelings of well-being (Chandler, Holden, & Kolander, 1992; Fredrickson, Cohn, Coffey, Pek, & Finkel, 2008; Singh, 2003a; Smith, Compton, & Beryl, 1995). Meditation has been used to treat and prevent substance abuse (Dakwar & Levin, 2009; Gelderloos, Walton, Orme-Johnson, & Alexander, 1991; Shafii, 1974, 1975;

Young, de Armas DeLorenzi, & Cunningham, 2011; Zgierska et al., 2009). Along with prayer, meditation is a key tool in the 12 steps of Alcoholics Anonymous. Meditation is utilized in about 60% of addiction treatment programs (Priester et al., 2009).

There are several forms of meditation, but we will talk about two: mantra meditation and mindfulness. Mantra meditation has a long history in Christian and Eastern thought. A mantra is a word or phrase repeated slowly and at intervals, mentally, not aloud but with the "tongue of thought" (Singh, 2003b). For those who are spiritually inclined, any name of God can be used. Others have found it effective to repeat a word such as "one" or "calm" (Benson, 1984). If you are interested in learning more about mantra meditation, read Rajinder Singh's book *Inner and Outer Peace through Meditation* (2003b). It contains complete and simple instructions for nondenominational spiritual meditation and exercises for getting started. For those who are not attracted to a spiritual meditation, Patricia Carrington's *The Book of Meditation* (1998) or *Meditation for Dummies* (Bodian, 2006) are good resources.

Mindfulness is a form of Theravadin Buddhist meditation that has found its way into a number of new therapies without its religious accoutrements. These include, mindfulness-based stress reduction (Kabat-Zinn et al., 1992), mindfulness-based cognitive therapy (Segal, Williams, & Teasdale, 2002), dialectical behavior therapy (Linehan, 1993), and acceptance and commitment therapy (Hayes, Luoma, Bond, Masuda, & Lillis, 2006). Mindfulness is not merely an activity conducted in a meditation sitting, but it is also a way of life. It involves paying strict attention to what is happening in the present moment without judging. Mindfulness as a therapeutic tool contrasts with traditional cognitive therapy because mindfulness does not challenge or replace negative thoughts. It substitutes "present awareness" for negative thinking. As a negative thought enters, it is noted without judgment and allowed to pass through. Mindfulness practitioners think that arguing with thoughts tends to strengthen them while allowing them to flow through consciousness reduces their potency.

Whether one uses mantra or mindfulness-based meditation, a noticeable benefit is a reduction in the constant chattering of the mind and the mental images that produce anxiety. For example, have you ever tried to sleep and found plans for the next day going around in your head? Meditation is a means of putting such thoughts to rest for a while. Unlike relaxation techniques, meditation has the effect of producing mental quietude, not just physical rest. Like relaxation, meditation must be practiced on a regular basis for at least 15 minutes per day for several weeks, before real benefits can be realized (Benson, 1984). After that, at least 30 minutes a day should be devoted to meditating. Regularity is crucial, and longer meditations are considered to be more beneficial than several short meditations. Like any skill, a teacher is helpful at all stages of training (Singh, 2003b).

Raising Emotional Arousal and Facilitating Expression

The patient only gets free from the hysterical symptom by reproducing
the pathogenic impressions that caused it and by giving utterance
to them with the expression of affect and thus the therapeutic task
consists solely in inducing him to do so.

BREUER AND FREUD, 1895/1955, P. 283

The earliest records of cathartic methods are found in ancient Greek drama. The word *katharsis* indicates a purging or purification experienced after the expression of emotions. The effectiveness of traditional uses of cathartic methods is documented in the history of religious rituals, confession of sins, mesmerism, and rituals of mourning. Helpers still use cathartic techniques to encourage clients to open up verbally and emotionally.

The basis for the modern approach to arousal and expression is found in the very roots of psychoanalysis (Bemak & Young, 1998; Young & Bemak, 1996). The quotation that opens this section is from the classic book *Studies on Hysteria*. It was in this publication that Breuer and Freud (1895/1955) presented their discovery that reliving past traumas, provoking emotional reactions and getting clients to express their feelings had healing power. Their famous client Anna O. called it "chimney sweeping."

Freud's idea was that relief from emotional suffering could be attained by releasing pools of stored emotions that were held in the unconscious. When freed, these stored emotions dissipate like water running down a drain. In all fairness to Freud, he modified his ideas about emotions later in his life, but this idea of releasing stockpiled emotions became popular and took root in many other therapeutic systems. Since Freud's time, the terms *catharsis, abreaction, emotional insight, corrective emotional experience, releasing blocked emotion,* and *experiencing* have been used to describe the release of emotions in the helping relationship (Nichols & Efran, 1985; Nichols & Zax, 1977).

Most helping professionals do not subscribe to Freudian principles today (Prochaska & Norcross, 2009; Young & Feiler, 1993). Still, emotional awareness and emotional expression are widely used in Gestalt therapy (Perls, 1977; Prochaska & Norcross, 2009), psychodrama (Moreno, 1958), and a number of group approaches, including encounter and marathon groups. Emotional arousal has been activated through hypnosis and drugs (Wolberg, 1977), psychodramatic methods (Moreno, 1958), guided imagery (Witmer & Young, 1985), reflective listening in client-centered therapy, confrontation, disparaging feedback in Synanon groups, free association in psychoanalysis, the empty-chair technique (Polster & Polster, 1973), focusing (Gendlin, 1969, 1978), flooding, implosive therapy (Stampfl & Levis, 1967), bioenergetics (Lowen, 1967), play therapy (Schaefer & Mattei, 2005), and many others. Research has generally supported the use of emotional expression as a therapeutic change technique (Rosner, Beutler, & Daldrup, 2000) even if many of the more radical approaches have been discredited (Norcross, Koocher, & Garofalo, 2006).

AROUSAL AND EXPRESSION The term **catharsis** is the most commonly used term in the context of arousal and expression, but it has become a catchall that actually encompasses two separate activities: (1) stimulating emotional arousal of the client and (2) encouraging emotional expression by the client (Young & Bemak, 1996). Arousing techniques frustrate, shock, anger, or evoke some other state of emotional arousal for the purpose of motivating change. Expressive techniques, on the other hand, help clients fully experience their feelings and allow them to communicate these emotions to the helper. Clients report "cathartic events" as extremely significant; however, several studies indicate that emotional arousal should be accompanied by a cognitive change or perspective shift to achieve maximum effectiveness. Furthermore, there is some indication that individuals who are underexpressive will benefit most from highly arousing and expressive techniques (Young & Bemak, 1996).

Be aware that emotionally stimulating techniques can be traumatic and potentially harmful to clients. Arousing techniques, in their simplest and most benign form, include encouraging clients to talk about troubling experiences and feelings rather than avoiding them. At the extreme, helpers may evoke powerful emotions that make the client feel out of control. Because some arousing techniques can produce harmful reactions, we will discuss moderately arousing methods that encourage clients to focus on their emotions but do not pressure them to do so. The more confrontational and cathartic methods are very advanced skills to be used only by experienced practitioners within strict ethical guidelines and in conjunction with close supervision (Young & Bemak, 1996). They are mentioned here because, sooner or later, every helper will see these methods on films or at conference workshops. Like a knife that cuts both ways, it is important to keep in mind that although these methods can produce strong reactions, the risks are substantial.

Besides the risks associated with arousing and expressive techniques, there is what Goleman (2006) calls a **ventilation fallacy.** Because expressing anger feels so good immediately, we are seduced into thinking that we have dispelled it. In fact, the opposite may be true (see Tavris, 1989). Expressing anger tends to arouse a person more, making him or her more likely to feel anger later, while managing or reducing anger may be more effective in preventing outbursts (LeCroy, 1988).

TECHNIQUES THAT STIMULATE EMOTIONAL AROUSAL AND EXPRESSION

Creative Arts

USING CREATIVE ARTS TO AROUSE Helpers expose clients to media such as music, films, art, or books that can bring out strong reactions (Gladding, 2010; Degges-White & Davis, 2011). For example, art therapists have used Beethoven's music because of its ability to stimulate strong feelings. Even observing paintings can evoke hidden emotions, and when a client can identify with the protagonist of a story or film, it enhances the emotional arousal; for example, a helper might suggest, the movie *The Great Santini* to a client from a military family. Later, helper and client discuss the film in terms of what feelings and thoughts were evoked. Obviously, clients for these treatments must be carefully selected and care must be taken so that they are not alone when these feelings are activated and that they have the opportunity to talk about what they are experiencing.

USING CREATIVE ARTS AS A MEANS OF EXPRESSION Helpers also use artistic media to facilitate expression of feelings. Arts as emotional catalysts differ from arousing methods in that clients are not passive, but actively create an artistic work that reflects an inner state. These media may include dance and movement, music performance, expressive writing of poetry, journaling, painting, drawing, sculpting, collages, sand tray work, and dramatic use of puppets and dolls. For example, a client who has trouble understanding his feelings about a past relationship could be asked to paint a picture or write a poem about the experience and share it during the next session.

STOP AND REFLECT

Journal writing is an activity that can be used in the helping relationship for the expression and release of emotions. Writing down our inner thoughts is a different activity from merely thinking about them or talking about them. In writing, we have the opportunity to really examine thoughts in detail, and to challenge them. We may record dreams, daily feelings, reflections on self-concept, or spiritual progress, or we may write about particularly troubling or significant periods of change in our lives. All these activities may help us become more deeply aware of emotional issues behind these events.

In this activity, called a "period log" (Gladding, 2010), you are asked (1) to indicate a particular interval of your life during which you experienced a number of changes or personal growth and (2) to reflect on your experiences at that time. Once you have identified a particular time period, begin writing and do not stop to edit your thoughts. Because you need not show this work to anyone, turn off the internal censor and try to write whatever comes up or emerges without stifling your thoughts or feelings. This is a free association, or stream-of-consciousness, method that psychodynamic therapists have found to be effective for uncovering underlying issues. Some practice is required before one can really let go and let thoughts and feelings flow. One way of doing this is to place your pen on a blank sheet of paper with a headline indicating the particular time period and write without picking up the pen for about 5 minutes. Start with the words "I felt . . ." and continue writing for the allotted time. When you have finished, answer the following questions.

- What were the major feelings you experienced during this period in your life? Did you reexperience any of them while writing?
- Did you find it hard to write in a stream-of-consciousness style?
- How did you block yourself from letting the ideas flow out?
- Do you think clients censor their true feelings about issues or a particular period in their lives?
- Did you encounter any personal reluctance to look at this period in your life?
- Do you see any value in reviewing the past, or would it be best to let these issues lie?
- What does your writing indicate about how comfortable you are now with this important period in your life?
- What other artistic media would you personally be most likely to use if it were suggested by a helper?
- How could you determine which methods would be best for a specific client?

CREATING POSITIVE EMOTIONS   *Positive psychology* is a term that was coined by Maslow in 1954. Maslow and other humanistic psychologists were concerned about the overemphasis on pathology and diagnosis. Since that time, focusing on strengths has remained alive in the work of Carl Rogers and many others who have studied "positive emotions, positive character traits and enabling institutions" (Seligman, Steen, Park, & Peterson, 2005, p. 410). More recently, positive psychologists have begun to accumulate a body of research supporting the use of strength-based helping techniques including gratitude, meditation, forgiveness, utilizing personal strengths, humor, creativity, optimism, humility, authenticity and many others. One of the most important voices in this movement is Barbara Frederickson (2001), who has found that these methods evoke positive emotions and that is why they work. She has found that creating positive emotions both broadens one's ability to see alternative solutions and builds resistance to negative feelings. Her book, *Positivity* (2009) is *not* about how to maintain a positive attitude but how to produce positive emotions as a bulwark against the stresses of the world and one's own negative emotions. She discovered that experiencing three positive emotions for every negative emotion helps us become more resilient in the face of problems. Let us focus on one specific tool for increasing positive emotions, the technique of gratitude.

GRATITUDE   Gratitude is a feeling that results when one recognizes a benefit that is unwarranted and unexpected. It involves feelings of wonder, thankfulness and appreciation (Emmons & McCullough, 2002). Gratitude may be directed towards others or a higher power. Inducing gratitude has been found to be associated with happiness, decreased depression, relationship satisfaction, improved sleep, and better social functioning (Young & Hutchinson, in press).

The timing of a gratitude intervention is important. Getting clients to focus on gratitude following a major calamity is a mistake. Gratitude is something to build into one's life over the long term, not something to distract or cheer someone up after a serious loss. Clients who are prescribed gratitude interventions should not be instructed to ignore or gloss over problems, but they should also be aware of good things that are happening in their lives. For example, we saw a client named Portia who had been out of work for some time, but recently found a job as a retail manager in an upscale shop. Although the pay is low, she receives good benefits, including health insurance and retirement. At her counseling visit, the client discussed the fact that she finds her job boring. She resents having to put up with rich clients whom she says do not respect her. She feels that her talents are not being recognized by her boss. I was aware that Portia had said two months ago that having a job was crucial to her happiness and financial well-being. She was elated when she signed on, but is now unhappy with her work. We discussed alternatives to her present situaton and developed a plan to help her look for a job. In the meantime, Portia was asked to keep a gratitude journal about the good things in her life in order to counteract some of the negative thoughts and feelings she was experiencing. Those negative thoughts could impede her present job functioning as well as her ability to find a new job.

Gratitude Techniques.   The journal is the most popular method for practicing gratitude. A client can be instructed to write daily or weekly record five things for which he or she is grateful. These can be simple things such as "no lines at Walmart." Sometimes, clients seem to write the same things and do not pay attention after a few entries. To counteract this, clients are instructed to use a different letter of the alphabet each day and write five things to be grateful for that begin with that letter. In addition, clients may need reminders to work on gratitude. These can be sticky notes, automated text messages, or e-mails. Clients can set up reminders and even journal on their smartphones using a number of available gratitude applications. Another widely used method is the *gratitude visit*. Clients are instructed to write and then deliver a letter to someone to whom they feel grateful but whom they have never acknowledged.

ACTIVATING CLIENT EXPECTATIONS, HOPE, AND MOTIVATION

Next we will take a closer look at the therapeutic factor involved in activating hope, increasing expectations, enhancing readiness, and helping clients find motivation to achieve their goals. Unlike the methods for dealing with negative and increasing positive emotions mentioned in the last section, here we look specifically at motivating the client within the helping process. Figure 14.2 shows this factor highlighted among the six therapeutic factors. Before learning the techniques for increasing hope, expectations, and motivation, it is important to recognize the discouragement, lack of confidence, and demoralization that most clients are experiencing when they first come for help.

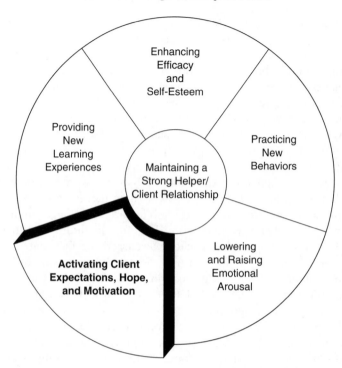

FIGURE 14.2 Therapeutic Factors in the REPLAN System: Activating Client Expectations, Hope, and Motivation

Beginning helpers are often surprised when clients fail to follow through with plans or seem unwilling to try anything new. Remember that seeking professional help is often a last resort. The clients have already tried several ways to solve their problems before coming to the helper, even seeking help from family and friends. They have come to believe that there is no way out of their difficulties. Therefore, before the clients can attack problems, they must first overcome the conviction that their situation is hopeless.

Another issue has to do with readiness. Steve de Shazer (1988) classified clients as *visitors, complainants,* or *customers.* The analogy is that clients who come to a professional helper are similar to retail clients. Some are browsing (visitors), others have a need to buy something and are checking out the prices (complainants), and some have come to the shop looking for a specific product, planning to buy something right away. Helpers who do not recognize these differences will try to force a client into a particular treatment. For example, not everyone is ready, in his or her own mind, to enter substance abuse treatment on day one. Some clients need education (visitors), while others need help thinking about the problem and weighing their options (complainants). Only customers need direct action to solve the problem.

One counseling approach that has shown considerable success is **motivational interviewing** (Miller & Rollnick, 2002; Miller, Rollnick, & Butler, 2008). It is a person-centered/cognitive approach that has been used most often with addictions. The method is based on the idea that clients come for help at different stages of readiness. Using a nonjudgmental, non-adversarial approach, practitioners try to help clients become more aware of the issue surrounding a problem behavior and explore the costs, benefits and risks associated with it. Special training is required to practice motivational interviewing, but you already know the first step—listen with empathy. After that, motivational interviewers carefully use confrontation, accept client resistance, and allow the client to be self-directing. As you can see, the process is composed of many of the building blocks you have already learned. As you acquire more complex skills, one of the ways to conceptualize them is in this fashion, by identifying the building blocks you have already mastered and then adding the specific components of the new strategy.

The Demoralization Hypothesis

According to Jerome Frank (de Figueiredo, 2007; Frank & Frank, 1991), those who seek counseling are demoralized. Demoralization is described by Frank as a "state of mind characterized by one or more of the following: subjective incompetence, loss of self-esteem, alienation, hopelessness (feeling that no one can help), or helplessness (feeling that other people could help but will not)" (p. 56). Frank also proposes that symptoms and mental demoralization interact. In other words, according to the **demoralization hypothesis** client problems and symptoms are worsened by the sense of discouragement and isolation. For example, sleeplessness may be seen as a minor annoyance by one person, whereas the demoralized individual sees it as another sign of the hopelessness of the situation. Seligman (1975) experimentally discovered an aspect of demoralization called *learned helplessness,* which is a state analogous to depression. Seligman found that dogs and people exposed to unsolvable problems became so discouraged that their later performance on *solvable* problems was negatively affected. Many clients do not give the helping process their full effort because they have little confidence that anything can be done. Thus, it is often a first task of the helper to instill some hope that the issues that motivated the client to seek help can be solved and that the client will be fully invested in that project.

Increasing Expectations

Many clients improve radically early in the helping process. Even those on waiting lists show improvement! This has been attributed to the *placebo effect,* a medical analogy that has been unfortunately applied to the psychological realm. The placebo effect implies that the helper is fooling the client with an imaginary treatment like a sugar pill. In actuality, the placebo effect, or expectancy effect, is tapping well-established factors in social influence, especially the attractiveness and trustworthiness of the helper as well as high expectations for treatment (Frank, Nash, Stone, & Imber, 1963; Greenberg, Constantino, & Bruce, 2006; Patterson, 1973). It is the expectation itself that is healing. Faith is powerful medicine (Siegel, 1986).

What can the helper do to increase the client's expectation that treatment will help without being unrealistic? One thing that helpers can do is inform their clients about the problem they are facing. They may have already looked at Internet sources and have conflicting ideas about treatment and the possibility of success. For example, if you have a client suffering from depression, it is important to let him or her know that there are effective treatments. In addition, by outlining the steps of treatment, the client understands the treatment ritual and does not develop expectations that the therapeutic relationship will take some time to develop. Many helpers have handouts for this purpose that explain the nature of the therapeutic process, how the client can make the most of the opportunity, and what background and training the helper has to assist with the client's problem.

ASKING CHANGE QUESTIONS Up to this point, we have largely discouraged informational or closed questions because they tend to put the client on the defensive and do not further the purpose of the nonjudgmental listening cycle, which is to establish the therapeutic alliance. But many questions are useful during the intervention and action phase of helping. These are special questions called *change questions* or *strategic questions* because they are not used for the purpose of gathering information but to influence or persuade (Tomm, 1988). There are literally scores of these but we will talk about only three: embedded questions, scaling questions, and the miracle question.

Embedded Questions. The embedded question has a hidden suggestion and an expectation that things are going to get better. Consider the following:

"When the problem is resolved, what will you be doing then that you are not doing now?"

"When you finally confront your ex-wife, will you feel that you have achieved something?"

"When you let go of your anger and forgive your father, what will change in your family?"

Can you see that these linguistic changes are future-oriented, optimistic messages that the client will change and that the client is expected to act?

Scaling Questions. These questions were devised and tested by solution-focused therapists. Their purpose is to encourage action and motivate change. Here is a dialogue with one member of a couple that illustrates how scaling questions might be used.

HELPER: "On a scale of 1 to 10, with 10 meaning that you believe that you can improve your couple relationship and 1 meaning that you think that it is hopeless, where are you right now?"

CLIENT: "Right now, I'd say about a 4, but I was at a 2 last week."

HELPER: "What was it that you did that moved your level of hope from 2 to 4?"

CLIENT: "I'm not sure, but I think that I put in more effort into trying to understand what she was saying."

HELPER: "And what would it take to move you from a 4 to a 5?"

CLIENT: "I guess I could continue to listen more and maybe we could take some time in the evenings, not just to talk but just be together."

The Miracle Question. The miracle question, like scaling questions, is designed to get clients moving toward their goals (de Shazer, 1988; O'Connell, 2005). The miracle question takes clients by surprise, and perhaps this makes it easier for them to talk about changes they need to make. Let's use the miracle question in the same example with a member of a couple who is complaining about communication problems in the relationship. To get the client to identify a course of action, the helper asks the following question slowly and carefully so that the client has time to think:

HELPER: "I want to ask you a question that's a little unusual. Just think about it before you respond. Let's suppose that tonight, when you get home, you go to bed and sleep and when you awake, the problem that brought you in here has been solved. Now here's the important part. Because you were asleep, you didn't know that the miracle had occurred. What would be the first thing you noticed that let you know that something had drastically changed?"

CLIENT: "I would go into the kitchen and my partner would smile at me."

HELPER: "Well, that would be different. And how would you respond to that smile?"

CLIENT: "I would probably smile, too, and ask if I could fix my partner a cup of tea."

HELPER: "How do you think your partner would react to that?"

CLIENT: "I think she would be shocked and not sure what to do."

This brief example shows that the miracle question gets the client on a new track. Instead of talking about the problem-saturated story of their discord, the client is now discussing changes in behavior that might lead to intimacy. The miracle question is not a miracle cure, but it is a tool that focuses clients on a world where the problem no longer exists. This helps the client envision such an outcome, enhancing expectations and suggesting ways to reach that world.

Encouragement

As we discuss demoralization, and enhancing client expectations, our thoughts naturally turn to *encouragement,* giving clients courage. Encouragement is a concept and a technique that is closely aligned with Alfred Adler's theory of individual psychology (1954). Yet, the use of encouragement is not limited to Adlerians (Watts & Pietrzak, 2000). In a national survey conducted by the author (Young & Feiler, 1993), encouragement was the second most frequently used counseling technique. It was utilized by 90% of the mental health counselors and counselor educators surveyed. We cannot be certain from these data that all respondents were operating under the same definition of encouragement; however, the survey supports the notion that encouragement is an essential therapeutic ingredient for most helpers. In addition, encouragement is probably integral to what most people today call "coaching." As we said earlier, our definition of coaching is "professional helping with a big dose of encouragement." If you learn to effectively utilize encouragement you will have learned a valuable and marketable skill.

ENCOURAGEMENT VERSUS PRAISE   Although, as we indicated earlier, **praise** can be a roadblock in the helping process, this idea goes against the grain for many beginning helpers, especially those who work with children. We sincerely want to uplift the client's spirits, and we want them to pay attention to their positive attributes, so we utilize one of our favorite social tools. There are times when praise is useful. However, praise definitely puts the helper in the role of a judging parent and the client in the role of obedient child. Most adults do not need a cheerleader; instead they need to develop faith in themselves. This is where encouragement comes in. Through encouragement, the helper focuses on respectfully pushing the client to develop a more positive view of life rather than merely giving the client approval.

To get a clearer idea about encouragement, look at Table 14.2, which compares the concepts of reinforcement from the behavioral tradition and the Adlerian concept of encouragement. The table makes the argument that praise (positive reinforcement) and encouragement both have important but distinct uses. In general, encouragement is designed to inspire, to foster hope, to stimulate, and to support (Pitsounis & Dixon, 1988), whereas praise is designed to increase the likelihood that a specific behavior will be repeated. Encouragement focuses on developing autonomy, self-reliance, cooperation rather than competition (it avoids comparisons), and an internal locus of control (Hitz & Driscoll, 1988). Praise is a reward that strengthens a behavior when it occurs. In summary, praise has several drawbacks in the helping relationship because it only recognizes success, not intentions, and it places the helper in a position of superiority.

TABLE 14.2 Comparison of Encouragement and Praise/Reinforcement

Dimension	Encouragement	Praise/Reinforcement
Purpose	To motivate, inspire, hearten, instill confidence	To maintain or strengthen a specific behavior
Nature	Focuses on inner direction and internal control; emphasizes personal appreciation and effort more than outcome	Focuses on outer direction and external control; tends to emphasize material appreciation; emphasizes outcome
Population	All ages and groups	Seems most appropriate for children, situations with limited self-control and development, and conditions of specific problem behavior
Thoughts/ Feelings/Actions	A balance of thinking, feeling, and actions with feeling underlying the responses; i.e., satisfaction, enjoyment, challenge	Attending primarily to an action (behavioral) response that is observable
Creativeness	Spontaneity and variation in how encourager responds; encouragee has freedom to respond in spontaneous and creative ways; however, it may be difficult to understand the expectations of the encourager	Reinforcer responds to very specific behavior in a specific way; reinforcee is expected to respond in a specific and prescribed way; little doubt about the expectations of the reinforcer; helpful in establishing goals
Autonomy	Promotes independence, less likelihood of dependency on a specific person or thing; more likely to generalize to other life situations	Tends to develop a strong association, perhaps dependence, between a specific reinforcer and a behavior; less likely to generalize to other life situations

Source: Witmer, J. M. (1985). *Pathways to personal growth.* Muncie, IN: Accelerated Development. Copyright J. M. Witmer. Reprinted with permission.

WHO BENEFITS MOST FROM ENCOURAGEMENT? According to Losoncy (1977), persons who are dependent, depressed, cut off from social support systems, or suffering from low self-esteem are best suited for encouragement. Encouragement also helps clients who have an excessive need for attention, for power, for control of situations and people, and for revenge. It is useful with clients who avoid participation and responsibility, who are perfectionistic, or who tend to be close-minded. If we analyze these situations, it may be obvious that these are clients who have given up on the world or other people or are fearful that things will spin out of control. Encouragement is helping someone discover the courage to be imperfect.

TYPES OF ENCOURAGING RESPONSES   Some of the major writers in the area of encouragement have been Dinkmeyer and Losoncy (1996), Losoncy (1977), Sweeney (2009), and Witmer (1985). Together, they identify 14 types of effective encouraging behaviors:

1. Acknowledging the client's efforts and improvement
2. Concentrating on the client's present capacities, possibilities, and conditions rather than on past failures
3. Focusing on the client's strengths
4. Showing faith in the client's competency and capabilities
5. Showing an interest in the progress and welfare of the client
6. Focusing on those things that interest or excite the client
7. Asking the client to evaluate his or her own performance rather than comparing it with another standard
8. Showing respect for the client and the client's individuality and uniqueness
9. Becoming involved with the client through honest self-disclosure
10. Offering assistance as an equal partner in the counseling process
11. Using humor
12. Providing accurate feedback on deeds rather than on personality
13. Confronting discouraging beliefs
14. Lending enthusiasm and asking for commitment toward goals

Summarizing these 14 interventions may oversimplify the Adlerian concept, but it may also give some general direction to helpers and improve the understanding of the method. I have divided these interventions into three major helper activities: focusing on the positive and the changeable, emphasizing equality and individuality, and pushing with enthusiasm.

Focusing on the Positive and the Changeable.

Optimism is the tendency to view the world as a benign, friendly source of support. Not everyone shares this view of life, but optimism can be learned (Carver, Scheier, Miller, & Fulford, 2009; Seligman, 1998). An optimistic point of view is also associated with good mental health and freedom from stress (Seligman, 1998; Witmer, 1985). On the other hand, research indicates that pessimism correlates with depression, lowered achievement, and health problems (Seligman, 1998).

In the preceding list, interventions 1 through 4 are grouped together into the encouraging helper behavior of focusing on *the positive* and *the changeable*. All foster development of an optimistic attitude by helping to shift the client's attention from the deficits to the strengths in his or her life. Such encouragement entails noticing the client's success as well as showing faith in the client's ability to succeed. Focusing on the positive and the changeable also includes redirecting the client's discussions from the past to the present. Note the positive, optimistic interventions in the following client/helper dialogue:

> CLIENT: "I feel like I've totally messed up my future. I don't like the job or the life I have right now, and I am not sure that I can turn things around."
>
> HELPER: "Tell me what you really enjoy doing." (focusing on the positive)
>
> CLIENT: "What? . . . Oh, well, I really enjoy working in the garden." (The client goes on to describe the feelings he enjoys, and the helper encourages him.)
>
> HELPER: "How do you feel now as you think about gardening?"
>
> CLIENT: "Better. But I always feel better when I think about good things like that."
>
> HELPER: "Yes, so do I. I prefer to feel good."
>
> CLIENT (LAUGHING): "Me too. But it isn't always easy."
>
> HELPER: "You're right. I was wondering what was going on in your life besides the problem areas, what is going well and what makes you feel optimistic."

This dialogue shows a helper who is a little abrupt in shifting the focus to the positive. This was done to help the client understand that he or she can push the positive button, not just the negative one. Encouragement should not be seen as trying to get the client to ignore difficult issues; instead, it asks the client to develop a balanced view that includes the positive aspects of life. In addition, it helps to focus the client on the parts of the problem that can be changed, rather than ruminating over the unchangeable. Here is an example:

> CLIENT: "We went to the picnic, and it was a total disaster just like I said it would be. Her mom started criticizing us again, so my wife and I ended up spending most of the time playing with the kids and talking to each other."
>
> HELPER: "It sounds like there were some uncomfortable moments, but it also sounds like you did something positive to deal with her mother's criticism."
>
> CLIENT: "What?"
>
> HELPER: "Well, instead of getting involved in the argument, you got away from it and spent some time with each other and some with the kids. It sounds like you hit on a good strategy. Do you agree?"

Emphasizing Equality and Individuality of the Client. The essence of interventions 5 through 10 on the list of encouraging responses is to communicate to the client that the helper and client are on equal footing and that each is unique. By self-disclosing, the helper takes away some of the artificiality of the helper role and connects with the client in a more genuine way. Finally, the helper teaches the client to challenge the idea that the worth of a person is judged by external standards. The client must come to evaluate performance against internal standards and to appreciate his or her personal strengths and unique approach to life, as in the following client/helper exchange:

CLIENT: "I finally got off drugs, got a job and an apartment. My life is back on track, but it's still not good enough."

HELPER: "What do you mean?"

CLIENT: "My mom won't let up about how I disappointed her, how I was supposed to finish college 2 years ago. Even though I'm back in school in the fall, all she can say is, 'Two years too late.'"

HELPER: "What about you—how do you look at it? Are you proud of what you've accomplished in the last 8 months?"

CLIENT: "Well, don't you think I've done a lot?"

HELPER: "You tell me." (asking the client to self-evaluate)

CLIENT: "I have. I have come a long way. It was hard, too."

Pushing with Enthusiasm.   Interventions 11 through 14 demonstrate that encouragement is not merely support; it does not mean believing that the situation should be accepted. There is an element of confrontation and a sincere effort to produce movement in the client. Discouragement is a defensive maneuver that seeks to maintain the status quo through inaction. Encouragement pushes the client by giving feedback, confronting the private logic of the client, asking for a commitment, and using humor to turn the client around (Mosak, 1987). The following example continues the client/helper dialogue from the previous section. Notice the confrontation and the helper pushing the client to make a commitment:

HELPER: "So although you know you've overcome a lot, sometimes you still use your mother's yardstick on your life rather than your own. Would you agree?"

CLIENT: "That's when I get depressed. I'm not sure I can ever please her, but that's not going to stop my recovery."

HELPER: "So how are you going to stop doing that?"

CLIENT: "Well, first of all, I will try to let it go in one ear and out the other. But really, I think I'll just spend less time over there."

HELPER: "That sounds like a good start. Let's consider that as a plan for this week, and when we get back together, you'll let me know, right?"

CLIENT: "Right."

How to Encourage

Following are general guidelines for encouraging a client. The accompanying example illustrates that encouragement consists of giving the client directives to pay attention to his or her strengths and to focus on what can be changed. Notice that the nonjudgmental listening cycle forms the foundation for the encouraging remarks of the helper.

Step 1:   The helper uses the nonjudgmental listening cycle to gain rapport and understand the problem. Encouraging responses will not be appropriate if the helper does not fully understand the client's problem. The nonjudgmental listening cycle is, in itself, an encouraging process because it promotes a relationship based on equality and respect.

Herb was a furniture salesman out of a job. He was very pessimistic about getting hired again after being out of work for 4 months. Although he had initially been rather active, recently he had spent more time driving around in his car than actually looking for a position. His wife accompanied him to the first session, but she refused to return for later appointments. During that session, she strongly expressed her worry, anger, and frustration. According to Herb, he had lost all ambition, was embarrassed, and he feared he would never be able to locate a new job.

HELPER: "So tell me, what it is like to be out of a job?"

HERB: "It is hell! Everyone blames me. I get depressed and resentful, but mostly I am angry."

HELPER: "You're mad at yourself for being in this situation."

HERB: "Exactly. What kind of a man am I? My father never lost a job. Neither did my father-in-law."

HELPER: "You mention your father and father-in-law. You seem to be saying that working is an important part of being a man."

HERB: "Of course, I am supposed to be the provider. Now my wife is taking care of me."

In this part of the dialogue, the helper begins with an open question, reflects feelings, and finally reflects meaning. These reflections of feeling and meaning convince the client that the helper understands the situation at a fairly deep level.

Step 2: The helper offers to be an ally.

HELPER: "Herb, my feeling is that what you really need right now is an ally in this process. You seem to have job-seeking skills, a good work history, and a positive attitude about your chosen profession. You've shown a lot of success in sales previously. Perhaps together we can help you find your enthusiasm again."

HERB: "I guess you're right that I have had success in the past, but I am at a dead end now. Sometimes I think it is hopeless."

HELPER: "My thought is that we begin to look at this thing from a different angle. Perhaps if we put our heads together, we might be able to find a solution."

Step 3: The helper focuses on the positive and notes client attempts, however small, to accomplish the goal.

CLIENT: "I still get up at 6:30 a.m. like I did when I was working. I get dressed and start out all right. First, I read the paper and start to make a call or two. That's when I start getting down. I end up driving around town, killing time until dinner, making my wife think that I am out looking for a job. Why am I doing this?"

HELPER: "Well, one of the things I notice is that the rhythm is still there. You are set to get back into a work routine, and you seem to like that. Even though you are not making the contacts, you are practicing, rehearsing for that day when you are back to work. That is a good sign and something we can build on."

Step 4: The helper offers feedback or confrontation and asks for commitment.

HELPER: "I've got some feedback for you if you want it."

HERB: "Okay."

HELPER: "It seems like one of the problems is that you are not being honest with yourself or your wife about what you do all day. I would like you to keep track of your activities a little better. I think this would help you feel better about yourself, and it might help the relationship, too."

HERB: "It is hard to do when I get nothing back."

HELPER: "I agree. It is difficult. But I am only asking that you begin to keep a log of what you're doing toward finding a job each day, and we will see if we can increase that or make some changes in the direction of your search."

HERB: "All right. I can do that."

Step 5: The helper shows continued enthusiasm for the client's goals and interest in the client's feelings and progress.

HERB (ONE WEEK LATER): "Since the last time we talked, I didn't do what we decided. I didn't make two calls per day looking for a job. I guess I averaged about one call per day. The first day I did three, then one, then one again, and I took the weekend off. I got no response."

HELPER: "I am very glad to hear about this. That kind of progress is what we've been looking for. It seems that getting off dead center is the hardest part, and you've gotten through that. Besides, by being honest about it, you've now included me in what's going on. Now what is needed is keeping up your efforts. Right?"

CLIENT: "I guess so. I'm afraid that this won't work, that it will be just like last time and fizzle out."

HELPER: "Yes, it can be scary, but let's try to focus on the present if we can, rather than look back. I have been hoping that you'd make this beginning and then hang in there until something breaks. Let's continue with this plan. I'll call you about Wednesday to see how things are going. Again, I feel good about these first steps."

PROVIDING NEW LEARNING EXPERIENCES

Education is not the filling of a pail, but the lighting of a fire.

WILLIAM BUTLER YEATS

In this section, we want to explore the techniques included under the final therapeutic factor—new learning experiences (Figure 14.3). As the quote from Yeats says, learning is not just instruction. New learning, in a therapeutic session, can be sparked through modeling, and it can also be stimulated through techniques such as humor, stories, metaphors, interpretation, and reframing. In addition, new learning is not merely acquiring facts. It may be a shift in perspective. According to research, gaining a new perspective is one of the most frequently mentioned therapeutic experiences cited by clients (Elliott, 1985). Clients have been able to recall insights and learning up to 6 months following therapy (Martin & Stelmaczonek, 1988).

Definitions of New Learning

A number of terms have been used to describe this therapeutic factor, such as *changing the worldview, redefining personal mythology, developing insight, developing outlook skills, perception transformation, cognitive restructuring, reframing, meaning attribution, perception shifts, the "aha!" experience, relabeling,* and *redecision.* All these terms seem to involve two basic helping techniques: (1) imparting to clients new information or skills and (2) helping clients to change inappropriate or ineffective beliefs, perceptions, and

FIGURE 14.3 Therapeutic Factors in the REPLAN System: Providing New Learning Experiences

outlooks. Let us look at a couple of client stories in order to demonstrate how these two types of new learning experiences are commonly embedded in a treatment plan.

- Maritza is a 23-year-old woman who was admitted for substance abuse problems following her arrest on a charge of driving while intoxicated. On the first day, the goal of the staff is to introduce clients to a "disease concept" model of alcoholism. Maritza attends a class where she learns that she is genetically predisposed to addiction based on her family history and that she cannot help the effect alcohol has on her. The result of this information is that Maritza begins to stop thinking of herself as "weak" or as morally unworthy. Instead, she starts to realize that she has a biological weakness. This new perspective has been stimulated by learning. It reduces guilt, changes her attitude about herself, and increases her hope for recovery.
- Dujuan is a 30-year-old man referred for help with panic attacks. During moments of high anxiety, he has been experiencing shortness of breath, rapid heart rate, and intense fear. At their first session, the helper identifies a core belief that seems to be at the root of his anxiety, "I could lose control over myself and go crazy." During the next 3 weeks, the helper encourages Dujuan to examine and modify this core belief. The goal is to help him to focus on the evidence for and against this belief and then to develop a more reasonable point of view. After a month, Dujuan is able to say, "Watching for danger actually increases my fear rather than reducing it. It is better to have a panic attack once a month than to spend every day worrying about it." Six months later Dujuan claims that he rarely finds himself falling into his old way of thinking and he has had fewer attacks. He feels that he has modified a core belief.

What Client Problems Are Helped Through New Learning?

A number of client problems are the result of inadequate training or lack of knowledge. In psychoeducational seminars and workshops, one can learn to cope with stress, hear about alternatives to addictive behavior, and develop better interpersonal, couples communication, and parenting skills. Clients can even change their thinking about painful remembered events and rethink their sense of guilt and failure. They can see themselves and others in a new light, and they can discover that situations that they have feared and avoided are not really so dangerous.

Resistance to New Learning

"The truth will set you free, but *first,* it will make you miserable." This saying from a humorous poster summarizes the experience of a person who is undergoing a significant change in perspective. Change brought about by new information may ultimately bring about enlightenment, but it can be extremely unsettling at first. Change is disquieting not only to the changing individual, but also to those in the client's sphere of influence. The story of Copernicus is a good example. He taught that the earth revolved around the sun and not the other way around. This upset the existing worldview so much that he was forced to recant, and his student Bruno was put to death 50 years later for spreading the news (Bernard & Young, 1996). On a much smaller scale, a helper tries to persuade a client to leave behind self-defeating ideas and teaches the client new skills and a way to construct a slightly different worldview. The result is that both the client and those close to the client experience discomfort and may actually try to resist or slow down the change.

For example, a social worker was seeing a client, a 65-year-old Italian woman whose husband had died a year ago. The client was lonely and depressed, but refused to go to social functions in her retirement community because going unaccompanied to such an event was, in her view, undignified and a sign to the world that she was looking for a new partner. She had grown up in a strictly religious, Italian community (40 years ago) where such behavior was frowned upon. No external force prevented her from enjoying the company and support of others, only her outdated ideas of propriety. The social worker's attempts to get this client to change her behavior or think about this in a different way met stiff resistance bolstered by years of experience and cultural reinforcement. The flip side of the coin is that when clients can change their outmoded concepts and self-imprisoning ideas, enormous growth occurs. The next section presents a few of the many tools helpers use to assist clients in seeing things in a different way and creating new visions of the future.

Common Methods Helpers Use to Provide New Learning Experiences for Clients

INTERPRETATION   *Interpretation* is one of the oldest therapeutic techniques (Clark, 1995; McHenry & McHenry, 2007). Interpretation consists of encouraging the client to look at the problem in the context of the theoretical orientation of the practitioner. Once the helper explains the reason for the problem, a client develops insight and is then presumably better able to change. For example, from a psychodynamic perspective, a client's reaction to his boss may be a carryover from his lifelong issues with his own father. Once this reaction is interpreted, confronted, and clarified, the client may start to see the unconscious motives behind his actions. Insight may occur (an *aha!* moment), or it may dawn gradually. Once insight occurs, that learning may be applied to other situations. In this example, the client may become aware of similar tendencies in his relationships with other authority figures. The psychodynamic technique of interpretation is an advanced method that cannot be grasped in a few paragraphs and must be learned in an extended training program.

Perhaps the most common use of the term interpretation is in the context of dream interpretation. Originally, the therapist listened to and then interpreted the meaning behind the client's dream. Today interpretation is a controversial technique because it firmly places the helper in the role of expert; thus it is not entirely compatible with an emphasis on collaboration in the helping process. A postmodern or constructivist point of view believes that it is often better to help the client find a viewpoint that works with the present system of understanding the world (Siegel, 2010).

MODELING AS NEW LEARNING   When we want to learn something, we watch others and copy them. Bandura (1971) is responsible for recognizing the potential power of modeling in the helping process. Modeling has been used extensively to help children learn prosocial behaviors, to assist developmentally delayed adults in skill development, to teach alcoholics methods of relapse prevention, to train helpers, to instruct parents, and to help clients deal with fearful situations (Perry & Furukawa, 1986; St Onge, 1995). In group therapy, it is common for members to copy the helper or other group members who are functioning more effectively. Clients learn to be more self-disclosing, assertive, and spontaneous by seeing examples of these behaviors and trying them in the safe environment of the group. Yalom (1995) found that group therapy participants identified interpersonal learning as one of the most important therapeutic factors.

Modeling takes place in the helping arena, either as an intentional process or as an unexpected by-product. An example of the latter occurs when clients take on the mannerisms or copy the clothing of the helper. Intentional modeling is exemplified by a helper of role-playing a specific behavior while the client watches or by exposing clients to symbolic, biographical, or fictional models in books, videos, and movies (Erford, Eaves, Bryant, & Young, 2010; Milan, 1985). Through modeling, clients are able to see a successful performance of a skill. The client then attempts to reproduce the skill, getting feedback from the helper (Mitchell & Milan, 1983).

STOP AND REFLECT

Think about three of your favorite teachers. Write their names in the following chart and describe them as best you can in the space provided:

Name	Personal Trait You Most Admired	Subject Taught	Values Held by Teacher	Most Important Thing You Learned	How Did Teacher Influence You?

- As you look over your answers, how do you think the teacher influenced or changed you? Was it primarily through modeling, or was it through the subject matter that he or she taught? Or was it something beyond the curriculum?
- Look over the list of personal traits. Are these traits you have tried to develop in yourself?
- Which of your favorite teachers would you consider to be a helper and not just an instructor? Why?

USING METAPHORS AND STORIES Metaphors, stories, and parables are common ways of stimulating new learning in clients (Barker, 1985; Gordon, 1978; Sims, 2003). For example, a helper once came up with this little aphorism for a client who was stewing about a situation over which he had no control: "You know, worry is like a rocking chair. It doesn't get you anywhere, but it's something to do." The purpose of the metaphor was to teach the client something about worry. It gently points out that the client might need to find another way of dealing with the problem rather than trying to solve it.

Metaphors and stories engage the listener with imagery, suspense, and humor. Consequently, the client is not always aware that he or she is learning something. A story bypasses some of a client's resistance to new ideas; the client is too engaged to fight.

This was true in the case of Judie, a 35-year-old woman living in New York City who had grown up on a farm. Judie had considered marriage to several different men while in her twenties. Each time, she had ended the relationship when marriage seemed to be the next step. Judie was an only child and was close to her parents, whose relationship with each other was quite poor. They had fought bitterly for years, and she believed that they had stayed together for her sake. She admitted that she saw love as "chains." Judie came for help because she had finally met a man whom she wanted to marry. She was filled with confusion and had changed the date of the wedding twice. In the first few counseling sessions, reflective listening uncovered her fears about relationships. She felt better about her decision to get married after these sessions, but one night (a week before the wedding), she telephoned the helper in a crisis of doubt about whether to go through with the ceremony. On the telephone, her helper told her the following story:

> "When I was a boy, we lived on a farm, and we had a very healthy and strong mare. She was high spirited, but gentle. She also had one peculiarity. She hated it when we closed the gate of the corral. In fact, she would run around in circles, rearing up, sometimes even hurting herself on the wooden fence. One day, we discovered by accident that if we left the gate open, she calmed down. And she never ran away. She didn't mind being in the corral. She just wanted to make sure that she could leave at any time."

The helper credited this story as the turning point in Judie's treatment and in restoring her sense of control. Although no interpretation was made, she apparently grasped that she did not have to feel imprisoned by her relationship and that she could retain a sense of freedom. The helper used the farm story because of his knowledge about Judie's background. He used the metaphor of the corral because she saw marriage as a form of prison. Through the image of the open gate, he was telling her that she could retain the option of leaving. Knowing that she had this option would help her stop worrying about being trapped. The story seemed to be much more effective than giving advice because it allowed her to decide for herself how to act. Stories such as these sometimes work like magic to help a client reconsider the problem situation. Of course, there is danger in overuse and in telling stories that clash with the client's worldview.

EXPOSURE TO AVOIDED STIMULI   There is a story about a woman who sees a man rubbing a rabbit's foot furiously and asks what he is doing. "I am keeping the tigers away," he replies.

"But there aren't any tigers around here," she argues.

"See," he says, "it's working."

Many clients come for help because of avoidance of social situations, fear of dogs, fear of airplanes, or a feeling of discomfort at being far from home. Like the man in the story, they are not willing to give up avoidance behaviors even when those behaviors are superstitious or ineffective. Because a client has learned to reduce anxiety by avoidance, he or she must be taught that the feared object or situation is not really harmful.

Exposure is the technique of helping clients to gradually face feared stimuli (Emmelkamp, 1982; Foa & Goldstein, 1978; Thomas, 2009). Helpers set up hierarchies of feared situations and, step-by-step, encourage clients to face more and more difficult scenarios. Clients learn important lessons from facing rather than avoiding. They learn that many of their fears are groundless and that their perception of how people will react to them may be erroneous. For example, many people fear that being more assertive will worsen relationships in their families. As they become more assertive, they find that most of the feared consequences of assertiveness never occur and that their relationships actually improve.

HUMOR   We know that learning is facilitated in a light atmosphere (Gardner, 1971). Humor also offers a subtle way to shift a client's viewpoint (Ansbacher & Ansbacher, 1956; Goldin et al., 2006; Mosak, 1987). Like a metaphor, a joke tells a story and sometimes contains a philosophical shift, interpretation, or message. It can also increase rapport if the client does not feel that the helper is trivializing his or her concerns (Goldin et al., 2006). Humor is often culturally defined (Maples et al., 2001), and this should be taken into consideration. Before using humor, it is imperative that you understand your client (Vereen, Butler, Williams, Darg, & Downing, 2006), but the very nature of humor is that it is spontaneous. Most humor is part of a conversation, not a planned joke. For this reason, humor that is inappropriate or that falls flat is quite likely. The helper can only hope that the therapeutic relationship is strong enough to sustain it.

LINGUISTIC CHANGES   *Linguistic changes* are helper suggestions that the client use different language in talking about the problem. Because language mirrors thought, what we say is a reflection of our worldview. Helpers often suggest that clients use new jargon or use specific words that reinforce the idea that the client is responsible for his or her own life, thoughts, and feelings. For example, when a client says, "I can't seem to get to work on time," the helper challenges the client's lack of responsibility by suggesting that the client rephrase as follows: "I won't go to work on time," or "I choose not to." Helpers also challenge clients when they engage in black-and-white thinking by using such terms as *always* and *never*.

DIRECT INSTRUCTION   *Direct instruction* is one of the most often used methods in helping. Direct instruction involves lecturing, discussion groups, modeling, and the use of films and demonstrations to provide new information to clients. Psychoeducational seminars are the stock-in-trade of parent education programs, stress reduction groups, anxiety management training, cognitive therapy for depression, couples enrichment seminars, substance abuse education, and a myriad of other programs. Besides the educational material that is presented, clients benefit from the support of others who are experiencing the problem, and they learn vicariously from the experiences of fellow learners.

Direct instruction can just as easily take place in the helper's office. For example, couples counseling may involve training in effective communication skills right in the office. Helpers often assign books and other reading material to educate clients about specific topics such as stress, substance abuse, anxiety or depression, sexual abuse, proper parenting procedures, and other social skills that a client needs to acquire.

In the next section, we discuss the technique of reframing, which contrasts with direct instruction in that the client is not being asked to learn new information and skills but learns to shift perspectives about events, others and themselves.

The Technique of Reframing

There was an advertisement for the Peace Corps that ran on television during the 1960s. It challenged viewers to determine whether they saw a glass as half empty or half full. This commercial points out that there are two ways of looking at a situation: in terms of its assets or in terms of its deficits. When a helper asks a client to see the problem situation in a new, more solvable or positive way, he or she is using the technique of *reframing*. An even better example of reframing comes from Mark Twain's story of Tom Sawyer, who convinces his friends that painting a fence is fun and a privilege, not work.

A more contemporary illustration comes from the movie *Moonstruck*. The hero of the story is rejected by his fiancée when his hand is severed by a bread slicer. The hero had always blamed his brother for distracting him at the crucial moment when the accident occurred. The reframing takes place when his new girlfriend convinces him that the real reason for the accident was his unconscious wish to stay single. She elegantly (but harshly) uses the metaphor of a lone wolf and accuses the hero of gnawing off his own leg to avoid the trap of commitment. Helpers use reframes like this to help the client see the problem in a more constructive and responsible way (Long & Young, 2007; Osborn, West, Kindsvatter & Paez, 2008). They move clients from blaming to taking responsibility from the victim's role to the survivor's role by gently urging them to look at the world through a different lens.

STOP AND REFLECT

The technique of reframing is based on the constructivist assumption that there are many different ways to understand a problem—there is not just one correct viewpoint. One easy way of understanding the idea of multiple viewpoints is a technique called *relabeling*. We use relabeling in career counseling to help clients recognize their personal strengths (see also Ward & Reuter, 2011). Have you ever noticed it is easier to get people to identify their weaknesses than their positive qualities? In this exercise, clients make a list of their own undesirable traits and a list of some undesirable traits of someone else they know. Then they try to think of another descriptor that puts a positive spin on the very same trait.

Take a look at these examples that have been given a "positive spin."

Negative Viewpoint	Positive Viewpoint
Compulsive	Organized
Sloppy	Casual, relaxed
Loud	Enthusiastic

Now make a list of your own negative traits and another list for someone you know. Relabel each trait in a more positive way as shown above. Then consider the following questions:

- Is reframing like this just putting a happy face on a negative trait, or does it really uncover something positive about the characteristic?
- As you look over your own list, would you really want to lose this quality? What would you be giving up?
- When you relabel another person's traits, do you see that person differently?

Discuss some of these issues and your own reactions with your classmates.

HOW TO REFRAME   According to Watzlawick, Weakland, and Fisch (1974), reframing means coming up with a new, more constructive definition of the problem that fits the facts just as accurately as the old definition. To reframe a client's problem, the helper must appreciate the client's worldview and then replace it with an acceptable alternative. Reframing fails when helpers do not take the time to make sure that the new viewpoint is accurate and that it does not clash with the client's perspective. For these reasons, it is best to proceed as follows:

Step 1:   Use the nonjudgmental listening cycle to fully understand the problem. The nonjudgmental listening cycle gives the helper a firm grasp of the details of the problem, including the people involved, their relationships, and the environment where the problem exists. Before reframing, it is especially helpful to reflect meaning to get a grasp of the client's worldview and values. In the following example, the helper summarizes a number of the feelings and meanings the client, Marlene, has expressed during the session.

MARLENE: "So that's the story. I have to move whether I like it or not. It's like being fired and I have no control over it. Either I move or I am out of work. I've never lost a job before. Sometimes I think it's their way of telling me they want me to quit."

HELPER: "From what I have heard so far, what bothers you the most is the lack of control over the decision. That makes you mad. But sometimes you see this situation as your failure and, at the same time, a personal rejection." (reflection of feeling and meaning)

Step 2:   Build a bridge from the client's viewpoint to a new way of looking at the problem. Develop a reframe that bridges the client's old view of the problem with a new viewpoint that stresses the positive aspects of the problem or presents it as solvable. The important point is to acknowledge some aspect of the client's viewpoint while, at the same time, suggesting another way of looking at it.

HELPER: "I wonder if you could start thinking about this move in a different way? You have always wanted to travel. A few months ago, you were even considering a new job or moving to another state. Although you feel uneasy about this because you don't like it when the decision is made for you, I wonder if this may not be a blessing in disguise. How might this job actually give you a little more freedom?" (reframe)

Step 3:   Reinforce the bridge. A shift in perspective, stimulated by reframing, is often something that develops slowly. One way of sustaining the shift is to assign homework that forces the client to see the problem in a new light. Marlene, for example, might be given a homework assignment to do more research on the positive aspects of the move.

PROBLEMS AND PRECAUTIONS OF REFRAMING   Reframing is most likely to be successful if the client is able to relate the significant aspects of the new frame of reference to corresponding features in the old frame of reference. For example, an algebra teacher used to try to reframe her examinations as "sharing experiences." The analogy was not successful, and everyone groaned because "sharing" is not a graded activity (an important feature). Unfortunately, it may be impossible to identify all aspects of a problem that might be important to the client, but every effort should be made to imagine those that could be crucial. In a metaphor or story told by the helper, the basic elements of the tale must conform to the client's situation, or else the reframe may be rejected.

MyCounselingLab™

Go to Topic 5, 7, and 10, *Cognitive Interventions*, *Humanistic Interventions*, and *Psychoeducational Interventions*, on the MyCounselingLab™ site (www.MyCounselingLab.com) for *Learning the Art of Helping: Building Blocks and Techniques*, Fifth Edition, where you can:

- Find learning outcomes for *Cognitive Interventions*, *Humanistic Interventions*, and *Psychoeducational Interventions*, along with the national standards that connect to these outcomes.
- Complete Assignments and Activities that can help you more deeply understand the chapter content.
- Apply and practice your understanding of the core skills identified in the chapter with the Building Counseling Skills unit.
- Prepare yourself for professional certification with a Practice for Certification quiz.
- Connect to videos through the Video and Resource Library.

MyCounselingLab™ Exercises

Go to the Video and Resource Library on the MyCounselingLab™ site for your text and search for the following clip: *Goal Setting: Linda*. Watch the video and then answer the following questions.

Assessing Level of Motivation

Goal Setting: Linda shows an interaction between Linda (helper) and Jennifer (client). We have looked at this segment previously. This time, let us consider Jennifer's level of motivation for change.

1. As you watch, jot down any instances where Jennifer indicates her motivation or lack thereof for change.
2. How would you classify her level of motivation?
3. How could you use encouragement to increase her level of motivation? What would you suggest she do next?
4. Can you recommend some activities to increase her readiness or to prepare her for the change? Do you think that role-playing or rehearsal through imagery might help?
5. Is it possible that she is considering "jumping ship" too quickly? If so, should the helper slow her down?

Summary

In this chapter, we looked at three therapeutic factors in the REPLAN model: Lowering and Raising Emotional Arousal (L); Activating Client Expectations, Hope, and Motivation (A); and providing New Learning Experiences (N). In so doing, we looked at the rationale for addressing each of these factors and examined, in more detail, the techniques of relaxation, encouragement, and reframing. We also discussed the methods of meditation for lowering arousal and also ways to stimulate emotional expression and create positive emotions. Finally, we touched on interpretation, modeling, use of metaphors and stories, exposure to avoided stimuli, humor, linguistic changes, and direct instruction as ways of providing new learning experiences.

As we bring this book to a close, it is apparent that we have only scratched the surface and that there are many more techniques to be learned on the journey. On the way, you will encounter books, articles, and conferences where some system or technique will be touted as the previously undiscovered panacea. If you believe that each person is unique, you must conclude that there will never be a perfect technique or a perfect theory that works for everyone. Instead, I encourage you to rely on the therapeutic relationship as your fundamental technique and to make your choice of tools based on what is respectful and what is likely to be effective for your client.

Exercises

GROUP EXERCISES

Exercise 1: Relaxation Training

For this exercise, the training group divides into dyads. Each person has a turn as either client or helper. Each dyad finds as quiet a spot as possible to practice the training. The helper takes the client through an abbreviated version of deep muscle relaxation given in Table 14.1. In this shorter variant, steps 2 and 5 are eliminated and the helper reads the instructions for steps 1, 3, 4, 6, and 7 only. For time considerations, each muscle group is to be tightened and relaxed only once rather than twice, as one would do in normal practice. Before starting the relaxation process, the helper should ask the client to rate the current level of present tension on a scale from 0 – 100 (0 = most relaxed you've ever been; 100 = extremely tense).

Following the relaxation sequence, take 5 minutes to discuss the effectiveness of the procedure. The client should answer the following questions:

- Using the 100-point scale (0, most relaxed you've ever been; 100, very tense), rate your present level of tension. Subtract this score from your original estimate. How deeply were you able to relax in this exercise?
- Were the helper's instructions presented in a calm and methodical way?
- Did the helper allow sufficient time for relaxation before proceeding to a new muscle group?

- What might the helper have done to deepen your relaxation?

After this feedback, client and helper switch roles and repeat the exercise.

QUICK TIPS: RELAXATION TRAINING

- Ask the client to rate tension based on a 100-point scale.
- Ask the client to move around slightly and find the most comfortable seating position before you begin the relaxation instructions.
- Keep your voice tone modulated and soothing.
- Watch the client for signs of tension or discomfort. When the procedure is complete, ask the client to do a body scan by returning to those areas where the client has difficulty relaxing, and ask the client to tense and relax those areas again.
- Make sure that you suggest deep **diaphragmatic breathing** as a transition between tensing and relaxing muscle groups.
- Ask the client to again rate himself or herself on the 100-point scale and compare this with the prerelaxation score.

Exercise 2: Reframing with a Reflecting Team

A recent innovation in family therapy is the reflecting team. A helper meets with a family and gets their perspective on the problem facing them. Midway through the session, the helper stops and consults with a group of observers who have been watching through a one-way mirror or on a monitor. The observers (the reflecting team) suggest alternative ways of looking at the family's problem. The helper then returns to the family and presents a reframe of their problem based on the suggestions he or she has heard. Of course, having a reflecting team is a luxury because most settings cannot afford to let six helpers see one individual, couple, or family.

Instructions

For this exercise, assemble a group of six to eight members to practice reframing. One person is designated as the helper, one acts as the client, and the remaining members form the reflecting team. The team makes suggestions but also allows the helper to think aloud and consider various ways to reframe the problem.

STEP 1: The client discusses a real or role-play situation with the helper, who uses the nonjudgmental listening cycle to understand the problem as completely as possible in the 5 to 10 minutes allotted for this activity. The team watches but does not interact with the client or the helper. Team members may take notes if they wish.

STEP 2: Once the helper feels that he or she has a good grasp of the client's viewpoint, the helper finishes with a summary. Then the client is asked to move out of earshot or leave the room for approximately 5 minutes. During this time, the team conducts a group discussion about alternative ways in which the client's problem might be viewed. The team is encouraged to identify reframes that are consistent with the client's worldview and values, but that are more positive and change encouraging than the client's current way of looking at the problem.

STEP 3: The helper brings the client back into the presence of the reflecting team and delivers a reframe to the client. The helper chooses the best reframe for the client based on his or her own thinking and the thoughts of the reflecting team. The client is encouraged to respond to the reframe. When this has been completed, the role play is over.

STEP 4: The client gives written feedback regarding the reframe that was presented by the helper and team using a 5-point scale, as shown in the Feedback Checklist.

    The exercise continues by changing roles and allowing several members the opportunity to play the role of the helper who makes the reframe.

Feedback Checklist: Reframing

Client Name: _____ Helper Name: _____

Use the following number codes to rate the four questions below:

1. Strongly disagree

2. Disagree somewhat

3. Neutral

4. Agree somewhat

5. Strongly agree

_____ 1. The helper understood my problem completely.

_____ 2. The reframe was a more positive viewpoint than the original statement of the problem.

_____ 3. The reframe was a more constructive way of looking at the problem.

_____ 4. The reframe fit with my own personal outlook and values.

SMALL GROUP DISCUSSIONS

Discussion 1: Motivation

Motivation is a knotty issue in helping. There are important ethical issues concerning treating clients who are unwilling or unmotivated to change. How would you feel about having a client who was forced to come to counseling but was unmotivated? What do you think about requiring counseling? Should children be forced to receive help by schools or by their parents? Should counseling be mandated if a college student develops problems with alcohol?

    Some helpers say that clients must be "ready, willing, and able" to participate in the helping process. That is, clients must be motivated (a customer), be voluntary, and possess the skills and abilities to participate in the helping process. If these criteria were applied, some clients would not participate in group, individual, couple, or family work. Discuss your thoughts on this topic with a small group.

WRITTEN EXERCISES

Exercise 1: Identifying Levels of Client Motivation

Review Steve de Shazer's classification of clients into visitors, complainants and customers described at the beginning of the section "Activating Client Expectations, Hope, and Motivation." Then, identify each of the following clients as either a visitor, complainant. Remember, they may not be customers for the specific problem that we identified here but they may be customers for other aspects of the problem or for other services. Discuss your answers with the class or small group.

1. _____ A client comes to the substance abuse treatment center on three occasions. Each time, he asks questions about the services, but does not wish to make an appointment. He says, "I'll think about it and call you back."

2. _____ A 16-year-old girl comes to her school counselor indicating that she is considering running away to California with her boyfriend. She recognizes the possible legal consequences and her parents' objections, but doesn't want to lose her boyfriend. She has talked to her friends, both about leaving and about staying.

3. _____ A man comes to couples counseling with his wife because he is having an affair. He wants to repair his relationship with his wife and will end the affair, but claims he should not have to give up his "friendship" with the other person.

4. _____ A couple comes to a school counselor concerning their son's argumentative behavior at school. During the session, the parents squabble and verbally abuse each other. When the school counselor suggests some couples counseling, they indicate that they only want help for their son.

5. _____ A client comes for help to learn better communication skills. He lost his previous job due to poor relationships with coworkers. His present boss has suggested some kind of training because he is encountering the same sorts of problems. Previously, he blamed his coworkers, now he is coming to the realization that the problem lies in the way he talks to people.

Exercise 2: Practicing Encouragement

Below are a number of client responses that suggest pessimism and discouragement. Review the list of encouraging responses and make a statement that reflects feelings or meanings. Then write down one or more encouraging responses that (1) focus on the positive and the changeable, (2) communicate equality in the helping relationship and respect the individuality of the client, or (3) push or confront the client, adding energy and enthusiasm for the goal.

Example

CLIENT: "I am having difficulties at work. My boss has hired a less experienced manager who now supervises me. I am a little bit afraid of him because he has been verbally abusive to some of my colleagues. A number of them have been let go, and the morale in our unit is very low. I am constantly worried about losing my job, and I feel that something should be done about the new manager. I am torn between reporting my new manager to Human Resources and just trying to sneak under the radar until I can find a new job."

HELPER, REFLECTING: "You feel trapped, and you don't know how to improve the situation."

HELPER, ENCOURAGING (FOCUSING ON THE POSITIVE AND THE CHANGEABLE): "You say that you are thinking of looking for a new job and have considered reporting your manager to Human Resources. I think you have two important avenues to explore, and I want to help you get started."

Now take this opportunity to practice an encouraging response. As in the example, first try a paraphrase or a reflection of feeling or meaning. Then try an encouraging response to the following client statements:

1. "I don't like talking about myself very much. For one thing, how will it really help? You just throw things out. That doesn't change them, and, besides, I was taught never to air dirty laundry in public."

2. "My partner feels I have problems with drinking. But I don't. She says she's at the end of her rope and is going to leave me unless I get help. I'm working every day. I bring home my paycheck. Lots of people drink more than I do."

3. "I've tried everything to quit smoking in the past. Why, 2 years ago, I went to hypnosis. Once when I was younger, I went to a seminar. Somebody said I should try nicotine gum or patches. But I've tried before. I know it's bad for my health and the kids are always nagging me, but some people just can't quit."

4. "I'm in a dead-end job. I know I should look for a new job. But maybe I'm too old to go back to school, learn a whole new way of doing things. When I see these young people on computers, they already know so much. Could I really keep up?"

In a small group, discuss your answers to these exercises. Note that these helping responses are designed to increase the client's sense of optimism and hope, not to solve the client's problem for him or her. Evaluate both your reflecting and your encouraging responses. When looking at your encouraging responses, think about whether the client might perceive these as patronizing, or not genuine, or whether the client might get the impression that you are ignoring the seriousness of the problem.

SELF-ASSESSMENT

Using Praise

Review the difference between praise and encouragement in Table 14.2. Do you tend to use praise in your sessions, saying "Good," and "That's great," when a client makes a positive step? When do you use praise in interacting with friends and family?

> I overuse praise, evaluating the client too much. _____
>
> I use praise about the right amount, maybe once during a session. _____
>
> I use encouragement rather than praise most of the time. _____
>
> I do not use much encouragement or praise at all. _____

Ask a classmate to rate you on your use of praise based upon the categories above. Get this information from a recent practice session.

Benefiting from Feedback

If you currently work as a helper, you will probably be supervised in both group and individual formats. If you are learning the art of helping as part of a class, you have probably already received verbal or written feedback from your teacher or other students. Consider the following questions concerning your ability to hear feedback, and change your behavior based on what you hear. Rate yourself from 1 to 10 on each of the following scales, with 1 being "not at all true of me" to

10 "very true of me." When you are finished, respond to the final scaling question.

1. I can accept feedback even when it hurts.
2. Feedback does not discourage me and make me feel like giving up.
3. I identify goals to work on when someone gives me feedback.
4. I know how to encourage myself when I feel that I have not done well.

Scaling Question

Now that you have rated yourself on the four questions above, what would you have to do to move yourself up one point on each of the questions? The answer to this might help you set a goal for your future development as a helper when you receive supervision.

HOMEWORK

Homework 1: A Collage as a Stimulus for Emotional Expression

A collage is a visual collection of words and images as a means of self-expression. Assemble two separate collages using photos, drawings, and words cut from newspapers, magazines, and other print media. The first collage should represent a time in your life when you were experiencing troubling or conflicting emotions. Prepare a second collage that represents your feelings and experiences during one of the best times of your life. Identify these feelings in writing beneath each picture. As you look back at each period of your life, does it reawaken any of these feelings in you? How might a collage such as this be useful for a client who is trying to deal with conflicting emotions from the past? Collages are often used with adolescent clients. How might you develop a conversation with an adolescent client using the collage as a stimulus?

Homework 2: Relaxation Techniques

The skill of relaxation requires the therapeutic factor of practice to make it a part of one's life. Find a way of building relaxation practice into your daily routine. Consider the following suggestions and then implement one in your own life. Report on your attempts in a paragraph or two.

• Every time you stop at a traffic light, do deep diaphragmatic breathing to lower your tension.

- Use small colored dots, available in office supply stores, to remind you to do a body scan. Place these dots on your computer screen, watch, or appointment book. Whenever you see one, tense and relax those muscles that seem the most uncomfortable.
- Before going to sleep each night, do a complete body scan and note the areas where the most tension resides. Keep a diary for a week and see if the same areas tend to hold much of your tension.
- Using the instructions in this chapter, meditate for 10 to 15 minutes each morning. What effects does it have on your level of tension and your mental attitude?

Homework 3: Keep a Gratitude Journal

Earlier we described how research has supported the use of a gratitude journal to improve mood and interpersonal functioning. In this homework assignment, keep a gratitude journal in which you count your blessings each night before bed. Try to identify five positive things in your life each night and note the effects. Record the results of your experience in a paragraph or two.

JOURNAL STARTERS

Reread one of your journal entries from the beginning and another from the middle of training. What do you notice about your development? Look again at Perry's stages in Chapter 1. They are dualistic, multiplistic, and relativistic. Have you noticed any such changes in your thinking during training? Review Table 1.1, which shows the levels of expertise, beginning with naivete and ending with master. Where do you place yourself on this chart? What training experiences will help you develop to the next level?

GLOSSARY

Affect Affect is the outward manifestation of a client's emotions. Affective is used in this book to denote those emotional excesses and deficits that should be noted during the assessment process.

Aides Aides are friends or family who serve as allies to the client in accomplishing a therapeutic goal. Aides supply both help and encouragement. For example, some clients use family members to help them remember to take medication regularly.

Alternate interpretation This building block skill involves helping the client generate an alternate interpretation of his or her experience.

Assessment Assessment is the general name for the interaction between client and helper wherein the helper is eliciting and recording data and the client is providing it. This can be achieved through conversation, observation, information from other sources, the use of assessment instruments, and formal testing.

Attentive silence These are small periods of silence when the helper remains present and attentive to the client. These periods of silence allow time for client and helper contemplation, and may encourage further disclosure from the client.

Baseline Baseline refers to the frequency of a behavior that a client wants to increase or decrease. This is the number at the beginning of treatment against which change can be measured.

Bibliotherapy Bibliotherapy refers to the use of books assigned for the client to read as a method of treatment. Bibliotherapy is a psychoeducational technique.

Blind spot Things others may know about us but we do not know about ourselves.

Body scan A body scan is a client's internal review of sensations in his or her body from head to toe to identify any areas of tension or disturbance. It is a part of relaxation training.

Boiling down the problem This skill involves reducing the problem into several subproblems and then further distilling it into a simple, clear goal statement.

Brainstorming This is a skill that originated in the advertising world to generate ideas in a group environment. It involves a free flow of ideas with an emphasis on quantity and creativity.

Catharsis Catharsis is an experience caused by stimulating emotional arousal and encouraging emotional expression.

Client acceptance scale A three-point scale that reflects the client's acceptance of a confronting response.

Closed questions These questions require short, factual responses or yes/no responses. Examples include, "How long were you married?" and "Are you angry?" Closed questions are not the most effective invitational skills but are important for eliciting key pieces of information.

Coaching Coaching is counseling with emphasis on encouragement.

Cognitive dissonance Discomfort caused by possessing conflicting values, attitudes, and beliefs. We are motivated to reduce the dissonance by resolving or ignoring the differences.

Cognitive therapy A theoretical position that states that emotions are mediated by thoughts. Change irrational or erroneous thinking and you improve emotional health.

Confrontation Presenting the discrepant elements of a client's story and asking the client to resolve the inconsistencies.

Congruence Being genuine in one's interactions with a client. One's thoughts, feelings, and actions all correspond.

Constructivism The philosophy that human beings construct their own view of the world. Humans actively reinterpret the world consistent with their beliefs.

Counseling The goals for counseling are usually to help clients overcome normal developmental hurdles. Counseling goals are growth oriented and emphasize the therapeutic relationship as a major factor. The distinction between counseling and psychotherapy, in practice, is difficult to draw because counseling may also involve helping people with mental disorders.

Countering Countering is a technique that teaches the client to challenge thoughts damaging to self-esteem and replace them with more productive and realistic messages.

Countertransference This refers to the helper's reactions to a client. These originate in past relationships or personal issues and are transferred to the client or on to the helping relationship. For example, the helper responds very passively toward the client, because he or she has had difficulty handling domineering people in an assertive manner.

Demoralization hypothesis The demoralization hypothesis is Jerome Frank's idea that the primary issues to address in the helping relationship are the client's sense of hopelessness, feelings of incompetence, alienation, and loss of self-esteem when they enter a helping relationship.

Developmental Developmental issues are those that are common to a particular period of life. They may be the result of physical, social, religious, value, or ego development. By assessing the client's stage of life, one can identify expected obstacles and resources for helping a client.

Diagnosis Diagnosis is the placing of a client's personality, symptoms, or problems into a category so that appropriate treatment can be applied. Normally, the term refers to a category in the *DSM-IV* list of mental disorders.

Diaphragmatic breathing This breathing practice consists of inhaling and exhaling below the ribs rather than in the upper chest. Diaphragmatic breathing is used to produce bodily relaxation.

Discrepancies Inconsistencies in thoughts, feelings, and behaviors in a client's story.

Door openers Door openers are invitations to talk. They are requests for the client to continue or expand. Examples include, "Help me understand more about that," and "Go on."

Dualistic stage This is Perry's first stage, during which learners evaluate their performances as either right or wrong.

Duration The amount of time a behavior is performed. Some client goals involve increasing the duration of a new behavior or decreasing the duration of a negative behavior. For example, a shy 15-year-old boy may set a goal of talking to a classmate for 2 minutes.

Efficacy Efficacy is a component of self-esteem identified by Bandura. It is the expectation that one can perform a specific task; that one is competent.

Emotional intelligence The ability to recognize your own emotions and also those of others. In addition, the emotionally intelligent person uses emotional knowledge to make decisions and determine behavior.

Empathy The ability to communicate understanding of a client's feelings and worldview. The ability to

grasp the facts, feelings, and significance of another's story and convey this understanding to them. It is the ability to "feel oneself into" another's experience.

Encouragement Encouragement involves helping another person gain faith in himself or herself. It is a very commonly utilized technique in which the helper gets involved with the client and enthusiastically pushes the client to achieve the established goals.

Facilitative body position A helper's body posture is facilitative when it communicates interest, relaxation, and openness. It encourages the client's communication and comfort. It is also referred to as a "posture of involvement."

Fading In this context, fading means reducing the number of sessions over time, finally extending them to 3- or 6-month intervals. These booster sessions help maintain gains.

Feedback Providing another person with information about how you perceive him or her.

Focusing on the client Focusing on the client is the skill of responding to the client by emphasizing the parts of the story that relate to the client's experience rather than the actions of other people or the environment.

Focusing summary The helper often uses this kind of summary in the beginning of a session to remind client and helper of previous sessions and goals. The focusing summary can also be used when it appears that the session has gotten off track.

Freewheeling Freewheeling is one of the rules for brainstorming. This means that ideas are not judged at the time they are generated. Practical considerations are put off until later. This allows for a free flowing atmosphere where creative and unusual solutions can emerge.

Frequency One way of determining a change in behavior is to note the number of times it occurs. When we have identified the frequency, we can set a goal to increase or decrease the frequency of the behavior.

Genogram The genogram is a pictorial family tree that can elicit useful information about the client's family and cultural background.

Gestures Gestures are facial expressions and hand and body movements when they are used as communication. Gestures can facilitate client communication or become distractions for the client.

Giving information Supplying data or facts to help the client attain his or her goals. It is recommended that this skill be used sparingly. It may be appropriate for correcting erroneous ideas around parenting, sexuality, or drug use, or to provide information regarding accessing social services.

Goal-attainment scaling A subjective worksheet in which client and helper evaluate the degree to which client goals have been reached.

Helping Helping is the broadest possible description of the relationship between any two people where one gives and the other receives assistance. This may occur within or outside of a professional environment.

Homework Homework is out-of-session, *in vivo,* practice by the client.

Inner-circle strategy A technique devised by Arnold Lazarus that asks the client to consider whether the therapeutic relationship is focusing on the deepest issues or remains superficial.

Intake form An intake form is the paperwork a helper completes after seeing the client for the first time. Intakes normally record contact and demographic information, a brief notation about the client's problems, historical data, and a preliminary diagnosis.

Intensity Intensity in the helping professions usually refers to the degree of discomfort that an individual experiences due to a symptom.

Internal critic "The voice in one's head" that finds fault and reproaches the self.

Interviewing Interviewing is not necessarily helping, and the interviewee is not necessarily a client of the interviewer. The client may be an entity other than the person being interviewed, such as an agency, corporation, or school. The purpose may not be to help the interviewee but to make a decision about treatment, hiring, or placement.

Irrational belief This is Albert Ellis's term for deeply entrenched, self-destructive ideas about the self or the world. Often developed in childhood, these ideas erode our self-esteem. Examples include "I must be competent in everything" and "I must be approved of by everyone."

Journaling Journaling is a homework assignment in which the client writes about specific topics as a way of solidifying learning. Sometimes journals are used to keep records of improvement in specific client behaviors or *in vivo* practice.

Minimal encouragers Minimal encouragers are short supportive statements that indicate that the helper is paying attention and understands the client. They are useful to nudge the client to continue yet they do not intrude and distract. Examples include "Okay" and "I'm with you."

Miracle question The miracle question was devised by solution focused therapists. It is particularly useful in getting clients off the problem-saturated story and onto the solution. The question is as follows: "Imagine that while you were asleep, a miracle occurred and the problem that brought you for help was completely solved. But because you were asleep, you did not know the problem had been solved. What are the first things that you would notice if the problem were gone?"

Motivational interviewing Motivational interviewing is a synthesis of person-centered and cognitive therapies that are aimed and enlisting the client in the treatment process and removing blockages by enhancing the therapeutic relationship and utilizing gentle confrontation. It is widely used in addictions treatment.

Multiplistic stage Perry's stage of development when learners realize that there are several right answers and multiple ways of accomplishing the task.

Nonjudgmental listening cycle (NLC) The NLC is the author's way of mapping helper responses in a typical progression, moving the client from factual issues to feelings and then to meanings. The NLC usually ends with a summary.

Observation Observation involves noticing and recording a client's verbal and nonverbal behaviors as these provide information that might be useful in helping the client.

Open questions Open questions direct the client to talk about a particular subject, but are less demanding in comparison to closed questions. While they may suggest an area for exploration, they give the client a wider range of possible responses. Because of this, they encourage the client to open up rather than supply a single piece of data. "Can you tell me about your marriage?" is an example of an open question.

Outcome evaluation Outcomes are the desired beneficial effects of helping. The new emphasis on outcome evaluation suggests that helpers need to be focusing their efforts on techniques that work to help clients make progress toward these identified outcomes.

Overshooting Overshooting is a common error of accuracy in reflecting feelings. It refers to a helper response that exaggerates the client's feeling beyond what the client is trying to communicate. For example, if a helper reflects anger when a client is only annoyed, the helper is overshooting.

Paraphrase A paraphrase is a distilled version of the content of the client's message. The content includes significant facts, thoughts, and intentions. Helpers use the skill of paraphrasing to allow clients to feel understood.

Parroting Parroting is the error of reflecting feelings by repeating the client's exact words. A good reflecting response uses slightly different language.

Planning summary Helpers usually make planning summaries at the end of a session. This type of summary includes a capsule version of the story but also identifies agreed-upon plans for future work.

Poor body image Poor body image is the perception of oneself as physically unattractive and therefore less worthy. A poor body image may cause low self-esteem and severe problems, including unhealthy and dangerous eating patterns.

Positive regard The ability to suspend judgment and accept a person regardless of his or her actions.

Practice-based evidence Using clinical evidence as a way of learning about what works and what does not work in helping.

Praise Praise means positively evaluating another person by giving compliments and noticing progress.

Problem ownership Problem ownership refers to the degree to which a person feels responsible for change. If a client "owns" a problem, he or she is disturbed by the situation and wants to make changes.

Professional helping The term describes a contractual relationship between a helper and client who agree on compensation for the helper and goals for the client. The client's goals are paramount and the helper abides by professional ethics.

Progress notes Written records completed by the helper after each session that name the client goals, record client progress toward goals, identify techniques used during the session toward the goal, and future plans and homework.

Psychodrama This powerful method, developed by Moreno, involves the re-creation of a scene in the individual's past, present, or future to explore his or her thoughts, dreams, and emotions as deeply as possible.

Psychoeducational Psychoeducational methods are treatments that involve educating a client about psychological issues such as better communication, stress, assertiveness, etc.

Psychotherapy Compared to counseling, psychotherapy is a type of helping that relies on accurate diagnosis, focuses on eliminating pathology, and is more concerned with treating mental disorders.

Readiness Readiness is a different way of looking at client obstructionism. From this vantage point, clients are not unwilling but unready. Helpers can increase client readiness by educating them, using encouragement, and examining the precursors to change that may be lacking in their preparation.

Reflecting feeling A reflection of feeling (ROF) is a helping response that accurately identifies the clients' emotions based on their verbal or nonverbal messages.

Reflecting meaning Reflecting meaning is an advanced reflecting skill in which the helper feeds back to the client the underlying meanings based on the client's worldview and values.

Reflective practitioner A reflective practitioner is a professional who makes a commitment to personal awareness by monitoring his or her thinking, automatic reactions, decisions, and prejudices by taking time to think back on these reactions and perhaps to record them in a journal or discuss them with a supervisor.

Relativistic stage The relativistic stage is Perry's final stage of cognitive development in which a learner recognizes that some answers are better than others. They can be evaluated on how well the answers fit a particular situation.

REPLAN System Each letter of REPLAN stands for a different therapeutic factor that underlies counseling techniques. It was devised by the author to allow helpers to select a general category of techniques based on the client's needs.

Role-playing Role-playing is a technique for recreating past events or enacting future events in a dramatic way. Clients can try out different roles and experiment with different behaviors before *in vivo* practice.

Self-disclosure Self-disclosure reveals information about the self to others. Deeper self-disclosure is thought to lead to greater self-knowledge, self-acceptance, and deeper interpersonal relationships.

Self-help groups Self-help groups are leaderless community groups that help clients maintain gains in areas such as sobriety, weight loss, etc. Examples are Weight Watchers and Alcoholics Anonymous.

Self-management Self-management means using behavioral principles to self-reward and self-punish in order to make and maintain desired changes. For example, clients will reward themselves with new clothes if they are able to lose 25 pounds.

Self-monitoring Self-monitoring means that the client is asked to become aware of some behavior or thought and keep records. For example, a client might write down each time during the day when engaging in self-downing thoughts.

Self-worth Self-worth is one aspect of self-esteem. It is the global feeling that one is good and has a right to exist. It can be summarized as a fundamental belief that one is "okay."

Signal summary Helpers use signal summaries to send a message to the client that the story has been grasped. When clients receive a signal summary, they feel free to go on and explore other issues.

SUDS Subjective Units of Discomfort Scale. Clients rate the intensity of their current general distress or the intensity of a specific symptom and then post-treatment, evaluate the effectiveness of the technique.

Summarizing Summarizing is a technique in which the helper provides a distilled version of facts, feelings, and meanings covering everything the client has said up to that point. Better summaries include all three domains.

Termination Termination is the ending of the helping relationship. This may be done unilaterally when either party is dissatisfied with the outcomes. Positive endings are usually jointly agreed upon when goals are accomplished.

Testing The formal process of testing involves assessment using standardized instruments such as an intelligence, achievement, or personality tests.

Thematic summary Sometimes the helper notices repeated experiences, feelings, and meanings in the client's story. A helper identifies a theme and feeds it back to the client.

Therapeutic building blocks The therapeutic building blocks are the basic or elementary skills that one learns in the beginning to build more complex techniques. There are 21 therapeutic building blocks described in this book.

Therapeutic factors These are the common curative forces that underlie the helping techniques. In this book, we recognize six therapeutic factors.

Therapeutic faux pas Therapeutic faux pas are helper responses that may weaken or disrupt the helping relationship. For example, criticizing the client is generally considered inappropriate.

Transference Transference refers to client feelings from past relationships or personal issues that are carried over to the helper or helping relationship. For example, the client feels anger toward a male helper due to past abusive experiences with men.

Treatment planning Treatment planning is the helper-guided activity of selecting effective treatments for agreed-upon goals.

Treatment planning list This is a simple list of the client's problems in priority order.

Ultimate meanings technique A technique created by Leontiev that uses questions to track down the most important meaning and values issues in a client's life.

Undershooting Undershooting is also an error of accuracy in reflecting feelings. Undershooting is underestimating a client's emotion and reflecting a feeling that is too mild. For example, if a client is shocked and the helper describes the reaction "mildly surprised."

Values These are assumptions about what is right and wrong. By understanding a client's values, we begin to grasp his or her internal struggles and moral dilemmas. Values are a person's basis for self-evaluation and the evaluation of others. A client's values tell us about what the client expects of himself or herself, how his or her ideals and aspirations are defined, and what is important.

Ventilation fallacy An erroneous belief that expressing emotions purges them from our system. The current thinking is that a cognitive change must accompany emotional expression for maximum therapeutic benefit.

Warm-up Warm-up refers to a client's state of readiness to engage in an activity. Warm-up can be enhanced by mental imagery and role-playing.

Worldview Worldview is the sum total of an individual's beliefs about self, others, and the world. The worldview is significantly influenced by an individual's experiences and culture.

REFERENCES

Ackerman, S. J., & Hilsenroth, M. J. (2003). A review of therapist characteristics and techniques positively impacting the therapeutic alliance. *Clinical Psychology Review, 23*(1), 1–33.

Adams, G. R. (1977). Physical attractiveness research: Toward a developmental social psychology of beauty. *Human Development, 20,* 217–239.

Adler, A. (1954). *Understanding human nature.* New York: Fawcett Premier.

Aftanas, L., & Golosheykin, S. (2005). Impact of regular meditation practice on EEG activity at rest and during evoked negative emotions. *International Journal of Neuroscience, 115*(6), 893–909.

Albeck, J. H., & Goldman, C. (1991). Patient-therapist codocumentation: Implications of jointly authored progress notes for psychotherapy practice, research, training supervision and risk management. *American Journal of Psychotherapy, 45,* 317–334.

Alyn, J. H. (1988). The politics of touch in therapy. *Journal of Counseling and Development, 66,* 155–159.

American Association of Suicidology. (2006). Know the warning signs. Retrieved July 20, 2011, from http://www.suicidology.org/web/guest/stats-and-tools/warning-signs.

American Psychiatric Association. (2000). *Diagnostic and statistical manual of mental disorders: Text revision* (4th ed.). Washington, DC: Author.

Anastasi, A., & Urbina, S. (1997). *Psychological testing* (7th ed.). New York: Macmillan.

Andersen, S. M., & Berk, M. S. (1998). The social-cognitive model of transference: Experiencing past relationships in the present. *Current Directions in Psychological Science, 7,* 109–115.

Anderson, C. M., & Stewart, S. (1983). *Mastering resistance: A practical guide to family therapy.* New York: Guilford.

Andrews, J., Clark, D. J., & Baird, F. (1997). Therapeutic letter writing: Creating relational case notes. *Family Journal, 5,* 149–158.

Ansbacher, H. L., & Ansbacher, R. R. (Eds.). (1956). *The individual psychology of Alfred Adler.* New York: Basic Books.

Antony, M. M., & Barlow, D. H. (Eds.). (2010). *Handbook of assessment and treatment planning for psychological disorders* (2nd ed.). New York: Guilford.

Apóstolo, J., & Kolcaba, K. (2009). The effects of guided imagery on comfort, depression, anxiety, and stress of psychiatric inpatients with depressive disorders. *Archives of Psychiatric Nursing, 23*(6), 403–411.

Archer, D., & Akert, R. M. (1977). Words and everything else: Verbal and nonverbal cues in social interpretation. *Journal of Personality and Social Psychology, 34,* 443–449.

Argyle, M. (1987). Functions of nonverbal communication. *Semiotica, 67,* 135–140.

Armstrong, K. L. (2004). Family theory applied in a group setting: The family issues group. *Family Journal, 12*(4), 392–395.

Armstrong, P. I., & Rounds, J. (2010). Integrating individual differences in career assessment: The Atlas Model of Individual Differences and the Strong Ring. *Career Development Quarterly, 59,* 143–153.

Armsworth, M. W., & Stronck, K. (1998). Intergenerational effects of incest on parenting: Skills, abilities, and attitudes. *Journal of Counseling and Development, 77,* 303–313.

Asay, T., Lambert, M., Gregersen, A., & Goates, M. (2002). Using patient-focused research in evaluating treatment outcome in private practice. *Journal of Clinical Psychology, 58*(10), 12–23.

Bachelor, A., & Horvath, A. (1999). The therapeutic relationship. In M. Hubble, B. Duncan, & S. Miller (Eds.), *The heart and soul of change: What works in therapy* (pp. 133–178). Washington, DC: American Psychological Association.

Baird, P., & Sights, J. R. (1986). Low self-esteem as a treatment issue in the psychology of anorexia and bulimia. *Journal of Counseling and Development, 64,* 449–451.

Bandura, A. (1971). Psychotherapy based on modeling principles. In A. E. Bergin & S. L. Garfield (Eds.), *Handbook of psychotherapy and behavior change: An empirical analysis* (pp. 653–708). New York: Wiley.

Bandura, A. (1982). Self-efficacy mechanism in human agency. *American Psychologist, 37,* 122–147.

Bandura, A. (1997). *Self-efficacy: The exercise of control.* New York: Freeman.

Bannikotes, P. G., Kubinski, J. A., & Purcell, S. A. (1981). Sex role orientation, self-disclosure, and gender related perceptions. *Journal of Counseling Psychology, 28,* 140–146.

Bar, M., Neta, M., & Linz, H. (2006). Very first impressions. *Emotion, 62,* 269–278.

Barbrack, C. R., & Maher, C. A. (1984). Effects of involving conduct problem adolescents into the setting of counseling goals. *Child and Family Behavior Therapy, 6,* 33–43.

Barker, P. (1985). *Using metaphors in psychotherapy.* New York: Brunner/Mazel.

Barkham, M., & Shapiro, D. A. (1986). Counselor verbal response modes and experienced empathy. *Journal of Counseling Psychology, 33,* 3–10.

Barlow, D. H., & Durand, V. (2005). *Abnormal psychology: An integrative approach* (4th ed.). Belmont, CA: Wadsworth Publishing.

Barrett, M. S., & Berman, J. S. (2001). Is psychotherapy more effective when therapists disclose information about themselves? *Journal of Clinical and Consulting Psychology, 69,* 597–603.

Barrow, J. C. (1987). Is student development "dissonance roulette"? *Journal of College Student Personnel, 28,* 12–13.

Basch, M. F. (1980). *Doing psychotherapy.* New York: Basic Books.

Bass, E., & Davis, L. (2008). *The courage to heal. A guide for women survivors of child sexual abuse* (20th anniversary edition). New York: Harper.

Bauer, S., de Niet, J., Timman, R., & Kordy, H. (2010). Enhancement of care through self-monitoring and tailored feedback via text messaging and their use in the treatment of childhood overweight. *Patient Education and Counseling, 79*(3), 315–319.

Beamish, P. M., Granello, D. H., & Belcastro, A. L. (2002). Treatment of panic disorder: Practical guidelines. *Journal of Mental Health Counseling, 24,* 224–243.

Beck, A. T., Rush, A. J., Shaw, B. F., & Emery, G. (1979). Integration of homework into therapy. In A. T. Beck, A. J. Rush, B. F. Shaw, & G. Emery (Eds.), *Cognitive therapy of depression* (pp. 272–294). New York: Guilford.

Beck, A. T., Steer, R. A., & Brown, G. K. (1996). Beck Depression Inventory–II (BDI–II). San Antonio, TX: Psychological Corporation.

Beck, E. S., & Hoppock, R. (1998). Vocational fantasy: An empowering technique. In H. G. Rosenthal (Ed.), *Favorite counseling and therapy techniques* (pp. 34–36). Washington, DC: Accelerated Development.

Bedi, R. P., Davis, M. D., & Williams, M. (2005). Critical incidents in the formation of the therapeutic alliance from the client's perspective. *Psychotherapy: Theory, Research, Practice, Training, 42*(3), 311–323.

Bednar, R. L., & Peterson, S. R. (1995). *Self-esteem: Paradoxes and innovations in clinical theory and practice.* Washington, DC: American Psychological Association.

Beier, E. G., & Young, D. M. (1998). *The silent language of psychotherapy* (3rd ed.). Hawthorne, NY: Aldine de Gruyter.

Belkin, G. S. (1980). *Introduction to counseling* (2nd ed.). New York: Brown.

Bem, S. L. (1975). Sex-role adaptability: One consequence of psychological androgyny. *Journal of Personality and Social Psychology, 31,* 634–643.

Bemak, F., & Young, M. E. (1998). Catharsis in group psychotherapy. *International Journal of Action Methods, 50,* 166–184.

Benjamin, A. (1969). *The helping interview.* Boston: Houghton Mifflin.

Benson, H. (1984). *Beyond the relaxation response.* New York: Berkley.

Berking, M., Holtforth, M. G., Jacobi, C., & Kroner-Herwig, B. (2005). Empirically based guidelines for goal-finding procedures in psychotherapy: Are some goals easier to attain than others? *Psychotherapy Research, 15,* 316–324.

Bernard, J. (1981). Women's educational needs. In A. W. Chickering (Ed.), *The modern American college* (pp. 256–278). New York: Jossey-Bass.

Bernard, J. M., & Goodyear, R. K. (2009). *Fundamentals of clinical supervision* (4th ed.). Boston, Allyn & Bacon.

Bernard, T., & Young, J. M. (1996). *The ecology of hope.* Easthaven, CT: New Society Press.

Berne, E. (1961). *Transactional analysis in psycho-therapy*. New York: Grove Press.

Berne, E. (1963). *Games people play*. New York: Ballantine.

Berne, E. (1972). *What do you say after you say hello?* New York: Grove Press.

Bernes, K. B., & Bardick, A. D. (2007). Conducting adolescent violence risk assessments: A framework for school counselors. *Professional School Counseling, 10,* 419–427.

Blatner, A. (1996). *Acting-in: Practical applications of psychodramatic methods*. New York: Springer.

Blatner, A. (2000). *Foundations of psychodrama: History, theory and practice*. New York: Springer.

Blocher, D. (1987). *The professional counselor*. New York: Macmillan.

Bloom, L. J., Weigel, R. G., & Trautt, G. M. (1977). Therapeutic factors in psychotherapy: Effects of office decor and subject-therapist sex pairing on the perception of credibility. *Journal of Consulting and Clinical Psychology, 45,* 867–873.

Blum, D. (1998). Face it! *Psychology Today, 31*(5), 32–70.

Bodian, S. (2006). *Meditation for dummies* (2nd ed.). New York: Wiley.

Bogart, G. (1991). The use of meditation in psychotherapy: A review of the literature. *American Journal of Psychotherapy, 45,* 383–412.

Bolton, R. (1979). *People skills: How to assert yourself, listen to others, and resolve conflicts*. Upper Saddle River, NJ: Prentice Hall.

Bonitz, V. (2008). Use of physical touch in the "talking cure": A journey to the outskirts of psychotherapy. *Psychotherapy Theory, Research, Practice, Training, 45,* 391–404.

Borbely, C. J., Graber, J. A., & Nichols, T. (2005). Sixth graders' conflict resolution in role plays with a peer, parent and teacher. *Journal of Youth & Adolescence, 34,* 279–291.

Borelli, B., & Mermelstein, R. (1994). Goal setting and behavior change in a smoking cessation program. *Cognitive Therapy and Research, 18,* 69–83.

Boyd, G. E. (2003). Pastoral conversation: Relational listening and open-ended questions. *Pastoral Psychology, 51,* 345–361.

Braaten, L. F. (1989). The self-development project list-90. A new instrument to measure positive life attainment. *Small Group Behavior, 20,* 3–23.

Brammer, L. (1973). *The helping relationship: Process and skills*. Upper Saddle River, NJ: Prentice Hall.

Brammer, L. M., Shostrom, E. L., & Abrego, P. J. (1989). *Therapeutic psychology: Fundamentals of counseling and psychotherapy* (5th ed.). Upper Saddle River, NJ: Prentice Hall.

Branden, N. (1969). *The psychology of self-esteem*. Los Angeles: Nash.

Branden, N. (1971). *The disowned self*. New York: Bantam.

Branden, N. (1994). *Six pillars of self-esteem*. New York: Bantam.

Brehm, M., & Back, W. (1968). Self-image and attitude towards drugs. *Journal of Personality, 36,* 299–314.

Breuer, J., & Freud, S. (1895/1955). *Studies on hysteria*. In J. Strachey (Ed.), *The complete works of Sigmund Freud,* Standard Edition (Vol. 2). London: Hogarth.

Brodsky, S. L., & Lichtenstein, B. (1999). Don't ask questions: A psychotherapeutic strategy for treatment of involuntary clients. *American Journal of Psychotherapy, 53,* 215–221.

Brooks, C. I., Church, M. A., & Fraser, L. (1986). Effects of duration of eye contact on judgments of personality characteristics. *Journal of Social Psychology, 126,* 71–78.

Brooks, J. S., & Scarano, T. (1985). Transcendental meditation in the treatment of post-Vietnam adjustment. *Journal of Counseling & Development, 64,* 212–215.

Browning, S., Collins, J. S., & Nelson, B. (2005). Creating families: A teaching technique for clinical training through role-playing. *Marriage & Family Review, 38,* 1–19.

Bruce, P. (1984). Continuum of counseling goals: A framework for differentiating counseling strategies. *Personnel and Guidance Journal, 62,* 259–263.

Burns, D. (1999a). *Feeling good*. New York: William Morrow.

Burns, D. (1999b). *Ten days to self-esteem*. New York: Quill.

Burns, J. L., Lee, R. M., & Brown, L. J. (2011). The effect of meditation on self-reported measures of stress, anxiety, depression, and perfectionism in a college population. *Journal of College Student Psychotherapy, 25(2)*, 132–144.

Butler, C. W., Potter, J., Danby, S., Emmison, M., & Hepburn, A. (2010). Advice-implicative interrogatives: Building "client-centered" support in a children's helpline. *Social Psychology Quarterly, 73*(3), 265–287.

Caffarella, R. S. (1993). Self-directed learning. *New Directions for Adult and Continuing Education, 57,* 25–35.

Cameron, S., & Turtle-Song, I. (2002). Learning to write case notes using the SOAP format. *Journal of Counseling & Development, 80,* 286–293.

Campbell, C. I., & Alexander, J. A. (2002). Culturally competent treatment practices and ancillary service use in outpatient substance abuse treatment. *Journal of Substance Abuse Treatment, 22,* 109–119.

Campbell, J., & Witmer, J. M. (1991). *Working with special populations: Guidelines for treatment and counselor education.* Unpublished manuscript.

Canipe, J. B., & Brockett, R. G. (2003). New perspectives on self-directed learning. *Adult Learning, 14,* 4.

Canfield, B. S., Low, L., & Hovestadt, A. (2009). Cultural immersion as a learning method for expanding intercultural competencies. *The Family Journal, 17,* 318–322.

Caproni, V., Levine, D., O'Neal, E., McDonald, P., & Garwood, G. (1977). Seating position, instructor's eye contact availability and student participation in a small seminar. *Journal of Social Psychology, 103,* 315–317.

Carkhuff, R. R. (1987). *The art of helping* (6th ed.). Amherst, MA: Human Resource Development Press.

Carkhuff, R. R., & Berenson, B. G. (1967). *Beyond counseling and psychotherapy.* New York: Holt, Rinehart, & Winston.

Carlock, C. J. (Ed.). (1999). *Enhancing self-esteem* (3rd ed.). Philadelphia, PA: Accelerated Development.

Carrington, P. (1998). *The book of meditation: The complete guide to modern meditation.* Boston: Element Books.

Carver, C. S., Scheier, M. F., Miller, C. J., & Fulford, D. (2009). Optimism. In S. J. Lopez, C. R. Snyder, S. J. Lopez, & C. R. Snyder (Eds.), *Oxford handbook of positive psychology* (2nd ed.) (pp. 303–311). New York: Oxford University Press.

Cashwell, C. S., Shcherbakova, J., & Cashwell, T. H. (2003). Effect of client and counselor ethnicity on preference for counselor disclosure. *Journal of Counseling & Development, 81,* 196–201.

Cavanagh, M. E. (1982). *The counseling experience.* Monterey, CA: Brooks/Cole.

Chandler, C. K., Holden, J. M., & Kolander, C. A. (1992). Counseling for spiritual wellness: Theory and practice. *Journal of Counseling & Development, 71,* 168–175.

Chapman, G. (1992). *The five love languages.* Chicago: Northfield Publishing.

Cheatham, H. E., & Berg-Cross, L. (1992). College student development: African Americans reconsidered. *College Student Development, 6,* 167–191.

Choate, L. H. (2007). Counseling adolescent girls for body image resilience: Strategies for school counselors. *Professional School Counseling, 10,* 317–326.

Choate, L. H. (2008). *Girls and women's wellness.* Alexandria, VA: American Counseling Association.

Claiborn, C. D. (1982). Interpretation and change in counseling. *Journal of Counseling Psychology, 29,* 439–453.

Clark, A. J. (1995). An examination of the technique of interpretation in counseling. *Journal of Counseling and Development, 73,* 483–490.

Clark, D. M., Ehlers, A., Hackmann, A., McManus, F., Fennell, M., Grey, N., Waddington, L., & Wild, J. (2006). Cognitive therapy versus exposure and applied relaxation in social phobia: A randomized controlled trial. *Journal of Consulting & Clinical Psychology, 74,* 568–578.

Clemence, A. J., Hilsenroth, M. J., Ackerman, S. J., Strassle, C. G., & Handler, L. (2005). Facets of the therapeutic alliance and perceived progress in psychotherapy: Relationship between patient and therapist perspectives. *Clinical Psychology & Psychotherapy, 12,* 443–454.

Cluss, P. A., Chang, J. C., Hawker, L., Hudson Scholle, S., Dado, D., Buranosky, R., & Goldstrohm, S. (2006). The process of change for victims of intimate partner violence: Support for a psychosocial readiness model. *Women's Health Issues, 16,* 262–274.

Combs, A. W., Avila, D. L., & Purkey, W. W. (1971). *Helping relationships: Basic concepts for helping professions.* Boston: Allyn & Bacon.

Connell, J., Grant, S., & Mullin, T. (2006). Client initiated termination of therapy at NHS primary care counseling services. *Counselling & Psychotherapy Research, 6,* 60–67.

Cooper, J., Zanna, M., & Taves, P. A. (1978). Arousal as a necessary condition for attitude change following induced compliance. *Journal of Personality and Social Psychology, 36,* 1101–1106.

Corey, G., Corey, M., & Callanan, P. (2007). *Issues and ethics in the helping professions* (7th ed.). Monterey, CA: Brooks/Cole.

Corey, G., Corey, M., & Callanan, P. (2010). *Issues and ethics in the helping professions* (8th ed.). Monterey, CA: Brooks/Cole.

Corey, M. S., & Corey, G. (2006). *Groups: Process and practice.* Belmont, CA: Thomson Brooks/Cole.

Corey, M. S., Corey, G., & Corey, C. (2010). *Groups: Process and practice* (8th ed.). Belmont, CA: Brooks/Cole.

Cormier, W. H., & Cormier, S. L. (1985). *Interviewing strategies for helpers: Fundamental skills and cognitive behavioral interventions* (2nd ed.). Pacific Grove, CA: Brooks/Cole.

Corradi, R. B. (2006). A conceptual model of transference and its psychotherapeutic application. *Journal of the American Academy of Psychoanalysis & Dynamic Psychiatry, 34,* 415–439.

Corrigan, J. D., Dell, D. M., Lewis, K. N., & Schmidt, L. D. (1980). Counseling as a social influence process: A review. *Journal of Counseling Psychology, 27,* 395–441.

Corsini, R. J. (Ed.). (2001). *Handbook of innovative psychotherapy* (2nd ed.). New York: Wiley.

Corsini, R. J., & Wedding, D. (2008). *Current psychotherapies* (8th ed.). Pacific Grove, CA: Brooks/Cole.

Couture, S. J., & Sutherland, O. (2006). Giving advice on advice-giving: A conversation analysis of Karl Tomm's practice. *Journal of Marital and Family Therapy, 32,* 329–344.

Covey, S. (1990). *The seven habits of highly effective people: Powerful lessons in personal change.* New York: Fireside.

Croyle, R. T., & Cooper, J. (1983). Dissonance arousal: Physiological evidence. *Journal of Personality and Social Psychology, 45,* 782–789.

Curtis, R., Field, C., Knaan-Kostman, I., & Mannix, K. (2004). What 75 psychoanalysts found helpful and hurtful in their own analyses. *Psychoanalytic Psychology, 21,* 183–202.

Dakwar, E., & Levin, F. R. (2009). The emerging role of meditation in addressing psychiatric illness, with a focus on substance use disorders. *Harvard Review of Psychiatry, 17*(4), 254–267.

Dalenberg, C. J. (2004). Maintaining the safe and effective therapeutic relationship in the context of distrust and anger: Countertransference and complex trauma. *Psychotherapy: Theory, Research, Practice, Training, 41,* 438–447.

Daly, M. J., & Burton, R. L. (1983). Self-esteem and irrational beliefs: An exploratory investigation with implications for counseling. *Journal of Counseling Psychology, 30,* 361–366.

Davis, M., Eshelman, E. R., & McKay, M. (2000). *The relaxation and stress reduction workbook.* Richmond, CA: New Harbinger.

de Figueiredo, J. M. (2007). Demoralization and psychotherapy: A tribute to Jerome D. Frank, MD, Ph.D. (1909–2005). *Psychotherapy & Psychosomatics, 76,* 129–133.

de Shazer, S. (1988). *Clues: Investigating solutions in brief therapy.* New York: Norton.

de Shazer, S. (1989, October). Brief therapy. Symposium conducted at Stetson University, Deland, FL.

de Shazer, S. (1990, May). Brief therapy. Symposium conducted at Stetson University, DeLand, FL.

de Waal, F. (2009). *The age of empathy.* New York: Random House.

Daniel, M., & Gurczynski, J. (2010). Mental status evaluation. In D. L. Segal & M. Hersen (Eds.), *Diagnostic Interviewing* (pp. 61–88). New York: Springer.

Deane, F. P., Spicer, J., & Todd, D. M. (1997). Validity of a simplified target complaints measure. *Assessment, 4,* 119–130.

Decety, J., & Ickes,W. (2009). *The social neuroscience of empathy.* Cambridge, MA: MIT Press.

Degges-White, S., & Davis, N. (Eds.). (2011). *Integrative the expressive arts into counseling practice.* New York: Springer Publishing.

Derogatis, L. R. (1975). *Brief symptom inventory.* Baltimore, MD: Clinical Psychometric Research.

Devoe, D. (1990). Feminist and nonsexist counseling: Implications for the male counselor. *Journal of Counseling and Development, 69,* 33–36.

Dickson, G. L., & Parmerlee, J. R. (1980). The occupational family tree: A career counseling technique. *School Counselor, 28,* 131–134.

Diehl, M., & Stroebe, W. (1991). Productivity loss in idea-generating groups: Tracking down the blocking effect. *Journal of Personality and Social Psychology, 61,* 392–403.

Dimberg, U., Andréasson, P., & Thunberg, M. (2011). Emotional empathy and facial reactions to facial expressions. *Journal of Psychophysiology, 25,* 26–31.

Dimond, R. E., & Havens, R. A. (1975). Restructuring psychotherapy: Toward a prescriptive eclecticism. *Professional Psychology, 6,* 193–200.

Dimond, R. E., Havens, R. A., & Jones, A. C. (1978). A conceptual framework for the practice of prescriptive eclecticism in psychotherapy. *American Psychologist, 33,* 239–248.

Dinger, U., Strack, M., Sachsse, T., & Schauenburg, H. (2009). Therapists' attachment, patients' interpersonal problems and alliance development over time in inpatient psychotherapy. *Psychotherapy: Theory, Research, Practice, Training, 46*(3), 277–290.

Dinkmeyer, D., Sr., & Losoncy, L. E. (1996). *The skills of encouragement: Bringing out the best in yourself and others.* Boca Raton, FL: St. Lucie Press.

Dixon, D. N., & Glover, J. A. (1984). *Counseling: A problem-solving approach.* New York: Wiley.

Dodgen, C. E. (2005). *Nicotine dependence: Understanding and applying the most effective treatment interventions.* Washington, DC: American Psychological Association.

Doverspike, W. F. (2009). Mental status examination. In J. B. Allen, E. M. Wolf, & L. VandeCreek, (Eds.), *Innovations in clinical practice: A 21st century sourcebook* (Vol. 1, pp. 213–216). Sarasota, FL: Professional Resource Press/Professional Resource Exchange.

Dowd, E. T. (1985). Self statement modification. In A. S. Bellack & M. Hersen (Eds.), *Dictionary of behavior therapy techniques* (p. 200). New York: Pergamon.

Doyle, A. C. (1929). *Conan Doyle's best books* (Vol. 2). New York: Collier.

Driscoll, M. S., Newman, D. L., & Seals, J. M. (1988). The effect of touch on perception of helpers. *Counselor Education and Supervision, 27,* 113–115.

Droney, J. M., & Brooks, C. I. (1993). Attributions of self-esteem as a function of duration of eye contact. *Journal of Social Psychology, 133,* 715–723.

Drummond, R. J., & Jones, K. D. (2010). *Appraisal procedures for counselors and helping professionals* (7th ed.). Upper Saddle River, NJ: Merrill/Prentice Hall.

DuBrin, A. J. (2005). *Coaching and mentoring skills.* Upper Saddle River, NJ: Prentice Hall.

Duncan, B. L., Miller, S. D., Wampold, B. E., & Hubble, M. A. (2009). *The heart and soul of change: Delivering what works in therapy* (2nd ed.). Washington, DC: American Psychological Association.

Dyer, W. W., & Vriend, J. (1977). A goal-setting checklist for counselors. *Personnel and Guidance Journal, 55,* 469–471.

Dyer, W., & Vriend, J. (1977). *Counseling techniques that work.* New York: Funk & Wagnall.

Edwards, C., & Murdock, N. (1994). Characteristics of therapist self-disclosure in the counseling process. *Journal of Counseling and Development, 72,* 384–389.

Eiden, B. (1998). The use of touch in psychotherapy. *Self & Society, 26,* 3–8.

Ekman, P. (1975). Universal smile: Face muscles talk every language. *Psychology Today, 9*(4), 35–39.

Ekman, P. (2009). *Telling lies: Clues to deceit in the marketplace, politics, and marriage.* New York: W. W. Norton & Co.

Elkind, S. N. (1992). *Resolving impasses in therapeutic relationships.* New York: Guilford.

Elliott, R. (1985). Helpful and nonhelpful events in brief counseling interviews: An empirical taxonomy. *Journal of Counseling Psychology, 32,* 307–322.

Elliott, R., Bohart, A. C., Watson, J. C., & Greenberg, L. S. (2011). In J. C. Norcross, *Psychotherapy relationships that work* (pp. 132–152). New York: Oxford.

Ellis, A. (1973). *Humanistic psychotherapy.* New York: McGraw-Hill.

Ellis, A. (1985). *Overcoming resistance: Rational-emotive therapy with difficult clients.* New York: Springer.

Ellis, A., & Velten, E. (1992). *When AA doesn't work for you: Rational steps to quitting alcohol.* New York: Barricade Books.

Emmelkamp, P. M. G. (1982). Exposure in vivo treatments. In A. Goldstein & D. Chambless (Eds.), *Agoraphobia: Multiple perspectives on theory and treatment*. New York: Wiley.

Emmons, R., & McCullough, M. (2003). Counting blessings versus burdens: An experimental investigation of gratitude and subjective well-being in daily life. *Journal of Personality and Social Psychology, 84*(2), 377–389.

Epperson, D. L. (1983). Client self terminations after one counseling session: Effects of problem recognition, counselor gender, and counselor experience. *Journal of Counseling Psychology, 30*, 307–315.

Epstein, M. H. (1998). Assessing the emotional and behavioral strengths of children. *Reclaiming Children and Youth, 6*(4), 250–252.

Epstein, M. H. (2004). *Behavioral and emotional rating scale* (2nd ed.). Austin, TX: PRO-ED.

Epstein, M. H., Harniss, M. K., Pearson, N., & Ryser, G. (1999). The Behavioral and Emotional Rating Scale: Test-retest and inter-rater reliability. *Journal of Child and Family Studies, 8*, 319–327.

Erford, B. T., Eaves, S. H., Bryant, E. M., & Young, K. A. (2010). *35 techniques every counselor should know*. Upper Saddle River, NJ: Merrill.

Erskine, R. G. (1998). Psychotherapy in the USA: A manual of standardized techniques or a therapeutic relationship? *International Journal of Psychotherapy, 3*, 231–234.

Evans, M. H. (1984). Increasing patient involvement with therapy goals. *Journal of Clinical Psychology, 40*, 728–733.

Evans, W. N. (1998). Assessment and diagnosis of substance abuse disorders (SUDS). *Journal of Counseling and Development, 76*, 332–336.

Eyckmans, S. (2009). Handle with care: Touch as a therapeutic tool. *Gestalt Journal of Australia and New Zealand, 6*(1), 40–53.

Fair, P. L. (1989). Biofeedback-assisted relaxation strategies in psychotherapy. In J. V. Basmajian (Ed.), *Biofeedback: Principles and practice for clinicians* (3rd ed., pp. 187–196). Baltimore: Williams & Wilkins.

Farber, B. A. (2006). *Self-disclosure in psychotherapy*. New York: Guilford Press.

Fedotchev, A. I. (2010). Efficacy of EEG biofeedback procedures in correcting stress-related functional disorders. *Human Physiology, 36*(1), 86–90.

Felix, E. D., Sharkey, J. D., Green, M. J., & Tanigawa, D. (2011). Getting precise and pragmatic about the assessment of bullying: The development of the California Bullying Victimization Scale. *Aggressive Behavior, 37*, 234–247.

Festinger, L. (1957). *A theory of cognitive dissonance*. Stanford, CA: Stanford University Press.

Fiedler, F. E. (1950). The concept of an ideal therapeutic relationship. *Journal of Consulting Psychology, 14*, 239–245.

Fisher, J. D., Rytting, M., & Heslin, R. (1976). Affective and valuative effects of an interpersonal touch. *Sociometry, 39*, 416–421.

Flükiger, C., Wüsten, G., Zinbarg, R. E., & Wampold, B. E. (2010). *Resource activation: Using clients' own strengths in psychotherapy and counseling*. Cambridge, MA: Hogrefe Publishing.

Foa, E. B., & Goldstein, A. (1978). Continuous exposure and complete response prevention in the treatment of obsessive compulsive neurosis. *Behavior Therapy, 9*, 821–829.

Fong, M. L., Borders, L. D., Ethington, C. A., & Pitts, J. H. (1998). Becoming a counselor: A longitudinal study of student cognitive development. *Counselor Education & Supervision, 38*, 100–114.

Frank, J. D. (1981). Therapeutic components shared by all psychotherapies. In J. H. Harvey & M. M. Parks (Eds.), *Psychotherapy research and behavior change* (pp. 175–182). Washington, DC: American Psychological Association.

Frank, J. D. (1971). Psychotherapists need theories. *International Journal of Psychiatry, 9*, 146–149.

Frank, J. D., & Frank, J. B. (1991). *Persuasion and healing* (3rd ed.). Baltimore: Johns Hopkins University Press.

Frank, J. D., Nash, E. H., Stone, A. R., & Imber, S. D. (1963). Immediate and long-term symptomatic course of psychiatric outpatients. *American Journal of Psychiatry, 120*, 429–439.

Frattaroli, J. (2006). Experimental disclosure and its moderators: A meta-analysis. *Psychological Bulletin, 132*, 823–865.

Fredrickson, B. L. (2001). The role of positive emotions in positive psychology: The broaden-and-build theory of positive emotions. *American Psychologist, 56*, 218–226.

Fredrickson, B. L. (2009). *Positivity: Groundbreaking research reveals how to embrace the hidden strength of positive emotions, overcome negativity, and thrive.* New York: Crown.

Fredrickson, B. L., Cohn, M. A., Coffey, K. A., Pek, J., & Finkel, S. M. (2008). Open hearts build lives: Positive emotions, induced through loving-kindness meditation, build consequential personal resources. *Journal of Personality and Social Psychology, 95*(5), 1045–1062.

Fremont, S., & Anderson, W. P. (1986). What client behaviors make counselors angry? An exploratory study. *Journal of Counseling and Development, 65,* 67–70.

Fretz, B. R., Corn, R., Tuemmler, J. M., & Bellet, W. (1979). Counselor nonverbal behaviors and client evaluations. *Journal of Counseling Psychology, 26,* 304–311.

Fromm-Reichmann, F. (1960). *Principles of intensive psychotherapy.* Chicago: University of Chicago Press.

Frydenberg, E., & Brandon, C. M. (2002). *The best of coping.* Melbourne: Oz Child.

Gaff, J. G., & Gaff, S. S. (1981). Student-faculty relationships. In A. W. Chickering (Ed.), *The modern American college* (pp. 642–657). New York: Jossey-Bass.

Galanti, G. (2004). *Caring for patients from different cultures.* Philadelphia, PA: University of Pennsylvania Press.

Galanti, G. (2008). *Caring for patients from different cultures* (4th ed.). Philadelphia, PA: University of Pennsylvania Press.

Gardner, R. A. (1971). *Therapeutic communication with children: Mutual story-telling technique.* New York: Science House.

Gass, C. S. (1984). Therapeutic influence as a function of therapist attire and the seating arrangement in an initial interview. *Journal of Counseling Psychology, 40,* 52–57.

Gatchel, R. J., & Baum, A. (1983). *An introduction to health psychology.* Reading, MA: Addison-Wesley.

Gelderloos, P., Walton, K. G., Orme-Johnson, D. W., & Alexander, C. N. (1991). Effectiveness of the transcendental meditation program in preventing and treating substance misuse: A review. *International Journal of the Addictions, 26*(3), 293–325.

Gelso, C. J., & Carter, J. A. (1985). The relationship in counseling and psychotherapy: Components, consequences and theoretical antecedents. *Counseling Psychologist, 13,* 155–243.

Gelso, C. J., & Woodhouse, S. S. (2002). The termination of psychotherapy: What research tells us about the process of ending treatment. In G. S. Tryon (Ed.), *Counseling based on process research: Applying what we know.* Boston, MA: Allyn & Bacon.

Gendlin, E. T. (1969). Focusing. *Psychotherapy: Theory, Research and Practice, 6,* 4–15.

Gendlin, E. T. (1978). *Focusing.* New York: Everest House.

Gilbert, L. A., & Scher, M. (1999). *Gender and sex in counseling and psychotherapy.* Boston: Allyn & Bacon.

Gilliland, B. E., James, R. K., & Bowman, J. T. (1989). *Theories and strategies in counseling and psychotherapy.* Upper Saddle River, NJ: Prentice Hall.

Gladding, S. T. (1995). Creativity in counseling. *Counseling and Human Development, 28,* 1–12.

Gladding, S. T. (2005). *Counseling as an art: The creative arts in counseling* (3rd ed.). Alexandria, VA: American Counseling Association.

Gladding, S. T. (2010). *Counseling as an art: The creative arts in counseling* (4th ed.). Alexandria, VA: American Counseling Association.

Gladding, S. T. (2007). *Counseling: A comprehensive profession* (5th ed.). Upper Saddle River, NJ: Merrill/Prentice Hall.

Gladding, S. T. (2008). *Counseling: A comprehensive profession* (6th ed.). Upper Saddle River, NJ: Merrill/Prentice Hall.

Gladding, S. T. (2010). *Family therapy: History, theory, and practice* (5th ed.). Upper Saddle River, NJ: Merrill/Prentice Hall.

Gladding, S. T., & Gladding, C. (1991). The ABCs of bibliotherapy for school counselors. *School Counselor, 39*(1), 7–13.

Gladstein, G. A. (1974). Nonverbal communication and counseling/psychotherapy. *Counseling Psychologist, 4,* 35–37.

Gladwell, M. (2005). *Blink: The power of thinking without thinking.* New York: Little Brown.

Gladwell, M. (2008). *Outliers: The story of success.* New York: Little, Brown & Co.

Goldberg, C., & Crespo, V. R. (2003). The personal-story approach. *American Journal of Psychotherapy, 57,* 337–347.

Goldberg, M. C. (1998). *The art of the question: A guide to short-term question-centered therapy.* New York: Wiley.

Goldin, E., Bordan, T., Araoz, D. L., Gladding, S. T., Kaplan, D., Krumboltz, J., & Lazarus, A. (2006). Humor in counseling: Leader perspectives. *Journal of Counseling & Development, 84,* 397–404.

Goldman, M., & Fordyce, J. (1983). Prosocial behavior as affected by eye contact, touch and voice. *Journal of Social Psychology, 121,* 125–131.

Goleman, D. (1998). *Vital lies, simple truths: The psychology of self-deception.* New York: Simon & Schuster.

Goleman, D. (2006). *Emotional intelligence: Why it can matter more than IQ.* New York: Bantam.

Goleman, D. (2003). Emotional intelligence: Issues in paradigm building. [Electronic version]. Retrieved August 30, 2003, from http://www.eiconsortium. org/research/ei_issues_in_paradigm_building.htm

Goleman, D. (2006). *Social intelligence.* New York: Bantam.

Goodman, M., & Teicher, A. (1988). To touch or not to touch. *Psychotherapy: Theory, Research and Practice, 25,* 492–500.

Goodyear, R. (1981). Termination as a loss experience for the counselor. *Personnel and Guidance Journal, 59,* 347–350.

Goodyear, R. K., & Bradley, F. O. (1986). The helping process as contractual. In W. P. Anderson (Ed.), *Innovative counseling: A handbook of readings* (pp. 59–62). Alexandria, VA: American Association for Counseling and Development.

Goodyear, R., & Schumate, J. (1996). Perceived effects of therapist self-disclosure of attraction to clients. *Professional Psychology, 27,* 613–616.

Gordon, C. (2004). Counsellor's use of reflective space. *Counselling & Psychotherapy Research, 4*(2), 40–44.

Gordon, D. (1978). *Therapeutic metaphors.* Cupertino, CA: Meta Publications.

Gordon, T. (1975). *PET: Parent effectiveness training.* New York: Wyden.

Gordon, T. (1975, 2000). *PET: Parent effectiveness training.* New York: Three Rivers Press.

Gordon, T. (1986). *Leadership effectiveness training, L.E.T.: The no-lose way to release the productive potential of people.* New York: Bantam.

Gottfredson, G. D., Holland, J. L., & Ogawa, D. K. (1996). *Dictionary of Holland occupational codes* (3rd ed.). Odessa, FL: Psychological Assessment Resources.

Gottman, J. (2000). *Seven principles for making marriage work.* London: Orion.

Granello, D. H. (2010). The process of suicide risk assessment: Twelve core principles. *Journal of Counseling & Development, 88,* 363–370.

Granello, D. H. (2002). Assessing the cognitive development of counseling students: Changes and epistemological assumptions. *Counselor Education & Supervision, 41,* 279–292.

Granello, D. H., & Granello, P. F. (2007). *Suicide: An essential guide for helping professionals and educators.* Boston: Allyn & Bacon.

Granello, P. F., & Granello, D. (1998). Training counseling students to use outcome research. *Counselor Education & Supervision, 37,* 224–238.

Granello, D. H., & Young, M. E. (2012). *Counseling today: Foundations of professional identity.* Upper Saddle River, NJ: Pearson.

Gray, J. (1992). *Men are from Mars, women are from Venus.* New York: HarperCollins.

Grayson, H. (1979). *Short term approaches to psychotherapy.* New York: Human Sciences Press.

Greenberg, R. P., Constantino, M. J., & Bruce, N. (2006). Are patient expectations still relevant for psychotherapy process and outcome. *Clinical Psychology Review, 26,* 657–678.

Greenspan, M. (1983). *A new approach to women and therapy.* New York: McGraw-Hill.

Griffith, B. A., & Frieden, G. (2000). Facilitating reflective thinking in counselor education. *Counselor Education & Supervision, 40,* 82–93.

Griner, D., & Smith, T. B. (2006). Culturally adapted mental health intervention: A meta-analytic review. *Psychotherapy: Theory, Research, Practice, Training, 43*(4), 531–548.

Guerney, B., Stollack, G., & Guerney, L. (1971). The practicing psychologist as educator: An alternative to the medical practitioner's model. *Professional Psychology, 11,* 276–282.

Guiller, J., & Durndell, A. (2007). Students' linguistic behaviour in online discussion groups: Does gender matter? *Computers in Human Behavior, 23,* 2240–2255.

Guterman, J. (2006). *Mastering the art of solution-focused counseling.* Alexandria, VA: American Counseling Association.

Haberstroh, S., Parr, G., Gee, R., & Trepal, H. (2006). Interactive E-Journaling in Group Work: Perspectives from Counselor Trainees. *Journal for Specialists in Group Work, 31*(4), 327–337.

Hackney, H. (1974). Facial gestures and subject expression of feelings. *Journal of Counseling Psychology, 21,* 173–178.

Hackney, H., & Cormier, L. S. (1979). *Counseling strategies and objectives.* Upper Saddle River, NJ: Prentice Hall.

Hackney, H., & Cormier, L. S. (2005). *Counseling strategies and interventions* (5th ed.). Upper Saddle River, NJ: Prentice Hall.

Haley, J. (1978). Ideas which handicap therapists. In M. Berger (Ed.), *Beyond the double blind: Communication and family systems, theories, techniques with schizophrenics* (pp. 24–36). New York: Brunner/Mazel.

Hall, C. (2006). Inside out: Exploring body image. *Therapy Today, 17,* 45–47.

Hall, J., Guterman, D. K., Lee, H. B., & Little, S. G. (2002). Counselor-client matching on ethnicity, gender, and language: Implications for counseling school-aged children. *North American Journal of Psychology, 4,* 367–381.

Hammond, D. C., Hepworth, D. H., & Smith, V. G. (1977). *Improving therapeutic communication.* San Francisco: Jossey-Bass.

Hannan, S. E., & Tolin, D. F. (2005). Acceptance and mindfulness-based behavior therapy for obsessive-compulsive disorder. In S. M. Orsillo & L. Roemer, *Acceptance and mindfulness-based approaches to anxiety: Conceptualization and treatment* (pp. 271–299). New York: Springer.

Hargie, O., & Dickson, D. (2004). *Skilled interpersonal communication: Research, theory and practice* (4th ed.). New York: London Taylor & Francis Routledge.

Harris, G. E. (2003). Progressive muscle relaxation: Highly effective but often neglected. *Guidance & Counseling, 18,* 142–148.

Hart, R. (1978). Therapeutic effectiveness of setting and monitoring goals. *Journal of Consulting and Clinical Psychology, 60,* 24–28.

Harvey, C., & Katz, C. (1985). *If I'm so successful, why do I feel like a fake? The imposter phenomenon.* New York: St. Martin's Press.

Hayes, S. C., Luoma, J., Bond, F., Masuda, A., & Lillis, J. (2006). Acceptance and commitment therapy: Model, processes, and outcomes. *Behavior Research and Therapy, 44*(1), 1–2.

Hazaleus, S. L., & Deffenbacher, J. L. (1986). Relaxation and cognitive treatments of anger. *Journal of Consulting and Clinical Psychology, 54,* 222–226.

Hazler, R. J. (1988). Stumbling into unconditional positive regard. *Journal of Counseling and Development, 67,* 130.

Hazlewood, M. G., & Schuldt, W. J. (1977). Effects of physical and phenomenological distance on self-disclosure. *Perceptual & Motor Skills, 45,* 805–806.

Herink, R. (1980). *The psychotherapy handbook: The A to Z guide to more than 250 different therapies in use today.* New York: New American Library.

Hermans, H. J. M., Fiddelaers, R., de Groot, R., & Nauta, J. F. (1990). Self-confrontation as a method for assessment and intervention in counseling. *Journal of Counseling & Development, 69,* 156–162.

Hersey, P., Blanchard, K. H., & Johnson, D. E. (2007). *Management of organizational behavior: Leading human resources* (9th ed.). Upper Saddle River, NJ: Prentice Hall.

Hill, C. E. (2004). *Helping skills: facilitating exploration, insight, and action* (2nd ed.). Washington, DC: American Psychological Association.

Hill, C. E., & Knox, S. (2002). Self-disclosure. In J. Norcross (Ed.), *Psychotherapy relationships that work* (pp. 255–265). New York: Oxford University Press.

Hill, C. E., Helms, J. E., Tichenor, V., Spiegel, S. B., O'Grady, K. E., & Perry, E. S. (1988). The effects of therapist response modes in brief psychotherapy. *Journal of Counseling Psychology, 35,* 222–233.

Hill, C. E., Thompson, B. J., & Ladany, N. (2003). Therapist use of silence in therapy: A survey. *Journal of Clinical Psychology, 59,* 513–524.

Hill, C. E., Thompson, B. J., Cogar, M. C., & Denman, D. W. (1993). Beneath the surface of long-term therapy: Therapist and client report of their own and each other's covert processes. *Journal of Counseling Psychology, 40,* 278–287.

Hinton, D. E., Hofmann, S. G., Rivera, E., Otto, M. W., & Pollack, M. H. (2011). Culturally adapted CBT (CA-CBT) for Latino women with treatment-resistant PTSD: A pilot study comparing CA-CBT to applied muscle relaxation. *Behaviour Research and Therapy, 49*(4), 275–280.

Hitz, R., & Driscoll, A. (1988). Praise or encouragement? New insights into praise: Implications for early childhood teachers. *Individual Psychology: Journal of Adlerian Theory, Research and Practice, 43,* 138–141.

Hoffman, R. R., Shadboldt, N. R., Burton, A. M., & Klein, G. (1995). Eliciting knowledge from experts: A methodological analysis. *Organizational Behavior and Human Decision Processes, 62,* 129–158.

Hohenshil, T. H. (1996). Role of assessment and diagnosis in counseling. *Journal of Counseling and Development, 75,* 64–67.

Holmes, T. H., & Rahe, R. H. (1967). The social readjustment rating scale. *Journal of Psychosomatic Research, 11,* 213–218.

Holroyd, J., & Brodsky, A. (1980). Does touching patients lead to sexual intercourse? *Professional Psychology, 11,* 807–811.

Holtz, L. (1998). *Winning every day.* New York: Harper Business.

Hood, A. B., & Johnson, R. W. (2006). *Assessment in counseling: A guide to the use of psychological assessment procedures* (4th ed.). Alexandria, VA: American Counseling Association.

Horvath, A. O., & Bedi, R. P. (2002). The alliance. In J. C. Norcross (Ed.), *Psychotherapy relationships that work: Therapist contributions and responsiveness to patients* (pp. 37–69). New York: Oxford University Press.

Horvath, A. O., & Greenberg, L. (Eds.). (1994). *The working alliance: Theory, research and practice.* New York: Wiley.

Horvath, A. O., Del Re, A. C., Flückiger, C., & Symonds, D. (2011). In J. C. Norcross, *Psychotherapy relationships that work: Evidence based responsiveness* (pp. 25–69). New York: Oxford University Press.

Hubbs, D., & Brand, C. F. (2005). The paper mirror: Understanding reflective journaling. *Journal of Experiential Education, 28,* 60–71.

Hubble, M. A., Duncan, B. L., & Miller, S. D. (Eds.). (1999). *The heart and soul of change: What works in therapy.* Washington, DC: American Psychological Association.

Hunter, M., & Struve, J. (1997). *The ethical use of touch in psychotherapy.* Thousand Oaks, CA: Sage.

Iacomboni, M. (2009). *Mirroring people: The science of empathy and how we connect with others.* New York: Picador.

Ilgen, M., Tiet, Q., & Finney, J. (2006). Quality of therapeutic relationship associated with better treatment outcomes. *Brown University Digest of Addiction Theory & Application, 25,* 1–7.

Ingham, J. G., Kreitman, N. B., Miller, P. M., & Sasidharan, S. P. (1986). Self-esteem, vulnerability and psychiatric disorder in the community. *British Journal of Psychiatry, 148,* 373–385.

Israelashvili, M. (1998). Preventive school counseling: A stress inoculation perspective. *Professional School Counseling, 1,* 21–25.

Ivey, A. E. (1971). *Microcounseling: Innovations in interviewing training.* Springfield, IL: Thomas.

Ivey, A. E. (1994). *Intentional interviewing.* Pacific Grove, CA: Brooks/Cole.

Ivey, A. E., & Mathews, J. W. (1986). A metamodel for structuring the clinical interview. In W. P. Anderson (Ed.), *Innovative counseling: A handbook of readings* (pp. 77–83). Alexandria, VA: American Counseling Association.

Ivey, A. E., & Simek-Downing, L. (1980). *Counseling and psychotherapy: Skills, theories and practice.* Upper Saddle River, NJ: Prentice Hall.

Ivey, A. E., Ivey, M. B., & Simek-Morgan, L. (1997). *Counseling and psychotherapy: A multicultural perspective.* Boston: Allyn & Bacon.

Izard, C. E. (1977). *Human emotions.* New York: Plenum.

Jackson, S. A. (2001). Using bibliotherapy with clients. *Journal of Individual Psychology, 57,* 289–297.

Jacobson, E. (1938). *Progressive relaxation.* Chicago: University of Chicago Press.

Johns Hopkins University. (1998). Why and how to ask questions. *Population Reports, 26,* 5–6.

Johnson, D. W. (2000). *Reaching out.* Boston: Allyn & Bacon.

Johnson, D. W., & Johnson, F. P. (2008). *Joining together* (10th ed.). Boston: Allyn & Bacon.

Johnson, D. W., & Matross, R. (1977). Interpersonal influence in psychotherapy: A social psychological view. In A. S. Gurman & A. M. Razin (Eds.), *Effective psychotherapy: A handbook of research* (pp. 395–432). Elmsford, NY: Pergamon.

Johnson, J. A. (1990). Empathy as a personality disposition. In R. C. McKay, J. R. Hughes, & E. J. Carver (Eds.), *Empathy in the helping relationship* (pp. 49–64). New York: Springer.

Jongsma, Jr., A. E., Peterson, L. M., & McInnis, W. P. (2000). *The child psychotherapy treatment planner* (2nd ed.). New York: Wiley.

Jourard, S. (1971). *The transparent self.* New York: Van Nostrand Reinhold.

Jouriles, E. N., Rowe, L. S., McDonald, R., Platt, C. G., & Gomez, G. S. (2011). Assessing women's responses to sexual threat: Validity of a virtual role-play procedure. *Behavior Therapy, 42,* 475–484.

Joyce, A. S., Piper, W. E., Ogrodniczuk, J. S., & Klein, R. H. (2007). Patient-Initiated Termination. In A. S. Joyce, W. E. Piper, J. S. Ogrodniczuk, R. H. Klien (Eds.), *Termination in psychotherapy: A psychodynamic model of processes and outcomes* (pp. 133–156). Washington, DC: American Psychological Association.

June, L., & Smith, E. (1983). A comparison of client and counselor expectancies regarding the duration of counseling. *Journal of Counseling Psychology, 30,* 596–599.

Juhnke, G. A., Granello, D. H., & Granello, P. F. (2011). *Suicide and violence in the schools.* New York: Wiley.

Junkhe, G. A., Granello, P. F., & Lebrón-Striker, M. A. (2007). IS PATH WARM? A suicide assessment mnemonic for counselors (ACAPCD-03). Alexandria, VA: American Counseling Association.

Kabat-Zinn, J., Massion, A. O., Kristeller, J., Peterson, L., Fletcher, K. E., Pbert, L., Lenderking, W. R., & Santorelli, S. F. (1992). Effectiveness of a meditation-based stress reduction program in the treatment of anxiety disorders. *American Journal of Psychiatry, 149,* 936–943.

Kakiuchi, K. S., & Weeks, G. R. (2009). The occupational transmission genogram: Exploring family scripts affecting roles of work and career in couple and family dynamics. *Journal of Family Psychotherapy, 20,* 1–20.

Kanfer, F. H. (1975). Self-management methods. In F. H. Kanfer & A. P. Goldstein (Eds.), *Helping people change* (pp. 309–355). New York: Pergamon.

Kanfer, F. H., & Goldstein, A. P. (1986). Introduction. In F. Kanfer & A. Goldstein (Eds.), *Helping people change: A textbook of methods.* New York: Pergamon.

Kanfer, F. H., & Schefft, B. K. (1988). *Guiding therapeutic change.* Champaign, IL: Research Press.

Kaplan, H. I., & Sadock, B. J. (1998). *Synopsis of psychiatry: Behavioral sciences, clinical psychiatry* (8th ed.). Baltimore, MD: Lippincott, Williams & Wilkins.

Kaplan, L. (1995). Self-esteem is not our national wonder drug. *School Counselor, 42,* 341–345.

Karson, M., & Fox, J. (2010). Common skills that underlie the common factors of successful psychotherapy. *American Journal of Psychotherapy, 64*(3), 269–281.

Kaufman, G. (1999). *Stick up for yourself: Every kid's guide to personal power and self-esteem.* Minneapolis, MN: Free Spirit.

Kazantzis, N., & L'Abate, L. (2011). *Handbook of homework assignments in psychotherapy: Research, practice & prevention.* New York: Springer.

Kazantzis, N., Busch, R., Ronan, K. P., & Merrick, P. L. (2007). Using homework assignments in psychotherapy: Differences by theoretical orientation and professional training? *Behavioural and Cognitive Psychotherapy, 35,* 121–128.

Kazdin, A. E. (1980). *Behavior modification in applied settings.* Homewood, IL: Dorsey Press.

Keen, E. (1976). Confrontation and support: On the world of psychotherapy. *Psychotherapy: Theory, Research & Practice, 13,* 308–315.

Kelly, A. E., & McKillop, K. J. (1996). Consequences of revealing personal secrets. *Psychological Bulletin, 120,* 450–465.

Kelly, A. E., & Yuan, K. (2009). Clients' secret keeping and the working alliance in adult outpatient therapy. *Psychotherapy: Theory, Research, Practice, Training, 46*(2), 193–202.

Kelly, E. W. (1994). *Relationship centered counseling: An integration of art and science.* New York: Springer.

Kerka, S. (1999). *Career development and gender, race, and class* (ERIC Digest No. 199). Columbus, OH: ERIC Clearinghouse on Adult Career and Vocational Education.

Kiesler, C. A., & Pallak, M. S. (1976). Arousal properties of dissonance manipulations. *Psychological Bulletin, 83,* 1014–1025.

Kiesler, D. J. (1988). *Therapeutic communication: Therapist impact disclosure as feedback in psychotherapy.* Palo Alto, CA: Consulting Psychologists Press.

Kim, B. S. K., Liang, C. T. H., & Li, L. C. (2003). Counselor ethnicity, counselor nonverbal behavior, and session outcome with Asian American clients: Initial findings. *Journal of Counseling and Development, 81,* 202–207.

Kipper, D. A. (1986). *Psychotherapy through clinical role-playing.* New York: Brunner/Mazel.

Kipper, D. A. (1996). The emergence of role playing as a form of psychotherapy. *Journal of Group Psychotherapy, 49,* 99–120.

Kipper, D. A., & Ritchie, T. D. (2003). The effectiveness of psychodramatic techniques: A meta-analysis. *Group Dynamics: Theory, Research and Practice, 7*(1), 13–25.

Kiresuk, R. J., & Sherman, R. E. (1968). Goal attainment scaling: A general method for evaluating community mental health programs. *Community Mental Health Journal, 4,* 443–453.

Kirk, S. A., & Hsieh, D. K. (2004). Diagnostic consistency in assessing conduct disorder: An effect on the effect of social context. *American Journal of Orthopsychiatry, 74,* 43–55.

Kiselica, M. S., & Englar-Carlson, M. (2010). Identifying, affirming, and building upon male strengths: The positive psychology/positive masculinity mode of psychotherapy with boys and men. *Psychotherapy: Theory, Research, Practice, Training, 47,* 276–287.

Kitchener, K. S. (1984). Intuition, critical evaluation and ethical principle: The foundation for ethical decisions in counseling psychology. *The Counseling Psychologist, 12,* 43–56.

Kleinke, C. L. (1986). Gaze and eye contact: A research review. *Psychological Bulletin, 100,* 78–100.

Kleinke, C. L. (1994). *Common principles of psychotherapy.* Pacific Grove, CA: Brooks/Cole.

Knox, S., Adrians, N., Everson, E., Hess, S., Hill, C., & Crook-Lyon, R. (2011). Clients' perspectives on therapy termination. *Psychotherapy Research, 21*(2), 154–167.

Knox, S., Hess, S., Petersen, D., & Hill, C. E. (1997). A qualitative analysis of client perceptions of the effects of helpful therapist self-disclosure in long-term therapy. *Journal of Counseling Psychology, 44,* 274–283.

Koltko-Rivera, M. E. (2004). The psychology of worldviews. *Review of General Psychology, 8*(2), 3–58.

Kopp, S. (1978). *If you meet the Buddha on the road, kill him!* New York: Bantam.

Kottler, J. (1997). *The language of tears.* San Francisco: Jossey-Bass.

Kottler, J. A. (2010). On being a therapist (4th ed.). San Francisco: Jossey-Bass.

Kottler, J. A. (Ed.). (2002). *Counselors finding their way.* Alexandria, VA: American Counseling Association.

Kottler, J. A., & Blau, D. S. (1989). *The imperfect therapist.* San Francisco: Jossey-Bass.

Kottler, J. A., & Carlson, J. (2011). *Duped: Lies and deception in psychotherapy.* New York: Routledge.

Kramer, S. A. (1986). The termination process in open-ended psychotherapy: Guidelines for clinical practice. *Psychotherapy, 23,* 526–531.

Kramer, S. A. (1990). *Positive endings in psychotherapy.* San Francisco: Jossey-Bass.

Krantz, P. L., & Lund, N. L. (1979). A dilemma of play therapy: Termination anxiety in the therapist. *Teaching of Psychology, 6,* 108–110.

Kupers, T. A. (2005). Toxic masculinity as a barrier to mental health treatment in prison. *Journal of Clinical Psychology, 61,* 713–724.

Kurpius, D., Rockwood, G. F., & Corbett, M. O. (1989). Attributional styles and self-esteem: Implications for counseling. *Counseling and Human Development, 21*(8), 1–12.

La Torre, M. (2005). Self-Reflection-An Important Process for the Therapist. *Perspectives in Psychiatric Care, 41*(2), 85–87.

Ladany, N., Hill, C. E., Thompson, B. J., & O'Brien, K. M. (2004). Therapist perspectives on using silence in therapy: A qualitative study. *Counselling & Psychotherapy Research, 4,* 80–89.

LaFrance, M., & Mayo, C. (1976). Racial differences in gaze behavior during observations: Two systematic observational studies. *Journal of Personality and Social Psychology, 33,* 47–52.

Lamb, D. H. (1985). A time frame model of termination in psychotherapy. *Psychotherapy, 22,* 604–606.

Lambert, M. J. (1986). Implications of psychotherapy outcome research for eclectic psychotherapy. In J. C. Norcross (Ed.), *Handbook of eclectic psychotherapy* (pp. 436–462). New York: Brunner/Mazel.

Lambert, M. J. (2005). Early response in psychotherapy: Further evidence for the importance of common factors rather than "placebo effects." *Journal of Clinical Psychology, 61,* 855–869.

Lambert, M. J., Hansen, N. B., Umphress, V., Lunnen, K., Okiishi, J., Burlingame, G. M., Huefner, J., & Reisinger, C. (1996). *Administration and scoring manual for the OQ 45.2.* Stevenson, MD: American Professional Credentialing Services.

Lane, J., Seskevich, J., & Pieper, C. (2007). Brief meditation training can improve perceived stress and negative mood. *Alternative Therapies in Health & Medicine, 13*(1), 38–44.

Last, C. G. (1985). Homework. In A. S. Bellack & M. Hersen (Eds.), *Dictionary of behavior therapy techniques* (pp. 140–141). New York: Pergamon.

Lawson, G., & Myers, J. E. (2011). Wellness, professional quality of life, and career-sustaining behaviors: What keeps us well? *Journal of Counseling & Development, 89*(2), 163–171.

Lazarus, A. A. (1971). *Behavior therapy and beyond.* New York: McGraw Hill.

Lazarus, A. A. (1981). *The practice of multimodal therapy.* New York: McGraw-Hill.

Lazarus, A. A. (1982). Counseling the Native American child: Acquisition of values. *Elementary School Guidance and Counseling, 17,* 83–88.

Lazarus, A. A. (1982). *Personal enrichment through imagery* (Cassette Recording). New York: BMA Audio Cassettes/Guilford.

Lazarus, A. A. (1985). Behavior rehearsal. In A. S. Bellack & M. Hersen (Eds.), *Dictionary of behavior therapy techniques* (p. 22). New York: Pergamon.

Lazarus, A. A. (1990). Can psychotherapists transcend the shackles of their training and superstitions? *Journal of Clinical Psychology, 46*(3), 351–358.

Leary, T. (1957). *Interpersonal diagnosis of personality.* New York: Ronald.

LeCroy, C. W. (1988). Anger management or anger expression: Which is most effective? *Residential Treatment of Children & Youth, 5,* 29–39.

Lee, D. Y., Uhlemann, M. R., & Haase, R. F. (1985). Counselor verbal and nonverbal responses and perceived expertness, trustworthiness and attractiveness. *Journal of Counseling Psychology, 32,* 181–187.

Lee, M. Y., Uken, A., & Sebold, J. (2007). Role of self-determined goals in predicting recidivism in domestic violence offenders. *Research on Social Work Practice, 17,* 30–41.

Lemberg, R. (1994). Couples journaling technique: A brief report. *Family Journal, 2*(1), 64–65.

Lent, J. (2009). Journaling enters the 21st century: The use of therapeutic blogs in counseling. *Journal of Creativity in Mental Health, 4*(1), 67–73.

Leontiev, D. A. (2007). Approaching worldview structure with ultimate meanings technique. *Journal of Humanistic Psychology, 47,* 243–266.

LeShan, L. (1996). *Beyond technique: Psychotherapy for the 21st century.* Northvale, NJ: Jason Aronson.

Lim, S., & Nakamoto, T. (2008). Genograms: Use in therapy with Asian families with diverse cultural heritages. *Contemporary Family Therapy, 30,* 199–219.

Lilliengren, P., & Werbart, A. (2005). A model of therapeutic action grounded in the patients' view of curative and hindering factors in psychoanalytic psychotherapy. *Psychotherapy: Theory, Research, Practice, Training, 42,* 324–339.

Little, B. R., Salmela-Aro, K., & Phillips, S. D. (2007). *Personal project pursuit: Goals, action, and human flourishing.* Mahwah, NJ: Lawrence Erlbaum.

Long, L. L., & Young, M. E. (2007). *Counseling and therapy for couples: An integrative approach* (2nd ed.). Pacific Grove, CA: Brooks/Cole.

Lopez, S. J., & Kerr, B. A. (2006). An open source approach to creating positive psychological practice: A comment on Wong's strength-centered therapy. *Psychotherapy: Theory, Research, Practice, Training, 43,* 147–150.

Lopez, S. J., & Snyder, C. R. (2009). *Positive psychological assessment: A handbook of models and measures.* Washington, DC: American Psychological Association.

Lopez, S. R., Grover, K. P., Holland, D., & Johnson, M. J. (1989). Development of culturally sensitive psychotherapists. *Professional Psychology: Research & Practice, 20,* 369–375.

Losoncy, L. E. (1977). *Turning people on: How to be an encouraging person.* Upper Saddle River, NJ: Prentice Hall.

Lowen, A. (1967). *The betrayal of the body.* New York: Collier.

Luft, J. (1969). *Of human interaction.* Palo Alto, CA: National Press.

Lukas, S. (1993). *Where to start and what to ask: An assessment handbook.* New York: Norton.

Lyddon, W. J., Yowell, D. R., & Hermans, J. M. (2006). The self-confrontation method: Theory, research and practical utility. *Counselling Psychology Quarterly, 19,* 27–43.

MacCluskie, K. C., & Ingersoll, R. E. (2001). *Becoming a 20th century agency counselor.* Pacific Grove, CA: Brooks/Cole.

MacDonald, F. F. (2005). Why do we talk so much? The art of silence in psychotherapy. *Annals of the American Psychotherapy Association, 8,* 43.

Mackrill, T. D. (2011). Differentiating life goals and therapeutic goals: Expanding our understanding of the working alliance. *British Journal of Guidance and Counselling, 39,* 25–39.

Macneil, C. A., Hasty, M. K., Conus, P., & Berk, M. (2010). Termination of therapy: What can clinicians do to maximise gains? *Acta Neuropsychiatrica, 22*(1), 43–45.

Madrid, S., & Kantor, R. (2009). Being kitties in a preschool classroom: Maintaining group harmony and acting proper in a female peer culture play routine. *Ethnography & Education, 4,* 229–247.

Magnuson, S., & Norem, K. (2002). Reflective counselor education and supervision: An epistemological declaration. *Reflective Practice, 3*(2), 167–173.

Mahalik, J. R., Good, G. E., & Englar-Carlson, M. (2003). Masculinity scripts, presenting concerns, and help seeking: Implications for practice and training. *Professional Psychology: Research and Practice, 34,* 123–131.

Maholick, L. T., & Turner, D. W. (1979). Termination: That difficult farewell. *American Journal of Psychotherapy, 33,* 583–591.

Mahoney, M. J. (2004). What is constructivism and why is it growing? *Contemporary Psychology, 49,* 360–363.

Majors, R. (1991). Nonverbal behaviors and communication styles among African Americans. In R. L. Jones, *Black psychology* (3rd ed., pp. 269–294). Berkeley, CA: Cobb & Henry.

Mallett, S. D., Spokane, A. R., & Vance, F. L. (1978). Effects of vocationally relevant information on the expressed and measured interests of freshman males. *Journal of Counseling Psychology, 25,* 10–15.

Malott, K. M., & Magnuson, S. (2004). Using genograms to facilitate undergraduate students' career development: A group model. *Career Development Quarterly, 53,* 178–186.

Maples, M. F., Dupey, P., Torres-Rivera, E., Phan, L. T., Vereen, L., & Garrett, M. T. (2001). Ethnic diversity and the use of humor in counseling: Appropriate or inappropriate. *Journal of Counseling & Development, 79,* 53–60.

Markell, K. A., & Markell, M. A. (2008). *The children who lived: Using Harry Potter and other fictional characters to help grieving children and adolescents.* New York: Routledge.

Marlatt, G. A. (1988). Matching clients to treatment: Treatment models and stages of change. In D. M. Donovan & G. A. Marlatt (Eds.), *Assessment of addictive behaviors* (pp. 474–483). New York: Guilford.

Marlatt, G. A., & Donovan, D. M. (Eds.). (2005). *Relapse prevention: Maintenance strategies in the treatment of addictive behaviors* (2th ed.). New York: Guilford.

Marsh, A. A., Elfenbein, H. A., & Ambady, N. (2003). Nonverbal "accents": Cultural differences in facial expressions of emotion. *Psychological Science, 14,* 373–377.

Martin, G. A., & Worthington, E. L. (1982). Behavioral homework. In M. Hersen, R. Eisler, & P. M. Miller (Eds.), *Progress in behavior modification* (Vol. 13, pp. 197–226). New York: Academic Press.

Martin, J., & Stelmaczonek, K. (1988). Participants' identification and recall of important events in counseling. *Journal of Counseling Psychology, 35,* 385–390.

Martinez, M. E. (2002). Effectiveness of operationalized Gestalt therapy role-playing in the treatment of phobic behaviors. *Gestalt Review, 6,* 148–167.

Marx, S. D. (1990). Phase I: On the transition from student to professional. *Psychotherapy in Private Practice, 8*(2), 57–67.

Mathews, B. (1989). Terminating therapy: Implications for the private practitioner. *Psychotherapy in Private Practice, 7,* 29–39.

Matsumoto, D. (2009). Culture and emotional expression. In R. S. Wyer, & C. Chiu, & Y. Hong (Eds.), *Understanding culture: Theory, research and application* (pp. 271–287). New York: Psychology Press.

Maurer, R. E., & Tindall, J. H. (1983). Effect of postural congruence on client's perception of helper empathy. *Journal of Counseling Psychology, 30,* 158–163.

McCarthy, P. (1979). Differential effects of self-disclosing versus self-involving statements. *Journal of Counseling Psychology, 26,* 538–541.

McCarthy, P. (1982). Differential effects of counselor self-referent responses and counselor status. *Journal of Counseling Psychology, 29,* 125–131.

McCarthy, P. (2001). Differential effects of self-disclosing versus self-involving counselor statements. In C. E. Hill (Ed.), *Helping skills: The empirical foundation* (pp. 389–396). Washington, DC: American Psychological Association.

McConnaughy, E. A. (1987). The person of the therapist in psychotherapeutic practice. *Psychotherapy, 24,* 303–314.

McEachern, A. G., & Kenny, M. C. (2002). A comparison of family environment characteristics among White (non-Hispanic), Hispanic, and African Caribbean groups. *Journal of Multicultural Counseling & Development, 30,* 40–58.

McHenry, B., & McHenry, J. (2007). What therapists say and why they say it: Effective therapeutic responses and techniques. Boston: Allyn & Bacon.

McKay, M., & Fanning, P. (1987). *Self-esteem.* Oakland, CA: New Harbinger.

McKenna, G., Hevey, D., & Martin, E. (2010). Patients' and providers' perspectives on bibliotherapy in primary care. *Clinical Psychology & Psychotherapy, 17*(6), 497–509.

McLennan, J. (1994). The skills-based model of counselling training: A review of the evidence. *Australian Psychologist, 29,* 79–88.

McLeod, J. (2007, May). Evaluating a pluralistic framework for counselling. Symposium conducted at the meeting of the British Association for Counselling and Psychotherapy, York, UK.

McMullin, R. E. (2000). *The new handbook of cognitive therapy techniques.* New York: Norton.

Meadow, A. (1982). Psychopathology, psychotherapy and the Mexican-American patient. In E. E. Jones & S. J. Korchin (Eds.), *Minority mental health* (pp. 331–362). New York: Praeger.

Mehrabian, A. (1972). *Nonverbal communication.* Chicago: Aldine.

Meichenbaum, D. H. (1993). Stress inoculation training: A twenty year update. In R. L. Woolfolk & P. M. Lehrer (Eds.), *Principles and practice of stress management* (pp. 373–406). New York: Guilford Press.

Mennicke, S. A., Lent, R. W., & Burgoyne, K. L. (1988). Premature termination from university counseling centers: A review. *Journal of Counseling and Development, 66,* 458–465.

Menninger, K. (1958). *Theory of psychoanalytic technique.* New York: Harper & Row.

Michalak, J., Teismann, T., Heidenreich, T., Ströhle, G., & Vocks, S. (2011). Buffering low self-esteem: The effect of mindful acceptance on the relationship between self-esteem and depression. *Personality and Individual Differences, 50*(5), 751–754.

Miller, J. (2010). Current views on the therapeutic value of homework in counselling and psychotherapy. *Counselling Psychology Quarterly, 23,* 235–238.

Miller, W. R. & Rollnick, S. (2002). *Motivational interviewing: Preparing people to change.* NY: Guilford Press.

Milan, M. (1985). Symbolic modeling. In M. Hersen & A. S. Bellack (Eds.), *Dictionary of behavior therapy techniques* (pp. 212–215). New York: Pergamon.

Miller, L., Berg, J. H., & Archer, R. L. (1983). Openers: Individuals who elicit intimate self-disclosure. *Journal of Personality and Social Psychology, 44,* 1234–1244.

Miller, S. D., Hubble, M. A., & Duncan, B. L. (Eds.). (1996). *Handbook of solution focused brief therapy.* San Francisco: Jossey-Bass.

Miller, W. R., & Rose, G. S. (2009). Toward a theory of motivational interviewing. *American Psychologist, 64,* 527–537.

Miller, W. R., & Rollnick, S. (1999). *Motivational interviewing: Preparing people to change addictive behavior*. New York: Guilford.

Miller, W. R., Benefield, R. G., & Tonigan, J. S. (1993). Enhancing motivation for change in problem drinking: A controlled comparison of two therapist styles. *Journal of Consulting and Clinical Psychology, 61*, 455–461.

Minuchin, S. (1974). *Families and family therapy*. Boston: Harvard University Press.

Mitchell, Z. P., & Milan, M. (1983). Imitation of high-interest comic strip models' appropriate classroom behavior: Acquisition and generalization. *Child and Family Behavior Therapy, 5*, 25–30.

Moffat, M. J., & Painter, C. (Eds.). (1975). *Revelations: Diaries of women*. New York: Vintage.

Moline, M. E., Williams, G. T., & Austin, K. M. (1998). *Documenting psychotherapy: Essentials for mental health practitioners*. London: Sage.

Moreno, J. L. (1958). *Psychodrama* (Vol. 2). New York: Beacon House.

Moreno, J. L. (1964). *Psychodrama* (Vol. 1, 3rd ed.). New York: Beacon House.

Mosak, H. H. (1987). *Ha ha and aha*. Muncie, IN: Accelerated Development.

Mullen, B., Johnson, C., & Salas, E. (1991). Productivity loss in brainstorming groups: A meta-analytic integration. *Basic and Applied Social Psychology, 12*, 3–25.

Munro, J. N., & Bach, T. R. (1975). Effect of time-limited counseling on client change. *Journal of Counseling Psychology, 22*, 395–398.

Murray, E. J. (1986). Possibilities and promises of eclecticism. In J. C. Norcross (Ed.), *Handbook of eclectic psychotherapy* (pp. 398–415). New York: Brunner/Mazel.

Myers, J. E., & Sweeney, T. J. (2005). *Counseling for wellness: Theory, research and practice*. Alexandria, VA: American Counseling Association.

Nayak, M. B., Byrne, C. A., Martin, M. K., & Abraham, A. G. (2003). Attitudes toward violence against women: A cross-nation study. *Sex Roles, 49*, 333–342.

Nelson, M. L. (1993). A current perspective on gender differences: Implications for research in counseling. *Journal of Counseling Psychology, 40*(2), 200–209.

Newton, M. (2002). Evaluating the outcome of counselling in primary care using a goal attainment scale. *Counselling Psychology Quarterly, 15*, 85–89.

Nichols, M. P., & Efran, J. S. (1985). Catharsis in psychotherapy: A new perspective. *Psychotherapy, 22*, 46–58.

Nichols, M. P., & Zax, M. (1977). *Catharsis in psychotherapy*. New York: Gardener Press.

Nickel, M. K. (2007). Behavioral/psychoeducational group training in therapy for overtaxed men. *Journal of Psychosomatic Research, 62*, 597.

Nietzsche, F. W. (1920). *The anti-Christ*. New York: Knopf.

Nilsson, D., Strassberg, D., & Bannon, J. (1979). Perceptions of counselor self-disclosure: An analog study. *Journal of Counseling Psychology, 26*, 399–404.

Norcross, J. C. (1990). Personal therapy for therapists: One solution. *Psychotherapy in Private Practice, 8*(1), 45–59.

Norcross, J. C. (2011). *Psychotherapy relationships that work: Evidence based responsiveness*. New York: Oxford University Press.

Norcross, J. C., Koocher, G. P., & Garofalo, A. (2006). Discredited psychological treatments and tests: A Delphi poll. *Professional Psychology: Research & Practice, 37*, 515–522.

Novaco, R. W. (1977). Stress inoculation: A cognitive therapy for anger and its application to a case of depression. *Journal of Consulting and Clinical Psychology, 45*, 600–608.

Novaco, R. W. (1983). Stress inoculation therapy for anger control. In P. A. Keeler & L. G. Rift (Eds.), *Innovations in clinical practice: A source book* (Vol. 2, pp. 181–201). Sarasota, FL: Professional Resource Exchange.

Nuttall, J. (2002). Modes of therapeutic relationship in brief dynamic psychotherapy. *Journal of Psychodynamic Process, 89*, 505–523.

O'Connell, B. (2005). *Solution-focused therapy*. London: Sage.

O'Hanlon, W. H., & Weiner-Davis, M. (1989). *In search of solutions: A new direction in psychotherapy*. New York: Norton.

Ogrodniczuk, J. S., Joyce, A. S., & Piper, W. E. (2005). Strategies for reducing patient-initiated premature termination of psychotherapy. *Harvard Review of Psychiatry, 13*, 57–70.

Okamoto, S. K. (2002). The challenges of male practitioners working with female youth clients. *Child & Youth Care Forum, 31,* 257–268.

Okiishi, R. W. (1987). The genogram as a tool in career counseling. *Journal of Counseling & Development, 66,* 139–143.

Older, J. (1982). *Touching is healing.* New York: Stein & Day.

Olson, P., & Claiborn, C. D. (1990). Interpretation and arousal in the counseling process. *Journal of Counseling Psychology, 37,* 131–137.

Ornston, P. S., Cichetti, D. V., Levine, J., & Freeman, L. B. (1968). Some parameters of verbal behavior that reliably differentiate novice from experienced therapists. *Journal of Abnormal Psychology, 73,* 240–244.

Osborn, C. J., West, J. D., Kindsvatter, A., & Paez, S. B. (2008). Treatment planning as collaborative care map construction: Reframing clinical practice to promote client involvement. *Journal of Contemporary Psychotherapy, 38*(4), 169–176.

Öst, L.-G. (1987). Applied relaxation: Description of a coping technique and review. *Behaviour Research and Therapy, 23,* 397–409.

Othmer, E., & Othmer, S. C. (2002). *The clinical interview using DSM-IV-TR.* Washington, DC: American Psychiatric Publishing.

Overholser, J. C. (1991). The use of guided imagery in psychotherapy: Modules for use with passive relaxation training. *Journal of Contemporary Psychotherapy, 21,* 159–172.

Palmer, S., & McMahon, G. (Eds.). (1997). *Client assessment.* London: Sage.

Paniagua, F. A. (2005). *Assessing and treating culturally diverse clients: A practical guide* (3rd ed.). Thousand Oaks, CA: Sage.

Parker, W. M. (1988). Becoming an effective multicultural counselor. *Journal of Counseling and Development, 67,* 93.

Parker, W. M., & Schwartz, R. C. (2002). On the experience of shame in multicultural counselling: Implications for white counsellors-in-training. *British Journal of Guidance and Counselling, 30,* 311–318.

Parloff, M. B. (1979, February). Shopping for the right therapy. *Saturday Review,* 135–142.

Patanaik, D. (2009). *Wired to care: How companies prosper when they create widespread empathy.* Upper Saddle River, NJ: FT Press.

Patterson, C. H. (1973). *Theories of counseling and psychotherapy* (2nd ed.). New York: Harper & Row.

Patterson, L. E., & Eisenberg, S. (1983). *The counseling process* (3rd ed.). Boston: Houghton Mifflin.

Paul, G. L. (1967). Strategy of outcome research in psychotherapy. *Journal of Consulting Psychology, 31,* 109–119.

Pearson, J. C., West, R. L., & Turner, L. H. (1995). *Gender and communication* (3rd ed.). Dubuque, IA: Brown & Benchmark Publishers.

Pedersen, P. B. (1987). Ten frequent assumptions of cultural bias in counseling. *Journal of Multicultural Counseling and Development, 14,* 16–24.

Pekarik, G. (1985). Coping with dropouts. *Professional Psychology: Research and Practice, 16,* 114–124.

Pennebaker, J. W. (1989). Confession, inhibition, and disease. In L. Berkowitz (Ed.), *Advances in experimental social psychology* (Vol. 22, pp. 211–214). New York: Academic Press.

Pennebaker, J. W. (1990). *Opening up: The healing power of confiding in others.* New York: William Morrow.

Pennebaker, J. W. (Ed.). (2002). *Emotion, disclosure and health.* Washington, DC: American Psychological Association.

Pennebaker, J. W. (2004). *Writing to heal: A guided journal for recovering from trauma & emotional upheaval.* Oakland, CA: New Harbinger Publications.

Perls, F. S. (1959). *Gestalt therapy verbatim.* New York: Bantam Books.

Perls, F. S. (1977). *The Gestalt approach: An eye witness to therapy.* Palo Alto, CA: Science and Behavior Books.

Perry, G. P., & Paquin, J. J. (1987). Practical strategies for maintaining and generalizing improvements from psychotherapy. In P. A. Keller & S. R. Heyman (Eds.), *Innovations in clinical practice: A source book* (Vol. 6, pp. 151–164). Sarasota, FL: Professional Resource Exchange.

Perry, M. A., & Furukawa, M. J. (1986). Modeling methods. In F. H. Kanfer & A. P. Goldstein (Eds.), *Helping people change* (pp. 66–110). New York: Pergamon.

Perry, W. G., Jr. (1970). *Forms of intellectual and ethical development in the college years.* New York: Holt, Rinehart, & Winston.

Phelan, J. E. (2009). Exploring the use of touch in the psychotherapeutic setting: A phenomenological review. *Psychotherapy Theory, Research, Practice, Training, 46*(1), 97–111.

Pierce, J. T. (2006). Efficacy of imagery rehearsal treatment related to specialized populations: A case study and brief report. *Dreaming, 16,* 280–285.

Pietrofesa, J. J., Hoffman, A., & Splete, H. H. (1984). *Counseling: An introduction*. Boston: Houghton Mifflin.

Piselli, A., Halgin, R. P., & MacEwan, G. H. (2011). What went wrong? Therapists' reflections on their role in premature termination. *Psychotherapy Research, 21*(4), 400–415.

Pitsounis, N. D., & Dixon, P. N. (1988). Encouragement versus praise: Improving productivity of the mentally retarded. *Individual Psychology: Journal of Adlerian Theory, Research and Practice, 44,* 507–512.

Pittman, T. S. (1975). Attribution of arousal as a mediator in dissonance reduction. *Journal of Experimental and Social Psychology, 11,* 53–63.

Polanski, P. J., & Hinkle, J. S. (2000). The mental status examination: Its use by professional counselors. *Journal of Counseling & Development, 78,* 357–364.

Polcin, D. L. (2006). Reexamining confrontation and motivational interviewing. *Addictive Disorders & Their Treatment, 5,* 201–209.

Pollak, J., Levy, S., & Breitholtz, T. (1999). Screening for medical and neurodevelopmental disorders for the professional counselor. *Journal of Counseling & Development, 77,* 350–355.

Polster, E., & Polster, M. (1973). *Gestalt therapy integrated*. New York: Brunner/Mazel.

Ponte-Allan, M., & Giles, G. M. (1999). Goal setting and functional outcomes in rehabilitation. *American Journal of Occupational Therapy, 53,* 646–649.

Powers, M. B, & Emmelkamp, P. M. G. (2008). Virtual reality therapy for anxiety disorders: A meta-analysis, *Journal of Anxiety Disorders, 22,* 561–569.

Pressly, P. K., & Heesacker, M. (2001). The physical environment and counseling: A review of theory and research. *Journal of Counseling & Development, 79,* 148–160.

Priester, P., Scherer, J., Steinfeldt, J., Jana-Masri, A., Jashinsky, T., Jones, J., & Vang, C. (2009).
The frequency of prayer, meditation, and holistic interventions in addictions treatment: A national survey. *Pastoral Psychology, 58*(3), 315–322.

Prochaska, J. O., & DiClemente, C. C. (1983). Stages and processes of self-change in smoking: Toward an integrative model of change. *Journal of Consulting and Clinical Psychology, 51,* 390–395.

Prochaska, J. O., & DiClemente, C. C. (1986). The transtheoretical approach. In J. C. Norcross (Ed.), *Handbook of eclectic psychotherapy* (pp. 163–200). New York: Brunner/Mazel.

Prochaska, J. O., & Norcross, J. C. (2009). *Systems of psychotherapy: A transtheoretical analysis* (7th ed.). Pacific Grove, CA: Brooks/Cole.

Prochaska, J. O., Norcross, J. C., & DiClemente, C. C. (1994). *Changing for good*. New York: William Morrow.

Purkey, W. W. (1987). *The inviting relationship: An expanded perspective for professional counseling*. Englewood Cliffs, NJ: Prentice Hall.

Purvis, J. A., Dabbs, J. M., & Hopper, C. (1984). The "Opener": Skilled use of facial expression and speech pattern. *Personality and Social Psychology Bulletin, 10,* 60–66.

Quimby, J. L., & O'Brien, K. M. (2006). Predictors of well-being among nontraditional female students with children. *Journal of Counseling & Development, 84,* 451–460.

Reik, T. (1968). *Listening with the third ear*. New York: Pyramid Books.

Ridley, N. C., & Asbury, F. R. (1988). Does counselor body position make a difference? *School Counselor, 35,* 253–258.

Ritchie, M. H. (1986). Counseling the involuntary client. *Journal of Counseling and Development, 64,* 516–518.

Ritter, A., Bowden, S., Murray, T., Ross, P., Greeley, J., & Pead, J. (2002). The influence of the therapeutic relationship in treatment for alcohol dependency. *Drug & Alcohol Review, 21,* 261–268.

Robbins, J. H. (1983). Complex triangles: Uncovering sexist bias in relationship counseling. *Women and Therapy, 2* (2–3), 159–169.

Robey, P. (2011). The terrible, awful, unspeakable secret—And how it changed me. In J. Kottler & J. Carlson (Eds.), *Duped: Lies and deception in psychotherapy* (pp.133–139). New York: Routledge.

Robins, R. W., Mendelsohn, G. A., Connell, J. B., & Kwan, V. S. Y. (2004). Do people agree about the causes of behavior? A social relations analysis of behavior ratings and causal attributions. *Journal of Personality & Social Psychology, 86,* 234–344.

Robinson, E. H., & Jones, K. D. (2001). Existential counseling. In D. C. Locke, J. E. Myers, & E. L. Herr (Eds.), *The handbook of counseling* (pp. 159–169). Thousand Oaks, CA: Sage.

Robinson, T. L., & Watt, S. K. (2001). "Where no one goes begging": Converging gender, sexuality, and religious diversity in counseling. In D. C. Locke, J. E. Myers, & E. L. Herr (Eds.), *The handbook of counseling* (pp. 589–600). Thousand Oaks, CA: Sage.

Roe, D., Dekel, R., Harel, G., & Fennig, S. (2006). Clients' reasons for terminating psychotherapy: A quantitative and qualitative inquiry. *Psychology and Psychotherapy: Theory, Research, and Practice, 29,* 529–538.

Rogers, C. R. (1957). The necessary and sufficient conditions of therapeutic personality change. *Journal of Consulting Psychology, 21,* 95–103.

Rogers, C. R. (1961). *On becoming a person.* Boston: Houghton Mifflin.

Rogers, C. R. (1967). *Person to person: The problem of being human.* Moab, UT: Real People Press.

Rogers, C. R. (1972). Client-centered therapy. In J. Huber & H. Millman (Eds.), *Goals and behavior in psychotherapy and counseling* (pp. 117–141). Columbus, OH: Merrill.

Rollnick, S., Miller, W. R., & Butler, C. C. (2008). *Motivational interviewing in health care: Helping patients change behavior.* NY: Guilford Press.

Rosen, S., & Tesser, A. (1970). On the reluctance to communicate undesirable information: The MUM effect. *Sociometry, 33,* 253–263.

Rosenberg, M. (1962). The association between self-esteem and anxiety. *Journal of Psychiatric Research, 1,* 135–152.

Rosenhan, D. L. (1973). On being sane in insane places. *Science, 180,* 250–258.

Rosner, R., Beutler, L. E., & Daldrup, R. J. (2000). Vicarious emotional experience and emotional expression in group psychotherapy. *Journal of Clinical Psychology, 56*(1), 1–10.

Rossi, E. (1980). *Collected papers of Milton Erickson on hypnosis* (Vols. 1–4). New York: Irvington.

Roth, A., & Fonagy, P. (2005). *What works for whom? A critical review of psychotherapy research* (2nd ed.). New York: Guilford.

Rotter, J. B. (1966). Generalized expectancies for internal versus external control of reinforcement. *Psychological Monographs: General & Applied, 80,* 1–28.

Rudestam, K. E. (1980). *Methods of self-change: An ABC primer.* Monterey, CA: Brooks/Cole.

Rule, W. R. (1982). Pursuing the horizon: Striving for elusive goals. *Personnel and Guidance Journal, 61,* 195–197.

Russell, M. N. (1984). *Skills in counseling women.* Springfield, IL: Thomas.

Salmela-Aro, K. (1992). Struggling with self: The personal projects of students seeking psychological counseling. *Scandinavian Journal of Psychology, 33,* 330–338.

Salovey, P., & Mayer, J. D. (1990). Emotional intelligence. *Imagination, Cognition, and Personality, 9,* 185–211.

Sattler, J. (1998). *Clinical and forensic interviewing of children and families.* San Francisco: Author.

Sattler, J. M., & Hoge, R. D. (2006). *Assessment of children: Behavioral, social and clinical foundations* (5th ed.). San Francisco: Jerome M. Sattler Publishers.

Sax, P. (2006). Developing preferred stories of identity as reflective practitioners. *Journal of Systemic Therapies, 25,* 59–72.

Schaefer, C. E., & Mattei, D. (2005). Catharsis: Effectiveness in children's aggression. *International Journal of Play Therapy, 14,* 103–109.

Schaub, M., & Williams, C. (2007). Examining the relations between masculine gender role conflict and men's expectations about counseling. *Psychology of Men & Masculinity, 8,* 40–52.

Schectman, Z., & Yanov, H. (2001). Interpretives (confrontation, interpretation, and feedback) in preadolescent counseling groups. *Group Dynamics, 5,* 124–135.

Scheel, M. J., Hanson, W. E., & Razzhavaikina, T. I. (2004). The process of recommending homework in psychotherapy: A review of therapist delivery methods, client acceptability, and factors that affect compliance. *Psychotherapy: Theory, Research, Practice, Training, 1,* 38–55.

Scher, M., & Stevens, M. (1987). Men and violence. *Journal of Counseling and Development, 65,* 351–354.

Schiraldi, G. R., McKay, M., & Fanning, P. (2005). *The self-esteem workbook*. Oakland, CA: New Harbinger.

Schön, D. A. (1983). *The reflective practitioner: How professionals think in action*. New York: Basic Books.

Schön, D. A. (1987). *Educating the reflective practitioner: Toward a new design for teaching and learning in the professions*. San Francisco: Jossey-Bass.

Schutz, W. (1981). *Holistic education*. In I. R. Corsini (Ed.), *Handbook of innovative psychotherapies* (pp. 378–388). New York: Wiley.

Schwarzbaum, S. E. (2004). Low-income Latinos and dropout: Strategies to prevent dropout. *Journal of Multicultural Counseling, 32,* 296–306.

Sciscoe, M. (1990). *The termination of therapy*. Unpublished manuscript.

Segal, Z. V., Williams, J. M. G., & Teasdale, J. (2002). *Mindfulness-based cognitive therapy for depression: A new approach to preventing relapse*. New York: Guilford Press.

Seligman, M. E. P. (1975). *Helplessness*. San Francisco: Freeman.

Seligman, M. E. P. (1991). *Helplessness: On depression, development, and death* (2nd ed.). New York: Freeman.

Seligman, M. E. P. (1998). *Learned optimism*. New York: Simon & Schuster.

Seligman, M. E. P., Steen, T., Park, N., & Peterson, C. (2005). Positive psychology progress: Empirical validation of intervention, *American Psychologist, 60,* 410–421.

Sermat, V., & Smythe, M. (1973). Content analysis of verbal communication in the development of a relationship: Conditions influencing self-disclosure. *Journal of Personality and Social Psychology, 26,* 332–346.

Sexton, T. (1996). The relevance of counseling outcome research: Current trends and practical implications. *Journal of Counseling & Development, 74,* 62–63.

Sexton, T. L., Whiston, S. C., Bleuer, J. C., & Walz, G. R. (1997). *Integrating outcome research into counseling practice and training*. Alexandria, VA: American Counseling Association.

Shafii, M. (1974). Meditation and marijuana. *American Journal of Psychiatry, 131,* 60–63.

Shafii, M. (1975). Meditation and the prevention of alcohol abuse. *American Journal of Psychiatry, 132,* 942–945.

Shannon, J., & Guerney, B. G., Jr. (1973). Interpersonal effects of interpersonal behavior. *Journal of Personality and Social Psychology, 26,* 142–150.

Shapiro, D. H. (1994). Examining the content and context of meditation: A challenge for psychology in the areas of stress management, psychotherapy and religion/values. *Journal of Humanistic Psychology, 34,* 101–135.

Sharpley, C. F. (2001). Standard posture, postural mirroring and client-perceived rapport. *Counselling Psychology Quarterly, 14,* 267–280.

Sharpley, C. F. (2005). Silence and rapport during initial interviews. *Counselling Psychology Quarterly, 18,* 149–159.

Shaughnessy, M. F. (1987). Cognitive techniques for "slippery" clients. *Techniques, 3,* 36–41.

Shelton, J. L., & Ackerman, J. M. (1974). *Homework in counseling and psychotherapy*. Springfield, IL: Thomas.

Shelton, J. L., & Levy, R. L. (1981). *Behavioral assignments and treatment compliance*. Champaign, IL: Research Press.

Shulman, L. (1979). *The skills of helping individuals and groups*. Itasca, IL: Peacock Press.

Siegel, A. B. (2010). Dream interpretation in clinical practice: A century after Freud. *Sleep Medicine Clinics, 5*(2), 299–313.

Siegel, B. (1986). *Love, medicine and miracles*. New York: William Morrow.

Simpson, D. E., Dalgaard, K. A., & O'Brien, D. K. (1986). Student and faculty assumptions about the nature of uncertainty in medicine and medical education. *Journal of Family Practice, 23*(5), 468–472.

Sims, P. A. (2003). Working with metaphor. *American Journal of Psychotherapy, 57,* 528–536.

Singer, E. (1970). *Key concepts in psychotherapy* (2nd ed.). New York: Basic Books.

Singer, J. (2006). *Expanding imagery in patient and therapist*. Washington, DC: American Psychological Association.

Singh, R. (2003a). *Empowering your soul through meditation*. London: HarperCollins.

Singh, R. (2003b). *Inner and outer peace through meditation*. London: HarperCollins.

Skovholt, T. M., & Ronnestad, M. H. (1992). Themes in therapist and counselor development. *Journal of Counseling and Development, 70,* 505–515.

Skovholt, T. M., Ronnestad, M. H., & Jennings, L. (1997). Searching for expertise in psychotherapy, professional psychology, and counseling. *Educational Psychology Review, 9,* 361–369.

Smith, E. W. L., Clance, P. R., & Imes, S. (1998). *Touch in psychotherapy*. New York: Guilford.

Smith, J. A., Hauenstein, N. M. A., & Buchanan, L. B. (1996). Goal setting and exercise performance. *Human Performance, 9,* 141–154.

Smith, W. P., Compton, W. C, & Beryl, W. (1995). Meditation as an adjunct to a happiness enhancement program. *Journal of Clinical Psychology, 51,* 260–273.

Smokowski, P. R. (2003). Beyond role-playing: Using technology to enhance modeling and behavioral rehearsal in group work practice. *Journal for Specialists in Group Work, 28,* 9–22.

Snyder, C. R., & Lopez, S. J. (2009). *Handbook of positive psychology* (2nd ed.). New York: Oxford.

Sommers-Flanagan, J., & Sommers-Flanagan, R. (2008). *Clinical interviewing* (4th ed.). New York: Wiley.

Spinhoven, P., Giesen-Bloo, J., van Dyck, R., Kooiman, K., & Arntz, A. (2007). The therapeutic alliance in schema-focused therapy and transference-focused psychotherapy for borderline personality disorder. *Journal of Consulting & Clinical Psychology, 75,* 104–115.

Spurling, L., & Dryden, W. (1989). The self and the therapeutic domain. In W. Dryden & L. Spurling (Eds.), *On becoming a psychotherapist*. London: Tavistock/Routledge.

Stampfl, T. G., & Levis, D. J. (1967). Essentials of implosive therapy: A learning-theory-based psychodynamic behavioral therapy, *Journal of Abnormal Psychology, 72,* 496–503.

St Onge, S. (1995). Modeling and role-playing. In M. Ballou & M. Ballou (Eds.), *Psychological interventions: A guide to strategies* (pp. 21–36). Westport, CT: Praeger Publishers/Greenwood Publishing Group.

Starr, A. (1977). *Psychodrama: Rehearsal for living*. Chicago: Nelson Hall.

Steiner, C. (1976, April). Radical psychiatry. Symposium conducted at the University of Dayton, Dayton, OH.

Stenzel, C. L., & Rupert, P. A. (2004). Psychologists' use of touch in individual psychotherapy. *Psychotherapy: Theory, Research, Practice, Training, 41*(3), 332–345.

Sternberg, K. J., Lamb, M. E., Hershkowitz, I., Yudilevitch, L., Orbach, Y., Esplin, P. W., & Hovav, M. (1997). Effects of introductory style on children's abilities to describe experiences of sexual abuse. *Child Abuse and Neglect, 21,* 1133–1146.

Stevens, S. E., Hynan, M. T., Allen, M., Beaun, M. M., & McCart, M. R. (2007). Are complex psychotherapies more effective than biofeedback, progressive muscle relaxation, or both? A meta-analysis. *Psychological Reports, 100,* 303–324.

Stone, G. L., & Morden, C. J. (1976). Effect of distance on verbal productivity. *Journal of Counseling Psychology, 23,* 486–488.

Stone, M. (1998). Journaling with clients. *Journal of Individual Psychology, 54,* 535–545.

Strong, T. (2009). Collaborative goal-setting: Counselors and clients negotiating a counseling focus. *Counselling Psychology Review, 24*(3–4), 24–37.

Strong, T., & Massfeller, H. F. (2010). Negotiating post-consultation 'homework' tasks between counselors and clients. *International Journal for the Advancement of Counselling, 32,* 14–30.

Strong, T., & Zeman, D. (2010). Dialogic considerations of confrontation as a counseling activity: An examination of Allen Ivey's use of confronting as a microskill. *Journal of Counseling & Development, 88,* 332–339.

Sue, D. W. (1978). Eliminating cultural oppression in counseling: Toward a general theory. *Journal of Counseling Psychology, 25,* 419–428.

Sue, D. W., & Sue, D. (2008). *Counseling the culturally diverse: Theory and practice* (5th ed.). New York: Wiley.

Sue, S. (2003). In defense of cultural competency in psychotherapy and treatment. *American Psychologist, 58,* 964–970.

Sue, S., & McKinney, H. (1975). Asian Americans in the community mental health care system. *American Journal of Orthopsychiatry, 45,* 111–118.

Sue, S., & Zane, N. (1987). The role of culture and cultural techniques in psychotherapy. *American Psychologist, 42,* 37–45.

Suinn, R. M. (1996). Imagery rehearsal: A tool for clinical practice. *Psychotherapy in Private Practice, 15,* 27–31.

Suiter, R. L., & Goodyear, R. K. (1985). Male and female counselor and client perceptions of four levels of counselor touch. *Journal of Counseling Psychology, 32,* 645–668.

Sullivan, H. S. (1954). *The psychiatric interview.* New York: Norton.

Sutton, S., & Gilbert, H. (2007). Effectiveness of individually tailored smoking cessation advice letters as an adjunct to telephone counseling and generic self-help materials: Randomized controlled trial. *Addiction, 102,* 994–1000.

Swade, T., Bayne, R., & Horton, I. (2006). Touch me never? *Therapy Today, 17,* 41–42.

Sweeney, T. J. (2009). *Adlerian counseling* (5th ed.). New York: Routledge.

Tannen, D. (2001). *You just don't understand: Women and men in conversation.* New York: Quill.

Tavris, C. (1989). *Anger: The misunderstood emotion.* New York: Touchstone.

Taylor, M. (1994). Gender and power in counselling and supervision. *British Journal of Guidance and Counselling, 22*(3), 319–326.

Tepper, D. T., Jr., & Haase, R. F. (1978). Verbal and nonverbal communication of facilitative conditions. *Journal of Counseling Psychology, 25,* 35–44.

Thomas, G. M. (2009). Cognitive behavioral treatment of traumatized adults: Exposure therapy. In A. Rubin, D. W. Springer, A. Rubin, D. W. Springer (Eds.), *Treatment of traumatized adults and children: Clinician's guide to evidence-based practice* (pp. 31–101). Hoboken, NJ: John Wiley & Sons.

Thompson, J. K., & Thompson, C. M. (1986). Body size distortion and self-esteem in asymptomatic, normal weight males and females. *International Journal of Eating Disorders, 5,* 1061–1068.

Thompson, S. C. (1991). Intervening to enhance perceptions of control. In C. R. Snyder & D. R. Forsyth (Eds.), *Handbook of social and clinical psychology* (pp. 607–623). New York: Simon & Schuster.

Timm, S., & Schroeder, B. L. (2000). Listening/nonverbal communication training. *International Journal of Listening, 14,* 109–128.

Tjeltveit, A. C. (2006). To what ends? Psychotherapy goals and outcomes, the good life and the principle of beneficence. *Psychotherapy: Theory, Research, Practice, Training, 43,* 186–200.

Tomm, K. (1988). Interventive interviewing: Part III. Intending to ask linear, circular, strategic or reflexive questions? *Family Process, 27,* 1–15.

Tracey, T. J., Hays, K. A., Malone, J., & Herman, B. (1988). Changes in counselor response as a function of experience. *Journal of Counseling Psychology, 35,* 119–126.

Trout, J. D. (2010). *Why empathy matters: The science and psychology of better judgment.* New York: Penguin.

Truant, G. S. (1999). Assessment of suitability for psychotherapy: II. Assessment based on process goals. *American Journal of Psychotherapy, 53,* 17–34.

Truax, C. B., & Carkhuff, R. R. (1967). *Toward effective counseling and psychotherapy: Training and practice.* Chicago: Aldine.

Tryon, G.S., & Winograd, G. (2011). Goal consensus and collaboration. In J. C. Norcross (Ed.), *Psychotherapy relationships that work* (pp. 153–167). New York: Oxford University Press.

Tsai, J. L., Levenson, R. W., & McCoy, K. (2006). Cultural and temperamental variation in emotional response. *Emotion, 6,* 484–497.

Tubesing, D. (1981). *Kicking your stress habits.* Duluth, MN: Whole Person Press.

Twenge, J. M., Konrath, S., Foster, J. D., Campbell, W. K., & Bushman, B. J. (2008). Egos inflating over time: A cross-temporal meta-analysis of the Narcissistic Personality Inventory. *Journal of Personality, 76,* 875–901.

Tymms, P., & Merrell, C. (2006). The impact of screening and advice on inattentive, hyperactive and impulsive children. *European Journal of Special Needs Education, 21,* 321–337.

Vera, E. M., Speight, S. L., Mildner, C., & Carlson, H. (1999). Clients' perceptions and evaluations of similarities to and differences from their counselors. *Journal of Counseling Psychology, 46,* 277–283.

Vereen, L. G., Butler, S. K., Williams, F. C., Darg, J. A., & Downing, T. K. E. (2006). The use of humor when counseling African American college students. *Journal of Counseling & Development, 84,* 10–15.

Vincent, P. J., Boddana, P., & MacLeod, A. K. (2004). Positive life goals and plans in parasuicide. *Clinical Psychology and Psychotherapy, 11,* 90–99.

Vogel, D. L., Epting, F., & Wester, S. R. (2003). Counselors' perceptions of female and male clients. *Journal of Counseling & Development, 81,* 131–140.

Vrij, A., Akehurst, L., Soukara, S., & Bull, R. (2004). Detecting deceit via analyses of verbal and nonverbal behavior in children and adults. *Human Communication Research, 30,* 8–41.

Wachtel, P. L. (2011). *Therapeutic communication* (2nd ed.). New York: Guilford.

Walz, G. (1990). *Counseling for self esteem.* Alexandria, VA: American Association for Counseling and Development.

Ward, C. C., & Reuter, T. (2011). *Strength-centered counseling: Integrating postmodern approaches and skills with practice.* Thousand Oaks, CA: Sage Publications.

Ward, D. E. (1984). Termination of individual counseling: Concepts and strategies. *Journal of Counseling and Development, 63,* 21–25.

Watkins, C. E., Jr. (1986). Transference phenomena in the counseling situation. In W. P. Anderson (Ed.), *Innovative counseling: A handbook of readings.* Alexandria, VA: American Association of Counseling and Development.

Watkins, C. E., Jr. (1990). The effects of counselor self-disclosure: A research review. *Counseling Psychologist, 18,* 477–500.

Watts, R. E., & Pietrzak, D. (2000). Adlerian 'encouragement' and the therapeutic process of solution-focused brief therapy. *Journal of Counseling & Development, 78(*4), 442–447.

Watzlawick, P., Weakland, J., & Fisch, R. (1974). *Change: Principles of problem formation and problem resolution.* New York: Norton.

Weiner, M. F. (1979). *Therapist disclosure: The use of self in psychotherapy.* Boston: Butterworth Press.

Weiner-Davis, M. (1992). *Divorce busting.* New York: Summit Books.

Weiner-Davis, M. (2001). *The divorce remedy.* New York: Simon & Schuster.

Wester, S. R., & Vogel, D. L. (2002). Working with the masculine mystique: Male gender role conflict, counseling self-efficacy and the training of male psychologists. *Professional Psychology: Research & Practice, 4,* 370–376.

Wester, S. R., Vogel, D. L., & Pressly, P. K. (2002). Sex differences in emotion: A critical review of the literature and implications for counseling psychology. *Counseling Psychologist, 30,* 630–652.

Whetworth, L., Kimsey-House, K., Kimsey-House, H., & Sandahl, P. (2007). *Co-active coaching* (2nd ed.). Mountain View, CA: CPP.

Whiston, S. C. (2004). *Principles and applications of assessment in counseling.* Belmont, CA: Wadsworth.

White, M. (2000). *Reflections on narrative practice: Essays and interviews.* Adelaide, Australia: Dulwich Centre Publications.

Wiggins-Frame, M. (2001). The spiritual genogram in training and supervision. *The Family Journal, 9,* 109–115.

Wierzbicki, M., & Pekarik, G. (1993). A meta-analysis of psychotherapy dropout. *Professional Psychology: Research and Practice, 24,* 190–195.

Williams, E. N., Polster, D., Grizzard, M. B., Rockenbaugh, J., & Judge, A. B. (2003). What happens when therapists feel bored or anxious? A qualitative study of distracting self-awareness and therapists' management strategies. *Journal of Contemporary Psychotherapy, 33,* 5–18.

Williams, P., & Davis, D. C. (2002). *Therapist as life coach: Transforming your practice.* New York: W. W. Norton.

Willison, B. G., & Masson, R. L. (1986). The role of touch in therapy: An adjunct to communication. *Journal of Counseling and Development, 64,* 497–500.

Willow, R. A., Bastow, E. K., & Ratkowski, E. M. (2007, March). *A model for reflective inquiry and constructivist learning in a counselor training program.* Symposium presented at the annual meeting of the American Counseling Association Conference, Detroit, MI.

Wilson, A., & Krane, R. (1980). Change in self esteem and its effect on symptoms of depression. *Cognitive Therapy and Research, 4,* 419–421.

Witmer, J. M. (1985). *Pathways to personal growth: Developing a sense of worth and competence.* Muncie, IN: Accelerated Development.

Witmer, J. M., & Sweeney, T. J. (1992). A holistic model for wellness and prevention over the life span. *Journal of Counseling and Development, 71,* 140–148.

Witmer, J. M., & Young, M. E. (1985). The silent partner: Uses of imagery in counseling. *Journal of Counseling and Development, 64,* 187–189.

Witmer, J. M., & Young, M. E. (1987). Imagery in counseling. *Elementary School Guidance and Counseling, 22,* 5–16.

Wohl, J. (1995). Traditional individual psychotherapy and ethnic minorities. In J. F. Aponte, R. Y. Rivers, & J. Wohl (Eds.), *Psychological interventions and cultural diversity* (pp. 74–91). Boston: Allyn & Bacon.

Wolberg, L. R. (1954). *The technique of psychotherapy.* New York: Grune & Stratton.

Wolberg, L. R. (1967). *The technique of psychotherapy* (2nd ed.). New York: Grune & Stratton.

Wolberg, L. R. (1977). *The technique of psychotherapy.* New York: Grune & Stratton.

Wolpe, J. (1958). *Psychotherapy by reciprocal inhibition.* Stanford, CA: Stanford University Press.

Wong, Y. (2006). Strength-centered therapy: A social constructionist, virtues-based psychotherapy. *Psychotherapy, 43,* 133–146.

Wong, E. C., Kim, B. S. K., Zane, N. W. S., Kim, I. J., & Huang, J. S. (2003). Examining culturally based variables associated with ethnicity: Influences on credibility perceptions of empirically supported interventions. *Cultural Diversity & Ethnic Minority Psychology, 9,* 88–96.

Wong, Y. J., Steinfeldt, J. A., LaFollette, J. R., & Tsao, S. (2010, November). Men's tears: Football players' evaluations of crying behavior. *Psychology of Men and Masculinity, 12*(4), 1–15.

Woody, S. R., Detweiler-Bedell, J., Teachman, B. A., & O'Hearn, T. (2003). *Treatment planning in psychotherapy: Taking the guesswork out of clinical care.* New York: Guilford.

Workman, W. J. (1993). Relationship of counselor variables to preference for type of response in counseling. *Counselor Education and Supervision, 32,* 178–188.

World Health Organization. (2002). *World report on violence and health.* Geneva, Switzerland: Author.

Yablonsky, L. (1976). *Psychodrama: Resolving emotional problems through role-playing.* New York: Basic Books.

Yalom, I. (1989). *Love's executioner.* New York: Basic Books.

Yalom, I. D. (1995). *Theory and practice of group psychotherapy* (4th ed.). New York: Basic Books.

Yalom, I. (1999). *Momma and the meaning of life.* New York: Basic Books.

Yalom, I. D. (2000). *Love's executioner and other tales of psychotherapy.* New York: HarperCollins.

Young, M. E. (1998). Skills-based training for counselors: Microskills or mega-skills. *Counseling & Human Development, 31*(3), 1–12.

Young, M. E., de Armas DeLorenzi, L. & Cunningham, L. (2011). Using meditation in addiction counseling. *Journal of Addiction and Offender Counseling, 32,* 58–72.

Young, M. E., & Bemak, F. (1996). Emotional arousal and expression in mental health counseling. *Journal of Mental Health Counseling, 18,* 316–332.

Young, M. E., & Feiler, F. (1993). Trends in counseling: A national survey. *Guidance and Counselling, 9,* 4–11.

Young, M. E., & Hutchinson, T. S. (in press). The rediscovery of gratitude. *Journal of Humanistic Counseling.*

Young, M. E., & Rosen, L. S. (1985). The retreat: An educational growth group. *Journal for Specialists in Group Work, 10,* 157–163.

Yznaga, S. D. (2008). Using the genogram to facilitate the intercultural competence of Mexican immigrants. *The Family Journal, 16,* 159–165.

Zanna, M. P., & Cooper, J. (1974). Dissonance and the pill: An attribution approach to studying the arousal properties of dissonance. *Journal of Personality and Social Psychology, 29,* 703–709.

Zgierska, A., Rabago, D., Chawla, N., Kushner, K., Koehler, R., & Marlatt, A. (2009). Mindfulness meditation for substance use disorders: A systematic review. *Substance Abuse, 30*(4), 266–294.

Zyromski, B. (2007). Journaling: An underutilized school counseling tool. *Journal of School Counseling, 5*(9), 1–30.

INDEX